(continued inside back cover)

INTRODUCTION TO DATA STRUCTURES AND ALGORITHM ANALYSIS

Second Edition

INTRODUCTION TO DATA STRUCTURES AND ALGORITHM ANALYSIS

Second Edition

Thomas L. Naps
Lawrence University

WEST PUBLISHING COMPANY
St. Paul   New York   San Francisco   Los Angeles

WEST'S COMMITMENT TO THE ENVIRONMENT

In 1906, West Publishing Company began recycling materials left over from the production of books. This began a tradition of efficient and responsible use of resources. Today, up to 95 percent of our legal books and 70 percent of our college texts are printed on recycled, acid-free stock. West also recycles nearly 22 million pounds of scrap paper annually—the equivalent of 181,717 trees. Since the 1960s, West has devised ways to capture and recycle waste inks, solvents, oils, and vapors created in the printing process. We also recycle plastics of all kinds, wood, glass, corrugated cardboard, and batteries, and have eliminated the use of styrofoam book packaging. We at West are proud of the longevity and the scope of our commitment to our environment.

Copyediting: Publication Services, Inc.
Composition: Publication Services, Inc.
Artwork: Publication Services, Inc. and Miyake Illustration
Text design: Wendy Calmenson
Cover image: Gregory MacNicol
Cover design: Diane Beasley
Indexing: Publication Services, Inc.

Library of Congress Cataloging-in-Publication Data

Naps, Thomas L.
    Introduction to data structures and algorithm analysis / Thomas L. Naps. — 2nd ed.
        p. cm.
    Rev. ed. of: Introduction to data structures / Bhagat Singh, Thomas L. Naps. c1985.
        Includes bibliographical references (p.   ) and index.
        ISBN 0-314-93309-3 (hard)
        1. Data structures (Computer science)   2. Computer algorithms.
    I. Singh, Bhagat, 1940–   Introduction to data structures.
    II. Title.
    QA76.9.D35N32   1992
    005.7'3—dc20   91-47570
                                                                    CIP

To

Joyce, Keith, and Joey

T.L.N.

PREFACE

Background and Objectives

The most exciting (and sometimes frustrating) aspect of computer science is its adherence to the maxim "Change is the only constant." Since publication of the first edition of *Introduction to Data Structures* in 1985, computer science curricula have continued to evolve. Recently, the Joint Curriculum Task Force of the Association for Computing Machinery (ACM) and the Institute of Electrical and Electronic Engineers—Computer Society (IEEE—CS) issued its report, *Computing Curricula 1991*. Central to this report are the recurring themes of theory, abstraction, and design in all areas of computer science. The structure of the second edition of *Introduction to Data Structures and Algorithm Analysis* reflects these themes.

Theory and abstraction are built into the text's formal definitions of all data structures as abstract data types (ADTs). Each ADT includes a set of operations that are specified in formal pre- and postcondition style. These strict definitions replace the more intuitive approach that was often used in the first edition. After an ADT has been defined, various implementations of it are studied. Here the theory and abstraction begin to mesh with the design theme. Different implementations of an ADT illustrate different design perspectives. These perspectives are reflected in the time and space efficiency of a particular implementation. Each implementation of an ADT that we present is accompanied by an analysis of its time and space efficiency. Such analyses typically combine mathematical theory with the empirical observation paradigm of the natural sciences.

The design theme in computer science runs much deeper than mere consideration of how to implement ADTs. Given an ADT and its implementation, students must recognize the role of that ADT in realistic, large-scale applications. This will prepare them for future careers in software engineering. For instance, to study queues without gaining some insight into how queues are used in scheduling and simulation applications would seriously shortchange the design theme. It is important that students see how to use complex data structures in other areas of computer science. In this respect, the second edition retains the first edition's emphasis on applications of data structures, which are viewed as an integrated component in the entire discipline of computer science.

Organization and Coverage of Topics

The text's organization makes it appropriate for several types of courses. It could be used for a student's second course in computer science, assuming the student has completed a very rigorous first course and, ideally, a discrete mathematics course. In such a course, the early chapters of the text would be covered thoroughly, and selected advanced topics from later chapters could be skipped as described below.

The text could also be used for a more advanced course in data structures and algorithms, assuming a previous course that included a survey of elementary data structures such as stacks, queues, linked lists, and binary trees. For this more advanced course in algorithms, some early chapters of the text could be covered quickly, allowing appropriate time for later treatment of advanced topics.

Chapters 1 and 2 of the text set the stage for the abstraction theme that will be emphasized throughout the rest of the text. The focus in Chapter 1 is on algorithmic abstraction. We establish a pseudocode that is used for implementing algorithms throughout the remainder of the text. This pseudocode emphasizes the formal specification of an algorithm in terms of its pre- and postconditions. It also encourages the use of procedural parameters as a means of increasing the degree of generality of an algorithm's interface. Students who have not previously used procedural parameters should thoroughly master this technique in the programming language they are using. Appendix C offers guidelines for using procedures and functions as parameters in a variety of languages. Chapter 1 also establishes the mathematical framework for analyzing the efficiency of algorithms.

In Chapter 2 the emphasis switches to data abstraction. A formalism for specifying ADTs is established. The formalism is thoroughly illustrated by presenting definitions of the matrix, string, pointer, and set ADTs. These four ADTs will recur throughout the remainder of the text as we study more sophisticated ways of implementing them. The material in Section 2.2 on the Knuth-Morris-Pratt implementation of the string search operation will be particularly appropriate for more advanced students. Conversely, if this is a student's initial exposure to ADTs, this material could be skipped without loss of continuity.

Chapter 3 establishes ADT definitions for a variety of list types, including general lists and ordered lists. Linked lists and physically ordered arrays are compared as two implementation strategies for list ADTs. Also discussed are implementations of the pointer ADT. These include implementation by arrays as well as the pointer type built into many programming languages. The implementation of pointers is an important topic for students at this level; it is explored more deeply in the final chapter's discussion of memory management strategies. Applications discussed in Chapter 3 include sparse matrices, strings, sets, and the union-find problem.

Chapters 4 and 5 treat specialized lists: queues, priority queues, and stacks. Since these ADTs are conceptually simple to define, the emphasis in these two chapters is on applications.

The radix sort algorithm and scheduling users of a shared resource are examined as applications of a queue. Parsing and evaluation of expressions are the stack applications. It is necessary to cover queues before stacks since the parsing application that involves stacks also assumes knowledge of the queue ADT.

Chapter 6 examines recursion in depth. A student who has already been introduced to recursion in a prior course may skim Section 6.1. Recurrence relations and recursive call trees are introduced as a means of analyzing recursive algorithms. Applications of recursion covered in later sections of the chapter include quick sort, merge sort, and recursive descent parsing. The section on recursive descent parsing could be skipped without loss of continuity.

Chapters 7 and 8 provide in-depth coverage of trees. Chapter 7 focuses on the binary tree ADT. Sections 7.3 and 7.4 examine applications of binary trees in the heap sort algorithm and in implementing ordered lists and priority queues. Sections 7.5 and 7.6 describe threading and height balancing as ways of enhancing the efficiency of a binary tree implementation of an ordered list. Chapter 8 defines the general tree as an ADT and then investigates applications of it in the implementation of ordered lists via 2-3 trees and in the union-find problem. Advanced search strategies using trees are covered in Section 11.1. The material in that section could be covered after completing Chapter 8.

Chapters 9 and 10 focus on graphs and networks. In Chapter 9, ADT definitions are provided for these structures. Algorithms for traversing graphs and networks (depth-first and breadth-first algorithms), finding paths (Dijkstra, Floyd, and Warshall algorithms), constructing minimum spanning trees (Prim and Kruskal algorithms), and sorting topologically are explored. Chapter 10 scrutinizes path finding from a slightly different perspective. The notion of a conceptual network is introduced, and heuristically guided search techniques are studied. Since such techniques are particularly relevant in artificial intelligence, the chapter concludes with a discussion of the minimax algorithm in searching game trees.

Search and sort algorithms that have not fit into earlier chapters are covered in Chapters 11 and 12, respectively. Chapter 11 investigates additional search strategies, including variations on trees (Section 11.1), hashing (Section 11.2), and indexing for file structures (Section 11.6). The applications described in Section 11.3 (implementation of ordered lists), Section 11.4 (implementation of sparse matrices), and Section 11.5 (Rabin-Karp string search) are all dependent only on hashing. Hence Sections 11.1 and 11.6 could readily be skipped if time does not allow coverage of them. Since the material in Section 11.1 examines the use of a variety of tree structures (splay trees, 2-3-4 trees, and red-black trees) in developing search algorithms, this section could be covered anytime after the presentation of 2-3 trees in Section 8.3.

Chapter 12 is relatively short because internal sorting algorithms are covered earlier in the text. It summarizes the sorting methods that have been previously studied and establishes an $n \log_2 n$ limit on the efficiency of comparison-based sorting algorithms. In Section 12.2 external sorting algorithms are discussed; these algorithms could be skipped without loss of continuity.

Chapter 13 illustrates the use of data structures in several memory management applications. From an operating systems perspective, the fragmentation problem and buddy systems are studied. From a programming language perspective, heap management for implementations of pointer variables is investigated.

Features of the Text

Topical coverage alone is certainly not enough in a text. Such coverage must be couched in style that integrates quality pedagogical features with sound principles of software engineering. Toward these ends we have integrated many unique features into the text:

1. *Presentation of all ADTs by formal specification of their operations.* This specification takes the form of procedure interfaces that combine a high degree of generality with a unique and consistent style of documentation. The documentation style incorporates the pre- and postconditions for the operation into the parameter list for the corresponding procedure. Students thus view the definition of pre- and postconditions as an indispensable component of the procedural interface. They are encouraged from the outset to develop ADT operations that are reusable in a variety of contexts. The rigor and abstraction built into these procedural interfaces makes them particularly well suited to object-oriented languages (such as C++ and Turbo Pascal).

2. *Extensive use of figures and graphic documentation.* This allows students to visualize the effect of algorithms on data structures. Algorithms are pictorially traced in a way that will bring them to life in the students' minds. It is our feeling that this visualization of data structures and algorithms represents true data abstraction, allowing students to understand at the conceptual level while also seeing the implementation of the algorithm in pseudocode.

3. *Relevant issues.* These asides provide glimpses of how the topic under discussion in a particular chapter finds application in a more advanced area of computer science, and some of them discuss potential societal impact of such an application.

4. *Exercises at the end of each section.* The exercises tend to be thought provoking and relatively short. They require the student to trace an algorithm studied in the chapter, provide a brief essay answer to a conceptual question, write a short procedure to accomplish a specific task, or analyze the efficiency of an algorithm.

5. *An extensive set of programming problems and projects at the end of each chapter.* Solutions to some of these should be implemented by the students in the programming language they are using for the course.

6. *Appendices and endsheets.* These provide hints and solutions to many odd-numbered exercises, random number algorithms that can be used in a variety of the experimentation-based problems, a review of important recurrence relations used in the analysis of recursive algorithms, guidelines for passing procedures as parameters in a variety of languages, and a taxonomy of ADTs covered in the text. The latter will be particularly helpful to students who are implementing ADTs in an object-oriented language since it corresponds to a hierarchy of object-oriented classes.

Ancillaries

Ancillary materials for the text include the following:

1. An *Instructor's Manual,* which provides useful hints on how to present the material in each chapter, solutions to even-numbered exercises, and additional ideas for programming problems and projects.

2. *Transparency masters,* which can be used to illustrate key concepts, are available to adopters from the publisher. A list of figures from the text available as transparency masters is in the Instructor's Manual.

3. *Software disk containing pseudocode and Pascal versions of the ADT interfaces and all other algorithms presented in the text.* Because of the text's heavy emphasis on reusable code, this can save instructors and students from having to "reinvent the wheel."

4. A *lab manual* will be available for use in conjunction with this text. The manual contains collections of lab exercises coordinated with the algorithms and data structures presented in the text. Each exercise centers around a (Pascal) program that implements the algorithm being studied. The student initially uses the program to discover and explore the nuances of the algorithm. The student then modifies the program to see how the performance of the algorithm is affected. Often the goal of such a modification is to make the algorithm more efficient. The programs produce output that allows the student to monitor this efficiency. For each exercise there is a series of questions the student must answer. Initial questions reinforce the student's understanding of the basic algorithm. Later questions have the student write up the results of his or her experimentation and exploration with the algorithm.

Acknowledgments

This text represents not so much a second edition as it does a completely new data structures book. As such, the patient support of our editors, Jerry Westby and Denis Ralling, has been a key ingredient in producing a quality work. They understood that the "quick and dirty" approach to producing a new edition would not be possible because of the tremendous advances in the discipline of computer science over the last six years. The production staff, including Melissa Madsen and Kirsten Stigberg at Publication Services and Jayne Lindesmith at West, have battled a variety of obstacles to keep the project on schedule. From the College of Charleston, George Pothering, coauthor of the Pascal version of the text, contributed many insights and refinements to the pseudocode version as well; Andrea Kellner assisted with the preparation of the hints and solutions; Jimmy Wilkinson offered helpful suggestions while using the text in various prepublication forms in his CSCI330 class. We greatly appreciate the efforts of Luegina Mounfield of Louisiana State University in preparing an excellent instructor's manual. As we revised and revised, the wisdom of many reviewers has woven itself into the text. They are Elizabeth Adams, Hood College; Robert P. Burton, Brigham Young University; Daniel E. Cooke, University of Texas at El Paso; David L. Doss, Illinois State University; Robert J. Douglas, San Francisco State University; Dan Everett, University of Georgia; Mark Fineup, University of Northern Iowa; Hugh Garraway, University of Southern Mississippi; Michael Henry, West Virginia University; Pentti A. Honkanen, Georgia State University; Peter Isaacson, University of Northern Colorado; David J. John, Wake Forest University; Allen Klinger, University of California, Los Angeles; Danny Kopec, University of Maine; Vijay Kumar, University of Missouri–Kansas City; Ronald A. Mann, University of Louisville; Andrea Martin, Louisiana State University; Luegina C. Mounfield, Louisiana State University; Jai K. Navlakha, Florida International University; Clifford L. Pelletier, Central Connecticut State University; Anita Read, Salem State College; James L. Richards, Bemidji State University; Richard Roiger, Mankato State University; Sally Sage, Southern College of Technology; Patricia A. Slaminka, Auburn University; Thiab R. Taha, University of Georgia; David T. Wang, New Jersey Institute of Technology; Gail W. Wells, Northern Kentucky University; Robert Zerwekh, Northern Illinois University. Of course, my greatest debt is to my family—Joyce, who did all the word processing; Keith, who did all the backups; and Joey, who gave me all those hugs!

CONTENTS

3   LISTS—OPERATIONS, IMPLEMENTATIONS, AND APPLICATIONS   100

7   BINARY TREES   290

12 SORTING—REVISITED AND EXTENDED 587

13 MEMORY MANAGEMENT TECHNIQUES 604

Appendix A RANDOM NUMBERS: GENERATION AND USE IN EVENTS BASED ON PROBABILITIES A-1

1 ALGORITHMS— ABSTRACTION AND EFFICIENCY

'Where shall I begin, please your Majesty?' he asked.
'Begin at the beginning,' the King said, gravely, 'and go on
till you come to the end: then stop.'

Lewis Carroll

CHAPTER OUTLINE

Perhaps no word has ever been used as much in computer science as abstraction. According to Webster's dictionary, that which is abstract is "dissociated from any specific instance." *Abstraction* is the process of identifying certain properties or characteristics of a material object and then using them to specify a new object, known as *an* abstraction, which represents a simplification of that object from which it was derived. Although for most computer scientists the true material "objects" of their world are the states of the electronic components of computers, it is safe to say that no computer scientist relies on direct contact with these components to pursue his or her work in this field. At worst something might work with an abstraction provided by the manufacturer of a computer—namely, the instructions and data types provided in the machine language of the computer—but even these abstractions are too cumbersome for most. Consequently, most computer scientists prefer to work with abstractions that are as free as possible from the constraints of any one architecture. This leads us logically into the realm of high-level languages such as FORTRAN, ALGOL, Pascal, C, Modula-2, and Ada (to name just a few of the historically more significant languages). Now if there were only one high-level language around, it might sufficiently specify a level of abstraction at which many people would be content to work. There are however, a great number of high-level languages, each with unique features. Computer scientists have attached themselves to a still higher level of abstraction in trying to remove themselves from the constraints imposed by these high-level languages. Two of the abstractions they deal with at this level are *algorithms* and *data structures*. Although we shall later define both terms more precisely, for now an *algorithm* can be considered an abstraction of a program and a *data structure* an abstraction of a collection of similarly typed variables in a program.

Our objective in this book is to explore the work that computer scientists have carried out at this higher level of abstraction. Our emphasis will be on providing thorough, understandable definitions of the concepts that are paramount in data structures and algorithms and on examining their application in a variety of areas. Once a concept is understood at an abstract level, *implementations* of the concept—that is, realizations of it using the tools provided by a particular computer language—will also be explored. We shall see that an abstraction may have many implementations. Some of these implementations are good; others are not. They are judged according to efficiency considerations. From a practical perspective, a measure of the efficiency of an algorithm's implementation is achieved by analyzing the efficiency with which it utilizes the computer's time and memory. To a certain extent, such an analysis can be carried out mathematically—by predicting the behavior of an algorithm's implementation before it even executes on a machine. Often, however, such an analysis leads only to very rough estimates of efficiency. A more detailed efficiency analysis may require controlled observation of the algorithm's implementation as it executes with a variety of data. From such empirical measurements, a more precise mathematical estimate of the algorithm's efficiency can often be made.

1.1 ALGORITHMS, DATA STRUCTURES, AND ABSTRACT DATA TYPES

There are as many different definitions of the term *algorithm* as authors who write about algorithms. Underlying all of these definitions, however, are some common premises:

- An algorithm is a sequence of instructions for solving a problem.

- The problem to be solved has specifiable goal conditions that, when met, stop the execution of the algorithm and allow one to categorize the problem as having been "solved" in accordance with a set of specifiable initial conditions. Furthermore, the goal conditions must be attainable from the initial conditions in a finite amount of time.
- The intent of each instruction in the algorithm must be apparent to and within the capabilities of the agent that will be carrying out the instruction.
- As soon as one instruction in the algorithm has been carried out, the next instruction to be performed is uniquely determined by the instruction just completed and the current status of the solution.

Assimilating these assumptions into our own definition, *we shall define an algorithm as an unambiguous sequence of clear instructions that will solve a given problem in a finite amount of time and then halt.*

Although the term *algorithm* is now closely linked with computer science, algorithms have been a part of our lives since the first time one person explained to another person how to do something. People use algorithms when they follow recipes in a cookbook, follow instructions for assembling a child's toy, or program a VCR. Scientists publish algorithms describing experiments they have carried out so that other scientists can duplicate their work and confirm their results. Space agencies follow elaborate algorithms—countdowns—for launching rockets. Considered in this light, all of us have had frustrations at one time or another in dealing with algorithms that were ambiguous or beyond our capabilities. One can therefore understand the need for clarity in an algorithm when the agent carrying out the instructions of the algorithm will be a computer—one that is incapable of the ingenious improvisations that often allow human agents to deal effectively and appropriately with unexpected circumstances.

Data Structures

As we noted in our opening remarks, a data structure represents an abstraction of the data types provided by a language. Elementary data types are characterized by the fact that the values they admit are atomic; that is, they admit no further decomposition. Integer, real, and character data types are among the elementary data types supported in most programming languages. If the values of a data type do admit a decomposition into several components, however, then the data type is called "structured" instead of elementary, and the organization of each component and the relationships between components constitute what is known as a *data structure*. Arrays and records are two examples of data structures that enjoy direct support in many programming languages and are suitable for effectively handling the representation of information in a great many applications. Computer scientists and insightful programmers have developed data structures besides arrays and records that are better suited to other applications. It is the primary goal of this book to describe some of these data structures and to show how they can be realized in languages that do not directly support them.

Abstract Data Types

In recent years an additional emphasis has been added to the study of data structures. If they are realistically to represent abstractions of the data types found in programming languages, then not only are the organization and interrelationships among the components of their values important, but the operations permitted on these values must also be considered. Although arithmetic operations and comparisons are among the operations one normally expects to be associated with numeric data values, one does not normally associate these operations with character or boolean values. Similarly, one does not expect arithmetic or comparison operations to be provided for record types. Consequently, when considering data types that go beyond those found in a high-level language, the abstraction would be incomplete if one discussed only the structure of the values of these types without considering as well the operations to be performed on data objects that can assume these values. The term *abstract data type* (ADT) is used to define those data abstractions that require not only a specification of the structure of the values for this new data type, but also a specification of the complete set of operations that can be performed on data objects of this type. The approach we have adopted in this book is to introduce all data structures as abstract data types. We shall then use algorithms to describe how these operations can be carried out for given implementations of these abstract data types.

Algorithms and Languages—PSEUDO

If an algorithm is a sequence of *instructions*, then a *language* must be used to express the algorithm's semantics with adequate precision and freedom from ambiguity. This requires us to use a language that is sufficiently formal to avoid the imprecision inherent in a natural language. Beyond this, we want our language to be sufficiently concise and compact to facilitate verification of an algorithm's correctness. This verification may take the form of mathematical proofs of correctness, or, more often, observations of the performance of the algorithm with a carefully selected set of test cases. These test cases should attempt to cover all of the exceptional circumstances likely to be encountered by the algorithm. Just what these exceptional circumstances are will depend upon the structures being used to represent and manipulate the data. However, certain generic circumstances must be verified for all algorithms manipulating data structures:

- Does the algorithm work when the data structure is empty? For instance, does the logic of the algorithm correctly allow data to be added to a structure that presently contains no data? Is an attempt to delete data from such a structure appropriately trapped?
- Does the algorithm work when the data structure is full? Is an attempt to add data to such a structure appropriately trapped?

- Does the algorithm work for all the classes of possibilities that can occur between an empty structure and a full structure?

The need for conciseness in algorithms becomes obvious when one considers the problem of verifying their correctness. The more an algorithm attempts to do, the more possibilities must be considered in its verification. Hence, we will take the view that *an algorithm should concern itself with one specific problem*. Each algorithm is a logical *module* designed to perform a particular operation on a data item or structure. Once defined and verified, such a module represents an abstraction in that it may be used by other algorithms, which need not be concerned with the details underlying the module's implementation. These other algorithms need only understand what the module does and how to call upon the module.

The algorithmic language we propose with these goals in mind is called PSEUDO. The definition of PSEUDO involves three aspects: data types, control constructs, and procedures/functions. PSEUDO borrows ideas from a variety of programming languages, including Pascal, Modula-2, Ada, and C. As such, it should be readily apparent how to convert PSEUDO algorithms into actual programs in your favorite language.

Data Types in PSEUDO All unstructured data described in PSEUDO must fit into one of five categories:

integer

real

boolean

character

pointer

Both **integer** and **real** data types are numeric. **Integer** data consist only of whole numbers (and their negatives), whereas **real** data have an appropriate exponential format. For example, 18 is **integer**, but 1.8E1 and 0.92E-2 are **real**. In this text, **real** data will be rarely used. **Boolean** refers to logical data that have **true** and **false** as their only possible values. **Character** data are single alphanumeric values enclosed in quotes, such as "S" or "r". A discussion of the **pointer** data type will be deferred until Chapter 2.

Variables represent instances of a data type and must be declared via a nonexecutable **var** statement. Thus we could have

```
var C1, C2, C3: integer;
var EndOfData: boolean;
var StatusCode: character;
```

To avoid confusion as to where one statement ends and another starts, PSEUDO requires all statements to be separated by semicolons, as illustrated in the above **var** statements.

Data items can be compared using the following relations:

=   equal to
<   less than
>   greater than
<=   less than or equal to
>=   greater than or equal to
<>   not equal to

We assume the standard arithmetic and logical operators $+$, $-$, $*$, $/$, **and, or,** and **not**. These operators can be applied to variables or constants to build up expressions that in turn belong to the same data type as their components. To avoid ambiguity, we will follow the convention that *no mixing of data types within an expression is allowed.* As an example, consider:

```
C3 := C1 + C2
```

Here C3 is assigned the integer sum of C1 plus C2 (:= indicates assignment of a value to a particular variable). When division is applied to integer operands, the resulting quotient is truncated to produce an integer result.

Structured types in PSEUDO are **arrays** and **records.** The range of each index of an array is from 1 to some integer specified in the declaration of the array. For example, the declarations

```
var Person: array [15] of integer;
var Job: array [5, 4] of integer;
```

specify a one-dimensional array Person with entries Person[1], Person[2], . . . , Person[15] and a two-dimensional array Job with entries Job[1, 1], Job[1, 2], . . . , Job[5, 4]. Records are aggregates of potentially heterogeneous data items in which field names are used instead of an index to refer to a particular item. For example, the declaration

```
var BirthDay: record
            Month, Day, Year: integer
          endrecord;
```

would allow access to the Month field of BirthDay by the notation BirthDay.Month.

It is also possible to declare structured types and then declare variables of that type, as in

```
type Date: record
          Month, Day, Year: integer
        endrecord;
var BirthDay: Date;
```

This allows us to nest conveniently arrays within records and use records as the base data type for arrays. Building on our prior declarations, we could thus declare an array of dates in the following fashion:

```
var Dates: array [10] of Date;
```

Finally, in PSEUDO we have no formal file-handling statements. Instead, when we discuss file structures, files will be viewed as arrays of infinite extent that exist on permanent storage devices. We will designate a particular record in a (direct access) file by referring to an index position in the infinite array. This will allow us to describe file-handling algorithms in PSEUDO without the cumbersome OPENs, CLOSEs, READs, and WRITEs necessary in compiled or interpreted languages.

Control Constructs in PSEUDO For specifying the order of execution of instructions (also known as *flow of control*), we use the following PSEUDO constructs:

> For decisions:
>> **if-then** statement
>> **if-then-else** statement
> For iteration:
>> Pretest **while** loop
>> Posttest **repeat** loop
>> Fixed iteration **for** loop

These constructs represent decisional and iterative logic with which you are familiar from your work in computer science. The particular semantics of each construct is given in the combination of flowcharts and code segments which follow.

Control Construct I—if-then
General form:

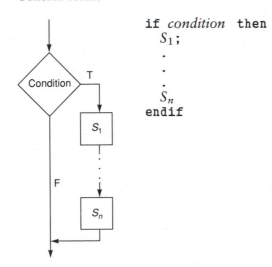

```
if condition then
    S₁;
    .
    .
    .
    Sₙ
endif
```

Example:

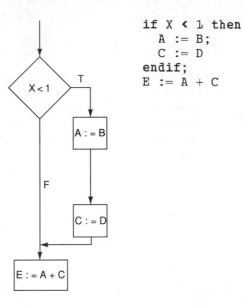

```
if X < 1 then
   A := B;
   C := D
endif;
E := A + C
```

Control Construct II—**if-then-else**
General form:

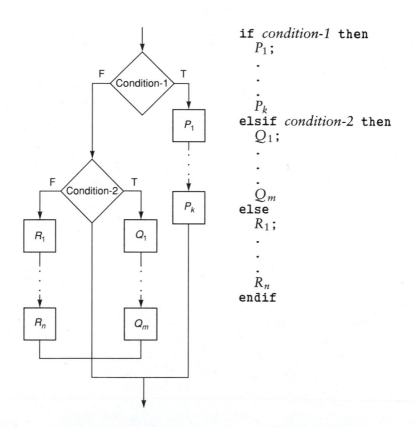

```
if condition-1 then
   P₁;
   .
   .
   .
   Pₖ
elsif condition-2 then
   Q₁;
   .
   .
   .
   Qₘ
else
   R₁;
   .
   .
   .
   Rₙ
endif
```

Although the pattern above shows one **elsif** clause in the **if-then-else**, the number of **elsif** clauses may be zero or more. No more than one **else** clause is ever used.

Example:

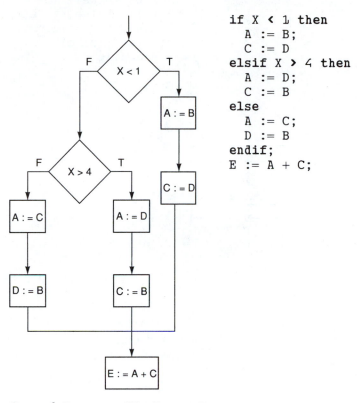

```
if X < 1 then
    A := B;
    C := D
elsif X > 4 then
    A := D;
    C := B
else
    A := C;
    D := B
endif;
E := A + C;
```

Control Construct III—Pretest Loop

General form:

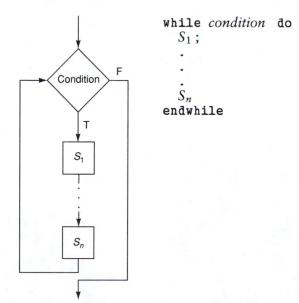

```
while condition do
    S₁ ;
    .
    .
    .
    Sₙ
endwhile
```

Example:

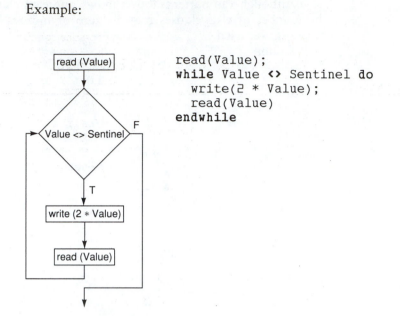

```
read(Value);
while Value <> Sentinel do
  write(2 * Value);
  read(Value)
endwhile
```

Note that the **read** and **write** procedures in the preceding example are PSEUDO's only input and output capabilities. For the purposes of the algorithms we will discuss, input and output are of minimal importance.

Control Construct IV—Posttest Loop
General form:

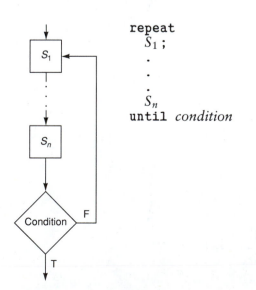

```
repeat
  S₁ ;
    .
    .
    .
  Sₙ
until condition
```

Example:

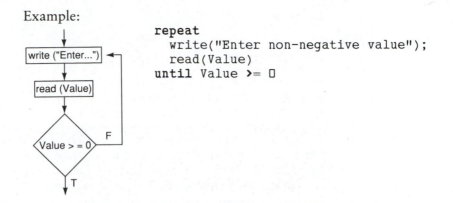

```
repeat
   write("Enter non-negative value");
   read(Value)
until Value >= 0
```

Note that a **repeat** loop essentially uses the logically opposite condition to perform the same sequence of actions that could be achieved with a **while** loop. That is, you execute the body of the loop when the condition is **true** in the **while** and when it is **false** in the **repeat-until**. There is, however, one fundamental difference: if the condition in a **while** loop is **false**, the body of the loop will not be executed at all. In a **repeat** loop, the body is executed once prior to the testing of the condition and hence will always be executed at least once. Thus, there are situations for which analogous **while** and **repeat** control structures will not be equivalent in their execution.

Control Construct V—Fixed Iteration Loop

General form:

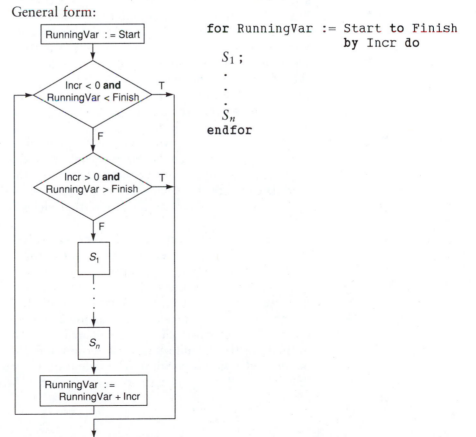

```
for RunningVar := Start to Finish
                        by Incr do
   S₁ ;
    .
    .
    .
   Sₙ
endfor
```

$S_1 ;$

S_n

Example:

```
for I := 1 to N do
  S := S + A[I];
  P := P * A[I]
endfor
```

This control construct is just PSEUDO's version of the automatic loop-ing mechanism found in all high-level languages—for example, Pascal's **for** loop. As do most of these high-level languages, we follow the convention that, if the increment is omitted, it is assumed to be +1. Note that the fixed iteration loop is actually a luxury, because it can always be replaced by an equivalent **while** loop (though not by a **repeat** loop).

Algorithmic Modules in PSEUDO—Procedures and Functions

No language structure is more critical to encouraging abstraction than the program *module*. Ideally, a module should be a structure that can be written and compiled apart from a program that uses it and whose specific task can be understood and activated solely through an interface, without requiring knowledge of its internal details. There are three important objectives to keep in mind when developing modules.

First, a module should be *functionally cohesive*: that is, it should be focused on solving one particular aspect of a problem. Since modules typically are used in concert with higher-level modules, there should be no unforeseen side effects from calling upon a module. It solves the problem it is designed to solve and does nothing else. In particular, it must not alter any data items or structures other than those that it is required to alter, according to the definition of the problem.

Second, when viewed as a name applied to a collection of instructions designed to solve a particular problem, a module encourages the abstract approach we emphasized at the beginning of the chapter. Once we have a module called **Sort**, which sorts a list, we have enabled ourselves to work at a higher level of abstraction—a level that views sorting as a given primitive operation.

Third, because one module typically solves a problem so that other modules at a higher level may be shielded from the details of that particu-lar problem's solution, it is important that a module have an *interface*. This interface represents lines of communication between a module and those that use it. For instance, a module that sorts an array must be given access to that array. The interface to a module is its parameter list. The skillful use of parameter lists can greatly enhance a module's degree of abstraction by making the module usable in more contexts and by hiding the details of the underlying algorithm. The definition of procedures and functions in PSEUDO will make it easy to develop such abstract interfaces to a mod-ule.

Here is the general form of a PSEUDO module:

```
⎧procedure⎫ module-name (parameter list);
⎩function ⎭

    Local var and type declarations

    start module-name
        .
        .
        .
    Executable statements
        .
        .
        .
    end module-name;
```

The parameter list specifies the preconditions and postconditions for the algorithm implemented in the module. A *precondition* is a condition that exists before the algorithm executes. A *postcondition* is a result of executing the algorithm. Hence, preconditions represent what the algorithm is *given* and postconditions what it *returns*. For example, in a module to sort an array of integers, one might have as preconditions the array, a parameter or parameters indicating a subrange of array indices over which to perform the sort, and perhaps a parameter indicating the ordering criterion to be used in the sort. The postcondition would be the original array modified so that the elements within the specified subrange were arranged according to the ordering criterion. Or, as in the following example, a module to swap the values of two storage locations, the preconditions would be the locations whose values are to be swapped, whereas the postconditions would be those same two locations, but with each holding what was formerly the other's value.

This notion of "given preconditions/return postconditions" is reflected in the parameter list structure of PSEUDO, which appears as follows.

```
( given parameter(s): parameter-type  (* Supporting documentation *);
    .
    .
    .
  return parameter(s): parameter-type (* Supporting documentation *);
    .
    .
    .
                        );
```

For instance, consider the following PSEUDO procedure to interchange the values of two locations storing values of a type ElementType.

```
procedure Swap
  ( given A, B: ElementType     (* Locations to be interchanged *);
    return A, B: ElementType     (* A with B's original value,
                                     B with A's original value *) );

  var Temp: ElementType;

  start Swap
    Temp := A;
    A  := B;
    B  := Temp
  end Swap;
```

From this discussion, it is evident that we will use the notation (*...*) for comments in PSEUDO. It is not evident how Swap would be called. One possibility would be

```
Swap(x, y, x, y)
```

Although the appearance of a variable twice in the formal parameter list of the procedure serves to clarify the preconditions and postconditions of the algorithm, such double listing is redundant and serves no purpose in the actual parameter list of the procedure call. Hence, we specify that the parameter appear only once in the actual parameter list. So

```
Swap(x, y)
```

is sufficient to invoke Swap. Though this way of matching up parameters in the formal and actual parameter lists may seem unusual initially, it is completely free of ambiguity. If effect, the second occurrence of a parameter in the postcondition of a formal parameter list is simply ignored when the actual parameter list is matched up with the formal. For example, a formal parameter list of

```
( given X, Y: character;
        A, B: integer;
  return B: integer;
        Y: character;
        P: real )
```

and an actual parameter list of

```
(P, Q, F, G, M)
```

would match up actual parameter P with formal parameter X, Q, with Y, F with A, G with B, and M with P (with the second occurrences of B and Y ignored).

What is to be gained by specifying formal parameter lists in this fashion? We can make the formal parameter list a very precise statement of the interface to the procedure. Moreover, this interface is presented in the form of preconditions followed by postconditions—a format that facilitates verification of the algorithm.

The formal parameter list for a **function** in PSEUDO may specify only one parameter type in its postcondition section. This parameter type appears without a corresponding parameter name since the value is returned as the function name. The value returned by a function may be any elementary or structured data type. Consider, for instance, the following PSEUDO function to compute the greatest common divisor of two positive integers.

```
function GCD
  ( given Value1, Value2: integer (* Value1 and Value2 are positive integers *);
    return: integer             (* Return the greatest common divisor of
                                   Value1 and Value2 *) );

  var Rem: integer;

  start GCD
    Rem := Value1 mod Value2;     (* Assume mod yields remainder *)
    while Rem <> 0 do
      Value1 := Value2;
      Value2 := Rem;
      Rem := Value1 mod Value2
    endwhile;
    GCD := Value2
  end GCD;
```

A function may be invoked within expressions and assignment statements; for example,

```
X := GCD(Y, Z) + GCD(P, Q)
```

Procedures and Functions as Parameters

We will allow the precondition section of a formal parameter list to contain procedures and functions as parameters. This capability is consistent with such high-level languages as Pascal, Modula-2, and C, although it is often omitted from the material covered in introductory courses. (See the Relevant Issue in Section 1.2 and Appendix C.) This feature can be a powerful tool in developing procedures and functions with a higher degree of generality than would otherwise be possible. To see how this generality can be attained, consider first the following PSEUDO function, which returns the index position of the smallest ("champion") value in a prescribed subrange of an array of integers.

```
type (* Assume IndexLimit is constant determining array size *)
  ElementArray: array [IndexLimit] of integer;

function FindChampionIndex
  ( given A: ElementArray   (* Array of integer values with at most
                               IndexLimit entries *);
          Lo, Hi: integer   (* Specify an array subrange. Assume that
                               1 <= Lo <= Hi IndexLimit *);
```

```
    return: integer          (* The index of the smallest ("champion") value
                                among A[Lo]...A[Hi]. If the smallest value
                                occurs more than once, the index returned is
                                that of the first occurrence. *) );

  var I, Tentative: integer;

  start FindChampionIndex
    Tentative := Lo;
    for I := Lo + 1 to Hi do
      if A[I] < A[Tentative] then
        Tentative := I
      endif
    endfor;
    FindChampionIndex := Tentative
  end FindChampionIndex;
```

In this algorithm we viewed the smallest entry as the "champion." Clearly the same algorithm would work to find the index of the largest as "champion," but we would have to code a new function with ">" replacing "<." Moreover, the same algorithm should work for finding the position of the "champion" in a subrange of an array of reals, strings, or any other data type on which we can define a "better than" comparison between two elements. That is, the current version of FindChampionIndex is not as abstract as we would like because it ties what should be a general algorithm to a particular data type and order relation. However, if we define a general ElementType and provide FindChampion with a BetterThan relation to apply to two data items of ElementType, we succeed in stating a more generalized algorithm. To provide FindChampion with a BetterThan relation we pass it in as a function parameter whose type is established in a declaration. The declaration serves to establish the function parameter's *signature*, that is, the number and type of its formal parameters. This is illustrated in the following version of the function.

```
type (* Assume IndexLimit is constant determining array size *)
  ElementType: (* May be anything with an order relationship between
                  elements *);
  ElementArray: array [IndexLimit] of ElementType;
  Comparison: function
            ( given A, B: ElementType
                          (* Values to compare *);
              return: boolean (* true if A better than
                                 B, false otherwise *) );
```
This establishes a function signature.

```
function FindChampionIndex
  ( given A: ElementArray        (* Array of values with at most
                                    IndexLimit entries *);
      Lo, Hi: integer           (* Specify an array subrange. Assume that
                                    1 <= Lo <= Hi <= IndexLimit *);
      BetterThan: Comparison    (* The function
                                   parameter for
                                   comparing values *);
```
Note function in parameter list.

```
    return: integer          (* The index of "best" value among A[Lo]...A[Hi]. If
                                the best value occurs more than once, the index
                                returned is that of the first occurrence. *) );

var I: ElementType;
    Tentative: integer;

start FindChampionIndex
  Tentative := Lo;
  for I := Lo + 1 to Hi do
    if BetterThan(A[I], A[Tentative]) then ┐——— Note use of
      Tentative := I                             function parameter.
    endif
  endfor;
  FindChampionIndex := Tentative
end FindChampionIndex;
```

If we now want FindChampionIndex to return the position of the largest entry in a subrange of a real array (instead of the smallest entry within an integer array), we need merely declare

```
type ElementType: real;
```

A sample call to FindChampionIndex would then appear as

```
FindChampionIndex(X, Low, High, GreaterThan)
```

Here X would be declared as an array of reals and Low and High as integers. GreaterThan would be the boolean function that has a signature of type Comparison and is determined by the > relationship:

```
function GreaterThan
  ( given V1, V2: ElementType (* Two arbitrary values *);
    return: boolean           (* true if V1 is greater than
                                 V2 by the ordering relation
                                 of ElementType *) );

  start GreaterThan
    GreaterThan := V1 > V2
  end GreaterThan;
```

The preceding FindChampionIndex function illustrates the syntax for a formal parameter that is a procedure or a function. Namely, first establish a signature for the parameter in a type declaration. Then merely insert a variable of that signature type into the formal parameter list of the procedure or function. When a procedure or function is invoked requiring that a procedure or function be supplied as an actual parameter, it is *only the name* of the procedure or function that is furnished in the actual parameter list—not the name along with parameters it may require. This is the reason we invoked our generalized FindChampionIndex function as

```
FindChampionIndex(X, Low, High, GreaterThan)
```

using only the name GreaterThan as the actual parameter.

There is one further (pedagogic) note we wish to make about the FindChampionIndex function. The commentary appearing to the right of the brace next to FindChampionIndex is illustrative of a technique called *graphic documentation*, which we will frequently use to clarify algorithms when purely textual commentary is not enough.

Example 1.1   Suppose that an array of customer records for a bank is defined by the following **type** and **var** declarations.

```
type
  CustomerRec: record
                 IDNumber: integer;
                 Balance: real
               endrecord;
  CustomerList: array [IndexLimit] of CustomerRec;
var
  Customers: CustomerList;
```

Indicate how the FindChampionIndex function could be used to find the index position of the bank customer with the largest balance.

Define ElementType to be equivalent to CustomerRec via the declaration:

```
type
  ElementType: CustomerRec;
```

Then define an appropriate function with signature of type Comparison to compare two customer records.

```
function BetterCustomer
  ( given C1, C2: CustomerRec (* Two arbitrary customer records *);
    return: boolean            (* True if customer C1 has a larger
                                  balance than C2 *) );
  start BetterCustomer
    BetterCustomer := C1.Balance > C2.Balance
  end BetterCustomer;
```

Finally, assuming that NumberOfCustomers is a variable that keeps track of the number of customer records currently in the array Customers, call on FindChampionIndex as follows:

```
FindChampionIndex(Customers, 1, NumberOfCustomers, BetterCustomer)
```

This completes our discussion of PSEUDO—the language we will be using to describe all the algorithms in the text. It places heavy emphasis on procedure/function interfaces stated in terms of pre- and postconditions. It also encourages procedural abstraction by allowing procedures and functions to appear as parameters. As you work with PSEUDO, do not worry about syntactical details. Concentrate instead on the problem you are trying to solve in the most general way possible—that's where the real challenge lies!

Exercises 1.1

1. Can a fixed-iteration (**for**) loop in PSEUDO always be replaced by a **repeat** loop that is guaranteed to be equivalent in its execution? If so, provide a general scheme. If not, provide a rationale.

2. Write a PSEUDO procedure that will invert the order of elements in an array.

3. Write a PSEUDO procedure that receives three values and returns them arranged with the "best" value first and "worst" value last. Here "best-worst" is determined by a parameter given to the procedure.

4. Write a PSEUDO procedure that will accumulate the entries in an array. To "accumulate" could mean to form a sum or a product. The caller of the procedure should be able to pass in the specified operation. Be sure to specify any assumptions in your preconditions for the procedure to allow for this generality.

5. Write a **repeat** loop that is always equivalent in its execution to the **while** loop given in the example accompanying Control Construct III. (Hint: Use an **if**.)

1.2 ALGORITHM EFFICIENCY AND THE SORTING PROBLEM

As we pointed out in the opening paragraphs of this chapter, from a practical perspective the measure of the efficiency of an algorithm is achieved by analyzing the efficiency with which its implementation utilizes a computer's time and memory (or space). By space efficiency, we mean the amount of memory an algorithm consumes when it runs. As for time efficiency, at first glance one would expect this to mean the amount of time it takes the algorithm to execute; however, there are several reasons why such an absolute measure is not appropriate:

- The execution time of an algorithm is sensitive to the amount of data that it must manipulate and typically grows as the amount of data increases.

- The execution times for an algorithm when run with the same data set on two different computers may differ because of the execution speeds of the processors.

- Depending on how an algorithm is implemented on a particular computer (choice of programming language, use of a compiler or interpreter, etc.), one implementation of an algorithm may run faster than another, even on the same computer and with the same data set.

In our opening remarks we observed that an algorithm is one of the *abstractions* that a computer scientist studies. Consequently, in assessing the efficiency of an algorithm's runtime we want to remove all implementation considerations from our analysis and focus on those aspects of the algorithm that most critically affect this execution time. We noted that one of these is the number of data items the algorithm manipulates. Typically, the rest of the analysis consists of trying to determine how often a critical operation (e.g., a comparison, data interchange, or addition or multiplication of values) or sequence of such operations gets performed in manipulating these data items. This count, expressed as a function of a variable N that provides an indicator of the size of the set of data items, is what represents the "running time" of the algorithm.

Consider the following two examples of nested loops intended to sum each of the rows of an $N \times N$ array A, storing the row sums in a one-dimensional array Sum and the overall total in GrandTotal.

Version 1

```
GrandTotal := 0;
for K := 1 to N do
  Sum[K] := 0;
  for J := 1 to N do
    Sum[K] := Sum[K] + A[K, J];
    GrandTotal := GrandTotal + A[K, J]
  endfor
endfor
```

Version 2

```
GrandTotal := 0;
for K := 1 to N do
  Sum [K] := 0;
  for J := 1 to N do
    Sum[K] := Sum[K] + A[K, J]
  endfor;
  GrandTotal := GrandTotal + Sum[K]
endfor
```

If we analyze the number of addition operations required by these two versions, we see that Version 2 is better in this respect. Because Version 1 incorporates the accumulation of GrandTotal into its inner loop, it requires $2N^2$ additions. That is, the additions Sum[K] + A[K, J] and GrandTotal + A[K, J] are each executed N^2 times, for a total of $2N^2$. Version 2, on the other hand, accumulates GrandTotal after the inner loop; hence it requires only $N^2 + N$, which is less than $2N^2$ for any N greater than 1. Version 2 is apparently guaranteed to execute faster than Version 1 for any nontrivial value of N. As a final observation, we point out that the variable N being used in our analysis is merely an indicator of the number of data items being manipulated (namely N^2) rather than giving the actual number of data items.

Note also that "faster" here may not have much significance in the real world of computing. Assuming a hypothetical computer that allows us to store a 1,000 by 1,000 array and that executes at a microsecond per instruction, Version 1 would require two seconds to perform its addition; Version 2 would require just over one second. On a 100,000 by 100,000 array, Version 1 would crunch numbers for slightly under six hours and Version 2 would take about three hours. Although Version 2 is certainly better from an aesthetic perspective, it may not be good enough to be appreciably different from a user's perspective. That is, in situations where one version will respond within seconds, so will the other. Conversely, when one is annoyingly slow, the other will be also. For the 1,000 by 1,000 array, both versions would be fast enough to allow their use in an interactive environment. For the 100,000 by 100,000 array, both versions would dictate an overnight run in batch mode since an interactive user will be no more willing to wait three hours than six hours for a response.

In terms of the order of magnitude of run time involved, these versions should not be considered significantly different. *Order of magnitude* is an expression used by scientists in loosely comparing two values. Traditionally, two positive values A and B are of the same order of magnitude if the ratio of the larger to the smaller is less than $10 : 1$. On the other hand, value A would be k orders of magnitude greater than value B if the ratio of A to B is between $10^k : 1$ and $10^k + 1 : 1$. However, the reliance on powers of 10 for determining the ranges for these ratios is frequently relaxed and other ranges used instead. For example, for time measurements, seconds, minutes, hours, days, months, and years could be used to assess orders of magnitude. Under this progression, an hour would be two orders of magnitude above a second rather than the three orders the traditional method would yield.

Considerations such as these have led computer scientists to use a method of algorithm classification that makes more precise the notion of order of magnitude as it applies to time and space considerations. This method of classification, typically referred to as *big-O notation* (in reference to "on the order of"), hinges on the definition given in the following section.

Big-O Notation

Suppose there exists a function $f(n)$ defined on the nonnegative integers such that the number of operations required by an algorithm for an input of size n, say $T(n)$, is less than some constant C times $f(n)$ for all sufficiently large values of n. That is, there is a positive integer M and a constant C such that for all $n \geq M$ we have $T(n) \leq Cf(n)$. Such an algorithm is said to be an $O(f(n))$ algorithm relative to the number of operations it requires to execute. Similarly, we could classify an algorithm as $O(f(n))$ relative to the number of memory locations it requires to execute. The constant C is known as the *constant of proportionality* of the order relationship.

Consider the algorithms discussed earlier for summing the elements of the $N \times N$ array. For the Version 1 algorithm we calculated its run time to be $T(N) = 2N^2$ for all N; hence, with $C = 2$ in the definition of big-O, we see that $T(N) = O(N^2)$. For the Version 2 algorithm, whose run time we calculated as $N^2 + N$, we note when $N \geq 1$, we have $N \leq N^2$, so that $N^2 + N \leq N^2 + N^2 = 2N^2$. Thus, this algorithm is also $O(N^2)$.

Essentially, the definition of $O(f(n))$ as applied to the run time of an algorithm states that, up to a constant factor, the function $f(n)$ gives an upper bound on how the algorithm is performing for large n; saying in effect that as n gets larger, the growth in execution time will be no worse than that shown by $f(n)$. What the definition does not say is how good this upper bound is. For example, though the Version 1 and Version 2 algorithms just analyzed were both $O(N^2)$, we could just as well have said they were $O(N^3)$, since when $N \geq 2$ we have $2N^2 \leq N^3$; similarly they are $O(N^4)$, or $O(N^2 \log_2 N)$, and so forth. In order for the statement $T(N) = O(f(N))$ to be meaningful, it must therefore be understood that f is the "smallest" such function that can be used. In practice, the manner in which f is determined in the analysis of an algorithm normally ensures this minimality, but there are algorithms for which such minimal functions are currently unavailable (see the discussion of the Shell sort in Section 1.4).

Two questions merit further discussion at this stage.

How well does the Big-O notation provide a way of classifying algorithms from a real-world perspective? To answer this question, consider Table 1.1. This table presents some typical $f(n)$ functions we will use to classify algorithms and their order of magnitude run time for an input of size 10^5 on our hypothetical computer. From this table, we can see that an $O(n^2)$ algorithm will take hours to execute for an input of size 10^5. The number of hours is dependent upon the constant of proportionality in the definition of the big-O notation. Regardless of the value of this constant of proportionality, however, a categorization of an algorithm as an $O(n^2)$ algorithm has achieved a very practical goal: we now know that, for an input of size 10^5, we cannot expect an immediate response for such an algorithm. Moreover, we know that, for a reasonably small constant of proportionality, we have an algorithm for which submission as an overnight job would be practical. That is, unlike an $O(n^3)$ algorithm, we could expect the computer to finish executing our algorithm in a time frame that would be acceptable, if it could be scheduled to not interfere with other uses of the machine. On the other hand, an $O(n^3)$ algorithm applied to a data set of this size would be completely impractical.

Two other observations on using big-O notation to classify algorithms should be mentioned. The first pertains to the use of the phrase "for all sufficiently large values of n," in our definition of big-O. This highlights the fact that there is usually little difference in the choice of an algorithm if n is reasonably small. For example, almost any sorting algorithm would sort 100 integers instantly. Second, the constant of proportionality used to establish that an algorithm's run-time efficiency is $O(f(n))$ is crucial only for comparing algorithms that share the same function $f(n)$; it makes almost no difference when comparing algorithms whose $f(n)$'s are of different magnitudes. It is therefore appropriate to say that the function $f(n)$ dominates

$f(n)$	Order of magnitude run time for input of size 10^5 (assuming proportionality constant $k = 1$ and one operation per microsecond)	
$\log_2 n$	2×10^{-5}	second
n	0.1	second
$n \log_2 n$	2	seconds
n^2	3	hours
n^3	32	years
2^n		centuries

TABLE 1.1
Some typical $f(n)$ functions.

the run-time performance of an algorithm and characterizes it in its big-O analysis. The following example should help clarify this situation.

Consider two algorithms L_1 and L_2 with run times equal to $2n^2$ and n^2 respectively. The constants of proportionality of L_1 and L_2 are 2 and 1 respectively. The dominating function $f(n)$ for both of these algorithms is n^2, but L_2 runs twice as fast as L_1 for a data set of n values. The different sizes of the two constants of proportionality indicate that L_2 is faster than L_1. Now suppose that the function $f(n)$ for L_2 is n^3. Then, even though its constant of proportionality is half of what it is for L_1, L_2 will be frustratingly slower than L_1 for large n. This latter comparison is shown in Figure 1.1.

How does one determine the function $f(n)$ that categorizes a particular algorithm? We will give an overview of that process here and later illustrate it more fully by doing actual analyses for two sorting algorithms. In general, the run-time behavior of an algorithm is dominated by its behavior in any loops it contains. Hence, by analyzing the loop structures of an algorithm, we can estimate the number of run-time operations required by the algorithm as a sum of several terms, each dependent on n, the indicator of the number of items being processed by the algorithm. That is, we are typically able to express the number of run-time operations (and, for that matter, the amount of memory) as a sum of the form

$$f_1(n) + f_2(n) + \cdots + f_k(n)$$

It is also typical that we identify one of the terms in this expression as the *dominant term*. A dominant term is one that for bigger values of n, becomes so large that it allows us to ignore all the other terms, from a big-O perspective. For instance, suppose that we had an expression involving two terms, such as $n^2 + 6n$. The n^2 term dominates the $6n$ term since, for $n \geq 6$, we have

$$n^2 + 6n \leq n^2 + n^2 = 2n^2$$

Thus, $n^2 + 6n$ would lead to an $O(n^2)$ categorization because of the dominance of the n^2 term. In general, the problem of big-O categorization reduces

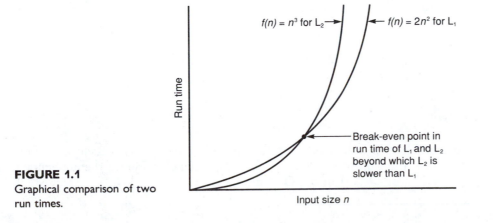

FIGURE 1.1

Graphical comparison of two run times.

to finding the dominant term in an expression representing the number of operations (or amount of memory) required by an algorithm.

Example I.2   Use big-O notation to analyze the time efficiency of the following PSEUDO fragment in terms of the integer N.

```
for K := 1 to N / 2 do
   .
   .
   .
   for J := 1 to N * N do
      .
      .
      .
   endfor;
   .
   .
   .
endfor;
```

   Since these loops are nested, the critical operations for this analysis will be those within the innermost loop—they are the ones that will execute most often. Operations within the innermost loop will each execute N^2 times whenever the innermost loop executes. We see in fact that this innermost loop will execute $N/2$ times. Consequently, the critical operations for this algorithm will execute $(N/2)(N^2)$, or $N^3/2$, times. It follows then that the run-time efficiency of this algorithm is $O(N^3)$ in big-O terms, with a constant of proportionality equal to $\frac{1}{2}$.

Example I.3   Use big-O notation to analyze the time efficiency of the following PSEUDO fragment in terms of the integer N.

```
for K := 1 to N / 2 do
   .
   .
   .
endfor;
for J := 1 to N * N do
   .
   .
   .
endfor;
```

Since one loop follows the other, the number of operations executed by both of them is the sum of the individual loop efficiencies. Hence the efficiency is $N/2 + N^2$, or $O(N^2)$ in big-O terms.

Example 1.4 Use big-O notation to analyze the time efficiency of the following PSEUDO fragment in terms of the integer N.

```
K := N;
while K > 1 do
    .
    .
    .
    K := K / 2      (* integer division *)
endwhile;
```

Since the loop control variable is cut in half each time through the loop, the number of times that statements inside the loop will be executed is measured by $\log_2 N$. For instance, if N is 64, then the loop will be executed for the following values of K.

$$64$$
$$32$$
$$16$$
$$8$$
$$4$$
$$2$$

Note that this yields six loop iterations, that is, $\log_2 64$. For values of N that are not precisely a power of 2, the number of loop iterations will be the smallest integer greater than $\log_2 N$. In any case, the run-time efficiency of this algorithm is $O(\log_2 N)$.

Table 1.2, which lists frequently occurring dominant terms, will prove helpful in our future big-O analyses of algorithms. It is worthwhile to characterize briefly some of the classes of algorithms that arise from the dominant terms listed in Table 1.2. Algorithms whose efficiency is dominated by a $\log_a n$ term (and hence are categorized as $O(\log_a n)$) are often called *logarithmic algorithms*. Since $\log_a n$ will increase more slowly than n itself, logarithmic algorithms are generally very efficient. Algorithms whose efficiency can be expressed in terms of a polynomial of the form

$$a_m n^m + a_{m-1} n^{m-1} + \cdots + a_2 n^2 + a_1 n + a_0$$

TABLE 1.2

Common dominant terms in expressions for algorithmic efficiency based on the variable n.

n dominates $\log_a n$; a is often 2
$n \log_a n$ dominates n; a is often 2
n^m dominates n^k when $m > k$
a^n dominates n^m for any values of a and m greater than 1

are called *polynomial algorithms*. Since the highest power of n will dominate such a polynomial, such algorithms are $O(n^m)$. The only polynomial algorithms we will discuss in this book have $m = 1$, 2, or 3; they are called *linear, quadratic*, and *cubic* algorithms, respectively.

Algorithms with efficiency dominated by a term of the form a^n are called *exponential algorithms*. These algorithms are of more theoretical than practical interest because they cannot reasonably be run on typical computers for moderate or large values of n. We will not encounter algorithms in the exponential and $n \log_a n$ categories until we study recursion in Chapter 6. At that time, we will develop some additional principles for analyzing such algorithms. The relationships between all of these various classes of algorithms are graphically summarized in Figure 1.2.

The Sorting Problem

Stated generally, the sorting problem requires that one take a given sequence of items (perhaps presented as an array or a sequential file) and reorder them so that an item and its successor satisfy a prescribed ordering relationship (for example, greater than or less than). Here we will apply the concepts of big-O analysis to determine the efficiency of two sorting algorithms.

For the purposes of discussion, we can use the following PSEUDO interface to specify the pre- and postconditions for the sorting problem when the items to be sorted appear in an array.

FIGURE 1.2

Relationships in run time required between commonly occuring classes of algorithms.

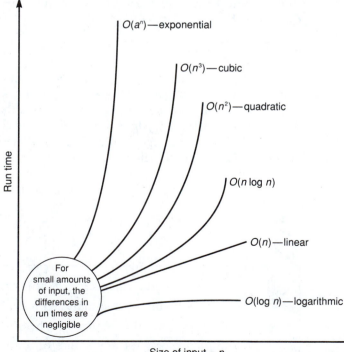

```
type (* Assume IndexLimit is constant determining array size *)
  ElementType: (* May be anything with an order relationship between
                 elements *);
  ElementArray: array [IndexLimit] of ElementType;
  Comparison: function
               ( given A, B: ElementType   (* Values to compare *);
                 return: boolean            (* true if A precedes B in the order
                                              relationship on ElementType, false
                                              otherwise *) );

procedure Sort
  ( given A: ElementArray          (* Array with at most IndexLimit
                                      entries *);

          N: integer               (* Number of entries. Assume
                                      1 <= N <= IndexLimit *);

          Precedes: Comparison     (* An order relationship on elements
                                      in A *);

    return A: ElementArray         (* The array of values arranged in
                                      order according to Precedes
                                      relation *) );
```

Selection Sort

A simple solution to the sorting problem specified above is the *selection sort* algorithm. This algorithm repeatedly finds the position of the entry that should come first from among array positions $K, K + 1, \ldots, N$. This entry is then exchanged with the entry in position K. Hence, as K runs from 1 to $N - 1$, we *select* the entry that belongs in the first position and swap it there, then the entry which belongs in the second position and swap it there, and so on (thus the name *selection sort*). The action of this sorting algorithm on a small array is illustrated in Figure 1.3. In this figure we assume that the Precedes relation is the usual *less than* relation between integers. Hence, the five-element array is arranged in ascending numerical order after four passes.

It is apparent from this figure that sorting an array of N elements will require $N - 1$ passes through the array, with one less comparison needed to select the appropriate entry on each successive pass. We may bury the internal logic of each pass in a call to the function FindChampionIndex discussed in Section 1.2, thereby enhancing the procedure's degree of abstraction.

```
procedure Sort (* Selection sort *)
  ( given  A: ElementArray         (* Array with at most IndexLimit
                                      entries *);

          N: integer               (* Number of entries. Assume 1 <= N
                                      <= IndexLimit *);

          Precedes: Comparison     (* An order relationship on elements
                                      in A *);

    return A: ElementArray         (* The array of values arranged in order
                                      according to Precedes relation *) );

  var K, FirstAmongRest: integer;
```

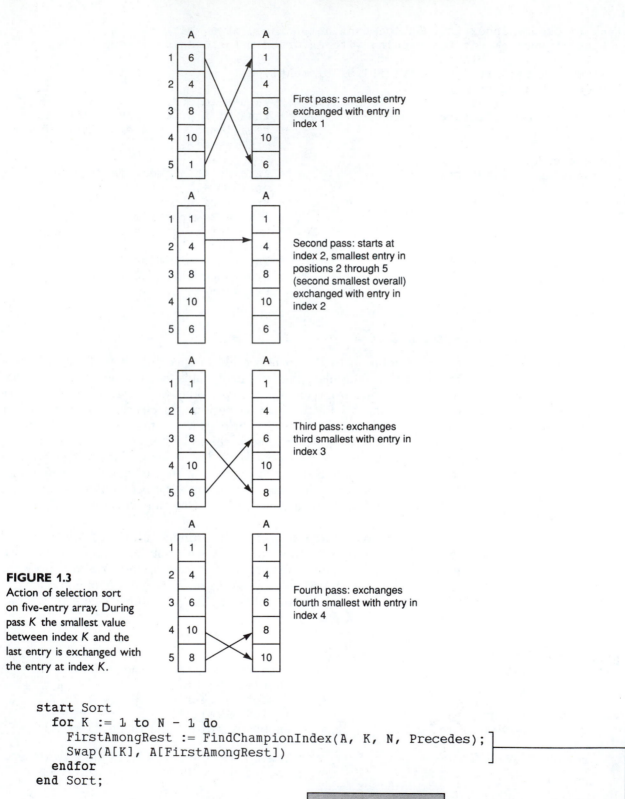

FIGURE 1.3
Action of selection sort on five-entry array. During pass *K* the smallest value between index *K* and the last entry is exchanged with the entry at index *K*.

First pass: smallest entry exchanged with entry in index 1

Second pass: starts at index 2, smallest entry in positions 2 through 5 (second smallest overall) exchanged with entry in index 2

Third pass: exchanges third smallest with entry in index 3

Fourth pass: exchanges fourth smallest with entry in index 4

```
start Sort
  for K := 1 to N - 1 do
    FirstAmongRest := FindChampionIndex(A, K, N, Precedes);
    Swap(A[K], A[FirstAmongRest])
  endfor
end Sort;
```

See the illustration at the top of page 29.

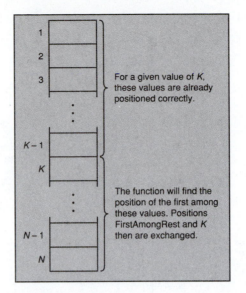

Insertion Sort

Selection sort is blind to the original order of the array being sorted. That is, the number of comparisons required to sort the array will be the same whether the array's initial state is sorted, almost sorted, randomized, or completely reversed. This property of selection sort is attributable to its use of **for** loops in both the Sort procedure and the subordinate FindChampionIndex function. Hence, neither of these loops can be short-circuited (i.e., terminated normally, but earlier than expected) when an array or a portion of an array is already ordered.

Insertion sort attempts to overcome this deficiency using logic similar to what we use in arranging a hand of playing cards dealt one card at a time. Given that we are holding $K - 1$ cards already arranged in order and are dealt a Kth card, we scan the $K - 1$ cards in our hand, seeking the position to insert the new card. This process is illustrated in Figure 1.4. With some luck we may not have to examine all (or even a significant portion) of the cards in our hand before finding the insertion slot for the new card. This will potentially reduce the number of comparisons made by insertion sort vis-à-vis selection sort. The action of insertion sort on the array of numbers from Figure 1.3 is portrayed in Figure 1.5. Here we scan the sorted portions of the array from bottom to top.

Note that only one comparison is made on the first, second, and third passes in Figure 1.5. Only in the final pass would the number being inserted have to be compared to all previous values in the array. This dependency of the number of comparisons on the original order of the data is reflected in the inner **while** loop of the following PSEUDO procedure for insertion sort.

FIGURE 1.4

Insertion sort logic in arranging playing cards.

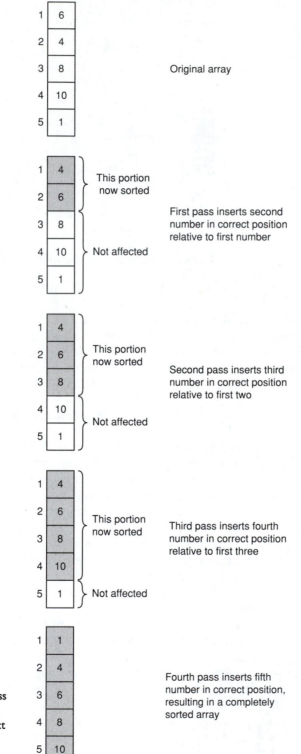

FIGURE 1.5
Tracing the action of insertion sort. During pass K the $(K+1)$th number is inserted into its correct position relative to the first K.

```
procedure Sort (* Insertion sort *)
  ( given A: ElementArray        (* Array with at most IndexLimit entries *);
         N: integer              (* Number of entries. Assume 1 <= N <= IndexLimit *);
         Precedes: Comparison    (* An order relationship on elements in A *);
    return A: ElementArray        (* The array of values arranged in order according
                                     to Precedes relation *) );

  var K, J: integer;
      Done: boolean;

  start Sort (* Insertion sort *)
    for K := 2 to N do            (* On pass K - 1, insert Kth element *)
      J := K;
      Done := false;              (* When (J - 1)th element precedes Jth element,
                                     we know it is appropriately positioned *)

      while J >= 2 and not Done do
        if Precedes(A[J], A[J - 1]) then
          Swap(A[J], A[J - 1]);
          J := J - 1
        else                      (* We know array is now sorted in first K
                                     positions *)

          Done := true
        endif
      endwhile
    endfor
  end Sort;
```

Array at beginning
of the *K*th stage

```
   1   2   3  · · ·  K–1  K
 ┌───┬───┬───┬───┬───┬───┬───┬───┬───┐
 │   │   │   │   │   │   │   │   │   │
 └───┴───┴───┴───┴───┴───┴───┴───┴───┘
```

Sorted   Unsorted
              *K*th element inserted in its
              rightful place among
              first *K* entries
              on (*K*–1)st pass

Big-O Analysis of Selection Sort Recall that the loop structure of the selection sort algorithm was given by

```
for K := 1 to N - 1 do
  FirstAmongRest := FindChampionIndex(A, K, N, Precedes);
  Swap(A[K], A[FirstAmongRest])
endfor
```

where N represents the number of values being sorted. Observe that the first time FindChampionIndex is executed, the comparison in the **if** statement of this subordinate procedure will be made $N - 1$ times. Then it will be made $N - 2$ times, $N - 3$ times, and, finally, just one time. Hence, the number of comparisons will be the sum of the sequence of numbers

$$N - 1$$
$$N - 2$$
$$\cdot$$
$$\cdot$$
$$\cdot$$
$$1$$

A well-known formula from algebra shows this sum to be

$$N(N - 1)/2$$

Thus we conclude that selection sort is an $O(N^2)$ algorithm, in terms of the number of comparisons it must make.

Although selection sort is $O(N^2)$, we note that it is $O(N)$ in the number of times it must swap data items because they are not swapped until after the internal loop of FindChampionIndex is executed. This minimization of data interchanges is one of selection sort's strengths and can be particularly important when the cost of an interchange is high vis-à-vis the cost of a comparison. For instance, this would be the case if we were sorting an array of large records and the Precedes relationship was determined by comparing integer key fields within two records. The integer comparison would be a very fast operation on all computers, but interchanging two large records would actually result in a machine language loop whose cost would not be apparent in the high-level, algorithmic language. This illustrates how the choice of an algorithm for an actual application must always be tied to the realities of the machine on which the algorithm will eventually run.

Big-O Analysis of Insertion Sort   Because selection sort is blind to the original order of data in an array, it is always $O(N^2)$ in the number of comparisons it makes, where N is the number of values being sorted. Insertion sort, on the other hand, may occasionally fare better because of its inner **while** loop. That is, for insertion sort, we expect different levels of performance for different original orderings of the array being sorted. Hence, an efficiency discussion of insertion sort should really analyze the behavior of the algorithm from three perspectives—the worst case, the best case, and the average case.

For insertion sort, it is evident that the worst case is an array that is completely reversed in its original order. Under these circumstances, the boolean variable Done, which controls insertion sort's inner loop, is never set to true. Hence, on the first pass through the inner loop one comparison is made, on the next pass two comparisons, then three, until $N - 1$ comparisons are made on the last pass. The sum of the number of comparisons is precisely the same as for selection sort, and we conclude that insertion sort is $O(N^2)$ in its worst case.

In its best case, insertion sort receives an array that is ordered to start with. Under these circumstances, the inner loop is always exited after one comparison. Hence only $N - 1$ comparisons are necessary to verify the sorted array, and the algorithm is determined to be $O(N)$ in this case.

However, the best and worst cases represent extremes. Perhaps a more relevant question is how we can expect insertion sort to behave on the average. An exact analysis of this case requires the use of probability theory; however, a satisfactory intuitive analysis can be achieved by starting with the quite reasonable expectation that on average an item being inserted would have to be compared to half of the already sorted items before finding its niche. This means that the number of comparisons in this average case is half of the number in the worst case. Since the average case is proportional to the worst case, we conclude that insertion sort is $O(N^2)$ in its average performance.

Selection	Insertion sort
Always performs $O(N^2)$ comparisons.	In its average case, $O(N^2)$ comparisons. However, its constant of proportionality is roughly half that of selection sort.
No best case; that is, no difference among cases.	$O(N)$ comparisons and interchanges in its best case.
No worst case; that is, no difference among cases.	Equivalent to selection sort in the worst-case number of comparisons, plus considerably more data interchanges.
Always $O(N)$ data interchanges.	$O(N^2)$ data interchanges in worst and average cases.

TABLE 1.3
Comparison of time efficiencies: selection sort and insertion sort.

Our big-O analysis of the selection and insertion sort algorithms has thus led us to the conclusion that, overall, there is no order-of-magnitude difference between the two algorithms. However, during the course of this analysis, we have also identified some relatively significant differences in the algorithms. These differences are summarized in Table 1.3.

Exercises 1.2

1. Trace the contents of the array

18	90	40	9	3	92	6

as the selection sort algorithm would manipulate it into ascending order. To "trace" means to show the contents of the array each time two values are interchanged.

2. Repeat Exercise 1 for the insertion sort algorithm.

3. An improved insertion sort algorithm can be obtained if, instead of employing element "swaps," one employs element "moves." In this latter case, one inserts the value of element K into its proper position with respect to the previous $K - 1$ elements by starting at element $K - 1$ and copying it and the values of each of its predecessors into their respective succeeding elements until one encounters an element, say at position J, whose value precedes that of the original value of element K. One then copies the original value at location K into location $J + 1$. Write a PSEUDO algorithm for this version of the insertion sort and do a big-O efficiency analysis as we did for the version of insertion sort that uses element swaps.

4. (Bubble Sort) The bubble sort is another sorting algorithm typically covered in introductory computer science courses. The general idea behind the bubble sort is to make repeated passes through the array and on each pass compare the value of each element in the array with that of its successor. If the

Procedure and Function Parameters in Actual Programming Languages

The use of procedures or functions as formal parameters to increase the generality of a module is a technique that is often skipped in introductory computer science courses. You may be wondering whether the ability to do this is available in real programming languages as well as purely algorithmic languages like PSEUDO. Fortunately, the answer to this question is yes. Most modern languages (for example, Pascal, C, C++, Modula-2, and Ada) offer some form of parameter that may be a procedure or function. For instance, the PSEUDO procedure Sort, which receives a Precedes function parameter to determine the sort order, could be incorporated into a standard Pascal program as follows:

```pascal
program ProcedureParameter(input, output);

   (* Demonstrate the use of procedure parameters in
      Pascal *)

const
   IndexLimit = 100;

type
   ElementType = integer;
   ElementArray = array [1..IndexLimit] of ElementType;

var
   Size, J: integer;
   Data: ElementArray;

function GreaterThan      (* Used as the actual parameter
                             for Precedes *)
   ( A, B: ElementType    (* Values to compare *) )
        : boolean         (* Return true if A > B *);
   begin
     GreaterThan := (A > B)
   end;  (* GreaterThan *)

procedure Sort            (* Insertion sort algorithm *)
   ( var A: ElementArray  (* Array of values to be returned
                             in order according to Precedes
                             relation *);
        N: integer        (* Number of values in array.
                             Assume 0 <= N <= IndexLimit *);
     (* In standard Pascal, the function parameter's
        signature appears within the formal parameter
        list, as illustrated below *)
     Precedes: function
               ( A, B: ElementType (* Values to
                                      compare *)
                    : boolean      (* Return true if A
                                      precedes B in
                                      order relationship
                                      on ElementType *) );
```

```pascal
var K, J, Temp: integer;
    Done: boolean;

begin  (* Insertion sort *)
  for K := 2 to N do
    begin
      J := K;
      Done := false;
      while (J >= 2) and not Done do
        if Precedes(A[J], A[J - 1])
          then
            begin
              Temp := A[J];
              A[J] := A[J - 1];
              A[J - 1] := Temp;
              J := J - 1
            end
          else
            Done := true
    end  (* for *)
end;  (* Sort *)

begin (* Main program to demonstrate procedure call to
         sort in descending order *)
  write('How many values to sort? ');
  readln(Size);
  for J := 1 to Size do
    read(Data[J]);
  readln;
    (* Sample call to produce a sort of integers in
       descending order *)
  Sort(Data, Size, GreaterThan);
  for J := 1 to Size do
    write(Data[J]);
  writeln
end
```

In the preceding example, we have illustrated how Pascal would allow a call to the generalized Sort procedure that would produce an integer array sorted in descending order. The array is sorted in descending order because GreaterThan is passed as the actual function parameter for the formal function parameter Precedes.

Appendix C briefly discusses, for several languages, the syntax governing passage of parameters that are procedures or functions. You will certainly find a more comprehensive treatment in any thorough text on your particular programming language. Our Pascal example has shown that such use of parameters is possible in actual programs as well as in PSEUDO descriptions of algorithms. We encourage you to use this powerful technique when developing modules in your favorite language. It will allow you to re-use such modules in a wider variety of contexts—thereby achieving a higher degree of procedural abstraction.

two values are not in the proper order, they are swapped. The array will be completely sorted when no swaps are made during a pass. Write a PSEUDO version of this algorithm. Then subject your PSEUDO procedure to a big-O efficiency analysis as we did for the selection and insertion sorts. Compare bubble sort's best, average, and worst case performance to those of the other two algorithms.

5. Do a big-O analysis for those statements inside each of the following nested loop constructs.

```
a. for K := 1 to N do
      for J := 6 to N do
         .
         .
         .
      endfor
   endfor
b. for K := 1 to N do
      J := N;
      while J >= 1 do
         .
         .
         .
         J := J / 2      (* integer division *)
      endwhile
   endfor
c. K := 1;
   repeat
      J := 1;
      repeat
         .
         .
         .
         J := 2 * J
      until J >= N;
      K := K + 1
   until K >= N
```

6. An algorithm has an efficiency $O(n^2|\sin(n)|)$. Is it any better than $O(n^2)$ for large integer n?

7. Suppose that each of the following expressions represents the number of logical operations in an algorithm as a function of n, the size of the list being manipulated. For each expression, determine the dominant term and then classify the algorithm in big-O terms.

a. $n^3 + n^2 \log_2 n + n^3 \log_2 n$

b. $n + 4n^2 + 4^n$

c. $48n^4 + 16n^2 + \log_8 n + 2^n$

8. Consider the following nested loop construct. Categorize its efficiency in terms of the variable N using big-O notation. Finally, suppose the statements represented by the ellipsis require four main memory accesses (each requiring one microsecond) and two disk file accesses (each requiring one millisecond).

Express in milliseconds the amount of time this construct would require to execute if N were 1,000.

```
X := 1;
repeat
  Y := N;
  while Y > 0 do
    .
    .
    .
    Y := Y - 1
  endwhile;
  X := X + X
until X > N * N;
```

9. A sorting algorithm is called *stable* if it does not change the relative order of array elements that are equal. For example, a stable sorting algorithm will not place 13_1 after 13_2 in the array

18	13_1	6	12	13_2	9

Are insertion sort and selection sort stable? If not, provide an example of an array with at least two equal elements that change in their order relative to each other.

1.3 ALGORITHM EFFICIENCY—THE SEARCH PROBLEM

In the previous section, we introduced big-O notation and used it to analyze two algorithmic solutions to the sorting problem. In this section we will examine a general strategy for solving the search problem—finding a particular value in an ordered array. As in Section 1.2, we may more formally state this problem as a PSEUDO interface expressed in precondition/postcondition form.

```
type (* Assume IndexLimit is constant determining array size *)
  ElementType: (* May be anything with an order relationship between elements *);
  ElementArray: array [IndexLimit] of ElementType;
  Comparison: function
                ( given A, B: ElementType    (* Values to compare *);
                  return: boolean            (* true if A precedes B in order
                                                relationship on ElementType;
                                                false otherwise *) );
  SplittingFunc: function
                ( given Hi, Lo: integer    (* 1 <= Lo <= Hi <= IndexLimit *);
                  return: integer          (* Lo <= returned value <= Hi *) );

procedure Search
  ( given A: ElementArray              (* Array with at most IndexLimit
                                          entries ordered by Precedes
                                          parameter *);
```

```
         N: integer              (* Number of values in array. Assume
                                     0 <= N <= IndexLimit *);
    Target: ElementType          (* Value being sought in array *);
    Precedes: Comparison         (* A function parameter for comparing
                                     values in ElementArray *);
       Split: SplittingFunc      (* A function parameter used to determine
                                     a splitting point in array A *);
  return Found: boolean          (* Set to true if Target can be found in A *);
         Place: integer          (* The index location of Target in A
                                     if Found is true. Undefined if
                                     Found is false *) );
```

The Precedes and Split parameters in the Search interface require some explanation. If we do not assume that the array being searched is ordered, these two parameters are not needed. However, we prefer to work under that assumption because it allows us to develop search strategies that are more efficient than a sequential search strategy. Recall that such a strategy merely examines successive locations (starting with the first) until it finds the Target or advances beyond index N.

By assuming an array that is ordered according to the Precedes relationship, we may develop a *divide-and-conquer* search strategy similar to what we use when searching for a name in a phone book. We do not search for "Smith, Sam" in a phone book by starting with the first page and examining successive pages. Rather, because the phone book is alphabetically ordered, we make a guess that the location of "Smith, Sam" will be roughly three-quarters of the way into the phone book. We open to the page designated by this guess. If "Smith, Sam" appears on this page, we are done. If the names on this page precede "Smith, Sam," we iterate this process with the portion of the phone book that follows. If the names on the page follow "Smith, Sam," we iterate with the front portion of the book. This divide-and-conquer strategy is highlighted in Figure 1.6. The Split function parameter that appears in our Search procedure interface represents the method on which our divide-and-conquer guess is based. The complete Pascal procedure for the divide-and-conquer search follows.

```
procedure Search
  ( given A: ElementArray       (* Array with at most IndexLimit entries *);
         N: integer             (* Number of values in array. Assume
                                    0 <= N <= IndexLimit *);
```

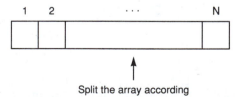

Split the array according
to some guess.

If the target follows the data at the splitting location,
work with the portion to the right of the splitting.

FIGURE 1.6

Divide-and-conquer search
strategy.

If the target precedes the data at the splitting location,
work with the portion to the left of the splitting.

```
          Target: ElementType  (* Value being sought in array *);
       Precedes: Comparison  (* A function parameter for comparing values
                                 in ElementArray *);
          Split: SplittingFunc (* A function parameter used to determine a
                                  splitting point in array A *);
  return Found: boolean      (* Set to true if Target can be found in A *);
          Place: integer      (* The index location of Target in A if Found
                                 is true. Undefined if Found is false *) );


var Hi, Lo, Guess: integer;


start Search
  Hi := N;
  Lo := 1;
  Found := false;
  while not Found and (Lo <= Hi) do
    Guess := Split(Lo, Hi);
    if A[Guess] = Target then
      Found := true;
      Place := Guess
    elsif Precedes(A[Guess], Target) then
      Lo := Guess + 1      (* Work with portion of
                              A that follows Guess *)
    else                   (* A[Guess] follows Target *)
      Hi := Guess - 1      (* So work with portion
                              of A that precedes Guess *)

    endif
  endwhile
end Search;
```

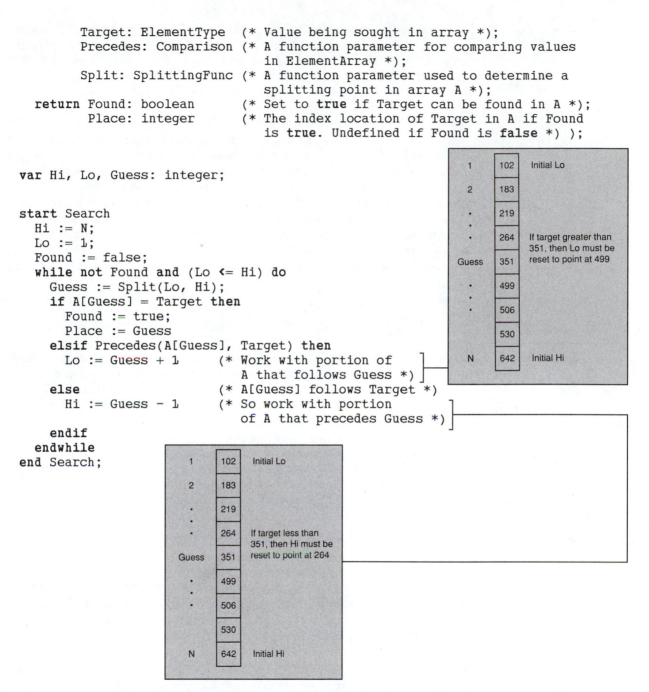

Big-O Analysis of the Divide-and-Conquer Search Strategy

Clearly the time efficiency of this search strategy is dependent on how well the Split function homes in on the Target being sought. One particular Split function that lends itself to an easy analysis is

```
Split := (Lo + Hi) / 2   (* integer division *)
```

This particular choice for a Split function is interesting because it doesn't make a truly guided guess at the location of Target but merely splits the array in half. The search algorithm that results from this choice of a Split function is called a *binary search*. From our discussion in Example 1.4, we know that such a repeated halving strategy will yield a worst-case efficiency of $O(\log_2 N)$, where N represents the number of values in the array being searched. As you will discover in the Exercises (1.3), an $O(\log_2 N)$ search algorithm will execute very quickly. This raises the question whether other divide-and-conquer strategies, which make a "better" guess based on the particular relationship between A[Lo], Target, and A[Hi], will actually outperform the binary search. Such strategies are called *interpolative*. Since these other strategies will be highly dependent on the distribution of values in the array, a comparison between them and the binary search requires more than formal big-O analysis. In the exercises you will explore some other possibilities for the Split function. The discussion in Section 1.4 will then provide you with means for analyzing these other schemes in comparison with the binary search.

Exercises 1.3

1. Suppose that you have a large database with 4 million items in an ordered array. How many probes into the list will the binary search require before finding its target or concluding that it cannot be found? Assuming it takes 1 microsecond to access an item, estimate the execution time of the binary search.

2. Why is it unrealistic to assume that the 4-million-item list of Exercise 1 would be stored in an array? More likely such a large list would have to reside in external storage, such as a random access disk file for which access times are much slower. Compute the execution time for the binary search if the list of Exercise 1 is stored in a random access file for which the time to access one record is 50 milliseconds.

3. Suppose the Split function for our search procedure is

   ```
   Split := Lo
   ```

   Describe the search strategy that results. What is its big-O time efficiency?

4. Develop a Split function that actually interpolates for an array of numerical data. That is, it should take into account the range of values between A[Lo] and A[Hi] and split the array a distance from Lo that is proportional to the relative distance between A[Lo] and Target.

5. Develop a Split function that actually interpolates for an array of alphanumeric data. That is, it should take into account the range of values between A[Lo] and A[Hi] and split the array a distance from Lo that is proportional to the relative distance between A[Lo] and Target.

6. (Fibonacci Search)   The Fibonacci sequence of numbers starts with two 1's. Thereafter, each number in the sequence is the sum of the preceding two numbers. Hence, the first seven terms of the Fibonacci sequence are

$$1, 1, 2, 3, 5, 8, 13, \ldots$$

If we suppose that the number of records N in the array being searched has the property that $N + 1$ is the kth Fibonacci number F_k for some k, then the array may be split at the F_{k-1}th record, dividing the array into subarrays of $F_{k-1} - 1$ and $F_{k-2} - 1$ records. For example, given an array of $N = 7$ records, we note that

$$N + 1 = 8 = F_6$$

whence we choose the $F_5 = 5$th record for our splitting point

$$1 \quad 2 \quad 3 \quad 4 \quad 5 \quad 6 \quad 7$$
$$\uparrow$$
Choose this as a splitting point

Notice that such a splitting strategy will result in two subarrays (index ranges 1...4 and 6...7), each of which also has the property that the number of elements in the subarray plus one is a perfect Fibonacci number. That is, if we iterate this choice of a splitting point, Hi and Lo from procedure Search will have the property that Hi − Lo + 2 is always a perfect Fibonacci number. The motivation for this splitting strategy is the hope that this iteration of splitting points will choose the smaller, right half of the array often enough to converge to the Target faster than a plain binary search. The resulting search is called a *Fibonacci search*. Discuss an appropriate initialization to ensure that the Fibonacci search works even when $N + 1$ is not a perfect Fibonacci number, and then write the Split function necessary for this search.

1.4 EMPIRICAL EFFICIENCY ANALYSIS OF ALGORITHMS

The insertion sort, selection sort, and binary search algorithms of the preceding two sections have lent themselves to a straightforward big-O analysis. Such analysis has been sufficient to categorize completely the behavior of these algorithms. However, as we study more complex algorithms, the results of merely doing a big-O analysis may not give us a sufficiently precise handle on predicting an algorithm's performance for the vast variety of data sets it will encounter. In such situations, our inability to conveniently package data sets into best-case, worst-case, and average-case categories may necessitate that we empirically observe the performance of the algorithm. For instance, strategies for developing interpolative Split functions for the Search procedure of the preceding section would have to be observed under actual run-time conditions to determine if they result in search times significantly faster than the binary search.

A sorting algorithm that similarly defies big-O analysis is the *Shell sort* algorithm. Originally conceived by D. L. Shell (*Communications of the Association of Computing Machinery*, 2, July 1959, pp. 30–32), this algorithm is inspired by the insertion sort's ability to work very fast on an array that is almost in order originally.

Instead of sorting the entire array at once, Shell sort first divides the array into smaller, noncontiguous segments, which are then separately sorted using the insertion sort. The advantage of doing this is twofold. First, whereas a comparison dictates a swap of two data items in a segment, this swap within a noncontiguous segment of the array moves an item a greater distance within the overall array than the swap of adjacent array entries in the usual insertion sort. This means that one swap is more likely to place an element closer to its final location in the array when using Shell sort than when using the simple insertion sort. For instance, a large-valued entry that appears near the front of the array will more quickly move to the tail end because each swap moves it a greater distance in the array. The second advantage of dividing the array into segments is tied to the first. That is, because early passes tend to move elements closer to their final destination than in a straight insertion sort, the array readily becomes partially sorted. The fact that the array is likely to become partially sorted earlier thus allows the embedded insertion sort logic to make more frequent use of its loop shut-off check. (Recall that this check makes the insertion sort particularly efficient for partially sorted arrays.) An example will help clarify this Shell sort rationale.

Example 1.5   Suppose we have an array A containing the following integers:

80	93	60	12	42	30	65	85	10

We first divide this into three segments of three elements each.

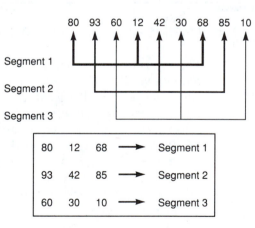

and sort each of the segments.

12	68	80	→	Segment 1
42	85	93	→	Segment 2
10	30	60	→	Segment 3

The original array, partially sorted, now appears as

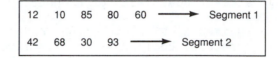

We divide this partially sorted array as

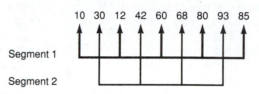

These segments are then sorted and the array A takes the form

10 30 12 42 60 68 80 93 85

Segment 1

Segment 2

Finally, this array is sorted as one segment; 12 and 30, and then 93 and 85 are swapped to give us the sorted array

10	12	30	42	60	68	80	85	93

The key to the Shell sort algorithm is that the whole array is first fragmented into segments whose elements are a distance K apart, for some number K. There will be K of these segments. If the size of the array A is N, then the segments are

$$A[1], \quad A[K + 1], \quad A[2 * K + 1], \quad \dots$$
$$A[2], \quad A[K + 2], \quad A[2 * K + 3], \quad \dots$$
$$\vdots$$
$$A[K], \quad A[2 * K], \quad A[3 * K], \quad \dots$$

Because each segment is sorted, the whole array is partially sorted after the first pass. For the next pass, the value of K is reduced, which increases the size of each segment, hence reducing the number of segments. Preferably, the next value of K is also chosen so that it is *relatively prime* to its previous value. (Two integers are said to be relatively prime to each other if they have no common factor greater than 1.) The process is finally repeated with

$K = 1$, at which point the array is sorted. The insertion sort is applied to each segment, so each successive segment is partially sorted. Consequently, the later applications of the insertion sort become very efficient, dramatically increasing the overall efficiency of the Shell sort.

To emphasize the fashion in which the Shell sort algorithm relies on the logic of insertion sort, we present a SegmentedInsertionSort procedure, which arranges segments with distance K between elements in an N-element array into ascending order.

```
type (* Assume IndexLimit is constant determining array size *)
  ElementType: (* May be anything with an order relationship between
                 elements *);
  ElementArray: array [IndexLimit] of ElementType;
  Comparison: function
              ( given A, B: ElementType (* Values to compare *);
                return: boolean        (* true if A precedes B in the order
                                          relationship on ElementType, false
                                          otherwise *) );

procedure SegmentedInsertionSort
  ( given A: ElementArray          (* Array with at most IndexLimit
                                      entries *);
         N: integer                (* Number of values. Assume
                                      1 <= N <= IndexLimit *);
         K: integer                (* Distance between elements of the
                                      same segment (as well as the number
                                      of segments). The Ith segment
                                      consists of A[I], A[I + K],
                                      A[I + 2 * K], and so on *);
         Precedes: Comparison      (* An order relationship on elements
                                      in A *);
    return A: ElementArray         (* The array with each of its K
                                      segments arranged in order according
                                      to the Precedes relationship *) );

  var
    L, J: integer;

  start SegmentedInsertionSort
    for L := K + 1 to N do
      J := L - K                            (* J counts down through
                                               current segment *)

      while J > 0 do
        if Precedes(A[J + K], A[J]) then
          (* Adjacent entries in current segment compared *)
          (* Interchange if out of order *)
          Swap(A[J + K], A[J]);
          J := J - K
        else
          J := 0                            (* To shut off J loop *)
        endif
      endwhile
    endfor
  end SegmentedInsertionSort;
```

See the illustration at the top of page 45.

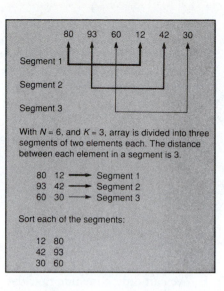

Given the SegmentedInsertionSort procedure, we now merely call on this with values of K that become successively smaller. Eventually, Segmented-InsertionSort must be called with $K = 1$ to guarantee that the array, viewed as one segment, is completely sorted.

The following procedure for Shell sort illustrates these successive calls to SegmentedInsertionSort for values of K that are repeatedly halved.

```
procedure Sort (* Shell sort *)
  ( given A: ElementArray        (* Array with at most IndexLimit entries *);
         N: integer              (* Number of entries.  Assume
                                    1 <= N <= IndexLimit *);
         Precedes: Comparison    (* An order relationship on elements in A *);
   return A: ElementArray        (* The array of values arranged in order
                                    according to Precedes relation *) );

  var K: integer;

  start Sort (* Shell sort *)
    K := N / 2;                  (* K represents current number of segments. *)
    while K > 0 do
      SegmentedInsertionSort(A, N, K, Precedes);
      K := K / 2                 (* Reduce number of segments *)
    endwhile
  end Sort;
```

Efficiency of the Shell Sort

The Shell sort is also called the *diminishing increment sort* because the value of K (the distance between elements of a segment) continually decreases. The sort will work with any decreasing sequence of values of K, as long as the last value of K is 1. There will clearly be $\log_2 N$ repetitions of Segmented-InsertionSort for the version of Shell sort that we have presented here. Within each of these repetitions, big-O analysis of the efficiency of Segmented-

InsertionSort is difficult. The outer loop of SegmentedInsertionSort is clearly $O(N)$, but the inner loop defies such a precise analysis because it is so dependent on the order of data within the segment—an order that we hope is closer to sorted as we progress through the diminishing increments. Thus, a big-O analysis of Shell sort is complicated by the following triple nested loop structure.

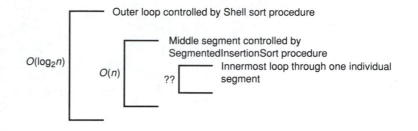

We can only conclude that the number of comparisons required by Shell sort is

$$O(A \times n \times \log_2 n)$$

where A is some unknown factor.

Experimentation with an algorithm can often be used to augment a purely formal mathematical analysis. By observing how an algorithm performs on a variety of data sets, we may be able to draw some statistical conclusions concerning its behavior. For instance, in the case of Shell sort, we counted the number of comparisons made by the algorithm for a variety of randomly generated data sets of 1,000, 3,000, and 5,000 items. We then averaged the number of comparisons required for data sets of each of these three sizes. Table 1.4 summarizes our results.

Although such results do not have the clout of a mathematical proof, they certainly lend credence to a claim that $O(N(\log_2 N)^2)$ and $O(N^{3/2})$ are reasonable estimates of the average-case behavior of Shell sort. Our results are consistent with those of many larger studies that have been done on Shell sort. (See Donald E. Knuth, *Searching and Sorting*, Vol. 3 of *The Art of Computer Programming* (Menlo Park, CA; Addison-Wesley, 1973).)

An important observation arises from the preceding discussion: computer science is *science* in the sense that we must often hypothesize a solution

Size of randomly generated data set	Average number of comparisons	Number of comparisons expressed in terms of $N \times (\log_2 N)^2$	Number of comparisons expressed in terms of $N^{(3/2)}$
1,000	14,702	$0.148 \times N \times (\log_2 N)^2$	$0.465 \times N^{(3/2)}$
3,000	57,958	$0.145 \times N \times (\log_2 N)^2$	$0.353 \times N^{(3/2)}$
5,000	109,065	$0.144 \times N \times (\log_2 N)^2$	$0.309 \times N^{(3/2)}$

TABLE 1.4   Results of Shell sort experimentation.

FIGURE 1.7
An inefficiency in the present sequence of diminishing increments: 4,2,1. Many values within the array will not be compared to each other until the increment size reaches 1.

1	2	3	4	5	6	7	8
80	70	60	50	40	30	20	10

As we attempt to sort into ascending order, none of [80, 60, 40, 20] are compared to any value in [70, 50, 30, 10] until final pass

to a problem and prove or disprove that hypothesis through experimental observation. Not all solutions can yet be verified by purely formal mathematical arguments. The exercises and programming problems/projects in this book will often encourage you to perform such exploratory analyses.

In the spirit of such exploration, we should note that the particular sequence of diminishing increments that we have chosen for our implementation of Shell sort may not be the best possible because many values within the entire array will never be compared to each other until the increment size reaches 1. This phenomenon is illustrated in Figure 1.7. In an attempt to make a greater variety of comparisons when the increment size is large (and hence array elements move a great distance), Knuth suggests choosing a sequence of diminishing increments in which successive values are relatively prime to each other. For instance, Knuth suggests a sequence of values such as $1, 3, 7, 15, \ldots$, for reverse values of K; that is, the $(J + 1)$th value is two times the Jth plus 1. You will experiment with this and other possible sequences in the exercises and programming problems that follow.

Exercises 1.4

1. Consider the Shell sort procedure given in this section. Suppose that we sort this array into ascending order and trace the contents of the array being sorted after each call to the procedure SegmentedInsertionSort. What would we see as output if we called Shell sort with the following array?

60	12	90	30	64	8	6

2. Repeat Exercise 1.4.1 for a six-element array that initially contains

1	8	2	7	3	6

3. Why is the Shell sort called by that name?

4. Why is the Shell sort more efficient when the original data are in almost-sorted order?

5. What advantage do the relatively prime values of the increments have over other values in a Shell sort?

6. What property must the sequence of diminishing increments in the Shell sort have to ensure that the method will work?

7. Provide examples of best-case and worst-case data sets for the Shell sort algorithm presented in this section.

8. Repeat Exercise 1.4.1 for the following sequence of diminishing increments: 5, 3, 1. Compare the performance of the algorithm for this sequence to that of the sequence used in this section.

9. Consider the eight-element array

80	70	60	50	40	30	20	10

   Suppose that we wish to sort this array into ascending order. Count the number of comparisons required to do this by insertion sort, by Shell sort with the sequence of diminishing increments given in this section, and by Shell sort with 5, 3, 1 as the sequence of diminishing increments.

10. Repeat Exercise 1.4.1 for the array

8	5	2	6	3	7	4	1

   using the sequence of diminishing increments 5, 3, 1.

11. Rewrite the Shell sort procedure of this section so that it works with the following sequences of diminishing increments

   a. 1, 3, 5, 9, . . . (reverse order)

   b. 1, 3, 7, 15, . . .

   c. 1, 3, 5, 11, . . .

   d. 1, 4, 13, 40, . . .

12. A sorting algorithm is called *stable* if it does not change the relative order of array elements that are equal. For example, a stable sorting algorithm will not place 13_1 after 13_2 in the array

18	13_1	6	12	13_2	9

   Is Shell sort stable? If not, provide an example of an array with at least two equal elements that change in their order relative to each other.

Chapter Summary

In this chapter we introduced the concepts that will be the foundation for the rest of our work in this book—abstraction, algorithms, data structures, abstract data types, and efficiency. *Abstraction* is the process of identifying certain properties of an object and then using these properties to specify a new object, which represents a simplification of the object from which it was derived. An *algorithm* is an abstraction of a computer program. It specifies a sequence of instructions for solving a problem in a way that is free from the constraints imposed by the architecture of any given computer. The instructions must be clear and unambiguous, must solve the problem in a finite amount of time, and must conclude when the problem has been solved.

A *data structure* is an abstraction of the data types supported by a language. Whereas the values of elementary data types are atomic, those of data structures are composites of values of both elementary data types and previously defined data structures. The definition of a data structure requires a specification of the organization of its composite values as well as any relationships that may exist between the components. An abstract data type (ADT) results when, in addition to specifying the organization and intercomponent relationships of a data structure, one specifies the complete set of operations that can be performed among objects admitting values with this structure.

The concepts of algorithms, data structures, and abstract data types come together in *implementing* an abstract data type; that is, in moving from the specification of the data type to a realization of it on a computer via the data types and instructions of a programming language for that computer. Choices must be made concerning which of the language's data types to use in representing the components of the data structure, how to represent the relationships among these components, and which algorithms to use for the operations associated with the abstract data type. To provide a means by which different implementations may be compared, *efficiency analysis*, in terms of the run time and memory utilizations of algorithms and structures, is introduced. Classifications of efficiency, in terms of the *big-O* analysis, are described.

The language in which algorithms and data structures will be described in this book is a pseudocode that reflects the features of many modern programming languages. Following a description of the PSEUDO constructs that we will need, PSEUDO algorithms for solving the sorting problem and the searching problem are given, together with a big-O analysis of each algorithm.

Key Words

abstract data type	divide-and-conquer	module
abstraction	exponential algorithms	order of magnitude
algorithm	functionally cohesive	polynomial algorithms
big-O notation	implementation	PSEUDO
binary search	insertion sort	selection sort
constant of	interface	Shell sort
proportionality	logarithmic algorithms	signature
data structure		

Programming Problems/Projects

1. Consider a list of records for students at a university. The list includes fields for student name, credits taken, credits earned, and total grade points. Write a program that, based upon a user's request, will sort the list of records in ascending or descending order keying on one of the four fields within the record. For instance, the user might specify that the sort should proceed in descending order according to credits earned. As much as possible, try to refrain from having to write a separate sort procedure for each particular ordering and field. Experiment by developing different procedures based on each of the three sorting strategies discussed in this chapter.

2. Consider the same list of records as in Problem 1. Now write a procedure to sort the records in descending order by credits earned. Records having

the same number of credits earned should be arranged in descending order by total grade points. Those with the same number of credits earned and total grade points should be arranged alphabetically by name. Incorporate this procedure into the complete program that you wrote for Problem 1. Experiment by developing different procedures based on each of the three sorting strategies discussed in this chapter.

For any or all of Problems 3–7, design a program to answer the question posed. Then analyze the time efficiency of your program in big-O terms. Run your program to try to see the relationship between big-O classification and actual run-time as measured by a clock.

3. In the first century A.D. numbers were separated into "abundant" (such as 12, whose divisors have a sum greater than 12), "deficient" (such as 9, whose divisors have a sum less than 9), and "perfect" (such as 6, whose divisors add up to 6). In all cases, the number itself is not included. For example, the only numbers that divide evenly into 6 are 1, 2, 3, and 6; and $6 = 1 + 2 + 3$.

   Write a program to list all numbers between 2 and N and classify each as abundant, deficient, or perfect. Keep track of the numbers in each class.

4. In the first century A.D. Nicomachus wrote a book entitled *Introduction Arithmetica*. In it the question "How can the cubes be represented in terms of the natural numbers?" was answered by the statement: "Cubical numbers are always equal to the sum of successive odd numbers and can be represented this way." For example,

$$1^3 = 1 = 1$$
$$2^3 = 8 = 3 + 5$$
$$3^3 = 27 = 7 + 9 + 11$$
$$4^3 = 64 = 13 + 15 + 17 + 19$$

Write a program to find the successive odd numbers whose sum equals K^3 for K having the values from 1 to N.

5. A conjecture, first made by the mathematician Goldbach, the proof of which has defied all attempts, is that "every even number larger than two can be written as the sum of two prime numbers." For example,

$$100 = 89 + 11$$
$$10 = 3 + 7$$
$$8 = 3 + 5$$
$$6 = 3 + 3$$
$$4 = 2 + 2$$

Write a program that determines for every even integer N with $2 < N$ two prime numbers P and Q such that $N = P + Q$.

6. A pair of numbers M and N are called "friendly" (or they are referred to as an "amicable pair") if the sum of all the divisors of M (excluding M) is equal to the number N and the sum of all the divisors of the number N (excluding N) is equal to $M (M \neq N)$. For example, the numbers 220 and 284 are an amicable pair because the only numbers that divide evenly into 220 (1, 2, 4, 5, 10, 11, 20, 22, 44, 55, and 110) add up to 284, and the only numbers that divide evenly into 284 (1, 2, 4, 71, and 142) add up to 220.

Write a program to find at least one other pair of amicable numbers. Be prepared to let your program search for some time.

7. A consequence of a famous theorem (of the mathematician Fermat) is the fact that

$$2^{(P-1)} \bmod P = 1$$

for every odd prime number P. An odd positive integer K satisfying

$$2^{(K-1)} \bmod K = 1$$

is called a pseudoprime. Write a program to determine a table of pseudoprimes and primes between 2 and N. How many pseudoprimes occur that are not prime numbers?

8. Design a program that allows you to experiment with the various Split functions discussed in Section 1.3. Your program should allow you to

   a. Enter an array interactively,

   b. Load an array from a text file, or

   c. Randomly generate data for an array.

   Sort the array so that the Search procedure of Section 1.3 applies. Then the program should allow you to search for specific Target values using the binary Split function, the Fibonacci Split function (see Exercise 6 from Section 1.3), and other interpolative Split functions (see Exercises 4 and 5 from Section 1.3; you may have to add the array as a parameter for the Split function). As the Search is conducted, your program should count the number of comparisons necessary to find the Target or it should conclude that the target is not in the array. Use the program to conduct an empirical comparative analysis between the various Split functions. Present the results of this analysis that includes a statistical table and a write-up in which you state your conclusions regarding the relative efficiencies of the methods. Save your program so that it can be extended as we discuss other solutions to the Search problem in future chapters.

9. Design a program that allows you to experiment with the selection, insertion, and Shell sort procedures described in this chapter. The program should allow you to

   a. Enter an array interactively,

   b. Load an array from a text file, or

   c. Randomly generate an array.

   You should be able to enter the method(s) by which the array should be sorted. If Shell sort is one of the methods chosen, allow entry of the sequence of diminishing increments. The program should then sort the array for each of the methods chosen and count the number of comparisons and data interchanges required for each method. Use the program to conduct an empirical comparative analysis that includes a statistical table and write-up in which you state your conclusions regarding the relative efficiencies of the algorithms. Pay particular attention to various sequences of diminishing increments for the Shell sort.

10. In Exercise 4 of Section 1.2, you developed a procedure to implement the bubble sort algorithm. The logic of this algorithm allows for an early loop exit as soon as the array under consideration falls into sorted order. Because

of this, Shell sort may also be implemented using array segments that are sorted by bubble sort instead of insertion sort.

Develop a version of Shell sort that uses an underlying bubble sort procedure on array segments. Run this version of Shell sort against that based on insertion sort for a variety of data sets, counting the number of operations performed by each version of the algorithm. Write a statement, backed by your empirical findings, in which you summarize the relative performance of the two algorithms. If one algorithm seems to perform better than the other, be sure to explain why.

2

DATA: ABSTRACTION AND STRUCTURE

Does it contain any abstract reasoning concerning quantity or number? No. Does it contain any experimental reasoning, concerning matter of fact and existence? No. Commit it then to the flames: for it can contain nothing but sophistry and illusion.

David Hume

CHAPTER OUTLINE

In the first chapter we emphasized an abstract approach to describing algorithms and how this approach increases the potential for an algorithm to be applicable in a variety of contexts. The question we raise in this chapter is the following: can an abstract approach in describing data yield a similar benefit? As an initial step in answering this question, in Section 2.1 we reexamine the concept of an abstract data type (ADT), which we introduced in Section 1.1. Examples of abstract data types—matrices, strings, pointers, and sets—are then discussed in Sections 2.1, 2.2, 2.3, and 2.4, respectively. For each of these examples, we show how to define that data type in a way that will allow many alternate implementations. Some of these implementations are discussed in this chapter. Other, more efficient implementations will be developed in subsequent chapters as we study more advanced techniques. It is critical to realize, however, that whatever implementation we use, it must fit the original definition of the particular abstract data type.

2.1 ABSTRACT DATA TYPES

In an age when we are increasingly dependent upon computer software, it is important that we design software systems that are reliable, flexible, expandable, efficient, and verifiable. Clearly, these are nontrivial goals. How can we have a reasonable chance of attaining them? The evolution of the answer to this question indicates how far the young discipline of computer science has progressed. In the late 1950s and early 1960s there was a widely held belief that designing effective software systems was something akin to an occult art. That is, those who succeeded in designing such systems did so by virtue of a variety of mysterious reasons. Their success, as opposed to the high percentage of software designers who failed, was somewhat mystical—similar to the spark of unfathomable inspiration that separates a great painter from a doodler.

Software Engineering

This view of successful software designers began to change in the latter part of the 1960s. We discovered that such designers seemed to use a methodology similar to an engineer's approach to problem solving. What characterizes this engineering approach? To answer the question, consider the various phases involved in the successful development of a complex structure such as a bridge. First, the engineer meets with the people (often laypersons) who want the bridge built and learns about its intended function: is it to be part of a heavily traveled urban freeway or a one-lane country road? From such meetings, the engineer develops a conceptual picture of the bridge. This picture is an abstract entity in the engineer's mind or perhaps exists in very rough form on paper. At this stage the engineer is working with ideas and ignoring most physical construction details.

The next steps allow the engineer to come successively closer to the tangible implementation of the bridge. A miniature prototype of the bridge will be built. This model will allow the engineer to come face-to-face with many potential construction problems. It also provides a way to check whether the bridge will serve the needs specified by those who originally wanted it built. This prototype will be followed by the development of detailed plans in blueprint form. Again, this represents a step away from the purely abstract bridge toward its actual implementation. These blueprints provide the essential details to the contractor, and the contractor completes the entire process by implementing the engineer's plans in the physical structure of the bridge.

As we review the engineering approach, three important points should be made.

1. The entire process that culminates in the building of the bridge is a series of refinements from an abstract view of the bridge to its tangible implementation. This process parallels closely the phases in the development of a successful software system, beginning with a purely conceptual view of the problem and culminating with the implementation of a solution in program code.

2. This engineering approach truly places the emphasis on design issues. The design process is a very creative endeavor. Typically, during the design process, engineers try out various combinations of possible options and frequently change their minds about many significant aspects of the overall design. The opportunity for such experimentation exists when the design is still in abstract form and when such creative considerations are possible—even encouraged—because of the openness of the conceptual model. As the model draws nearer to actual implementation, a myriad of details specific to the chosen implementation make similar "what-if" reasoning expensive and often impossible, for all practical purposes.

3. The engineering approach encourages prototyping—building systems that, from outward appearances, appear to be finished. But why do such prototypes rely on underlying modules that may perform a task in some relatively inefficient way? Because developing such a prototype can be achieved easier and faster than developing a completely efficient system and a prototype has the advantage of allowing prospective users to interact with the system and to voice their pleasure or displeasure with it. This allows the engineer to get some early feedback on the system—a factor critical in the overall design process. If users are pleased with the prototype, the engineer can then concentrate on replacing the quickly developed, inefficient modules with modules that optimize the overall performance of the system. Critical in this fine-tuning phase is the ability to "plug in" a new module for a particular function in a way that doesn't require tampering with the rest of the system.

As early software developers analyzed frequent programming failures, they looked to the already established field of engineering for a paradigm. The engineering methodology of successively refining abstract models toward an eventual implementation made sense as an approach to developing complete data structures. A system designer who decides too quickly how to implement a data structure in the code of a particular computer language is analogous to an engineer who allows construction of a bridge to begin before adequate planning has been done. Both are heading for final results that are inelegant and riddled with serious flaws. However, because of the more rigorous design methodology intrinsic for years to their profession, engineers have not found themselves in this predicament as often as did programmers. The solution seemed obvious: attempt to apply a similarly rigorous methodology to the discipline of computer science. Hence, software engineering has developed into an important area of study within computer science. It represents an attempt to apply the structured methods of engineering to software development. Its goal is to ensure that software is produced in a way that is cost-effective and sufficiently reliable to deserve the increasing trust we are placing in it.

Abstract Data Types—Concepts and the Matrix ADT

If we are to approach the development of a complex data structure as an engineer would approach the development of a bridge, it is critical that we initially view the data from an abstract perspective. We want to specify the data types apart from considerations regarding their implementation. This separation of a data type's specification from declarations that implement the data type in a particular language is the essence of data abstraction. It turns out that some abstract data types will have very easy implementations in your favorite language. For others, their implementations will be much less direct. At this stage of our problem analysis, we don't want language considerations to influence our solution to the problem. Such considerations should come later, after we have accurately described the problem. The specification of an *abstract data type* involves three factors.

1. A description of the elements that compose the data type.
2. A description of the relationships between the individual components in the data type.
3. A description of the operations that we wish to perform on the components of the data type.

Note that all three factors are language-independent. An abstract data type is a formal description of data elements and relationships as envisioned by the software engineer; it is thus a conceptual model. Ultimately this model must be implemented in an appropriate computer language via declarations for the elements and relationships and via instructions (often in the form of procedure/function calls) for the operations. At an even deeper level, the implementation is translated by the compiler into a representation in an assembler language. An assembler then translates this representation into a physical, electronic representation on a particular computer.

This hierarchy of levels of abstraction is illustrated in Figure 2.1. As much as possible, each level in this hierarchy should be shielded from details of the levels that appear below it. Consider, for instance, the separation between the definition of an abstract data type and its implementation in a computer language. There may be several ways to implement a given abstract data type. Each implementation will carry its own collection of declarations, instructions, and, possibly, limitations. This collection should form a cohesive package that meets all the specifications in the definition of the abstract data type. From the perspective of the abstract data type, we are not concerned with the details of how the data relationships and instructions are implemented in this package; we are concerned only that they meet the specification of the definition. Indeed, keeping implementation details of an abstract data type out of its specification as much as possible (known as information hiding) will make it relatively easy to interchange one package of declarations and instructions with another package implementing the same abstract data type. Such interchangeability is desirable when we want to evaluate and compare the performance characteristics of several implementation strategies for

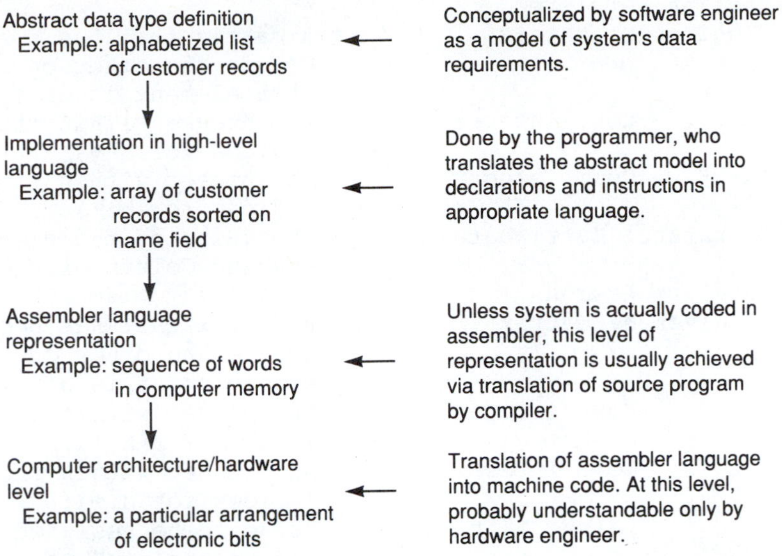

FIGURE 2.1
Levels of abstraction in
specifying data.

a given abstract data type. Similarly, in situations where a prototype system
has been developed quickly to obtain user feedback, interchangeability is
critical as the prototype is transformed into an efficiently running system
based on more complex implementations of the critical data structures. Thus,
the term *information hiding* describes the ability of a package to meet the
specifications of an abstract data type in a self-contained fashion, allowing use
of the package without having to know how it achieves the implementation.

Example 2.1 To illustrate the separation between the specification of an ADT and its implementations, we will begin by considering the familiar notion of a matrix.

• **Definition:** The ADT *matrix* is a collection of data items of the same type,
MatrixData, arranged as a rectangular grid. Any entry in the grid may be
specified by giving its row and column position. The rows and columns
themselves are each indexed by a separate contiguous range of the integers.
The operations performed on a matrix are

```
procedure Create
  ( given M: Matrix        (* An arbitrary matrix variable M in an
                              unknown state *);
    return M: Matrix       (* The matrix M returned as an initialized
                              empty matrix, that is, no defined values
                              assigned to any row/column locations *) );

procedure Destroy
  ( given M: Matrix        (* An arbitrary matrix variable M that has
                              been acted upon by Create and other
                              operations *);
    return M: Matrix       (* The matrix M returned in an undefined
                              state, with storage dynamically
                              allocated for M now available for future
                              invocations of Create *) );
```

```
function Retrieve
  ( given M: Matrix          (* A matrix that has been acted upon by
                                Create and other operations and in which
                                each element is of type MatrixData *);
          Row: integer       (* An integer within the range of row
                                indices for M *);
          Col: integer       (* An integer within the range of column
                                indices for M *);
       return: MatrixData    (* The value of the element at the specified
                                Row and Column of M *) );
procedure Assign
  ( given M: Matrix          (* A matrix that has been acted upon by
                                Create and other operations and in which
                                each element is of type MatrixData *);
          Row: integer       (* An integer within the range of row
                                indices for M *);
          Col: integer       (* An integer within the range of column
                                indices for M *);
          Value: MatrixData  (* Value to be assigned to designated row
                                and column of M *);
       return M: Matrix      (* The matrix M with Value assigned to
                                designated row and column *) );
```

Observe from this example that the three factors involved in an ADT's definition have all been carefully specified.

- Description of elements—only restriction is that all elements be of the same type
- Relationships between individual components—specified by row-column coordinate system
- Operations—specified as set of PSEUDO interfaces

All ADT definitions should appear in this three-factor format. From the perspective of some application that uses the ADT, the interfaces to the ADT operations are of paramount importance. They define *everything* that the application can do with the ADT. The Create and Destroy operations are provided for virtually all ADTs. The Create operation is used to initialize each ADT variable and should always be called prior to using any other operations on such a variable. The Destroy operation is called when an application is finished with a particular ADT variable. This operation will release storage that was dynamically allocated to the variable, thereby enabling such storage to be reallocated to other variables.

From the perspective of implementing an ADT, we must work below the level of the interface. That is, the interface tells us the preconditions and postconditions that the operation must satisfy. In our implementation, we are free to do anything provided that the end result meets the specified conditions in a way that is transparent to an application using the particular operation. This is the essence of information hiding. The implementation completely shields users of the ADT from any hint of how the details of the ADT definition are being fulfilled. Users of the ADT are able to work at a completely conceptual level, only concerning themselves with the formal definition of the ADT.

Implementing the Matrix ADT

The matrix ADT has a straightforward implementation in most programming languages. According to our description of PSEUDO in Chapter 1, we could merely declare a two-dimensional array such as

```
var
   Numbers: array [6, 5] of MatrixData;
```

If MatrixData is integer, then a sample assignment of values to the matrix Numbers is pictured in Figure 2.2.

From the perspective of a programmer in a high-level language, the preceding PSEUDO declaration gives us a direct way to implement a matrix. Through the notation Numbers[Row, Col] we can write the Retrieve and Assign operations as

```
Retrieve := Numbers[Row, Col]
```

and

```
Numbers[Row, Col] := Value
```

respectively. However, from the perspective of the compiler writer, a matrix declaration represents a level of abstraction because, internally, computer memory is not arranged as a rectangular grid. Instead, computer memory locations are arranged in a linear sequence beginning with location 0, and then 1, 2, 3, and so on. Because of this, there must be manipulations made behind the scenes when a program requests the entry in the fifth row and fourth column of a matrix (as highlighted in Figure 2.2). Essentially, the coordinates of the fifth row and fourth column must be transformed into an address within this linear sequence of memory locations. The nature of the transformation is dependent upon how the designers of the compiler have chosen to implement the application programmer's mental image of rows and columns within the linear sequence of memory locations.

	1	2	3	4	5
1	10	18	42	6	14
2	13	19	8	1	44
3	63	80	12	90	51
4	16	13	9	8	4
5	12	11	12	14	83
6	1	4	18	99	90

FIGURE 2.2

Values in the matrix Numbers.

Suppose that our compiler has chosen to store the 30 entries in the two-dimensional array Numbers as indicated in Figure 2.3. According to this arrangement, the first row would take up the first five locations; the second row, the next five locations; and so on. The entry in the fifth row and fourth column would in fact be located in the twenty-fourth position within the list.

In this array the Kth row and the Jth column must be transformed into the (NumCols × (K − 1) + J)th entry in the linear list, where NumCols represents the number of columns. At an even deeper level, this position in the linear list of Figure 2.3 must be transformed into the address of a particular word within the memory of the computer. This latter translation will be highly dependent upon the addressing techniques of the computer and the nature of the data elements in the matrix. Most high-level computer languages implement two-dimensional (and higher) arrays in the manner just described (known as *row-major* form, since the rows are stored one after the other) and do so in a way largely hidden from the applications programmer. However, all programmers should be aware that multidimensional arrays are inherently less efficient than one-dimensional arrays because of the computations required by the transformation from row/column coordinates to linear address each time an entry in the array is accessed. Such a transformation is often called a *mapping function*.

If you have programmed in FORTRAN, you will recall that when initializing a two-dimensional array via a DATA statement, the entries for the array must be listed by column; that is, first column, second column, and so on. FORTRAN is one of the few high-level languages to store a multidimensional array in column-major order (that is, the columns are stored one after the other), as indicated in Figure 2.4.

To access the entry in the Kth row and the Jth column of a two-dimensional array stored in column-major order, the transformation

$$\text{NumRows} \times (J - 1) + K$$

is required; NumRows represents the number of rows in the array. The fact that this transformation requires the number of rows but not the number of columns explains why many FORTRAN compilers insist that a subroutine be

| 10 | 18 | 42 | 6 | 14 | 13 | 19 | 8 | 1 | 44 | 63 | 80 | 12 | 90 | 51 | 16 | 13 | 9 | 8 | 4 | 12 | 11 | 12 | 14 | 83 | 1 | 4 | 18 | 99 | 90 |

FIGURE 2.3   Linear storage of data from the matrix Numbers of Figure 2.2. The data is stored in row-major form. This means the first row of Numbers takes up the first five locations; the second row the next five locations; and so on.

| 10 | 13 | 63 | 16 | 12 | 1 | 18 | 19 | 80 | 13 | 11 | 4 | 42 | 8 | 12 | 9 | 12 | 18 | 6 | 1 | 90 | 8 | 14 | 99 | 14 | 44 | 51 | 4 | 83 | 90 |

FIGURE 2.4   Column-major storage of data from the matrix Numbers of Figure 2.2. Here, the first column of Numbers takes up the first six locations; the second column, the next six; and so on.

informed of the number of rows in an array passed from a calling program but not the number of columns.

The Sparse Matrix Problem

From what has been said about the compiler's possible implementation strategy for a two-dimensional array, it should be clear that we might be paying a very high price in memory when the matrix manipulated by our program has a large percentage of locations that are one uniform value. Such matrices are said to be *sparse matrices*. This happens in many scientific and economic applications. Often the nonzero values in such matrices tend to cluster around the diagonal, resulting in a *band matrix* such as that illustrated in Figure 2.5.

The drawback of the standard row- and column-major implementations of such matrices is that a large percentage of space used in storing the matrix is dedicated to storing many copies of the uniform value that makes the matrix sparse. For large matrices, this may result in the compiler's allocation of memory for the matrix extending beyond the space limitation of the actual machine. In such situations we may have to resort to an alternate implementation of the matrix ADT. However, regardless of the implementation we choose, we are still working with a matrix at the abstract level.

An Alternate Implementation of a Sparse Matrix Let us assume that the value occurring a large percentage of time in a sparse matrix is zero. We are seeking an implementation that will conserve memory by not actually storing the high percentage of zero entries that appear in the conceptual matrix. One possibility is simply to store a list of ordered triples: the first entry in the triple is a row number, the second is a column number, and the third is the value at that row and column of the matrix. One of these triples is on the list for each nonzero entry in the conceptual matrix. Conversely, a zero entry in the conceptual matrix does not get a triple (row, column, value) on the list. Hence, a probe into the Kth row and the Jth column of the conceptual matrix returns the associated nonzero value if an appropriate search algorithm can find the pair (K, J) on the list representing the matrix; it returns zero otherwise. What have we gained? For each nonzero value in the conceptual matrix we now must store three values—so there is actually a loss in this regard. However, for the much higher percentage of zero values, we now store absolutely nothing on the list.

FIGURE 2.5

Example of sparse band matrix. Note how the nonzero values are clustered around the diagonal.

	1	2	3	4	5	6	7	8	9	10	11	12	13	14
1	0	83	19	40	0	0	0	0	0	0	0	0	0	0
2	0	0	0	91	0	42	12	0	0	0	0	0	0	0
3	0	0	0	0	0	18	4	0	0	0	0	0	0	0
4	0	0	0	0	0	0	0	0	71	64	0	13	0	0
5	0	0	0	0	0	0	0	0	0	0	0	0	21	40

The example, exercises, and problems that follow have you explore this suggested implementation for a sparse matrix. In designing a system based on this implementation, you will discover certain run-time inefficiencies that can be at least partially overcome by the implementations we will introduce in Chapters 3 and 11.

Example 2.2   The following declarations would provide a suitable basis for implementing the sparse matrix of mostly zeroes in the fashion just discussed. The constant MaxNonZeroEntries represents the maximum number of nonzero entries that this implementation will allow.

```
type
  MatrixData: (* A numeric data type *);
  SparseMatrixRec: record
                    R, C: integer;        (* Row and column *)
                    Value: MatrixData   (* Non-zero value at that
                                           row and column *)
              endrecord;
  Matrix: record
          Count: integer;                 (* Stores number of nontrivial
                                             values *)
          Entry: array [MaxNonZeroEntries] of MatrixData
        endrecord;
```

Assuming an appropriate implementation of the Create operation, which initialized the Count field to zero, the following function could be used to implement the Retrieve operation for the sparse matrix.

```
function Retrieve
  ( given M: Matrix       (* A matrix that has been acted upon by Create
                            and other operations and in which each
                            element is of type MatrixData *);
          Row: integer    (* An integer within the range of row indices
                            for M *);
          Col: integer    (* An integer within the range of column indices
                            for M *);
       return: MatrixData (* The value of the element at the specified Row
                            and Column of M *) );

  var K: integer;
      Found: boolean;

  start Retrieve
    Found := false;
    K := 1;
    while not Found and K <= M.Count do
      if M.Entry[K].R = Row and M.Entry[K].C = Col then
        Found := true
```

```
    else
       K := K + 1
    endif
 endwhile;
 if Found
    then
       Retrieve := M.Entry[K].Value
    else
       Retrieve := 0
 endif
end Retrieve;
```

Exercises 2.1

1. Explain the meaning of the term *information hiding*. In what sense does the sparse matrix implementation of Example 2.2 hide information?

2. Show by an example how the row-major and column-major implementations for a two-dimensional array would differ.

3. What would the mapping function be for a three-dimensional matrix implemented in row-major form? Can you generalize this to matrices of higher dimensions?

4. Is a two-dimensional M by M array more efficient or less efficient than a one-dimensional array of extent M^2? Explain your answer.

   Exercises 5–9 refer to the alternate implementation for a sparse matrix, discussed at the end of this section and in Example 2.2.

5. Given the declarations and implementation of the Retrieve operation in Example 2.2, write the procedure for the Create, Destroy, and Assign operations.

6. Rewrite the implementation of the Retrieve operation in Example 2.2 to use a version of the binary search algorithm. How must your answer to Exercise 5 change to accommodate this?

7. Using big-O notation, analyze the time efficiency of the Retrieve and Assign operations you have implemented in Exercise 6.

8. Analyze the space efficiency of the sparse matrix implementation you have provided in your answers to Exercise 6 versus a row-major implementation of the same matrix. What percentage of values would have to be zero for your implementation to be more space-efficient than a row-major implementation?

9. How should the sparse matrix implementation discussed at the end of this section be adjusted for boolean data?

10. Suppose that PSEUDO did not have a **record** data type, but only an **array** type. Explain how you could still implement the record as an abstract data type under such circumstances. To do this, you must first provide an adequate definition of **record** as an ADT and then specify how your implementation would allow all of the record operations you have specified in your definition. (Hint: any elementary data type can be represented as a sequence of characters that are transformed to the appropriate internal data representation when operations such as arithmetic are performed with the data.)

2.2 THE STRING ADT

In the previous section we considered the matrix ADT—a data type for which most programming languages provide a complete implementation. We will now consider an ADT for which a full set of operations is not provided by most languages. This is the string ADT, defined as follows:

- **Definition:** A *string* is a sequence of characters. The characters in a string are related in linear fashion with an identifiable first element, second element, and so on. The operations associated with the string ADT are

```
procedure Create
  ( given S: String              (* An arbitrary string variable S in an unknown
                                     state *);
    return S: String             (* S as an initialized empty string *) );

procedure ReadAString
  ( given S: String              (* A previously created string S with
                                     arbitrary contents *);
    return S: String             (* S, with contents read from some input source;
                                     assume that the characters from this input
                                     source are terminated by some standard
                                     delimiter, which is not stored as part of the
                                     string *) );

procedure WriteAString
  ( given S: String              (* A previously created string S with arbitrary
                                     contents. The contents are written to some
                                     standard output source *) );

procedure Assign
  ( given Source: String         (* A string whose contents are to be copied
                                     to Destination *);
    return Destination: String   (* Contains a copy of Source *) );

function Length
  ( given S: String              (* An arbitrary string S *);
    return: integer              (* The number of characters in S *) );

procedure Concatenate
  ( given S, T: String           (* Two arbitrary strings *);
    return S: String             (* The result of appending the contents of
                                     T to S *) );

procedure Substring
  ( given S: String              (* An arbitrary string *);
        Start: integer           (* Represents a position within S *);
        Len: integer             (* A length for a substring of S *);
    return T: String             (* That portion of S beginning at Start
                                     and ending at Start + Len - 1. If
                                     Start + Len - 1 > Length(S), then stop at
                                     last character in S. If Start > Length(S)
                                     or Len = 0, then T is empty *) );

function Search
  ( given Master,
        Sub: String              (* Two strings with Sub potentially contained
                                     in Master *);
```

```
         Start:integer           (* Represents a character position in Master;
                                     Master is to be searched for Sub from this
                                     position onward *);
   return: integer               (* The position of the first occurrence of Sub
                                     in Master at position Start or after. Zero
                                     returned if Sub is not found in this portion
                                     of Master *) );

procedure Insert
   ( given S, T: String          (* Two arbitrary strings *);
         Place: integer          (* The position where T is to be inserted in
                                     S *);
   return S: String              (* S, with T inserted at position Place; if
                                     Place is greater than Length(S), S is not
                                     altered *) );

procedure Delete
   ( given S: String             (* An arbitrary string *);
         Start, Number: integer  (* A starting position in S and a number
                                     of characters to delete from S,
                                     beginning at that position *);
   return S: String              (* The given string with the designated
                                     characters removed; if the number of
                                     characters specified extends beyond
                                     Length(S), delete only through the
                                     end of the string *) );

function Equal
   ( given S, T: String          (* Two arbitrary strings *);
   return: boolean               (* true if S and T match, character for
                                     character; false otherwise *) );

function LessThan
   ( given S, T: String          (* Two arbitrary strings *);
   return: boolean               (* true if S precedes T in alphabetical order;
                                     false otherwise *) );

function GreaterThan
   ( given S, T: String          (* Two arbitrary strings *);
   return: boolean               (* true if S follows T in alphabetical order;
                                     false otherwise *) );
```

Figure 2.6 portrays examples of some of the operations specified for strings. Strings find wide-spread application in such diverse areas as text editing, computer-assisted instruction, and language processing.

Example 2.3   To give some idea of how the string ADT and its operations could be used in a program, consider an application in which a user is to enter a master string and a target string, and the program is to print the master string with *all* occurrences of the target string removed. Hence, if the master string were "BAA-BAA BLACK SHEEP" and the target string were "BAA", the program should respond with "- BLACK SHEEP". A main program that uses string operations to achieve this is given by the following:

```
var
   Master, Target: String;
   Pos: integer;
```

Concatenate: The contents of string T are appended to those of string S

S	T	yields	S
"BIRD"	"DOG"	$\longrightarrow$	"BIRDDOG"

Substring: T comprises the five characters of string S between locations three and seven.

S	Start	Len	yields	T
"TALE OF TWO CITIES"	3	5	$\longrightarrow$	"LE OF"

Search: Returns the position of the first occurrence of the string Sub in string Master at position Start or after.

Master	Sub	Start	yields	
"MODERN BASEBALL HISTORY"	"BASEBALL"	1	$\longrightarrow$	8

Insert: Inserts the contents of string T into string S, starting at location 5 of S.

S	T	Place	yields	S
"SALT PEPPER"	"AND "	5	$\longrightarrow$	"SALT AND PEPPER"

Delete: Removes nine characters from string S, starting with the fifth character of S.

S	Start	Number	yields	S
"SALT AND PEPPER"	5	9	$\longrightarrow$	"SALTER"

FIGURE 2.6

Examples of string operations.

```
start Main
  Create(Master);
  Create(Target);
  ReadAString(Master);
  ReadAString(Target);
  Pos := Search(Master, Target, 1);
  while Pos <> 0 do
    Delete(Master, Pos, Length(Target));
    Pos := Search(Master, Target, Pos)
  endwhile;
  WriteAString(Master)
end Main;
```

This example illustrates an important point about abstract data types. It is entirely possible to discuss an application that uses abstract data types without ever knowing anything about how those ADTs are implemented. This is the essence of information hiding—*complete* separation of the use of an ADT from its implementation. This separation is so critical that we specify the following rule:

ADT Use Rule

Applications that use an ADT may access variables of that type only through the operations provided in the ADT definition.

Compliance with this rule ensures that the application can use *any* implementation of the ADT because implementations must obey a corresponding rule:

ADT Implementation Rule

An implementation of an ADT must provide an interface that is entirely consistent with the operations specified in the ADT's definition.

In the discussion that follows, we shall show how two different implementations of the string Search operation can be developed in accordance with this ADT Implementation rule. Because they are developed in accordance with the rule and because the main program of Example 2.3 obeys the ADT Use rule, either of these implementations could be invoked from the main program without the need to alter the main program *at all*.

Fixed-Length Implementation of the String ADT

One way of implementing a string is to store the sequence of characters in an array. Thus, we seemingly could declare

```
type
    String: array [MaxStringSize] of character;
```

where MaxStringSize is an appropriately defined constant. There are several problems with this implementation, however.

First, since most strings will likely not have MaxStringSize as their length, computing the length of a string could be a costly operation—one

---

A RELEVANT ISSUE

Object-Oriented Programming—The Evolution of ADTs

The programming paradigm that emerged during the 1970s was *structured programming*. This included emphasis on the use of procedures and the elimination of GOTO statements. It is reflected in the programming languages presently in widespread use—for example, Pascal, C, and Modula-2.

The programming paradigm that emerged during the 1980s is often called *object-oriented programming*. This style of programming places heavy emphasis on the use of libraries of procedures/functions that embody operations on various abstract data types. Once developed, these libraries can be used in many applications, so that the code for these ADT implementations never needs to be reinvented. In applications using these ADTs, specific instances of an ADT are called *objects*—hence, the terminology *object-oriented*.

Object-oriented programming also places great emphasis on the ability to interchange implementations of an ADT without having to change the applications. As programmers develop more complex data structures that inherit operations from one ADT to use in implementing another ADT (as we suggest in the union-find ADT of this chapter), the capacity of a programming language to provide complete and transparent interchangeability among implementations of an ADT becomes a very sophisticated issue in language design. Some of the languages that have emerged under the object-oriented paradigm are Object-Oriented Pascal, C++, Objective C, Smalltalk, Eiffel, Actor, and Trellis-Owl. Stay tuned! In the 1990s, you'll no doubt have to become familiar with such languages to remain current. A good source to begin your exploration of such languages is Brad Cox's *Object-Oriented Programming: An Evolutionary Approach*, (Reading, MA: Addison-Wesley, 1986).

that involves padding the array with spaces after the end of the string and then searching backward through the array for the first nonspace character. To avoid this inefficiency in the Length function, it is better to continually maintain a counter that stores the number of characters currently in the string. In effect, the string itself is now two items—the array of characters and the length counter. Since the interface to a String provided by the ADT definition will not allow us to require two parameters in passing information for one string, we must *encapsulate* this information in the data type; that is, we must bundle into a record all data items necessary to implement the string in this fashion.

```
type
  String: record
            CharData: array [MaxStringSize] of character;
            Length: integer
          endrecord;
```

Only through encapsulation can we provide an interface that meets the specifications of the ADT definition.

A second problem persists with this implementation despite the encapsulation of the data type. The length of strings is limited by MaxStringSize. Moreover, if most strings are considerably shorter than MaxStringSize, a large amount of space will be wasted in each string. That is, the implementation can be very space-inefficient. These drawbacks are inherent in the method; it represents an imperfect implementation of the ADT. Because of the limitations on string length, this implementation is called the *fixed-length implementation of strings*. You are charged for a fixed amount of space regardless of the length of your string. To overcome these particular space inefficiences, we will need to examine different implementations in Programming Problem 7 and Section 3.6.

Fixed-Length Strings and the Search Operation

You will explore writing most of the string operations for this implementation in the exercises. However, the Search operation merits some special discussion because it has spawned several interesting algorithms. We will first consider a straightforward approach to this algorithm and then examine how we can dramatically improve its worst-case efficiency.

Straightforward String Search

The general flavor of the algorithms we will discuss is given by the following loop structure.

Initially, align Sub string against leftmost portion of Master string;
repeat
    Do *a character-by-character comparison of Sub against Master*
        until you can conclude match or no match;
    if *no match* **then**
      realign Sub to the right against a new portion of Master
    endif
until *match found or no match possible*;

Before refining this statement of the algorithm, we will use Figure 2.7 to trace its execution for the straightforward approach. In this figure, we are searching the master string "KOKOMO" for the Sub string "KOM". Aligning "KOM" against the leftmost portion of Master, we realize that they do not match after three individual character comparisons. Realignment in the straightforward approach is simply sliding the Sub string one position to the right in the Master string. This is done in the second snapshot of Figure 2.7. We compare "OKO" from Master with "KOM" and realize that they do not match after one individual character comparison. Once more Sub is realigned one position to the right in Master, and this time a match is found.

The complete PSEUDO algorithm for this straightforward approach is

```
function Search              (* Straightforward algorithm *)
  ( given Master,
          Sub: String        (* Two strings with Sub potentially contained
                                in Master *);
          Start:integer      (* Representing a character position in Master. Master
                                is to be searched for Sub from this position onward *);
      return: integer        (* The position of the first occurrence of Sub in Master
                                at position Start or after; zero returned if Sub is
                                not found in this portion of Master *) );

  var
    M, S: integer;

  start Search
    M := Start;
    S := 1;
    while S <= Length(Sub) and Length(Sub) <= (Length(Master) - Start  + 1) do
      if Master.CharData[M] = Sub.CharaData[S] then (* Current characters match *)
        M := M + 1;
        S := S + 1
```

FIGURE 2.7
Straightforward version of Search ("KOKOMO", "KOM", 1). If after a character-by-character comparison of Sub against its current alignment in Master a mismatch occurs, Sub is realigned by moving it one position to the right in Master. This is repeated until a complete match occurs (here, beginning at position three in Master) or until we conclude that no match is possible.

```
                                      1 2 3 4 5 6
                 Snapshot 1   Master : K O K O M O
                              Sub    : K O M
                                          ↑
                              Mismatch in
                              position 3

                                      1 2 3 4 5 6
                 Snapshot 2   Master : K O K O M O
                              Sub    :   K O M
                                          ↑
                              Mismatch in
                              position 2

                                      1 2 3 4 5 6
                 Snapshot 3   Master : K O K O M O
                              Sub    :     K O M
                              Successful match,
                              return position 3
```

```
      else            (* No match, so realign *)
        Start := Start + 1;
        M := Start;
        S := 1
      endif
   endwhile;
   if S > Length(Sub) then
      (* A match was found *)
      Search := Start
   else
      Search := 0
   endif
end Search;
```

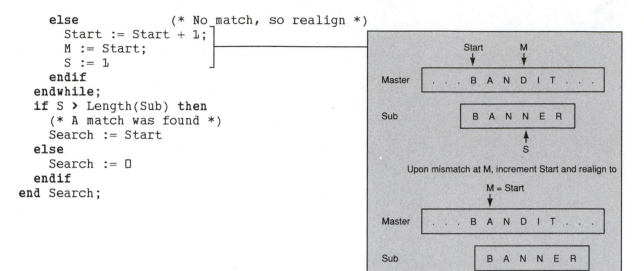

Analysis of Straightforward Search The average performance of the straightforward search is highly dependent on the nature of the text being processed. In normal English text, we would not expect to proceed too far into Sub before determining that realignment was necessary. However, in the worst case, we may have to proceed all the way to the last character of Sub before determining that realignment is necessary. This would require Length(Sub) comparisons. This worst case is illustrated in Figure 2.8. Here we would make Length(Sub) comparisons for each of the Length(Master) − Length(Sub) + 1 alignments of Sub against Master, for a total of

$$\text{Length(Master)} \times \text{Length (Sub)} - (\text{Length(Sub)})^2 + \text{Length(Sub)}$$

comparisons. Since Length(Master) > Length(Sub), the term Length(Master) × Length(Sub) dominates this expression, and we therefore conclude that in the worst case the efficiency of Search for the straightforward implementation is O(Length(Master) × Length(Sub)).

Knuth-Morris-Pratt Search Algorithm (Optional)

The worst case for the straightforward string search illustrates a drawback. Namely, after it realigns the Sub string it may make many comparisons whose outcome was really determined in a previous alignment of Sub. To see why it makes these unnecessary comparisons, trace the action of the straightforward approach in Figure 2.9. In Snapshot 3 of this figure, we see that five of the six comparisons that match A against A are in a sense unnecessary, since we know that we have matched the five A's preceding H during the first

```
Master : AAAAAAAAAAAAH
Sub    : AAAAAAH
```
We must repeatedly compare characters
all the way to H before realigning

FIGURE 2.8

Worse case for straightforward search.

pass through Sub in Snapshot 1. This phenomenon is highlighted in Figure 2.10.

According to this figure, the character comparison of Sub against Master could actually start at the point of the mismatch in Master from the previous alignment. The reason for this is that the five-character pattern immediately preceding H in Sub matches the five-character pattern that starts Sub. Since that five-character pattern preceding H matched positions 2 through 6 in Master before the mismatch at H was detected, it will certainly match again when we shift Sub one position to the right in its alignment and compare the leading five characters in Sub against positions 2 through 6 in Master.

We will now illustrate that this ability to use a partial match from the preceding alignment can be generalized apart from the worst-case scenario. Suppose we invoke Search with

```
Search("KOKOKOMO", "KOKOMO",1)
```

Figure 2.11 portrays how this search would proceed. This figure indicates that when a mismatch occurs in a particular alignment at index P of

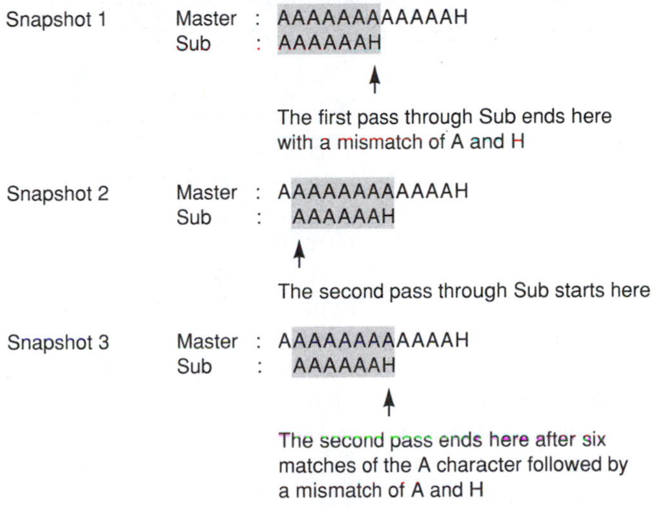

Snapshot 1   Master : AAAAAAAAAAAAH
              Sub   : AAAAAAH
                             ↑
              The first pass through Sub ends here
              with a mismatch of A and H

Snapshot 2   Master : AAAAAAAAAAAAH
              Sub   : AAAAAAH
                         ↑
              The second pass through Sub starts here

Snapshot 3   Master : AAAAAAAAAAAAH
              Sub   : AAAAAAH
                             ↑
              The second pass ends here after six
              matches of the A character followed by
              a mismatch of A and H

FIGURE 2.9
Action of straight forward Search for data of Figure 2.8.

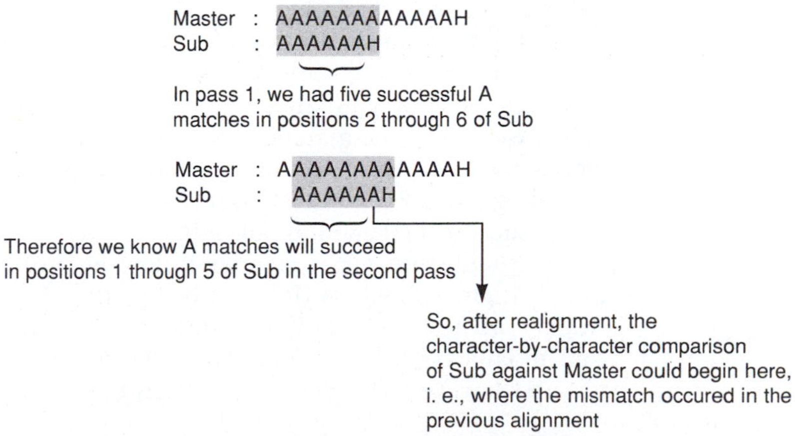

              Master : AAAAAAAAAAAAH
              Sub   : AAAAAAH
                        ‿‿‿‿‿
              In pass 1, we had five successful A
              matches in positions 2 through 6 of Sub

              Master : AAAAAAAAAAAAH
              Sub   : AAAAAAH
                         ‿‿‿‿‿
Therefore we know A matches will succeed
in positions 1 through 5 of Sub in the second pass

So, after realignment, the
character-by-character comparison
of Sub against Master could begin here,
i. e., where the mismatch occured in the
previous alignment

FIGURE 2.10
Unnecessary comparisons in straight-forward search of Figure 2.9. By failing to observe that the five A's preceding H in Sub match the first five A's of Sub, the straightforward search algorithm will make five unnecessary comparisons with each realignment against Master.

Snapshot 1   Master : K O K O K O M O
                   Sub   : K O K O M O

In first alignment, first
mismatch occurs here,
at index P of Sub

Snapshot 2   Master : K O K O K O M O
                   Sub   :   K O K O M O

Because the two characters preceding the mismatch in Snapshot 1
match the first two characters of Sub, we can align the first K in Sub
against the third K in Master and begin making character-by-character
comparisons from the point of the previous mismatch

FIGURE 2.11   In performing Search (Master, Sub, 1) with Master = "KOKOKOMO" and Sub = "KOKOMO" we observe that there is a substring of Sub (the second "KO") leading up to a point of mismatch with Master that will match a leading substring of Sub (the first "KO"). This tells us that Sub may be realigned with Master so that this leading substring will automatically match a substring in Master immediately preceding the position of the prior mismatch.

Sub, then we must look to the character matches that occurred in the portion of Sub preceding index P. We are seeking a substring of Sub in the portion of Sub immediately prior to index P that matches a leading substring of Sub. Once found, Sub may be realigned so that this leading substring overlays what had been the matching substring immediately prior to index P. The character-by-character comparison can then proceed from the position of the prior mismatch. Figure 2.12 illustrates this concept in its most general setting.

This apparently more efficient string search algorithm was discovered in the 1970s by D. E. Knuth, J. H. Morris, and V. R. Pratt. Consequently, it is known as the Knuth-Morris-Pratt (or KMP) algorithm. Its use requires an initial pass through the string Sub to determine the appropriate amount of realignment when a mismatch occurs at position P in Sub. Note that this determination is dependent only on Sub, not at all on Master. In effect, for each index P, we seek the longest sequence of characters immediately preceding position P that matches a sequence at the beginning of Sub. We must qualify this slightly to avoid problems in the degenerate case, in which all characters preceding position P are the same. When this occurs (as exemplified in Figure 2.10), we restart the matching pass through Sub at position $P - 1$. In other words, we specifically seek the maximum sequence of characters immediately preceding index P *with length less than $P - 1$* such that this sequence matches a sequence at the beginning of Sub.

We will store, for each index P, the length of such a sequence in an array called Align. Since Align[P] must be less than $P - 1$, we start by initializing Align[1] to -1 and Align[2] to 0. Figure 2.13 illustrates that for $P \geq 3$ we can initially try to determine Align[P] by comparing Sub.CharData[$P - 1$] to Sub.CharData[Q] where Q = Align[$P - 1$] + 1. Since the Align array is

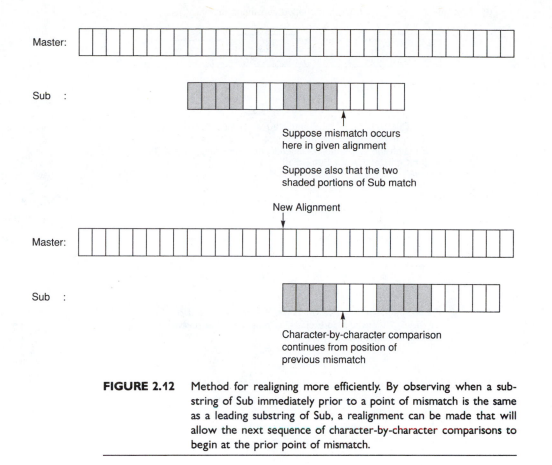

Master:

Sub :

Suppose mismatch occurs
here in given alignment

Suppose also that the two
shaded portions of Sub match

New Alignment

Master:

Sub :

Character-by-character comparison
continues from position of
previous mismatch

FIGURE 2.12 Method for realigning more efficiently. By observing when a substring of Sub immediately prior to a point of mismatch is the same as a leading substring of Sub, a realignment can be made that will allow the next sequence of character-by-character comparisons to begin at the prior point of mismatch.

computed for successive values of P, Align[P − 1] will have been computed by the time we attempt to compute Align[P].

If the test indicated in Figure 2.13 fails, we will then seek a leading substring of the shaded portion on the left of Figure 2.13 that matches a substring ending at position P − 1. Working within the shaded portion on the left of Figure 2.13 (that is, with the characters at the beginning of Sub) we know that the leading Align[Q] characters on the left of this shaded portion exactly match the characters in the Align[Q] positions preceding Q. This follows from the definition of the values already stored in the Align array. We also know that the two shaded substrings in Figure 2.13 must match. Combining these facts, we conclude that the first Align[Q] characters in Sub exactly match the sequence of Align[Q] characters preceding position P − 1 in Figure 2.13. Consequently, if we reassign Q := Align[Q] + 1, then Align[P] will equal Q *provided* Sub.CharData[Q] = Sub.CharData[P − 1]. This logic is iterated until Sub.CharData[Q] = Sub.CharData[P − 1] or Q reaches 0, as indicated in Figure 2.14.

The resulting algorithm for the computation of Align is given by the following PSEUDO procedure:

```
type
  AlignArray: array [MaxStringSize] of integer;
```

General case:

By definition of Align[P − 1], the two shaded substrings match.

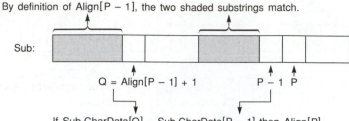

Q = Align[P − 1] + 1   P − 1   P

If Sub.CharData[Q] = Sub.CharData[P − 1] then Align[P]
is Q since we then know that the first Q characters in
Sub match the Q characters immediately preceding position P.
If Sub.CharData[Q] <> Sub.Data[P − 1], further checking is
required.

Specific example:

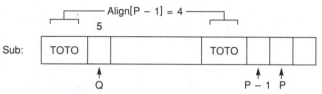

If Sub.CharData[5] = Sub.CharData[P − 1] then Align[P]
will be 5. Otherwise, more checking must be done before
we can determine Align[P].

FIGURE 2.13

Initial attempt at computing
Align[P] for P ≥ 3. In the
lower figure the substring
"TOTO" appears in the
first four positions of Sub
and in the four positions
preceding position P − 1.
This substring represents the
contents of the two shaded
areas of Sub appearing in the
upper figure.

General case:

Since the larger shaded substrings in Figure 2.13 match, these smaller
substrings must match also.

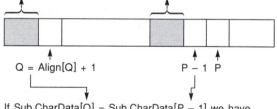

Q = Align[Q] + 1   P − 1   P

If Sub.CharData[Q] = Sub.CharData[P − 1] we have
determined Align[P] to be Q.

Otherwise continue reassigning Q := Align[Q] + 1 to work
with a smaller leading sequence of characters.

Specific example:

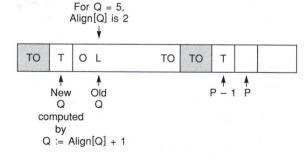

Since Sub.CharData[Q] = Sub.CharData[P − 1], Align[P]
is determined to be 3

If Sub.CharData[Q] were different from Sub.CharData[P − 1],
Q would have to be reduced again.

FIGURE 2.14

Continuation of logic from
Figure 2.13.

74

```
procedure ComputeAlignArray
  ( given  Sub: String       (* An arbitrary string *);
    return Align: AlignArray  (* Will be computed so that the value at position P
                                 indicates the length of the longest sequence of
                                 characters immediately preceding position P that
                                 matches a sequence at the beginning of given
                                 string Sub *) );
  var
    P, Q: integer;

  start ComputeAlignArray
    Align[1] := -1;
    Align[2] := 0;
    for P:= 3 to Length(Sub) do
      Q := Align[P - 1] + 1;  (* Move into Sub one position past the number of
                                 characters that are matched leading up to
                                 position P - 1 *)
      while Q > 0 and Sub.CharData[Q] <> Sub.CharData[P - 1] do
        (* Keep looking for substrings in the positions leading up to position
            P - 1 that match those at the beginning of Sub using values at earlier
            positions of Align to determine how long the matching substrings
            leading up to position P - 1 are (telling us where in Sub to locate
            the character to compare to the character in position P - 1) *)
        Q := Align[Q] + 1
      endwhile;
      (* In addition to telling us where to look for a match with the character
          at position P - 1, the index tells us how long a potential matching
          substring would be; if Q becomes 0 we reached the first character in Sub
          and failed to get a match; hence, there is no matching substring *)
      Align[P] := Q
    endfor
  end ComputeAlignArray;
```

The computation of the Align array is quite tricky. The following example should help to clarify its logic.

Example 2.4   Trace the computation of the Align array for the string "AHAHHAHAHAA".

```
                  P
                  ↓
 Align [1]  : -1 by definition.
 Align [2]  : 0 by definition.
 Align [3]  : Set Q := Align[2] + 1 = 1.
              Since Sub.CharData[Q] <> Sub.CharData[P - 1],
              reset Q := Align[1] + 1 = 0, exit
              while loop and conclude Align[P] = 0.
 Align [4]  : Set Q := Align[3] + 1 = 1.
              Since Sub.CharData[Q] = Sub.CharData[P - 1],
              conclude Align[P] = 1.
 Align [5]  : Set Q := Align[4] + 1 = 2.
              Since Sub.CharData[Q] = Sub.CharData[P - 1],
              conclude Align[P] = 2.
```

```
Align [6]  : Set Q := Align[5] + 1 = 3.
             Since Sub.CharData[Q] <> Sub.CharData[P - 1],
             reset Q := Align[3] + 1 = 1.
             Since Sub.CharData[Q] <> Sub.CharData[P - 1],
             reset Q := Align[1] + 1 = 0, exit
             while loop and conclude Align[P] = 0.
Align [7]  : Set Q := Align[6] + 1 = 1.
             Since Sub.CharData[Q] = Sub.CharData[P - 1],
             conclude Align[P] = 1.
Align [8]  : Set Q := Align[7] + 1 = 2.
             Since Sub.CharData[Q] = Sub.CharData[P - 1],
             conclude Align[P] = 2.
Align [9]  : Set Q := Align[8] + 1 = 3.
             Since Sub.CharData[Q] = Sub.CharData[P - 1],
             conclude Align[P] = 3.
Align [10] : Set Q := Align[9] + 1 = 4.
             Since Sub.CharData[Q] = Sub.CharData[P - 1],
             conclude Align[P] = 4.
Align [11] : Set Q := Align[10] + 1 = 5.
             Since Sub.CharData[Q] <> Sub.CharData[P - 1],
             reset Q := Align[5] + 1 = 3.
             Since Sub.CharData[Q] = Sub.CharData[P - 1],
             conclude Align[P] = 3.
```

We are now prepared to provide a complete implementation of the string search operation using the KMP algorithm. The computation of the Align array is hidden from the search algorithm in the ComputeAlignArray procedure that we developed earlier.

```
function Search (* Knuth-Morris-Pratt *)
  ( given Master,
          Sub: String    (* Two strings with Sub potentially contained
                            in Master *);
          Start:integer (* Representing a character position in Master. Master is
                            to be searched for Sub from this position onward *);
    return: integer      (* The position of the first occurrence of Sub in
                            Master at position Start or after. Zero returned
                            if Sub is not found in this portion of Master *) );
  var
    M, S: integer;
    StillAChance: boolean;
    Align: array [MaxStringSize] of integer;

  start Search
    ComputeAlignArray(Sub, Align);
    M := Start;
    S := 1;
    StillAChance := (Length(Sub) - S) <= (Length(Master) - M);
    while S <= Length(Sub) and StillAChance do
      if Master.CharData[M] = Sub.CharData[S] then (* Sub and Master still match,
                                                       so move to next character *)
        M := M + 1;
        S := S + 1
```

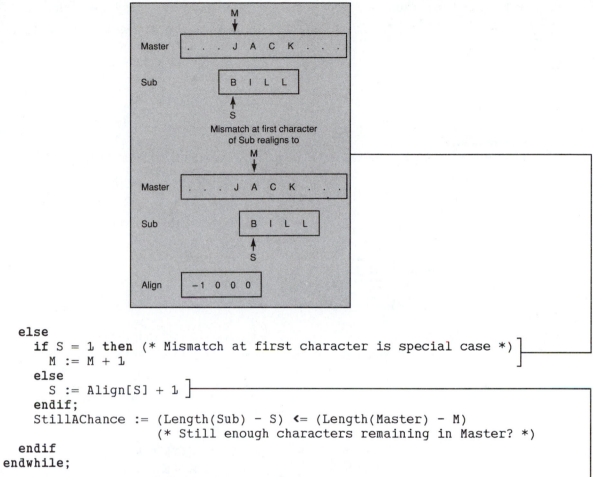

```
else
   if S = 1 then (* Mismatch at first character is special case *)
      M := M + 1
   else
      S := Align[S] + 1
   endif;
   StillAChance := (Length(Sub) - S) <= (Length(Master) - M)
                   (* Still enough characters remaining in Master? *)
endif
endwhile;
```

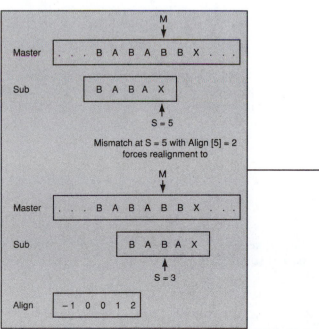

```
  if S > Length(Sub) then
    Search := M - Length(Sub)
  else
    Search := 0
  endif
end Search;
```

Example 2.5   Trace the action of the KMP string search algorithm for the call

Search("KOKOKOMO", "KOKOMO", 1)

This is portrayed as follows:

Align $\boxed{-1\ 0\ 0\ 1\ 2\ 0}$

		M=1
		↓
Start of first	Master	: K O K O K O M O
pass through Sub:	Sub	: K O K O M O
		↑
		S=1

		M=5
		↓
End of first	Master	: K O K O K O M O
pass through Sub:	Sub	: K O K O M O
		↑
		S=5

		M=5
		↓
Start of second	Master	: K O K O K O M O
pass through Sub:	Sub	: K O K O M O
		↑
		S=3

Since Align[5] = 2,
S is reset to 2 + 1
and M does not change

		M=9
		↓
End of second	Master	: K O K O K O M O
pass through Sub:	Sub	: K O K O M O
		↑
		S=7

Return M − Length(Sub) = 3

Example 2.6   Trace the action of the KMP string search algorithm for the call

Search("AAAAAAAH", "AAAAAH", 1)

This is portrayed as follows:

Align $\boxed{-1\ 0\ 0\ 1\ 2\ 3\ 4}$

		M = 1 ↓
Start of first pass through Sub:	Master :	AAAAAAAH
	Sub :	AAAAAH
		↑ S = 1

		M = 6 ↓
End of first pass through Sub:	Master :	AAAAAAAH
	Sub :	AAAAAH
		↑ S = 6

		M = 6 ↓
Start of second pass through Sub:	Master :	AAAAAAAH
	Sub :	AAAAAH
		↑ S = 5 (Since Align[6] = 4)

		M = 7 ↓
End of second pass through Sub:	Master :	AAAAAAAH
	Sub :	AAAAAH
		↑ S = 6

		M = 7 ↓
Start of third pass through Sub:	Master :	AAAAAAAH
	Sub :	AAAAAH
		↑ S = 5 (Since Align[6] = 4)

		M = 9 ↓
End of third pass through Sub:	Master :	AAAAAAAH
	Sub :	AAAAAH
		↑ S = 7 Return M − Length(Sub) = 3

Analysis of KMP String Search Intuition tells us that the KMP algorithm becomes more efficient for Sub strings that contain frequently recurring patterns. In such cases, comparisons between characters in Sub and a portion of Master are quite likely to proceed a considerable distance into Sub before a mismatch occurs. The Align array may then allow a substantial leap forward in the realignment of Sub against Master—a leap bypassing many comparisons made by the straightforward implementation of StringSearch.

A more formal analysis of KMP's efficiency hinges on the fact that we never back up in the Master string. Examining the **while** loop in the algorithm, we see that M, the index for Master, either advances or remains fixed each time through the loop. When it remains fixed, we set S back to Align[S] + 1. However, as Figure 2.15 shows, the resetting of S in this fashion implies that we have a sequence of matching characters in Master and Sub prior to reaching position M. In particular, the length of this preceding sequence of matches (during which M advanced) will be at least as great as the number of times S must be reset via Align values while we are stuck at the current value of M. Hence, although for some index positions the character at position M in Master may have to be compared to numerous characters in Sub, this will always be offset by other positions M that had to be compared to only one character in Sub. Due to this balancing, the overall number of comparisons in the **while** loop of KMP Search must be O(Length(Master)). A similar argument shows that the number of comparisons in ComputeAlignArray will be O(Length(Sub)). Hence, the overall efficiency of KMP Search will be O(Length(Master) + Length(Sub))—a considerable improvement over the O(Length(Master) × Length(Sub)) worst-case efficiency of the straightforward approach.

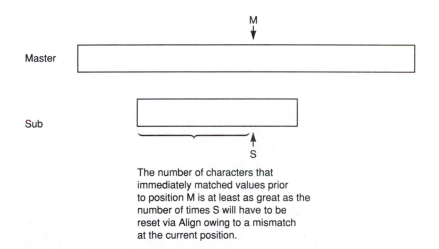

The number of characters that immediately matched values prior to position M is at least as great as the number of times S will have to be reset via Align owing to a mismatch at the current position.

FIGURE 2.15   Preceding matching characters offset the backup of S in Sub. The worst case occurs when all the characters preceding S and matching characters in Master are the same, but do not match the character at location M of Master. S will have to back up as many times as there are characters that precede S, while M stays fixed. Sometimes, however, S may have to back up only once, such as when the lack of matching substrings prior to location S causes S to be reset to the beginning of Sub.

For searching in normal English text, the KMP algorithm is not likely to improve much upon the straightforward algorithm because the worst case for the straightforward method rarely occurs in English text; usually a mismatch in characters between Master and Sub occurs before we have progressed very far into the strings. Another algorithm, known as the Boyer-Moore search algorithm, will generally be more effective on normal English text. You will explore this algorithm in the exercises.

The KMP algorithm is particularly well suited to strings consisting of relatively few different characters—such as binary strings. In such strings, the recurring patterns that heighten the efficiency of KMP are more likely to occur. Because the KMP algorithm never has to back up in the Master string, it is also the method of choice for applications in which the master string is a text file being read one character at a time.

Exercises 2.2

1. Explain what encapsulation is. Why is encapsulation necessary if we are to obey the ADT Use and Implementation rules formulated in this section?

2. In this section we have presented two algorithms for the string Search operation to be used with the fixed-length string implementation. Formulate PSEUDO procedures/functions for each of the other string operations using this implementation.

3. In both the straightforward and KMP search algorithms presented in this section, the Length function for a string is called quite often. Given the implementation of the Length function that you wrote for Exercise 2, do these calls to Length add appreciably to the time efficiency of the string Search algorithm? Explain.

4. In the style of Example 2.4, trace the computation of the KMP Align array for each of the following strings:

   a. ABBADABBADOO

   b. ABRACADABRA

   c. UMBOMUMBOJUMBO

5. In the Align array of the KMP search algorithm

   $$0 \le \text{Align}[P] < P - 1$$

   for $1 < P \le \text{Length(Sub)}$. Is the KMP algorithm most efficient when the Align[P] values tend to be close to $P - 1$ or when they tend to be close to 0? Justify your answer with a written explanation.

6. In the style of Examples 2.5 and 2.6, trace the action of both the straightforward and KMP string searches for the following invocations of the operation:

   a. Search ("ABBADABBADOO", "ADO", 1)

   b. Search ("AAAHAAAHAAHAHAAA", "HAHA", 1)

   c. Search ("PHILS FROM PHILADELPHIA", "PHILADELPHIA", 8)

   d. Search ("IFFIFFIFFIFFFIIIF", "IFFIFFF", 1)

7. Suppose that in a particular application you know that Master and Sub strings will consist only of combinations of two letters. Explain how computation, under these conditions, of the Align array could be altered to make the resulting KMP search slightly more efficient.

8. Provide an argument that the computation of the Align array for the KMP search algorithm is $O(Length(Sub))$. (Hint: apply logic similar to that used in our argument that the **while** loop in KMP Search is $O(Length(Master))$.

9. In a particular application, suppose that the KMP Search procedure is likely to be called often with the same string for the Sub argument. In that case the present version of KMP Search will continually recompute the Align array for this particular value of Sub. Specify a way to avoid this in a fashion that does not violate the ADT Use and Implementation rules formulated in this section. Rewrite all the string operations from Exercise 2 in a fashion consistent with the method you have specified to solve this problem.

10. (Boyer-Moore String Search Algorithm) Like the KMP algorithm, a string search algorithm developed by Boyer and Moore in 1977 initially examines the structure of the Sub string to see if it can be realigned a considerable distance to the right, when a mismatch occurs. Unlike the KMP algorithm, the Boyer-Moore algorithm compares the characters of the Sub string to that of the Master string in a right-to-left fashion. The hope is that this will allow realignments of considerable magnitude when a mismatch occurs early in the comparison of Sub against a portion of Master. For instance, suppose that, at the beginning of a right-to-left scan of Sub aligned against a portion of Master, we find the character "L" in Master and some other nonmatching character in the rightmost position of Sub. Then, if "L" does not occur anywhere else in Sub, Sub may be realigned $Length(Sub)$ characters to the right. (Why?) Analogously, if the first "L" to the left of the final position occurs at position I of Sub, then Sub may be realigned $(Length(Sub) - I)$ characters to the right. (Why?) Thus, when a mismatch occurs at the rightmost (that is, the first examined) position of Sub, the character in Master that caused the mismatch can be used to tell us how much Sub can be realigned to the right. A preprocessing pass through Sub could be used to determine the amount of realignment for any possible character that could occur in Master. This information could then be used in a fashion similar to the Align array in the KMP algorithm. (The full-blown version of the Boyer-Moore algorithm actually takes into account possible realignments when the mismatched character does not occur at the rightmost position of Sub. We omit the details of such a refinement here.)

    a. Write a PSEUDO procedure to compute the Align array for the Boyer-Moore algorithm.

    b. Using your answer to part **a**, write a PSEUDO version of the Boyer-Moore algorithm.

    c. Would you expect the Boyer-Moore or KMP algorithm to perform better on typical English text? Explain why.

    d. Would you use Boyer-Moore or KMP when the Master string is a text file being read one character at a time? Explain why.

2.3   THE POINTER ADT

In Chapter 1, when we indicated the primitive types in PSEUDO that we use in this text, we included the type *pointer*. Unlike the case with the other primitive types, however, objects typed as pointers are used to reference other data objects, usually (but not necessarily) of another type. Consequently, not only is their role in a program often less apparent than that of data objects of the other primitive types, but the programmer who employs them must exercise further care in order to avoid newer kinds of errors in logic (which are normally harder to track down).

For those readers who may be unfamiliar with pointers or for those who wish a review of them, we now discuss pointers more fully, treating them as an abstract data type. You may be wondering why we are once again (as we did with the matrix ADT) going through the trouble of describing a feature that many languages support directly. There are several reasons for this. First, even though pointers are implemented in many languages (Pascal, Modula-2, Ada, and C), they are not implemented in all languages, including some that are still widely used (such as FORTRAN, COBOL, and BASIC). Thus, it is important for you to have a precise specification of pointers and how they might be implemented in the event that you want to use them while working in a language that does not support them directly. It is important to realize that, just because a language does not have pointers, you need not completely avoid data structures that require pointers—you merely have to provide your own implementation of the pointer ADT.

Second, even in languages that provide pointers, you may run into situations where the implementation is not suitable for your application. For instance, in many languages, you cannot display the values of a pointer with a direct output statement. Often it would be useful to see the value, especially when you have a bug in a program that you suspect may be caused by a pointer having an improperly assigned value. By implementing your own pointers, you can provide them with additional features suitable for debugging purposes and then easily switch back to the language's implementation of pointers once you are convinced that your program is working properly. Likewise, should you need to map a data structure such as a linked list onto a random access file, you will not be able to use a programming language's implementation of memory-resident pointer variables. To cite one more instance, when we study hashing in Chapter 11 we will explore a situation where supplied pointer variables will not meet our needs. Hence, an understanding of what lies below the abstract-level pointer variables will likely be valuable regardless of your future endeavors in computer science.

• **Definition of the Pointer ADT:** A pointer is a data object that provides only the location in memory of another data object. A specification of the operations for the Pointer ADT assumes that the pointers refer to data objects of type ObjectType. That is, ObjectType is the type of a data object whose *location* may be the value of a pointer variable.

```
type
   ObjectType: (* The type of a data object which pointers may reference *);

procedure GetNode
   ( given P: pointer to ObjectType    (* An arbitrary pointer variable to
                                           objects of type ObjectType *);
```

```
    return P: pointer to ObjectType      (* P is now assigned a specific location
                                             where we may store an object of type
                                             ObjectType *) );

procedure ReturnNode
  ( given P: pointer to ObjectType        (* A pointer to a data object that is no
                                             longer needed by an algorithm *);
    return P: pointer to ObjectType       (* The data node referenced by P has been
                                             returned to the space management system
                                             for later re-use when GetNode is called;
                                             P itself is now unreliable *) );

function Ref                              (* A special dereferencing function, used to
                                             access the object being pointed to by P *)
  ( given P: pointer to ObjectType        (* A pointer variable assumed to have been
                                             assigned a valid object location *);
    return: ObjectType                    (* The data object at the location
                                             referenced by P *) );
```

Some remarks are in order concerning the pointer ADT. To declare pointer variables and types, we use the expression **pointer to**. Hence, the following declarations would allow the variables P and Q to store the locations in memory of data objects of type EmployeeRecord.

```
type
  EmployeeRecord: record
                     IDNumber: integer;
                     WageRate: real
                   endrecord;
  EmployeePointer: pointer to EmployeeRecord;
var
  P, Q: EmployeePointer;
```

By invoking GetNode(P), we give the variable P a value that is a memory address where we may store an object of type EmployeeRecord. Ref(P) can then be used to dereference the pointer, that is, to refer to the contents of the record at this memory address (as opposed to the value of the address itself or a copy of the contents of the record at this address). Hence, the PSEUDO statement

```
Ref(P).WageRate := 5.50
```

could be used to assign the value 5.50 to the WageRate field of the object referenced by the pointer P. Finally, invoking ReturnNode(P) indicates that we are done with the data currently referenced by P and that the space at this address could be reused by a later invocation of New. These conceptual operations are portrayed in Figure 2.16.

We can assign one pointer variable to another via a simple assignment statement Q := P. The effect of this is to aim the pointer Q at the object also referenced by P. That is, P and Q now reference the same object. We will also assume that two pointers can be tested to see if they are equal or not. The test P = Q is **true** if and only if P and Q reference the same object, that is, contain the same memory address.

Computer Memory

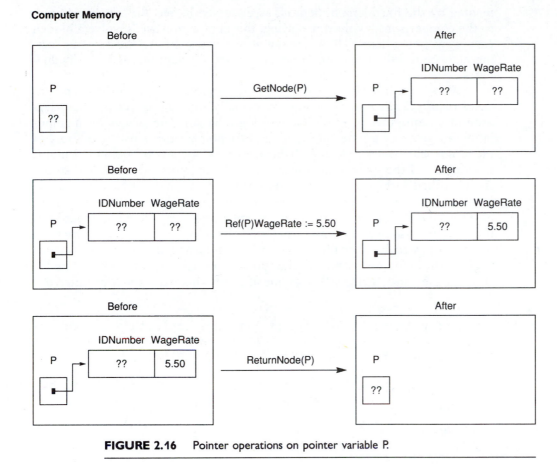

FIGURE 2.16   Pointer operations on pointer variable P.

Finally, we will assume the existence of a sentinel value NULL, which can be thought of as a memory address at which no object can be stored. Pointer variables may be assigned the value NULL to allow later conditional testing for this sentinel value, for example P = NULL. Since no data can be stored at the NULL location, Ref(P) is an unreliable function call when P is NULL. You should not assume that a pointer variable will be NULL prior to its being assigned a specific non-NULL pointer value (through GetNode or other means). Nor should you assume that a pointer variable will be NULL after ReturnNode is called with it. Rather, the value of a pointer P is unpredictable after invoking ReturnNode(P).

We shall not discuss the implementation of the pointer ADT at this time because the most common implementation, using arrays, relies on a structure known as a linked list—a topic we discuss in Chapter 3. Nevertheless, we now discuss an application that uses the pointer ADT. By so doing we further emphasize the effectiveness of an ADT because we will be using one without having any knowledge of the details of its implementation.

Pointer Sort Algorithms

To illustrate the use of pointers, consider an application in which we wish to sort an array of potentially long strings. Suppose that the strings are implemented by the fixed-length method, as discussed in Section 2.2. In addition to the comparisons involved in sorting, this application will involve a hidden cost in swapping items. The swapping of two strings necessitated by our sorting algorithm will, at the machine level, involve swapping many individual bytes.

We wish to use pointers to lessen the impact of these costly swaps. Instead of *physically sorting* strings by actually moving arrays of characters around in computer memory, we will logically sort the strings by manipulating an array of pointers so that the first pointer contains the address of the string that comes first in alphabetical order, the second pointer contains the address of the string that comes second in alphabetical order, and so on. As illustrated in Figure 2.17, the end result will be that we have the capacity to process the strings in alphabetical order even though the strings have never exchanged positions in computer memory. The following procedures illustrate the use of our pointer operations by allowing the user to enter the list of strings to be logically sorted and then sorting the pointers. First we begin with the necessary type declarations and then define the procedure for entering the list of strings. We assume at most MaxStrings will be entered.

```
type
    StringPointer: pointer to String; (* Suitable implementation of
                                          string ADT *)
    StringPtrArray: array [MaxStrings] of StringPointer;
```

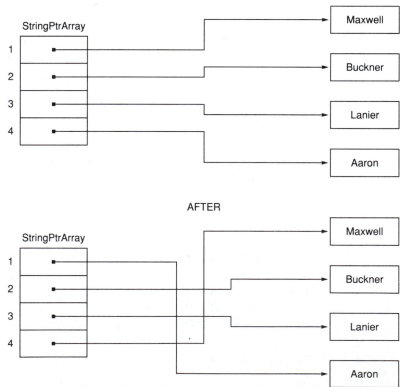

FIGURE 2.17

Before and after snapshots for pointer sort algorithm. The "array of strings" is actually implemented as an "array of pointers to strings." Thus, physically swapping two pointer values (in this figure, the pointers at locations 1 and 4 of the StringPtrArray array) corresponds to logically swapping the positions of two strings (here, the strings "MAXWELL" and "AARON").

```
      procedure LoadStrings
        ( given S: StringPtrArray    (* An array of pointer variables *);
          return S: StringPtrArray   (* The original array, with the first
                                        N pointers now referencing
                                        strings *);

                   N: integer        (* The number of strings entered by
                                        the user *);

          var
            I: integer;

          start LoadStrings
            read(N);
            for I := 1 to N do
              GetNode(S[I]);          (* Get space to put the string *)
              Create(Ref(S[I]));      (* Create the string referenced by
                                         S[I] *)

              ReadAString(Ref(S[I]))  (* Enter data at location referenced
                                         by S[I] *)

            endfor
          end LoadStrings;
```

We now define the PointerSort procedure. We shall take advantage of our existing Sort procedures from Chapter 1 by establishing appropriate type equivalences, by establishing an appropriate Precedes function (which we call ComesBefore), and then by invoking the Sort procedure. The constant declarations and type equivalences can be established by

```
(* Establish the type equivalences that will allow us to invoke the Sort
   procedure by the generic interface established in Chapter 1 *)

type
  ElementType: StringPointer;
  ElementArray: StringPtrArray;

(* Then establish the function parameter that will be passed to the Sort
   procedure. Note that this comparison function must compare strings,
   although it is given pointers to strings. *)

function ComesBefore
  ( given A, B: StringPointer             (* Pointers to strings to compare *);
    return: boolean                       (* true if string referenced by A
                                             precedes string referenced by B
                                             in the order relationship on
                                             Strings; false otherwise *) );


  start ComesBefore
    ComesBefore := LessThan(Ref(A), Ref(B));  (* Invoke String LessThan operation
                                                 on the data objects referenced by
                                                 pointers A and B *)

  end ComesBefore;

(* Finally, the pointer sort procedure itself *)
```

```
procedure PointerSort
  ( given S: StringPtrArray        (* Array of pointers to strings  *);
          N: integer               (* Number of strings to be sorted *);
    return S: StringPtrArray       (* Array of pointers leading to
                                       logically ordered list *) );

  start PointerSort
    Sort(S, N, ComesBefore)
  end PointerSort;
```

Not only does the pointer sort example illustrate one of the many uses of the pointer ADT, but it also allows us to take advantage of an existing Sort procedure, rather than code a new one to accommodate new circumstances. We shall return to the pointer ADT frequently in future chapters and use it in the implementation of other data structures.

Exercises 2.3

1. Let us suppose that the array S passed into the PointerSort procedure of this section initially contains

1	3094
2	4016
3	4492
4	5138
5	5232
6	5300

where
- The string "ZAPPA" is stored at location 3094
- The string "MILLER" is stored at location 4016
- The string "BUTTER" is stored at location 4492
- The string "ALPHA" is stored at location 5138
- The string "GREEN" is stored at location 5232
- The string "CARSON" is stored at location 5300

Trace the status of the array S as it is manipulated by PointerSort using the LessThan function for strings. That is, show the new contents of the array each time two pointers are swapped. Assume that an insertion sort implementation of the Sort procedure is used.

2. Write the PSEUDO procedure WriteStrings, which could be called after invoking PointerSort to print the list of strings in alphabetical order.

3. Why would a pointer sort technique achieve relatively less performance improvement if it were incorporated into selection sort instead of insertion sort?

4. Suppose P and Q are pointer variables.
   a. If P <> Q is **true**, then is it possible that Ref(P) = Ref(Q)? Explain.
   b. If P = Q is **true**, then is it possible that Ref(P) <> Ref(Q)? Explain.

2.4   THE SET ADT

In the previous two sections, we introduced the string and pointer ADTs. The pointer ADT is one that will be used to implement many other ADTs. The string is an ADT for which we will consider a variety of implementations in the remainder of the text. The ADT we introduce in this section—the set—is similar to the string ADT in that there are a variety of ways to implement it. We will discuss one implementation of the set in this section and later examine numerous other implementations that may be more effective for other applications. As with strings, the key factor to remember in developing any implementation of sets is to keep the interface to your implementation completely compatible with the specifications for operations on the ADT. That is, you must obey the Use and Implementation rules for ADTs presented earlier in this chapter. The definition of a set as an ADT is a direct consequence of the way sets are typically used in the disciplines of mathematics and logic.

• **Definition of the Set ADT:** A *set* is a collection of objects from some specified universe. The objects in a set are not necessarily ordered by any relationship. The operations we can perform on sets are the following:

```
type
   Universe:   (* Some domain from which potential set members are drawn; often
               assumed to be an ordinal data type such as characters or
               integer *);
procedure Create
   ( given S: Set        (* A set S in an arbitrary, perhaps uninitialized
                             state *);
     return S: Set       (* S initialized to the empty set *) );

function IsElementOf
   ( given S: Set        (* An arbitrary set *);
          E: Universe    (* A member of the universe of items that may
                             compose S *);
     return: boolean     (* true if E is a member of S; false otherwise *) );

procedure Assign
   ( given S: Set        (* An arbitrary set S *);
     return T: Set       (* T should contain a copy of the contents of S *) );

function Empty
   ( given S: Set        (* An arbitrary set *);
     return: boolean     (* true if S is the empty set; false otherwise *) );

function Equal
   ( given S, T: Set     (* Two arbitrary sets S and T *);
     return: boolean     (* true if S and T are equal, that is, contain
                             precisely the same members; false otherwise *) );
function SubsetOf
   ( given S, T: Set     (* Two arbitrary sets S and T *);
     return: boolean     (* true if S is a subset of T, that is, every element of
                             S is also a member of T; false otherwise *) );
```

```
procedure Union
   ( given R, S: Set        (* Two arbitrary sets R and S *);
     return T: Set          (* The union of R and S, that is, the set whose elements
                               are those members of the Universe that are in R or
                               S *) );
procedure Intersection
   ( given R, S: Set        (* Two arbitrary sets R and S *);
     return T: Set          (* The intersection of R and S, that is, the set whose
                               elements are those members of the Universe in both R
                               and S *) );
procedure Difference
   ( given R, S: Set        (* Two arbitrary sets R and S *);
     return T: Set          (* The difference of R and S, that is, the set whose
                               elements are in R but not in S *) );
procedure Add
   ( given S: Set           (* An arbitrary set *);
           U: Universe      (* A member of the Universe to be added as an element
                               of S *);
     return S: Set          (* S, with U added as an element *) );
procedure Remove
   ( given S: Set           (* An arbitrary set *);
           U: Universe      (* A member of the Universe to be removed from S *);
     return S: Set          (* S, with U removed if U is in S;  S will be
                               unaffected otherwise *) );
```

Although many programming languages provide direct implementations of sets, such implementations usually place significant restrictions on the potential size of the universe of objects from which set elements are drawn. Hence, as with sparse matrices and pointers, you may often be forced into developing your own implementation of sets.

Implementation of Sets by Boolean Arrays

In this implementation of sets, we must place some restrictions on the Universe of elements from which set members are drawn. In particular, we specify that the Universe must be a finite subrange of some ordinal data type. We will call the first element in that subrange *FirstValueInUniverse* and the last element *LastValueInUniverse*. Thus, we do not allow sets whose elements are reals or values of a structured data type. This restriction allows us to view the members of the Universe as indices for an array of booleans. Each set will be implemented by such a boolean array. In practice, these booleans are ideally represented by a bit so that the set requires the minimal possible storage. In case the Universe is not a subrange of the integers starting at 1, we assume the existence of the following functions.

```
function Index
   ( given X: Universe       (* An arbitrary value of the Universe *);
     return: integer         (* A value in a contiguous subrange of the integers
                               starting at 1 with the property that X < Y implies
                               Index(X) < Index(Y) *) );
function Successor
   ( given X: Universe       (* Any member of the Universe except the last *);
     return: Universe        (* The value that immediately follows X *) );
```

```
function Predecessor
  ( given X: Universe      (* Any member of the Universe except the first *);
    return: Universe        (* The value that immediately precedes X *) );
```

Clearly, such functions are trivial to write for integers and characters. Given these functions, the criterion for whether or not a value X is in the set SampleSet is whether SampleSet[Index(X)] is **true** or **false**.

Example 2.7   Write the IsElementOf function for this implementation of sets.

```
type  (* Assume SizeOfUniverse is constant that establishes size of
          Universe *);
  Set: array [SizeOfUniverse] of boolean;

function IsElementOf
  ( given S: Set          (* An arbitrary set *);
          E: Universe      (* A member of the Universe of items that may
                              compose S *);
    return: boolean        (* true if E is a member of S; false
                              otherwise *) );

  start IsElementOf
    IsElementOf := S[E]
  end IsElementOf;
```

Example 2.8   Using the declaration of Set in Example 2.7, write the Union procedure for this implementation of sets.

```
procedure Union
  ( given R, S: Set        (* Two arbitrary sets R and S *);
    return T: Set          (* The union of R and S, that is, the set whose
                              elements are those members of the Universe
                              that are in R or S *) );

  var
    U: Universe;

  start Union
    U := FirstValueInUniverse;
    repeat
      T[Index(U)] := R[Index(U)] or S[Index(U)];   (* U in T if in R
                                                        or S *)

      U := Successor[U]
    until U = LastValueInUniverse;
    T[Index(LastValueInUniverse)] := R[Index(LastValueInUniverse)]
                                     or S[Index(LastValueInUniverse)]

  end Union;
```

You will explore writing the rest of the operations for this implementation of sets in the exercises at the end of this section.

The Union-Find Problem

Before closing this chapter, we will examine one more problem derived from the set ADT. It is called the *union-find problem* and could be thought of as a problem that might arise in a large, complex transportation network. In such a network, we could group cities into sets according to whether or not a route exists between them. Thus, in Figure 2.18, Atlanta, Orlando, and Birmingham would be in one set; New York, Washington, Philadelphia, and Boston in a second set; Milwaukee and Chicago in a third set; Phoenix, Sacramento, San Francisco, and Los Angeles in a fourth set; and Boise in a fifth set all by itself. In effect the sets divide the fourteen members of this universe into disjoint groups. This is one of the preconditions for the union-find problem—the members of the universe must be partitioned into sets such that each member is in one and only one set. The two operations we require in such a situation are the following:

1. The Find operation: given X and Y in the Universe, determine whether or not there is a route between them. That is, are they in the same set?
2. The Union operation: Given X and Y in the Universe, link them by a direct route. That is, form the union of the sets that contain X and Y.

Interestingly, we may actually formulate the union-find problem as an abstract data type.

• Definition of the Union-Find ADT: Consider objects in a finite Universe. At all times these objects are partitioned into disjoint subsets. Each subset

FIGURE 2.18
Partitioning of Universe of cities for union-find problem. Each set of the partition represents a group of cities for which routes exist between them in a transportation network. Since Boise is the only member of its set, no routes exist between it and the other cities.

is of type Set, and the collection of disjoint subsets is of type Partition. The operations we perform on these objects and the disjoint subsets into which they are partitioned are shown here:

```
procedure UFCreate
  ( given P: Partition        (* P, uninitialized *);
    return P: Partition        (* P, initialized as a collection of disjoint sets in
                                  which each member of the Universe is a member of a
                                  one-element set; that is, P is a partition of the
                                  Universe into sets with only one element each *) );

function UFFind
  ( given X, Y: Universe       (* X and Y, arbitrary members of the Universe *);
           P: Partition        (* A partition of the Universe *);
    return: boolean            (* true if X and Y are in the same set in P;
                                  false otherwise *) );

procedure UFUnion
  ( given X, Y: Universe       (* X and Y, arbitrary members of the Universe *);
           P: Partition        (* A partition of the Universe *);
    return P: Partition        (* The sets containing X and Y in P are unioned;
                                  if the union is different from the original
                                  sets containing X and Y, this union must be
                                  added to P and the original sets removed *) );
```

Example 2.9   To illustrate the union-find operations, suppose that our Universe consists of six integer objects 1, 2, 3, 4, 5, and 6. Consider the following sequence of union-find operations and their results.

1. UFCreate(P)
   P returned as {{1}, {2}, {3}, {4}, {5}, {6}}
2. UFUnion(1, 4, P)
   P returned as {{1, 4}, {2}, {3}, {5}, {6}}
3. UFUnion(4, 6, P)
   P returned as {{1, 4, 6}, {2}, {3}, {5}}
4. UFUnion(2, 5, P)
   P returned as {{1, 4, 6}, {2, 5}, {3}}
5. UFFind(1, 6, P)
   Returns **true** since 1 and 6 are in same set.
6. UFFind(5, 3, P)
   Returns **false** since 5 and 3 are in different sets.

The union-find problem and its associated ADT form a classic problem in computer science. Although it is possible to develop an implementation for it using the tools we have presented in this chapter, such an implementation will not be highly efficient. We leave it for you to fathom such an implementation in the exercises. We will frequently return to this problem in future chapters to discuss more efficient implementation strategies.

One other interesting aspect of the union-find problem is that it illustrates some of the complexity surrounding ADTs. The union-find ADT is an ADT that requires another ADT, the set, for its definition. Hence, implementations of the union-find ADT will be highly dependent upon the implementation of sets being used.

Exercises 2.4

1. Example 2.7 provided the IsElementOf operation for the boolean array implementation of the set ADT, and Example 2.8 did the same for the Union operation. Write PSEUDO procedures/functions for each of the other set operations under this implementation.

2. Using big-O notation, analyze the time efficiency of each of the Set ADT operations you implemented in Exercise 1.

3. Discuss the space efficiency of the boolean array implementation of sets. Can you identify conditions under which this implementation would be highly space-inefficient? Highly space-efficient?

4. Discuss how the boolean array implementation of sets could be extended to sets of strings. What restrictions would you put on the strings?

5. Devise a strategy for implementing the union-find ADT that uses only the ideas presented in this chapter. (Hint: one way involves making Partition an array of pointers.)

6. Write PSEUDO versions of the UFCreate, UFFind, and UFUnion operations for the implementation you devise in Exercise 5.

Chapter Summary

We have expanded upon the notion of an ADT and its implementation. An ADT is specified by describing its elements, the relationships between them, and the operations that can be performed on them. These operations can be thought of as a collection of PSEUDO interfaces in pre- and postcondition form. Any implementation of an ADT must provide a procedure or function for each operation. Moreover, the implementation's procedures/functions must obey the interfaces established in the formal definition of the ADT. This makes it painless to switch from one implementation to another in a given application.

In particular, we have defined the matrix, string, pointer, set, and union-find ADTs in this chapter. We have discussed some simple implementations for these ADTs. We will be looking at applications and more efficient implementations in future chapters.

Key Words

abstract data type	mapping function	set
column-major	matrix	sparse matrix
dereferencing	pointer	string
encapsulate	row-major	union-find problem
information hiding		

Programming Problems/Projects

1. Extend the definition of the matrix ADT from Section 1 to include the usual linear algebra operations on matrices of reals—for example, matrix sum, matrix product, transpose, determinant, and inversion. Write appropriate interfaces (as PSEUDO procedure/function headers) for each of these operations. First develop an implementation of these operations by using the assign and retrieve operations for matrices built into your programming language. Then develop an implementation that inherits the matrix Assign and Retrieve operations for sparse matrices developed in Example 2.2 and Exercise 6 of Section 1. Test the performance of your new matrix operations under these two implementations of matrix Assign and Retrieve. Which provides better performance? Why? Under what conditions does the performance difference become noticeable?

2. Due to factors such as type of airplane, amount of pilot experience, and pilot geographic location, each of the pilots employed by the Wing-and-a-Prayer Airline Company qualifies to fly on only a relatively small percentage of flights offered by this growing company. The information concerning which flights a given pilot is qualified to fly could be stored as a large Boolean array.

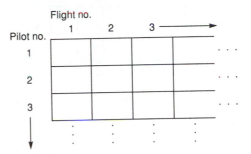

Help Wing-and-a-Prayer by developing a program that will accept as input a flight or pilot number and then print all pilots or flights, respectively, that correspond to the input. Because a given pilot qualifies for only a small percentage of flights, the sparse matrix technique from Section 2.1 should be used to store the data. (Note: is it necessary to store ordered triples (row, column, value) in the list associated with this technique when the data in the matrix is boolean?)

3. In the programming language of your choice, provide a complete solution to the problem for which a main program is given in Example 2.3. Provide string operations for this program in such a way that the implementation of the string data type could be changed without changing the main program *at all*.

4. *The Game of Life* was invented by mathematician John H. Conway (*Scientific American,* October 1970, p. 120). This game models the growth and changes in a complex collection of living organisms. The model can be interpreted as applying to a collection of microorganisms, an ecologically closed system of animals or plants, or an urban development.

   Start with an $N \times N$ checkerboard on which "counters" are to be placed. Each location that is not on a border has eight neighbors. The counters are born, survive, or die during a "generation" according to the following rules:

- *Survival:* Counters with two or three neighboring counters survive to the next generation.

- *Death:* Counters with four or more neighbors die from overcrowding and are removed for the next generation. Counters with zero or one neighbor die from isolation and are removed for the next generation.

- *Birth:* Each empty location that has exactly three counters in the eight neighboring locations is a birth location. A counter is placed in the location for the next generation. For example, on a 6 × 6 space, the pattern on the left would look like the one on the right in the next generation:

Certain patterns are stable:

Other patterns repeat a sequence:

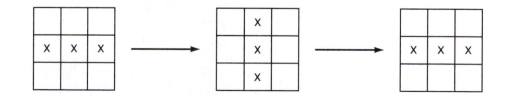

Because two $N \times N$ matrices are required to implement *The Game of Life*, it is clear that memory limitations could easily become a problem for a large N.

After initializing the first generation, print it out. Then calculate the next generation in another array and print this too. Repeat for a specified number of generations. Your output should be an "X" for live cells and a blank otherwise.

Develop the high-level logic of your program by employing the fundamental Assign and Retrieve operations for matrices. First use your compiler's implementation of these operations. Then switch to the implementation of sparse matrices described in Section 2.1. Your high-level logic should not need to change at all. In a written statement, describe the performance differences you observe with these two implementations. Explain why these differences occur.

5. Write a program that allows a user to enter a target string to be searched for in a file of text. Your program should then count the number of occurrences of this target string in the file. Your program should make absolutely no assumptions about the line structure of the file; that is, do not assume that all lines in the file are shorter than some specified maximum length.

6. Provide a complete fixed-length implementation of strings. Then use this implementation to write a high-level program that is a small-scale text editor. Your high-level program should access strings only through the provided operations.

7. Although the fixed-length method for strings is very easy to implement, it leads to two potential problems. First, what about the string longer than MaxStringSize characters? The fixed-length method simply cannot accommodate such a string. Second, since most strings will be considerably shorter than MaxStringSize characters, the fixed-length method will waste a sizeable amount of memory. This memory waste is shown in Figure 2.19.

The alternate implementation method we propose here is known as the *workspace-index* method. We will look at another possible implementation for strings in the next chapter, when we discuss linked lists. The idea behind the workspace-index method is that one large memory workspace is allocated to storing all strings. Additionally, an index table of records with two fields for each string is maintained. One field contains the address in the workspace at which a particular string starts, and the other contains the length of each string. This principle is illustrated in Figure 2.20.

Suppose now that we add a third string to the collection in Figure 2.20. All that we need to know is where the free portion of the workspace begins (in this case, it begins at location 10). We place the string starting at that location, add appropriate entries to our index table, and adjust the pointer to the beginning of the free memory. This threefold process is illustrated in Figure 2.21 for the addition of the string CREAM.

The storage advantages of the workspace-index method should be evident. By associating two indexing integers with each string, we are trading off the storage required for two integers against the potentially large number of wasted characters that pad strings in the fixed-length method. Moreover, the only restraint on maximum string length is the amount of storage left in the workspace.

Begin your work on this problem by writing a workspace-index implementation of all string operations. Then, plug this new implementation into the high-level text editor you developed for the previous problem.

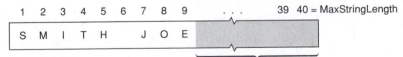

FIGURE 2.19

Example of wasted memory with fixed-length implementation of strings.

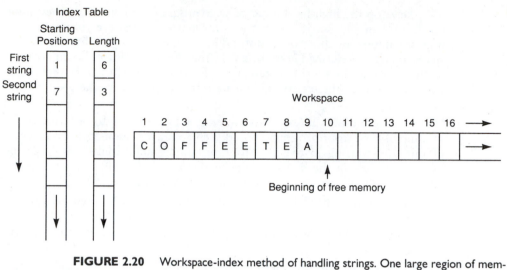

FIGURE 2.20   Workspace-index method of handling strings. One large region of memory, the *workspace,* is allocated to storing all strings. An *index table* maintains the starting address in the workspace of each string that has been stored as well as the length of the string. In this figure the first string stored was "COFFEE" and the second string stored was "TEA". When a third string is stored, its first character will go in location 10.

(Note: this is a good problem for working in teams of three. One person should develop the high-level text editor, another the fixed-length string implementation, and a third the workspace-index implementation. If you obey the Use and Implementation rules for ADTs given in Section 2.2, no changes to the high-level text editor should be required when an alternate implementation is plugged in.)

8. Write a program that allows a user to enter a string. The program should then output the following:

    a. All letters that appear in this string (letters as distinguished from other possible characters)

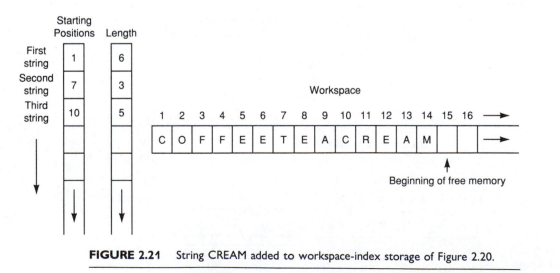

FIGURE 2.21   String CREAM added to workspace-index storage of Figure 2.20.

b. A count of how many letters appear in the string

For example, suppose the input string is

```
The numbers -2, 5, 20, and symbols "?", ":" should be
ignored.
```

Then output from your program should be

```
The letters in this string are

T a b d e g h i l m n o r s u y

There are 16 letters in this string.
```

Your program should use a boolean array implementation of sets to keep track of the sets of all upper- and lowercase letters and the set of letters that actually occur in the string. Access these sets only through the provided operations so that it will be easy to change the implementation of sets in the future.

9. Write a program that allows input of a string Master and a string Sub to be sought in the master. Your program should then use both the straightforward and KMP Search procedures to locate Sub in Master. Add statements to these procedures that count the number of comparisons made by each method.

Once your program is developed, use it to conduct an experiment. Run it for a variety of strings—strings entered interactively, strings generated randomly, strings from famous passages of English prose, strings composed from a reduced number of letters. In a separate write-up summarize the results of your findings. Include charts, tables, and graphs as appropriate.

10. Add the Boyer-Moore string search (Exercise 10 of Section 2.2) to your work from the previous problem.

11. Exercises 4 and 5 of Section 2.4 suggest an implementation for the union-find ADT. Develop this implementation by writing procedures/functions for each of the union-find operations. Now, use your procedures/functions in a high-level program that allows a user to manipulate cities in a transportation network in the fashion described in Section 2.4. Assume the cities are identified by a single letter.

3

LISTS—OPERATIONS, IMPLEMENTATIONS, AND APPLICATIONS

List, list, O, list!

Shakespeare, *Hamlet*

CHAPTER OUTLINE

The variety of information we store in lists is mind-boggling. From the records of students at a university to the items we need on our weekly trip to the grocery store, we organize data into lists. In general, we can subdivide these lists into two types: those that are ordered according to some criterion and those that are not. The list of student records at a university would likely fit into the first category since it is typically ordered by some identifier such as name or identification number. The record in the first position of the list is there because the associated name alphabetically precedes the names of the other students. The criterion of alphabetical precedence dictates the position of an item in this ordered list.

Unless you are an incredibly organized person, your weekly shopping list of grocery items is probably not ordered by any inherent property of the items. Here the item first on the list is there simply because it was thought of first. Hence, in an unordered list there is no logical relationship between the first and second items, second and third items, and so on. In Sections 3.1 and 3.2, we will focus our attention on ordered lists—leaving unordered lists for the exercises.

We will explore two different implementations of ordered lists: an ordered-array implementation and a linked-list implementation. The linked-list implementation will require a more detailed consideration of the pointer data type, introduced in Chapter 2. We will show how the pointer data type itself can be implemented using arrays in Section 3.3.

Several variations on the basic linked-list theme will be studied in Section 3.4. A discussion of three applications of linked lists close the chapter: sparse matrices in Section 3.5, strings in Section 3.6, and sets with the union-find problem in Section 3.7.

3.1 DEFINITIONS OF LIST ADTs

To introduce our definition of an *ordered list,* consider the problem faced by many small businesses—organizing their database of customer records. Further suppose that each customer record in such a database consists of the following information:

Customer last name
Customer first name
Street address
ZIP code
Amount owed to company

One way the company might organize these records is in a list, kept in alphabetical order by last name. An example of such a list is shown in Figure 3.1.

Now consider the operations such a business will want to perform upon its customer list. New customers must be *added* to the list. Customers who take their business elsewhere must be *deleted* from the list. The records of

FIGURE 3.1
Ordered list of four customer records. The ordering is alphabetical according to last name.

	LastName	FirstName	StreetAddress	ZIP	AmountOwed
1	ALLEN	RICHARD	419 N. 5TH ST.	34819	400.16
2	CARSON	NATHAN	812 E. 2ND ST.	26814	12.32
3	SMITH	ELLEN	333 W. 4TH ST.	91815	0.00
4	WILSON	ELIZABETH	687 S. 12TH ST.	44615	90.14

customers who move, pay a bill, or make a purchase must be *updated*. When a particular customer has an inquiry about her bill, her record must be *retrieved* and displayed. Finally, a variety of monthly reports require that the entire list be *traversed,* with a particular operation applied to each customer's record. These five list operations are highlighted in Figures 3.2 through 3.6. They form the basis of the following definition of an *ordered list* as an ADT.

	LastName	FirstName	StreetAddress	ZIP	AmountOwed
1	ALLEN	RICHARD	419 N. 5TH ST.	34819	400.16
2	CARSON	NATHAN	812 E. 2ND ST.	26814	12.32
3	SMITH	ELLEN	333 W. 4TH ST.	91815	0.00
4	WILSON	ELIZABETH	687 S. 12TH ST.	44615	90.14

ADD record for MILLER JEAN

FIGURE 3.2
Add operation on list from Figure 3.1. A customer with last name "MILLER" has been added, and the ordering by last name preserved.

	LastName	FirstName	StreetAddress	ZIP	AmountOwed
1	ALLEN	RICHARD	419 N. 5TH ST.	34819	400.16
2	CARSON	NATHAN	812 E. 2ND ST.	26814	12.32
3	MILLER	JEAN	496 E. WABASH	62843	0.00
4	SMITH	ELLEN	333 W. 4TH ST.	91815	0.00
5	WILSON	ELIZABETH	687 S. 12TH ST.	44615	90.14

	LastName	FirstName	StreetAddress	ZIP	AmountOwed
1	ALLEN	RICHARD	419 N. 5TH ST.	34819	400.16
2	CARSON	NATHAN	812 E. 2ND ST.	26814	12.32
3	SMITH	ELLEN	333 W. 4TH ST.	91815	0.00
4	WILSON	ELIZABETH	687 S. 12TH ST.	44615	90.14

FIGURE 3.3
Delete operation on list from Figure 3.1. The customer with last name "CARSON" has been deleted.

DELETE record of CARSON NATHAN

	LastName	FirstName	StreetAddress	ZIP	AmountOwed
1	ALLEN	RICHARD	419 N. 5TH ST.	34819	400.16
3	SMITH	ELLEN	333 W. 4TH ST.	91815	0.00
4	WILSON	ELIZABETH	687 S. 12TH ST.	44615	90.14

FIGURE 3.4
Retrieve Operation on list of Figure 3.1. A search for the customer with last name "SMITH" was conducted. Once located, a copy of the entire record was made.

	LastName	FirstName	StreetAddress	ZIP	AmountOwed
1	ALLEN	RICHARD	419 N. 5TH ST.	34819	400.16
2	CARSON	NATHAN	812 E. 2ND ST.	26814	12.32
3	SMITH	ELLEN	333 W. 4TH ST.	91815	0.00
4	WILSON	ELIZABETH	687 S. 12TH ST.	44615	90.14

RETRIEVE record of SMITH ELLEN

LastName	FirstName	StreetAddress	ZIP	AmountOwed
SMITH	ELLEN	333 W. 4TH ST.	91815	0.00

FIGURE 3.5
Update Operation on list of Figure 3.1. A search for the record of the customer with the last name "SMITH" was conducted, and when found, was given a new value for amount owed.

	LastName	FirstName	StreetAddress	ZIP	AmountOwed
1	ALLEN	RICHARD	419 N. 5TH ST.	34819	400.16
2	CARSON	NATHAN	812 E. 2ND ST.	26814	12.32
3	SMITH	ELLEN	333 W. 4TH ST.	91815	0.00
4	WILSON	ELIZABETH	687 S. 12TH ST.	44615	90.14

UPDATE AmountOwed in record of SMITH ELLEN

	LastName	FirstName	StreetAddress	ZIP	AmountOwed
1	ALLEN	RICHARD	419 N. 5TH ST.	34819	400.16
2	CARSON	NATHAN	812 E. 2ND ST.	26814	12.32
3	SMITH	ELLEN	333 W. 4TH ST.	91815	63.94
4	WILSON	ELIZABETH	687 S. 12TH ST.	44615	90.14

FIGURE 3.6
Traverse operation on list of Figure 3.1.

	LastName	FirstName	StreetAddress	ZIP	AmountOwed
1	ALLEN	RICHARD	419 N. 5TH ST.	34819	400.16
2	CARSON	NATHAN	812 E. 2ND ST.	26814	12.32
3	SMITH	ELLEN	333 W. 4TH ST.	91815	0.00
4	WILSON	ELIZABETH	687 S. 12TH ST.	44615	90.14

TRAVERSE list, applying procedure that reduces AmountOwed of each customer by amount paid by that customer.

	LastName	FirstName	StreetAddress	ZIP	AmountOwed
1	ALLEN	RICHARD	419 N. 5TH ST.	34819	294.16
2	CARSON	NATHAN	812 E. 2ND ST.	26814	0.00
3	SMITH	ELLEN	333 W. 4TH ST.	91815	0.00
4	WILSON	ELIZABETH	687 S. 12TH ST.	44615	50.00

• **Definition of an Ordered List:** An *ordered list* is a collection of objects, called *nodes,* arranged in a linear sequence according to some ordering criterion between data in the nodes. Given that each node is of type ListNode, and contains data of type ListData, the following operations are provided for the ADT List.

```
type
  ListData: (* The type of data in each node of the list *);
  ListNode: (* Data type giving the structure of each node of the list.  In
              the simplest case it will be equivalent to ListData *);
  Comparison: function (* The signature of a function that
                          determines the ordering of the list *)
              ( given Item1, Item2: ListData (* Two data items to be
                                                compared *);
                return: boolean               (* true if Item1 is to be
                                                 considered as preceding Item2
                                                 in ordering for L, false
                                                 otherwise *) );
  MatchCriterion: function (* The signature of a function that determines
                             whether two list items match each other *)
                  ( given Target, AnyData: ListData (* Two data items with
                                                       Target containing
                                                       a value to be matched
                                                       in some sense as
                                                       determined by Match
                                                       function *);
                    return: boolean                 (* true if Target and
                                                     AnyData satisfy
                                                     the Match criterion *) );
  NodeOperation: procedure (* The signature of a procedure that can be
                             applied to an individual list node *)
                 ( given Item: ListNode  (* Arbitrary node in list L *);
                   return Item: ListNode (* Item as affected by
                                            ProcessNode *) );
procedure Create
  ( given L: List                        (* An arbitrary list variable L in an
                                            unknown state *);
    return L: List                       (* L as an initialized empty List *) );

procedure Destroy
  ( given L: List                        (* An arbitrary list variable L that has
                                            been acted upon by Create and other
                                            operations *);
    return L: List                       (* L returned in undefined state, with
                                            storage allocated for L now available for
                                            future invocations of Create *) );
procedure Assign
  ( given Source: List                   (* A list whose contents are to be copied to
                                            Destination *);
    return Destination: List             (* Contains a copy of Source *) );

procedure Add
  ( given L: List                        (* A list L ordered by Precedes
                                            relationship *);
```

```
        Item: ListData              (* A data item to be added to L *);
        Precedes: Comparison        (* The relationship between nodes that
                                       determines the ordering of L *);
   return L: List                   (* L with Item inserted according to the
                                       order determined by Precedes * );
           Success: boolean         (* Set to true if Item successfully
                                       inserted. Set to false if Item could not
                                       be inserted because L is full *) );

procedure Delete
   ( given L: List                  (* A list L *);
         Target: ListData           (* Data to be matched for deletion *);
         Match: MatchCriterion      (* This function determines which node
                                       is to be deleted from L *);
   return L: List                   (* The first ListNode in L whose data satisfy
                                       the Match criterion is deleted. Only the
                                       first such ListNode is deleted. *);
           Success: boolean         (* false if nothing in list L satisfied the
                                       Match criterion; true otherwise *) );

procedure Retrieve
   ( given L: List                  (* A list L *);
         Target: ListData           (* Data to be matched for retrieval *);
         Match: MatchCriterion      (* This function determines which node is
                                       being sought *);
   return Item: ListData            (* The data in the first node in L
                                       satisfying the criterion established by
                                       Match *);
           Success: boolean         (* false if nothing in L satisfied the Match
                                       criterion; true otherwise *) );

procedure Update
   ( given L: List                  (* A list L *);
         Target: ListData           (* Data to be matched for updating *);
         Match: MatchCriterion      (* This function determines the node
                                       to be updated *);
         NewValue: ListData         (* The new value to be assigned to the first
                                       node in L which satisfies the Match
                                       criterion. Assume that NewValue does not
                                       alter the logical position of the node in
                                       L. See Exercise 1 for a more detailed
                                       explanation of this assumption. *)
   return L: List                   (* The list L with the first ListNode whose
                                       data satisfy the Match criterion replaced
                                       by NewValue *);
           Success: boolean         (* false if nothing satisfied the Match
                                       criterion; true otherwise *) );

procedure Traverse
   ( given L: List                  (* A list L *);
         ProcessNode: NodeOperation (* Some process to be applied to each
                                       node *);
   return L: List                   (* L with each node in it affected by
                                       ProcessNode *) );
```

The definition given above for the ADT List makes considerably more use of procedure/function parameters than the ADT definitions discussed in Chapter 2. The reason for this is threefold. First, since the list ADT we are specifying here is ordered, we must allow the user of the Add operation to pass in the ordering relation that is appropriate for the given list. Second, since the Delete, Retrieve, and Update operations all require finding a data value that meets a certain criterion, we can achieve a high degree of generality in these operations by allowing the user to pass in a Match function that defines the criteria for deleting, retrieving, or updating in a particular application. Finally, the role of the Traverse operation is to walk through the list in an ordered fashion, applying some procedure to each node in the list. The particular procedure that is applied is independent of the Traverse operation itself. By allowing the user of Traverse to pass in a ProcessNode operation, we achieve this independence. One Traverse procedure works for whatever operation we want to do at each node. We do not have to write a separate Traverse procedure for each particular process that we might apply to a node. The examples below illustrate how procedure/function parameters allow our list operations to be used in a variety of contexts.

Example 3.1   Suppose we have a list structure with list nodes similar to those appearing in Figure 3.1:

```
type
   ListData: record
               LastName: String;
               FirstName: String;
               Street: String;
               Zip: integer;
               AmountOwed: real
             endrecord;
```

Assuming a suitable implementation for the ADT string, write a procedure that will allow a user to add a customer record to a list L being maintained in alphabetical order by customer last name.

```
procedure AddCustomer
  ( given L: List  (* A previously created list of customer records *);
    return L: List (* L with the addition of a new data node entered
                       interactively by the user *) );

  var NewData: ListData;
      Success: boolean;

  function CustomerRelationship      (* Used to establish ordering for
                                        list L *)
    ( given Cust1, Cust2: ListData (* Customer records to be compared *);
      return: boolean                (* true if the last name of Cust1
                                        alphabetically precedes the last
                                        name of Cust2 *) );

    start CustomerRelationship
      CustomerRelationship := LessThan(Cust1.LastName, Cust2.LastName)
    end CustomerRelationship;
```

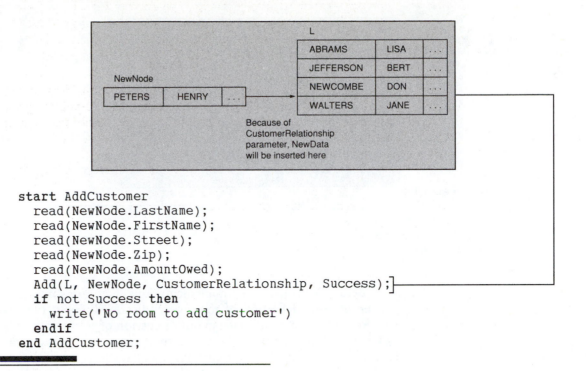

```
start AddCustomer
   read(NewNode.LastName);
   read(NewNode.FirstName);
   read(NewNode.Street);
   read(NewNode.Zip);
   read(NewNode.AmountOwed);
   Add(L, NewNode, CustomerRelationship, Success);
   if not Success then
      write('No room to add customer')
   endif
end AddCustomer;
```

Example 3.2   Suppose that we have the same list structure as in Example 3.1. Assuming a suitable implementation for the ADT string, write a procedure that will allow deletion of all list nodes that have a last name matching a target name entered by a user.

```
procedure DeleteByName
   ( given L: List    (* A previously created list of customer records *);
     return L: List  (* L, with all occurrences of records matching a
                          user-specified last name removed *) );

   var Target: ListData;
       Success: boolean;

   function Match
      ( given Target, Cust: ListData (* A Target record containing the
                                         particular last name we seek and
                                         an arbitrary list data item Cust
                                         to be compared to Target *);
        return: boolean                (* true if Cust.LastName equals
                                         Target.LastName *) );

      start Match
         Match := Equal(Cust.LastName, Target.LastName)
      end Match;

start DeleteByName
   read(Target.LastName);
```

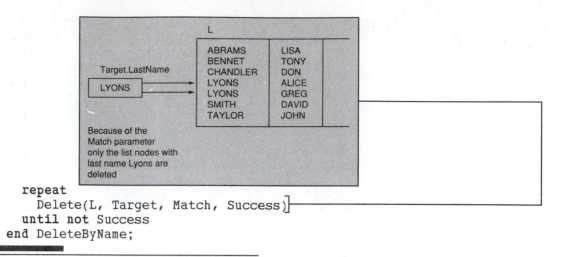

```
repeat
   Delete(L, Target, Match, Success)
until not Success
end DeleteByName;
```

Before we consider its implementations, here are some final comments concerning our definition of the ordered-list ADT. First, the two examples should reinforce a point made in our discussion of sort and search algorithms in Chapter 1: use of procedures and functions as parameters can add a potent degree of generality to algorithms and data structures. In these examples we have been able to use the list ADT operations in the context of the customer list of Figure 3.1 by passing procedure/function parameters particular to that application. In the exercises you will see that exactly the same ADT operations can be used in completely different contexts by passing in other suitably defined procedures/functions.

Second, it is important to note that Examples 3.1 and 3.2 have used the operations provided by the ordered-list ADT without making any assumptions about how that ADT would be implemented. This is consistent with the ADT Use rule, formulated in Section 2.2. Accessing an ADT only through its provided operations allows us to discuss algorithms involving that ADT before ever considering how it is implemented.

Third, the ADT approach we are emphasizing allows a large degree of creativity and flexibility in defining the operations associated with an ADT. It would be a gross overstatement to maintain that the operations we have provided for an ordered list in this section will be sufficient for all applications. In the exercises you will explore ways of extending and altering our collection of operations in ways that might provide a better list ADT for certain situations. Indeed, formulating the definition of operations for a complex ADT is an endeavor that truly tests the creative abilities of any computer scientist.

Exercises 3.1

1. In the preconditions for the update operation on an ordered-list ADT, we specified that the NewValue being assigned to the node in the list could not alter the logical position of the node in the list. For instance, given the list of Figure 3.1 which is ordered by customer last name, this precondition is equivalent to the assumption that a customer's last name cannot be altered by the Update operation. We shall see in Section 3.2 that the reason for this

limitation is one of efficiency. Does the assumption mean that it is impossible for a customer to change his name? If not, write a procedure to perform this type of change using list operations other than Update.

2. In this exercise you are to work with the customer list of Figure 3.1 and Example 3.1. Write a procedure that will print the names of all customers who owe more than $100.00. (Hint: design an appropriate procedure to pass to the Traverse operation.)

3. In this exercise you are to work with the customer list of Figure 3.1 and Example 3.1. Write a procedure for use when a customer has paid a portion of her bill. The procedure should read in the customer's last name and the amount paid and should appropriately adjust the amount owed by that customer.

4. Suppose that the database of the registrar's office at High Plains University consists of records with the following fields:

StudentName

  Last

  First

TotalCreditsTaken   (including courses failed)

TotalCreditsEarned   (only those courses passed)

TotalGradePoints   (based on 4 for A, 3 for B, and so on)

The database is ordered by student name. Students with the same last name are ordered alphabetically by first name. Declare an appropriate type ListData for the registrar's application. Then write the following procedures:

a. Allow the registrar to add a new student.

b. Allow the registrar to delete a student's record. (Make sure that the correct student is deleted when more than one student share a last name.)

c. Allow the registrar to display the grade point average of a student specified by input of first and last name. (Grade point average is TotalGradePoints divided by TotalCreditsTaken.)

d. Allow the registrar to enter a student's courses and grades received for the term just ended, and have the student's record appropriately adjusted.

e. Allow the registrar to print a list of all graduating seniors, defined to be those students with 120 credits or more and a GPA of 1.8 or above.

5. An ordered-list ADT may be defined without a Traverse operation if a collection of more primitive operations is provided that allows you to write your own traversal algorithm for each particular application. Write an alternative definition for the ordered-list ADT that takes this approach. (Hint: think about the operations provided by a programming language that allow you to proceed through a sequential file by continually accessing the next record in the file.) Then use your new definition to provide answers for Exercises 2 and 4e.

6. An alternative to passing functions as parameters to determine the ordering and matching criteria for an ordered list is to specify that ListData always have a designated *key field* used for ordering the list and determining whether a value in the list matches a given target. Provide a complete alternate definition for an ordered list with this approach. In what ways is this approach less general that the approach taken in the definition of this section?

7. In an *unordered list* there is no ordering relationship between nodes at position N and N + 1 in the list. In other words, the nodes in an unordered list are ordered only by their absolute position in the list (that is, first node, second node, etc.), not by any intrinsic property of the nodes. Write a complete ADT specification for an unordered list. The criterion by which nodes are added, deleted, and so on is to be specified as an absolute position within the list instead of a functional parameter that defines a particular ordering or match. Finally, give some examples of applications where the unordered list you have defined may be a more appropriate ADT than an ordered list.

8. As in Exercise 7, write a complete ADT specification for an unordered list; this time, however, the criterion by which nodes are added, deleted, and so on is to be specified as a position relative to that of another node in the list, instead of a functional parameter defining a particular ordering or match. Thus, your parameter list will have to include the address of a node in the list and an integer specifying the position after that of the given node where a node is to be added, deleted, and so on. If the relative position is a negative integer, it refers to a node before the given node.

9. Write a function Sum to sum the integers in an ordered list of integers. Show how it is called from the main program.

3.2   IMPLEMENTATIONS OF THE LIST ADT

In the previous section we developed some algorithms that use the list ADT. Consequently, it is now imperative that we implement this ADT by strictly adhering to the ADT Implementation rule of Section 2.2. This will ensure that the list algorithms we have already developed will not have to be altered to fit our implementations. We will discuss two implementations of an ordered list: a sorted array with binary search and a linked list.

Ordered Array with Binary Search

The techniques behind this implementation should be familiar to you. We will merely maintain the data values in an array such that the value first in the logical order of the list is stored in the node in the first physical position of the array, the value second in logical order in the node in the second physical position, and so on. This array will then be encapsulated with a counter that keeps track of the number of nodes currently in the list, up to a maximum of MaxListSize. Hence, the ADT List will be implemented as follows:

```
type (* Constant MaxListSize establishes limit on list size *)
   ListData: (* The type of data in each node of the list *);
   ListNode: ListData;
   List: record
           Node: array [MaxListSize] of ListNode;
           NumberOfNodes: integer
         endrecord;
```

Example 3.3   Using the previous declaration for a List, write the implementation of the Add operation.

```
procedure Add
  ( given L: List              (* A list L ordered by Precedes
                                   relationship *);
          Item: ListData       (* A data item to be added to L *);
          Precedes: Comparison (* The relationship between nodes that
                                   determines the ordering of L *);
    return L: List             (* L with Item inserted according to the
                                   order determined by Precedes *);
           Success: boolean    (* Set to true if Item successfully
                                   inserted; set to false if Item could
                                   not be inserted because L is full *) );
  var K, PositionToAdd: integer;

  function FindSlot
    ( given L: List              (* A list L ordered by Precedes
                                     relationship *);
            Item: ListData       (* A data item to be added to L *);
            Precedes: Comparison (* This function determines the
                                     ordering of the list *);
      return: integer            (* The physical position in L.Node
                                     where Item must be inserted to
                                     maintain order according to the
                                     Precedes relationship *) );
    start FindSlot
      (* Implementation of the FindSlot function is left for the
         exercises *)
    end FindSlot;

  start Add
    if L.NumberOfNodes = MaxListSize then
      Success := false
    else
      Success := true;
      PositionToAdd := FindSlot(L, Item, Precedes);
      for K := L.NumberOfNodes to PositionToAdd by -1 do
        L.Node[K + 1] := L.Node[K]
      endfor;
```

		Name	Other fields
To be inserted	1	ALLEN ELIZABETH	
BAKER FRANK →	2	BOWEN CHARLES	
	3	COOPER PAMELA	
	4	DAVIS WARREN	
	.	.	.
	.	.	.
	.	.	.
NumberOfNodes		WARDEL EVE	
MaxListSize			

These records must be moved down one slot to make room for the insertion

```
      L.Node[PositionToAdd] := Item;
      L.NumberOfNodes := L.NumberOfNodes + 1
    endif
  end Add;
```

Completion of the other list operations for the ordered-array implementation of a list is left for the exercises. Note that because of the physical ordering of the array, the search efficiency to find a node or insertion slot for this implementation can be $O(\log_2 NumberOfNodes)$ comparisons. A hint of the price paid for this very fast search efficiency is given in the graphic documentation accompanying Example 3.3. Here we see that the Add operation for this implementation of an ordered list requires an excessive amount of data movement. For instance, the addition of BAKER FRANK, as indicated in the graphic documentation, will force all nodes beginning at the second index to be moved down one slot. In a realistic situation where your database may have 10,000 records, each consisting of 500 bytes, this will mean shuffling 5,000,000 bytes of data around in computer storage. If the storage involved is a magnetic disk instead of primary memory, this "pushing down" of all records starting with the second one could well leave the system in a loop that would require several minutes to execute.

An analogous problem occurs when a node near the top of the list is deleted. All the nodes below it must rise one slot to maintain the physical order. Thus, the implementation we are proposing here will not fare particularly well with respect to all of the operations defined for the list ADT. In particular, this implementation is well suited only for those lists that are **stable,** that is, not undergoing frequent additions and deletions.

Linked List

The linked-list implementation of the ordered-list ADT addresses the shortcomings of the previous implementation by not requiring that an item's physical position in the list match its logical position. The central motivation behind the linked-list data structure is eliminating the data movement associated with insertions into and deletions from the middle of the list. Of course, we might suspect that efficiency in eliminating such data movement can only come by trading off other efficiency factors. One of the crucial questions to ask yourself as we study linked lists is, "What price are we paying to handle additions and deletions effectively?" One way of conceptually understanding a linked list is to think of the game some parents use to make the opening of the holiday gifts particularly exciting for their children. One feature of the game, which helps to build children's anticipation, ensures that minor gifts are opened first, gradually building up to the most substantial gift. (Recall from your own childhood experience the partial letdown that occurred when you opened a gift package containing a mere pair of socks after having already unwrapped something significantly more exciting, such as a baseball glove or new doll!) Thus, the premises of this gift-giving game are that gifts may be ranked according to their desirability and that the game is more fun when the most desirable gifts are opened last.

To achieve this end, parents will hide a child's wrapped gifts at various locations throughout the home. For instance, let us suppose a scenario in which parents have the following four gifts for their child, ranked and hidden as indicated.

Ranking	Gift	Hiding place
least desirable	pair of socks	under bed
↓	box of candy	kitchen drawer
	video game	basement cabinet
most desirable	bicycle	garage

The parents will then tell the child *only* the location of the least desirable gift; for instance, they would give instructions to look under a bed for the first gift. Upon opening that gift, the child will find the uninspiring pair of socks plus a more intriguing note with the information that the next gift will be in a kitchen drawer. The pattern should now be obvious. From the box of candy, the child follows an informational pointer to a basement cabinet, where the video game is discovered along with a similar informational link to the garage as a location where something bigger and better may be found. The now eager child will uncover a bike along with a final (and no doubt disappointing) note indicating that the end of the chain of gifts has been reached.

A conceptual picture of this chain of gifts is presented in Figure 3.7. This same picture applies to the *linked-list* data structure we are about to study. In this figure, the arrows connecting packages represent the informational note in each package, telling us the location of the next package. Conceptually, the form taken by this informational pointer is not important. However, it is crucial that we have a reliable pointer to the leading gift (often called a *head pointer*) and, thereafter, a reliable pointer in each package to the next package. Should any pointer be flawed, the remaining gifts on the chain become essentially inaccessible (much to the dismay of the child who wanted that bike so desperately).

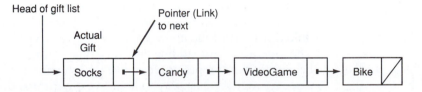

FIGURE 3.7   Linked chain of gifts. The pointers represent information stored with each gift telling us the location of the next gift. The *head* pointer tells us where to find the first gift, while the pointer with value / (NULL) tells us (alas) there are no more gifts.

In addition to introducing us to much of the vernacular that comes with linked lists, this review of a simple childhood game can also give us a hint of the ease with which such a linked chain of nodes can handle additions and deletions. For instance, suppose that a sudden windfall allows the parents to buy a baseball glove in addition to the four gifts they had already purchased. Assuming that this new gift is ranked between the video game and the bicycle in desirability, consider what must be done to link it into the gift chain. We must do as follows:

1. Find a place to hide it—for example, the attic.
2. Take the informational linking note from the video game package and put it in the baseball glove package. (Why?)
3. Insert a new informational pointer in the video game package, indicating the attic as the location of the next node. (Why?)

The important aspect to note in this series of moves is that no gift that was already in place had to be moved to accommodate adding the new gift. From a conceptual perspective, this is the reason linked lists are able to avoid the movement of data associated with an insertion into an ordered-array.

Along the same lines, let us now suppose that our shameless parents devour all of their child's candy before the holiday arrives. Clearly they must remove this package from the chain to hide this disgusting behavior from their child. Convince yourself that the following steps will accomplish this deletion:

1. Remove the now empty candy package from the kitchen drawer.
2. Before throwing away the empty package, remove the linking note from it and put this note in the package containing the socks.
3. Dispose of the incriminating candy container and the linking note that originally was in the package with the socks.

It is important to note again that no package remaining on the chain had to be physically moved to a new location: a situation much different from what happened when we removed a name from an array-implemented list. A *formalization* of this intuitive notion of a linked list is the following: a *linked list* is a collection of nodes, each containing a data portion and a pointer. The data portion of each node is of the same type. The pointer in a given node contains the location of the node that logically follows the given node in the ordering of the list. The entire list is referenced by a separate head pointer to the first element in the linear ordering.

According to our definition of a linked list, an alphabetically ordered linked list with four nodes could be logically viewed as shown in Figure 3.8. The operations of adding and deleting a node from such a list may also be conveniently represented in such a schematic form. In fact, you will soon discover that the best way to conceive algorithms that manipulate linked lists is to draw what you want to happen via such logical pictures. Such a picture of a linked list is completely at the abstract level; it implies nothing about how the linked list will finally be implemented. Once you understand the concept from such a graphic representation, it is usually a straightforward matter to implement it.

FIGURE 3.8
Alphabetically ordered linked
list with four nodes.

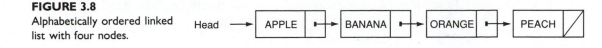

For instance, we now wish to add a node containing GRAPE to the list shown in Figure 3.8; all we need to do is to store GRAPE in an available memory location outside the list, such as the one pointed to by P in Figure 3.9. We then reset the pointer link of the node containing BANANA to point to the node containing GRAPE, and the pointer link of the node containing GRAPE to point to the node containing ORANGE. This logically maintains the alphabetical order of the data in the nodes without physically moving any of the existing nodes.

Similarly, should you then wish to delete an existing node from the linked list, a graphic representation of the list can again indicate how the pointers should be altered to reflect such a change. For example, given the list of Figure 3.9, the diagram of Figure 3.10 pictorially outlines what must be done to delete the node containing BANANA. Notice in this figure that, as was the case for insertion, only pointers must be changed to delete a node. Again, no movement of data occurs.

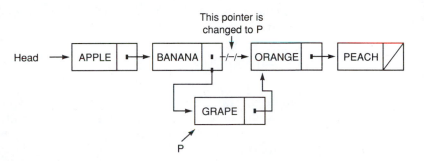

FIGURE 3.9 Insertion of node containing GRAPE into linked list of Figure 3.8. The pointer of the node containing the data BANANA has been reset to point to the new node, containing the data GRAPE. The pointer field of the new node, on the other hand, has been set to the node formerly referenced by the pointer of BAANANA's node.

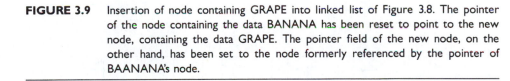

FIGURE 3.10 Deletion of node containing BANANA from linked list of 3.9. The pointer of the node preceding BANANA has been reset to bypass BANANA's node, and instead to point to the node following BANANA's in the list. Had BANANA's node been last in the list, the pointer field of APPLE's node would have been given the special value, NULL, here represented by the symbol /.

To implement these schematics, we will use the pointer ADT introduced in Section 2.3. Thus a linked list may be implemented using the following structures:

```
type
  List: pointer to ListNode;
  ListNode: record
              Data: ListData;
              Link: List
          endrecord;
```

Suppose that we are given variables P and Q declared by

```
var
  P, Q: List;
```

and that we want to "aim" the Link field in the node referenced by P to another node referenced by Q, as indicated in Figure 3.11. The statement

```
Ref(P).Link := Q
```

will achieve this. Similarly, if we wish to advance P from one node to the next, the statement

```
P := Ref(P).Link
```

is required. This action is highlighted in Figure 3.12.

We are now prepared to write PSEUDO code for a linked-list implementation of the Add and Delete operations. For both of these operations, it is important to note the following two points.

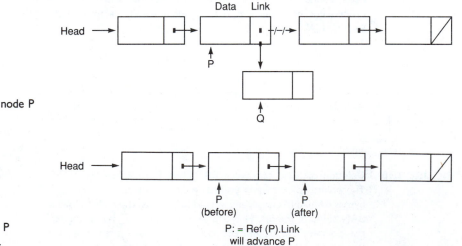

FIGURE 3.11

Aiming Link field in node P at node Q.

FIGURE 3.12

Advancing a pointer P through a linked list.

1. A linked list L is initialized to the empty list by setting L to the NULL pointer value. (Hence, the Create operation is defined.)

2. Both the Add and Delete operations require a pointer to the node that precedes the node to be inserted or removed. As Figures 3.9 and 3.10 indicate, it is the Link field in this preceding node that must be altered. The only exception to this occurs when the node being inserted/removed is located at the head of the list. We will signal this special case in our procedures by having the pointer to the previous node set to NULL.

Example 3.4

```
(* Linked-list implementation of Add operation for lists *)

procedure Add
  ( given L: List              (* A list L ordered by Precedes
                                  relationship *);
         Item: ListData        (* A data item to be added to L *);
         Precedes: Comparison  (* The relationship between nodes that
                                  determines the ordering of L *);
    return L: List             (* L with Item inserted according to the
                                  order determined by Precedes *);
         Success: boolean      (* Set to true if Item successfully
                                  inserted; set to false if Item
                                  could not be inserted because L is
                                  full *) );

  var
    P, Prev: List; (* P used to point at the node to be inserted. Prev
                     points at the node that logically precedes Item
                     referenced by P *)

  procedure FindSlot
    ( given L: List              (* A list L ordered by Precedes
                                    relationship *);
           Item: ListData        (* A data item to be added to L *);
           Precedes: Comparison  (* This function determines the
                                    ordering of the list *);
      return Prev: List          (* A pointer to the node in L whose
                                    value logically precedes Item. If
                                    Item precedes all nodes in L, then
                                    Prev is set to NULL *) );

    var Q: List;

    start FindSlot
      Prev := NULL;
      Q := L;
```

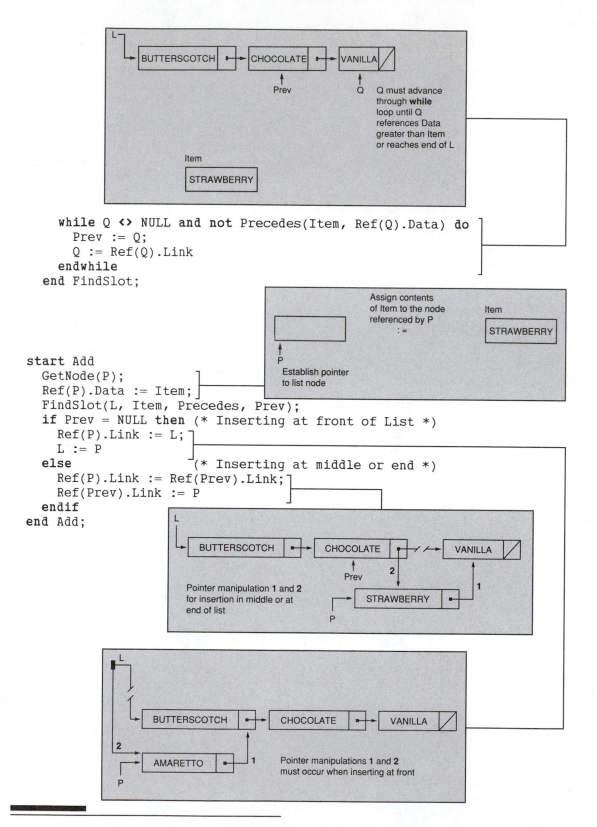

```
    while Q <> NULL and not Precedes(Item, Ref(Q).Data) do
      Prev := Q;
      Q := Ref(Q).Link
    endwhile
  end FindSlot;
```

```
start Add
  GetNode(P);
  Ref(P).Data := Item;
  FindSlot(L, Item, Precedes, Prev);
  if Prev = NULL then (* Inserting at front of List *)
    Ref(P).Link := L;
    L := P
  else              (* Inserting at middle or end *)
    Ref(P).Link := Ref(Prev).Link;
    Ref(Prev).Link := P
  endif
end Add;
```

Q must advance through **while** loop until Q references Data greater than Item or reaches end of L

Assign contents of Item to the node referenced by P

:=

Establish pointer to list node

Pointer manipulation 1 and 2 for insertion in middle or at end of list

Pointer manipulations 1 and 2 must occur when inserting at front

Before implementing the Delete procedure for a linked list, we should note the compound condition in the **while** loop of the preceding FindSlot procedure:

```
while Q <> NULL and not Precedes(Item, Ref(Q).Data) do
```

In formulating this **while** statement, we have made the assumption that the evaluation of an **and** will be short-circuited upon the first **false** value encountered in a left-to-right evaluation. This assumption is critical for the above **while** loop to function properly in all circumstances since, if Q is NULL and the right-hand component of the **and** is evaluated, a run-time error may result from referencing a NULL pointer. You should check the specifics of how your programming language evaluates **and**s before blindly following the PSEUDO code version of this procedure. A similar situation does not arise in the FindNodeToDelete procedure nested within the following implementation of the Delete operation because a boolean variable is used to control the analogous **while** loop.

Example 3.5

```
(* Linked-list implementation of Delete operation for Lists *)

procedure Delete
  ( given L: List              (* A list L *);
         Target: ListData       (* Data to be matched for deletion *);
         Match: MatchCriterion  (* This function determines which node
                                   is to be deleted from L *);
    return L: List              (* The first ListNode in L whose data
                                   satisfy the Match criterion is
                                   deleted. Only the first such ListNode
                                   is deleted. *);
           Success: boolean     (* false if nothing in list L satisfied
                                   the Match criterion; true
                                   otherwise *) );
  var
    P, Prev: List (* P will reference node to be deleted, and Prev will
                     reference the preceding node. Prev is NULL if node
                     to be deleted is first node in list L. *)

  procedure FindNodeToDelete
  ( given L: List              (* A list L *);
         Target: ListData       (* Data to be matched for deletion *);
         Match: Comparison      (* This function determines which ListNode
                                   is to be deleted from L *);
    return P: List              (* References node to be deleted *);
           Prev: List           (* References node prior to P; NULL if P
                                   references first node *);
           Success: boolean     (* false if cannot find node to be
                                   deleted *) );
    start FindNodeToDelete
      Prev := NULL;
```

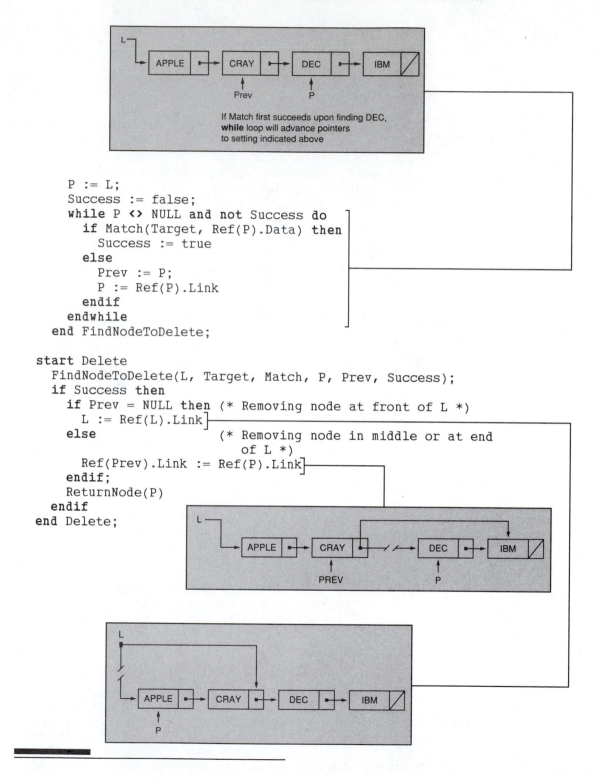

```
      P := L;
      Success := false;
      while P <> NULL and not Success do
        if Match(Target, Ref(P).Data) then
          Success := true
        else
          Prev := P;
          P := Ref(P).Link
        endif
      endwhile
    end FindNodeToDelete;

start Delete
  FindNodeToDelete(L, Target, Match, P, Prev, Success);
  if Success then
    if Prev = NULL then (* Removing node at front of L *)
      L := Ref(L).Link
    else                (* Removing node in middle or at end
                           of L *)
      Ref(Prev).Link := Ref(P).Link
    endif;
    ReturnNode(P)
  endif
end Delete;
```

The specifics for the rest of the operations in the list ADT will be left for you to ponder in the exercises.

Comparison of Efficiencies for the Two Implementations

Add/Delete considerations may make a linked list an attractive alternative to an ordered-array implementation of a list. Figures 3.9 and 3.10 indicate that adds and deletes merely require the exchange of two pointers, an $O(1)$ operation, since it requires the same amount of time to execute no matter how many nodes are in the list. Since pointers are merely locations of other nodes, this means that we are usually manipulating mere integers or similarly simple data in doing such pointer operations. Hence, for linked lists, both additions and deletions would appear to be $O(1)$ operations in terms of data movement. This compares very favorably to the massive movement of entire records forced by an addition or deletion on an array implementation of a list.

In general, in an array implementation, such insertion and removal operations will be $O(n)$ in terms of data movement. Despite this substantive advantage, you should proceed cautiously and not be too quick to adopt the linked list as a cure-all for the ills involved with list-oriented systems. Your experience should make you suspicious that there must be a trade-off involved to get this superior efficiency for add and delete operations. The price we pay is giving up random access to the nodes. For example, to access the fourth node, we must follow the head pointer to the first node, the first node's pointer to the second, and so on, until we reach the fourth node. Hence, any operation that requires finding a particular node on the list will essentially have to invoke a sequential search algorithm.

The superb $O(\log_2 n)$ search efficiency possible with an array implementation of a list cannot be approached with a linked implementation of the same list because the binary search algorithm we used to achieve this efficiency requires random access into the list. Instead we must settle for the $O(n)$ efficiency of the sequential search. Note that this is even a deterring factor in add and delete operations because, typically, an appropriate spot in the list must be found before the add or delete can occur. Although the add or delete itself may require only $O(1)$ data movements, an $O(n)$ search must usually precede it.

Despite this search inefficiency, linked lists can be used to tremendous advantage when implementing lists that are highly volatile, that is, frequently undergoing insertions and deletions. If the number of these operations is sufficiently great in relation to the number of requests for retrieving and updating nodes, then the linked implementation will probably pay off.

Exercises 3.2

1. Provide PSEUDO code for the FindSlot procedure nested within the Add procedure of Example 3.3.

2. The definition of the ordered-list ADT in Section 3.1 involves eight operations: Create, Destroy, Assign, Add, Delete, Retrieve, Update, and Traverse. For the ordered-array implementation of this ADT, only one of these operations was actually provided in PSEUDO code form in Section 3.2. Provide implementations for the other seven.

3. Analyze in big-O terms the number of comparisons and number of data interchanges for each of the eight list operations in the ordered-array implementation you provided in Exercise 2.

Storage of Disk Files and Computer Security

Operating systems typically grant their users disk storage in units called blocks. On the magnetic disk itself, a block is a contiguous area capable of storing a fixed amount of data. For example, a block in DEC's well-known VAX/VMS time-sharing system is 512 bytes. As a user enters data into a disk file, the system must grant additional blocks of storage as they are needed. In such a timesharing environment, although each block represents physically contiguous storage area on the disk, it may not be possible for the operating system to give a user blocks that are physically next to each other. Instead, when a user needs an additional storage block, the operating system may put information into the current block about where the next block is located. In effect, a link is established from the current block to the next block. By the time a naive user has completed entering a four-block file, it may be scattered over the entire disk surface, as indicated in the following diagram.

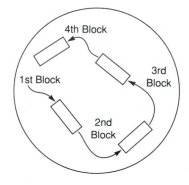

Scattered allocation
of disk file blocks.

Although this may seem like an ingenious way of extending files indefinitely, one pays in several ways for such scattered blocks. Namely, the read-write head that seeks and puts data on the disk surface is forced to move greater distances, thereby slowing system performance. To combat such inefficiencies, shrewd users can often take advantage of options that allow them to preallocate the contiguous disk storage that will be required for a file. Also, blocks may be released to users in clusters of contiguous blocks—similar to the way in which we shall describe clusters of characters for a linked list representation of strings in Section 3.6. In the event that file access remains sluggish in spite of such measures, systems managers may occasionally shut down the entire system to rebuild disks, a process that entails copying all files that are presently scattered over the disk onto a new disk in physically contiguous form.

Yet another more serious price that may be paid for storing disk files in this fashion revolves around the issue of data security and what the operating system does with blocks that are no longer needed by a user. From our discussion in Section 3.3, it is clear that the disk blocks used to store a file are returned to some type of available block list when a user deletes that file from his or her directory. When these blocks are returned to that available space list, the data in them may remain intact until another user's request to extend a file results in the block's being reallocated to that new user. This means that, if clever users ("hackers") know how to access the available space list, they may be able to scavenge through data that other users once owned and then released (assuming it was not destroyed upon being released).

One of the authors was actually involved in an incident in which a clever student was able to "find" old versions of a test that a professor had typed in on the computer and then discarded to this available block list. Needless to say, the professor whose tests were being explored by the student was somewhat alarmed upon discovering what had happened. As a protection against this type of scavenging, many operating systems will, by default or as an option, actually destroy data returned to the available block list.

4. For an ordered-array implementation of a list, write a PSEUDO version of the Update procedure that does not require the assumption that the new value of the node being updated will not alter the node's logical position in the list. How does this version of Update affect your answer to Exercise 3?

5. Repeat Exercise 2 for a linked-list implementation of an ordered list.

6. Repeat Exercise 3 for a linked-list implementation of an ordered list.

7. Repeat Exercise 4 for a linked-list implementation of an ordered list.

8. In procedure Add for a linked-list implementation of a list, the following two statements appear in the **else** clause of the **if** statement:

```
Ref(P).Link := Ref(Prev).Link;
Ref(Prev).Link := P
```

Describe the effect, using an appropriate picture, of switching the order of these two statements.

9. Consider the linked list pictured in Figure 3.13. What would be the output of the following loop?

```
P := L;
while Ref(P).Link <> NULL do
  write(Ref(P).Data);
  P := Ref(P).Link
endwhile;
```

10. The definition of a list ADT allows an operation Assign, which makes a copy of a Source list in a Destination list. For a linked-list implementation, consider the following strategy for implementing this operation: merely assign the head pointer for the Source list to the pointer representing the Destination list. Is this a foolproof, $O(1)$ method of achieving this end? If not, explain why. (Hint: consider the consequences of a Update operation following such an assignment.)

11. Summarize the advantages and disadvantages of a linked-list implementation of a list compared to an ordered-array implementation.

12. Consider the following ordered list required in a postal service application. A list of all five-digit ZIP codes in the United States is maintained along with a counter for the number of letters mailed to each ZIP code. At the post office, letters are electronically scanned by an optical character-recognition system.

FIGURE 3.13
Linked list for Exercise 9.

For each scanned letter, the ZIP code is read, and the corresponding counter increased by one, hence, tallying destinations of letters passing through that post office. How should this list of ZIP codes be implemented? Justify your answer.

13. In Exercise 5 of Section 3.1 you provided an alternate definition for the ordered-list ADT. Now provide PSEUDO code procedures to implement the operations of that ADT as an ordered array with binary search. Finally, use big-O notation to analyze the efficiency of each operation in terms of comparisons and data interchanges.

14. Repeat Exercise 13 for a linked-list implementation.

15. In Exercise 7 of Section 3.1 you provided a definition for the unordered-list ADT. Now provide PSEUDO code procedures to implement the operations of that ADT using an array. Finally, use big-O notation to analyze the efficiency of each operation in terms of comparisons and data interchanges.

16. Repeat Exercise 15 for a linked-list implementation of the unordered-list ADT.

17. In what way is the data structure involved with the pointer sort algorithm in Section 2.3 not a linked list?

18. Write a PSEUDO procedure to reverse a linked list L.

3.3 IMPLEMENTATION OF POINTER VARIABLES USING ARRAYS

To implement linked lists in the previous section, we had to assume the existence of operations for the pointer ADT. Following up our discussion from Section 2.3 as to why it may be useful or even necessary to know how pointers may be implemented, we now take up this topic. The implementation of pointers discussed in this section will not mesh perfectly with the definition of the pointer ADT presented in Section 2.3. The reason for this is twofold. First, the concept of a pointer presented in Section 2.3 would allow us to declare two different pointers to different types of objects via a declaration such as

```
var
  P: pointer to ObjectType1;
  Q: pointer to ObjectType2;
```

Our implementation will instead require different pointer data types to reference different object types. For example,

```
var
  P: Pointer1;    (* Where Pointer1 is the type of pointer
                     variables that reference ObjectType1 *)
  Q: Pointer2;    (* And Pointer2 is the type of pointer
                     variables that reference ObjectType2 *)
```

Second, the Ref operation, which we used in our ADT definition of pointer, will not map conveniently *as a notation,* to the scheme we will use to implement pointers. Instead we will employ a different array-based notion for operation Ref. This notation will emerge and will be carefully examined later in our discussion.

Hence, our implementation of pointer variables will admittedly violate the ADT Implementation rule of Section 2.2. This is the price we must pay for keeping our discussion relatively simple. Providing a pointer implementation as comprehensive as that required by our ADT definition (and as nice as that provided by full-scale programming languages) is beyond our scope at this point of study. We will return to the implementation of pointers in Section 13.3, providing additional insight into the advanced techniques behind a more comprehensive implementation.

Pointers as Addresses

The most important idea behind a pointer is that it represents the address of a piece of data in computer memory. This address is relative to the particular *word* of memory that begins the storage allocation for this data. Typically such memory words are just identified by integer addresses, which proceed sequentially from some designated starting address. This means that a pointer variable is essentially equivalent to a (nonnegative) integer variable where the integer contents of the variable represent an address instead of other data. We can also designate the value 0 to represent the special value NULL described in Section 2.3.

Thus, we can implement pointers using integers. The only question is, where will the memory "words" referenced by these integers reside? The answer is simple. We can simulate computer memory using an array (or random access file) in which each location is capable of storing one data node of the type being referenced by our pointers. The head pointer for the list would merely contain the integer index of the first item in the list. Each node would contain an integer link to the index of the item that follows. Hence, the linked list of names in Figure 3.14 might be realized in the array picture in Figure 3.15.

In Figure 3.15, all array slots are currently being used to store data. That is, no slots are available should we request one via a GetNode operation. The question that arises is, how should we keep track of array indices that

FIGURE 3.14
Logical representation of linked list.

FIGURE 3.15
Array realization of linked list in Figure 3.14. Pointers are represented by indices to an array component.

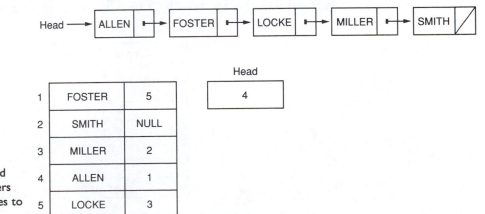

are available for allocation to data items through GetNode? The answer is to weave another linked list among the slots in the array. This linked list joins together those nodes that are not currently in use storing data. The linked list of available nodes is not in any particular logical order, since these nodes do not contain any reliable data values. All that is important is that they are reliably linked together in a list kept separate from the actual data list. An example should help to clarify this.

Example 3.6   Consider an eight-node pool of available memory. The following snapshots indicate the status of the available space list (referenced by the pointer Avail) and a data list (referenced by the pointer Head), as the following data items,

> WAGNER
> ELLIS
> GORDON
> NIEMAN
> HILLER

arrive for insertion into the data list.
Before first insertion—all nodes linked together in available node list:

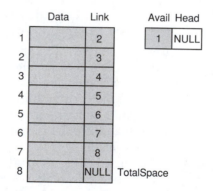

After first insertion—first node on available list has been allocated to store WAGNER, being replaced by a new first node on available list.

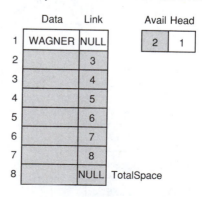

After second insertion

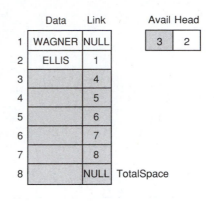

After third insertion

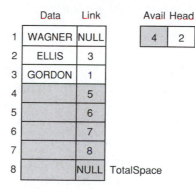

After fourth insertion

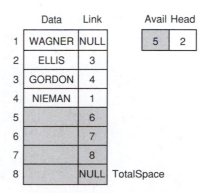

After fifth insertion

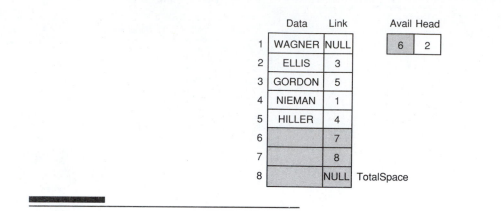

As nodes are deleted from the data list, they are returned to available storage by putting them at the front of the available space list. Example 3.7 traces such a sequence.

Example 3.7   Assume that the following operations occur on the list developed in Example 3.6.

Delete WAGNER
Delete NIEMAN
Add ZARDA

Then the available and data lists are traced by the following snapshot sequence.
After first deletion

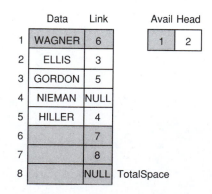

After second deletion

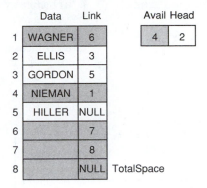

After insertion of ZARDA

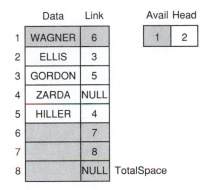

Note that data contained in nodes that are returned to the available space pool are not actually destroyed until the nodes are reused via a call to GetNode.

It is evident that, if we are to use a global array to emulate memory that would be allocated and deallocated by the GetNode and ReturnNode operations on pointers, then we must initialize the available space structure via the following procedure.

```
type (* Assume TotalSpace is constant limiting overall available space *)
  ObjectType: ListData;
  Pointer: integer (* Assumed to be in range 0...TotalSpace, where 0
                represents NULL *);
  SpaceNode: record
              Data: ObjectType;
              Link: Pointer
           endrecord;
  SpaceStruct: record
              Nodes : array [TotalSpace] of SpaceNode;
              Avail : Pointer (* Head of available space list *)
           endrecord;
```

```
procedure InitializeSpace
  ( given Space: SpaceStruct    (* A arbitrary structure of nodes that are to
                                    be made available to an application *);
    return Space: SpaceStruct   (* Avail pointer indicates first
                                    available node and all other nodes are linked
                                    together in available space list *) );

    var K: Pointer;

    start InitializeSpace
      for K := 1 to TotalSpace - 1 do
        Space.Nodes[K].Link := K + 1
      endfor;
      Space.Nodes[TotalSpace].Link := NULL;
      Space.Avail := 1
    end InitializeSpace;
```

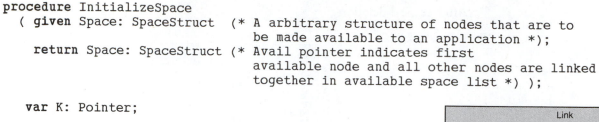

For GetNode and ReturnNode to act in concert with the structure established by InitializeSpace, they must receive the available space structure from which nodes are being allocated or deallocated. You should verify that the following versions of GetNode and ReturnNode perform their operations in a fashion consistent with that indicated in Examples 3.6 and 3.7.

```
procedure GetNode
  ( given Space: SpaceStruct    (* An available space structure *);
    return Space: SpaceStruct   (* The available space structure
                                    with one node removed from the
                                    available list and allocated
                                    to the calling application *);
           P: Pointer           (* A pointer to the node allocated
                                    to the calling application *) );
    start GetNode
      if Space.Avail = NULL then
        write ('No space available')
      else
        P := Space.Avail;
        Space.Avail := Space.Nodes[Avail].Link
      endif
    end GetNode;
```

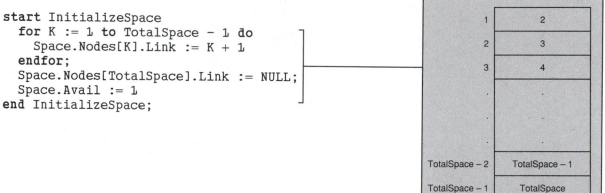

```
procedure ReturnNode
  ( given Space: SpaceStruct  (* An available space structure *);
         P: Pointer          (* A pointer to the node to be
                                 returned to Space *);
    return Space: SpaceStruct (* The available space structure
                                 with the node referenced by P
                                 returned to the available
                                 list *) );
  start ReturnNode
    Space.Nodes[P].Link := Space.Avail;
    Space.Avail := P
  end ReturnNode;
```

To complete our implementation of the pointer ADT, we must supply the Ref operation. As we noted in Section 2.3, Ref is somewhat unusual in that Ref(P) returns the actual contents of the node at memory address P. That is, Ref(P) gives its caller access to the data located at P, not just a copy of that data. The usual mechanism used to return a function's value in most programming languages returns a copy of the value computed by the function; it does not allow us direct access to the computed value itself. This means that programming languages that provide pointers are implementing the Ref operation by means outside the normal semantics of the language, using addressing techniques available in the assembly language of a particular machine.

For the implementation of pointers we are developing in this section, the interpretation of Ref(P) is merely the node at index P of the space structure under consideration. That is, Ref(P), relative to a space structure called Space, is simply Space.Nodes[P]. To get at the data in the node referenced by P, we would use the array notation Space.Nodes[P].Data. To access the link field in the same node, Space.Nodes[P].Link is the appropriate notation. The following example will clarify how the array-based implementation of pointers that we have developed here could be used for the linked-list operations developed in Section 3.2.

Example 3.8   Assuming a space structure designated by Space, that is,

```
var
  Space: SpaceStruct;
```

adapt the Add procedure for a linked list from Example 3.4 to an array-based implementation of pointers.

```
(* Linked-list implementation of Add operation for List, with
   array-based implementation of pointers *)

type List: Pointer;

procedure Add
  ( given L: List              (* A list L ordered by Precedes
                                   relationship *);
          Item: ListData       (* A data item to be added to L *);
          Precedes: Comparison (* The relationship between nodes that
                                   determines the ordering of L *);
    return L: List             (* L with Item inserted according to the
                                   order determined by Precedes * );
           Success: boolean    (* Set to true if Item successfully
                                   inserted; set to false if Item could
                                   not be inserted because L is full *) );
    var P, Prev: List; (* P used to point at the node to be inserted. Prev
                          points at the node that logically precedes Item
                          referenced by P *)
  procedure FindSlot
    ( given L: List              (* A list L ordered by Precedes
                                     relationship *);
            Item: ListData       (* A data item to be added to L *);
            Precedes: Comparison (* This function determines the
                                     ordering of the list *);
      return Prev: List          (* A pointer to the node in L whose
                                     value logically precedes Item. If
                                     Item precedes all nodes in L, then
                                     Prev is set to NULL *) );

    var Q: List;

    start FindSlot
      Prev := NULL;
      Q := L;
      while Q <> NULL and not Precedes(Item, Space.Nodes[Q].Data) do
        Prev := Q;
        Q := Space.Nodes[Q].Link
      endwhile
    end FindSlot;

  start Add
    GetNode(Space , P);
    Space.Nodes[P] .Data := Item;
    FindSlot(L, Item, Precedes, Prev);
    if Prev = NULL then (* Inserting at front of List *)
      Space.Nodes[P] .Link := L;
      L := P
    else
      Space.Nodes[P] .Link := Space.Nodes[Prev].Link;
      Space.Nodes[Prev] .Link := P
    endif
  end Add;
```

The italicized portions of code in the preceding example represent textual changes that had to be made in the code of Example 3.4 because our pointer variables were implemented in the array Space. In this sense we were forced to bend the ADT Implementation rule of providing pointer operations in a fashion that would not necessitate changes in higher-level code that uses those operations. This was unavoidable because we had to provide an array to allocate space for the objects being referenced by pointers. In Chapter 13 we shall see that programming languages that provide pointer variables allocate and deallocate storage in a more general area, often called the *heap*. However, for the time being, we have provided an implementation of the pointer ADT that can be easily adapted to any programming language—whether the particular application is manipulating a pointer-based data structure in main memory or random access file storage.

Exercises 3.3

1. Suppose that you are given the following initial state of an array implementation of a linked list.

	Data	Link
1	47	3
2	89	5
3	66	7
4	100	2
5	13	10
6	55	2
7	112	4
8	178	0
9	79	6
10	19	8

   a. Indicate the nodes on the lists if the head pointer is 9 and 0 is used to indicate the value NULL.

   b. Indicate the final state of the Data and Link fields after the following program segment is executed.

```
J := 4;
Data[J] := 883;
J := Link[J];
while Link[J] <> 0 do
   J := Link[J];
   Data[J] := 912
endwhile;
```

2. Consider the array implementation of a linked list of names that appears in Figure 3.14. Suppose that the physical order of the five names in that list was given by the illustration at the top of page 134.

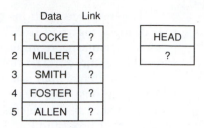

Fill in the Head and Link fields so that the list could be traversed in logical alphabetical order.

3. Indicate the changes in the Link and Head fields from Exercise 2 if MILLER is deleted from the list.

4. Indicate the changes in the Link and Head fields from Exercise 2 if ALLEN is deleted from the list.

5. Consider an array implementation of a linked list of names that is to be maintained in alphabetical order. Trace the status of the Data and Link fields and the Head and Avail pointers as the following operations are performed on the list:

   Add JAMES

   Add CHILTON

   Add SEFTON

   Add LEE

   Delete CHILTON

   Add WAGNER

   Delete JAMES

   Add AARON

6. Suppose that X, Y, and Z are pointers and the following sequence of commands is executed.

```
GetNode(Space, X);
Y := X;
Space.Node[X].Data := 42;    (* Assume integer data *)
ReturnNode(Space, X);
GetNode(Space, Z);
GetNode(Space, X);
Space.Nodes[Z].Data := 64;
Space.Nodes[X].Data := 128;
write(Space.Nodes[X].Data);
write(Space.Nodes[Y].Data);
write(Space.Nodes[Z].Data);
```

   Does this sequence of commands contain a potential run-time error? If so, what is it? If not, describe the output produced by this sequence of commands. If you work in a language that provides an implementation of pointer variables, develop an analogous sequence of commands, run it in a test program, and describe what happens.

7. Use big-O notation to analyze the efficiency of the GetNode and ReturnNode operations.

8. Example 3.8 provided the code for the linked-list Add operation using an array-based implementation of pointers. Develop code for each of the other seven list operations using this implementation of pointers.

9. Using an array-based implementation of pointers, reformulate each of the procedures/functions you developed for Exercise 14 in Section 3.2.

10. Using an array-based implementation of pointers, reformulate each of the procedures/functions you developed for Exercise 16 in Section 3.2.

3.4 VARIATIONS ON LINKED-LIST STRUCTURES

Linked lists provide a tremendously useful tool in situations where a highly volatile general list must be maintained in some prescribed logical order. Their widespread use has led to the development of several "tricks of the trade" suitable in certain applications. These are ways of fine-tuning the basic linked-list structure to meet the needs of particular situations. Four such variations on the linked list are presented in this section: dummy headers, circular lists, doubly linked lists, and multilinked lists.

Dummy Headers

A *dummy header* node in the list before the first actual data node can often contain useful information about the structure (for example, if ListData is numeric or a variant type, the Data element of the header node can store the number of nodes). A query algorithm can then determine the status of the list by examining the contents of the dummy header node without having to traverse the entire list. This amounts to adding one more node to the list. Figure 3.16 illustrates this concept. Additions to and deletions from the list require changing this information-keeping field in the dummy header node of the list.

There is another distinct advantage of the dummy header node. If the list becomes empty and a dummy header node is not used, then the Head pointer for the list must be set to NULL. But if the dummy header node is

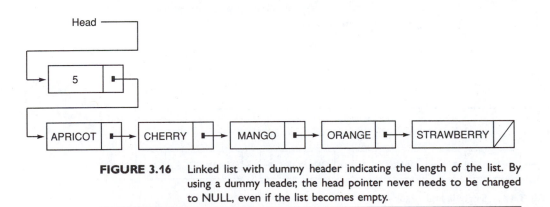

FIGURE 3.16 Linked list with dummy header indicating the length of the list. By using a dummy header, the head pointer never needs to be changed to NULL, even if the list becomes empty.

present, then the Head pointer never needs to be changed to NULL because it always points to this dummy header. That is, the empty list is only empty in a logical sense. Physically, it still contains the dummy header. This convention can serve to simplify the coding involved in procedures Add and Delete by removing the special handling previously required for inserts and deletes at the beginning of the list. (You will write these simplified procedures as an exercise at the end of this section.) This convenience factor alone provides substantial practical motivation for always using dummy headers. Moreover, in real-world applications, you will find that you can almost always use the extra data space in the dummy header to store some valuable items of information.

Linked Circular Lists

Although linked lists are satisfactory in many instances, the presence of a NULL value at the end of the list makes this structure most efficient only if the entire list is to be processed. The efficiency of such list-processing algorithms decreases when the linked list is to be processed beginning at an arbitrary point in the list. In such situations, it would be desirable to be able to enter the list anywhere and process it efficiently independent of the entry point. In other words, we need a linked list that has no beginning or end.

Linked circular lists are precisely such data structures. A singly linked circular list is a linked list in which the last node of the list points to the first node in the list. Notice that in circular list structures there are no NULL values. Figure 3.17 depicts a singly linked circular list.

As an example of the utility of such a circular list in the area of operating systems, suppose the nodes in Figure 3.17 represent current users on a time-sharing computer. In such an environment, the operating system schedules each user for a small time slice on the central processing unit (CPU) and then proceeds to devote its momentary attention to the next user. When the final user has completed his or her time slice, ownership of the CPU must again revert to the first user, and the scheduling cycle starts again. Because of the speed of the CPU, this cyclic scheduling creates the illusion for each user that the computer is dedicated to his or her particular process. Clearly, a circular linked list is made to order for this type of scheduling. The circularity ensures no unnecessary interruptions in restarting the scheduling cycle when the end of the user list is reached. The linked nature of the structure enables the operating system to quickly process new users who log on and users who complete their work and log off.

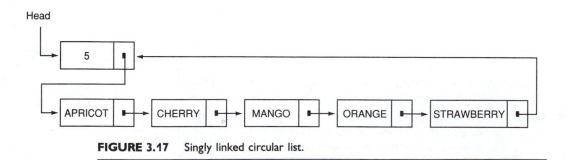

FIGURE 3.17   Singly linked circular list.

Doubly Linked Circular Lists

In the previously developed procedure Delete, we found the node to remove by calling a routine that searched the entire list. Because search algorithms require time proportional to half the length of the list, run time can be substantial if the list is very long. As an example, suppose we have a singly linked list in which we wish to delete a node A, pointed to by P; but we do not know the address of (that is, a pointer to) the node preceding A. If we are to depend upon the current structure of the list, then we must search the list for the node preceding A—an inefficient procedure. In other words, even in situations where we may be able to locate A by other means (such as a hashing strategy to be studied in Chapter 11), we must traverse the list up to A in order to find the preceding node. Figure 3.18 portrays this predicament.

A satisfactory way of getting around the difficulty presented in Figure 3.18 is a *doubly linked circular list* in which each node has two pointers: a forward link and a backward link. The forward link is a pointer to the next node in the list; the backward link points to the preceding node. The circular nature of the list, along with a special dummy header node, can be used to conveniently avoid special conditional checking when adding to or deleting from the beginning or end of the list.

Figure 3.19 illustrates a doubly linked circular list. This list has five nodes (plus a dummy header), each having a forward link (FLink) and a backward link (BLink). FLink points to the successor node, whereas BLink

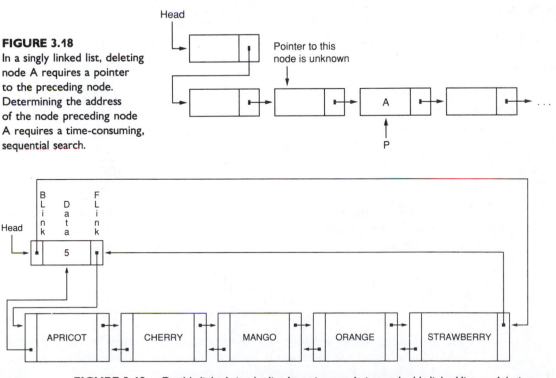

FIGURE 3.18
In a singly linked list, deleting node A requires a pointer to the preceding node. Determining the address of the node preceding node A requires a time-consuming, sequential search.

FIGURE 3.19   Doubly linked circular list. Inserting a node into a doubly linked list, or deleting one from it, is easier than for singly linked lists because we do not need a separate pointer to a preceding node.

points to the predecessor node. Because the list is circular, BLink of the header node must point to the last node, and FLink of the last node must point to the header node. Inserting a node into a doubly linked list, or deleting one from it, is potentially a much easier task because we do not need a separate pointer to a preceding node. Hence, we may be able to avoid the time inefficiency inherent in finding such a pointer in situations where the insertion or deletion point can be found by means faster than traversing the list. The following procedure InsertNodeDouble inserts a node, pointed to by Point1 (already obtained via GetNode), into a doubly linked circular list with a dummy header. The node is inserted just before a node pointed to by Point2.

```
type
   DoublyLinkedPtr: pointer to DoublyLinkedNode;
   DoublyLinkedNode: record
                  Data: ListData;
                  FLink, BLink: DoublyLinkedPtr
              endrecord;

procedure InsertNodeDouble
  ( given Point1: DoublyLinkedPtr    (* Pointer to a node, already containing
                                         data, that is to be inserted into a
                                         circular doubly linked list *);
          Point2: DoublyLinkedPtr    (* Pointer to a node, within circular doubly
                                         linked list, which is to follow node
                                         referenced by Point1 *);
    return Point1: DoublyLinkedPtr   (* FLink and BLink pointers are altered to link
                                         node referenced by Point1 into the list *);
           Point2: DoublyLinkedPtr   (* BLink pointer now referencing Point1 *) );

  var Prev: DoublyLinkedPtr;

  start InsertNodeDouble
    Prev := Ref(Point2).BLink;
    Ref(Point1).FLink := Point2;
    Ref(Point1).BLink := Prev;
    Ref(Prev).FLink := Point1;
    Ref(Point2).BLink := Point1
  end InsertNodeDouble;
```

See the illustration at the top of page 139.

Note that the **procedure** InsertNodeDouble illustrates how streamlined insert and delete operations become when a dummy header is used. In particular, because the empty list appears as

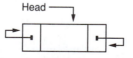

Head

the procedure works without any awkward checking of whether the list is empty or whether the insertion is being made at the front of the list. Clearly a dummy header simplifies procedures in this situation.

The following procedure DeleteNodeDouble deletes a node pointed to by Point1 from a doubly linked list and returns the node to the storage pool of available nodes.

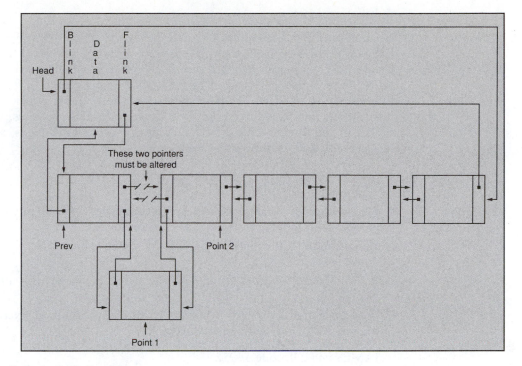

```
procedure DeleteNodeDouble
  ( given Point1: DoublyLinkedPtr  (* Pointer to a node that is to be deleted
                                      from a circular doubly linked list *);
    return Point1: DoublyLinkedPtr (* The node it references is deleted from the
                                      list and returned to available storage *) );

  var
    Save: DoublyLinkedPtr;

  start DeleteNodeDouble
    Save := Ref(Point1).BLink;
    Ref(Save).FLink := Ref(Point1).FLink;
    Save := Ref(Point1).FLink;
    Ref(Save).BLink := Ref(Point1).BLink;
    ReturnNode(Point1)
  end DeleteNodeDouble;
```

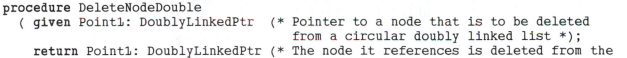

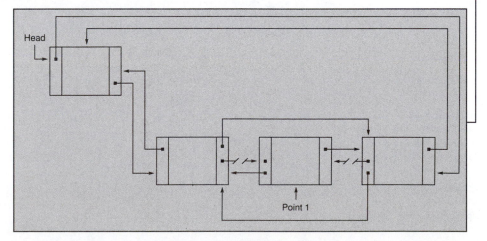

Multilinked Lists

We shall end this discussion of variations on the linked-list theme by noting that a doubly linked list is a special case of a structure known as a *multilinked* list. Because each link field determines an order in which the nodes of a list are to be processed, we can in fact establish a different link field for every different order in which we wish to process the nodes in a list. Figure 3.20 illustrates such a multilinked list. By following the IDLink fields, we traverse the list in IDNumber order; by following the NameLink fields, we traverse the list in alphabetical order by Name.

Exercises 3.4

1. Repeat Exercise 5 from Section 3.3, this time using a linked list with a dummy header.

2. Repeat Exercise 5 from Section 3.3 for a singly linked circular list with a dummy header.

3. Repeat Exercise 5 from Section 3.3 for a doubly linked list with a dummy header.

4. Suppose that we wish to be able to go through the list of Exercise 5 from Section 3.3 in ZIP code order where

   JAMES has ZIP code 54952

   CHILTON has ZIP code 48649

   SEFTON has ZIP code 22111

   LEE has ZIP code 84682

   WAGNER has ZIP code 11843

   AARON has ZIP code 99218

   Trace the status of all fields (including headers and available space pointer) in an array-based, multilinked implementation of this list of names and ZIP codes.

5. What are some advantages of storing information about a list in a dummy header node?

6. What coding advantage does a dummy header node provide in linked lists?

	IDHead	NameHead
	4	3

FIGURE 3.20
Link fields for processing nodes. By following the IDLink fields we traverse the list in IDNumber order; by following the NameLink we traverse the list in alphabetical order by name.

	Name	IDNumber	NameLink	IDLink
1	PEMBROOK	8316	4	NULL
2	DOUGLAS	4212	5	5
3	ATWATER	6490	2	1
4	WITHERS	1330	NULL	2
5	LAYTON	5560	1	3

Multilinked List

7. What main convenience does a doubly linked list offer in comparison with a singly linked list when adding or deleting?

8. Assuming a linked-list implementation in which a dummy header is used, write PSEUDO versions of each of the eight operations on the ordered-list ADT defined in Section 3.1.

9. Repeat Exercise 8 assuming the implementation is a doubly linked circular list.

3.5 APPLICATION: SPARSE MATRICES

Now that we have studied lists from an abstract perspective and have discussed some of their implementations, we are ready to examine several applications. The applications we will explore in the last three sections of this chapter—sparse matrices, strings, and sets—are all ADTs we introduced in Chapter 2. The idea will now emerge that each of these ADTs can be implemented by a form of list. Thus, we will essentially use the operations provided with one ADT to implement the operations of another. Sometimes we may have to augment the list operations by providing some new operations on lists expressly for the application at hand.

This interaction among ADTs reinforces the notion of levels of abstraction that lies at the core of a comprehensive treatment of data structures. The data structures themselves may be categorized as a complex hierarchical structure of ADTs with their implementations. In this section, the sparse matrix will be the ADT that we will implement using ordered lists. The efficiency will largely be dependent upon the deeper-level question of how we choose to implement the ordered-list ADT. This hierarchy is illustrated in Figure 3.21. At the base level of this hierarchy, we will see that a linked list provides a better implementation than an ordered array because of the frequent insertions and deletions on the lists, which are used to represent rows of the sparse matrix.

To illustrate how we will use linked lists to implement a sparse matrix, consider the sparse matrix of integers pictured in Figure 3.22. In Section 2.1 we described a strategy for implementing such a matrix that would have us

FIGURE 3.21
Hierarchy of ADTs and their implementations in representation of sparse matrices.

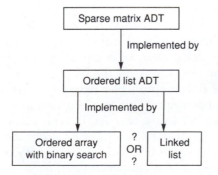

	1	2	3	4	5	6	7	8	9	10	11	12	13	14
1	0	83	19	40	0	0	0	0	0	0	0	0	0	0
2	0	0	0	91	0	42	12	0	0	0	0	0	0	0
3	0	0	0	0	0	18	4	0	0	0	0	0	0	0
4	0	0	0	0	0	0	0	0	71	64	0	13	0	0
5	0	0	0	0	0	0	0	0	0	0	0	0	21	40

FIGURE 3.22

Sparse matrix of integer data.

store a list of those row and column coordinates that do not resolve to zero. Along with each such coordinate pair we would store its associated nontrivial value. The drawback of this approach stems from the implementation of the list of nonzero coordinates via an array. The array implementation will result in an extremely inefficient solution for any volatile matrix of data. The reasons for this inefficiency parallel those that made an array implementation of an ordered list inadequate. Namely, if we somehow order the nonzero data in the matrix to enable use of the binary search, then assigning a nonzero value to a matrix component that was previously zero requires inserting a value into this ordered array. On the other hand, assigning zero to a matrix location that was previously nonzero requires deleting a value from the ordered array. Both operations will involve shifting large amounts of data. Conversely, if we neglect to order the data, then changing values can be done efficiently, but search efficiency will deteriorate.

The implementation method we now propose uses linked lists to ensure no data shifting occurs when a zero value is changed to nonzero (or vice versa). Moreover, by employing many linked lists (one for each row), it reduces the length of sequential searches to the number of nonzero column coordinates in a particular targeted row, instead of all nonzero row-column coordinates for the entire matrix. The method is completely dynamic and requires an array of pointers, each leading to a linked list storing the nonzero data in a given row of the sparse matrix. Each node in one of these linked lists would need to contain not only an entry from the matrix but also an indication of which column within that particular row is occupied by the data in this node. We further stipulate that, for efficiency in processing, each linked list be arranged in ascending order of column numbers within that row. Given these conventions, the 5×14 matrix from Figure 3.22 would be represented by Figure 3.23.

By using list operations with appropriate Precedes and Match parameters, we may now write a function Retrieve to implement the retrieval of the value from the Kth row and Jth column of a matrix and a procedure Assign to implement the assignment of a particular value to the Kth row and Jth column. Since the operations on the list ADT also include a Retrieve operation, we use the dot notation List.Retrieve to distinguish the list operation from the matrix operation. This is a convention we will follow throughout the text when we are using two ADTs with identically named operations. Depending upon the capabilities of your programming language, you may have an analogous notation to remove ambiguity or (at worst) may have to rename one of the conflicting operations.

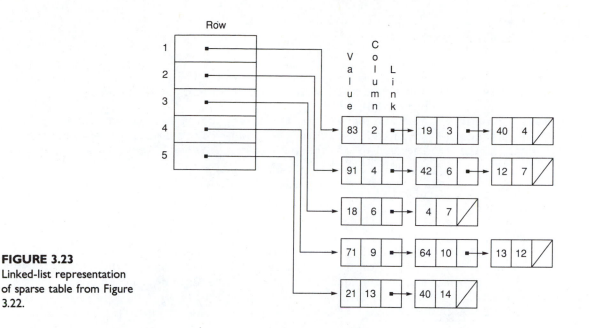

FIGURE 3.23
Linked-list representation of sparse table from Figure 3.22.

```
type (* Assume that NumberRows is a constant that limits number of rows *)
  ListData: record
              Value: MatrixData; (* Nonzero value at particular row and column *)
              Column: integer    (* Column coordinate *)
            endrecord;
  List: pointer to ListNode;
  ListNode: record
              Data: ListData;
              Link: List
            endrecord;
  Matrix: array [NumberRows] of List;

(* Before writing Retrieve and Assign for sparse matrices, establish the
   Match and Precedes functions that will be used with the list routines. *)

function Match (* This function dictates that the list representing the
                  row of the matrix is searched for a match on Column *)
  ( given Target,                (* ListData containing the Column being sought *)
          MatrixEntry: ListData  (* Data in a node on the list for the row *);
    return: boolean              (* true if the Column in MatrixEntry matches
                                    the Column in Target *) );
  start Match
    Match := MatrixEntry.Column = Target.Column
  end Match;

procedure Precedes (* This function determines that entries in the list
                      for a given row are arranged in ascending order
                      according to column number *);
  ( given Entry1, Entry2: ListData  (* List entries to have Column fields
                                       compared *);
    return: boolean                 (* true if the Column of Entry1 is less
                                       than that of Entry2 *) );
```

```
start Precedes
  Precedes := Entry1.Column < Entry2.Column
end Precedes;

function Retrieve (* Retrieve value from sparse matrix *)
  ( given M: Matrix     (* A matrix M in which each element is of type
                           MatrixData *);
          Row: integer (* An integer within the range of row indices for M *);
          Col: integer (* An integer within the range of column indices for M *);
     return: MatrixData (* The value of the entry at the specified row and
                           column of M *) );
  var
    DataSought, Target: ListData;
    Success: boolean;
  start Retrieve
    Target.Column := Col;
    List.Retrieve(M[Row], Target, Match, DataSought, Success);
      (* Call on Retrieve operation for the List ADT, here denoted by
         List.Retrieve to avoid ambiguity with Retrieve for Matrix *)
    if Success then
      Retrieve := DataSought.Value
    else
      Retrieve := 0   (* The value comprising most matrix entries *)
    endif
  end Retrieve;

procedure Assign (* Assign value to particular row and column of sparse matrix *)
  ( given M: Matrix        (* A matrix M in which each element is of type
                              MatrixData *);
          Row: integer     (* An integer within the range of row indices for M *);
          Col: integer     (* An integer within the range of column
                              indices for M *);
          Value: MatrixData (* Value to be assigned to designated row and
                              column of M *);
     return M: Matrix      (* The matrix M with Value assigned to the
                              designated row and column *) );
  var
    NewData, Target: ListData;
    Success: boolean;
  start Assign
    Target.Column := Col;
    if Value = 0 then
      Delete(M[Row], Target, Match, Success)
```

If assigning 0 to Column 3,
this node must be deleted

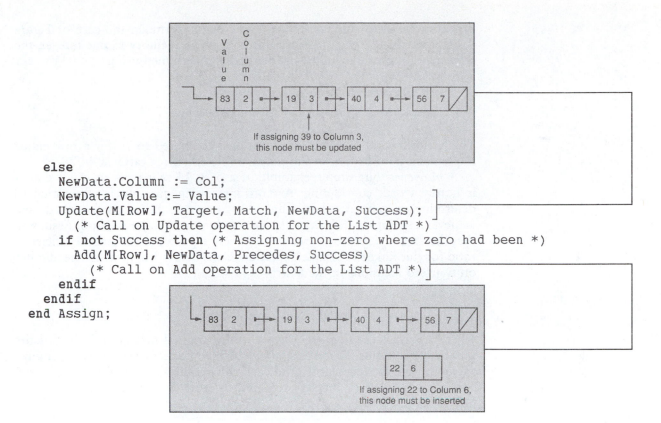

```
else
   NewData.Column := Col;
   NewData.Value := Value;
   Update(M[Row], Target, Match, NewData, Success);
     (* Call on Update operation for the List ADT *)
   if not Success then (* Assigning non-zero where zero had been *)
     Add(M[Row], NewData, Precedes, Success)
       (* Call on Add operation for the List ADT *)
   endif
  endif
end Assign;
```

Efficiency Considerations

The above PSEUDO routines provide a nice illustration of the advantages (and, as we shall see, disadvantages) of abstract data typing. The two primary advantages illustrated here are the hiding of the list's implementation from the sparse matrix routines and the relative simplicity of the logic within the **start–end** blocks of both Retrieve and Assign. The former advantage means that we could plug in a different list implementation and the sparse matrix routines would not need to change at all. The latter advantage enhances the reliability of these routines. Given a well-tested, reliable implementation of lists, the logic is so simple that there is very little that can go wrong with these routines. This is the essence of abstract data typing; by shielding one level of logic from the implementation details of another level of logic, we greatly reduce the chance of errors.

Since the main motivation for an implementation of a sparse matrix is to save memory space, a more important efficiency consideration is the amount of space we have saved. To determine this, we define the efficiency ratio of a sparse matrix implementation by the fraction

$$\frac{\text{Number of storage locations used by a sparse matrix implementation method}}{\text{Number of storage locations used by standard row-major form}}$$

Clearly, the smaller we can make this ratio, the better our implementation. Moreover, this ratio must drop below 1 before a particular method can even begin to surpass standard row-major form. In the case of Figure 3.22, if we assume that a pointer takes as much memory as one integer, the efficiency ratio of our linked-list method is determined using

> five locations for head-of-list pointers
>
> three locations for each of 13 nonzero values

This yields a total of 44 storage locations, compared to 70 for a row-major implementation; hence, we have a desirable efficiency ratio of 44/70.

However, our simple example of a 5×14 matrix is so small that it is hardly worth considering. A more interesting question is attempting to determine, in general, when a linked-list implementation as described here achieves a savings in memory over the standard row-major method. Assuming that the data in a sparse matrix are of integer type, we claim that the efficiency ratio for this linked-list implementation drops below 1 only when the number on nonzero locations in the matrix is less than

$$\text{NRow} \times (\text{NCol} - 1)/3$$

where NRow is the number of rows in the original matrix and NCol is the number of columns. To see this, note that each nonzero matrix entry requires three integers to represent it. And each row requires an integer head pointer. The total number of integers required to store N nonzero entries via the linked-list method is

$$\text{NRow} + \text{N} \times 3$$

Since we want to force the efficiency ratio

$$\frac{\text{NRow} + \text{N} \times 3}{\text{NRow} \times \text{NCol}}$$

to be less than 1, we conclude that

$$\text{NRow} + \text{N} \times 3 < \text{NRow} \times \text{NCol}$$
$$\text{N} \times 3 < \text{NRow} \times \text{NCol} - \text{NRow}$$
$$\text{N} < \text{NRow} \times (\text{NCol} - 1)/3$$

Similar types of efficiency analyses can be carried out for different base data types and implementation schemes.

Our earlier comments indicated that the time efficiency of the sparse matrix operations for this implementation are dependent upon the implementation used for lists. If we assume that a linked list is used, then, with respect to run time, the efficiency of this implementation of a sparse matrix will require no wholesale data movement when values are assigned to the array. Moreover, since accessing a particular value in the matrix requires a sequential search along one of the many linked lists that contain a row, we essentially have a retrieval time of $O(\text{NumberColumns})$.

To a certain extent, however, we pay a price in run-time efficiency by accessing our linked lists only through the provided ADT operations. For example, in the **else** clause of the Assign procedure, the Add procedure for a list is potentially called after the Update procedure is called. This results in two partial list traversals when the task could actually be performed with one partial traversal *if* the sparse matrix Assign procedure were allowed to directly manipulate the underlying linked-list implementation. This trade-off between the reliability achieved by allowing access to an ADT only through provided operations versus the increased efficiency that may result from an application's directly accessing the implementation of the ADT is one that must be carefully weighed in the context of a particular situation.

A similar trade-off arises if the application using the sparse matrix must frequently process data along a given row or column. The data items along a given row of the matrix could be processed much more efficiently if the application simply traversed the linked list for that row instead of repeatedly invoking the Retrieve operation for the succession of columns along the row. The reason is that the linked-list implementation we have described is oriented toward conveniently traversing a row instead of a column. In order to allow convenient traversals of *both* rows and columns, we must employ a multilinked implementation: not only must we link the nodes representing the nontrivial data along a given row, but also along each column. The picture of such a structure emerging from the data of Figure 3.22 is given in Figure 3.24. In the exercises at the end of the section, you will continue to explore ways of enhancing efficiency by directly manipulating the linked-list implementation of a sparse matrix.

Exercises 3.5

1. Retrieve and Assign routines have been developed in this section for a linked-list implementation of a sparse matrix. Complete this package by writing appropriate Create and Destroy routines. Create should initialize a sparse matrix containing a common uniform value (such as zero) in all cells. Destroy should return to available space all memory associated with a given sparse matrix.

2. Using big-O notation, analyze the time efficiency of the Retrieve and Assign operations for the sparse matrix implementation discussed in this section. Consider both the number of comparisons and number of data interchanges required for each operation, expressing your answer in terms of the number of rows and number of columns in the matrix. First, provide answers that assume the underlying list operation is a linked list. Then provide analogous answers, assuming an ordered array with binary search is used.

3. Suppose you have an application requiring you to form the sums of the entries along each row of a sparse matrix implemented by a linked list of values and columns for each row. Write a PSEUDO version of an algorithm to form these sums, accessing the matrix values only by the provided matrix Retrieve operation. Use big-O notation to analyze the time efficiency of your algorithm.

4. Repeat Exercise 3, but now bypass the matrix Retrieve operation and directly manipulate the linked lists that represent rows within the matrix. Can you make your new procedure significantly more efficient than the one in Exercise 3?

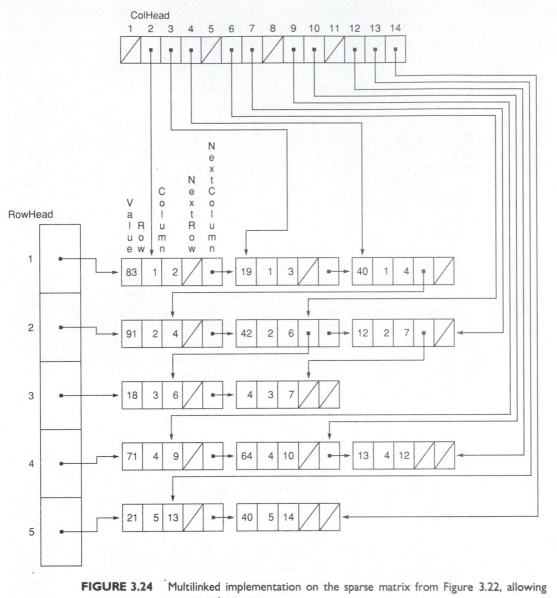

FIGURE 3.24 Multilinked implementation on the sparse matrix from Figure 3.22, allowing row or column access.

5. Suppose you have an application requiring you to form the sums of the entries along each column as well as along each row of a sparse matrix. Using a multilist structure, devise a method to implement a sparse matrix that makes the column access needed by this application as efficient as row access. Finally, provide PSEUDO procedures to compute the row and column sums respectively.

6. In the linked-list implementation of a sparse matrix described in this section, the array of head pointers is space-efficient only if most rows contain nonzero values. Discuss a strategy for storing head pointers that would be more space-efficient in a situation where only a few rows contained nonzero values.

3.6   APPLICATION: STRINGS

In Section 2.2 we introduced the string ADT and examined two implementations of it: the fixed-length implementation and the workspace-index implementation (see Programming Problem 7 in Chapter 2). Both of these implementations allow highly efficient versions of the string search operation. Moreover, the workspace-index method gracefully solves the problem of having to declare a maximum possible string length and then wasting memory when strings are shorter than that length. However, neither of these methods adequately solve the problem of having to move a tremendous amount of data when insertions and deletions occur on a larger scale. On the other hand, the linked implementation of strings we are about to describe handles both of these problems. Of course, as we have now come to expect in this world of tradeoffs, we shall see that it is not without its own set of problems.

We shall view each string as a doubly linked circular list fitting the description in Section 3.4. Each node in the list contains a backward pointer, a forward pointer, and a data portion consisting of (for the moment) a single character. Clearly, for each such string, we need a pointer to the dummy header node for the list, and, for later use, we want to keep track of the length of each string. The following conventions will be assumed throughout this section:

- Data of type String is a record that contains a Head pointer to the dummy header of a string.

- Each data item of type String also contains a Len field, which stores the length of the string referenced by the Head pointer in the record.

- The backward pointer for each node within a string will be referred to as BLink, the forward pointer as FLink, and the data portion as Data.

Figure 3.25, which pictures the three strings "COFFEE", "TEA", and "CREAM". with the length and dummy header location of each string, should help to clarify these conventions.

Let us consider how the string operations we have specified would be performed in such an implementation. The assignment of one string to another could be achieved in very slick and efficient (perhaps somewhat deceptive) fashion. That is, instead of physically creating two identical strings, we will simply have two separate Head pointers referencing the same string. This particular strategy does have some potential repercussions that might have to be avoided in certain applications (as we will see in the Exercises). String *searching,* as defined in the ADT operations, presents no real problem other than a potential reduction in efficiency. This is examined in an exercise at the end of the chapter. *Substring operations* do present a problem and will be discussed in detail later in this section. *Insertion, deletion,* and *concatenation* (which may be viewed as a special case of insertion) can be handled elegantly and efficiently using the linked-list method.

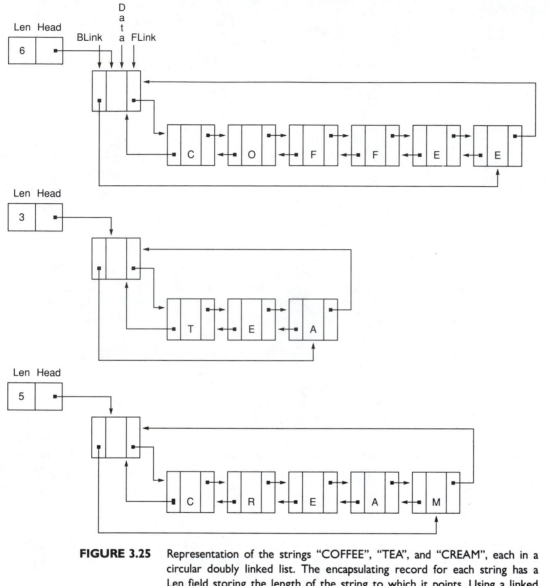

FIGURE 3.25   Representation of the strings "COFFEE", "TEA", and "CREAM", each in a circular doubly linked list. The encapsulating record for each string has a Len field storing the length of the string to which it points. Using a linked structure allows insertions and deletions to be made in the strings without moving large amounts of data.

Example 3.9   The following procedure implements the Insert operation for a linked list implementation of the string ADT.

```
type
  StringPtr: pointer to StringNode;
  StringNode: record
              BLink: StringPtr;
              Data: char;
              FLink: StringPtr
          endrecord;
```

```
String: record
           Head: StringPtr;
           Len: integer
        endrecord;

procedure Insert
  ( given S, T: String       (* Two arbitrary strings *);
        Place: integer       (* The position where T is to be inserted
                                into S *);
     return S: String        (* S, with T inserted at position Place. If
                                Place is greater than Length(S), S is not
                                altered *) );
  var
    K: integer;
    FirstInT, LastInT, P: StringPtr;

  start Insert
    if Place <= S.Len then
      P := S.Head;
      (* First find Place by traversing list *)
      for K := 1 to Place do
        P := Ref(P).FLink
      endfor;
      (* Now link in T *)
      FirstInT := Ref(T.Head).FLink;
      LastInT  := Ref(T.Head).BLink;
      Ref(FirstInT).BLink := Ref(P).BLink;      (* 1 *)
      Ref(LastInT).FLink := P;                  (* 2 *)
      Ref(Ref(P).BLink).FLink := FirstInT;      (* 3 *)
      Ref(P).BLink := LastInT;                  (* 4 *)
```

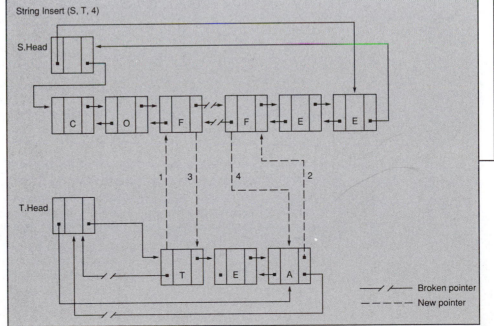

```
        (* Finally update length *)
        S.Len := S.Len + T.Len
    endif
end Insert;
```

Note that this procedure is doing a slightly more complicated task than our previous insertion algorithm for a linked list. Earlier, we were concerned only with inserting one node. As the above graphic documentation indicates, here we are inserting an entire collection of nodes; we are inserting one linked list within another. This is done with relative ease because our implementation of a doubly linked list gives us convenient pointers to both the first and last nodes in the list. Hence, our linked-list implementation of strings has provided a rather neat illustration of the utility of double linking.

Efficiency Considerations for the Linked-List Method

In this string-handling application we have seen that the linked-list method allows both dynamic string allocation with no practical limit on string length and extremely efficient insertion and deletion operations. However, the linked-list method is not a cure-all, for use in all applications.

Three general problem areas exist. First, you may have already noticed that, although the procedure Insert in Example 3.9 achieves a very efficient insertion, it renders string T thereafter inaccessible as a separate entity. This happens because the pointers within T had to be altered to chain it into S (See graphic documentation for Example 3.9).

Second, consider an application in which operating with substrings is of more importance than insertion and deletion. With both the fixed-length and the workspace-index table methods, the substring consisting of the Jth through the Kth characters could be directly accessed because the characters within any given string are physically next to each other. Accessing the same substring via the linked-list implementation requires beginning at the initial character in the string and traversing the entire string until the Jth character is reached. Our implementation of a string as a doubly linked list allows this process to be somewhat more efficient. In particular, the length of the string from which we want to extract a substring could be checked to determine if the substring occurs in the front or back half. If in the back half, the pointer to the last character in the string could be used to begin a traversal from the rear of the list that stops when we reach the desired substring. However, this would still require sequential processing of the list until the desired substring is found. Hence, for substring operations, the linked-list method does not stack up to either of the other two methods.

A third problem arises in the efficiency of memory utilization for the linked-list method as we have described it. If the data portion of a node in the linked list contains only one character, then the two pointers associated with that node could require four to eight times more memory than the data. That is, only 11 to 20 percent of memory is being utilized to store the data in which we are really interested; the rest of the memory is storing data about data.

This memory utilization problem may be alleviated by making the data portion of a node a cluster of characters. Suppose, for instance, we choose a cluster size of four characters. Then the same strings given in Figure 3.25 would appear as shown in Figure 3.26. Here we have used the symbol ~ to represent a null character, one that is always ignored when the string is processed.

Notice that, although this technique has enabled us to devote a greater percentage of memory for storage of data, a significant complication has been added: our code must now always account for null characters. For example, if we wish to insert the second string from Figure 3.26 in the first string beginning at position 4, the scheme pictured in Figure 3.27 emerges.

Here the node containing "COFF" had to be split into the two nodes "COF~" and "F~~~" in order to achieve an effective insertion. As you might expect, we have had to trade-off one feature for another. To gain more effective memory utilization, we have had to make our program code more cumbersome and less efficient in its execution time.

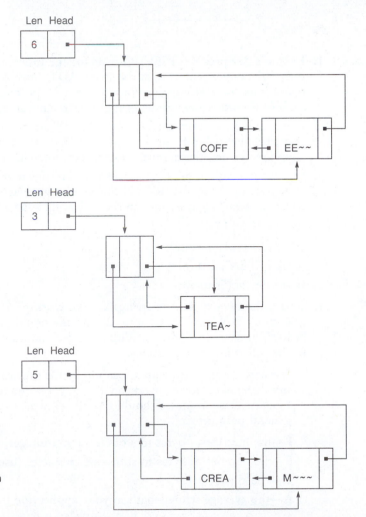

FIGURE 3.26

Strings from Figure 3.25 with a cluster size of four. By storing a cluster of characters in each node, the amount of memory used can be decreased since fewer pointers have to be used.

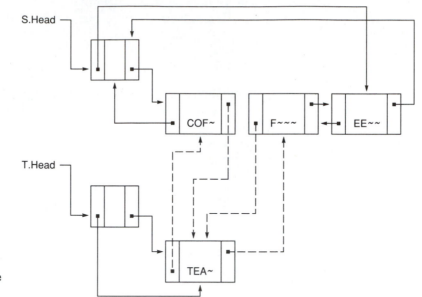

FIGURE 3.27
After insertion of string T into S beginning at position 4. The node containing the characters COFF from the COFFEE's representation in Figure 3.26 had to be split into two nodes—"COF~" and "F~~~" to achieve the designed insertion.

Exercises 3.6

1. Example 3.9 provides PSEUDO code for the Insert operation using a doubly linked list implementation of the string ADT. Complete the package of string operations for this implementation. That is, provide PSEUDO versions for each of the other operations in the ADT definition appearing in Section 2.2.

2. Using big-O notation, analyze the time efficiency of each of the operations you implemented in Exercise 1. In your analysis, include both the number of comparisons and the number of character interchanges.

3. Discuss some of the potential unsuspected results that might occur if the string assignment strategy discussed in this section were actually used. In particular, consider what might happen in the following situation:

   Assign("COFFEE", String1);

   Assign(String1, String2);

   Assign("TEA", String1);

   WriteAString(String2);

4. Two techniques of storing strings are the workspace-index method (see Programming Problem 7 in Chapter 2) and the doubly linked list (with dummy header) of character clusters. With these techniques in mind, provide answers to the following two questions.

   a. For each method, develop a formula that expresses the percentage of memory devoted to storing overhead data (as opposed to actual character data). Each of these formulas should be expressed as a function of the following general parameters:

   P—the number of bytes to store a pointer/integer

   S—the number of bytes to store one character (usually $S = 1$)

   C—the cluster size

   A—the average string length in your application

   For each formula you develop, explain how you derive it.

    b. Your answer to part **a** should indicate that the workspace-index method is generally more space-efficient than the doubly linked list. However, suppose your application calls for frequently inserting one string in another. For this application, the doubly linked list method is more time-efficient. Explain why. If it will help, include diagrams in your explanation. Your explanation should also make it evident why a doubly linked list with a dummy header is a more effective structure for this type of application than a singly linked list.

5. Refine the PSEUDO code of Example 3.9 to remedy the side effect that string T is rendered useless after calling the procedure. What is the cost in efficiency of your remedy?

6. In Section 2.2, two sophisticated string search algorithms were discussed: the Knuth-Morris-Pratt algorithm and the Boyer-Moore algorithm (see Exercise 10 in Section 2.2). Which of these algorithms is more readily adaptable to a doubly linked list implementation of the string ADT? Explain why. Then provide PSEUDO code for this algorithm adapted to the doubly linked list implementation. Finally, discuss whether the algorithm remains as efficient for the doubly linked list implementation as it was for the fixed-length implementation of strings.

3.7 APPLICATION: SETS

Just as we have in the preceding two sections, we will again return to Chapter 2 for a final application of linked lists. In Section 2.4 we introduced the set ADT and discussed an implementation of it that used boolean arrays. We remarked that a shortcoming of the boolean array implementation is that it is limited to sets drawn from a universe that is a finite subrange of some ordinal data type. We will now develop two alternate implementations for sets using linked lists. One of these implementations uses an ordered linked list.

Ordered Linked List Implementation of Sets

The first implementation we consider uses an ordered linked list. Like the boolean array implementation, this implementation is somewhat limited in its universe of elements. In particular, the universe must be an ordered universe, though it need not be a finite subrange of an ordinal type as required by the boolean array implementation. Thus, we could represent a set of reals or strings. The representation scheme used by this implementation is illustrated on a set of reals in Figure 3.28. The linked list corresponding to the conceptual set contains exactly those elements that are in the set, linked together in the order determined by the universe. We suggest that the linked list representing such a set be a doubly linked circular list with a dummy header. Such a representation offers a built-in pointer to the last list node as well as the first. The utility of having this pointer can be seen in the following example.

Head

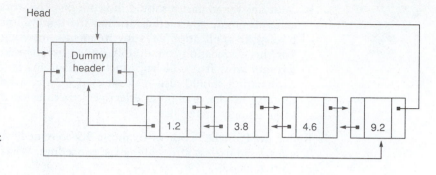

FIGURE 3.28
Set of reals {4.6, 9.2, 3.8, 1.2} and a corresponding ordered (doubly) linked list implementation.

Example 3.10   The following procedure implements the Union operation for the ordered linked list representation of sets. Essentially two ordered lists must be merged, employing logic we will see again when the merge sort algorithm is studied in Chapter 6.

```
type
   Universe: (* A data type whose values have an order relation *);
   Set: pointer to SetNode;
   SetNode: record
            BLink: pointer to SetNode;
            Data: Universe;
            FLink: pointer to SetNode
         endrecord;

procedure Union
   ( given R, S: Set    (* Two arbitrary sets, R and S *);
      return T: Set      (* The union of R and S, that is, the set whose
                            elements are those members of the Universe that
                            are in R or S *) );

   var
      RPtr, SPtr: Set;   (* Used to traverse R and S *)

   procedure AttachToEndOfSet
      ( given T: Set       (* An arbitrary set, represented by doubly
                              linked list *);
             V: Universe   (* A value greater than any other value
                              in T *);
         return T: Set      (* T with V inserted at the end of its
                              list *) );

      var P: Set;

      start AttachToEndOfSet
         GetNode(P);
         Ref(P).Data := V;
```

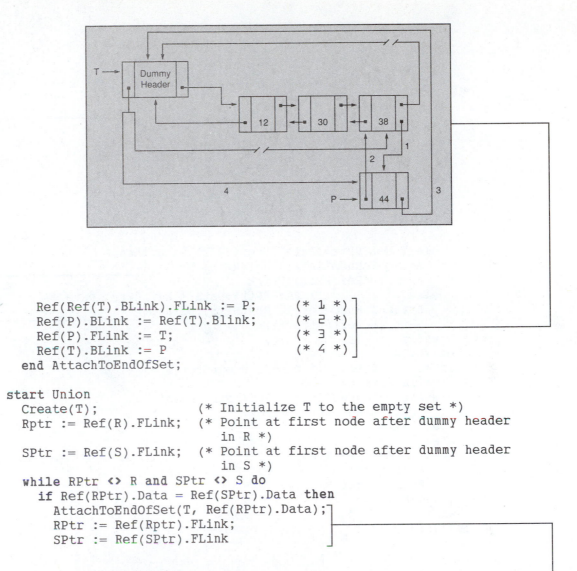

```
        Ref(Ref(T).BLink).FLink := P;        (* 1 *)
        Ref(P).BLink := Ref(T).Blink;        (* 2 *)
        Ref(P).FLink := T;                   (* 3 *)
        Ref(T).BLink := P                    (* 4 *)
    end AttachToEndOfSet;

start Union
    Create(T);                (* Initialize T to the empty set *)
    Rptr := Ref(R).FLink;     (* Point at first node after dummy header
                                    in R *)
    SPtr := Ref(S).FLink;     (* Point at first node after dummy header
                                    in S *)
    while RPtr <> R and SPtr <> S do
      if Ref(RPtr).Data = Ref(SPtr).Data then
        AttachToEndOfSet(T, Ref(RPtr).Data);
        RPtr := Ref(Rptr).FLink;
        SPtr := Ref(SPtr).FLink
```

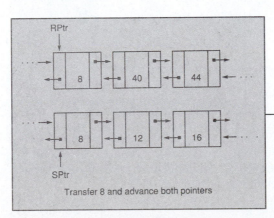

Transfer 8 and advance both pointers

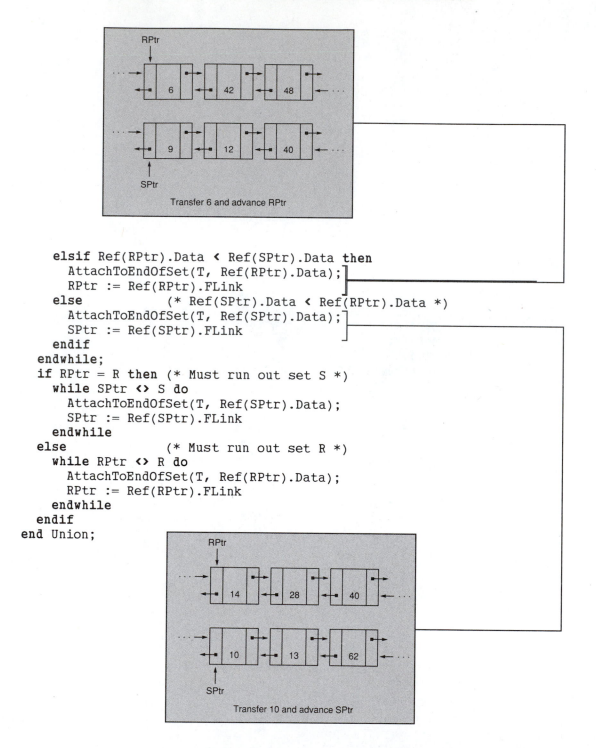

Transfer 6 and advance RPtr

```
    elsif Ref(RPtr).Data < Ref(SPtr).Data then
      AttachToEndOfSet(T, Ref(RPtr).Data);
      RPtr := Ref(RPtr).FLink
    else            (* Ref(SPtr).Data < Ref(RPtr).Data *)
      AttachToEndOfSet(T, Ref(SPtr).Data);
      SPtr := Ref(SPtr).FLink
    endif
  endwhile;
  if RPtr = R then (* Must run out set S *)
    while SPtr <> S do
      AttachToEndOfSet(T, Ref(SPtr).Data);
      SPtr := Ref(SPtr).FLink
    endwhile
  else             (* Must run out set R *)
    while RPtr <> R do
      AttachToEndOfSet(T, Ref(RPtr).Data);
      RPtr := Ref(RPtr).FLink
    endwhile
  endif
end Union;
```

Transfer 10 and advance SPtr

Note how the existence of a pointer to the end of set T allows us to attach a new value to T (in procedure AttachToEndOfSet) without a costly traversal of all elements already in T.

Efficiency Considerations for Ordered Linked List Implementation of Sets

Because the merge logic of Example 3.10 necessitates only one traversal of the lists representing R and S, the efficiency of the union operation is $O(N_R + N_S)$ where N_R and N_S denote the number of elements in R and S, respectively. As you will discover in the exercises, the intersection and difference operations can also be achieved in $O(N_R + N_S)$ time. The only operation where we pay a penalty for ordering the list that represents the set is the Add operation. Because this operation is essentially an insertion into an ordered linked list, Add is an $O(N)$ operation in terms of the number of comparisons that must be performed. A hidden cost in all of the set operations accrues when the universe consists of structured elements. In that case, determining whether two universe elements are equal or which precedes the other may itself be a nontrivial operation whose efficiency depends on the size of the elements.

Unordered Linked List Implementation of Sets

In this implementation, a set is represented as a linked list of its elements in arbitrary order. For space efficiency we insist that no element appear more than once in such a linked list, as illustrated in Figure 3.29. Because ordering is not considered in the lists, we can use this technique to represent sets of arbitrary types. Thus, we could have a set of arrays, matrices, or even a set of sets. This latter type of set will prove extremely useful when we reexamine the union-find problem at the end of this section.

Efficiency Considerations for the Unordered Linked List Implementation

Specific coding for set operations is left for the exercises. However, some conclusions on the efficiency of the operations are evident. Because we can add any element to the front of the list, the Add operation is $O(1)$ instead of $O(N)$ as it was for an ordered list representation. A similar savings is not achieved in the union, set, and difference operations. This is due to the requirement that no element appear twice in the list corresponding to set. Hence, when taking the union of R and S, we must search S for each element of R (or vice versa). Consequently, the efficiency of these operations is $O(N_R \times N_S)$ instead of $O(N_R + N_S)$.

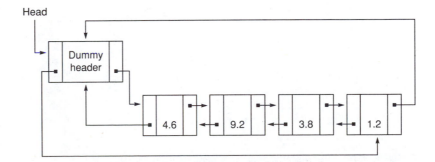

FIGURE 3.29
Set of reals {4.6, 9.2, 3.8, 4.6, 1.2, 9.2} and a corresponding unordered (doubly) linked list implementation.

The Union-Find Problem Revisited

The implementation of sets by an unordered list gives us a convenient way of representing the information needed in the union-find problem, which we introduced in Section 2.4. Consider again the partitioning of cities given in Figure 2.18. Each disjoint subset in this partition may be represented by a linked list as indicated in Figure 3.30. The partition itself, which is nothing but a set of disjoint sets, may be similarly represented via a linked list. The only difference is that the nodes in this linked list do not contain cities but rather pointers to linked lists of cities as indicated in Figure 3.31. That is, since a partition is a set of sets, our representation of sets by linked lists results in a partition being a linked list of linked lists!

Given this implementation, the algorithm for the UFFind operation (see Section 2.4) requires that each disjoint set be searched for the pair of cities

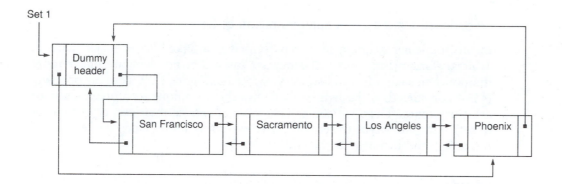

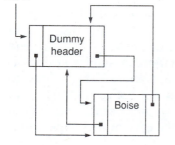

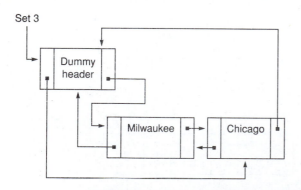

FIGURE 3.30   Representation of sets of cities from Figure 2.18.

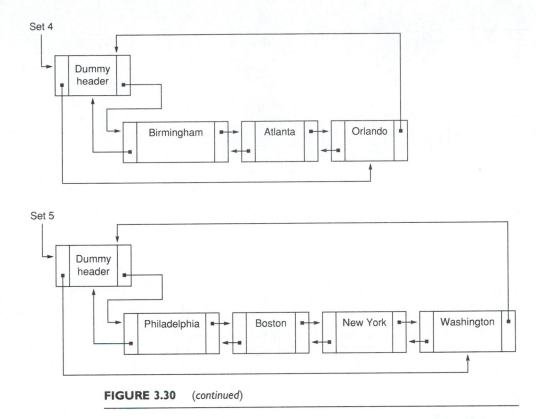

FIGURE 3.30 (continued)

given to UFFind. Clearly this will be $O(N)$ (where N is the number of elements in the universe) in both its worst and average efficiency.

The algorithm for the UFUnion operation will be $O(N)$ in its number of comparisons since the pair of cities it is given, X and Y, must first be found in the partition. Once found, the actual union of the two sets containing elements X and Y respectively can be achieved in $O(1)$ time. For instance, a call to UFUnion(Boise, Atlanta, P) for the partition P in Figure 3.31 results in the partition P of Figure 3.32.

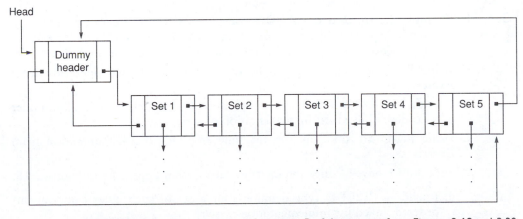

FIGURE 3.31 Representation of partition P of disjoint sets from Figures 2.18 and 3.30.

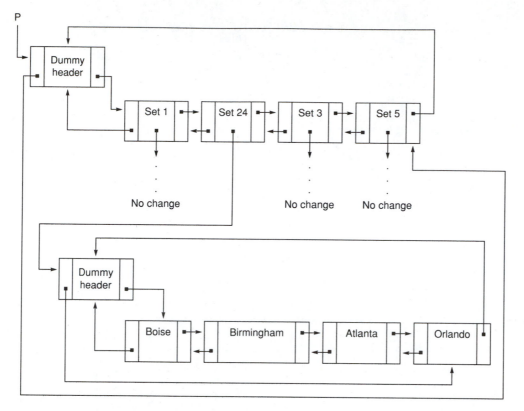

FIGURE 3.32   Partition P from Figures 3.30 and 3.31 after UFUnion(Boise, Atlanta, P).

As we proceed in our study of data structures, we shall return several times to the union-find problem. We will see that, by using more sophisticated implementations, we significantly enhance the $O(N)$ efficiency of the UFFind and UFUnion operations.

Exercises 3.7

1. Example 3.10 provided PSEUDO code for the Union operation under an ordered linked list implementation of sets. Provide PSEUDO code for each of the other set operations (as defined in Section 2.4) under this implementation.

2. Using Big-O notation, analyze the time efficiency of each operation from Exercise 1.

3. Provide PSEUDO code for each set operation (as defined in Section 2.4) under an unordered linked list implementation of sets.

4. Using Big-O notation, analyze the time efficiency of each operation from Exercise 3.

5. Suppose we have a collection of cities such as that appearing in Figure 2.18.

   a. Provide a PSEUDO type definition for a Set of such cities using an unordered linked list implementation of sets.

b. Given your definition of a Set type in part **a**, provide a PSEUDO definition of the type Partition as required in the union-find problem.

c. Given your type definitions in parts **a** and **b**, provide PSEUDO code for the three union-find ADT operations as defined in Section 2.4.

6. Suppose that the Set of cities you defined in Exercise 5a were implemented as an ordered linked list instead of unordered. What would be gained by such an implementation? What would be lost?

7. In discussing the unordered list implementation of sets in this section, we stated that the efficiency of the Union operation would be $O(N_X \times N_Y)$ where N_X and N_Y represent the number of elements in the sets X and Y respectively. Then, in discussing the unordered list implementation of sets for the union-find problem, we stated that the efficiency of the UFUnion operation would be $O(1)$. Does this contradict our earlier claim of $O(N_X \times N_Y)$? Explain. (Hint: what do we know about sets in the union-find problem that makes the union operation "easier" for this problem?)

Chapter Summary

In this chapter we discuss the *list* ADT, which is based on a data structure known as an *ordered list*. An ordered list is a collection of data nodes arranged in a linear sequence according to some ordering criterion between nodes. Two implementations for the list ADT are given: an implementation using an ordered array with binary search and an implementation using a linked list. As applications for the list ADT we give alternative implementations for the sparse matrix ADT, the string ADT, the set ADT, and the union-find ADT, which were introduced in Chapter 2.

Since the linked list implementation of the list ADT requires the use of pointers, we discuss an implementation of the pointer ADT using arrays. Such an implementation is worthwhile so that one can implement other ADTs that require pointers even while working in a language that has no pointer type. Additionally, knowing how to implement pointer types can be useful in situations where a particular language's implementation of pointers is not suitable.

The widespread use of linked lists has led to the development of several variations suitable in certain applications. Four such variations presented in this chapter were linked lists with dummy headers, circular lists, doubly linked lists, and multilinked lists.

Key Words

circular linked list	head pointer	multilinked list
doubly linked list	heap	ordered list
dummy header	linked list	

Programming Problems/Projects

1. Wing-and-a-Prayer Airlines maintains four scheduled flights per day, identified by the numbers 1, 2, 3, and 4. For each of these flights, they keep an alphabetized list of passengers. The data base for the entire airline could hence

be viewed as four linked lists. Write a program that sets up and maintains this data base by handling commands of the following form:

Command → Add
Flight number → 3
Passenger name → BROWN
Command → Delete
Flight number → 1
Passenger name → JONES
Command → List
Flight number → 2
(List alphabetically all passengers for the specified flight)

Use an appropriate string storage strategy for the passenger names.

2. In order to take care of their growing business, the Fly-by-Night credit card company would like to update their customer data field. Write a program in a high-level language that sets up a doubly linked list into which a record is

    a. inserted into the list in the correct place, sorted according to the social security number of the customer.
    b. updated if the customer record exists.
    c. deleted if the customer no longer wishes to patronize the company.

    In the preceding data manipulation activities, the list should always remain in order sorted by the social security number.

3. As a struggling professional football team, the Bay Area Brawlers have a highly volatile player roster. Write a program that allows the team to maintain its roster as a linked list in alphabetical order by player last name. Other data items stored for each player are the following:

    • Height

    • Weight

    • Age

    • University affiliation

    As an added option, allow your program to access players in descending order of weight or in descending order of age.

4. Develop a line-oriented text editor that assigns a number to each line of text and then maintains the lines in a linked list in line number order (similar to the way in which BASIC programs are maintained on many systems). Your program should be able to process the following commands:

I line-number 'text'
    (instruction to insert text at specified number)
L line1-line2
    (instruction to list line1 through line2)

D line1-line2

(instruction to delete line1 through line2)

If you feel really ambitious, incorporate into your program a string storage strategy that will allow the user to perform editing operations such as inserting and deleting characters within a given line.

5. Write a program that, given a file of text, will add to an index to those words in the text that are marked by special delimiting brackets [ ]. The words in the index will be printed after the text itself has been formatted and printed. Words in this index should be listed alphabetically and should have a page-number reference for each page of text on which they are delimited by the special brackets. Note that this program would be part of a word processing system an author could use when developing a book with an index of terms.

6. A data structure sometimes used to facilitate searching a list of values is that of a *self-organizing list*. The idea here is that the list is searched sequentially for a given data item. If the data item does not appear in the list, then a node with the data item is inserted at the beginning of the list; otherwise, after the data item has been found, its node is moved from its current position to the beginning of the list.

    This structure could be useful for situations in which the data items involved exhibit a phenomenon known as *locality of reference*, which is characterized by situations wherein a data item is referenced frequently for a while; then over time it exhibits less and less usage, only to reappear again frequently for a while, and so on. References to identifiers of variables in a program are one example of items that exhibit such locality of reference.

    For this problem you are to specify a self-organizing list as an abstract data type with the usual list operations Create and Destroy, with a modified Retrieve operation that causes the list to function in the self-organizing manner described above, and with a Traverse procedure to visit each node of the list sequentially from the beginning of the list, displaying the value of the data item for that node. Now write a program that accepts a stream of strings (perhaps representing program identifiers) as input and traverses the list each time the order of the nodes in the list changes. You should use an appropriate string storage strategy for the input strings.

7. Write a program that allows input of an arbitrary number of polynomials as coefficient and exponent pairs. Store each polynomial as a linked list of coefficient-exponent pairs arranged in descending order by exponent. Note that the pairs need not be input in descending order; it is the responsibility of your program to do that. Your program should then be able to evaluate each of the polynomials for an arbitrary argument X and be able to output each of the polynomials in the appropriate descending exponent order. Be sure that your program works for all "unusual" polynomials such as the zero polynomial, polynomials of degree one, and constant polynomials.

8. Extend the polynomial evaluation program you developed for Problem 7 to perform polynomial arithmetic. That is, develop procedures to perform polynomial addition, subtraction, multiplication, and division.

9. Consider the following memorandum from the registrar at the renowned Lowcountry University.

MEMORANDUM
Lowcountry University

TO : Director of Data Processing
FROM : Head Registrar
DATE : July 29, 1994
RE : Automation of record keeping on students

Records for students at our school consist of a university identification number, a last name, a first name, a middle initial, a Social Security number, a list of courses the student has taken along with the grade received in each course, and a list of extracurricular activities in which the student has indicated an interest. A university identification number for a student consists of a six-digit number: the first two digits represent the year a student entered the university. The remaining four digits are simply assigned on a sequential basis as students are admitted to the school. For instance, the student with ID number 910023 is the twenty-third student admitted in the class that entered L.U. in 1991.

Given this data base, we frequently need to work with it in the following ways:

- Find and display all data for a particular student, as identified by university ID number.
- Add and delete student records from the data base.
- Print records for all students in Social Security number order, starting with the most recent class and working back.
- Add, change, or delete the information in a course for a particular student. For instance, change the grade received by student 910023 in CompSci2 from C to B.
- Find all students with an extracurricular interest that matches a particular target interest. Students extracurricular interests are viewed as arbitrarily long strings. These strings are entered into our records directly from information provided by students on their registration forms. For instance, a given student may have indicated PLAYING BASKETBALL and GOING TO PLAYS as her two interests. We would want to be able to find this student (as well as students who indicated an interest such as WATCHING BASKETBALL or SHOOTING BASKETBALLS) if we were to search our data base for students who had an interest matching BASKETBALL.

In what sense could the overall data base described in this memo be viewed as a list? As lists embedded within another list? As a two-dimensional matrix? As lists embedded within a two-dimensional matrix?

Finally, implement a solution based on linked lists for the system requested by the registrar at L.U.

10. (Josephus Problem) Consider the following problem—often referred to as the Josephus problem. Imagine that a class of N students decided to choose one from among themselves to approach a curmudgeonly professor about

postponing for a week an upcoming examination. They elect to arrange themselves in a circle and excuse the Mth person around the circle—with the size of the circle being reduced by one each time a person is excused. The problem is to find out which person will be the last remaining, or more generally, to find the order in which the people are excused. For example, if $N = 9$ and $M = 5$, then the people are excused in the order 5 1 7 4 3 6 9 2. Hence the eighth person is left to face the professor. To solve the Josephus problem, write a program that inserts persons 1 through N into a list and then appropriately deletes them from the list until only one is left.

11. In Exercise 4 of Section 3.1, you developed PSEUDO procedures for the information-processing needs of the registrar's office at High Plains University (a primary competitor of the Lowcountry University of Problem 9). Now incorporate these procedures into a complete, functioning system for the registrar.

12. Computers can only store and do arithmetic with integers of limited size. When integers surpass that limiting value, *overflow* occurs and the results will either be unreliable or cause your program to die with a run-time error. However, by altering the implementation of an integer, you can develop algorithms to do virtually limitless integer arithmetic. The basis of such an implementation is to store each digit of an integer in a list; that is, to represent an integer as a list of digits. Then develop algorithms to do integer arithmetic operations on a digit-by-digit basis, taking carries, borrows, and so forth into account as you do when performing these operations by hand. After carefully considering which list implementation best suits the problem, develop procedures to perform extended integer addition, subtraction, multiplication, and division (quotient and remainder).

13. Incorporate the procedures you developed for the union-find problem in Exercise 5 of Section 3.7 into a complete program that allows a user to manipulate cities in a transportation network in the manner described in Section 2.4. Unlike Problem 11 in Chapter 2, you should no longer assume that the cities are identified by a single letter.

14. Write a text editor program as described in Problem 6 of Chapter 2, but use a linked list implementation of strings. If you did Problem 6 of Chapter 2, formulate in writing a performance comparison of the two string implementations for this text editing application.

15. Write a *Game of Life* program (see Problem 4 of Chapter 2), using a linked list implementation of the sparse matrix. If you did Problem 4 of Chapter 2, formulate in writing a performance comparison of the two sparse matrix implementations for this application.

16. Write a program for the Wing-and-a-Prayer Airline application described in Problem 2 of Chapter 2—using a linked list implementation of the sparse matrix involved. If you did Problem 2 in Chapter 2, formulate in writing a performance comparison of the two sparse matrix implementations for this application.

4 QUEUES

Will the line stretch out to the crack of doom?

Shakespeare, *Macbeth*

CHAPTER OUTLINE

In Chapter 3 we introduced the linked list as a data structure specifically designed to handle conveniently the insertion and deletion of entries in an ordered list. In this chapter, we shall discuss another data structure, called a *queue*, which is a special type of general list as defined in Chapter 3. In particular, the *queue* is a list with restrictions imposed upon the way in which entries may be inserted and removed. Another name for a queue is a *first-in, first-out* (FIFO) list. This latter name comes close to completely characterizing the restricted types of adds and deletes that can be performed on a queue. Insertions are limited to one end of the list, whereas deletions may occur only at the other end; thus an item cannot be deleted from a queue until all items previously placed in the queue have been deleted. Conceptually a queue resembles a waiting line; for example, jobs waiting to be serviced by a computer or cars forming a long line at a busy tollbooth. As highlights of this chapter we shall use the queue structure to implement a new sorting algorithm, the radix sort, and then explore the application of queues in the scheduling of processes in a time-sharing environment.

4.1   THE QUEUE ADT

The following definition specifies the queue as an abstract data type.

• **Definition of Queue:** a queue is merely a restricted form of a list. In particular, all additions to a queue occur at one end, the *rear*, and all removals occur at the other end, the *front*. The effect of these restrictions is to ensure that the earlier an item enters a queue, the earlier it will leave the queue. That is, items are processed on a first-in, first-out basis. The six basic operations performed on a queue follow in the form of PSEUDO pre- and postconditions.

```
type
   QueueData: (* The type of each data item in the queue *);
   QueueNode: (* Data type giving the structure of each node
               in the queue; in the simplest case will be
               equivalent to QueueData *);
procedure Create
   ( given Q: Queue            (* An arbitrary queue variable Q in unknown state *);
     return Q: Queue           (* Q initialized to the empty queue *) );

procedure Destroy
   ( given Q: Queue            (* An arbitrary queue *);
     return Q: Queue           (* All dynamically allocated storage associated
                               with Q is returned to available space; Q itself
                               is in unreliable state *) );

function Empty
   ( given Q: Queue            (* A previously created queue *);
     return: boolean           (* true if no removal can be made from queue;
                               false otherwise *) );

function Full
   ( given Q: Queue            (* A previously created queue *);
     return: boolean           (* true if no addition can be made to queue; false
                               otherwise *) );

procedure Enqueue
   ( given Q: Queue            (* A previously created queue *);
         Item: QueueData       (* An item to be added to the rear of the queue *);
     return Q: Queue           (* Q with Item added to the rear of the queue. If
                               the queue is full, it is left unchanged *) );

procedure Dequeue
   ( given Q: Queue            (* A previously created queue *);
     return Q: Queue           (* Q with its front value removed *) );
         Item: QueueData       (* Contains the value that was at the front of
                               queue. If Q is empty, contents of Item are
                               unreliable *) );
```

The conceptual picture that emerges from this definition is given in Figure 4.1. From this definition of a queue, it is evident that two pointers will suffice to keep track of the data in a queue: one pointer to the front of the queue and one to the rear. This premise underlies all of the queue implementations discussed in the next section.

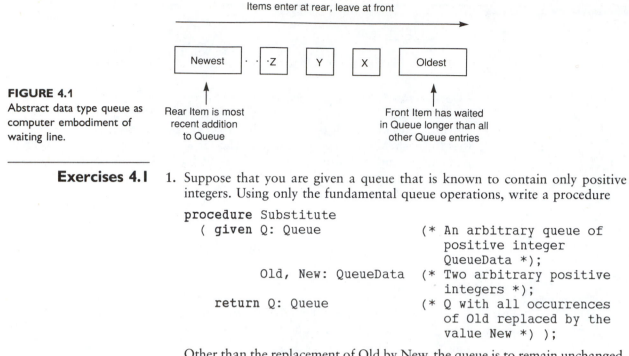

Items enter at rear, leave at front

FIGURE 4.1
Abstract data type queue as
computer embodiment of
waiting line.

Rear Item is most
recent addition
to Queue

Front Item has waited
in Queue longer than all
other Queue entries

Exercises 4.1

1. Suppose that you are given a queue that is known to contain only positive integers. Using only the fundamental queue operations, write a procedure

```
procedure Substitute
  ( given Q: Queue            (* An arbitrary queue of
                                  positive integer
                                  QueueData *);
         Old, New: QueueData  (* Two arbitrary positive
                                  integers *);
    return Q: Queue           (* Q with all occurrences
                                  of Old replaced by the
                                  value New *) );
```

Other than the replacement of Old by New, the queue is to remain unchanged. Avoid passing through the queue more than once.

2. Suppose that you are given a queue of real numbers. Using only the fundamental queue operations, write a function that returns the average value of the entries in the queue.

4.2 IMPLEMENTATIONS OF THE QUEUE

We will discuss three implementations of a queue here: array, circular, and linked list. Additionally, in Section 4.5 we will discuss a variation of a queue, known as a priority queue, and suggest possible implementations for it.

Array Implementation

Let us consider computer jobs being scheduled in a batch processing environment, a good example of a queue in use. Suppose further that jobs are scheduled strictly in the order in which they arrive. An array and two pointers can then be used to implement the scheduling queue.

```
type (* Assume that constant MaxQueueSize establishes maximum
        number of elements that queue may contain *)
  QueueData: String;
  QueueNode: QueueData;
  Queue: record
           Node: array [MaxQueueSize] of QueueNode;
           Front, Rear: integer
         endrecord;
```

As we noted above, MaxQueueSize is a constant declared to be the maximum number of entries that the Node array may contain. We shall see, however, that normally this is different from the actual number of entries that the queue may contain at a given time in processing.

If the Front and Rear pointers are initially set to 1 and 0, respectively, the state of the queue before any insertions or deletions appears as shown in Figure 4.2. Here the pointer Rear points to the location last occupied, not the one where the next addition will take place. The pointer Front, conversely, points to the location from which the next removal will take place. Thus, as additions are made to the queue, the value of Rear will first match and then exceed the value of Front. To understand this, suppose that in the queue of Figure 4.2 the job NEWTON arrives to be processed. The queue then changes to the state pictured in Figure 4.3. If job NEWTON is followed by job PAYROLL, the queue's status changes to that of Figure 4.4. These illustrations show that the addition of any Item to the queue requires two steps:

```
Q.Rear := Q.Rear + 1;
Q.Node[Q.Rear] := Item;
```

If the system is now ready to process NEWTON, the front entry must be removed from the queue to an appropriate location designated by Item in Figure 4.5. Here the instructions

```
Item := Q.Node[Q.Front];
Q.Front := Q.Front + 1;
```

achieved the desired effect.

It should be clear that the conditions in Table 4.1 signal the associated boundary conditions for an array implementation of a queue. The conditions

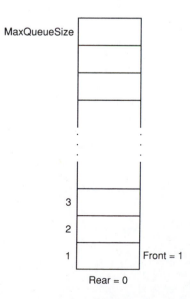

FIGURE 4.2

Empty queue.

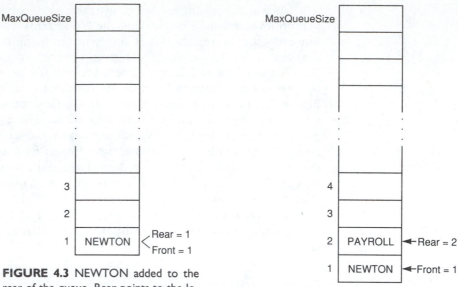

FIGURE 4.3 NEWTON added to the rear of the queue. Rear points to the location last occupied, Front points to the location from which the next removal will take place.

FIGURE 4.4 PAYROLL added after NEWTON.

allow us to develop into full-fledged procedures our brief two-line sequences for adding and removing. These in turn assume the existence of the boolean-valued functions Empty and Full to check whether or not the Dequeue and Enqueue operations are possible. In the exercises, you will be asked to write the Empty and Full functions for this implementation of the queue ADT.

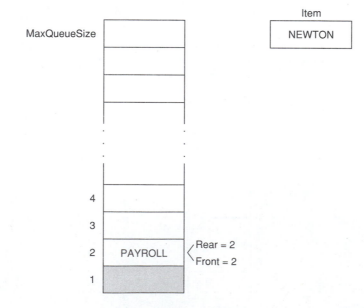

FIGURE 4.5
NEWTON removed from the queue.

Condition	Special situation
Rear < Front	Empty queue
Front = Rear	One-entry queue
Rear = MaxQueueSize	No more entries may be added to queue

TABLE 4.1
Boundary condition checks for array implementation of queue.

```
type (* Assume that constant MaxQueueSize establishes maximum number of
        elements that queue may contain *)
   QueueData: (* Any data appropriate for the queue *);
   QueueNode: QueueData;
   Queue: record
            Node: array [MaxQueueSize] of QueueData;
            Front, Rear: integer
          endrecord;

procedure Enqueue
   ( given Q: Queue          (* A previously created queue *);
          Item: QueueData    (* An item to be added to the rear of the queue *);
     return Q: Queue         (* Q with Item added to the rear of the queue. If
                                the queue is full, it is left unchanged *) );

   start Enqueue
     if not Full(Q) then
       Q.Rear := Q.Rear + 1;
       Q.Node[Q.Rear] := Item
     endif
   end Enqueue;
```

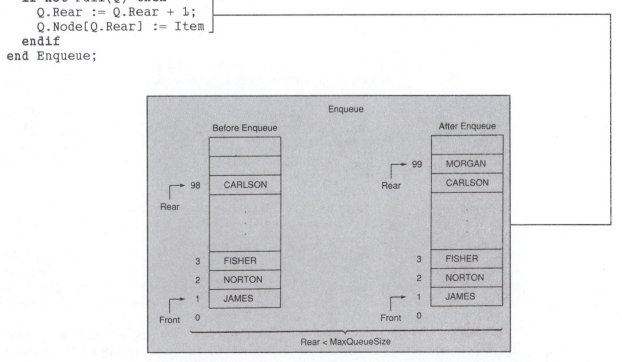

```
procedure Dequeue
  ( given  Q: Queue           (* A previously created queue *);
    return Q: Queue           (* Q with its front value removed *);
           Item: QueueData    (* Contains the value that was at front of queue.
                                 If Q is empty, contents of Item are
                                 unreliable *) );

  start Dequeue
    if not Empty(Q) then
      Item := Q.Node[Q.Front];
      Q.Front := Q.Front + 1
    endif
  end Dequeue;
```

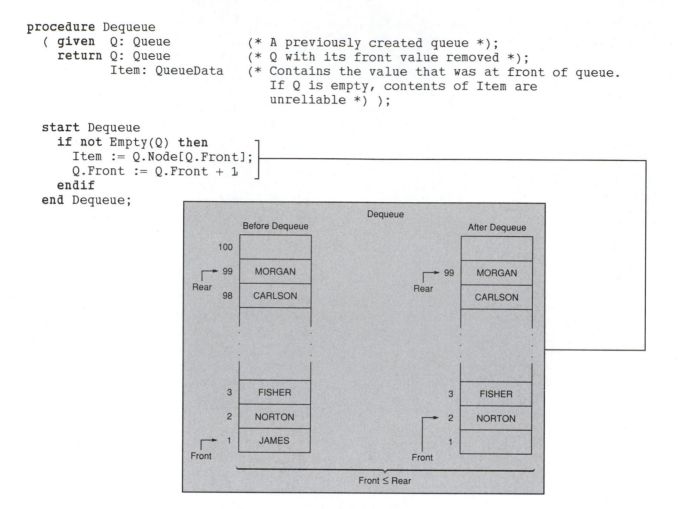

As it now stands, our implementation of a queue as a scheduling structure for jobs in a batch environment functions effectively until Rear matches MaxQueueSize. Then a call to Enqueue fails, even though only a small percentage of slots in the array may actually contain data items currently in the queue structure. In fact, given the queue pictured in Figure 4.6, we should be able to use slots 1–997 again.

This is not necessarily undesirable. For example, it may be that the mode of operation in a given batch environment is to process 1,000 jobs, then print a statistical report on these 1,000 jobs, and finally clear the queue to start another group of 1,000 jobs. In this case, the queue in Figure 4.6 is the ideal structure because data about jobs are not lost, even after they have left the queue. However, if the goal of a computer installation were to provide continuous scheduling of batch jobs, without interruption after 1,000 jobs, then the queue of Figure 4.6 would not be effective. One strategy that could be employed to correct this situation is to move the active queue down the array upon reaching the condition Rear = MaxQueueSize, as illustrated in Figure 4.7.

If the queue contains a large number of items, however, this strategy would not be satisfactory because it would require moving all of the individ-

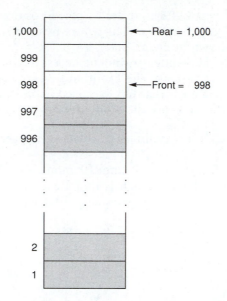

FIGURE 4.6
A full queue. The shaded region represents slots that were once used but no longer contain data items currently in the queue.

ual data items. We will discuss two other strategies that allow the queue to operate in a continuous and efficient fashion: a circular implementation and a linked-list implementation.

Circular Implementation

The circular implementation essentially allows the queue to wrap around upon reaching the end of the array. This transformation is illustrated by the addition of the item UPDATE to the queue in Figure 4.8. The technique is called a *circular* implementation of a queue because if we redraw the right-

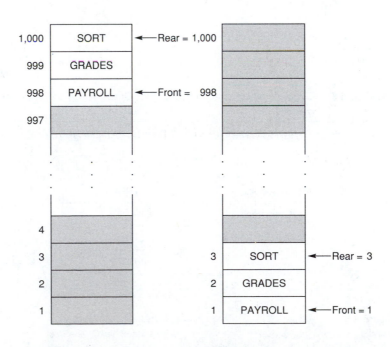

FIGURE 4.7
Active queue moved down. The shifting of the queue to the lower-indexed positions in the array was triggered upon reaching the condition Rear = MaxQueue Size (here, MaxQueueSize = 1,000).

hand array of Figure 4.8 in order to place position 1 immediately after the position MaxQueueSize as well as before position 2, then we get the circular arrangement shown in Figure 4.9.

To handle the pointer arithmetic necessary for such an implementation of a queue, we must make the Front and Rear pointers behave analogously to an odometer in a car that has exceeded its mileage capacity. A convenient way of doing this is to use the **mod** operator:

$$M \bmod N = \text{remainder of dividing integer } M \text{ by integer } N$$

(for example, $5 \bmod 3 = 2$ and $10 \bmod 7 = 3$). An immediate consequence of taking this approach is that Rear < Front will no longer suffice as a condition to signal an empty queue. To derive the empty queue condition,

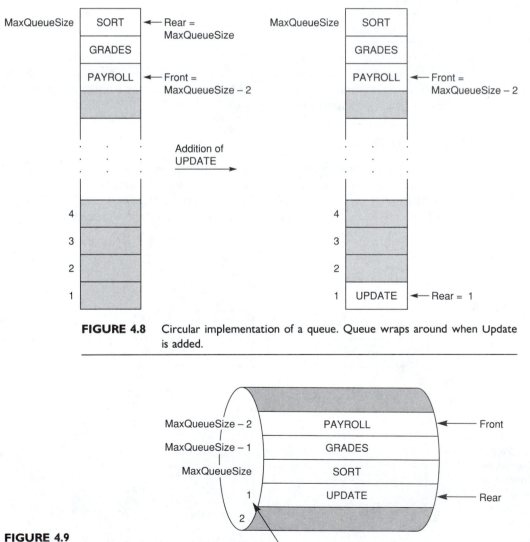

FIGURE 4.8   Circular implementation of a queue. Queue wraps around when Update is added.

FIGURE 4.9
Reillustration of Figure 4.8
to show wrap-around.

consider what remains after we remove an item from a queue that has only one item in it. There are two possible situations, as illustrated in Figure 4.10.

An inspection of both cases reveals that after the lone entry has been removed, the relationship

$$(\text{Rear } \textbf{mod } \text{MaxQueueSize}) + 1 = \text{Front}$$

holds between the pointers. There is a problem, however, with immediately adopting this as a check for an empty queue. As Case 1 in Figure 4.10 illustrates, if we allow all slots in the array to be occupied at any one time, this same relationship between pointers also exists when the queue is full. The apparent contradiction can be avoided easily if one memory slot is sacrificed; that is, if we view a queue with MaxQueueSize − 1 entries as a full queue. Then the test for fullness is met when the Rear pointer lags two behind Front (including considerations for wrapping around). These results are summarized in Table 4.2.

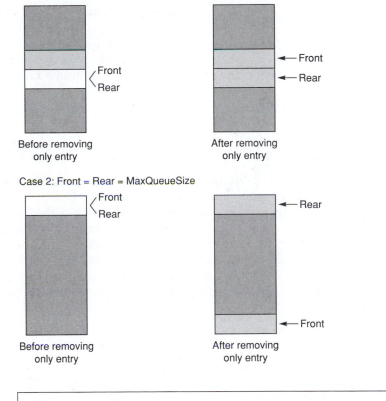

FIGURE 4.10

Removing from one-entry queue. Since the queue is being represented circularly in the array, deleting a single node at MaxQueueSize presents a special case.

Condition	Special situation
Front = Rear	One-entry queue
(Rear **mod** MaxQueueSize) + 1 = Front	Empty queue
[(Rear + 1) **mod** MaxQueueSize] + 1 = Front	Full queue

TABLE 4.2   Boundary condition checks for a circular queue, at most MaxQueueSize − 1 entries.

Example 4.1   Explain why the check for a full queue in Table 4.2 cannot be replaced by the boolean condition

$$(\text{Rear} + 2) \bmod \text{MaxQueueSize} = \text{Front}$$

This condition would work for all but one special case of a full queue. In particular, it would fail when Rear is MaxQueueSize − 2 and Front is MaxQueueSize. In that instance, the condition's value would be **false** even though the queue is full.

Example 4.2   Explain why the check for a full queue in Table 4.2 cannot be replaced by the boolean condition

$$(\text{Rear} \bmod \text{MaxQueueSize}) + 2 = \text{Front}$$

This condition would work for all but one special case of a full queue. In particular, it would fail when Rear is MaxQueueSize − 1 and Front is 1. In that instance, the condition's value would be **false** even though the queue is full.

Linked-List Implementation

The linked-list method allows the queue to be completely dynamic—with size restrictions imposed only by the pool of available nodes. Essentially, the queue is represented as a linked list with an additional rear pointer to the last node so that the list need not be traversed to find this node. To reduce the necessity of handling special cases, we follow the strategy described in Section 3.4 of having a dummy header, which carries no actual data, as the first node in the list. Hence, the linked-list implementation of the queue containing PAYROLL, GRADES, and SORT would appear as in Figure 4.11.

FIGURE 4.11   Linked representation of a queue with three data nodes. This representation uses a dummy header for the front of the queue and an additional rear pointer to the last node. By using the rear pointer, the list need not be traversed to locate the last node.

Condition	Special situation
Rear = Front	Empty queue
Rear = Ref(Front).Link	One-entry queue
Handled by space management system?	Full queue

TABLE 4.3

Conditional checks for special situations in linked-list implementation.

Table 4.3 lists the boundary conditions for a linked-list implementation of a queue. Unfortunately, depending upon the language in which you work, it may be difficult to define the Full function because many compilers treat the exhaustion of the pool of available nodes as a run-time error and terminate the program that generated it. Unless you have a way to circumvent this premature termination of your program (an action known as *exception handling*) and instead use the occurrence of the run-time error to set Full to **true**, you may have to use an alternate implementation of pointers—for example, one similar to the one we described in Chapter 3, but augmented with a function to indicate when the pool of available nodes is empty.

Appropriate procedures for handling additions to and removals from the queue follow. Notice that from a calling module's perspective, it would make little difference whether these low-level procedures used an array or a linked list to implement the queue. For each implementation, we have bundled all the information involved with the queue into a single record of type Queue. Hence, the calling protocol for these modules is the same regardless of the implementation being used. That is the essence of data abstraction: the details of how a data structure is actually implemented are hidden as deeply as possible in the overall program structure.

```
type  (* Declarations for linked list implementation of queue *)
  QueuePointer: pointer to QueueNode;
  QueueNode: record
              Data: QueueData;
              Link: QueuePointer
            endrecord;
  Queue: record
          Front, Rear: QueuePointer
        endrecord;

procedure Enqueue
  ( given Q: Queue         (* A previously created queue Q *);
          Item: QueueData  (* An item to be added to the rear of the
                              queue *);
    return Q: Queue        (* Q with Item added to the rear of the queue. If
                              the queue is full, it is left unchanged *) );

  var
    P: QueuePointer;
```

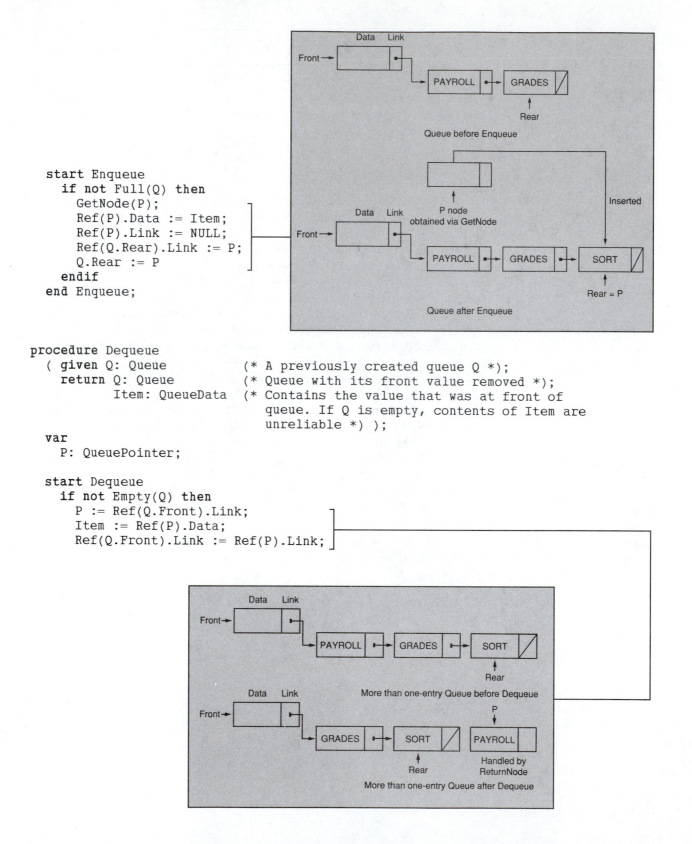

```
start Enqueue
  if not Full(Q) then
    GetNode(P);
    Ref(P).Data := Item;
    Ref(P).Link := NULL;
    Ref(Q.Rear).Link := P;
    Q.Rear := P
  endif
end Enqueue;
```

```
procedure Dequeue
  ( given Q: Queue          (* A previously created queue Q *);
    return Q: Queue         (* Queue with its front value removed *);
           Item: QueueData  (* Contains the value that was at front of
                               queue. If Q is empty, contents of Item are
                               unreliable *) );
  var
    P: QueuePointer;

  start Dequeue
    if not Empty(Q) then
      P := Ref(Q.Front).Link;
      Item := Ref(P).Data;
      Ref(Q.Front).Link := Ref(P).Link;
```

Data   Link

Front →

Queue before Enqueue

Inserted

Data   Link

Front →

P node
obtained via GetNode

PAYROLL   GRADES   SORT

Rear = P

Queue after Enqueue

Data   Link

Front →

PAYROLL   GRADES   SORT

Rear

More than one-entry Queue before Dequeue

Data   Link

Front →

GRADES   SORT

Rear

P

PAYROLL

Handled by
ReturnNode

More than one-entry Queue after Dequeue

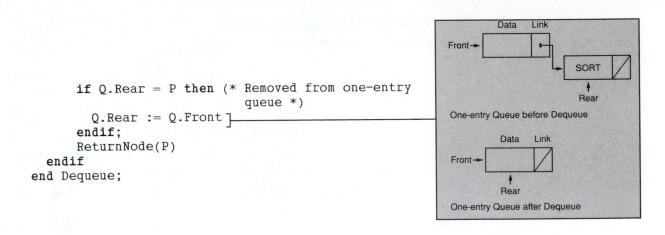

```
        if Q.Rear = P then (* Removed from one-entry
                             queue *)
          Q.Rear := Q.Front
        endif;
        ReturnNode(P)
    endif
end Dequeue;
```

Exercises 4.2

1. Consider a circular array implementation of a queue in which the array is declared to have MaxQueueSize = 5. Trace the status of the array and the front and rear pointers after each of the following successive operations.

   Enqueue SMITH
   Enqueue JONES
   Enqueue GREER
   Dequeue
   Enqueue CARSON
   Dequeue
   Enqueue BAKER
   Enqueue CHARLES
   Enqueue BENSON
   Dequeue
   Enqueue MILLER

2. Given the discussion of circular queues presented in this section, determine a valid initial setting for the front and rear pointers in a circular queue.

3. In the array implementation of a circular queue as described in this section what are the conditions to be satisfied by the pointers Rear and Front for a full queue, an empty queue, and a one-entry queue?

4. For a circular queue implemented by a linked list, it is necessary to separate and maintain only one queue pointer—which one: Front or Rear? Justify your answer, using a drawing to help.

5. Suppose that we adopt the following conventions for the front and rear pointers associated with a queue. Front is to point at the next item to be removed from the queue. Rear is to point at the first available location, that is, the next location to be filled. Explain how this change in convention would affect the operations Create, Empty, and Full for

   a. a noncircular array implementation.

b. a circular array implementation.

c. a linked list implementation.

6. Explain how a continuously maintained count of the number of elements in a circular queue could be used to implement the Create, Empty, and Full operations (instead of checking the relationship between Front and Rear). Write a record structure for such a queue. Then write PSEUDO procedures to implement each of the six basic queue operations.

7. Write procedures (or functions) to implement the Create, Destroy, Empty, and Full operations for a noncircular array implementation of a queue.

8. Write procedures (or functions) to implement all six queue operations for a circular array implementation of a queue.

9. Write procedures (or functions) to implement the Create, Destroy, and Empty operations for a linked-list implementation of a queue.

10. Consider all of the queue implementations suggested in Exercises 5 through 9. Would *any* operation for *any* of these implementations have a time efficiency that is *not* $O(1)$? If so, which operation for which implementation? What would be the efficiency of these operations?

4.3   APPLICATION: RADIX SORT

The *radix sort* algorithm is also called the *bin sort*, a name derived from its origin as a technique used on (now obsolete) machines called card sorters. These machines would sort a deck of key-punched cards by shuffling the cards into small bins, then collecting the cards from the bins into a newly arranged deck, and repeating this shuffling-collection process until the deck was magically sorted. There was, as we shall see, a very clever algorithm behind this rapid shuffling.

For integer data, the repeated passes of radix sort focus on the ones digit of each number, then on the tens digit, the hundreds digit, and so on until the highest-order digit of the largest number is reached. For string data, the first pass hinges on the rightmost character in each string with successive passes always shifting attention one character position to the left. To illustrate the algorithm, we will trace it on the following list of nine integers:

459 254 472 534 649 239 432 654 477

On each pass through this data, radix sort will arrange it into ten sublists (bins), one sublist for each of the digits, 0 through 9. Hence, on the first pass, all the numbers with the ones digit equal to 0 are grouped in one sublist, all those with the ones digit equal to 1 are grouped into another sublist, and so on. The resulting sublists follow.

Digit	Sublist
0	
1	
2	472 432
3	
4	254 534 654
5	
6	
7	477
8	
9	459 649 239

First pass of radix sort

The sublists are then collected into a single large list with the numbers in the sublist for 0 coming first, then those in the sublist for 1, and so on up to the sublist for 9. Hence, we would have a newly arranged list:

472 432 254 534 654 477 459 649 239

This new list is again partitioned into sublists, this time keying on the tens digit. The result is shown below.

Digit	Sublist
0	
1	
2	
3	432 534 239
4	649
5	654 254 459
6	
7	472 477
8	
9	

Second pass of radix sort

Note that in each sublist the data are arranged in order by their last two digits. The sublists would now be collected in a new master list:

432 543 239 649 654 254 459 472 477

Now focusing on the hundreds digit, the master list would be classified into ten sublists one more time. These final sublists are shown below. When the sublists are collected from this final partitioning, the data are arranged in ascending order.

Digit	Sublist
0	
1	
2	239 254
3	
4	432 459 472 477
5	543
6	649 654
7	
8	
9	

Third (final) pass of radix sort

The final order for the list is

239 254 432 459 472 477 543 649 654

A rough, top-level statement of the radix sort algorithm follows.

Begin with the current digit as the one's digit;
while *there is still a digit on which to classify data* **do**
  for *each number in the master list* **do**
    Add that number to the appropriate sublist, keying on the current digit
  endfor;
  for *each sublist (from 0 through 9)* **do**
    for *each number in the sublist* **do**
      Remove the number from the sublist and append it to a newly arranged master list
    endfor
  endfor;
  Advance the current digit one place to the left
endwhile;

If the radix sort is being applied to character strings instead of integers, this algorithm would have to proceed from the rightmost character to the leftmost character instead of from the ones digit to the highest-order digit.

At this point, you may be asking yourself what the radix sort has to do with the subject for this chapter, that is, queues. For the answer to this question, look at the nature of the master list and sublists manipulated by this algorithm. They are all first-in, first-out lists. In other words, queues are the ideal "bins" into which we categorize numbers by digits for the radix sort. In terms of queues, the preceding rough pseudocode statement of the algorithm can be refined to:

```
procedure RadixSort
  ( given  MasterList: Queue       (* A list of integers *);
    return MasterList: Queue       (* Arranged in ascending order *) );
  var
    SubList: array [10] of Queue;  (* A sublist for each possible digit *)
    K, Digit, Value, BinNumber: integer;
```

```
start RadixSort
  Digit := 1;                        (* Represents digit position within number, 1
                                        for one's digit, 10 for ten's digit, etc. *)

    while StillNonZero(Digit) do     (* Assume existence of a test to determine
                                        if there is still a non-zero digit in
                                        current position or any position to its
                                        left *)

      for K := 1 to 10 do
        Create(SubList[K])
      endfor;
      while not Empty(MasterList) do
        Dequeue(MasterList, Value);
        BinNumber := Isolate(Value, Digit) + 1;   (* Assume the existence of a
                                                      function that returns the
                                                      appropriate isolated Digit
                                                      from Value. That Digit,
                                                      plus one, yields correct
                                                      bin for Value. *)

        Enqueue(SubList[BinNumber], Value)
      endwhile;
```

```
    Destroy(MasterList);
    Create(MasterList);
    for K := 1 to 10 do
      while not Empty(SubList[K]) do
        Dequeue(SubList[K], Value);
        Enqueue(MasterList, Value)
      endwhile;
      Destroy(SubList[K])
    endfor;
    Digit := Digit * 10
  endwhile
end RadixSort;
```

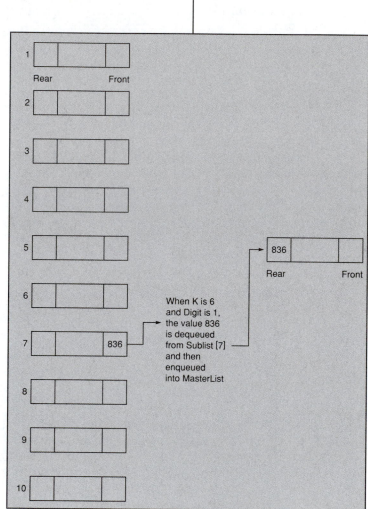

When K is 6 and Digit is 1, the value 836 is dequeued from Sublist [7] and then enqueued into MasterList

Efficiency of Radix Sort

An examination of the loop structure in the preceding PSEUDO code for radix sort indicates that, for each pass through the outer **while** loop, $O(n)$ operations must be performed. These $O(n)$ operations consist of the arithmetic necessary to isolate a particular digit within a number and the data swap necessary to attach it to the proper sublist and then collect it again into a new master list. The outer **while** loop will execute C times where C is the number of digits (or characters) in the integer (or string), making radix sort an $O(Cn)$ algorithm. If no duplicate values are permitted among those being sorted then we must have $\log_{10} n \leq C$ in the case of nonnegative integers, or $\log_s n \leq C$, in the case of strings, where s is the size of the set from which the characters used in the strings may be chosen. At the same time, practicality will dictate that there is an upper bound on the size of C (for example, rare is the application that requires one to sort 20-digit integers or 1,000-character strings); hence one can find a constant H so that $C \leq H \log_{10} n$ (or $C \leq H \log_s n$). Consequently, where unique values are being sorted, radix sort is $O(n \log n)$. If duplicate values are allowed, on the other hand, then the C times that the outer **while** loop executes is independent of n, so that in this case radix sort has an $O(n)$ run-time efficiency.

On the surface, our analysis of radix sort would so far seem to make it a significantly faster and better choice for sorting than the methods we studied in Chapter 1 and a choice comparable to, if not significantly better than, the more sophisticated methods we will study in Chapters 6 and 7. However, caution is urged. There is an old computer adage: you get nothing for nothing. We must examine the trade-offs before we jump too quickly on the radix-sort bandwagon. With radix sort, these trade-offs include the following:

1. Although radix sort may qualify as an $O(n)$ algorithm in some cases, remember that this merely means that the number of operations can be bounded by $k \times n$ for some constant k. With radix sort, this constant k can often be large enough that radix sort will be less efficient than $O[n(\log_2 n)^2]$ and $O(n \log_2 n)$ algorithms for reasonable values of n. How large k is depends to some degree on the efficiency of the methods you use to implement some of the operations within the outer **while** loop of the algorithm—operations such as the fundamental queue operations, checking if there are any numbers in the list that still have a nonzero digit in the current digit position (or any position to its left), and isolating the current digit within a given value. You will explore some of these ways to enhance the algorithm's efficiency in the exercises and problems.

2. Since you must keep track of the sublists as well as the master list, there is the potential that this algorithm will be much less space-efficient than sorting algorithms that directly manipulate a single array. How much less space-efficient is again dependent upon your implementation techniques and will be explored in the exercises.

3. To a degree, the algorithm is more dependent on the type of data being sorted than other sorting algorithms. Hence, it is more difficult to write a general-purpose version of radix sort—that is, a version that will work for integers, strings, reals, and even more complex objects that can be compared. The reason for this is simple—radix sort does not make any comparisons between values in the list being sorted. Hence, we cannot pass it a comparison parameter as we did to add generality to the sorting algorithms studied in Chapter 1. In a sense, this puts radix sort in a class by itself among sorting algorithms—a fact that is alluded to in our discussion on the inherent limits of sort efficiencies in Chapter 12.

Exercises 4.3

1. Consider again the data set given below. How many passes would be made through the outer **while** loop of the radix sort algorithm for these data? Trace the contents of the list after each of these passes.

Front ⟶
| 9438 |
| 3216 |
| 416 |
| 9021 |
| 1142 |
| 3316 |

Rear ⟶
| 94 |

2. Consider the following list of strings:

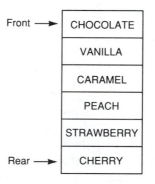

Front ⟶
| CHOCOLATE |
| VANILLA |
| CARAMEL |
| PEACH |
| STRAWBERRY |

Rear ⟶
| CHERRY |

How many passes would be made through the outer **while** loop of the radix sort algorithm for these data? Trace the contents of the list after each of these passes.

3. In the PSEUDO version of the RadixSort procedure presented in this section, we assume the existence of a test to check if any value in the list still has a nonzero digit in the current digit position (or any position to its left). Describe how you would implement this test, modifying the PSEUDO code for RadixSort or developing a subordinate function as appropriate. Then describe how the implementation you have chosen would affect the time efficiency of radix sort for integers. Be as explicit as possible in this description. That is, we know that radix sort should remain an $O(n)$ algorithm, but what effect will your implementation have on the constant k which bounds the number of radix sort operations by $k \times n$?

4. In the PSEUDO version of the RadixSort procedure presented in this section, we assume the existence of a function that will isolate a specific digit within

an integer. Describe how you would implement this function, modifying the PSEUDO code for RadixSort or developing a subordinate function as appropriate. Then describe how the implementation you have chosen would affect the time efficiency of radix sort for integers. Be as explicit as possible in this description. That is, we know that radix sort should remain an $O(n)$ algorithm, but what effect will your implementation have on the constant k, which bounds the number of radix sort operations by $k \times n$?

5. Radix sort as presented in this section uses a queue ADT. What implementation would you choose for the queue ADT in this algorithm? Explain why.

6. The version of radix sort presented in this section accesses queues only by the provided ADT operations. Given your answer to Exercise 5, could you make radix sort more time-efficient by accessing the queue implementation directly? If so, modify radix sort in this fashion and describe the degree to which this enhances the time efficiency of the algorithm.

7. Suppose you have 1,000 records to be sorted. Would the run-time efficiency of an $O(n^2)$ sort algorithm increase significantly if the 1,000 records were broken into four groups, each group sorted, and then appended together as one large sorted array instead of sorting the initial unsegmented array? Why or why not?

8. Write a PSEUDO procedure to sort a queue of strings using the radix sort algorithm.

9. Can you write a radix sort procedure to sort a queue of reals? If so, do it. If not, explain why.

10. A multiple key sort will sort a list of records giving highest priority to one field, secondary priority according to another field, and so on. For instance, to sort a list of dates in the form

```
record
   Month: integer;   (* Assume between 1 and 12 *)
   Day: integer;     (* Assume between 1 and 31 *)
   Year: integer
endrecord;
```

we would view Year as the primary field, Month as the secondary field, and Day as the tertiary field. Explain how you would adapt the radix sort algorithm to sort a list of records that include a date in the above form. Then implement your explanation in a complete PSEUDO procedure.

4.4 APPLICATION: SCHEDULING USERS OF A SHARED RESOURCE (OPTIONAL)

Queues find extensive application in operating system software for multiuser, timesharing environments. Consider the situation pictured in Figure 4.12—multiple point-of-sale terminals accessing a common inventory file. Suppose that point-of-sale terminal #1 records a sale of four items with ItemID 36481 at the same time that point-of-sale terminal #2 records a sale of six items with ItemID 36481. Suppose also that, prior to these two sales, the quantity in inventory of item 36481 is 640. Then, if we assume that the sale at point-of-

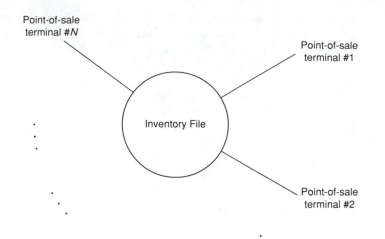

FIGURE 4.12

Point-of-sale terminals
sharing an inventory file.

sale terminal #1 occurs momentarily before that at terminal #2, the scenario pictured in Figure 4.13 could occur.

The flaw in this scenario is obvious. After all updates are completed, the inventory record for ItemID 36481 shows a quantity of 634 instead of the correct value of 630. What has caused this error? The two processes associated with terminal #1 and terminal #2, respectively, are allowed simultaneous access to the file record belonging to ItemID 36481. Consequently, the actions of process #2 inadvertently negate the work already done by process #1.

One solution to this problem often used by operating system designers is simply to block any other process from accessing the record associated with ItemID 36481 while that record is being worked with by process #1. In their accessing a particular record from the inventory file, any two processes associated with point-of-sale terminals are said to be *mutually exclusive*—one process cannot access this resource (for updating) while it is being used by another. The method for implementing this solution in a timesharing system is from Dijkstra (Dijkstra, E. W., "Cooperating Sequential Processes," Technological University, Eindhoven, Netherlands, 1965; reprinted in F. Genys (ed.), *Programming Languages,* New York: Academic Press, 1968). The method employs queues and a special flagging variable known as a *semaphore.*

To understand Dijkstra's solution, we must first define a *ready queue* of processes in a timesharing environment. In such an environment, the central processor dedicates a small *time slice* to each process before moving on to the next process. The ideal ADT to schedule processes in this fashion is a queue. The processor dequeues a process, dedicates a time slice to the dequeued process, and then enqueues that process before dequeuing another process. However, once mutually exclusive processes enter into this scenario, it becomes a bit more complicated. Now the processor cannot dedicate a time slice to a process unless that process has access to all the resources (such as file records) it needs for execution. So we shall restrict this notion of a queue of processes waiting to be serviced by the central processor to contain only

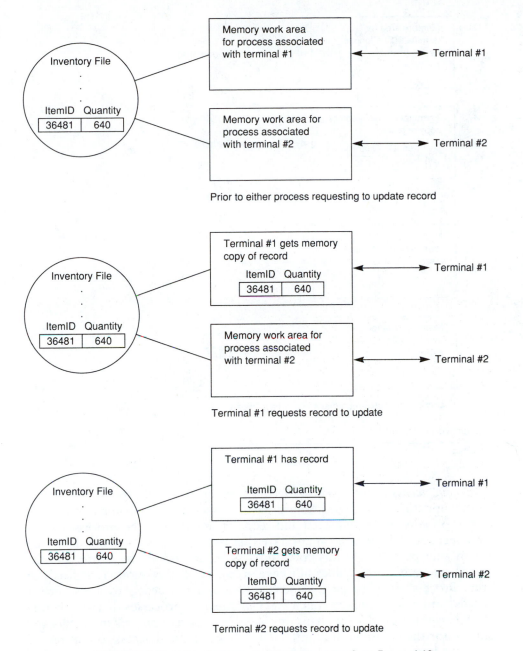

FIGURE 4.13   Possible scenario of events arising from Figure 4.12.

those processes that currently have access to all required resources. Because every process in this queue has access to every resource it needs, all of these processes are "ready" to execute. Consequently, this queue is known as the *ready queue* of processes.

Now, returning to the second snapshot in the scenario of Figure 4.13, suppose that the processor grants the process associated with terminal #1

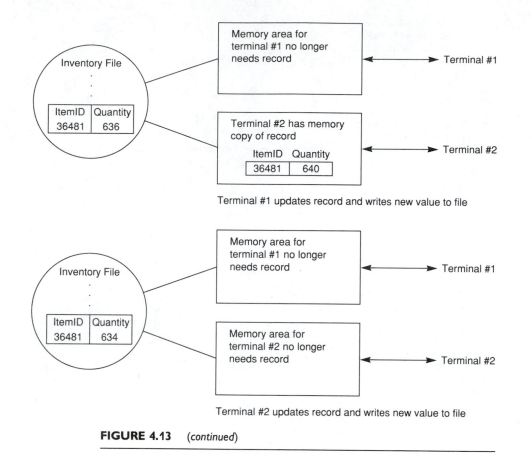

Terminal #1 updates record and writes new value to file

Terminal #2 updates record and writes new value to file

FIGURE 4.13   *(continued)*

exclusive access to the inventory record ItemID 36481. If process #1 doesn't finish updating this record before its time slice runs to completion, then, when process #2 is dequeued and requests this record, the processor must in effect say, "Sorry, you cannot have that resource, it is currently dedicated to another process." At this point, process #2 should not be returned to the ready queue because it does not have access to all the resources it needs to run. Process #2 is to be considered *blocked* (from access to a resource it needs) and will be enqueued in a *blocked queue* of processes that are waiting to access this record (or perhaps this file). Hence, every process in the blocked queue for the record with ItemID 36481 has requested access to that record and has been told by the processor that another process already owns it. The multiqueue picture is shown in Figure 4.14.

A semaphore is a special boolean variable used to control enqueuing/dequeuing for the queues in Figure 4.14. For each shared resource, we have a semaphore boolean variable associated with the blocked queue for that resource. The semaphore is **true** when its associated resource is available and **false** otherwise. Moreover, the semaphore variable is to be accessed only through two special operations—the Pause operation and the Signal operation (called the P and V operations by Dijkstra, from the first letters of the

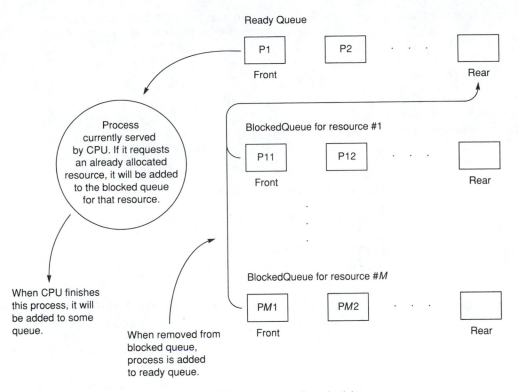

FIGURE 4.14   Ready and blocked queues for scheduling processes.

Dutch words *proberen,* "to test" and *verhogen,* "to increment," respectively). The definition of these operations is as follows:

```
type
   QueueData: record                  (* Record for process on a queue *)
              HasResources: boolean;  (* Set to true if process has access
                                         to all required resources *)

           (* Other fields as needed *)
          endrecord;

procedure Pause  (* Called when currently running process requests
                    resource R *)
  ( given R: boolean            (* Semaphore associated with resource R *);
         BlockedR: Queue        (* Blocked queue for resource R *);
         Process: QueueData     (* Data associated with currently running
                                   process *);

    return R: boolean           (* Semaphore for R must be set to false since
                                   R will certainly be allocated after call to
                                   Pause *);

         BlockedR: Queue        (* If resource R is not available when
                                   requested by currently running process,
                                   that process must be added to blocked
                                   queue for R *);
```

```
          Process: QueueData        (* Potentially the currently running process
                                        will no longer have resources it needs *) );

    start Pause
      if R then (* R is available *)
        R := false
      else        (* R is not available *)
        Process.HasResources := false;
        Enqueue(BlockedR, Process)
      endif
    end Pause;


  procedure Signal (* Called when currently running process is done with
                        resource R *)
    ( given R: boolean              (* Semaphore associated with resource R *);
           BlockedR: Queue          (* Blocked queue for resource R *);
           Ready:Queue              (* Ready queue of processes *);
      return R: boolean             (* Semaphore for R must be set according to
                                        whether or not another process is
                                        waiting for it *);

           BlockedR: Queue          (* If another process is waiting for R, the
                                        first such process must be removed from
                                        the blocked queue *);

           Ready: Queue             (* And that process can then be added to the
                                        ready queue *) );

    var
      Process: QueueData;

    start Signal
      if not Empty(BlockedR) then
        Dequeue(BlockedR, Process);
        Process.HasResources := true;
        Enqueue(Ready, Process)
      else
        R := true
      endif
    end Signal;
```

Relating these operations to Figure 4.14, the Pause operation will be invoked when the process currently served by the CPU requests resource R. At that point, one of two possibilities occurs. If resource R is available, the CPU allocates it to the currently running process. Otherwise, this process cannot continue since it cannot be granted access to a resource (namely R) that it needs. Consequently, the CPU will enqueue the process to the blocked queue of processes waiting for resource R.

The Signal operation will be invoked when the process currently serviced by the CPU finishes using a shared resource R. When this occurs, the CPU must check the blocked queue for resource R. If there is a process waiting in this queue, it can be dequeued, granted access to the resource R, and then enqueued to the ready queue. If the blocked queue for R is empty, the CPU need merely set the semaphore to true so that the resource will be viewed as available when it is next requested.

Simulation of Mutually Exclusive Processes Sharing a Resource

One of the ways in which queues find frequent application is in the simulation, or modeling, of activities. Such simulation allows us to "experiment in the abstract." That is, we can introduce situations that could be very costly (or dangerous) to create in real life and then use a computer model to predict how such situations affect the critical parameters by which we monitor the activity being observed. For instance, with respect to mutually exclusive processes sharing a resource, it would be useful to explore the relationship between given input conditions such as

- The likelihood that a new process will be enqueued to the ready queue in a given time slice.
- The average number of time slices required by a new process to complete its task(s) before logging off.
- The likelihood that the currently running process will request a shared resource.
- The average amount of time that the shared resource is tied up by the process to which it is allocated.

and the effect of these inputs upon monitoring parameters such as

- The average length of the blocked queue for that resource.
- The average amount of time a process must spend in the blocked queue waiting for the resource it requests.

The top-level logic for such a simulation is expressed in the following PSEUDO code. We assume that the data associated with a process is encapsulated in a QueueData record described by

```
type QueueData: record   (* Data associated with a process *)
             HasResources: boolean; (* For use by semaphore procedures *)
             SystemTime: integer;   (* Contains the number of time
                                       slices of processing time yet
                                       required by this process *)
             ResourceTime: integer  (* If owner of shared resource, the
                                       number of time slices that it will
                                       continue to use that resource *)

         endrecord;
         .
         .
         .

(* Top-level logic *)

Create(Ready);
Create(BlockedR);
SystemIsIdle := true;
ResourceSemaphore := true;
for TimeSlice := 1 to LengthOfSimulation do
   (* Does a new process log on during this time slice? *)
```

```
     if Logon(ProbabilityOfLogon) then           (* Call on function to determine
                                                     if a new process is logging on
                                                     during this time slice *)
       DetermineTime(AverageTime, NewProcess);   (* Call on procedure to determine
                                                     the amount of time the new
                                                     process will use the system,
                                                     based on the average amount of
                                                     time needed by a process *)
       Enqueue(Ready, NewProcess)                (* Enqueue the NewProcess to ready
                                                     queue *)
     endif;
     (* Prepare for another current process in the next time slice *)
     if not SystemIsIdle then                    (* Check if any process is
                                                     using the system *)

       if FinishedWithSystem(CurrentProcess) then (* Is current process about
                                                     to log off? CurrentProcess
                                                     will have its SystemTime
                                                     reduced by 1 *)

         if not Empty(Ready) then
           Dequeue(Ready, CurrentProcess)        (* Bring new current process
                                                     from Ready queue *)

         else
           SystemIsIdle := true
         endif
       else                                      (* Current process is not yet
                                                     done with system *)

         Enqueue(Ready, CurrentProcess);
         Dequeue(Ready, CurrentProcess)
       endif
     elsif not Empty(Ready) then                 (* System is currently idle *)
       Dequeue(Ready, CurrentProcess);
       SystemIsIdle := false
     endif;
     (* Will the currently running process relinquish or request the
        shared resource? *)
     if not SystemIsIdle then
       (* Call on function to determine if current process is done with shared
          resource. CurrentProcess will have its ResourceTime reduced by 1 if it
          owns the shared resource *)
       if FinishedWithResource(CurrentProcess) then
         Signal(ResourceSemaphore, BlockedR, Ready)
       (* Call on function to determine if current process will request shared
          resource during this time slice, based on probability of such a
          request *)
       elsif RequestSharedResource(ProbabilityOfRequest) then
         (* Call on procedure to determine the amount of time this process will
            require the shared resource, based on average time this resource is
            used by a process *)
         DetermineAvailableTime(AverageUseTime, CurrentProcess);
         Pause(ResourceSemaphore, BlockedR, CurrentProcess);
         SystemIsIdle := not CurrentProcess.HasResources
       endif
     endif
   endfor;
```

In the exercises and problems, you will explore the logic driving this simulation and complete a program to implement it. In particular, the procedure/functions Logon, DetermineTime, FinishedWithSystem, FinishedWithResource, RequestSharedResource, and DetermineAvailableTime must be developed to meet the following pre- and postconditions.

```
procedure Logon
  ( given ProbabilityOfLogin: real      (* The probability that a new process will
                                           log on to the system in a given time
                                           slice *);

    return: boolean                      (* true if a new process does log on,
                                           otherwise false *) );

procedure DetermineTime
  ( given AverageTime: real;            (* The average amount of CPU time
                                           slices required by a new process *);

    return NewProcess: QueueData        (* An initialized process record for
                                           a new process, with its SystemTime
                                           determined *) );

function FinishedWithSystem
  ( given Process: QueueData            (* The process record for the currently
                                           running process *);

    return Process: QueueData           (* The process record, with its
                                           SystemTime reduced by 1 *);

           : boolean                     (* true if Process is finished with
                                           the system; otherwise false *) );

function FinishedWithResource
  ( given Process: QueueData            (* The process record for the currently
                                           running process *);

    return Process: QueueData           (* The process record with its
                                           ResourceTime reduced by 1 if it
                                           owns the shared resource *);

           : boolean                     (* true if Process owns and is finished
                                           with the shared resource; otherwise
                                           false *) );

procedure DetermineAvailableTime
  ( given AverageTime: real             (* The average number of CPU time
                                           slices that a process will use the
                                           shared resource *);

         Process: QueueData            (* The record for the currently
                                           running process *);

    return Process: QueueData           (* The record for the currently
                                           running process, with its
                                           ResourceTime field determined.
                                           This value cannot be longer than
                                           the process will be on the
                                           system *) );

function RequestSharedResource
  ( given ProbabilityOfRequest: real   (* The probability that a process will
                                           request the shared resource in a
                                           given CPU time slice *);

    return: boolean                      (* true if the process requests the
                                           shared resource; false otherwise *) );
```

Several of these procedures will require using a random number generator and probability distributions. If you are not familiar with random number generation, this topic is discussed, along with its use in generating events according to specified probabilities, in Appendix A. Note also that in addition to returning a boolean value, the functions FinishedWithSystem and FinishedWithResource potentially alter the parameter Process. If your favorite language does not allow a function to do this, these functions can be recast as procedures.

Exercises 4.4

1. Suppose we have the following sequence of events in the first 10 time slices of the simulation discussed in this section:

   Time slice

   1: Process A logs on to system, with a job that will require six CPU time slices

   2: Process B logs on to system, with a job that will require four CPU time slices

   3: Current process requests shared resource for three CPU time slices

   4: Process C logs on to system, with job that will require six CPU time slices

   5–10: No new activity except each process that does not own the shared resource requests it for two time slices in its first time slice during this period

   Trace the status of the ready and blocked queues in each of the first 10 time slices. Also, indicate when the Pause and Signal semaphores would be executed during this period of the simulation.

2. Explain how the top-level logic for the simulation discussed in this section would change if the likelihood that a process would request a shared resource were process-dependent. That is, instead of this likelihood being a probability that applied to all processes, it would be a potentially different probability for each process. This is more characteristic of a true multiuser operating system environment, where many users would not use a particular shared resource at all, but others would have a very high probability of using the resource.

3. Suppose that we had more than one of a particular shared resource; that is, we have a pool of $n > 1$ identical resources. The situation would occur for such shared resources as line printers, tape drives, or memory buffers. Explain how you could extend the notion of a semaphore to apply to such a shared resource. Your explanation should include an appropriate rewrite of the Pause and Signal operations.

4. Define an appropriate QueueData node and design top-level logic for the simulation of

   a. Airplanes arriving at and departing from an airport with multiple runways.

   b. Customers waiting for service at an auto bank with multiple service windows.

   What are the similarities and differences between each of these simulations and the scheduling of computer users as discussed in this section?

A RELEVANT ISSUE

Mutually Exclusive Processes Sharing More Than One Resource

In this chapter we have seen how a semaphore and blocked queue can be used effectively to control mutually exclusive processes sharing a single resource. However, this solution is not without complications of its own, as the following example will show. Suppose that we have two separate shared resources—Resource A and Resource B. Note that A and B are not identical copies of the same resource in the sense of Exercise 3 in Section 4.4. Suppose also that both these resources are presently available and that we have two processes—Process 1 and Process 2—that might potentially request both of these resources. During its time slice, Process 1 requests Resource A. Since Resource A is available, Process 1 receives access to this resource and is placed on the ready queue when Process 2 begins it time slice. Process 2 requests Resource B and is similarly granted access to it. Now Process 1 starts its time slice again, and it requests Resource B in addition to Resource A, which it already owns. Since Process 2 owns Resource B, Process A must be put on the blocked queue for Resource B. Process 2 begins execution during its time slice and finds that it needs Resource A in addition to Resource B, which it already owns. Since Resource A is owned by Process 1, Process 2 must be put on the blocked queue for Resource A.

The dilemma in which we find ourselves is highlighted in Figure 4.15. Both Process 1 and Process 2 are stymied in blocked queues, waiting for a resource owned by the other process. Since neither process can run, neither can complete what it must do with the resource it already owns. The processes are hung in a situation known as deadlock, or fatal embrace.

Hence, solving one problem—mutually exclusive processes accessing a shared resource—has led to another. The deadlock problem is dreaded by all operating system designers. For a discussion of strategies for coping with it, see Harvey M. Deitel's *An Introduction to Operating Systems,* 2nd edition (Reading, Mass.: Addison-Wesley, 1990).

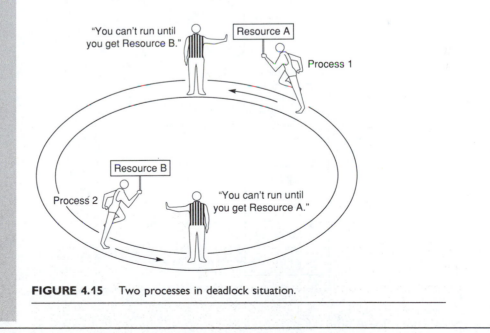

FIGURE 4.15   Two processes in deadlock situation.

4.5 PRIORITY QUEUES

Many multiuser operating systems attach priorities to processes that run on the system. Assume that processes with a higher priority will always be serviced before those with a lower priority. Then an appropriate structure for scheduling processes in such an environment is the priority queue abstract data type. We may think of a priority queue as a collection of mini-queues—one such mini-queue for each priority value of an item in the queue. When an item is added to a priority queue, it is added at the end of the mini-queue associated with that item's priority value. When an item is removed from a priority queue, it is removed from the mini-queue belonging to those items that have the highest priority among all items in the priority queue. This concept is illustrated in Figure 4.16. In this figure, we have a priority queue containing eight processes waiting to be serviced by the CPU of a computer system. STATS, PRINT, and BANK are the priority-3 (highest) jobs awaiting service; COPY and CHECK the priority-2 jobs; and UPDATE, AVERAGE, and TEST the priority-1 (lowest) jobs. If a new priority-3 job PROB1 arrived for service, it would be inserted at the end of the priority-3 queue, between BANK and COPY. Because jobs can be serviced only by leaving the front of the queue, PROB1 would be processed before any of the priority-2 or priority-1 jobs.

A formal definition of the priority queue ADT is given below, along with pre- and postconditions for priority queue operations.

• **Definition of Priority Queue:** A priority queue is a restricted list of items arranged by their priority values. When an item is removed from a priority

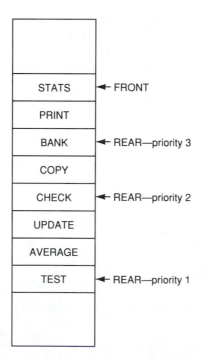

FIGURE 4.16

A priority queue with eight jobs at three priority levels.

queue, it must be an item of the highest priority value of all items in the priority queue. If there is more than one such item, then the item of highest priority value that has been in the priority queue for the longest time is the item removed.

```
type
    PriorityQueueData: (* The type of each data item in the priority queue *);
    PriorityQueueNode: (* Structure of each node in the priority queue *);
    PriorityType: (* A numeric type that defines the priority on which the
                    queue is based *);
    PriorityFunc: (* The signature of a function which determines the
                    priority level of a queue item *)
                function
                  ( given Item: PriorityQueueData  (* An item whose priority
                                                    is needed *);
                    return: PriorityType          (* The priority value of
                                                    Item *) );

procedure Create
    ( given Q: PriorityQueue              (* An arbitrary priority queue in an
                                          unknown state *);
      return Q: PriorityQueue            (* Q initialized to an empty priority
                                          queue *) );

procedure Destroy
    ( given Q: PriorityQueue              (* An arbitrary priority queue *);
      return Q: PriorityQueue            (* All dynamically allocated storage
                                          associated with Q returned to
                                          available space; Q itself is in
                                          unreliable state *) );

function Empty
    ( given Q: PriorityQueue              (* A previously created priority queue *);
      return: boolean                    (* true if Q is empty; false
                                          otherwise *) );

function Full
    ( given Q: PriorityQueue              (* A previously created priority queue *);
      return: boolean                    (* true if Q is full; false otherwise *) );

procedure PriorityEnqueue
    ( given Q: PriorityQueue              (* A previously created priority queue *);
            Item: PriorityQueueData      (* An item to be added to Q *);
            Priority: PriorityFunc       (* A function that determines the priority
                                          level of the item to be enqueued *);
      return Q: PriorityQueue            (* Q with Item added, according to its
                                          priority value *) );

procedure PriorityDequeue
    ( given  Q: PriorityQueue            (* A previously created priority queue *);
             Priority: PriorityFunc      (* A function that determines the priority
                                          level of the item to be dequeued *);
      return Q: PriorityQueue            (* Q with an item removed, according to
                                          its priority value *);
             Item: PriorityQueueData     (* The item removed from Q *) );
```

Implementation Strategies for Priority Queues

The priority queue presents some interesting implementation options. We will discuss these options conceptually and leave the details of each suggested implementation, along with its efficiency analysis, to the exercises.

Option 1: store the priority queue as a circular array, ordered by priority of items. Removal of an item is now easy and quick, but insertion could be costly.

Option 2: store the priority queue as an unordered circular array. This implementation reverses the pluses and minuses of Option 1. Removing an item now becomes quite costly.

Option 3: store the priority queue as an ordered linked list, or variation thereof. Think about whether double linking or maintaining special pointers to nodes within the list could be used to enhance the efficiency of the priority queue operations for this implementation.

Option 4: store the priority queue as an unordered linked list, or variation thereof. Again consider how double linking or maintaining auxiliary pointers could enhance efficiencies.

Option 5: if the priority function associated with the priority queue can only take on a finite number of values, the priority queue may be stored as a list of subordinate queues—one for each value assumed by the priority function. This would allow one to "inherit" an implementation of the ADT queue and then incorporate this queue implementation into an implementation of the priority queue. This inheritance concept is illustrated in Figure 4.17. It provides a nice example of the power of abstraction—the ability to create an implementation of a new ADT from the implementation of a previously existing ADT. Of course, in this situation, you must be careful to make a judicious choice of an implementation for the underlying ADT. Making an unwise choice could result in an implementation of the new ADT that is grossly time- or space-inefficient.

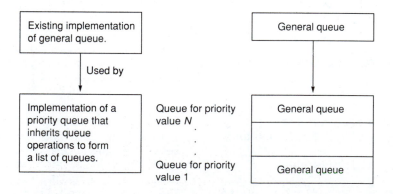

FIGURE 4.17

Inheriting an implementation of queues to build an implementation of priority queues.

The priority queue is a tremendously versatile ADT—one which we have just begun to explore. We shall return to this ADT in Chapter 7, where will discuss a more efficient implementation of it, and in Chapter 10, where we use it to guide some sophisticated search techniques.

Exercises 4.5

1. Using the suggestion in Option 1 of this section, develop a complete implementation for the priority queue ADT. Then analyze the efficiency of the operations for your implementation.

2. Repeat Exercise 1 for the suggestion offered in Option 2 of this section.

3. Repeat Exercise 1 for the suggestion offered in Option 3 of this section.

4. Repeat Exercise 1 for the suggestion offered in Option 4 of this section.

5. Repeat Exercise 1 for the suggestion offered in Option 5 of this section.

6. For each of the implementations in Exercises 1 through 5, discuss how the number of possible values taken on by the priority function affects the time and space efficiency of the implementation.

7. The operations PriorityEnqueue and PriorityDequeue each have a Priority function for one of their parameters. Is this parameter needed for each of these two operations in each of the five implementations in Exercises 1–5? If not, identify the particular operation and implementation(s) for which it is not necessary and explain why it is not necessary. Is there an argument for retaining the Priority function as a parameter even though it is not required for a particular implementation of an operation? If so, what is it?

8. Suppose that the priority function associated with a priority queue were real-valued instead of integer-valued. How does this complicate the implementation of a priority queue? Does it render impossible any of the implementations you developed in Exercises 1 through 5? If so, explain why. If not, convert that implementation so that it appropriately handles a real-valued priority function.

9. In scheduling prioritized processes that share time on a multiuser operating system, it may not be desirable to always let a higher-priority process have the CPU before a lower-priority process. We may wish simply to give higher-priority processes proportionally more time slices than lower-priority process. For instance, we may wish to give a priority-4 process four time slices of CPU time for each time slice dedicated to a priority-1 process and, in general, a priority-N process N time slices for each time slice dedicated to a priority-1 process. Can a priority queue still be used to schedule processes in such an arrangement? If so, provide a detailed explanation of how it would be done.

Chapter Summary

Chapter 4 introduces the first of two special types of general lists—the *queue* and the stack, which we discuss in Chapter 5. A queue is a list with restrictions imposed on the way in which entries may be inserted and removed. In particular, insertions may be made only from one end of the queue, known as the *rear*, while deletions are limited to the other end of the queue, called the *front*. The resulting behavior these restrictions impose on a queue with respect to the insertions and deletions of values give rise to another name for queues, *first-in, first-out* (FIFO) lists.

Three methods for implementing a queue are discussed, those based on arrays, circular lists, and linked lists. The circular implementation is a variation on the array-based implementation and avoids a situation where insertions and deletions cause the pointers to the rear and front of the queue to move strictly toward the upper-index end of the array. This prevents an array location from being used for more than one insertion. By going to a circular implementation, the front and rear pointers can wrap around the array, allowing a reuse of locations.

Two applications for queues are given—in the *radix sort*, and in the scheduling of users of a shared resource. In certain circumstances, radix sort qualifies as a $O(n)$ algorithm, though implementations of some of the operations its uses may degrade this efficiency significantly. Queues find extensive application in multiuser, time-sharing operating systems, especially through their association with semaphores, which are special boolean variables that control enqueuing and dequeuing for a corresponding queue. They are used to *block* or grant access to a resource being shared among several processes. This is examined via a simulation of several simultaneously executing processes which must be given mutually exclusive access to a shared resource.

The chapter concludes with an introduction of a *priority queue*, which is a restricted list of items arranged by priority values. Several options for implementing priority queues are described, with analyses left for exercises.

Key Words

blocked queue	priority queue	rear
circular queue	queue	semaphore
first-in, first-out list	radix sort	simulation
front	ready queue	

Programming Problems/Projects

1. Implement fully the simulation of mutually exclusive processes sharing a resource, as described in Section 4.4.

2. In Exercise 3 of Section 4.4 you discussed a strategy for extending semaphores to control shared resources of which there is a pool of $n > 1$ identical resources. Add this feature to the simulation you developed for Programming Problem 1.

3. In Exercise 9 of Section 4.5 you discussed a strategy that would allow users in a time-sharing environment to have their processes scheduled according to a priority system. Add this feature to the simulation you developed for Programming Problem 1.

4. A deque (double-ended queue) is a queue in which insertions and deletions can occur at either end. Write an implementation of the deque ADT that uses a circular array. Analyze the efficiency of each operation in this implementation.

5. Write an implementation of the deque ADT (see Programming Problem 4) that uses a linked list. Analyze the efficiency of each operation in this implementation.

6. Develop a program that sorts an array of records on multiple keys using the method you described in your answer to Exercise 10 of Section 4.3

7. In your answer to Exercise 6 of Section 4.3 you described how radix sort could be made more efficient if it were to access the implementation of a queue directly, instead of accessing the queue only via the provided ADT operations. Now develop a program that empirically tests how much more efficient this technique would be. Implement radix sort by both methods and time the two implementations under comparable conditions with identical data sets. In a written report, summarize the results of your experimentation.

8. Develop a program that empirically races radix sort against the shell sort algorithm, discussed in Chapter 1. Have your program sort data by both methods, keeping track of the number of data interchanges, comparisons (for shell sort), and determinations of appropriate bin (for radix sort). Use your program for experimentation. Race the two sorting methods on a variety of data. Recall that, although radix sort is $O(n)$, the constant of proportionality in determining its $O(n)$ efficiency can be quite large. How large does n have to be for various kinds of data (for example, integers and strings) before radix sort actually becomes faster than the $O[n(\log_2 n)^2]$ efficiency of shell sort? Summarize the results of your experimentation in a written report.

9. A bank has asked you to develop a program to simulate the arrival of customers in a waiting line at the bank. Factors to consider are the average time it takes to service one customer, the average number of customers that arrive in a given time period, and the number of service windows maintained by the bank. Statistics such as the length of time the average customer has to spend in the waiting line could be very helpful in the bank's future planning.

10. Here is a problem typically encountered in text formatting applications. Given a file of text, any text enclosed in brackets is to be considered a footnote. Footnotes, when encountered, are not to be printed as normal text but are instead stored in a footnote queue. Then, when the special symbol # is encountered, all footnotes currently in the queue are printed and the queue should be returned to an empty state. What you learn in solving this problem will allow you to make good use of string storage techniques discussed in earlier chapters.

11. In order to improve their services, the Fly-by-Night credit card company has decided to give incentives to their customers for prompt payment. Customers who pay their bill two weeks before the due date receive top priority and a 5 percent discount. Customers who pay their bills within one week of the due date receive next priority and a 1 percent discount. Third priority is given to customers who pay their bills on or within two days after the due date. The customers who pay their bills thereafter are assigned the lowest priority. Write a program to set up a priority queue to access customer records accordingly.

12. The Bay Area Brawlers professional football team has been so successful in recent weeks that the team management is considering the addition of several ticket windows at the team's stadium. However, before investing a sizable amount of money in such an improvement, they would like to simulate the operation of ticket sales with a variety of ticket window configurations. Develop a computer program that allows input of such data as number of ticket windows, average number of fans arriving each hour as game time approaches, and average length of time to process a ticket sale. Output

from your program should include statistics such as the average waiting-line length each hour as game time approaches and the amount of time the average fan has to wait in line. Use queues to represent each of the waiting lines.

13. The management of a grocery store is thinking about expanding the number of check-out lanes in their store (currently there are three). To help them decide what to do, they hire you to write a program to simulate the current activity of their check-out lanes as well as the activity that would ensue if they added a fourth lane. Currently, none of their check-out lanes are "express" lanes, so they would like for your simulation to account for two possible setups for the additional lane—either exclusively as an express lane or general patronage.

    For this project you are to write a program that produces at least the following statistics for the store's current and potential check-out arrangements (i.e., three-lane, four-lane, and three-lane plus express):

    • The mean number of people served per hour for each lane
    • The mean number of items processed per hour by each lane
    • The mean number of customers at a lane each time a new customer comes to that lane
    • The maximum number of customers who were at a given lane when a customer came to that lane

    You may add any additional statistics that you feel may be useful to the store managers. Your program should take into account the following patterns:

    • The intervals between the arrivals of customers at the check-out area
    • The service times required for each customer at a register
    • The number of items each customer brings to the check-out area
    • The choice of check-out lanes for a customer (assume the express lane limit will be strictly enforced)

    A suggestion for implementing the check-out behavior would be to use a uniform random number generator to generate the next arrival time and number of items for a customer and to determine the service time as a function of the number of items. Limits for the ranges of random numbers to be generated for arrival times and number of items can be entered as input, as can express lane limits and coefficients needed to calculate service times. For choosing a check-out lane, assume a customer will go to the lane that offers the shortest overall waiting time, in case of a tie, choose the lowest numbered lane (assuming the lanes are numbered 1, 2, 3, 4).

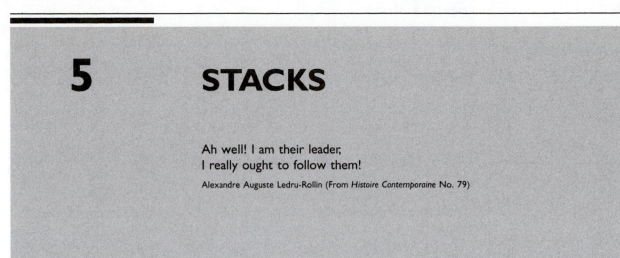

5 STACKS

Ah well! I am their leader,
I really ought to follow them!

Alexandre Auguste Ledru-Rollin (From *Histoire Contemporaine* No. 79)

CHAPTER OUTLINE

Although a first-in, first-out structure such as a queue seems to be the obvious way of storing items that must wait to be processed, there are many natural instances in which a last-in, first-out (LIFO) strategy is more appropriate. Consider, for example, the order in which a smart traveler will pack a suitcase. To minimize shuffling, the last item packed should be the first worn. Another familiar example of such a storage strategy is that of the pop-up mechanism used to store trays for a cafeteria line. Those trays that are the first ones loaded into the mechanism may be stored a long time before they are picked up by a passing diner.

A list of data items processed via a last-in, first-out scheduling strategy is called a *stack*. As we shall see in this chapter, stacks are an extremely useful data structure. They find extensive application in the processing of subroutine calls and in the syntactical checking and translation of programming languages by compilers. In Chapter 6, we will see that the stack ADT supports the powerful programming technique called recursion.

5.1 THE STACK ADT

The queue data structure presented in the previous chapter is a special type of list in which all data processing activity occurs at the two ends: the front and the rear. A stack may also be viewed as such a specialized list. However, a stack is even more restricted in that all activity occurs at one designated end called the *top*.

• **Definition of Stack:** A stack is a restricted list in which entries are added to and removed from one designated end called the top. The operations to be performed on a stack are shown in the following PSEUDO pre- and postconditions.

```
type
   StackData: (* The type of each data item in the stack *);
   StackNode: (* The structure of each node in the stack; in the simplest
              case is equivalent to StackData *);

procedure Create
   ( given S: Stack          (* An arbitrary stack variable in unknown
                                 state *);
     return S: Stack         (* S initialized to the empty stack *) );

procedure Destroy
   ( given S: Stack          (* An arbitrary stack *);
     return: Stack           (* All dynamically allocated storage associated
                                with S is returned to available space, S itself
                                is in unreliable state *) );

function Empty
   ( given S: Stack          (* A previously created stack *);
     return: boolean         (* true if S is empty; false otherwise *) );

function Full
   ( given S: Stack          (* A previously created stack *);
     return: boolean         (* true if S is full; false otherwise *) );

procedure Push
   ( given S: Stack          (* A previously created stack *);
         Item: StackData     (* An item to be added to the top of the stack *);
     return S: Stack         (* S with Item added to the top of the stack. If
                                S is full, it is left unchanged *) );

procedure Pop
   ( given S: Stack          (* A previously created stack *);
     return S: Stack         (* S with its top value removed *);
         Item: StackData     (* Contains the value that was on the top of the
                                stack S. If S is empty, contents of Item are
                                unreliable and S is unchanged. *) );
```

```
function OnTop
   ( given S: Stack          (* A previously created stack *);
     return: StackData        (* The value on the top of the stack. Unlike Pop,
                                 OnTop leaves the stack unchanged. If the stack S
                                 is empty, the value returned by OnTop is
                                 unreliable *) );
```

Conceptually, it is easiest to develop a mental image of the push and pop operations if you picture a stack as a vertical list with the first entry at the bottom and the last at the top. Then, as indicated in Figure 5.1, adding to the stack—that is, pushing—essentially makes this stack become taller and removing from the stack—that is, popping—results in a shorter stack.

Stacks and Subroutine Calls

Before we discuss methods of implementing a stack, we shall give some hint of their importance in the processing of subroutine calls. Of key importance to the processing of subroutines in any language is that the return from a

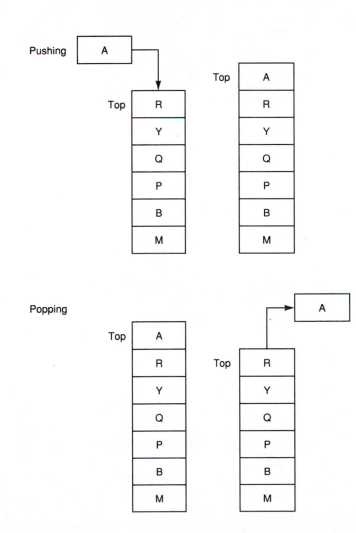

FIGURE 5.1

Pushing onto and popping from the stack.

subroutine must be to the instruction immediately following the call that originally transferred control to the subroutine. For example, in the partial coding that follows:

```
program Main;
   .
   .
   .
   procedure Sub3;
      .
      .
      .
      start Sub3
         .
         .
      end Sub3;

   procedure Sub2;
      .
      .
      .
      start Sub2
         .
         .
         .
         Sub3;         (* Call Sub3 *)
         P := P - Q;
         .
         .
      end Sub2;

   procedure Sub1;
      .
      .
      .
      start Sub1
         .
         .
         .
         Sub2;         (* Call Sub2 *)
         A := A + B;
         .
         .
         .
      end Sub1;

   start Main
      .
      .
      .
      Sub1;            (* Call Sub1 *)
      write(Q);
      .
      .
      .
   end Main;
```

the order of operations would be

1. Leave Main and transfer to Sub1.
2. Leave Sub1 and transfer to Sub2.
3. Leave Sub2 and transfer to Sub3.
4. Return from Sub3 to the instruction P := P − Q in Sub2.
5. Return from Sub2 to the instruction A := A + B in Sub1.
6. Return from Sub1 to the instruction write(Q) in Main.
7. End of Main.

Each time a call is made, the machine must remember where to return upon completion of that procedure.

A stack is precisely the structure capable of storing the data necessary to handle calls and returns in this sequence. Hence, the preceding partial coding would generate a stack that develops as illustrated in Figure 5.2. (The numbers in the figure correspond to the order of operations just shown.) Each time a call to a procedure is made, a return address is pushed on top of the stack. Each time a procedure is completed, the top item on the stack is popped

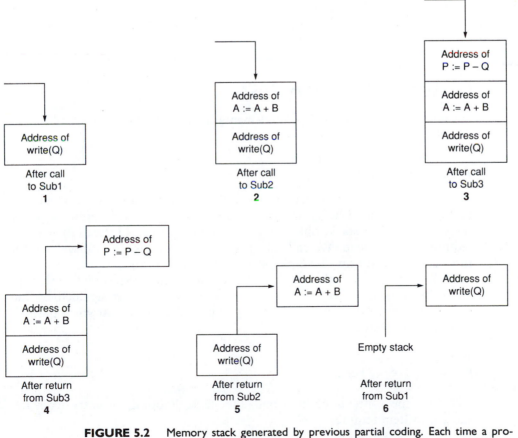

FIGURE 5.2   Memory stack generated by previous partial coding. Each time a procedure is called, a return address is pushed onto the stack. When the procedure completes, the stack is popped to obtain a return address.

to determine the memory address to which the return operation should be made. The nature of the leave-return sequence for procedures makes it crucial that the first return address accessed be the last one that was remembered by the computer. Because there is only one point, the top, at which data may enter or exit a stack, it is the ideal data structure to be used for this "last-stored, first-recalled" type of operation.

This description of the method by which a compiler actually implements procedure calls is just one illustration of the utility of stacks. In the next chapter we'll discuss a different type of procedure usage called recursion and examine in detail the role of the stack in handling such a recursive call. In the next section, however, we will consider two ways of implementing a stack.

Exercises 5.1

1. What is a stack structure?
2. The OnTop operation described in the definition of the stack as an abstract data type is actually unnecessary since it can be defined in terms of other stack operations. Provide such a definition of the OnTop operation.
3. Explain the role of a stack in processing procedure and function calls.
4. Explain how the stack used in processing subroutine calls could also be used as memory space for the parameters and local variables of a procedure or function.

5.2 IMPLEMENTATIONS OF A STACK

We now discuss two possible implementations of stacks: arrays and linked lists.

Array Implementation

A strategy similar to that used for an array implementation of a queue can be followed for a stack. However, because insertions and deletions occur at the same end of a stack, only one pointer will be needed instead of the two required for a queue. We call that pointer *Top*. In Figure 5.3, we trace it through the subroutine example of the previous section.

As in Figure 5.2, the numbers below each array correspond to the operations performed (see Section 5.1). The empty stack is signaled by the condition Top = 0. If we think of Top as pointing to the last entry pushed, then the two instructions

```
Top := Top + 1;
Node[Top] := Item;
```

will push the contents of Item onto the stack. Popping an entry from the stack into Item requires

```
Item := Node[Top];
Top := Top - 1;
```

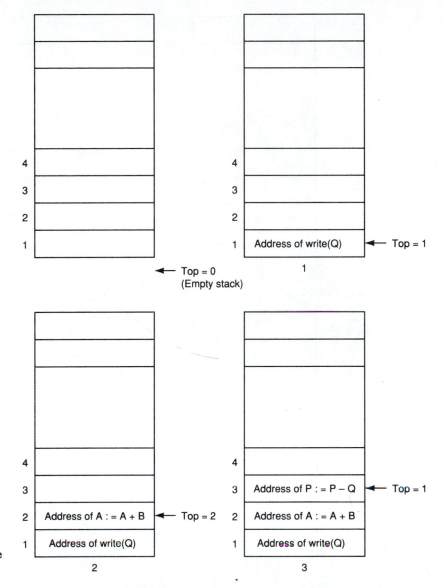

FIGURE 5.3
Array implementation of the
stack from Figure 5.2.

Complete procedures for the Push and Pop operations follow. These procedures use a record to bundle the top pointer and data array into one unified Stack type. These procedures also assume the existence of Empty and Full functions to test for these special boundary conditions. You will be asked to write these functions in the exercises at the end of this section.

```
type (* Assume MaxStackSize is constant limiting the number of elements
        that the stack may contain *);
   StackData: (* The type of each data item in the stack *);
   StackNode: StackData;
   Stack: record
           Node: array [MaxStackSize] of StackNode;
           Top: integer
        endrecord;
```

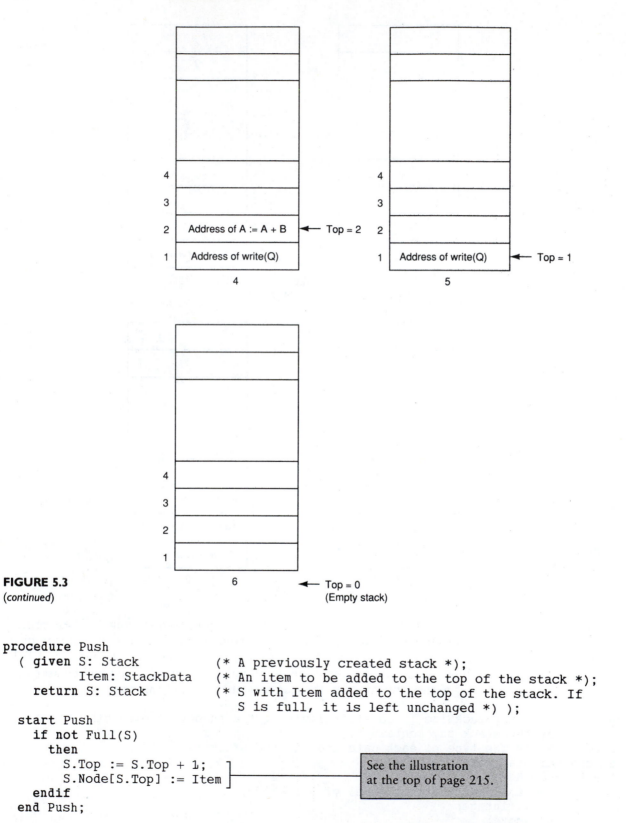

FIGURE 5.3
(*continued*)

```
procedure Push
   ( given S: Stack           (* A previously created stack *);
         Item: StackData      (* An item to be added to the top of the stack *);
     return S: Stack          (* S with Item added to the top of the stack. If
                                 S is full, it is left unchanged *) );

   start Push
     if not Full(S)
       then
         S.Top := S.Top + 1;
         S.Node[S.Top] := Item
     endif
   end Push;
```

See the illustration
at the top of page 215.

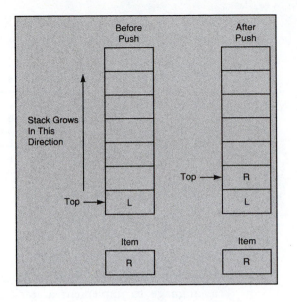

```
procedure Pop
  ( given S: Stack          (* A previously created stack *);
    return S: Stack          (* S with its top value removed *);
           Item: StackData   (* Contains the value that was on the top of the
                                stack S. If S is empty, contents of Item are
                                unreliable and S is unchanged *) );

  start Pop
    if not Empty(S)
      then
        Item := S.Node[S.Top];
        S.Top := S.Top - 1
    endif
  end Pop;
```

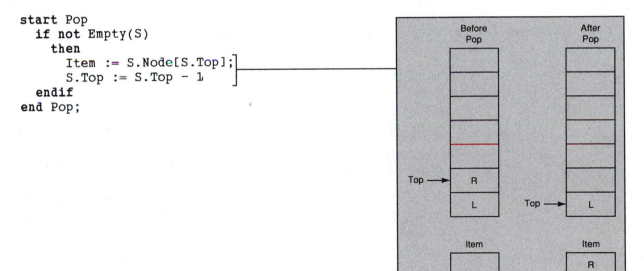

Linked-List Implementation

When we choose a linked-list implementation of a stack, we are paying the price of a relatively small amount of memory space needed to maintain linking pointers for the dynamic allocation of stack space. Assuming that we do not use a dummy header for the linked list, a stack with the three integer entries 18, 40, and 31 would appear as follows:

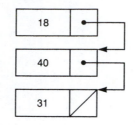

The Top pointer must be initialized to NULL, and, thereafter, the condition

Top = NULL

could be used to test for an empty stack. A full stack occurs only when there is no available space. Consequently, in using the pointers provided by a language to implement a stack as a linked list, one may encounter the same problems implementing the Full operation for a stack that arose in implementing the Full operation for a linked-list implementation of a queue.

Stack procedures to push and pop the stack now become nothing more than insertions at and deletions from the beginning of a linked list. As such, they are special cases of the procedures already developed in Chapter 3. You will write them in the following exercises.

Exercises 7.2

1. Write procedures or functions to implement each of the following operations for an array implementation of a stack.

   a. Create
   b. Full
   c. Empty
   d. OnTop

2. Write procedures or functions to implement each of the following stack operations for a linked-list implementation of a stack.

   a. Create
   b. Empty
   c. Push
   d. Pop
   e. OnTop

3. Design and implement an algorithm that utilizes a stack to print a line of text in reverse order.

4. Design and implement an algorithm that utilizes a stack to check whether an arithmetic expression such as

$$(5 \ / \ (3 - 2 * (4 + 3) - (8 \ / \ 2)))$$

has appropriately balanced left and right parentheses.

5.3 AN APPLICATION OF STACKS: PARSING AND EVALUATING ARITHMETIC EXPRESSIONS

Often the logic of problems for which stacks are a suitable data structure involves the necessity to backtrack, to return to a previous state. For instance, consider the problem of finding your way out of a maze. One approach to take would be to probe a given path in the maze as deeply as possible. Upon finding a dead end, you would need to backtrack to previously visited maze locations in order to try other paths. Such backtracking would require recalling these previous locations in the reverse order from which you visited them.

Not many of us need to find our way out of a maze. However, the designers of compilers are faced with an analogous backtracking situation in the evaluation of arithmetic expressions. As you scan the expression

$$A + B / C + D$$

from left to right, it is impossible to tell upon initially encountering the plus sign whether or not you should apply the indicated addition operation to A and the immediately following operand. Instead, you must probe further into the expression to determine whether an operation with a higher priority occurs. While you undertake this probing of the expression, you must stack previously encountered operation symbols until you are certain of the operands to which they can be applied.

Compounding the backtracking problem just described, there are often many different ways of representing the same algebraic expression. For example, the assignment statements

```
Z := A * B / C + D;
Z := (A * B) / C + D;
Z := ((A * B) / C) + D;
```

should all result in the same order of arithmetic operations even though the expressions involved are written in distinctly different form. The process of checking the syntax of such an expression and representing it uniquely is called *parsing* the expression. One frequently used method of parsing relies heavily upon stacks.

Infix, Postfix, and Prefix Notation

Usual algebraic notation is often termed *infix* notation; the arithmetic operator appears between the two operands to which it is being applied. Infix notation may require parentheses to specify a desired order of operations. For example, in the expression A/B + C, the division will occur first. If we want the addition to occur first, the expression must be parenthesized as A/(B + C).

Using *postfix* notation (also called *reverse Polish* notation after the nationality of its originator, the Polish logician Jan Lukasiewicz), the need for parentheses is eliminated because the operator is placed directly after the two operands to which it applies. Hence, A/B + C would be written as AB/C+ in postfix form, which says

1. Apply the division operator to A and B.
2. To that result, add C.

The infix expression A/(B + C) would be written as ABC+/ in postfix notation. Reading this postfix expression from left to right, we are told to

1. Apply the addition operator to B and C.
2. Then divide that result into A.

Although relatively short expressions such as the preceding ones can be converted from infix to postfix via an intuitive process, a more systematic method is required for complicated expressions. We propose the following algorithm for humans (and will soon consider a different one for computers):

1. Completely parenthesize the infix expression to specify the order of all operations.
2. Move each operator to the space held by its corresponding right (i.e., closing) parenthesis.
3. Remove all parentheses.

Consider this three-step method as it applies to the following expression in which ↑ is used to indicate exponentiation:

$$A/B \uparrow C + D * E - A * C$$

Completely parenthesizing this expression yields

$$(((A/(B \uparrow C)) + (D * E)) - (A * C))$$

Moving each operator to its corresponding right parenthesis,

and removing all parentheses, we are left with

$$ABC \uparrow /DE * + AC * -$$

Had we started out with

$$A/B \uparrow C - (D * E - A * C)$$

our three-step procedure would have resulted in

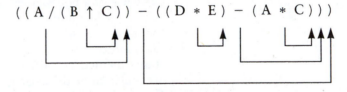

$$((A / (B \uparrow C)) - ((D * E) - (A * C)))$$

Removing the parentheses would then yield

$$ABC \uparrow /DE * AC * - -$$

In a similar way, an expression can be converted into *prefix* form, in which an operator immediately precedes its two operands. The conversion algorithm for infix to prefix specifies that, after completely parenthesizing the infix expression according to order of priority, we move each operator to its corresponding left (i.e., opening) parenthesis. Applying the method to

$$A/B \uparrow C + D * E - A * C$$

gives us

$$((A / (B \uparrow C)) + ((D * E)) - (A * C))$$

and finally the prefix form

$$+/A \uparrow BC - *DE * AC$$

The importance of postfix and prefix notation in parsing arithmetic expressions is that these notations are completely free of parentheses. Consequently, an expression in postfix (or prefix) form is in unique form. In the design of compilers, this parsing into postfix form is crucial because having a unique form for an expression greatly simplifies its eventual evaluation. Thus, in handling an assignment statement, a compiler must

1. Parse into postfix form
2. Apply an evaluation algorithm to the postfix form

We limit our discussion here to postfix notation. The techniques we cover are easily adaptable to the functionally equivalent prefix form.

Converting Infix Expressions to Postfix

First consider the problem of parsing an expression from infix to postfix form. Our three-step procedure is not easily adaptable to machine code. Instead, we will use an algorithm that has as its essential data structures the following:

1. A queue, Infix, containing the infix expression. This expression consists of individual *tokens,* which may be subdivided into the following categories:

a. Operator tokens, such as +, −, *, and /. We will assume the existence of a boolean-valued ValidOperator function, which receives a token and returns **true** if that token is a valid operator for the expressions we are considering.

b. Operand tokens. These may be thought of as variables and constants defined according to the rules of a particular language. We will assume the existence of a boolean-valued function Valid-Operand, which receives a token and returns **true** if that token is a valid operand.

c. Left and right parentheses tokens, denoted by LeftParen and RightParen, respectively.

d. A special EndToken, which delimits the end of the infix expression.

2. A stack, OperatorStack, which may contain operator tokens, LeftParen, RightParen, and EndToken.

3. A queue, Postfix, which contains the final postfix expression.

For the moment, we will consider only expressions that involve the operands +, −, /, and *. In the exercises and programming problems, you will consider some variations introduced by allowing additional operators. The description of the algorithm is as follows:

1. Define a function InfixPriority, which takes an operator, parenthesis, or EndToken as its argument and returns an integer as specified below:

Token	*	/	+	−	LeftParen	RightParen	EndToken
Returned value	2	2	1	1	3	0	0

This function reflects the relative position of an operator in the arithmetic hierarchy and is used with the function StackPriority (defined in step 2) to determine how long an operator waits in the stack before being enqueued on the postfix expression.

2. Define another function StackPriority, which takes the same possibilities for an argument and returns an integer as specified below:

Token	*	/	+	−	LeftParen	RightParen	EndToken
Returned value	2	2	1	1	3	undefined	0

This function is applied to operators in the operator stack and returns their priority in the arithmetic hierarchy—a value that is to be compared to the infix priorities of incoming operators from the infix queue. The result of this comparison determines whether or not an operator waits in the stack or is enqueued on the postfix expression.

3. Initialize OperatorStack by pushing EndToken.

4. Dequeue the next Token from the infix expression.

5. Test Token and

   5.1 If Token is an operand, enqueue it on the Postfix expression.

   5.2 If Token is a RightParen, then pop entries from OperatorStack and enqueue them on Postfix until a matching LeftParen is popped. Doing this ensures that operators within a parenthesized portion of an infix expression will be applied first, regardless of their priority in the usual arithmetic hierarchy. Discard both left and right parentheses.

   5.3 If Token is EndToken, pop all entries that remain on the stack and enqueue them on the Postfix queue.

   5.4 Otherwise, pop from the stack and enqueue on the Postfix queue operators whose StackPriority is greater than or equal to the InfixPriority of Token. This comparison, keying on the priority of Token from the Infix queue and operators that have previously been pushed onto the OperatorStack, ensures that operators are applied in the right order in the resulting Postfix queue. After popping these operators, push Token.

6. Repeat 4 and 5 until Token is the delimiting EndToken.

The key to the algorithm is the use of the stack to hold operators from the infix expression that appear to the left of another given operator even though that latter operator must be applied first. The defined functions InfixPriority and StackPriority are used to specify this priority of operators and the associated pushing and popping operations. This entire process is best understood by carefully tracing through an example.

Example 5.1   Parse the infix expression

$$A * B + (C - D/E) \#$$

into its equivalent postfix form. Trace the contents of the operator stack and the postfix string as each token is processed. Here the symbol # is used for EndToken. The solution to this problem is presented in Table 5.1. In this table, the parenthesized numbers in the Commentary column refer to subcases of step 5 in the preceding algorithm. We only show the content of a data structure when it changes.

The following PSEUDO procedure fully implements our algorithm. Note how the use of functional parameters ValidOperator, ValidOperand, InfixPriority, and StackPriority make the algorithm completely general. That is, by passing in appropriately defined functions for these parameters, we can control the parse in a variety of different ways—allowing different definitions for operators, operands, and the hierarchy of operations. You will explore ways of doing this in the exercises and problems.

Token	OperatorStack	Postfix	Commentary
	#		Push #
A			Dequeue Token
		A	Enqueue Token on Postfix (5.1)
*			Dequeue Token
	*		Push Token (5.4)
	#		
B			Dequeue Token
		AB	Enqueue Token on Postfix (5.1)
+			Dequeue Token
	+	AB*	Pop *, enqueue * on Postfix,
	#		push Token (5.4)
(			Dequeue Token
	(		Push Token (5.4)
	+		
	#		
C			Dequeue Token
		AB*C	Enqueue Token on Postfix (5.1)
−			Dequeue Token
	−		Push Token (5.4)
	(		
	+		
	#		
D			Dequeue Token
		AB*CD	Enqueue Token on Postfix (5.1)
/			Dequeue Token
	/		Push Token (5.4)
	−		
	(		
	+		
	#		
E			Dequeue Token
		AB*CDE	Enqueue Token on Postfix (5.1)
)			Dequeue Token
	+	AB*CDE/−	Pop and enqueue on Postfix until
	#		LeftParen reached (5.2)
#			Dequeue Token
		AB*CDE/−+#	Pop and enqueue rest of stack on Postfix (5.3)

TABLE 5.1 Parsing of infix expression A * B + (C − D / E)#.

```
type
   TokenType: (* Appropriate type for expressions being parsed, e.g.,
              character or string *);
   QueueData: TokenType;
   StackData: TokenType;
   TokenValidator: (* Establishes the signature of a function that can be used
                    to test whether a token is an operator or an operand *)
                 function
                    ( given Token: TokenType (* An arbitrary token *);
                      return: boolean       (* true if Token meets the criterion
                                              being tested; false otherwise *) );
   PriorityFunc: (* Establishes the signature of a function used to
                  evaluate the infix or stack priority of a token *)
                 function
                    ( given Token: TokenType (* A non-operand token *);
                      return: integer       (* The priority value associated with
                                              Token *) );

procedure ConvertInToPost
  ( given Infix: Queue             (* Queue of tokens representing infix
                                     expression *);

          ValidOperand: TokenValidator  (* Used to test whether a token is a
                                          valid operand *);

          ValidOperator: TokenValidator  (* Used to test whether a token is a
                                           valid operator *);

          InfixPriority: PriorityFunc   (* The infix priority function *);
          StackPriority: PriorityFunc   (* The stack priority function *);
    return PostFix: Queue          (* Queue of tokens representing postfix
                                     form of infix expression *) );


   var
      Item, NewToken: TokenType;
      OpStack: Stack;


   start ConvertInToPost
      Stack.Create(OpStack);
      Queue.Create(Postfix);
      Push(OpStack,EndToken);
      repeat
         Dequeue(Infix, NewToken);
         if ValidOperand(NewToken) then
            Enqueue(Postfix, NewToken)
         elsif NewToken = RightParen then
            Pop(OpStack, Item);
            while Item <> LeftParen do
               Enqueue(Postfix, Item);
               Pop(OpStack, Item)
            endwhile
```

NewToken is Operand

Postfix   Q   New Token from Infix

Opstack

In this case, transfer NewToken to Postfix

NewToken is RightParen

Postfix   )   New Token from Infix

(

Opstack

In this case, pop stack until encounter matching left parenthesis

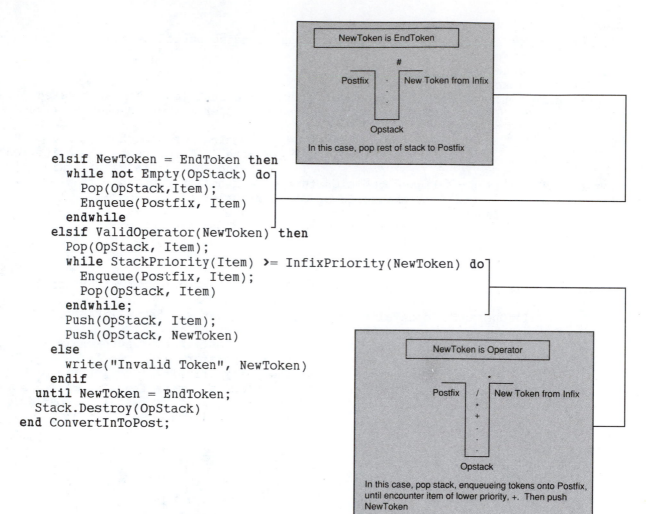

```
    elsif NewToken = EndToken then
      while not Empty(OpStack) do
        Pop(OpStack,Item);
        Enqueue(Postfix, Item)
      endwhile
    elsif ValidOperator(NewToken) then
      Pop(OpStack, Item);
      while StackPriority(Item) >= InfixPriority(NewToken) do
        Enqueue(Postfix, Item);
        Pop(OpStack, Item)
      endwhile;
      Push(OpStack, Item);
      Push(OpStack, NewToken)
    else
      write("Invalid Token", NewToken)
    endif
  until NewToken = EndToken;
  Stack.Destroy(OpStack)
end ConvertInToPost;
```

Note the elegant generality of this parsing algorithm. The types of expressions it parses and how it parses them is controlled completely by the four functional parameters. By passing in functions that define differently the structure of and relationships between operands and operators, you can guide the parse in a variety of directions without ever altering the code in procedure ConvertInToPost. Thus, the algorithm again illustrates the power of abstraction—being able to apply a technique in many situations by merely changing low-level, subordinate procedures and functions that are used by the top-level algorithm.

Evaluating Postfix Expressions

Once an expression has been parsed and represented in postfix form, another stack plays an essential role in its final evaluation. As an example, consider the postfix expression from Example 5.1.

$$AB * CDE/ - + \#$$

A RELEVANT ISSUE	Automating the Writing of Compilers

A RELEVANT ISSUE

Automating the Writing of Compilers

To a certain extent, programming language compilers view the entire source program they are translating as a large expression to be parsed and transformed into a suitable data structure (such as postfix notation). For instance, a **while** control structure could be thought of as a two-operand expression: one operand being the boolean condition following **while** and the other operand being the sequence of statements to be executed as long as the first operand is **true.** Similarly, an **if-then-else** statement could be viewed as an expression requiring three operands: a boolean condition following the **if,** a sequence of statements following **then,** and a sequence of statements following **else.**

Although the generation of machine code from such expressions is certainly a more complicated algorithm than the evaluation of algebraic expressions as discussed in this chapter, there are, nonetheless, many similarities between the two tasks. One such similarity is that, like our parsing algorithm for algebraic expressions, many compilers use a generic technique that applies to any source language provided that suitable "priority functions" are available to the algorithm. This technique, known as *LR parsing,* relies on another program called a *parser generator* to compute the appropriate priority tables for a given language. Such a parser generator is thus a program that takes as input the formal definition of a programming language's syntax and then computes the priority information necessary to drive the generic LR parser algorithm. One of the primary advantages of the LR algorithm is that, given the correct priority values for the language being parsed, it is guaranteed to work—just as our infix-to-postfix algorithm is *guaranteed* to work if the correct priority functions are supplied to it.

In the next chapter, we shall explore formal grammars as a means of precisely describing the syntax of a programming language. A more complete treatment of grammars, LR parsing, and parser generators can be found in *Crafting a Compiler* by Charles N. Fischer and Richard J. LeBlanc (Menlo Park, CA: Benjamin/Cummings, 1988).

Let us suppose that the symbols A, B, C, D, and E had associated with them the following values:

Symbol	Value
A	5
B	3
C	6
D	8
E	2

To evaluate such an expression, we repeatedly get tokens from the postfix expression. If the token is an operand, push the value associated with it onto the stack. If it is an operator, pop two values from the stack, apply the operator to them, and push the result back onto the stack. The technique is illustrated for our postfix expression in Figure 5.4.

In the following PSEUDO version of an algorithm to evaluate a postfix expression, we assume the existence of three functions:

1. ValidOperand—defined as it was for the procedure ConvertInToPost
2. ValueOf—a function that will return the real numeric value associated with an operand token
3. Eval—a function that will return the result of applying a particular operator to two real numeric operands

```
type
  TokenType: (* Appropriate type for expressions being evaluated, e.g.,
              character or string *);
  QueueData: TokenType;
  StackData: real;
  TokenValidator: (* Establishes the signature of a function that can
                   be used to test whether a token is an operator
                   or an operand *)
```

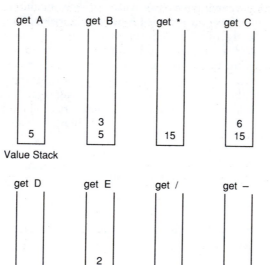

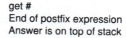

FIGURE 5.4
Evaluation of
AB*CDE/ −+#. If a token taken from the postfix expression is an operand, its value is pushed onto a stack. If the token is an operator, two values are popped, the operator applied to them, and the result pushed onto the stack.

```
            function
              ( given Token: TokenType  (* An arbitrary token *);
                return: boolean         (* true if Token meets the criterion
                                           being tested; false otherwise *) );
 ValueAssociator: (* Establishes the signature of a function that
                   associates a token with its numeric value *)
            function
              ( given Token: TokenType (* A token that is an operand *);
                return: real            (* The numeric value associated
                                           with Token *) );
 Evaluator: (* Establishes the signature of a function that applies an
             operation to two values *)
            function
              ( given V1, V2: real      (* Two real numeric operands *);
                  Operator: Token       (* A token that is an operator *);
                return: real            (* The result of applying Operator
                                           to V1 and V2 *) );

function Evaluate
  ( given Postfix: Queue                (* Queue of tokens representing postfix
                                           form of expression *);

        ValidOperand: TokenValidator    (* Function used to test tokens for
                                           being operands *);

        ValueOf: ValueAssociator        (* Function used to determine the
                                           numeric value of a token *);

        Eval: Evaluator                 (* Used to apply an operator to values
                                           in stack *);

    return: real                        (* The real numeric value obtained by
                                           evaluating the Postfix expression *) );

  var
    Token: TokenType;
    ValueStack: Stack;
    V1, V2: real;

  start Evaluate
    Create(ValueStack);
    Dequeue(Postfix, Token);
    while Token <> EndToken do
      if ValidOperand(Token) then
        Push(ValueStack, ValueOf(Token))
      else (* Token must be an operator *)
        Pop(ValueStack, V2);
        Pop(ValueStack, V1);
        Push(ValueStack, Eval(V1, V2, Token))
      endif;
      Dequeue(Postfix, Token)
    endwhile;
    Evaluate := OnTop(ValueStack);
    Destroy(ValueStack)
  end Evaluate;
```

When we explore symbol table methods in Chapters 7 and 11, we shall see how compilers handle expressions with operands far more complex than those involving the mere one-character "variables" we have traced in our examples. However, because of the generality of the procedures we have developed in this chapter, the conversion of such expressions to postfix notation and their resulting evaluation will require only that we pass different functional parameters to our existing ConvertInToPost and Evaluate routines.

Exercises 5.3

1. What are the infix, postfix, and prefix forms of the expression

$$A + B * (C - D) / (P - R)$$

2. Trace the contents of the stack as the postfix form of the expression in Exercise 1 is evaluated. Assume that A = 6, B = 4, C = 3, D = 1, P = 12, and R = 11.

3. Consider the expression with the infix notation

$$P + (Q - F) / Y$$

Using the algorithm discussed in this section to transform this into postfix expression, trace the state of both the operator stack and postfix queue as each token of the infix expression is processed.

	Operator Stack Bottom → Top	Postfix Queue
After 1st token		
After 2nd token		
After 3rd token		
After 4th token		
After 5th token		
After 6th token		
After 7th token		
After 8th token		
After 9th token		

4. Using the postfix expression you have obtained in Exercise 3, trace the stack of real values that would develop as the postfix expression is evaluated. You should indicate the numeric values on the stack as each token in the postfix expression is processed. Assume the values P = 10, Q = 18, F = 4, and Y = 2.

5. Parse the infix expression

$$P * (Q / Y) + A - B + D * Y$$

using the following definitions of InfixPriority and StackPriority:

Priority	*	/	+	−	LeftParen	RightParen	EndToken
Infix	2	2	4	4	5	0	0
Stack	1	1	3	3	0	undefined	0

Trace this parsing operation by filling in the table below to indicate the contents of the operator stack and postfix queue after each character is read in.

	Operator Stack Bottom ⟶ Top	Postfix Queue
After 1st token		
After 2nd token		
After 3rd token		
After 4th token		
After 5th token		
After 6th token		
After 7th token		
After 8th token		
After 9th token		
After 10th token		
After 11th token		
After 12th token		
After 13th token		
After 14th token		
After 15th token		
After 16th token		

6. Using the postfix expression you have obtained in Exercise 5, trace the stack of real numeric values that would develop as the postfix expression is evaluated. You should indicate the value of the stack as each token in the postfix expression is processed. Assume the values A = 4, B = 3, D = 2, P = 1, Q = 4, and Y = 2.

7. Explain how the relationship between the stack priorities and infix priorities of *, /, +, −, LeftParen, RightParen, and EndToken controls the parsing of an infix expression.

8. Using the rationale you developed in Exercise 7, explain how the InfixPriority and StackPriority functions would be extended to allow the exponentiation operator ↑. Remember that the laws of algebra typically dictate that

$$3^{2^3}$$

evaluates to 6,561, not 729.

9. Based on your work in Exercise 8, write a paragraph explaining why two priority functions are needed: one for operators in the infix expression and another for operators on the stack.

10. Discuss how the ConvertInToPost and Evaluate routines of this section would have to be modified to allow expressions to contain unary minus (that is, the negative of a single number) and trigonometric, logarithmic, and exponential functions. Implement these changes.

11. How would the functions InfixPriority and StackPriority be extended to include the boolean operators <, >, <=, >=, =, <>, AND, OR, and NOT?

Chapter Summary

Although a first-in, first-out structure such as a queue seems to be the obvious way of storing items that must wait to be processed, there are many natural instances in which a last-in, first-out (LIFO) strategy is more appropriate. A list of data items that enforces such a last-in, first-out strategy is called a *stack*. More specifically, a stack is a restricted list in which additions or deletions are permitted only from one designated end, called the *top*. The importance of stacks is emphasized by first considering the role they play in the processing of subroutine calls. Two methods for implementing stacks are considered, one using arrays, and another using linked lists.

Following a discussion of the *infix, prefix,* and *postfix* notations for algebraic expressions, stacks are used in parsing expressions from infix to postfix form and for evaluating postfix expressions.

Key Words

infix	postfix	stack
last-in, first-out	prefix	tokens
parsing	recursion	top

Programming Projects/Problems

1. Write a program that will parse infix expressions into prefix form.

2. In the Programming Problems for Chapter 3, you developed a passenger list processing system for the various flights of Wing-and-a-Prayer Airlines. Wing-and-a-Prayer management would now like you to extend this system so that it processes logical combinations of flight numbers. For example, the command

   LIST 1 OR 2

   should list all passengers whose name appears on the flight 1 or the flight 2 lists. Your program should also accept the logical operators **AND** and **NOT** and allow parenthesized logical expressions obeying the standard logical hierarchy

   NOT
   AND
   OR

3. A tax form may be considered a sequence of items, each of which is either a number or defined by an arbitrary mathematical formula involving other items in the sequence. To assist them in their tax-planning strategy, top management at the Fly-by-Night credit card company desire a program that would allow them to interactively enter numbers or formulas associated with given lines of a tax form. Once all such lines have been defined, users of the program may redefine the number or formula associated with a particular line, and all other lines dependent upon that one should be appropriately updated. Note that, since formulas may be entered interactively, your program will have to use a stack to evaluate them. In effect you will have written a small-scale spreadsheet program.

4. Write a program that will accept commands of the following form:

   • **INPUT** *variable name*
   • *variable name* = infix expression involving variable names and arithmetic operators +, −, *, /

- **PRINT** *variable name*
- **GO**

These commands are to be stored in an array of strings until the **GO** command is entered. Once **GO** is entered, your program should execute the previously stored commands. "Execute" here means

- For an **INPUT** command: send a question mark to the terminal and allow the user to enter a real number; this real number is then stored in *variable name*.
- For an assignment statement: parse the expression into postfix form and then evaluate it, storing the results in the *variable name* on the left of the equality sign.
- For a **PRINT** instruction: write to the terminal the numerical contents of the specified *variable name*.

To make things relatively easy you may assume a syntax that

- allows only one variable name following **INPUT** or **PRINT**
- allows one blank space after the keywords **INPUT** and **PRINT** and no blank spaces anywhere else

For an additional challenge, enable your program to handle successfully the exponentiation operator ↑ within assignment statement expressions. The following example should illustrate the need for care in handling this exponentiation operator:

$$3^{2^3} = 3^8 \quad \text{not } 9^3$$

5. This problem is an extension of Problem 4 to a "compiler" for a primitive programming language. Write a program that will accept commands of the following form:

- **INPUT** *variable name*
- **PRINT** *variable name*
- *variable name* = infix arithmetic expression involving variable names and arithmetic operators +, −, *, /
- **GOTO** *line* $\begin{cases} \textbf{ALWAYS, or} \\ \textbf{IF } \textit{infix logical expression} \text{ involving variable names} \\ \quad \text{and operators } +, -, *, /, \uparrow, \& \text{ (for \textbf{AND})}, ! \text{ (for \textbf{OR})}, \\ \quad \sim \text{ (for \textbf{NOT})}, <, >, = \end{cases}$
- **STOP**
- **RUN**

These commands are to be stored in an array of strings until the **RUN** command is entered. Upon encountering **RUN**, your program should execute the previously stored commands. "Execute" here means

- For an **INPUT** command: send a question mark to the terminal and allow the user to enter a real number, which is stored in variable name.
- For a **PRINT** command: write to the terminal the numerical contents of the specified variable name.
- For an assignment command: parse the expression into postfix form and then evaluate it. Store the result in the variable name on the left of the equality sign.

- For a **GOTO** command: branch to the line number specified when **ALWAYS** follows the line number or when the infix expression that follows the **IF** evaluates to **true.** Here "line number" refers to the relative position of the line in the sequence of lines that were entered prior to the **RUN** command. The first line number in this sequence is "00."
- For a **STOP** command: halt execution.

To make things relatively easy, you may assume a syntax that

- specifies that one and only one blank space follows **INPUT, PRINT, GOTO,** and line number. No other blanks appear anywhere.
- allows only one variable name to follow **INPUT** or **PRINT.**
- only allows variable names consisting of one uppercase alphabetical character.
- only allows line numbers consisting of two digits: 00 through 99.

The usual hierarchy for operators is assumed.

6. If you are familiar with the concept of integration from calculus, design and implement a program that will evaluate the integral of a function $f(x)$. The left and right endpoints of the interval over which integration is to occur *and* the definition of the function $f(x)$ should be entered interactively by the user. In particular, interactive entry of the function definition (in infix notation) will require you to parse the function into postfix form for later evaluation of $f(x)$ for various values of x. Approximate the integral by summing up the areas of a suitable number of rectangles bounded by the graph of the function between the endpoints entered by the user. Recall that the formal definition of the integral is nothing more than the limit of this sum of rectangular areas as the number of rectangles approaches infinity.

7. In propositional logic, elementary propositions may be combined by five logical connectives:

$P \leftrightarrow Q$: P if and only if Q
$P \rightarrow Q$: P implies Q, that is, if P then Q
$P \wedge Q$: P and Q
$P \vee Q$: P or Q
$\sim P$: not P

The truth tables for each of these logical connectives are given by

P	Q	$P \leftrightarrow Q$	$P \rightarrow Q$	$P \wedge Q$	$P \vee Q$	$\sim P$
T	T	T	T	T	T	F
T	F	F	F	F	T	F
F	T	F	T	F	T	T
F	F	T	T	F	F	T

Logical expressions involving these connectives may combine many connectives applied according to the following conventions:

all $\sim$ connectives are applied first

then all $\wedge$ connectives

FIGURE 5.5

Representation of a maze by a two-dimensional boolean table. Cells marked as **false** are blocked; those marked as **true** are open.

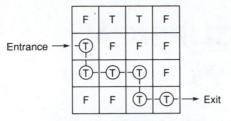

then all $\vee$ connectives

then all $\rightarrow$ connectives

finally, all $\leftrightarrow$ connectives

Of course, parentheses may be used to override this hierarchy of operations.

A *tautology* is a logical proposition that is always true, regardless of the truth values of its elementary components. For instance, the proposition

$$(P \rightarrow Q) \leftrightarrow (\sim P \vee Q)$$

is a tautology since it is always true—for any possible combination of true/false values of P and Q. Write a program that allows a logician to enter interactively a logical proposition and that then reports whether or not the proposition is a tautology. You may assume that all elementary propositions are represented by one of the letters P, Q, R, S, or T.

8. A maze may be represented by a two-dimensional boolean table in the form illustrated in Figure 5.5. Those cells marked by **false** are blocked; those cells marked by **true** are open. When exploring a maze, you may move north, south, east, or west from a given cell—provided that the cell in the direction you choose is open. Hence, the dotted line in Figure 5.5 represents one possible path from the entrance to the exit.

Write a program that allows a user to enter interactively a maze and that then searches for a path through the maze. Guide this search by pushing a record of each move made onto a stack. Whenever the search algorithm reaches a dead end, it can return to the previous position by popping the stack of prior moves and trying an alternative direction from that previous position. Eventually, your algorithm will either find a path to the exit or try all possibilities and find that none of them lead to such a path. In the latter case, have your program report that the maze is impossible to solve. Comment on the efficiency of your program in terms of the size of the maze that is searched.

6 RECURSION

Simple style is like white light. It is complex,
but its complexity is not obvious.

Anatole France

CHAPTER OUTLINE

In the *Pascal User Manual and Report* (Berlin: Springer-Verlag, 1974), Kathleen Jensen and Niklaus Wirth made famous a graphic way of representing the syntax of the Pascal language. By way of example, a syntax diagram that defines a Pascal statement is presented in Figure 6.1. One interesting feature to note about this diagram is that the term *statement* is used eight times in defining statement. Yet this definition is not ambiguous or circular since, ultimately, a statement must resolve to one of the following:

- Assignment statement
- Procedure call
- GOTO statement

Such a language definition illustrates beautifully the expressive power of *recursion*—defining the solution to a problem in terms of a simpler version of

234

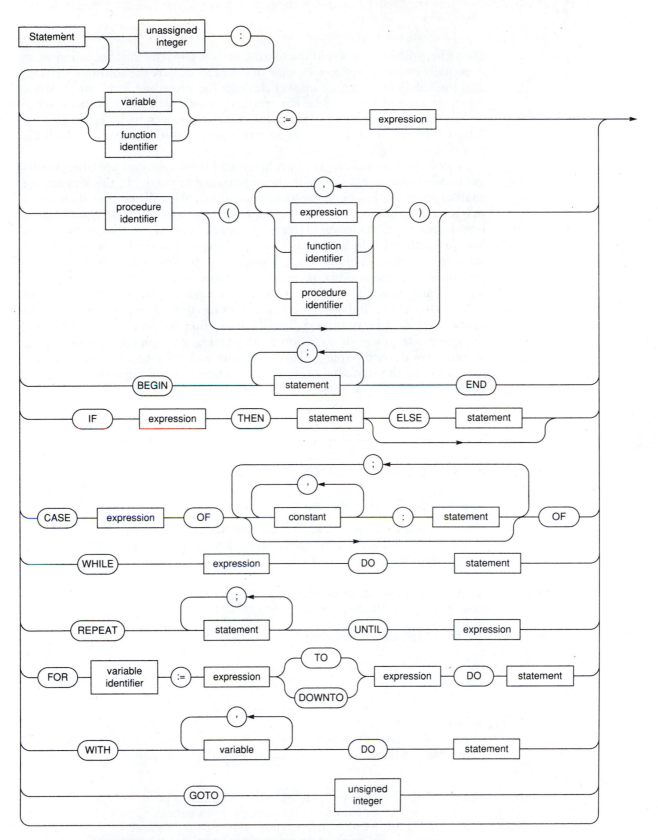

FIGURE 6.1 Recursive definition of a Pascal statement.

the same problem. To avoid circularity, such a self-referential solution must eventually end in a version so simple that we can declare the solution "trivial" and immediately return an answer through the preceding levels of recursive logic. At each of these levels, the returned answer will often be involved in computations resulting in a yet more complex answer to be returned to a different logical level. Finally, an answer is returned to the level at which the problem was originally posed.

Recursive formulations of problems and their solutions are often so elegant and compact that they give the appearance of magic. In this chapter we shall explore the basics of recursive algorithms. We will see that there is no magic involved but rather that the implementation of recursive algorithms is based upon intricate manipulations of a stack used in processing procedure and function calls. In Section 6.1 we shall explore in detail the role of this stack in recursive programming. Through introductory examples, we will begin to develop the notions of recurrence relations and recursive call trees as ways of analyzing the efficiency of recursive algorithms. In Sections 6.2 and 6.3 two recursive and highly efficient sorting algorithms—merge sort and quick sort—will be examined. Finally, in Section 6.4, we will demonstrate the expressive power of recursion by examining a parsing technique known as *recursive descent* parsing. This technique will offer an alternative implementation to the stack-based, priority function parsing algorithm discussed in Chapter 5.

6.1   INTRODUCTORY EXAMPLES

The Search Problem Revisited

The divide-and-conquer search algorithm we developed in Section 1.3 can be neatly formulated via recursive logic. Recall that the PSEUDO interface to this algorithm was given by

```
type (* Assume IndexLimit is constant determining array size *)
  ElementType: (* May be anything with an order relationship between
               elements *);
  ElementArray: array [IndexLimit] of ElementType;
  Comparison: function
              ( given A, B: ElementType   (* Values to compare *);
                return: boolean           (* true if A precedes B in order
                                             relationship on ElementType; false
                                             otherwise *) );
  SplitttingFunc: function
              ( given Hi, Lo: integer (* 1 <= Lo <= Hi <= IndexLimit *);
                return: integer        (* Lo <= returned value <= Hi *) );

procedure Search
  ( given A: ElementArray      (* Array with at most IndexLimit entries
                                  ordered by Precedes parameter *);
          N: integer           (* Number of values in array. Assume
                                  0 <= N <= IndexLimit *);
```

```
        Target: ElementType      (* Value being sought in array *);
        Precedes: Comparison     (* A function parameter for comparing values
                                    in ElementArray *);
        Split: SplittingFunc     (* A function parameter used to determine a
                                    splitting point in array A *);
 return Found: boolean           (* Set to true if Target can be found in A *);
        Place: integer           (* The index location of Target in A if Found
                                    is true; undefined if Found is false *) );
```

If we assume that Lo is initialized to 1 and Hi is initialized to N, then a high-level, recursive statement of the divide-and-conquer algorithm is the following.

```
if Lo > Hi then
    the Target cannot be located between Lo and Hi inclusive, so return
    Found  as false
else
    compute Guess position to be Split point of Lo and Hi
    if A[Guess] = Target then
        the Target has been located, so return Found as true and  Guess
        as location of match
    elsif Precedes(A[Guess], Target) then
        recursively invoke the same logic, except now use Guess + 1
        as the new Lo
    else
        recursively invoke the same logic, except now use Guess − 1
        as the new Hi
    endif
endif
```

The essence of the recursive paradigm is to recognize that the solution to a problem may be stated in terms of the solution to the same problem at a simpler level. For the divide-and-conquer search, Figure 6.2 indicates that this search within a search uses a continually smaller index range within which Target may be found. Equally important to the recursive paradigm is recognizing that this problem-within-a-problem theme cannot recur infinitely. Ultimately, conditions must exist that allow us to leave the recursion and return an answer. For the divide-and-conquer search, these termination conditions are either

The Target has been located (success).

or

Further narrowing of the index range is impossible (failure).

As you gain experience with recursion, you will acquire a feel for the type of problem that lends itself to a recursive expression. Usually you will recognize the problem-within-a-problem phenomenon first and then develop the specific conditions that allow the recursion to halt.

To formalize the recursive implementation of the divide-and-conquer search, we must allow two parameters Lo and Hi to specify the current range of index possibilities for the location of the Target. Thus, in the recursive

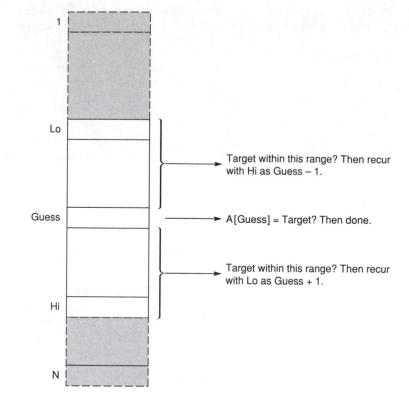

Target within this range? Then recur with Hi as Guess − 1.

A[Guess] = Target? Then done.

Target within this range? Then recur with Lo as Guess + 1.

FIGURE 6.2
Recurring search with narrowing index range.

version of the algorithm, Lo and Hi are incorporated into the parameter list of the search that appeared in Section 1.3.

```
procedure RecursiveSearch
  ( given A: ElementArray      (* Array with at most IndexLimit entries *);
         Lo, Hi: integer        (* An index range for A within which the Target
                                   will be sought *);

         Target: ElementType    (* Value being sought in array *);
         Precedes: Comparison   (* A function parameter for comparing values
                                   in ElementArray *);

         Split: SplittingFunc   (* A function parameter used to determine a
                                   splitting point in array A *);

    return Found: boolean       (* Set to true if Target can be found in A *);
           Place: integer       (* The index location of Target in A if
                                   Found is true; undefined if Found
                                   is false *) );

var
  Guess: integer;

start RecursiveSearch
  if Lo > Hi then
    Found := false
  else
    Guess := Split(Lo, Hi);
    if A[Guess] = Target then
      Found := true;
      Place := Guess
```

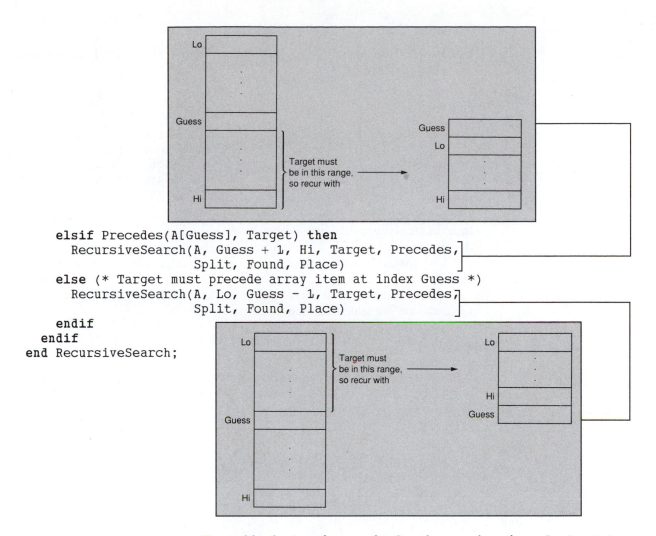

```
      elsif Precedes(A[Guess], Target) then
        RecursiveSearch(A, Guess + 1, Hi, Target, Precedes,
                  Split, Found, Place)
      else (* Target must precede array item at index Guess *)
        RecursiveSearch(A, Lo, Guess - 1, Target, Precedes,
                  Split, Found, Place)
      endif
    endif
end RecursiveSearch;
```

To enable the interface to the Search procedure from Section 1.3 to remain the same, the Search procedure itself now becomes a trivial front-end to the RecursiveSearch procedure.

```
procedure Search
  ( given A: ElementArray        (* Array with at most IndexLimit entries
                                     ordered by Precedes parameter *);
          N: integer             (* Number of values in array. Assume
                                     0 <= N <= IndexLimit *);
          Target: ElementType    (* Value being sought in array *);
          Precedes: Comparison   (* A function parameter for comparing values
                                     in ElementArray *);
          Split: SplittingFunc   (* A function parameter used to determine a
                                     splitting point in array A *);
    return Found: boolean         (* Set to true if Target can be found in A *);
          Place: integer         (* The index location of Target in A if Found
                                     is true; undefined if Found is false *) );
  start Search
    RecursiveSearch(A, 1, N, Target, Precedes, Split, Found, Place)
  end Search;
```

Traversal Operation for Ordered Lists

In Chapter 3 our definition of the (ordered) list ADT included an operation Traverse, specified by

```
procedure Traverse
  ( given L: List                    (* A list *);
         ProcessNode: NodeOperation (* Some process to be applied
                                       to each node *);
    return L: List                   (* L with each node in it
                                       affected by ProcessNode *) );
```

The purpose of Traverse is to allow one to walk through the list in an ordered fashion, applying procedure ProcessNode at each node; that is, starting with the first item in the list as determined by the Precedes relationship used in the Add operation, one applies ProcessNode successively to each node in the list.

If the ordered list is implemented using a (singly) linked list, then Traverse can be implemented recursively as follows:

```
procedure Traverse
  ( given L: List                    (* A list *);
         ProcessNode: NodeOperation (* Some process to be applied
                                       to each node *);
    return L: List                   (* L with each node in it
                                       affected by ProcessNode *) );

  start Traverse
    if L <> NULL then
      ProcessNode(Ref(L));
      Traverse(Ref(L).Link, ProcessNode)
    endif
  end Traverse;
```

Note that if L = NULL, then the call Traverse(L, ProcessNode) simply returns, having done nothing.

Suppose now that we wish to modify our definition of the List ADT so that it includes an operation ReverseTraverse to process the list in the reverse order, that is, starting at the last node in the list (again as determined according to the Precedes relationship) and stopping after the first node has been processed. Here again, for a singly linked list representation we can use a recursively defined implementation.

```
procedure ReverseTraverse
  ( given L: List                    (* A list *);
         ProcessNode: NodeOperation (* Some process to be applied
                                       to each node *);
    return L: List                   (* L with each node in it
                                       affected by ProcessNode,
                                       starting with the last node
                                       and ending with the
                                       first *) );
```

```
start ReverseTraverse
  if L <> NULL then
    ReverseTraverse(Ref(L).Link, ProcessNode);
    ProcessNode(Ref(L))
  endif
end ReverseTraverse;
```

Here again, if L = NULL then the call ReverseTraverse(L, ProcessNode) simply returns, without doing anything. What the algorithm says at each node is "put off processing this node until the rest of the list has been processed or until L = NULL (in which case, consider the node as having been processed)." A moment's reflection should be sufficient to convince you that such a sequence of deferred processing of each node does in fact yield the desired order of processing.

This last routine also provides us with our first hint at the potential elegance and simplicity of recursively defined algorithms. To see this, you should write a nonrecursive algorithm for procedure ReverseTraverse, assuming a singly linked list representation of the list data structure.

Writing and Verifying Recursive Algorithms

For many programmers, it takes some time until they acquire the insight for recognizing problems that might admit a recursive solution, that is, recognizing problems whose solutions can be expressed using a "simpler" version of the original. Often this insight comes when programmers simply remind themselves to *think recursively* when pondering a solution to a problem.

After having recognized the potential for a recursive solution, the programmer must ensure the following conditions when coding the solution as a procedure or function in a language that allows recursion:

1. There must be at least one simple (or base) case of the problem being solved that does not require recursion. Such cases will normally lead directly to a completion of the routine's task and a return to the point at which it was invoked.

   In our divide-and-conquer solution to the searching problem, the two cases Hi < Lo and A[Guess] = Target are sufficient to deduce that we should return Found = **false** and Found = **true**, respectively—no further calls to RecursiveSearch are needed. In Traverse and ReverseTraverse, the case L = NULL serves as the base case, requiring simply that nothing further be done.

2. Any recursive use of the procedure or function must move the problem closer to one of the base cases.

   In our divide-and-conquer solution to the searching problem, the recursive call depends on the outcome of the conditional test Precedes(A[Guess], Target). Either the recursive call RecursiveSearch(A, Guess + 1, Hi, Target, Precedes, Split, Found, Place) will be made, or the call RecursiveSearch(A, Lo, Guess − 1, Target, Precedes, Split, Found, Place) will be made. In either case, the parameter Lo used by RecursiveSearch will be at least one value closer to Hi (or one value beyond it if Lo = Hi when RecursiveSearch was called), thereby taking us at least one step closer to the base case Hi < Lo. At the same time, a new value for Guess will be calculated, which, if Target is in the array, will move us closer to the position where Target will be found.

In Traverse and ReverseTraverse, the recursive calls are made with the ListNode pointer Ref(L).Link, which takes us one node closer to the last node of the list, whose link field has the value NULL needed for our base case.

Verifying the correctness of a recursive procedure or function now becomes a matter of verifying that the following conditions have been satisfied:

1. That the procedure or function contains the requisite base cases and that they work

2. That all recursive calls of the procedure or function involve a case of the problem that is closer to one of the base cases

3. That, under the assumption that all recursive invocations do indeed solve the "simpler" cases represented in their invocation, the use made of the results of those invocations correctly solves the general problem with which the procedure or function is concerned

Let us see how we can verify the correctness of the RecursiveSearch algorithm.

1. RecursiveSearch has two base cases:
   a. Hi < Lo: here the assumed precondition Lo ≤ Hi, which specifies the index range within which to search, will be violated, allowing us to conclude that there is no value for Place such that Lo ≤ Place ≤ Hi, and Found must be **false**. Note also that following the assignment associated with the success of the test Hi < Lo, we go immediately to the end of the procedure, and hence return to the statement after the point of invocation.
   b. A[Guess] = Target: here, of course, the sought-after target value has been found; hence, Found and Place are the values **true** and Guess, after which we again go immediately to the end of the procedure, thus returning to the statement after the point of invocation.

2. RecursiveSearch uses two recursive calls:
   a. RecursiveSearch(A, Guess + 1, Hi, Target, Precedes, Split, Found, Place): this case solves a simpler case of the given problem because the range of indices has been reduced from Lo .. Hi to Guess + 1 .. Hi. The value of Guess was calculated by the function Split, which by assumption returns a value in the range Lo .. Hi (verifying that Split works correctly is a separate problem).
   b. RecursiveSearch(A, Lo, Guess − 1, Target, Precedes, Split, Found, Place): this case solves a simpler case of the given problem because the range of indices has been reduced from Lo .. Hi to Lo .. Guess − 1, where once again the value of Guess was calculated by the function Split, and is assumed to be in the range Lo .. Hi.

3. The Search problem for a value Target among the elements of an array A having indices in the range Lo..Hi can be broken down into four mutually exclusive cases: (a) Hi < Lo; (b) Lo ≤ Hi and A[Guess] = Target for some index Guess dependent upon Lo and Hi and in the subrange Lo..Hi; (c) Lo ≤ Hi and Precedes(A[Guess], Target); and (d) Lo ≤ Hi and Precedes(Target, A[Guess]), or equivalently Lo ≤ Hi, A[Guess] <> Target and not Precedes(A[Guess], Target). The RecursiveSearch algorithm tests for each case and takes an action that properly solves the Search problem since the first two involve base cases that were already verified and the last two cases involve the recursive calls of condition 2 (above), which we assume correctly solve the Search problem for their simpler cases.

Why Does Recursion Work?

We have thus far approached recursion as an intuitive concept well suited to expressing solutions for certain kinds of problems. We will now turn our attention to the question of how recursive procedure/function calls are implemented by programming languages. Such a discussion will serve two purposes. First, it will enhance our understanding of recursion as a problem-solving paradigm, thereby enabling us to approach more complex recursive problems with confidence. Second, a thorough understanding of how recursion works is necessary if we are to perform detailed time/space efficiency analyses of recursive algorithms.

In Section 5.1 we alluded to the existence of a general system stack onto which return addresses are pushed each time a function or procedure call is made. Let us now explain the role of that stack more fully. Each time a procedure or function call is made, an item called a stack frame will be pushed onto the system stack. The data in this stack frame consist of the return address (that is, where program execution is to resume after the procedure or function is completed) and a copy of each local variable for the procedure or function.

Figure 6.3 illustrates how stack frames are pushed and popped from the system stack when the procedure RecursiveSearch is invoked from the front-end procedure Search, with the Split function computed by (Lo + Hi) / 2. We can see from this example that a recursive call creates an entirely new collection of variables that a procedure can manipulate. These variables exist in the stack frame allocated for the current call to the procedure. While work is done in this topmost stack frame, the values of variables in prior, unfinished levels of recursive calls are protected within the stack. When the current level of recursion is completed, the return address in the topmost stack frame is examined to determine where processing is to resume. Then this stack frame is popped, in effect uncovering the values of variables that had existed at a prior recursive level.

The notion of *levels* is critical in recursive problem solving and, consequently, in recursive programming. Each recursive invocation of a procedure or function involves a view that is one degree simpler than the view at an earlier level. The fact that new space is allocated in the stack frame for parameters and other local variables can make recursion a space-inefficient technique. For those parameters that are given to a procedure, space to store

A	Lo	Hi	Target	Found	Place	Return point
Given Below	1	15	37	Undefined	Undefined	Search

RecursiveSearch called from Search

A	Lo	Hi	Target	Found	Place	Return point
Given Below	1	7	37	Undefined	Undefined	Recursive Search
Given Below	1	15	37	Undefined	Undefined	Search

RecursiveSearch called from RecursiveSearch

A	Lo	Hi	Target	Found	Place	Return point
Given Below	5	7	37	**true**	6	Recursive Search
Given Below	1	7	37	**true**	6	Recursive Search
Given Below	1	15	37	**true**	6	Search

RecursiveSearch called from RecursiveSearch

A	Lo	Hi	Target	Found	Place	Return point
Given Below	1	7	37	**true**	6	Recursive Search
Given Below	1	15	37	**true**	6	Search

Target Found, so return to prior level of RecursiveSearch

A	Lo	Hi	Target	Found	Place	Return point
Given Below	1	15	37	**true**	6	Search

Return to prior level of RecursiveSearch

System stack space for RecursiveSearch now empty: **true** and 6 returned to Search as Found and Place parameters

	A
1	14
2	19
3	24
4	29
5	33
6	37
7	41
8	45
9	49
10	55
11	59
12	63
13	72
14	77
15	84

FIGURE 6.3 Sequence of pushes and pops required by RecursiveSearch when called by Search to locate 37 in array A using Split function (Lo + Hi) / 2.

a complete copy of the parameter must be allocated. For instance, in Figure 6.3, space for the array A would, in theory, be allocated in each recursive stack frame. (This is one argument for passing such an array parameter by reference instead of by value.) For those parameters that are returned from a procedure, the procedure must be passed the address of the actual argument. This is the reason the assignment of **true** to Found and 6 to Place in the top stack frame of Figure 6.3 affects the values of Found and Place in prior levels buried deeper in the stack.

   An analysis of the time and space efficiency of a recursive algorithm is dependent upon two factors. The first of these is the depth, that is, the number of levels to which recursive calls are made before reaching the condition that triggers a return without making another recursive call. Clearly, the greater the depth, the greater the number of stack frames that must be allocated and the less space-efficient the algorithm becomes. It is also clear that recursive calls to a greater depth will consume more computer time. The second factor affecting the efficiency analyses (particularly time efficiency) of recursive algorithms is the amount of resource (time or space) consumed at any given recursive level. Figure 6.4 highlights this notion of recursive programs as a hierarchy of potential recursive calls through successively deeper

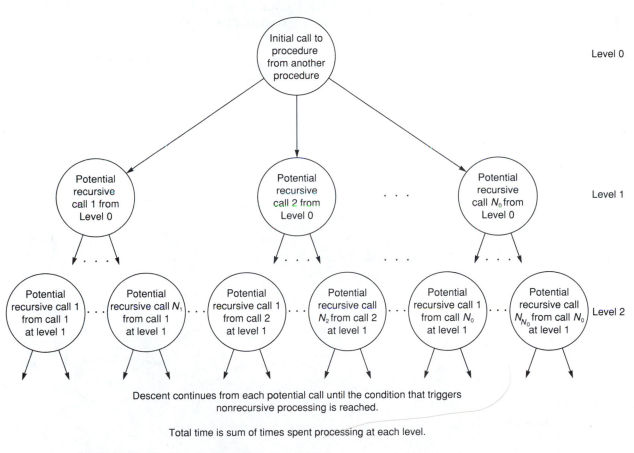

Descent continues from each potential call until the condition that triggers nonrecursive processing is reached.

Total time is sum of times spent processing at each level.

FIGURE 6.4   Generalized tree of recursive calls.

levels. A hierarchy of recursive calls such as that appearing in Figure 6.4 is called a *tree of potential recursive calls*. We shall use such trees often in analyzing recursive algorithms. Because a stack frame must be allocated at each level, the space efficiency of a recursive algorithm will be proportional to the deepest level at which a recursive call is made for a particular set of given parameter values. The time efficiency will be proportional to the sum, over all levels, of the times spent processing at each individual level. The following examples will clarify how such a tree of recursive calls can be used to analyze the time and space efficiencies of the procedure RecursiveSearch for two different choices of the Split function.

Example 6.1   Use a tree of potential recursive calls to analyze the space and time efficiency of procedure RecursiveSearch when the Split function is (Lo + Hi) / 2.

For this choice of a Split function, we have the tree of potential recursive calls that appears in Figure 6.5. For an array with 15 data items, this tree stops at level 3, as indicated in Figure 6.6. The OR's appearing in these two figures indicate that, at any given level, we will make at most one recursive call or the other, but not both. This is important (and, as we shall see, not the case for all recursive algorithms) since it implies that the work done at any given level is simply the work done at one node along that level. Clearly, the work done at any node is O(1) since we are merely comparing the Target item

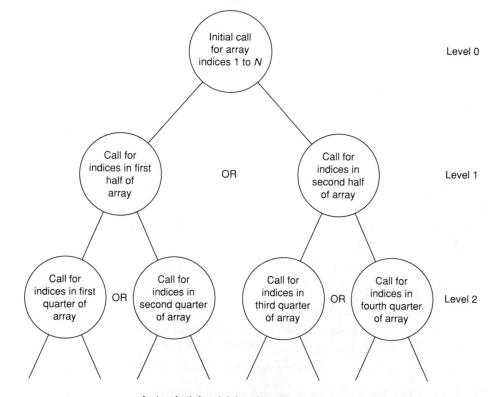

FIGURE 6.5

Tree of potential recursive calls for RecursiveSearch with Split function (Lo + Hi) / 2.

And so forth for eighths, sixteenths . . .

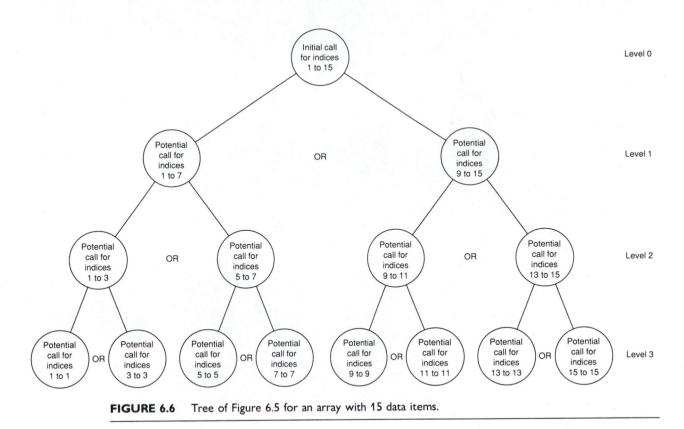

FIGURE 6.6   Tree of Figure 6.5 for an array with 15 data items.

to the data at the Guess position determined by the Split function. Hence, the time efficiency of the RecursiveSearch algorithm for this Split function will merely be proportional to the number of levels in the recursive call tree for an array with N items. From Figure 6.5 and 6.6 it is evident that doubling the number of items in the array will merely add one level to the recursive call tree. That is, the number of levels in the recursive call tree is $\log_2 N + 1$ (truncated). With the $O(1)$ work done at each level, we can thus conclude that the time efficiency of RecursiveSearch for this Split function is $O(\log_2 N)$. Similarly, since a stack frame will be allocated for each recursive level, the additional space requirements of the algorithm (beyond the array itself) are $O(\log_2 N)$.

Example 6.2   Repeat Example 6.1, but now use a Split function defined by

```
Split := Lo
```

The tree of recursive calls is shown in Figure 6.7. Note that, potentially, the number of levels in this tree will be N instead of the $\log_2 N$ figure that emerged in Example 6.1. Hence, this new choice of a Split function generates time and space efficiencies of $O(N)$.

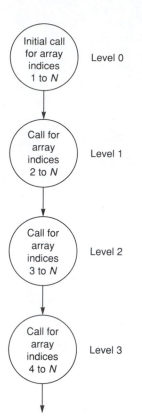

FIGURE 6.7
Tree of recursive calls
for RecursiveSearch with
Split = Lo.

The algorithm efficiency analyses carried out in the two preceding examples can also be achieved using *recurrence relations*. A recurrence relation is an equation that expresses the time or space efficiency of an algorithm for a data set of size N in terms of the efficiency of the algorithm on a smaller data set. For instance, the efficiency analysis we performed in Example 6.1 reported that the efficiency of the RecursiveSearch algorithm for the specified Split function on a data set of size N was 1 larger than the efficiency on a data set of half that size. In terms of an equation, we have

$$\text{Efficiency}(N) = \text{Efficiency}(N/2) + 1$$

Using techniques to solve explicitly such a recurrence relation, you can establish that $\text{Efficiency}(N)$ is proportional to $\log_2 N$ from the above equation—exactly the result that we obtained by our analysis of the recursive call tree. The techniques to solve explicitly such recurrence relations are covered briefly in Appendix B. We will not cover such techniques here, but we will give results arising from such techniques as needed.

Example 6.3   Develop a recurrence relation to describe the time and space efficiencies for RecursiveSearch with the Split function described in Example 6.2.

In this example, the recursive call tree implied that the efficiency of the algorithm on a data set of N items is one greater than on a data set of $N - 1$ items. That is,

$$\text{Efficiency}(N) \ = \ \text{Efficiency}(N - 1) \ + \ 1$$

Explicitly solving that recurrence relation yields the result that

$$\text{Efficiency}(N) \ = \ N$$

Again note that this approach is consistent with the efficiency we obtained directly from the recursive call tree.

Why Recursion?

At this point you could argue effectively that we have not achieved much with recursion so far in this chapter. Why? In the first two cases, at least, we merely provided recursive implementations of what we could have implemented just as easily with an iterative control structure. Moreover, these new implementations are less efficient than our previous implementation because they consume stack space without providing any savings in time. Similarly, even though our recursive algorithm for ReverseTraverse had the advantage of simplicity, an implementation that used an iterative control structure could easily have been given. Such objections are well taken. Recursion, as an alternative to straightforward iteration, is not a wise choice for an implementation strategy. What we have gained, however, by our treatment of a recursive version of the divide-and-conquer search and the Traverse operation is an initial understanding of how recursion works and how to analyze a recursive algorithm.

We shall now embark upon a discussion of some algorithms for which an ordinary iterative control structure would not be sufficient. These algorithms employ a recursive pattern that generates an intricate mix of calls and returns instead of an uninterrupted sequence of calls followed by their associated returns. In examining how such algorithms interact with the system stack, we shall observe a subtle ebb and flow as frames are pushed and popped for each recursive level. In effect, such algorithms are using recursion to gain access to the system stack operations that are associated with procedural calls and returns. In doing so, they often provide a compact and elegantly stated solution to a very complex problem.

There is an additional argument that can be made for recursion that relates to the costs of hardware and software development. In the early days of computing, the hardware was expensive, processing was slow, and computer memory was expensive and scarce. Consequently, when programmers wrote programs they did so with an inclination toward using algorithms that stressed speed of execution and economy of storage utilization over simplicity and clarity of code. Thanks to astounding advances in technology and manufacturing since those early times, the costs of hardware have continually dropped and processing rates dramatically increased. Computers having megabytes of primary memory have become commonplace—even in personal computers. At the same time, however, the human costs associated with using these computing resources (including the costs of writing, debugging, and maintaining programs) have increased to the point that they typically outweigh the costs of the hardware. One consequence of the convergence of these two economic trends was that algorithms placing a premium on execution speed and storage utilization at the expense of clarity, simplicity, maintainability, and ease of verification are not prized as they once were. It should not be surprising therefore that recursion is now seen as an important programming technique and that virtually every modern programming language supports the use of recursion.

The Towers of Hanoi Problem

The solution to the Towers of Hanoi problem represents a classic recursive algorithm. We will discuss it now to illustrate the more intricate stack manipulations that arise in a nontrivial recursive procedure. According to legend, there existed in ancient Hanoi a monastery where the monks had the painstaking task of moving a collection of N stone disks from one pillar, designated as pillar A, to another, designated as pillar C. Moreover, the relative ordering of the disks on pillar A had to be maintained as they were moved to pillar C. That is, as illustrated in Figure 6.8, the disks were to be stacked from largest to smallest, beginning from the bottom. Additionally, the monks were to observe the following rules in moving disks:

- Only one disk could be moved at a time.
- No larger disk could ever be placed on a pillar on top of a smaller disk.

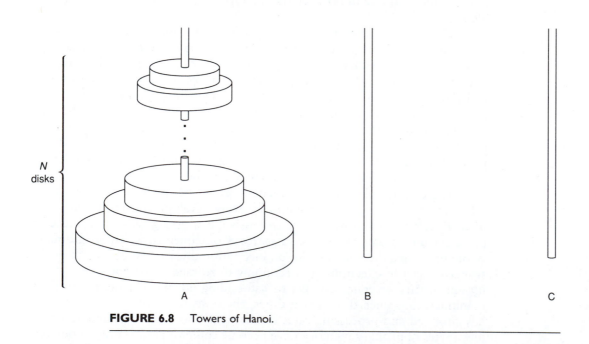

FIGURE 6.8   Towers of Hanoi.

- A third pillar B could be used as an intermediate to store one or more disks as they were being moved from their original source A to their destination C.

Consider the following recursive solution to this problem:

1. If $N = 1$, merely move the disk from A to C.
2. If $N = 2$, move first disk from A to B. Then move second disk from A to C. Then move first disk from B to C.
3. If $N = 3$, call upon the technique already established in step 2 to move the first two disks from A to B, using C as intermediate. Then move the third disk from A to C. Then use the technique in step 2 to move the first disks from B to C, using A as an intermediate.

$$\vdots$$

N. For general N, use the technique in the previous step to move $N - 1$ disks from A to B, using C as an intermediate. Then move one disk from A to C. Then use the technique in the previous step to move $N - 1$ disks from B to C, using A as an intermediate.

Notice that the technique described here calls upon itself but switches the order of parameters in so doing. This can be formalized in the following Pascal procedure. The return-point labels in the procedure are included only for later discussion purposes.

```
procedure Hanoi
  ( given N: integer            (* The number of disks to move; must be
                                   greater than or equal to 1 *);
          Source: character     (* A letter identifying the pillar disks
                                   are being moved from *);
          Destination: character (* A letter identifying the pillar disks
                                   are to be moved to *);
          Intermediate: character (* A letter identifying the pillar to be
                                   used for temporary storage *) );
  start Hanoi
    if N = 1 then
      write("Move disk from ", Source, " to ", Destination)
    else
      Hanoi(N - 1, Source, Intermediate, Destination);
      (* Return Point 1 *)
```

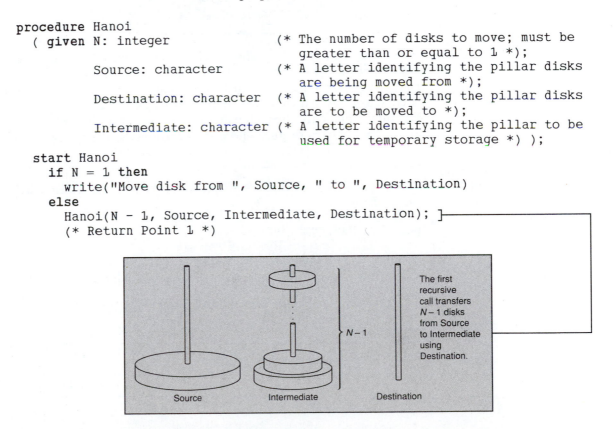

$N-1$

The first recursive call transfers $N-1$ disks from Source to Intermediate using Destination.

Source   Intermediate   Destination

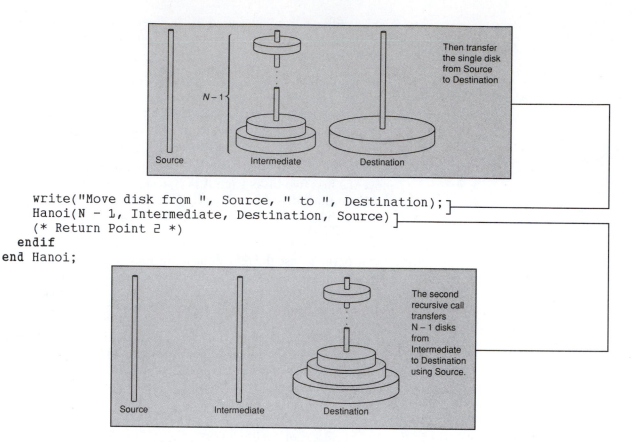

```
        write("Move disk from ", Source, " to ", Destination);
        Hanoi(N - 1, Intermediate, Destination, Source)
        (* Return Point 2 *)
    endif
end Hanoi;
```

Unlike the procedure RecursiveSearch, in which only one recursive call was made each time the procedure was invoked, procedure Hanoi will reinvoke itself twice each time it is called nontrivially. The result is a more complicated algorithm that cannot be implemented by using mere iterative control structures. Implicitly, through its recursive calls, procedure Hanoi is weaving an intricate pattern of push and pop operations on the system stack.

Example 6.4   To illustrate, we trace through the actions affecting the system stack when a call of the form

```
Hanoi(3, "A", "C", "B")
```

is initiated. The values in the return-address portion of the stack are the documentary statement labels in our Hanoi procedure.

1. We enter Hanoi with the following stack frame: N is not 1, so the condition in the **if** statement is **false**.

Original call	3	A	C	B
Return	N	Source	Destination	Intermediate

Parameters

StackFrame

2. We encounter Hanoi(N−1, Source, Intermediate, Destination) with A, B, and C as first, second, and third arguments. Because this represents a recursive call, some stacking must be done:

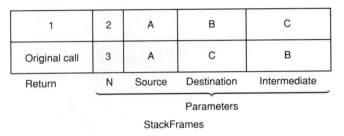

1	2	A	B	C
Original call	3	A	C	B
Return	N	Source	Destination	Intermediate

Parameters

StackFrames

3. Reenter Hanoi. Notice that as we enter this time, the procedure's view of the parameters is N = 2, Source = A, Destination = B, and Intermediate = C. Because N is not 1, the condition in the **if** statement is **false**.

4. We encounter Hanoi(N − 1, Source, Intermediate, Destination). Because this is a recursive call, stacking occurs.

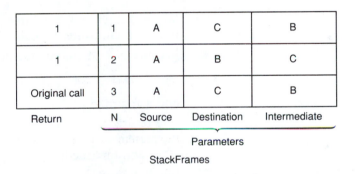

1	1	A	C	B
1	2	A	B	C
Original call	3	A	C	B
Return	N	Source	Destination	Intermediate

Parameters

StackFrames

5. We reenter Hanoi with N = 1, Source = A, Destination = C, and Intermediate = B. Because N = 1, the condition in the **if** statement is **true**.

6. Hence

```
Move disk from A to C
```

is printed and a return triggers a popping of a return address (1) and four parameters, leaving the system stack as pictured below.

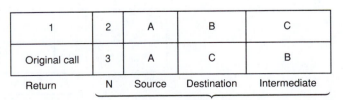

1	2	A	B	C
Original call	3	A	C	B
Return	N	Source	Destination	Intermediate

Parameters

StackFrames

7. Because the return address popped was 1

   ```
   Move disk from A to B
   ```

   is printed and

   ```
   Hanoi(N - 1, Intermediate, Destination, Source)
   ```

   is encountered with $N = 2$, Source = A, Destination = B, and Intermediate = C.

8. The call pushes a return address and four parameters onto the stack system.

   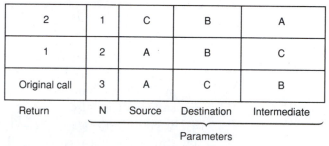

Return	N	Source	Destination	Intermediate
2	1	C	B	A
1	2	A	B	C
Original call	3	A	C	B

   Parameters

   StackFrames

9. We reenter Hanoi, this time with $N = 1$, Source = C, Destination = B, and Intermediate = A.

10. Because $N = 1$, the **if** statement generates the output

    ```
    Move disk from C to B
    ```

    and a return.

11. The return pops a frame from the system stack and we return to the statement labeled by 2 with $N = 2$, Source = A, Destination = B, and Intermediate = C.

12. But statement 2 is the end of the procedure and triggers a return itself, so a stack frame is popped again and we return to statement 1 with $N = 3$, Source = A, Destination = C, Intermediate = B.

13. Statement 1 triggers the output

    ```
    Move disk from A to C
    ```

    and we are immediately at another call:

    ```
    Hanoi(N - 1, Intermediate, Destination, Source)
    ```

    Hence, the status of the system stack is changed to

Return	N	Source	Destination	Intermediate
2	2	B	C	A
Original call	3	A	C	B

    Parameters

    StackFrames

14. We reenter Hanoi with N = 2, Source = B, Destination = C, and Intermediate = A. Because N is not 1, another call is executed and more values are stacked.

Return	N	Source	Destination	Intermediate
1	1	B	A	C
2	2	B	C	A
Original call	3	A	C	B

| | Parameters | |
| | StackFrames | |

15. Reenter Hanoi, with N = 1, Source = B, Destination = A, and Intermediate = C. Because N = 1, we print

```
Move disk from B to A
```

and return.

16. The return prompts the popping of the system stack. The return address popped is the statement labeled 1. Statement 1 causes output

```
Move disk from B to C
```

with the stack frames left at

Return	N	Source	Destination	Intermediate
2	2	B	C	A
Original call	3	A	C	B

| | Parameters | |
| | StackFrames | |

17. The output from statement 1 is followed by

```
Hanoi(N - 1, Intermediate, Destination, Source)
```

Hence, pushed onto the stack is

Return	N	Source	Destination	Intermediate
2	1	A	C	B
2	2	B	C	A
Original call	3	A	C	B

| | Parameters | |
| | StackFrames | |

18. Reenter (for the last time) Hanoi, with N = 1, Source = A, Destination = C, and Intermediate = B. Because N = 1, output

```
Move disk from A to C
```

and return.

19. But now the return pops return-address 2 from the stack, so return to statement 2 with the system stack given by

2	2	B	C	A
Original call	3	A	C	B
Return	N	Source	Destination	Intermediate

Parameters

StackFrames

20. Statement 2 is another return, so pop the stack again. The return address popped is 2, the same return statement. But this time the return will transfer control back to the original calling location and *we are done!*

Long-winded as this example is, you must understand it. Recursive procedures are crucial to many of the algorithms used in computer science, and you can acquire the necessary familiarity with recursion only by convincing yourself that it really works. If you have some doubt or are not sure you understand, we recommend that you trace through the Hanoi procedure with N = 4 (and be prepared to go through a lot of paper).

The analysis carried out in the next example will demonstrate that the Hanoi algorithm falls into the class of exponential algorithms defined in Section 1.2. This is the first exponential algorithm we have encountered. Recall from our discussion of algorithm efficiency in Section 1.2 that such algorithms are impractical to run for even moderate values of N. We shall return to a consideration of exponential algorithms in Chapter 10, where we will explore attempts at using *heuristics* to transform such algorithms into nonexponential $O(N^k)$ algorithms for a reasonable choice of k.

Example 6.6   Use the tree of recursive calls generated by procedure Hanoi to analyze the time and space efficiency of the algorithm.

A graphic of this tree is given in Figure 6.9. The most important difference between this tree and those used to analyze the procedure RecursiveSearch in Figures 6.5 and 6.6 is that the two nodes (representing calls) descending from each node are linked by an AND instead of an OR. This is to emphasize that, when N is not 1, *both* recursive calls will be made instead of just one, as was the case with RecursiveSearch. This difference has a rather

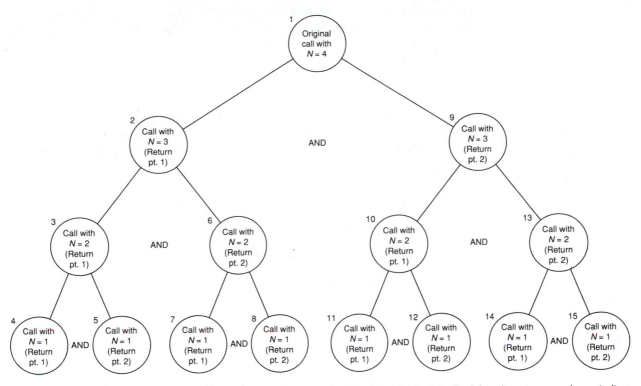

FIGURE 6.9   Tree of recursive calls for procedure Hanoi with N originally 4 (numbers in parentheses indicate order of recursive calls).

dramatic effect on the time efficiency of the algorithm. In particular, calling Hanoi initially with N = 4 results in a total of 15 calls in the recursive call tree. The numbers outside the circles in Figure 6.9 indicate the order in which these 15 call are made. Increasing to N = 5 would add a level with 16 nodes to the recursive call tree. In general, adding one disk adds only one level to the recursive call tree but doubles (plus 1) the number of nodes in the tree. This implies that the space efficiency of Hanoi relative to the system stack is $O(N)$, but, since *every* call in the recursive call tree will be made, the time efficiency is $O(2^N)$.

The recurrence relation to express the time efficiency of the Hanoi algorithm is

$$\text{Efficiency}(N) = 2 \times \text{Efficiency}(N - 1) + 1$$

An explicit solution of this relation with Efficiency (1) = 1 is $2^N - 1$. As in Example 6.3, observe that explicitly solving a recurrence relation yields an efficiency result consistent with that obtained by examining the recursive call tree.

In this section, our primary goal has been to establish a high degree of confidence in recursion as a problem-solving technique. As such, our examples have not been chosen with practical application in mind but rather to illustrate, in detail, how recursion works. We have also discussed how recursive call trees or, alternately, recurrence relations may be used to analyze the efficiency of recursive algorithms. Given the foundation established in this section, we shall now examine applications of recursion to sorting and parsing in the remainder of the chapter.

Exercises 6.1

1. Write a nonrecursive PSEUDO algorithm for the procedure ReverseTraversal, defined in this section. Assume a singly linked list implementation of an ordered list.

2. Consider the following two versions of the parameterless procedure Forever. Provide implementations of both versions of Forever in your favorite programming language. Then call on each version from a program that you run on your system. Do you observe any differences in run-time behavior of the two versions? Explain your observations in a written statement.

   Version 1

   ```
   procedure Forever;
    start Forever
       while true do
       endwhile
    end Forever;
   ```

   Version 2

   ```
   procedure Forever;
    start Forever
       Forever
    end Forever;
   ```

3. Consider the following recursive function and associated top-level call. Comments of the form (* Return Point N *) label possible return points from recursive calls. What would a stack frame for this function contain? By means of a series of stack "snapshots," show how the stack would be manipulated for the calls indicated. Finally, provide the recursive call tree and output that would be generated as this function was called from the top level.

   ```
   function Weird
     ( given M, N: integer (* Two non-negative integers *);
       return: integer );
     start Weird
       write (M, N);
       if M = 0 then
         Weird := N + 1
       elsif N = 0 then
         Weird := Weird(M - 1, 1)
                  (* Return Point 1 *)
       else
         Weird := Weird(M - 1,        Weird(M, N - 1))
                  (* Return Point 3 *)  (* Return Point 2 *)
       endif
     end Weird;
   ```

   Top-level call

   ```
   write(Weird(1, 3))
   (* Identify this as Return Point 0 *)
   ```

4. Write a recursive PSEUDO procedure that reads characters from an input line and prints the characters reversed from their order of entry.

5. Write a recursive version of the insertion sort algorithm.

6. The *Fibonacci sequence* is a sequence of integers, starting with two 1's, such that each member of the sequence is the sum of the two previous numbers. Thus, the first seven terms in the Fibonacci sequence are

$$1\ 1\ 2\ 3\ 5\ 8\ 13\dots$$

Use a tree of recursive calls to analyze the time and space efficiency of the following function to compute the Nth Fibonacci number. What is the recurrence relation that describes this efficiency? Try to explicitly solve this recurrence relation (provided that you have studied techniques to solve recurrence relations in a discrete mathematics course).

```
function Fibonacci
( given N: integer (* A positive integer *);
  return: integer  (* The Nth number in the Fibonacci
                      sequence *) );
start Fibonacci
  if N = 1 or N = 2 then
    Fibonacci := 1
  else
    Fibonacci := Fibonacci(N - 1) + Fibonacci(N - 2)
  endif
end Fibonacci;
```

7. Write a *recursive* function to compute the Nth Fibonacci number in a fashion that is significantly more time-efficient than the function provided in the preceding exercise. Analyze the time and space efficiency of your function.

8. Euclid devised a clever algorithm for computing the greatest common divisor of two integers. According to Euclid's algorithm,

$$GCD(M, N) = \begin{cases} GCD(M, N) & \text{if } N > M \\ M & \text{if } N = 0 \\ GCD(N, M \bmod N) & \text{if } N > 0 \end{cases}$$

Write a recursive function to compute greatest common divisors via Euclid's method. Analyze the time and space efficiency of your algorithm.

9. Using the operations for the string ADT discussed in Section 2.2, write a recursive function that is given a string S and returns the reversal of S. For example, given S = "PEACH", your function should return the string "HCAEP". Analyze the time and space efficiency of your function.

6.2 QUICK SORT

In Section 1.3 we introduced the divide-and-conquer technique and applied it in searching an ordered array. Then, in Section 6.1, we saw how that same divide-and-conquer search strategy could be implemented recursively. With searching, the recursive implementation proved to be less efficient than a straightforward iterative implementation. However, we are now ready to take a recursive leap. We shall see that by considering divide-and-conquer strategies for sorting we can break the $O(n^2)$ and $O(n\,(\log_2 n)^2)$ barriers we encountered when studying the insertion, selection, and Shell sort algorithms in Chapter 1. Moreover, because such divide-and-conquer techniques applied to sorting are considerably more complex than their searching counterparts, there is no choice other than to implement them recursively. (Actually, any recursive algorithm can be converted to a nonrecursive implementation using your own stack and the technique discussed in Problem 15 at the end of this chapter. However, essentially, such nonrecursive versions replace the system stack with a programmer-implemented stack and consequently achieve no real savings in time or space efficiency.)

The first such divide-and-conquer sorting algorithm we will examine is *quick sort*. The essence of the quick sort algorithm is to rely on a subordinate algorithm to partition the array. The process of partitioning involves moving a data item, called the *pivot,* in the correct direction just enough for it to reach its final place in the array. The partitioning process, therefore, reduces unnecessary interchanges and potentially moves the pivot a great distance in the array without forcing it to be swapped into intermediate locations.

Once the pivot item is chosen, moves are made so that data items to the left of the pivot are less than (or equal to) it; whereas those to the right are greater (or equal). The pivot item is thus in its correct position. The quick sort algorithm then recursively applies the partitioning process to the two parts of the array on either side of the pivot until the entire array is sorted. In the next example, we illustrate the mechanics of this partitioning logic by applying it to an array of numbers.

Example 6.7   Suppose the array A contains integers initially arranged as

15 20 5 8 95 12 80 17 9 55

Figure 6.10 shows a partition pass applied to this array. The following steps are involved:

1. Remove the first data item, 15, as the pivot, mark its position, and scan the array from right to left, comparing data item values with 15. When you find the first smaller value, remove it from its current position and put it in position A[1]. (This is shown in line 2.)
2. Scan line 2 from left to right beginning with position A[2], comparing data item values with 15. When you find the first value greater than 15, extract it and store it in the position marked by parentheses in line 2. (This is shown in line 3.)
3. Begin the right-to-left scan of line 3 with position A[8] and look for a value smaller than 15. When you find it, extract it and store it in the position marked by the parentheses in line 3. (This is shown in line 4.)
4. Begin scanning line 4 from left to right at position A[3]. Find a value greater than 15, remove it, mark its position, and store it inside the parentheses in line 4. (This is shown in line 5.)

Line number	A[1]	A[2]	A[3]	A[4]	A[5]	A[6]	A[7]	A[8]	A[9]	A[10]
1	15*	20	5	8	95	12	80	17	9	55 ←
2	9	20 →	5	8	95	12	80	17	( )	55
3	9	( )	5	8	95	12	80	17 ←	20	55
4	9	12	5 →	8	95	( )	80	17	20	55
5	9	12	5	8	( ) ←	95	80	17	20	55
6	9	12	5	8	15	95	80	17	20	55

Pivot 15

FIGURE 6.10
Each call to QuickSort partitions an array segment. The asterisk indicates the pivot value (here 15), and the arrows indicate the starting place for a scan and the direction of the scan. The parenthesis indicate where a value will be placed following a scan.

5. Now, when you attempt to scan line 5 from right to left, you are immediately at a parenthesized position—A[5]. This is the location to put the first data item, 15. (This is shown in line 6.) At this stage, 15 is in its correct place relative to the final sorted array.

Notice that all values to the left of 15 are less than 15, and all values to the right of 15 are greater than 15. The method will still work if two values are the same. The process can now be applied recursively to the two segments of the array on the left and right of 15.

Notice that these recursive calls eventually result in the sorting of the entire array. The result of any one call to procedure QuickSort is merely to partition a segment of the array so that the pivotal item is positioned with everything to its left being less than or equal to it and everything to its right being greater than or equal.

The procedure Partition that follows achieves one partitioning pass in the overall QuickSort algorithm as described in Example 6.7. The indices Lo and Hi represent the pointers that move from the left and right, respectively, until they meet at the appropriate location for the pivot. The pivotal value is initially chosen to be Key[Lo]. Later we will discuss the possible implications of choosing a different pivotal value. Note that it is crucial for Partition to return in PivotPoint the position where the pivotal value was finally inserted. This information will allow the QuickSort procedure that calls upon Partition to determine whether or not a base case has been reached.

```
type  (* Assume IndexLimit is constant determining array size *)
   ElementType: (* May be anything with an order relationship between elements *);
   ElementArray: array [IndexLimit] of ElementType;
   Comparison: function
             ( given A, B: ElementType  (* Values to compare *);
              return: boolean            (* true if A precedes B in the order
                                            relationship on ElementType; false
                                            otherwise *) );
```

```
procedure Partition
  ( given A: ElementArray        (* Array with at most IndexLimit entries *);
          Lo, Hi: integer        (* Array indices with  0 <= Lo <= Hi
                                     <= IndexLimit *);
          Precedes: Comparison   (* Order relationship on ElementType *);
    return A: ElementArray        (* Using A[Lo] as the pivotal value, array A is
                                     returned in partitioned form. That is, entries
                                     between indices Lo and Hi inclusive are
                                     arranged so that all values to the left
                                     of the pivot precede (or equal) the pivot
                                     according to Precedes parameter, and the
                                     pivot precedes (or equals) all value located
                                     to its right *);
          PivotPoint: integer    (* Contains final location of pivot value *) );
```

```
var Pivot: ElementType;

start Partition
  Pivot := A[Lo];
  while Lo < Hi do
    (* Begin right-to-left scan *)
    while Precedes(Pivot, A[Hi]) and Lo < Hi do
      Hi := Hi - 1
    endwhile;
    if Hi <> Lo then  (* Move entry indexed by Hi to left side of partition *)
      A[Lo] := A[Hi];
      Lo := Lo + 1
    endif;
    (* Begin left-to-right scan *)
    while Precedes(A[Lo], Pivot) and Lo < Hi do
      Lo := Lo + 1
    endwhile;
    if Hi <> Lo then (* Move entry indexed by Lo to right side of
                        partition *)
      A[Hi] := A[Lo];
      Hi := Hi - 1
    endif
  endwhile;  (* while Lo < Hi *)
  (* Lo and Hi met somewhere between their initial setting *)
  A[Hi] := Pivot;
  PivotPoint := Hi
end Partition;
```

See the illustration at the top of page 263.

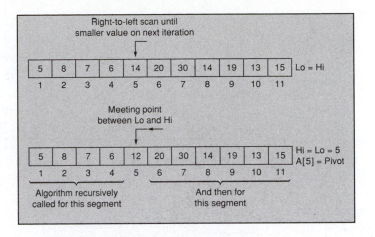

Given the previous Partition procedure, QuickSort itself must call on Partition and then use the returned value of PivotPoint to decide whether or not recursive calls are necessary to perform more refined partitioning of the segment to the left and right of PivotPoint. The recursive logic for this decision is given in the following procedure QuickSort. Partition would be incorporated as a subordinate local procedure within QuickSort.

```
procedure QuickSort
   ( given A: ElementArray       (* Array with at most IndexLimit entries *);
          Lo, Hi: integer        (* Array indices with 0 <= Lo <= Hi
                                    <= IndexLimit *);
          Precedes: Comparison   (* An order relationship on ElementType *);
     return A: ElementArray       (* The array of values between indices Lo and Hi
                                    arranged in order according to Precedes
                                    relation *) );

   var PivotPoint: integer;

   start QuickSort
      Partition(A, Lo, Hi, Precedes, PivotPoint);
      (* Recursive calls partition left and right segments *)
      if Lo < PivotPoint then
         QuickSort(Key, Lo, PivotPoint - 1, Precedes)
      endif;
      if Hi > PivotPoint then
         QuickSort(Key, PivotPoint + 1, Hi, Precedes)
      endif
   end QuickSort;
```

For instance, after the first call to QuickSort for a partitioning pass on the data in Figure 6.10, we would then recursively call on QuickSort with Lo = 1 and Hi = 4. This would trigger deeper-level recursive calls from which we would ultimately return, knowing that the segment of the array between indices 1 and 5 is now sorted. This return would be followed by a recursive call to QuickSort with Lo = 6 and Hi = 10.

The entire tree of recursive calls to QuickSort for the data of Figure 6.10 is given in Figure 6.11. Trace through the procedure to verify this call-return pattern.

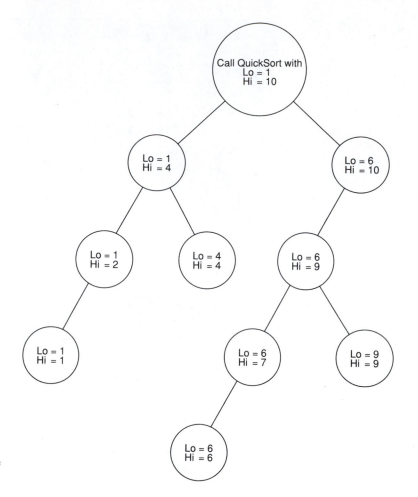

FIGURE 6.11
Tree of (recursive) calls to
QuickSort for data in Figure
6.10.

Finally, to maintain compatibility with the Sort interface established in Section 1.2, the Sort procedure itself now becomes a trivial front end that passes an index range of 1 to N to QuickSort.

```
procedure Sort (* Quick sort implementation *)
  ( given A: ElementArray      (* Array with at most IndexLimit entries *);
          N: integer           (* Number of entries. Assume 1 <= N
                                   <= IndexLimit *);
        Precedes: Comparison   (* An order relationship on elements in A *);
    return A: ElementArray      (* The array of values arranged in order
                                   according to Precedes relation *) );

  start Sort
    QuickSort(A, 1, N, Precedes)
  end Sort;
```

Efficiency of the Quick Sort

The average run-time efficiency of the quick sort is $O(n \log_2 n)$. In Chapter 12, we will demonstrate that, in a sense, no sort can do better than this.

In the best case, it is quite easy to provide a rationale for this $O(n \log_2 n)$ figure. This best case occurs when each array segment recursively passed to QuickSort partitions at its midpoint; that is, the appropriate location for each pivotal value in the series of recursive calls is the midpoint of the segment being partitioned. In this case,

1 call to QuickSort (the first) is made with a segment of size n.
2 calls to QuickSort are made with segments of size $n/2$.
4 calls to QuickSort are made with segments of size $n/4$.
8 calls to QuickSort are made with segments of size $n/8$.
.
.
.
n calls to QuickSort are made with segments of size 1.

overall $\log_2 n$ levels

Since each call with a segment of size m requires $O(m)$ comparisons, it is clear that k calls with segments of size n/k will require $O(n)$ comparisons. Hence, the total number of comparisons resulting from the preceding sequence of calls will be $O(n \log_2 n)$.

If segments partition away from the midpoint, the efficiency of quick sort begins to deteriorate. In the worst-case situation, when the array is already sorted, the efficiency of the quick sort may drop down to $O(n^2)$ owing to the continuous right-to-left scan all the way to the last left boundary. That is, the recursive call tree will appear as in Figure 6.12. In the exercises at the end of the section, you will explore how the worst-case situation is affected by your choice of the pivotal element.

The recurrence relation that expresses the best-case efficiency is

$$\text{Efficiency}(N) = 2 \times \text{Efficiency}(N/2) + N$$

That is, to quick sort N values when they partition at the midpoint, we must make N comparisons during a partitioning pass and then (recursively) quick sort two segments of size $N/2$. An explicit solution of this recurrence relation yields an $O(n \log_2 n)$ result—consistent with the analysis we obtained from the recursive call tree.

Exercises 6.2

1. Consider the procedure QuickSort given in this section. Suppose that we were to insert the following tracer output immediately at the beginning of this procedure.

```
write(Lo, Hi);
for K := Lo to Hi do
   write(A[K])
endfor;
```

What would we see as output from these tracers if we were to call on Quick-Sort with the array initially containing the following seven entries?

60 12 90 30 64 8 6

Draw the tree of recursive calls that results from this particular data.

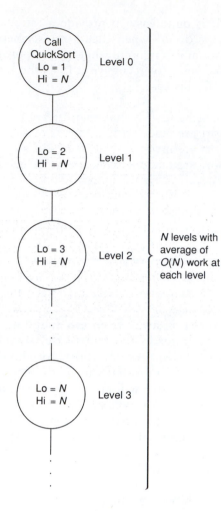

FIGURE 6.12

Recursive call tree for the quick sort's worst case.

2. Repeat Exercise 1 for a six-element array that initially contains

1 8 2 7 3 6

3. When is insertion sort better than quick sort as presented in this section?

4. When is selection sort better than quick sort as presented in this section?

5. Under what circumstances would you not use the quick sort from this section?

6. How does the choice of the pivotal value affect the efficiency of the quick sort algorithm? Suppose that the middle value or the last value in a segment to be partitioned were chosen as the pivotal value. How would this alter the nature of best-case and worst-case data sets? Give examples to illustrate your answer.

7. Develop trees of procedure calls to QuickSort for a variety of test data sets (analogous to what was done in Figure 6.11). Use these trees to analyze the efficiency of QuickSort. What types of data sets yield $O(n \log_2 n)$ efficiency? What types yield $O(n^2)$ efficiency? Can you reach a conclusion about how "far" from the best case a data set may wander before it becomes closer to $O(n^2)$ than $O(n \log_2 n)$? You will explore this last question experimentally in the problems/projects at the end of the chapter.

8. In Section 2.3, PointerSort used an index of pointers to sort data logically without rearranging it. Adapt the pointer sort procedure to the quick sort algorithm.

9. Suppose that the index for the pivot value is chosen at random between Lo and Hi, inclusive. How does this affect the efficiency of the quick sort algorithm? Do best-case and worst-case data sets exist for this strategy? Explain.

10. A sorting method is called *stable* if two data items of the same value are guaranteed not to be rearranged with respect to each other as the algorithm progresses. For example, in the four-element array

$$60 \ 42_1 \ 80 \ 42_2$$

a stable sorting method would guarantee a final order of

$$42_1 \ 42_2 \ 60 \ 80$$

Classify each of the insertions, selection, radix, Shell, and quick sort algorithms as to their stability. If you claim that a particular algorithm is not stable, be sure to provide an example data set to justify your claim. (To see why stability may be important, see Programming Problems 4 and 5 at the end of the chapter.)

11. Using trees of recursive calls, analyze the best- and worst-case space efficiency of the quick sort algorithm presented in this section.

6.3 MERGE SORT

Another recursive sorting algorithm is *merge* sort. Unlike quick sort, merge sort can guarantee $O(n \log_2 n)$ efficiency. However, in its average run time, it is usually somewhat slower than quick sort. Moreover, as we shall see, it is considerably less space-efficient than quick sort.

The essential idea behind *merge sort* is to make repeated use of a procedure that merges two lists, each already in ascending order, into a third list, also arranged in ascending order. The merge procedure itself only requires sequential access to the lists. Its logic is similar to the method you would use if you were merging two sorted piles of index cards into a third pile. That is, start with the first card from each pile. Compare them to see which one comes first, transfer that one over to the third pile, and advance to the next card in that pile. Repeat the comparison, transfer, and advance operations until one of the piles runs out of cards. At that point, merely move what is left of the remaining pile over to the third merged pile.

This logic is reflected in the generalized Merge procedure that follows. For reasons that will become apparent when we incorporate it into a full sorting procedure, this version of Merge begins with the two sorted lists stored in one array. The first list runs from subscript Lower to Mid of array Source. The second runs from subscript Mid + 1 to Upper of the same array. The merging of the two lists is generated in a second array Destination.

```
type  (* Assume IndexLimit is constant determining array size *)
  ElementType:  (* May be anything with an order relationship between
                   elements *);
  ElementArray: array [IndexLimit] of ElementType;
  Comparison: function
                  ( given A, B: ElementType (* Values to compare *);
                    return: boolean         (* true if A precedes B in the order
                                               relationship on ElementType; false
                                               otherwise *) );

procedure Merge
  ( given Source: ElementType        (* Array with at most IndexLimit entries.
                                         Assume that array is arranged in order
                                         by Precedes parameter between indices
                                         Lower...Mid and Mid + 1...Upper,
                                         respectively *);
          Lower, Mid, Upper: integer (* Array indices with 1 <= Lower
                                         <= Mid <= Upper <= IndexLimit *);
          Precedes: Comparison       (* An order relationship on
                                         ElementType *);
    return Destination: ElementArray (* Merged array containing the values from
                                         Source arranged in order according to
                                         Precedes relation *) );

  var S1, S2, D: integer; (*  Pointers into two Source lists and
                              Destination *)

start Merge
  (* Initialize pointers *)
  S1 := Lower;
  S2 := Mid + 1;
  D := Lower;
  (* Repeat comparison of current item from each list *)
  repeat
    if Precedes(Source[S1], Source[S2]) then
      Destination[D] := Source[S1];
      S1 := S1 + 1
    else
      Destination[D] := Source[S2];
      S2 := S2 + 1
    endif;
    D := D + 1
  until S1 > Mid or S2 > Upper;
  (* Move what is left of remaining list *)
  if S1 > Mid then
    repeat
      Destination[D] := Source[S2];
      S2 := S2 + 1;
      D := D + 1
    until S2 > Upper
  else
    repeat
      Destination[D] := Source[S1];
```

```
      S1 := S1 + 1;
      D := D + 1
    until S1 > Mid
  endif
end Merge;
```

Clearly, Merge is an $O(n)$ algorithm where n is the number of items in the two lists to be merged. A question remains: how can Merge be used to actually sort an entire array? To answer this we need another procedure called MergeSort that will take the values in indices Lower through Upper of an array Source and arrange them in ascending order in subscripts Lower through Upper of another array called Destination. Notice that MergeSort is itself almost a sorting procedure except that it produces a sorted list in a second array instead of actually transforming the array it originally receives. Our recursive use of MergeSort will be to obtain two sorted half-length sequences from our original array.

Then we will use the Merge procedure we have already developed to merge the two sorted half-length sequences back into the original array. Of course, this merely defers our original question of how to use Merge to sort, because now we are faced with the question of how MergeSort will be able to produce two sorted half-length sequences. This is where recursion enters the picture. To produce a sorted half-length sequence, we use Merge-Sort to produce two sorted quarter-length sequences and apply Merge to the results. Similarly, the quarter-length sequences are produced by calling on MergeSort to produce sorted eighth-length sequences and apply Merge to the results. The terminating condition for this descent into shorter and shorter ordered sequences is reached when MergeSort receives a sequence of length 1.

Given the crucial MergeSort procedure, the Sort procedure itself is almost trivial. It need merely create a copy of the array to be sorted and then call on MergeSort to sort the elements of the copy into the original. Note that because MergeSort continually calls on Merge and Merge cannot do its work within one array, the need to create a copy of the original array is unavoidable. Complete PSEUDO versions of Sort and MergeSort follow:

```
procedure MergeSort
  ( given  Source: ElementArray      (* Array with at most IndexLimit entries *);
           Destination: ElementArray (* Array with values identical
                                         to those in Source *);

           Lower, Upper: integer     (* Array indices with 1 <= Lower <= Upper
                                         <= IndexLimit *);

           Precedes: Comparison      (* An order relationship on ElementType *);
    return Destination: ElementArray (* Array containing the values from
                                         Source arranged in order according to
                                         Precedes relation *) );

  var Mid: integer;

  start MergeSort
    if Lower <> Upper then (* Recursively call to get smaller sorted segments,
                              which are then merged *)
```

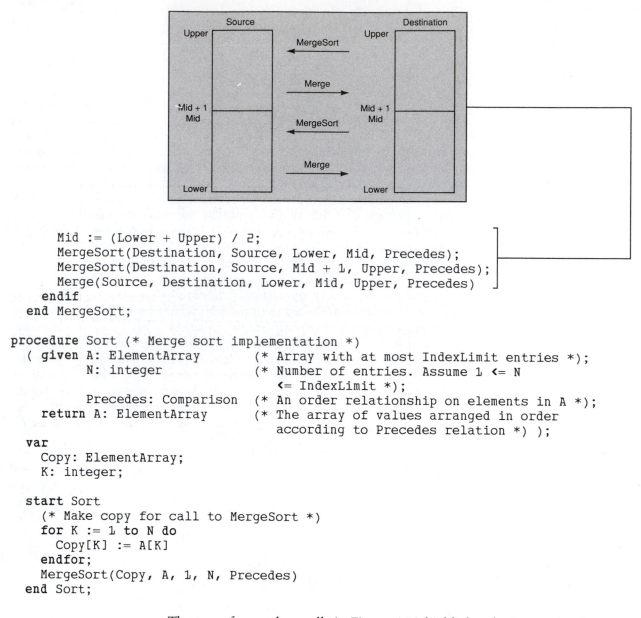

```
        Mid := (Lower + Upper) / 2;
        MergeSort(Destination, Source, Lower, Mid, Precedes);
        MergeSort(Destination, Source, Mid + 1, Upper, Precedes);
        Merge(Source, Destination, Lower, Mid, Upper, Precedes)
    endif
end MergeSort;

procedure Sort (* Merge sort implementation *)
  ( given A: ElementArray       (* Array with at most IndexLimit entries *);
         N: integer             (* Number of entries. Assume 1 <= N
                                    <= IndexLimit *);
         Precedes: Comparison   (* An order relationship on elements in A *);
   return A: ElementArray       (* The array of values arranged in order
                                    according to Precedes relation *) );

  var
    Copy: ElementArray;
    K: integer;

  start Sort
    (* Make copy for call to MergeSort *)
    for K := 1 to N do
      Copy[K] := A[K]
    endfor;
    MergeSort(Copy, A, 1, N, Precedes)
  end Sort;
```

The tree of procedure calls in Figure 6.13 highlights the interaction between MergeSort and Merge triggered by calling Sort with a simple array of size N = 11. The leaf nodes in this tree represent the recursive termination condition reached when Lower = Upper.

Efficiency Analysis of Merge Sort

From a tree of procedure calls such as that appearing in Figure 6.13, it is quite easy to deduce that merge sort requires $O(n \log_2 n)$ comparisons. The reasoning required for this deduction is as follows. All the merge operations across any given level of the tree will require $O(n)$ comparisons. There are $O(\log_2 n)$ levels to the tree of procedure calls. Hence, the overall efficiency

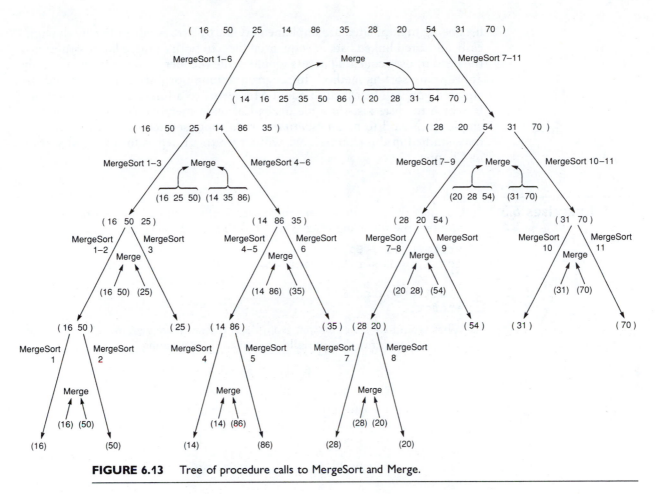

FIGURE 6.13   Tree of procedure calls to MergeSort and Merge.

is the product $O(n \log_2 n)$. Notice that, unlike the quick sort, the merge sort can guarantee this efficiency regardless of the original data. That is, there is no worst case that can cause its efficiency to deteriorate (as there is for quick sort). The tree of recursion calls will always have the same shape.

The price paid for using merge sort is in the memory space it requires. Of course, there is the stack space associated with recursion. More important, however, is the need for a duplicate copy of the array being sorted. In applications where the original array barely fits in memory, this space requirement will make merge sort totally impractical.

As steep as the memory price is, there is an added benefit to merge sort that makes it the only possible choice for certain applications: merge sort may be written in a way that necessitates only sequential access to the lists being manipulated. As we have presented it here, random access is required at only one point in the algorithm, namely, in the Merge procedure to access the second list beginning at index (Mid + 1) of Source. The need for this could have been eliminated by having Merge work with two separate source arrays. That is, we would merge ordered arrays Source1 and Source2 into Destination. This would be very costly with arrays because it would necessitate using three arrays to sort one array. However, it is less costly when the lists being manipulated are implemented not by arrays but rather by dynamically allocated linked lists or sequential files. In both of these latter situations, the need to use sequential access would make the merge sort strategy the only appropriate sorting method. In the programming problems at the end of the chapter, you will be asked to adapt MergeSort to a linked list. For situations in which the list exists in a file instead of main memory, the sorting method employed is said to be an *external sort* (as opposed to the *internal sorts* we have studied in this chapter). We will return to strategies for external sorting in Chapter 12.

Exercises 6.3

1. Consider the procedure MergeSort given in this section. Suppose that we were to insert the following tracer output at the beginning of this procedure.

```
write(Lower, Upper);
for K := Lower to Upper do (* K declared as scratch
                                        variable *)
   write(Source[K])
endfor;
```

   What would we see as output from these tracers if we were to call on Merge-Sort with an array that initially contained the following?

   60 12 90 30 64 8 6

   Provide the tree of recursive calls for this data set.

2. Repeat Exercise 1 for a six-element array that initially contains

   1 8 2 7 3 6

3. In Section 2.3, PointerSort used an index of pointers to sort data logically without rearranging it. Adapt the pointer sort procedure to the merge sort algorithm.

4. Identify and give an example of best-case and worst-case data sets for the merge sort algorithm.

5. Exercise 9 in Section 6.2 defined the notion of a stable sorting method. Is merge sort a stable sorting method? Justify your answer.

6. You are to sort an array in a program in which the following considerations are to be taken into account. First, there is a large amount of data to be sorted. The amount of data to be sorted is so large that frequent $O(n^2)$ run times will prove unsatisfactory. The amount of data will also make it impossible to use a large amount of overhead data (for example, stack space) to make the sort efficient in its run time because the overhead data would potentially take up space needed by the array. Second, you are told that the array to be sorted is often nearly in order to start with. For each of the six sorting methods listed, specify whether or not that method would be appropriate for this application and, in a brief statement, explain why your answer is correct.

   a. Insertion sort
   b. Selection sort
   c. Shell sort
   d. Quick sort
   e. Radix sort
   f. Merge sort

6.4 RECURSIVE DESCENT PARSING

In Section 5.3 we studied the parsing of infix algebraic expressions by the use of a stack and appropriate infix and stack priority functions. However, that parsing algorithm emphasized the conversion of the infix expression into a postfix expression and assumed that it had been given a syntactically valid infix expression. A problem equally important in parsing is the detection of syntax errors in the expression to be processed. One method of error detection, called *recursive descent parsing,* relies heavily upon recursive procedures. The inspiration for such recursive procedures comes from the linguistic concept of a *context-free grammar,* which provides a rigorous formalism for defining the syntax of expressions and other programming-language constructs, a formalism similar to that found in the syntax diagram of Figure 6.1. The scope of context-free grammars goes far beyond what we will cover in one section of this text. If your interest is aroused by the following discussion, we encourage you to consult *Crafting a Compiler* by Charles N. Fischer and Richard J. LeBlanc, Benjamin/Cummings, Menlo Park, CA, 1988.

A context-free grammar is composed of the following three elements.

1. A set of *terminals.* These terminals represent the *tokens*—characters, or groups of characters that logically belong together, such as operator symbols, delimiters, keywords, variable names—that ultimately compose the expression being parsed. In the case of infix algebraic expressions, the terminals would be variables, numeric constants, parentheses, and the various operators that are allowed.

2. A set of *nonterminals.* These nonterminals represent the various grammatical constructs within the language we are parsing. In particular, one nonterminal is designated as the *start symbol* for the grammar.

3. A set of *productions.* The productions are formal rules defining the syntactical composition of the nonterminals from point 2. The productions take the form:

Nonterminal → String of terminals and/or nonterminals

We say that the nonterminal on the left of such a production *derives* the string on the right.

An example of a context-free grammar should help to clarify this three-part definition.

Example 6.8   Provide a context-free grammar for infix algebraic expressions involving addition and multiplication and show how the particular expression A + B * C is derived from it.

1. Set of terminals:

```
{ '+', '*', '(', ')', identifier, number }
```

2. Set of nonterminals:

    { **<expression>**, **<factor>**, **<add-factor>**, **<mult-factor>**, **<primary>** }

    where <expression> is designated as the start symbol. Note that, by convention, nonterminals are enclosed in angle brackets to distinguish them from terminals.

3. Set of productions:
    a. <expression>   → <factor><add-factor>
    b. <factor>   → <primary><mult-factor>
    c. <add-factor>   → '+' <factor><add-factor>
    d. <add-factor>   → NULL
    e. <mult-factor> → '*' <primary><mult-factor>
    f. <mult-factor> → NULL
    g. <primary>   → identifier
    h. <primary>   → number
    i. <primary>   → '(' <expression> ')'

The symbol NULL is used to indicate the empty string. In effect, this implies that one defining option for <add-factor> and <mult-factor> is the empty string. We shall see why this is necessary in the derivation of A + B * C, which follows. As shown in Figure 6.14, the expressions defined by this set of productions could also have been presented using syntax diagrams.

To derive a particular infix expression, we begin with the start symbol <expression>. The production that defines <expression> says that <expression> must be <factor> followed by <add-factor>. Hence, we must

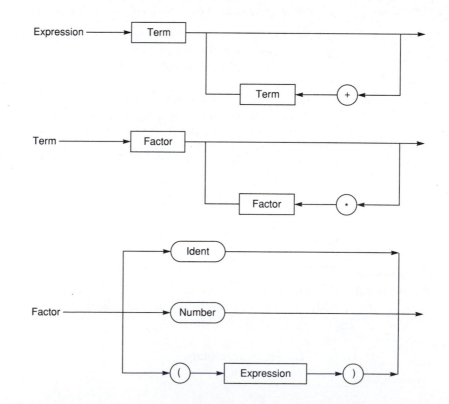

FIGURE 6.14

Expressions defined by the grammar of Example 6.8 depicted with syntax diagrams.

now try to derive these two nonterminals. This process of involving nonterminals in the definition of other nonterminals continues until we finally reach those nonterminals that are defined by the terminals in the infix expression being parsed. Thus, a formal derivation of A + B * C is given by

<expression> → <factor><add-factor>	By production a
→ <primary><mult-factor><add-factor>	By production b
→ A <mult-factor><add-factor>	By production g
→ A <add-factor>	By production f
→ A + <factor><add-factor>	By production c
→ A + <primary><mult-factor><add-factor>	By production b
→ A + B <mult-factor><add-factor>	By production g
→ A + B * <primary><mult-factor><add-factor>	By production e
→ A + B * C <mult-factor><add-factor>	By production g
→ A + B * C	By productions d and f

Note that there is a hint of recursion in the grammar of Example 6.8 in that some of the productions defining <add-factor> and <mult-factor> use these same nonterminals in their definitional pattern on the right of the production being defined. As the next example will show, it is this recursive portion of the definition that allows us to add arbitrarily many identifiers in one expression. That is, by the recursive appearance of <add-factor> and <mult-factor> in productions 3 and 5 respectively, we are able to keep introducing '+' and '*' into the expression being parsed.

Example 6.9 Provide a derivation of the infix expression A + B + C.

<expression> → <factor><add-factor>
→ <primary><mult-factor><add-factor>
→ A <mult-factor><add-factor>
→ A <add-factor>
→ A + <factor><add-factor>
→ A + <primary><mult-factor><add-factor>
→ A + B <mult-factor><hadd-factor>
→ A + B <add-factor>
→ A + B + <factor><add-factor>
→ A + B + <primary><mult-factor><add-factor>
→ A + B + C <mult-factor><add-factor>
→ A + B + C <add-factor>
→ A + B + C

You are encouraged to justify each step in the derivation by determining the production applied.

Just as we were able to describe recursive procedure processing with a tree of recursive calls, the formal derivation of an expression via the productions of a grammar can be represented by a diagram called a *parse tree*. (Parse trees for the derivation in Examples 6.8 and 6.9 are given in Figures 6.15 and 6.16, respectively.) Note that implicit in these parse trees is the order of operations in the algebraic expressions. That is, these parse trees are constructed, top-down, starting at each nonterminal within the tree and, from that nonterminal, descending to those nodes containing the terminals and nonterminals from the right side of the production applied in the derivation of the original nonterminal. Eventually, as we descend deeper into the tree, only terminals are left, and no nodes descend deeper from these terminals. In Figure 6.15, since the <factor> node on Level 2 of the tree encompasses all of B * C below it, we have an indication that B * C must be first evaluated as a <factor> and then added to A. On the other hand, in the parse tree

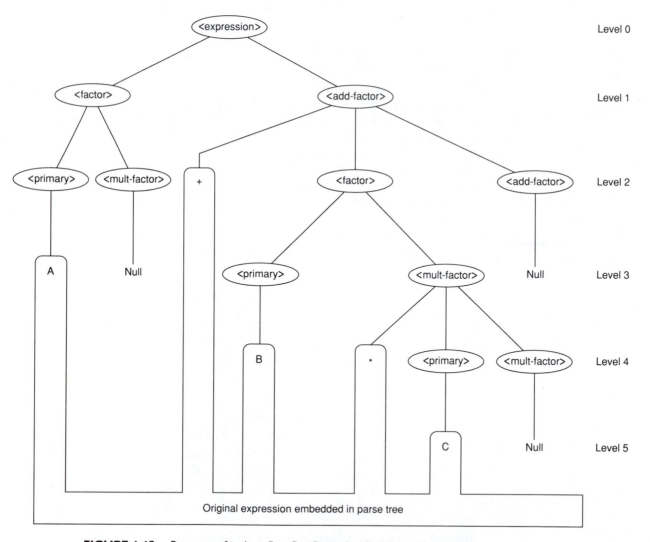

FIGURE 6.15   Parse tree for A + B * C reflects that B * C is evaluated first.

of Figure 6.16, the <factor> node at Level 2 encompasses only the B term. Hence, B is to be added to A, with C (below the <factor> node at Level 3) then added to that result. In the exercises and problems, you will continue to explore the relationships between context-free grammars, derivations, parse trees, and orders of evaluation in infix expressions.

   We now turn our attention to the problem of transforming the formal grammar that specifies the syntax of a language into a program that determines whether or not the tokens stored in an incoming queue constitute a valid string. The process is surprisingly easy. It begins with a front-end procedure called from an external module. This front-end procedure will eventually return an error flag indicating the success or failure of the parse. To do so, it performs necessary initializations and then calls on the first in a suite of "verifying" procedures. We write a separate verifying procedure for each nonterminal in the grammar. The responsibility of each procedure is simply

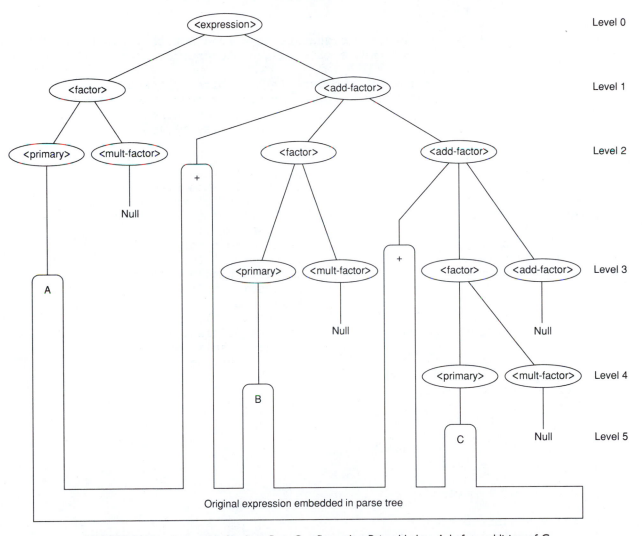

FIGURE 6.16   Parse tree for A + B + C reflects that B is added to A before addition of C.

to verify the particular grammatical construction after which it is named. The subordinate procedures called upon by a given procedure are dictated by the right sides of productions defining that procedure's associated nonterminal in the context-free grammar. Since typically many of these productions will have the terminal being defined on the left reappearing on the right, many of the associated procedures will be recursive in nature. Consequently, the general algorithmic technique is termed *recursive descent parsing*. The tree of recursive calls will parallel the parse tree for the expression. We will illustrate the method by developing a suite of procedures to parse expressions defined by the grammar of Example 6.8. The front-end procedure in this suite is the procedure TopLevelExpression. If it returns **true** in its SyntaxError parameter, the expression in the queue is not valid. Otherwise, it is syntactically correct.

```
type
  TokenType: (* Appropriate type for expressions being parsed, e.g., character
              or string *);
  QueueData: TokenType;
  TokenValidator: (* Establishes the signature of a function that can be used
              to test whether a token is an operator or an operand *)
            function
              ( given Token: TokenType (* An arbitrary token *);
                return: boolean          (* true if Token meets the
                                          criterion being tested; false
                                          otherwise *) );

procedure TopLevelExpression            (* This procedure called once from a
                                          program that wants an expression
                                          parsed. It sets stage for further
                                          calls to "verify" procedures *)

  ( given Infix: Queue                  (* Queue of tokens representing infix
                                          expression *);
        ValidOperand: TokenValidator  (* Used to test for valid operand *);
        ValidOperator: TokenValidator (* Used to test for valid operator *);
    return Infix: Queue               (* The remaining portion of the infix
                                          expression if the parse fails.
                                          Will be empty if the parse is
                                          successful *);

        SyntaxError: boolean          (* true if original Infix did not
                                          contain a valid expression;
                                          false otherwise * ) );
  var
    CurrentToken: TokenType;

  start TopLevelExpression
    if not Empty(Infix) then
      Dequeue(Infix, CurrentToken);
      SyntaxError := false
    else
      SyntaxError := true
    endif;
    if not SyntaxError then
      VerifyExpression(Infix, CurrentToken, ValidOperand, ValidOperator,
                      SyntaxError)
    endif;
```

```
   if not SyntaxError then
     if not Empty(Infix) then  (* There should be no more tokens *)
       SyntaxError := true
     endif
   endif
 end TopLevelExpression;

procedure VerifyExpression
  ( given Infix: Queue                (* Queue of tokens representing infix
                                          expression *);

          CurrentToken: TokenType     (* The token currently being
                                          processed *);

          ValidOperand: TokenValidator (* Used to test for valid operand *);
          ValidOperator: TokenValidator (* Used to test for valid operator *);
          SyntaxError: boolean        (* Initially false, indicating no
                                          syntax error has yet occurred *);

    return Infix: Queue               (* The remaining portion of the infix
                                          expression *);

          CurrentToken: TokenType     (* The token to be processed upon
                                          returning from this procedure *);

          SyntaxError: boolean        (* true if Infix does not begin with a
                                          valid Expression; false otherwise *) );

  start VerifyExpression
    VerifyFactor(Infix, CurrentToken, ValidOperand, ValidOperator,
              SyntaxError);
    if not SyntaxError then
      VerifyAddFactor(Infix, CurrentToken, ValidOperand, ValidOperator,
                  SyntaxError)
    endif
  end VerifyExpression;
```

<expression> → <factor><add-factor>

```
procedure VerifyFactor
  ( given Infix: Queue                (* Queue of tokens representing infix
                                          expression *);

          CurrentToken: TokenType     (* The token currently being
                                          processed *);

          ValidOperand: TokenValidator (* Used to test for valid operand *);
          ValidOperator: TokenValidator (* Used to test for valid operator *);
          SyntaxError: boolean        (* Initially false, indicating no
                                          syntax error has yet occurred *);

    return Infix: Queue               (* The remaining portion of the infix
                                          expression *);

          CurrentToken: TokenType     (* The token to be processed upon
                                          returning from this procedure *);

          SyntaxError: boolean        (* true if Infix does not begin with
                                          a valid Factor; false otherwise *) );

  start VerifyFactor
    VerifyPrimary(Infix, CurrentToken, ValidOperand,
              ValidOperator, SyntaxError);
    if not SyntaxError then
      VerifyMultFactor(Infix, CurrentToken, ValidOperand,
                  ValidOperator, SyntaxError)
    endif
  end VerifyFactor;
```

<factor> → <primary><mult-factor>

```
procedure VerifyAddFactor
   ( given Infix: Queue                    (* Queue of tokens representing infix
                                              expression *);
           CurrentToken: TokenType         (* The token currently being processed *);
           ValidOperand: TokenValidator    (* Used to test for valid operand *);
           ValidOperator: TokenValidator   (* Used to test for valid operator *);
           SyntaxError: boolean            (* Initially false, indicating no
                                              syntax error has yet occurred *);
     return Infix: Queue                   (* The remaining portion of the infix
                                              expression *);
            CurrentToken: TokenType        (* The token to be processed upon
                                              returning from this procedure *);
            SyntaxError: boolean           (* true if Infix does not begin with a
                                              valid AddFactor; false otherwise *) );
   start VerifyAddFactor
      (* Note: if we don't enter this procedure with the valid operator +
         as CurrentToken, we automatically have a valid AddFactor because of
         NULL production *)
      if ValidOperator(CurrentToken) then
        if CurrentToken = '+' then
          if not Empty(Infix) then
            Dequeue(Infix, CurrentToken);
            VerifyFactor(Infix, CurrentToken, ValidOperand,
                        ValidOperator, SyntaxError)
          else
            SyntaxError := true
          endif;
          if not SyntaxError then
            VerifyAddFactor(Infix, CurrentToken, ValidOperand,
                           ValidOperator, SyntaxError)
          endif
        endif
      endif
   end VerifyAddFactor;
```

<add-factor> → '+' <factor><add-factor>

```
procedure VerifyMultFactor
   ( given Infix: Queue                    (* Queue of tokens representing infix
                                              expression *);
           CurrentToken: TokenType         (* The token currently being
                                              processed *);
           ValidOperand: TokenValidator    (* Used to test for valid operand *);
           ValidOperator: TokenValidator   (* Used to test for valid operator *);
           SyntaxError: boolean            (* Initially false, indicating no syntax
                                              error has yet occurred *);
     return Infix: Queue                   (* The remaining portion of the infix
                                              expression *);
            CurrentToken: TokenType        (* The token to be processed upon
                                              returning from this procedure *);
            SyntaxError: boolean           (* true if Infix does not begin with a
                                              valid MultFactor; false otherwise *) );
   start VerifyMultFactor
      (* Note: if we don't enter this procedure with the valid operator *
         as CurrentToken, we automatically have a valid MultFactor because of
         NULL production *)
```

```
    if ValidOperator(CurrentToken) then
      if CurrentToken = '*' then
        if not Empty(Infix) then
          Dequeue(Infix, CurrentToken);
          VerifyPrimary(Infix, CurrentToken, ValidOperand,
                        ValidOperator, SyntaxError)
        else
          SyntaxError := true
        endif;
        if not SyntaxError then
          VerifyMultFactor(Infix, CurrentToken, ValidOperand,
                           ValidOperator, SyntaxError)
        endif
      endif
    endif
  end VerifyMultFactor;
```

<mult-factor> → '*' <primary><mult-factor>

```
procedure VerifyPrimary
  ( given Infix: Queue                  (* Queue of tokens representing infix
                                            expression *);
         CurrentToken: TokenType        (* The token currently being processed *);
         ValidOperand: TokenValidator   (* Used to test for valid operand *);
         ValidOperator: TokenValidator  (* Used to test for valid operator *);
         SyntaxError: boolean           (* Initially false, indicating no
                                            syntax error has yet occurred *);

    return Infix: Queue                 (* The remaining portion of the infix
                                            expression *);

           CurrentToken: TokenType      (* The token to be processed upon
                                            returning from this procedure *);

           SyntaxError: boolean         (* true if Infix does not begin with a
                                            valid Primary; false otherwise *) );

  start VerifyPrimary
    if ValidOperand(CurrentToken) then
      if not Empty(Infix) then
        Dequeue(Infix, CurrentToken)
      endif
    elsif CurrentToken = '(' then
      if not Empty(Infix) then
        Dequeue(Infix, CurrentToken);
        VerifyExpression(Infix, CurrentToken, ValidOperand,
                         ValidOperator, SyntaxError)
      else
        SyntaxError := true
      endif;
      if not SyntaxError then
        if CurrentToken <> ')' then
          SyntaxError := true
        else
          if not Empty(Infix) then
            Dequeue(Infix, CurrentToken)
          endif
        endif
      endif
    endif
```

<primary> → identifier
<primary> → number

<primary> → '(' expression ')'

```
    else  (* Not ValidOperand and not left paren *)
      SyntaxError := true
  endif
end VerifyPrimary;
```

The large amount of code in this suite of procedures belies the ease with which each procedure can be written, provided that we start with a sound grammatical description of the expressions being parsed. As indicated by the graphic documentation, each verifying procedure merely calls on subordinate verifying procedures in the order dictated by the right side of a production in the context-free grammar. For nonterminals that have more than one defining production, the CurrentToken parameter is examined to determine which production to follow.

As easy as the process seems, there are some negatives to the recursive descent parsing method. First, it applies only for context-free grammars that have their productions in a suitable form. The productions from Example 6.8 are in that form, but in the exercises you will explore context-free grammars that are not appropriate for the recursive descent method. Thus, to use recursive descent parsing, you must learn to write "correct" grammars. A second negative is the rigidity of a recursive descent parser once it has been implemented. Should you have a change of heart about the syntactical rules of the language being parsed, the resulting changes in productions may lead to widespread and dramatic changes in the code for the parser itself because the code is directly tied to the productions. Hence, maintainability of the code in a recursive descent parser can be a problem. This places a real premium on getting the grammar right the first time, before you begin generating code from it. Compare this to the ease with which one can alter a parse by changing the priority functions in the parsing method discussed in Section 5.3.

Exercises 6.4

1. Using the context-free grammar of Example 6.8, provide formal derivations and parse trees for the following expressions:

   a. A * B * C * D + E
   c. A + B * C * (D + E)
   d. ((A + B) * C) * (D + E)

2. Extend the grammar of Example 6.8 to

   a. Allow minus (−) and division (/) as algebraic operators.
   b. Allow exponentiation (↑) as an algebraic operator. Be sure that your grammar yields parse trees that imply that the order of consecutive exponentiations is right-to-left instead of left-to-right (as it is with other operators).
   c. Allow **or** (|), **and** (&), and **not** (~) as logical operators so that boolean as well as algebraic expressions are allowed by the grammar.

A RELEVANT ISSUE

Recursion, Lisp, and the Practicality of Artificial Intelligence

Artificial intelligence, the science of implementing on computers the problem-solving methods used by human beings, is one of the most rapidly expanding fields within computer science. Research in this field includes enabling computers to play games of strategy, to understand natural languages, to prove theorems in logic and mathematics, and to mimic the reasoning of human experts in fields such as medical diagnosis. Only recently has artificial intelligence become a commercially viable area of application, capable of solving some real-life problems apart from the idealized setting of a pure research environment. More and more, we are seeing artificial intelligence systems that perform such practical functions as aiding business executives in their decision-making processes and providing a near-English user-interface language for data base management software.

What has sparked the sudden emergence of artificial intelligence? Why was it not possible to produce commercially feasible programs in this field until recently? One of the primary answers to these questions is tied to the language in which most artificial intelligence programming is done. This language is called Lisp (for LISt Processor). Interestingly, the control structures of Lisp are based almost entirely on recursion. What a Pascal, C, or Modula-2 programmer would view as normal iterative control structures (for example, **while**, **repeat**, and **for** loops) appear in various versions of Lisp only as infrequently used extensions made to the language.

One of the reasons that a recursively based language such as Lisp is so ideally suited to this field is that most problem-solving methods in artificial intelligence involve developing rules for solving a complex problem. These rules formally describe the reasoning process used by humans when they solve such a problem. Frequently these rules are formulated in what is called a *production system*—a formalism analogous to the productions that are part of a context-free grammar. Just as a recursive descent parser tracks through productions as it tries to successfully parse an expression, so an artificial intelligence program in Lisp will (recursively) track through the rules in its production system as it attempts to find a solution to a problem.

The complexity of problems studied in artificial intelligence leads to recursive call trees of enormous size. Historically, Lisp has been available as a recursive language ideally suited to such tree searches. It is one of the oldest high-level programming languages, having been first developed by John McCarthy in the late 1950s. Researchers who work in artificial intelligence have long realized that Lisp's ability to recursively process general data structures was, on a theoretical basis, exactly what they needed. The problem through the years has been that, because of the very high overhead associated with recursion (and some other features built into Lisp), computer hardware has not been fast enough to run Lisp programs in practical applications. Thus, researchers were restricted not by Lisp itself but rather by the ability of computer hardware to execute Lisp programs in reasonable times. One of the major reasons for the recent expansion in the study of artificial intelligence has been the increase in speed of computer hardware and the decrease in cost of this same hardware. This has made it possible for users to have dedicated computer resources capable of meeting the demands of Lisp's recursive style. As hardware continues to improve, so will applications in Lisp improve, and artificial intelligence will become increasingly sophisticated.

3. Consider the following alternative, context-free grammar for the expressions defined by the grammar of Example 6.8.

```
<expression>   →<mult-factor>
<expression>   →<mult-factor> '+' <expression>
<mult-factor>  →<primary>
<mult-factor>  →<primary> '*' <mult-factor>
<primary>      → identifier
<primary>      → number
<primary>      → '(' <expression> ')'
```

    a. Does this grammar allow the same set of expressions as that in Example 6.8?

    b. Provide parse trees for any of the expressions in Exercise 1 that are accepted by the above grammar.

    c. What are differences in the parse trees produced by this grammar versus those produced by the grammar of Example 6.8?

    d. How would the differences you described in part c affect the order in which operators are applied?

    e. Which grammar—Example 6.8 or the one defined in this exercise—more accurately reflects the order of operations in standard programming languages?

4. (Left-Recursive Grammar) Consider the following alternative, context-free grammar for the expressions defined by the grammar of Example 6.8.

```
<expression>   → <mult-factor>
<expression>   → <expression> '+' <mult-factor>
<mult-factor>  → <primary>
<mult-factor>  → <mult-factor> '*' <primary>
<primary>      → identifier
<primary>      → number
<primary>      → '(' <expression> ')'
```

This grammar is an example of a *left-recursive grammar*—one that admits a derivation of the form.

$$< a > \rightarrow < a > X$$

where <a> is a nonterminal and X is a string of terminals and/or nonterminals. For the grammar of this exercise, productions associated with the nonterminals <expression> and <mult-factor> fit this criterion, so the grammar is left-recursive.

    a. Does this grammar allow the same set of expressions as that of Example 6.8?

    b. Provide parse trees for any of the expressions in Exercise 1 that are accepted by the above grammar.

    c. What are differences in the parse trees produced by this grammar versus those produced by the grammars of Example 6.8 and Exercise 3?

    d. How do the differences you described in part c affect the order in which operators are applied?

   e. What is the difficulty arising when you attempt to implement a recursive descent parser that reflects directly the grammar given in this exercise?

5. Provide a context grammar for the **if-then** and **if-then-else** structures of a conventional programming language like Pascal. Assume that nonterminals <condition> and <statement> are suitably defined elsewhere and, hence, can be used as primitives in your grammar. How many parse trees will your grammar allow for the following Pascal statement?

```
if A < B then
  if C < D then
    A := D
  else
    B := C
```

Which, if any, of your parse trees correspond to the fashion in which standard Pascal interprets this statement?

6. The programming language Lisp works with *S-expressions*. They may be defined as follows:

   a. NIL is a special S-expression denoting the empty S-expression.

   b. Any string composed of letters and/or digits with no other embedded characters is an S-expression.

   c. If $L_1, L_2, \ldots, L_k$ are S-expressions for $k \geq 0$, then $(L_1 \ L_2 \cdots L_k)$ is an S-expression.

   Construct a context-free grammar for S-expressions. Then draw parse trees for the following S-expressions.

   a. ((GLARP))
   b. (GLARP (GLARP) (((GLARP GLARP))) ( ))
   c. (((GLARP GLARP) NIL ( )) GLARP)

Chapter Summary   In this chapter we explored the basics of recursive algorithms, which are algorithms that define a solution to a problem in terms of a simpler version of the same problem. In Section 6.1 we introduced recursive algorithms by revisiting the divide-and-conquer search algorithm from Chapter 1 and by examining an implementation of the Traverse operation for ordered lists (introduced in Chapter 3). We also saw in this section that the implementation of recursive algorithms is based upon intricate manipulations of a stack used in processing procedure and function calls. We began to develop the notions of recurrence relations and recursive call trees as a means of analyzing the efficiency of recursive algorithms. Having first argued that nothing much was gained by a recursive divide-and-conquer algorithm over an iterative version, we then examined the run-time costs versus programmer costs of using recursion and followed this with a discussion of the Towers of Hanoi problem. Towers of Hanoi provided an example of a problem with a nontrivial recursive solution that could not be implemented merely by using iterative control structures. It also provided us with our first example of an exponential algorithm.

In Sections 6.2 and 6.3 we showed that by considering divide-and-conquer solutions to the sorting problem, namely quick sort in 6.2 and merge sort in 6.3, we can improve on the $O(n^2)$ and $O(n(\log_2 n)^2)$ sorting efficiencies of the insertion, selection, and Shell sorts, respectively.

Finally, in Section 6.4 we followed up on our discussion of parsing from Chapter 5 by examining the problem of detecting syntax errors in an expression being parsed. Following an introduction to context-free grammars, we examined the technique of recursive descent parsing for transforming a formal grammar that specifies the syntax of a language into a program that determines whether or not a given set of tokens, submitted to the parser as a queue, constitutes a valid string.

Key Words

context-free grammar	recursion	quick sort
merge sort	recursive descent parsing	terminals
non-terminals	parse tree	token
pivot	parsing	tree of recursive calls
recurrence relations	productions	

Programming Problems/Projects

1. Write a program to call for input of a decimal number and convert it to its binary equivalent using the method described in the following flow-chart.

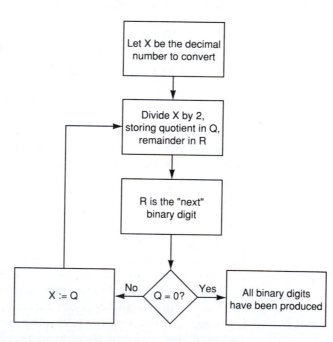

Note that this method produces the binary digits for the given number in reverse order. One strategy for printing out the digits in the correct order would be to store them in an array as they are produced and then print out the array. However, this strategy would have the drawbacks of allocating unnecessary storage for an array and limiting the size of the binary number to the size of the array. Your program is not to employ this strategy. Instead call for input of the decimal number in your main program and then immediately transfer control to a procedure that in turn is called recursively, stacking the binary digits as they are produced. Once division by 2 yields 0, the succession of returns can be used to print out the digits one by one as they are popped from the system stack.

2. Suppose that you have N thousand dollars and can use it to buy a combination of Orange computers (which cost $1,000 each), HAL computers (which cost $2,000 each), or MAX computers (which cost $4,000 each). How many different combinations of Orange, HAL, MAX computers could be bought with your N thousand dollars?

Write a program that receives N as input and responds with the number of possible combinations. Hint: if N were 100, then the number of combinations is

The number of combinations totaling $100,000
and involving Orange and HAL computers only

plus

The number of combinations totaling $96,000
and involving potentially all three brands

Think about this hint for a while and extend it to a recursive function that answers this question.

3. Write a *recursive* version of a Fibonacci function that is *significantly* faster than that given in Exercise 6 of Section 6.1.

4. The Bay Area Brawlers professional football team has stored the records of all the players who have played on the team throughout its history. One player's record consists of

Name
Total points scored
Number of touchdowns
Number of field goals
Number of safeties
Number of extra points

Write a program that lists players in order from the highest scorer in the team's history down to the lowest. Those players who have scored the same number of points should then be arranged in alphabetical order. Perform two sorts to achieve this—one sort by points scored and one sort by name. (Which one should be done first?) At least one of your sorts should be implemented as quick sort or merge sort. Can they both be quick or merge sort? (Hint: Think about your answers to Exercise 10 in Section 6.2 and Exercise 5 in Section 6.3.)

5. Consider a list of records, each containing four fields.

Name
Month of birth
Day of birth
Year of birth

Write a program to sort this list in oldest-to-youngest order as fast as possible. People with the same birth date should be arranged alphabetically. One strategy you could employ would be to concatenate strategically the four fields into one—sorting just that one field. Another strategy would be to sort the list four times, each time by a different field. (Think carefully about which field to sort first.) Which of the strategies would require that you choose a stable sorting algorithm? (See Exercises 10 and 5 in Sections 6.2 and 6.3, respectively.)

6. Modify MergeSort so that it will sort a linked list instead of an array.

7. Add statements to quick sort that count the number of comparisons made by the algorithm. Then run your program on a variety of randomly generated data sets, printing out N^2, $N \times \log_2 N$, and the number of comparisons made by your program for each data set. Observe the results of your program's runs and write a report in which you make conclusions about the average run-time efficiency of quick sort. Be sure to back up your conclusions by citing the empirical results of your program's runs.

8. Repeat Problem 7, making modifications in how the pivot is chosen. See the exercises in Section 6.2 for some suggestions. Also, try selecting the pivot as the median of three values—the first, last, and middle values in the segment of the array being partitioned.

9. Repeat Problem 8, but use insertion sort when the array segment becomes "sufficiently small" to avoid the overhead of recursion as the array becomes nearly sorted. Experiment with a suitable choice of an index range to find the optimal value for "sufficiently small." Be sure to include the results of your experimentation in your report.

10. Design a program that allows you to experiment with any or all of the sorting methods we have studied so far (selection, insertion, Shell, radix, quick, and merge). The program should allow you to do any or all of the following:

a. Enter an array interactively

b. Load an array from a text file

c. Randomly generate an array

You should be able to enter the method(s) by which the array is to be sorted. If Shell sort is one of the methods chosen, allow entry of the sequence of diminishing increments. If quick sort is chosen, provide some options in terms of how the pivot should be chosen and whether a nonrecursive method should be invoked when the array segment becomes sufficiently small. Your program should then sort the array for each of the methods chosen and count the number of comparisons and data interchanges required for each method. Use the program to conduct an empirical comparative analysis among the various sorting methods. Present the results of this analysis in a statistical table and a write-up in which you state your conclusions regarding the relative efficiencies of the algorithms.

11. Extend the recursive descent parser from Section 6.4 by

a. Providing descriptive error messages when a syntax error is encountered

b. Returning a queue of tokens representing the postfix form of the expression

c. Allowing any or all of the additional operators suggested in Exercise 2 of Section 6.4

12. Repeat Problem 11, but develop the recursive descent parser from the context-free grammar in Exercise 3 in Section 6.4.

13. Develop a recursive descent parser for the S-expression grammar you provided as an answer to Exercise 6 in Section 6.4.

14. (Removal of Tail Recursion via Iteration) An algorithm is said to be tail-recursive if the only recursion takes place in the algorithm's last step. The RecursiveSearch and Traverse algorithms given in Section 6.1 are both tail-recursive. The recursion can easily be removed from tail-recursive algorithms and replaced by an iterative control structure that yields a more time- and space-efficient algorithm. The key to the removal of the tail recursion is the simple observation that since the recursive call takes place as the last step in the algorithm, its effect is the same as looping back to the beginning of the algorithm and going through it again—this time, however, with new parameter values. In the iterative rewrite of the algorithm the looping back to the beginning of the algorithm can be controlled by a **while** statement, and local variables can assume the role of formal parameters. A model for such a rewrite can be found by comparing the RecursiveSearch procedure of Section 6.1 with its iterative-version Search in Section 1.3.

 a. Apply the techniques outlined here to rewrite the Traverse procedure of Section 6.1 so that it uses a nonrecursive algorithm.

 b. Write a nonrecursive algorithm based on Euclid's method (see Exercise 8 in Section 6.1) to find the GCD of two positive integers.

15. (Recursion Removal via System Stack Simulation) Implement the following strategy to remove recursion from a recursive algorithm. Simulate the system stack by declaring your own stack structure. Each time a recursive call is made in the algorithm, push the necessary information (including some form of return address) onto your stack. When you complete processing at this deeper level, pop the simulated stack frame and continue processing in the higher level at the point dictated by the return address popped from the stack. In languages that have a **goto** statement, the label following the **goto** can be used to direct processing to continue at a return address. In languages without a **goto**, the return address can be specific **case** labels in a **case** control structure. This **case** structure is then nested in an iterative control structure that loops until there are no return addresses left to pop from the stack.

 Use the strategy to write a nonrecursive version of quick sort or the function defined in Problem 2.

7

BINARY TREES

A fool sees not the same tree that a wise man sees.

William Blake

7.6 **Height-Balancing Trees**
AVL-Rotations
Why Does the AVL Height-Balancing Technique Work?
Height Balancing—Is It Worth It?

In Chapter 6 we used two types of diagrams called trees—a tree of recursive calls to analyze a recursive program's execution and a parse tree to analyze the syntactical structure of an expression. Both of these diagrammatic techniques were hierarchical in nature. That is, a node at level $n + 1$ in some sense belonged to or descended from a node at level n. From the opposite perspective, a node at level n of the tree diagram in some sense owned or controlled all nodes connected to it at levels deeper than n.

Our using a hierarchical scheme to describe recursion and parsing is not surprising. Human beings organize much of the world around them in hierarchies. For instance, an industrial or governmental body functions effectively only by defining a collection of supervisor-subordinate relationships among its participants. Computer scientists design a software system by breaking it down into modules and defining hierarchical boss-worker relationships among those modules. Parent-child relationships allow a natural categorization of a family's history with the use of a genealogical tree. In computer science, a *tree* is a data structure that represents such hierarchical relationships between data items.

To introduce some of the terminology of tree structures, consider the record of a student at a typical university. In addition to the usual statistical background information such as social security number, name, and address, a typical student record contains listings for a number of courses, exams and final grades in each course, overall grade point average, and other data relating to the student's performance. Figure 7.1 is a tree structure representing such a student record. As in genealogical trees, at the highest *level* (0) of a tree is its *root* (also called the *root node*). Here STUDENT is the root node. The nodes NAME, ADDRESS, SSN, COURSE, and GPA, which are directly connected to the root node, are the *child nodes* of the *parent node* STUDENT. The child nodes of a given parent constitute a set of *siblings*. Thus NAME, ADDRESS, SSN, COURSE, and GPA are siblings. In the hierarchy represented by a tree, the child nodes of a parent are one level lower than the parent node. Thus NAME, ADDRESS, SSN, COURSE, and GPA are at level 1 in Figure 7.1.

A link between a parent and its child is called a *branch*. Each node in a tree except the root must descend from a parent node via a branch. Thus LASTNAME, FIRSTNAME, and MIDDLENAME descend from the parent node NAME. The root of the tree is the *ancestor* of all nodes in the tree. Each node may be the parent of any number of nodes in the tree.

A node with no children is called a *leaf node*. In Figure 7.1, GPA is a leaf node. LASTNAME, FIRSTNAME, MIDDLENAME, EXAM1, and EXAM2 also are leaf nodes.

A *subtree* is a subset of a tree that is itself a tree; the tree in Figure 7.2 is a subtree of the tree in Figure 7.1. This subtree has the root node NAME. Similarly, the tree in Figure 7.3 is another subtree of the tree in Figure 7.1. Notice that the tree in Figure 7.3 is a subtree of the tree in Figure 7.1 and of the tree in Figure 7.4.

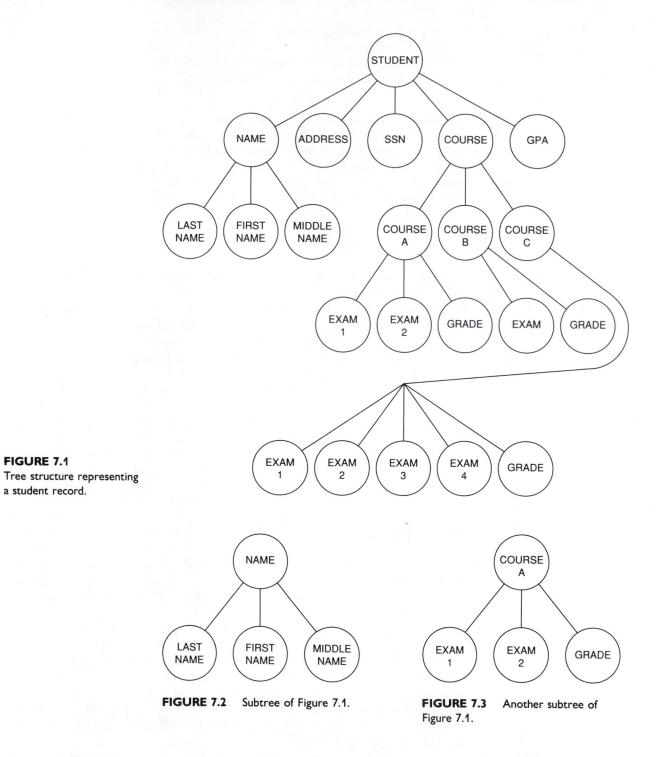

FIGURE 7.1
Tree structure representing
a student record.

FIGURE 7.2   Subtree of Figure 7.1.

FIGURE 7.3   Another subtree of
Figure 7.1.

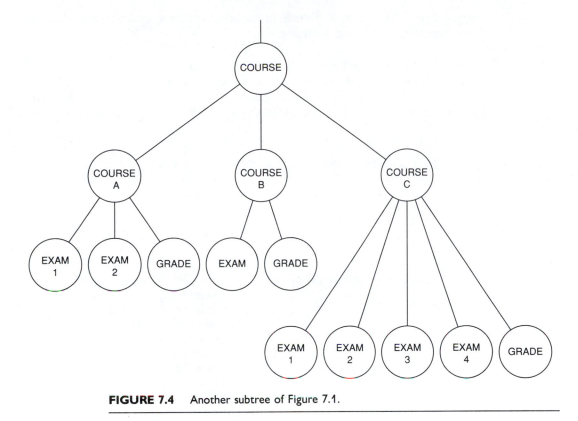

FIGURE 7.4 Another subtree of Figure 7.1.

7.1 THE BINARY TREE ADT

It is evident from the preceding discussion that a tree has the following interesting property: any given node within a tree is itself the root node of a completely analogous tree structure. That is, a tree is composed of a collection of substructures, each of which also meets the criteria for being a tree. This sounds dangerously circular, and, to formally describe a tree in this fashion, we must be sure to give ourselves a terminating condition for the recursion. This is done via the following partial definition of a tree as an abstract data type.

• **Definition (Partial) of Tree:** A *general tree* is a set of nodes that is either empty (the recursive terminating condition) or has a designated node, called the root, from which zero or more subtrees (hierarchically) descend. Each subtree itself satisfies the definition of a tree.

At the moment, we will refrain from providing a set of operations for the general tree ADT. Temporarily, we shall restrict ourselves to a more limiting definition that will be easier to work with and, at the same time, provide a surprisingly vast spectrum of applications. The primary restriction of this limited tree ADT is that any node in the tree will have exactly two subtrees. Consequently, it is called a binary tree.

• **Definition of Binary Tree:** A *binary tree* is a tree in which each node has exactly two subtrees, designated the *left subtree* and *right subtree*, either or both of which may be empty. The operations to be performed on a binary tree are shown in terms of the following PSEUDO pre- and postconditions.

```
type
   BinaryTreeData: (* The type of data item in each node of the binary tree *);
   BinaryTreeNode: (* Data type giving the structure of each node in the binary
                      tree. In the simplest case, will be equivalent to
                      BinaryTreeData *);
   MatchCriterion: function (* The signature of a function that determines
                              whether two binary tree data items match each
                              other *)
               ( given Target,
                       AnyData: BinaryTreeData (* Two data items, with
                                                  with Target containing
                                                  data to be matched in
                                                  some sense as
                                                  determined by Match
                                                  function *);
                 return: boolean            (* true if Target and
                                               AnyData satisfy the
                                               Match criterion *) );
   NodeOperation: procedure (* The signature of a procedure that can be
                              applied to an individual tree node *)
              ( given Item: BinaryTreeNode  (* Arbitrary node in binary
                                               tree *);
                return Item: BinaryTreeNode (* Item as affected by
                                               ProcessNode *) );

procedure Create
   ( given B: BinaryTree              (* An arbitrary binary tree variable in
                                         unknown state *);
     return B: BinaryTree             (* B initialized to the empty binary
                                         tree *) );

procedure Destroy
   ( given B: BinaryTree              (* An arbitrary binary tree B *);
     return B: BinaryTree             (* All dynamically allocated storage
                                         associated with B is returned to
                                         available space; B itself is in an
                                         unreliable state *) );

function Empty
   ( given B: BinaryTree              (* A previously created binary tree B *);
     return: boolean                  (* true if B is empty; false
                                         otherwise *) );

function Full
   ( given B : BinaryTree             (* A previously created binary tree B *);
     return: boolean                  (* true if there is no space to insert
                                         additional nodes in B; false
                                         otherwise *) );
```

```
procedure Assign
  ( given Source: BinaryTree         (* A binary tree whose contents are to be
                                         copied to Destination *);

    return Destination: BinaryTree   (* Contains a copy of Source *) );

procedure Retrieve
  ( given B: BinaryTree              (* A binary tree *);
         Target: BinaryTreeData      (* Data to be matched *);
         Match: MatchCriterion       (* This function determines which binary
                                         tree node is being sought *);

    return Item: BinaryTreeData      (* The data associated with the "first"
                                         node in B satisfying the criterion
                                         established by Match *);

         Success: boolean            (* false if no data in B satisfied the
                                         Match criterion; true otherwise *) );

procedure Update
  ( given B: BinaryTree              (* A binary tree *);
         Target: BinaryTreeData      (* Data to be matched *);
         Match: MatchCriterion       (* This function determines which node in
                                         B is to be updated *);

         NewValue: BinaryTreeData    (* The new value to be assigned to the
                                         first node in B that satisfies the
                                         Match criterion. Assume that NewValue
                                         does not alter the logical position of
                                         the node in B *);

    return B: BinaryTree             (* The binary tree B with the "first" node
                                         whose data satisfy the Match criterion
                                         replaced by NewValue *);

         Success: boolean            (* false if no data in B satisfied the
                                         Match criterion; true otherwise *) );

procedure PreOrderTraversal
  ( given B: BinaryTree              (* A binary tree *);
         ProcessNode: NodeOperation  (* This procedure determines the process
                                         applied to each BinaryTree node *);

    return B: BinaryTree             (* B with its root affected by
                                         ProcessNode, then with each node in
                                         its left subtree recursively affected
                                         by ProcessNode, and finally each node
                                         in its right subtree recursively
                                         affected by ProcessNode *) );

procedure PostOrderTraversal
  ( given B: BinaryTree              (* A binary tree *);
         ProcessNode: NodeOperation  (* This procedure determines the process
                                         applied to each BinaryTree node *);

    return B: BinaryTree             (* B with each node in its left subtree
                                         recursively affected by ProcessNode,
                                         then each node in its right subtree
                                         recursively affected by ProcessNode,
                                         and finally its root affected by
                                         ProcessNode *) );

procedure InOrderTraversal
  ( given B: BinaryTree              (* A binary tree *);
         ProcessNode: NodeOperation  (* This procedure determines the process
                                         applied to each BinaryTree node *);
```

```
    return B: BinaryTree              (* B with each node in its left subtree
                                         recursively affected by ProcessNode,
                                         then its root affected by ProcessNode,
                                         and finally each node in its right
                                         subtree recursively affected by
                                         ProcessNode *) );
```

```
(* Add and Delete operations incompletely specified *)

procedure Add
  ( given B: BinaryTree              (* A binary tree *);
         Item: BinaryTreeData        (* A data item to be added to B *)

    (* Additional parameters may be needed here, depending on the
       hierarchical relationship on which the tree is based *)

    return B: BinaryTree              (* B with Item inserted according to the
                                         hierarchical relationship upon which
                                         the tree is based *);
           Success: boolean          (* Set to true if Item successfully
                                         inserted; set to false if Item could
                                         not be inserted because there is no
                                         space in B *) );

procedure Delete
  ( given B: BinaryTree              (* A binary tree *);
         Target: BinaryTreeData      (* Data to be matched for deletion*);
         Match: MatchCriterion       (* This function determines which
                                         BinaryTreeNode is to be deleted from
                                         B *);

    (* Additional parameters may be needed here, depending on the
       hierarchical relationship on which the tree is based *)

    return B: BinaryTree              (* Binary tree with the "first" node
                                         whose data satisfy the Match criterion
                                         deleted. Only the first such
                                         BinaryTreeNode is deleted *);
           Success: boolean          (* false if no BinaryTreeNode in B
                                         satisfied the Match criterion; true
                                         otherwise *) );
```

Some similarities and differences between the binary tree ADT and the ordered-list ADT introduced in Section 3.1 should be noted. Aside from the traversal operations, there is a one-to-one correspondence between the operations for the two ADTs. This reflects the fact that, conceptually, we perform the same types of operations on individual nodes within the structures—add a node to the structure, delete a node from the structure, update a node in the structure, retrieve a node from the structure according to some match criterion, and so forth.

But this one-to-one correspondence between the operations on the structures cannot be carried too far. The correspondence certainly falls apart at the traversal operations. Essentially, all ordered lists are the same in that, given the Precedes relation on which their orderings are based, there is only one way to proceed through the list. With a binary tree, there are two directions to proceed from any node, which leads to several possible traversals. In the definition above we have identified three possible orders for traversing a binary tree. More are possible, but these three are the most frequently used.

Another critical difference between the ordered-list ADT and the binary tree ADT is that the hierarchical relationship that bonds a parent with its left and right subtrees in a binary tree is much more complex than the precedes relationship underlying an ordered list. In the three examples that follow, you will see how this hierarchical relationship can vary greatly in concept from one kind of binary tree to another. The complexity is both a blessing and a curse. On the plus side, it means that a binary tree is a much more powerful structure than an ordered list and can find application in a much broader range of problems. On the negative side, each such problem brings a unique hierarchical relationship to the binary tree used. Because of this, it is impossible to view the binary tree ADT as a specification that provides a complete package for every application. Rather, the binary tree ADT represents a generic starting point from which other more specific ADTs may be developed. Defining one ADT as an extension of another ADT will become increasingly important as we begin to study more complex data structures in the remainder of this text. The more specific ADT can be viewed as inheriting the features of the generic ADT and providing additional features unique to a particular application. Examples 7.1, 7.2, and 7.3 illustrate three such extensions of the generic binary tree. Each example is based on a completely different hierarchical scheme than the others.

Example 7.1   The tree of Figure 7.5 is a binary tree. Each node of this tree has two subtrees (empty or nonempty), designated as left and right. The particular hierarchy for this tree dictates that the data in any given node are greater than or equal to all the data in its left and right subtrees. A tree with this property is said to be a *heap* and to have the *heap property*. A heap will prove particularly important in our discussion of a nonrecursive, $O(n \log_2 n)$

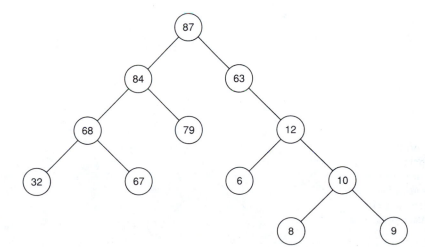

FIGURE 7.5
Binary tree with the heap property. The data in any given node are greater than or equal to the data in its left and right subtrees.

sorting method in Section 4 of this chapter. We will also see how a heap may be used to implement the priority queue ADT introduced in Chapter 4. The heap property is an example of a hierarchical relationship for a tree and is a property that must be preserved when various operations such as Add and Delete are performed upon the tree.

Example 7.2   A second example of a hierarchical relationship underlying a binary tree structure is shown in Figure 7.6. This binary tree exhibits the *ordering property:* the data in each node of the tree are greater than all of the data in that node's left subtree and less than or equal to all the data in the right subtree. We shall see the importance of trees possessing this property when we explore binary trees as a means of implementing an ordered list in Section 3 of this chapter.

We can also use this tree to illustrate the effect of the InOrderTraversal operation. Since the InOrderTraversal is recursively applied on the left subtree before applying ProcessNode to the root or recursively visiting the right subtree, 32 will be the first node affected by the ProcessNode procedural parameter. Thereafter, ProcessNode will be applied to 68, that is, the root of the subtree having 32 as its left subtree. After processing 68, the right subtree of 68, rooted at 74, will be visited in the order 70 74 80. Overall, you should confirm that the order in which nodes are visited by InOrderTraversal is

32 68 70 74 80 84 86 87 88 90 97 103 109

Note that an InOrderTraversal of a binary tree with the ordering property will visit the nodes of the tree in ascending order with respect to their data values.

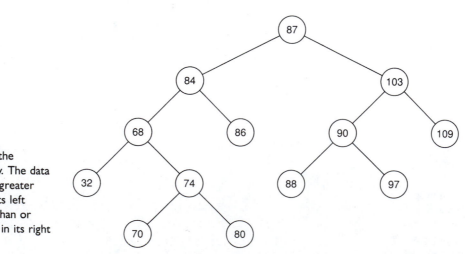

FIGURE 7.6

Binary tree with the ordering property. The data in each node are greater than the data in its left subtree and less than or equal to the data in its right subtree.

Example 7.3 As a final example of a hierarchical relationship that can determine the arrangement of data in a binary tree, consider Figure 7.7. Here we have a binary tree representation of the infix algebraic expression

$$(A - B) + C * (E / F)$$

The hierarchical relationship of parent to children in this tree is that of algebraic operator to its two operands. Note that an operand may itself be an expression (that is, a subtree) that must be evaluated before the operator in the parent node can be applied. Note also that if the order of evaluation in the expression changes to

$$(A - B) + C * E / F$$

then the corresponding binary expression tree must also change, as reflected in Figure 7.8.

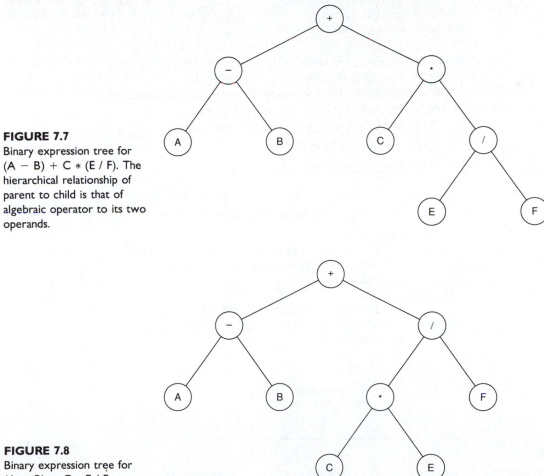

FIGURE 7.7
Binary expression tree for
$(A - B) + C * (E / F)$. The
hierarchical relationship of
parent to child is that of
algebraic operator to its two
operands.

FIGURE 7.8
Binary expression tree for
$(A - B) + C * E / F$.

Using the tree of Figure 7.7, you should confirm that the PostOrder-Traversal (applied recursively on the left subtree, then the right subtree, and finally the root) will visit nodes in the order

$$A\ B\ -\ C\ E\ F\ /\ *\ +$$

This is exactly the postfix representation of the expression. Similarly, the PreOrderTraversal yields the prefix form of the expression

$$+\ -\ A\ B\ *\ C\ /\ E\ F$$

Not surprisingly, the link between these traversals and standard forms of representing expressions makes the expression tree an important data structure in contemporary compilers. You will explore the binary expression tree more in the exercises and problems of this chapter.

These three examples indicate that the binary tree ADT is really just a starting point for an entire collection of ADTs. Each of these more specific ADTs in effect inherits the general properties and operations of the binary tree ADT and then extends these by providing operations unique to its hierarchical relationship. This inheritance phenomenon is highlighted in Figure 7.9. The Relevant Issue section from this chapter gives some indication of how the new paradigm called object-oriented programming has been influenced by inheritance.

Exercises 7.1

1. Draw a binary tree for the following expression:

$$A\ *\ B\ -\ (C\ +\ D)\ *\ (P\ /\ Q)$$

2. Represent the following StudentRec as a binary tree:

```
Name: record
        FirstName: array [10] of character;
        LastName: array [10] of character
      endrecord;
Year: record
        FirstSem: array [2] of character;
        SecondSem: array [2] of character
      endrecord;
```

FIGURE 7.9
A hierarchy of ADTs all inheriting generic properties of the binary tree.

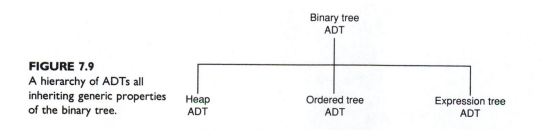

A RELEVANT ISSUE

More on Object-Oriented Programming—Inheritance and Polymorphism

In the Relevant Issue section of Chapter 2, we identified object-oriented programming (OOP) as an exciting new paradigm, which may well dominate the 1990s. The discussion on binary trees in the present chapter provides us with the background necessary to go a bit more deeply into what separates an OOP language from a conventional procedural language. One key difference is that object-oriented languages support *inheritance* among data types. That is, object-oriented languages make it simple for you to achieve a hierarchy of data structures such as that in Figure 7.9. You can declare a generic BinaryTree data type (often called a *class* in object-oriented languages) and then declare subclasses of the BinaryTree class—subclasses such as Heap, OrderedTree, and ExpressionTree. Because they are subclasses of the generic BinaryTree class, objects in these subclasses automatically inherit every operation defined for generic BinaryTrees. Hence, you do not have to "reinvent" implementations of the operations that your subclass shares with the generic "root class." You have such operations defined for you via inheritance from the ancestor class.

However, you may want to recode some of the operations to make them more efficient for the specific subclass with which you are working. For instance, you can redefine the Add and Delete operations for the Heap subclass instead of using the generic Add and Delete from the ancestor BinaryTree class. In traditional languages such redefinition of an operation will cause syntax problems with name clashes, forcing you to rename the operations. That is, there would be two Add and Delete operations; you would have to change the names of these operations for the Heap class to something like HeapAdd and HeapDelete. A feature of OOP languages called *polymorphism* (from the Greek for *many shapes*) eliminates the need for such messy and artificial renaming. A program that you code in an OOP language will be able to decide at runtime which of the two Add procedures is more appropriate for the particular object it is manipulating.

The goal of inheritance and polymorphism is to accelerate program development by making it very easy to incorporate previously developed software modules into a variety of new programs. In his excellent feature article "Object-Oriented Programming," (*Byte,* 15, February 1990, pp. 257–66), Dick Pountain writes:

> Designing good inheritance hierarchies is the essence of good OOP. If you choose sufficiently flexible and generic types for the root of the tree [of data classes], you can reuse a large percentage of your code. Writing new programs reduces to merely creating a few child types.

```
StudentRec: record
               StudentName: Name;
               YearOfStudy: Year
            endrecord;
```

3. What, in an abstract sense, does a tree structure represent?

4. Indicate which of the following are binary trees with the ordering property. Explain what is wrong with those that are not.

a.

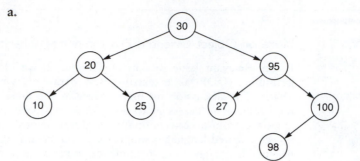

b.

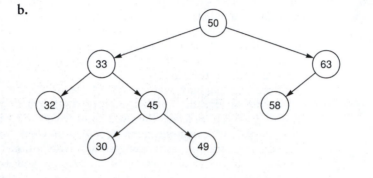

c.

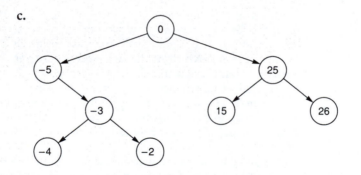

d.

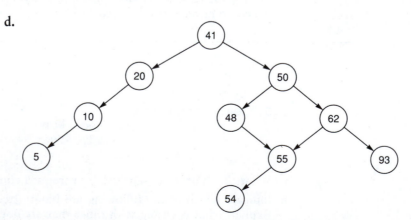

A RELEVANT ISSUE

More on Object-Oriented Programming—Inheritance and Polymorphism

In the Relevant Issue section of Chapter 2, we identified object-oriented programming (OOP) as an exciting new paradigm, which may well dominate the 1990s. The discussion on binary trees in the present chapter provides us with the background necessary to go a bit more deeply into what separates an OOP language from a conventional procedural language. One key difference is that object-oriented languages support *inheritance* among data types. That is, object-oriented languages make it simple for you to achieve a hierarchy of data structures such as that in Figure 7.9. You can declare a generic BinaryTree data type (often called a *class* in object-oriented languages) and then declare subclasses of the BinaryTree class—subclasses such as Heap, OrderedTree, and ExpressionTree. Because they are subclasses of the generic BinaryTree class, objects in these subclasses automatically inherit every operation defined for generic BinaryTrees. Hence, you do not have to "reinvent" implementations of the operations that your subclass shares with the generic "root class." You have such operations defined for you via inheritance from the ancestor class.

However, you may want to recode some of the operations to make them more efficient for the specific subclass with which you are working. For instance, you can redefine the Add and Delete operations for the Heap subclass instead of using the generic Add and Delete from the ancestor Binary-Tree class. In traditional languages such redefinition of an operation will cause syntax problems with name clashes, forcing you to rename the operations. That is, there would be two Add and Delete operations; you would have to change the names of these operations for the Heap class to something like HeapAdd and HeapDelete. A feature of OOP languages called *polymorphism* (from the Greek for *many shapes*) eliminates the need for such messy and artificial renaming. A program that you code in an OOP language will be able to decide at runtime which of the two Add procedures is more appropriate for the particular object it is manipulating.

The goal of inheritance and polymorphism is to accelerate program development by making it very easy to incorporate previously developed software modules into a variety of new programs. In his excellent feature article "Object-Oriented Programming," (*Byte*, 15, February 1990, pp. 257–66), Dick Pountain writes:

> Designing good inheritance hierarchies is the essence of good OOP. If you choose sufficiently flexible and generic types for the root of the tree [of data classes], you can reuse a large percentage of your code. Writing new programs reduces to merely creating a few child types.

```
StudentRec: record
               StudentName: Name;
               YearOfStudy: Year
            endrecord;
```

3. What, in an abstract sense, does a tree structure represent?

4. Indicate which of the following are binary trees with the ordering property. Explain what is wrong with those that are not.

a.

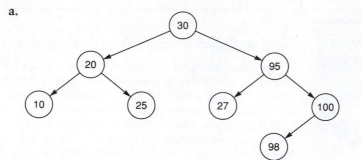

b.

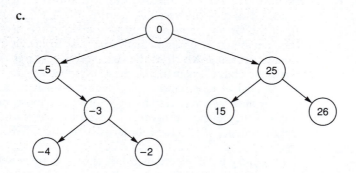

c.

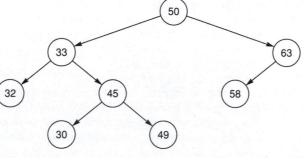

d.

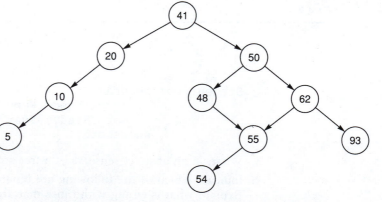

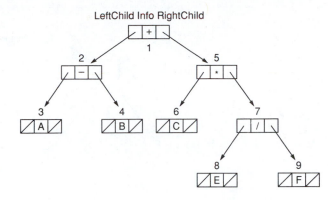

FIGURE 7.11

Linked representation of the binary expression tree of Figure 7.7. (The numbers on top of the cells represent addresses used in the LeftChild and RightChild fields in Figure 7.12.)

pointer fields are NULL. Figure 7.11 is a linked representation of the binary expression tree of Figure 7.7. The LeftChild and RightChild fields are pointers to (that is, memory addresses of) the left child and the right child of a node.

For the moment, we will consider a detailed description of the linked representation of the binary tree of Figure 7.7 using an array of records. This is similar to the way in which we first discussed linked lists in Section 3.3. By doing this, we will actually be able to trace the values of the pointers. Once the concept is thoroughly understood, we will then return to using abstract pointer variables for the actual implementation of binary trees. For example, we can implement the tree of Figure 7.11 as shown in Figure 7.12, using the strategy of building the left subtree for each node before considering the right subtree. The numbers on top of the cells in Figure 7.11 represent the addresses given in the LeftChild and RightChild fields.

In the linked representation, insertions and deletions involve no data movement except the rearrangement of pointers. Suppose we wish to modify the tree in Figure 7.7 to that of Figure 7.13. (This change might be required by some recent modification in the expression represented by Figure 7.7.) For instance, the insertion of nodes containing − and P into the tree structure can easily be achieved by simply adding the nodes containing − and P in the next available spaces in the array and adjusting the corresponding pointers.

For the implementation of the tree shown in Figure 7.12, the effect of this insertion is given by Figure 7.14. The adjusted pointers have been underscored. Notice that the change in location 1 of RightChild and the additional locations 10 and 11 are all that is necessary. No data were moved.

Location	Info	LeftChild	RightChild
1	+	2	5
2	−	3	4
3	A	NULL	NULL
4	B	NULL	NULL
5	*	6	7
6	C	NULL	NULL
7	/	8	9
8	E	NULL	NULL
9	F	NULL	NULL

FIGURE 7.12

Implementation of Figure 7.11 using an array of records.

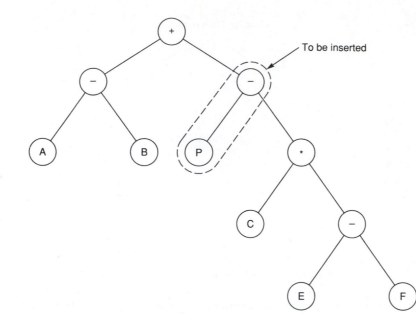

FIGURE 7.13

Desired modification of Figure 7.7.

FIGURE 7.14

Modification of Figure 7.12 by insertions into the tree of Figure 7.7. Values underscored represent changes from Figure 7.12.

Location	Info	LeftChild	RightChild
1	+	2	10
2	–	3	4
3	A	NULL	NULL
4	B	NULL	NULL
5	*	6	7
6	C	NULL	NULL
7	/	8	9
8	E	NULL	NULL
9	F	NULL	NULL
10	–	11	5
11	P	NULL	NULL

Similarly, if we wish to shorten the tree in Figure 7.7 by deleting the nodes * and C, then all we must do is rearrange the pointers to obtain the altered tree, as shown in Figure 7.15. The effect of this deletion is given in Figure 7.16. As before, the adjusted pointers have been underscored.

A more formal statement of an algorithm underlying such insertions and deletions will be given later in this chapter, when we discuss algorithms for maintaining a binary tree. Now that we have explained the linked representation of a binary tree by using arrays to contain pointer values that can be explicitly traced, we will use the following general record description with abstract pointer variables to implement this structure in the remainder of the chapter.

```
type
  BinaryTreeData: (* The type of each data item in the
                     binary tree *);
  BinaryTree: pointer to BinaryTreeNode;
```

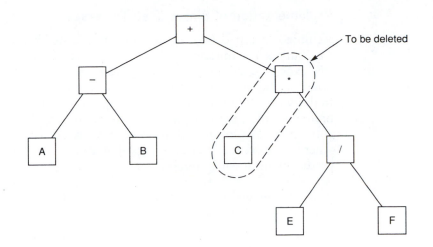

To be deleted

FIGURE 7.15
Another modification of
Figure 7.7.

Location	Info	LeftChild	RightChild	Modified tree
1	+	2	7	
2	–	3	4	
3	A	NULL	NULL	
4	B	NULL	NULL	
5	*			unused space after
6	C			deletion of * and C
7	/	8	9	
8	E	NULL	NULL	
9	F	NULL	NULL	

FIGURE 7.16
Modification of Figure 7.12
by deletions from the tree of
Figure 7.7.

```
BinaryTreeNode: record
                   LeftChild: BinaryTree;
                   Info: BinaryTreeData;
                   RightChild: BinaryTree
                endrecord;
```

Efficiency Considerations for the Linked Representation

As far as processing efficiency is concerned, the linked representation seems to be more efficient, particularly where frequent insertions and deletions are required. Although for most purposes the linked representation of a binary tree is very efficient, it does have certain disadvantages, namely:

1. Wasted memory space in NULL pointers. For instance, the representation in Figure 7.11 has 10 NULL pointers.

2. Given a node, it is difficult to determine its parent.

The first disadvantage can be offset by threading the tree, a technique discussed in Section 5 of this chapter. The second drawback can be easily overcome, at the expense of more memory, by adding a parent pointer field to each node.

Implementation of Binary Tree Traversals

As noted in our definition of a binary tree as an abstract data structure, a *tree traversal* requires an algorithm that visits (and processes) each node of a tree exactly once. Just as the only way into a linked list is through the head node, so the only way into a tree is through the root. However, any attempt to draw an analogy between traversing a singly linked list and a binary tree is limited to the preceding statement. Although both structures have only one entry point, from any given node in a linked list there is no choice about where to proceed. After entering a binary tree, we are faced with a threefold predicament at each node:

1. Do we process the data contained in the node at which we are currently located?

2. Do we remember the location of the current node (so that we can return to process it) and visit (and process) all nodes in its left subtree?

3. Do we remember the location of the current node (so that we can return to process it) and visit (and process) all nodes in its right subtree?

Here the generic term *process* applies to whatever operation is to be performed on the data at a given node—for example, print it or update it. What is actually done to the data is not as relevant to our discussion as the order in which the nodes are processed. Each of the three preceding choices represents a valid choice. The route chosen out of the threefold predicament dictates the order in which the nodes are visited and processed.

Although various arrangements of these three choices allow for many different traversals, three particular traversal techniques have come to be regarded as standard and hence are included in our ADT definition of the binary tree. They are the preorder traversal, inorder traversal, and postorder traversal. As alluded to in Examples 7.2 and 7.3, these three traversals correspond to visiting all nodes in ascending order for trees with the ordering property (inorder traversal) and to obtaining prefix and postfix representations of binary expression trees (preorder and postorder traversals, respectively). However, it is important to realize that the three traversals apply broadly to all binary trees, regardless of the hierarchical relationship underlying their structure.

Preorder Traversal

In a *preorder traversal,* the three options are combined in the following order:

1. First, process the root node.
2. Then, recursively visit all nodes in the left subtree.
3. Finally, recursively visit all nodes in the right subtree.

These three ordered steps are recursive. Once the root of the tree is processed, we go to the root of the left subtree, and then to the root of the left subtree of the left subtree, and so on until we can go no farther. Following these three steps, the preorder traversal of the tree of Figure 7.7 would process nodes in the order

$$+ - A B * C / E F$$

which is the prefix form of the expression

$$(A - B) + C * (E / F)$$

Hence, we conclude that, if to process a node means to print it, then a preorder traversal of a binary expression tree would output the prefix form of the expression.

The preorder traversal of an existing binary tree implemented via the linked representation and with a root node at location B can be accomplished recursively using the following procedure:

```
procedure PreOrderTraversal
  ( given B: BinaryTree              (* A binary tree *);
        ProcessNode: NodeOperation (* This procedure determines the process
                                      applied to each BinaryTree node *);
    return B: BinaryTree            (* B with its root affected by
                                      ProcessNode, then with each node in
                                      its left subtree recursively affected
                                      by ProcessNode, and finally each node
                                      in its right subtree recursively
                                      affected by ProcessNode *) );

  start PreOrderTraversal
    if B <> NULL then
      ProcessNode(Ref(B));
      PreorderTraversal(Ref(B).LeftChild,
                    ProcessNode);
      PreorderTraversal(Ref(B).RightChild,
                    ProcessNode)
    endif
  end PreOrderTraversal;
```

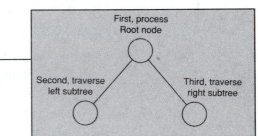

Inorder Traversal

The inorder traversal of a binary tree proceeds as outlined in the following three ordered steps:

1. First, recursively visit all nodes in the left subtree.
2. Then, process the root node.
3. Finally, recursively visit all nodes in the right subtree.

By carefully following these steps for the tree of Figure 7.7 and assuming "process" means "print," we obtain the readily recognizable infix expression

$$A - B + C * E / F$$

Unless we add parentheses, this infix expression is not algebraically equivalent to the order of operations reflected in the tree of Figure 7.7. The fact that prefix and postfix notations do not require parentheses to avoid such ambiguities makes them distinctly superior to infix notation for evaluation purposes.

A more formal statement of the recursive algorithm for an inorder traversal is given in the following procedure for a linked representation of a binary tree:

```
procedure InOrderTraversal
  ( given B: BinaryTree              (* A binary tree *);
        ProcessNode: NodeOperation   (* This procedure determines the process
                                        applied to each BinaryTree node *);
    return B: BinaryTree             (* B with each node in its left subtree
                                        recursively affected by ProcessNode,
                                        then its root affected by ProcessNode,
                                        and finally each node in its right
                                        subtree recursively affected by
                                        ProcessNode *) );
```

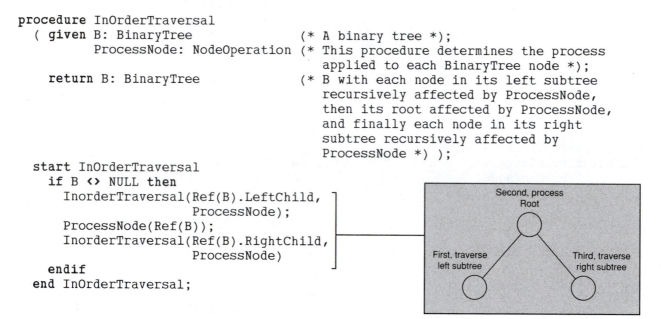

```
    start InOrderTraversal
      if B <> NULL then
        InorderTraversal(Ref(B).LeftChild,
                  ProcessNode);
        ProcessNode(Ref(B));
        InorderTraversal(Ref(B).RightChild,
                  ProcessNode)
      endif
    end InOrderTraversal;
```

Postorder Traversal

The third standard traversal of a binary tree, the *postorder traversal,* entails an arrangement of options that postpones processing the root node until last.

1. First, recursively visit all nodes in the left subtree of the root node.
2. Then, recursively visit all nodes in the right subtree of the root node.
3. Finally, process the root node.

The postorder traversal can be implemented recursively by the following procedure

```
procedure PostOrderTraversal
  ( given B: BinaryTree              (* A binary tree *);
        ProcessNode: NodeOperation   (* This procedure determines the process
                                        applied to each BinaryTree node *);
    return B: BinaryTree             (* B with each node in its left subtree
                                        recursively affected by ProcessNode,
                                        then each node in its right subtree
                                        recursively affected by ProcessNode,
                                        and finally its root affected by
                                        ProcessNode *) );
```

```
start PostOrderTraversal
  if B <> NULL then
    PostorderTraversal(Ref(B).LeftChild,
              ProcessNode);
    PostorderTraversal(Ref(B).RightChild,
              ProcessNode);
    ProcessNode(Ref(B))
  endif
end PostOrderTraversal;
```

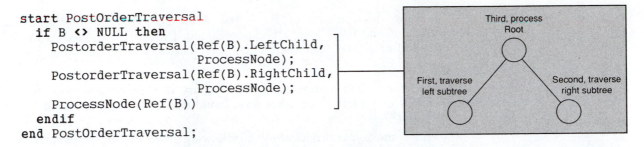

Although here we have illustrated the three traversal algorithms using binary expression trees, we emphasize that the traversals apply in general to *any* binary tree. Indeed, as we shall see in the next section, when used in combination with a tree exhibiting the hierarchical ordering property, the inorder traversal will neatly allow us to implement a general list using a binary tree.

Exercises 7.2

1. You are writing a program that uses a binary tree. To make it easy to trace the structure, you implement pointers using an array of records as described in Section 3.3. Consider the following binary tree:

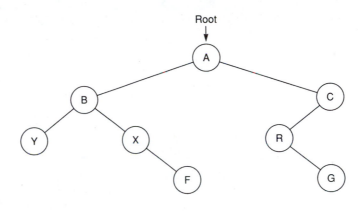

a. Indicate the contents of Root and Avail pointers and LeftChild and RightChild fields in the array Tree that follows:

Tree

Location	Info	LeftChild	RightChild
1	C		
2	R		
3	G		
4	F		
5	X		
6	Y		
7	B		
8	A		
9			

Root

Avail

b. Show the contents of Root and Avail pointers and LeftChild and RightChild fields after a node containing J has been inserted as the left child of X and then after R has been deleted with G becoming the left child of C.

2. How is a linked representation of a binary tree an improvement over its linear representation? In what ways could the linked representation be less efficient?

3. What is the output produced by the following procedure for the pictured tree?

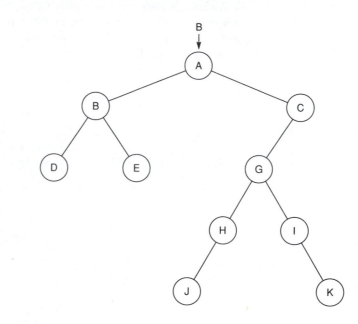

```
procedure TreeWalk
  ( given B: BinaryTree);

  start TreeWalk
    if B = NULL then
      write('OOPS')
    else
      TreeWalk(Ref(B).RightChild);
      TreeWalk(Ref(B).LeftChild);
      write(Ref(B).Info)
    endif
  end TreeWalk;
```

4. How does the output from Exercise 3 change if the statement

   `write(Ref(B).Info)`

   is moved ahead of the recursive calls to TreeWalk?

5. How does the output from Exercise 3 change if the statement

   `write(Ref(B).Info)`

   is located between the recursive calls to TreeWalk?

6. Repeat Exercises 3, 4, and 5 for the tree at the top of page 313.

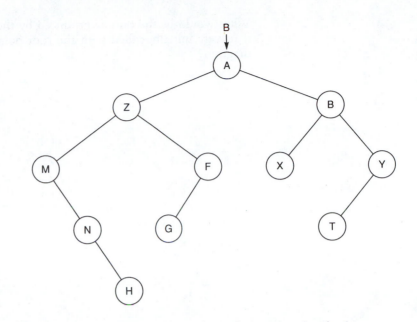

7. Given the following postorder and inorder traversals of a binary tree, draw the tree

   Postorder: A B C D E F I K J G H

   Inorder: C B A E D F H I G K J

   Attempt to deduce your answer in a systematic (and recursive) fashion, not by trial-and-error methods.

8. How could the inorder traversal of a binary tree be used to logically sort data?

9. A *ternary tree* is a tree in which each node may have at most three children. A pointer/record structure for a linked implementation of such a tree could thus be given by the following declarations:

```
type
  TernaryTree: pointer to TernaryTreeNode;
  TernaryTreeNode: record
                    LeftChild: TernaryTree;
                    MiddleChild: TernaryTree;
                    RightChild: TernaryTree;
                    Data: character
                  endrecord;
procedure TreeWalk
  ( given T: TernaryTree);

  start TreeWalk
    if T = NULL then
      write("NULL")
    else
      write(Ref(T).Data);
      TreeWalk(Ref(T).LeftChild);
      TreeWalk(Ref (T).MiddleChild);
      TreeWalk(Ref(T).RightChild)
    endif
  end TreeWalk;
```

What would be the output produced by the preceding TreeWalk procedure if it were initially called with the root pointer to the tree in the following diagram?

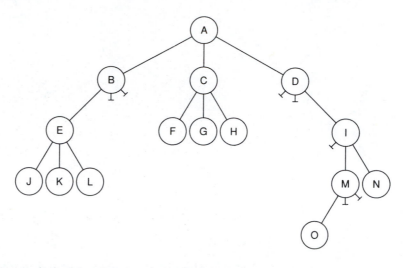

10. Given a linked implementation of a binary tree as described in this section, provide PSEUDO code for the following binary tree operations:

    a. Create

    b. Destroy

    c. Empty

    d. Full

    e. Assign

    f. Retrieve
    g. Update   Hint: in the absence of knowledge about the hierarchical relationship structuring the tree, use a modified traversal to locate the desired node.

11. Provide an encapsulated record definition for a linear representation of a binary tree. Then, using your definition, write PSEUDO code for the following binary tree operations.

    a. Create

    b. Destroy

    c. Empty

    d. Full

    e. Assign

    f. Retrieve
    g. Update   Hint: in the absence of knowledge about the hierarchical relationship structuring the tree, use a modified traversal to locate the desired node.

    h. PreOrderTraversal

    i. PostOrderTraversal

    j. InOrderTraversal

12. Given a linked implementation of a binary tree, analyze the time and space efficiencies of the traversal algorithms developed in this section. Upon what factors do these efficiencies depend?

7.3   BINARY TREE IMPLEMENTATION OF AN ORDERED LIST

The two implementations we considered for an ordered list in Section 3.2 have both been found lacking in certain respects. The ordered array implementation allowed the fast inspection of records via the binary search algorithm but necessitated excessive data movement when records were added to or deleted from the list. The linked-list implementation handled additions and deletions nicely but presented us with an undesirable $O(n)$ search efficiency due to the lack of random access, which forces a sequential search strategy. In this section, we shall see that by implementing a general list using a binary tree, we can achieve efficiency in both searching and adding or deleting while keeping the list in order. Moreover, we do not have to pay too great a price in other trade-offs to achieve this best of both worlds.

A binary tree implementation of a list is organized via the hierarchical ordering property discussed in Example 7.2. Recall that this ordering property stipulates the following:

> *For any given data item X in the tree, every node in the left subtree of X contains only items that are less than X with respect to a particular type of ordering. Every node in the right subtree of X contains only items that are greater than or equal to X with respect to the same ordering.*

For instance, the tree of Figure 7.17 illustrates this property with respect to alphabetical ordering. You can quickly verify that an inorder traversal of this

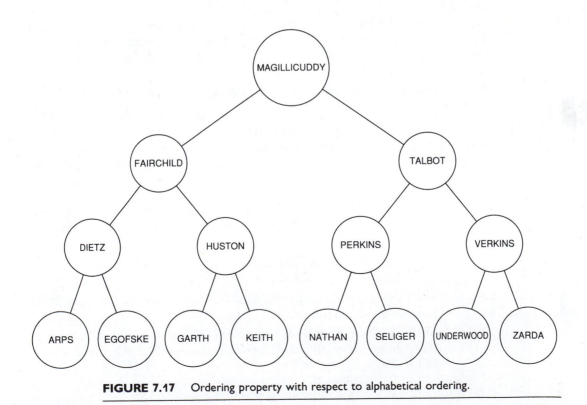

FIGURE 7.17   Ordering property with respect to alphabetical ordering.

tree (in which the processing of each node consists merely of printing its contents) leads to the following alphabetized list:

ARPS

DIETZ

EGOFSKE

FAIRCHILD

GARTH

HUSTON

KEITH

MAGILLICUDDY

NATHAN

PERKINS

SELIGER

TALBOT

UNDERWOOD

VERKINS

ZARDA

This reinforces the important conclusion of Example 7.2. That is, an inorder traversal of a binary tree that has the ordering property will visit nodes in ascending order with respect to their data values. Hence, such a tree may be viewed as an ordered general list. The first list element is the first node visited by the inorder traversal. More generally, the nth node visited by the inorder traversal corresponds precisely to the nth element in the list. Given this view of a binary tree as an implementation of a general list, let us now consider the operations of adding, deleting, and finding nodes in the list.

Adding Nodes to the Binary Tree Implementation of a List

Insertion of a new string into the ordered tree of Figure 7.17 is a fairly easy process that may well require significantly fewer comparisons than insertion into a linked list. Consider, for example, the steps necessary to insert the string SEFTON into this tree in a way that maintains the ordering property. We must

1. Compare SEFTON to MAGILLICUDDY. Because SEFTON is greater than MAGILLICUDDY, follow the right child pointer to TALBOT.

2. Compare SEFTON to TALBOT. Because SEFTON is less than TALBOT, follow the left child pointer to PERKINS.

3. SEFTON is greater than PERKINS. Hence, follow the right child pointer to SELIGER.

4. SELIGER is a leaf node, so SEFTON may be added as one of its children. The left child is chosen because SEFTON is less than SELIGER.

The resulting tree for this insertion is given in Figure 7.18.

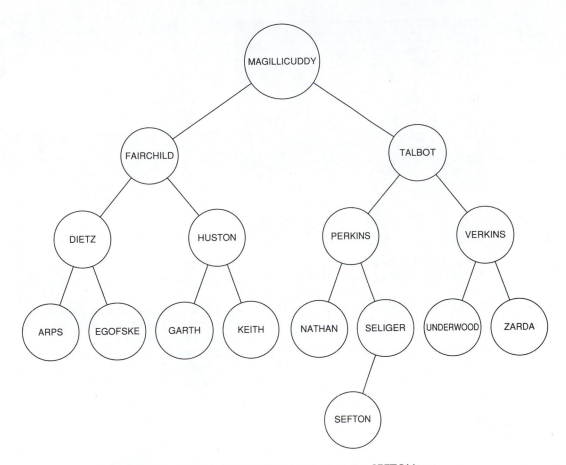

FIGURE 7.18   Tree in Figure 7.17 with the insertion SEFTON.

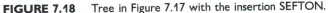

Example 7.4   Develop a complete procedure to add a data item to a binary tree with the ordering property. The procedure should receive a Precedes parameter that can be used to specify the ordering relationship between any two binary tree nodes.

```
type
   Comparison: function (* The signature of a function that
                          determines the ordering of the binary tree *)
              ( given Item1, Item2: BinaryTreeData (* Two data items to
                                                     be compared *);
                return: boolean              (* true if Item1 is
                                                to be considered
                                                as preceding
                                                Item2 in
                                                ordering for
                                                the tree; false
                                                otherwise *) );

procedure Add  (* for binary tree with ordering property *)
   ( given B: BinaryTree      (* A binary tree ordered by Precedes
                                 relationship *);
```

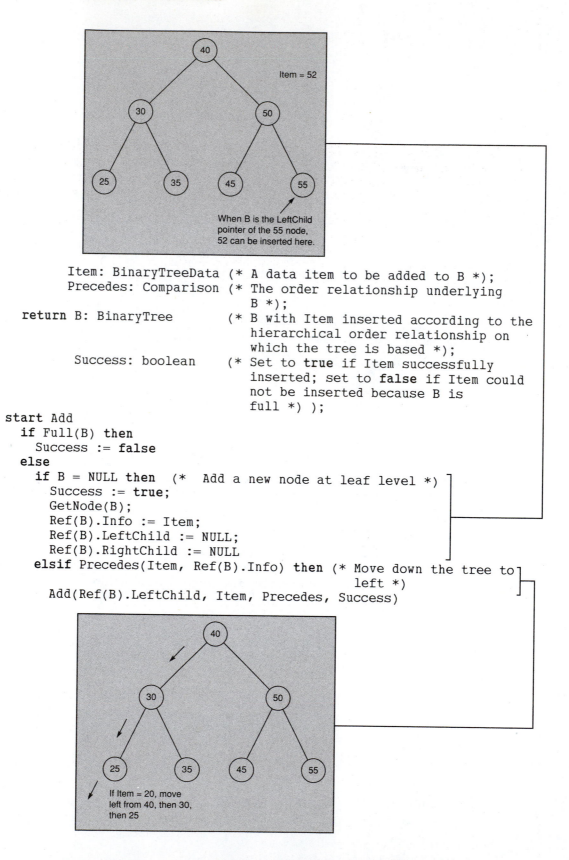

```
        Item: BinaryTreeData (* A data item to be added to B *);
        Precedes: Comparison (* The order relationship underlying
                                 B *);
 return B: BinaryTree        (* B with Item inserted according to the
                                 hierarchical order relationship on
                                 which the tree is based *);

        Success: boolean     (* Set to true if Item successfully
                                 inserted; set to false if Item could
                                 not be inserted because B is
                                 full *) );
start Add
  if Full(B) then
    Success := false
  else
    if B = NULL then  (*  Add a new node at leaf level *)
      Success := true;
      GetNode(B);
      Ref(B).Info := Item;
      Ref(B).LeftChild := NULL;
      Ref(B).RightChild := NULL
    elsif Precedes(Item, Ref(B).Info) then (* Move down the tree to
                                              left *)
      Add(Ref(B).LeftChild, Item, Precedes, Success)
```

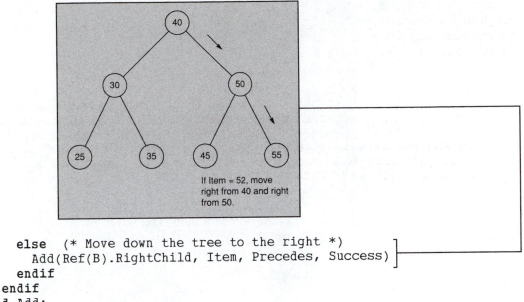

If Item = 52, move right from 40 and right from 50.

```
      else   (* Move down the tree to the right *)
        Add(Ref(B).RightChild, Item, Precedes, Success)
      endif
   endif
end Add;
```

The result of applying this Add procedure to the succession of items given by

> JEPHTHAH
> GILLIAN
> ALMA
> LETITIA
> PERCY
> TYBALT
> DUNSTAN
> HEDWIG
> KASPAR

is the binary tree of Figure 7.19.

The algorithm of Example 7.4 implies that insertion of new nodes will always occur at the leaf nodes of a tree. As with insertion into a linked list, no data are moved; only pointers are manipulated. However, unlike the steps required by a linked list representation, we do not have to traverse the list sequentially to determine where a new node belongs. Instead, using the *insertion rule*—if less than, go left; otherwise, go right—we need merely traverse one branch of the tree to determine the position for a new node. Provided that the tree maintains a full shape, the number of nodes on a given branch will be at most

$$\log_2 n + 1$$

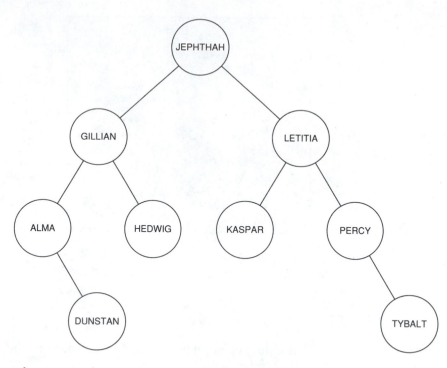

FIGURE 7.19

Binary tree resulting from procedure Add with sample data from Example 7.4.

where n is the total number of nodes in the tree. By *full* we mean that all nodes with fewer than two children must occur at level m or $m - 1$ where m is the deepest level in the tree. In other words, all nodes above level $m - 1$ must have exactly two children. Hence, adding ROBERTS to the tree of Figure 7.18 by the insertion rule would destroy its fullness.

Given this definition of full, the ($\log_2 n + 1$) figure for the maximum number of nodes on a branch emerges immediately upon inspection or, more formally, using a proof by mathematical induction. Our purpose, however, is not to give the details of such a proof but rather to emphasize that a binary tree with the ordering property presents an alternative to a linked list structure for the type of processing involved in maintaining ordered lists. Moreover, it is a particularly attractive alternative when the tree is full, because substantially fewer comparisons are needed to locate where in the structure an insertion is to be made. For instance, if n is 1024, the linked list may require as many as 1024 comparisons to make an insertion. Because $\log_2 1024$ is 10, the full binary tree will require at most 11 comparisons. This difference becomes even more dramatic as n gets larger. For an ordered list with 1,000,000 entries, a linked list may require that many comparisons, but the full binary tree requires a mere 21 comparisons.

What happens when the tree is not full? We comment on that situation at the end of this section, when we discuss the overall efficiency considerations for this implementation of a list. Before that, however, we consider the operations of finding and deleting data in a binary tree with the ordering property.

Searching for Data in the Binary Tree Implementation of a List

The insertion rule also dictates the search path followed through an ordered binary tree when we are attempting to find a given data item. Interestingly, if we trace the nodes visited on such a search path for a full binary tree, we will probe exactly the same items that we would in conducting a binary search on a physically ordered array containing the same data. For instance, if we are searching for SMITH in the tree of Figure 7.17, we will have to probe MAGILLICUDDY, TALBOT, and PERKINS. These are precisely the items that would be probed if the binary search algorithm were applied to the physically ordered list associated with Figure 7.17. Because of this, an ordered binary tree representation of a list is often called a *binary search tree*. Our analysis of such a tree has allowed us to conclude that, as long as the binary tree remains full, search efficiency for this method of implementing a list matches that of the ordered array implementation. That is, the best case search efficiency is $O(\log_2 n)$.

Deleting Data in the Binary Tree Implementation of a List

The deletion algorithm for an ordered binary tree is conceptually more complex than that for a linked list. Suppose, for instance, that we wish to remove TALBOT from the list represented by the tree of Figure 7.17. Two questions arise.

1. Can such a deletion be achieved merely by manipulating pointers?
2. If so, what does the resulting tree look like?

To answer these questions, begin by recalling that all that is necessary to represent an ordered list with a binary tree is that, for each node in the tree,

1. The left subtree must contain only items less than that node.
2. The right subtree must contain only items greater than or equal to that node.

With the preservation of this ordering property as the primary goal in processing a deletion, one acceptable way of restructuring the tree of Figure 7.17 after deleting TALBOT appears in Figure 7.20; essentially, SELIGER moves up to replace TALBOT in the tree. The choice of SELIGER to replace TALBOT is made because SELIGER represents the greatest data item in the left subtree of the node containing TALBOT. As long as we choose this greatest item in the left subtree to replace the item being deleted, we guarantee preservation of the crucial ordering property that enables the tree to represent the list accurately.

Given this general motivation for choosing a node to replace the one being deleted, let us now outline a case-by-case analysis of the deletion algorithm. Throughout this analysis, we assume that we have a pointer P to the item that we wish to delete. The pointer P may be one of the following:

1. The root pointer for the entire tree.
2. The left child pointer of the parent of the node to be deleted.
3. The right child pointer of the parent of the node to be deleted.

Figure 7.21 highlights these three possibilities; the algorithm applies whether 1, 2, or 3 holds. We now examine three cases of node deletion on a binary tree.

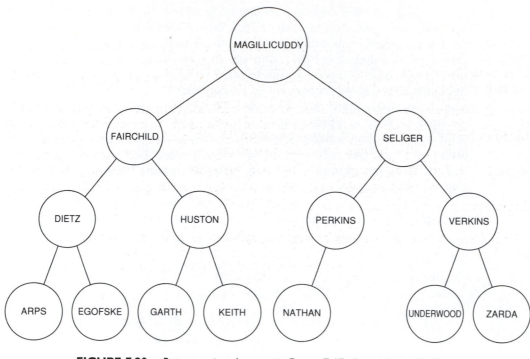

FIGURE 7.20   Restructuring the tree in Figure 7.17 after deleting TALBOT.

1. The node to be deleted has a left child.
2. The node to be deleted has a right child but no left child.
3. The node to be deleted has no children.

Case I The node pointed to by P, that is, the node to be deleted, has a left child. In Figure 7.22, node M is to be deleted and has left-child K. In this case, because we have a nonempty left subtree of the node to be deleted, our previous discussion indicates that we must find the greatest node in that left subtree. If the node pointed to by Ref(P).LeftChild (node K in the figure) has no right child, then the greatest node in the left subtree of P

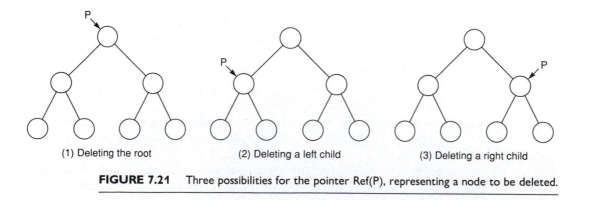

(1) Deleting the root   (2) Deleting a left child   (3) Deleting a right child

FIGURE 7.21   Three possibilities for the pointer Ref(P), representing a node to be deleted.

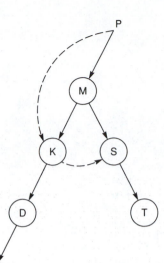

FIGURE 7.22

Case 1 with Ref(P).LeftChild (node K) having no right children.

is Ref(P).LeftChild itself. Figure 7.22 pictorially describes this situation; the dotted lines indicate new pointer values.

The partial coding to achieve this pointer manipulation is given by

```
X := P;
P := Ref(X).LeftChild;
Ref(P).RightChild := Ref(X).RightChild;
ReturnNode(X);
```

where LeftChild and RightChild refer to the left and right child pointers described earlier in this chapter.

If the node pointed to by Ref(P).LeftChild does have a right child, then to find the greatest node in the left subtree of P we must follow the right branch leading from Ref(P).LeftChild as deeply as possible into the tree. In Figure 7.23, node R is the one chosen to replace the deleted node. This figure gives the schematic representation, with the pointer changes necessary to complete the deletion. The coding necessary for this slightly more complicated version of Case 1 is

```
X := P;
Q := Ref(Ref(X).LeftChild).RightChild;
QParent := Ref(X).LeftChild;
(* Q will eventually point to node that will replace P.
   QParent will point to Q's parent. The following loop
   forces Q as deep as possible along the right branch
   from Ref(P).LeftChild. *)
while Ref(Q).RightChild <> NULL
  Q := Ref(Q).RightChild;
  QParent := Ref(QParent).RightChild
endwhile;
```

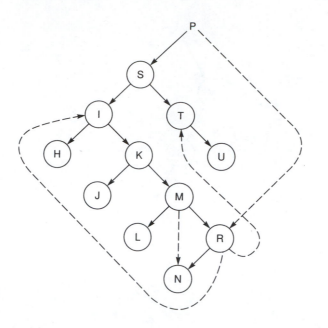

FIGURE 7.23
Case 1 with Ref(P).LeftChild
having a right child.

```
(* Having found node Q to replace P, adjust pointers to
   appropriately link it into the tree. *)
Ref(Q).RightChild := Ref(X).RightChild;
P := Q;
Ref(QParent).RightChild := Ref(Q).LeftChild;
Ref(Q).LeftChild := Ref(X).LeftChild;
ReturnNode(X);
```

Case 2 The node pointed to by P, that is, the node to be deleted, has a right child but no left child. This case is substantially easier than Case 1 and is described in Figure 7.24. The node to be deleted is merely replaced by its right child. The necessary PSEUDO code is

```
X := P;
P := Ref(X).RightChild;
ReturnNode(X);
```

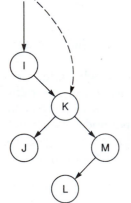

FIGURE 7.24
In Case 2 the node pointed
to by P has a right but no
left child.

Case 3 The node pointed to by P, that is, the node to be deleted, has no children. This is the easiest of all the cases. It can be compactly handled by the same coding used for Case 2 or, more directly, by

```
X := P;
P := NULL;
ReturnNode(X);
```

Efficiency Considerations for Binary Tree Implementation of a List

It is important to note that, in all three cases, the deletion of a node from the tree involved only pointer manipulation and no actual data movement. Hence, in a list maintained with a binary tree, we are able to process both insertions and deletions by the same pure pointer manipulation that makes linked lists so desirable. Moreover, the binary tree approach apparently allows us to locate data for inspection, insertion, or deletion much faster than a linked-list representation would. However, there are aspects of the binary tree method that tarnish its performance in comparison to a linked list:

- The binary tree implementation requires more memory in two respects. First, each node has two pointers instead of the one required in a singly linked list. This proliferation of pointers is particularly wasteful because many of the pointers may be NULL. Second, we presently can traverse the tree inorder only by using recursive techniques. Even in a language that allows recursion, a substantial amount of overhead is needed to maintain the stack used by recursive calls.

- The $O(\log_2 n)$ efficiency of the binary tree method is only an optimal, not a guaranteed, efficiency. It is contingent upon the tree's remaining nearly full. The tree's remaining full is in turn contingent upon the order in which data are added and deleted. In the worst case, data entering the tree structure in the wrong order can cause the tree to degenerate into a glorified linked list with a corresponding $O(n)$ efficiency. (The exercises at the end of this section have you explore this relationship between the order in which data arrive for insertion and the resulting search efficiency of the ordered binary tree.)

Both of these drawbacks can be overcome. We shall see in Section 5 of this chapter that we can actually avoid the overhead associated with recursion if we use a technique known as *threading*, which puts to good use the pointers that are otherwise wasted as NULL.

Moreover, by using a technique known as *height balancing,* the binary tree may be maintained in a fashion that approaches fullness at all times, regardless of the order in which data arrive for entry. We will examine this technique in Section 6 of this chapter. However, be forewarned that both threading and height balancing add a considerable measure of complexity to the algorithms manipulating ordered binary search trees. Consequently, we will first turn our attention to the somewhat easier topic of binary trees with the heap property.

Exercises 7.3

1. Suppose that integers arrive in the following order for insertion into a binary tree with the ordering property.

   100   90   80   70   60   50   40   30   20   10

   Draw the resulting tree, discuss its fullness, and categorize its search efficiency in big-O terms.

2. Repeat Exercise 1 but assume that the numbers arrive in the following order:

   60   80   30   90   70   100   40   20   50   10

3. Repeat Exercise 1 but assume that the numbers arrive in the following order:

   60   50   70   40   80   30   90   20   100   10

4. Describe a full binary tree.

5. Discuss the relative merits of maintaining an ordered list by a binary tree, a singly linked list, and a doubly linked list.

6. Discuss how the order in which data are entered into a binary tree representation of a list affects the fullness of the tree. Identify the best and worst possible cases.

7. In the style of Example 7.4, implement a procedure Retrieve to search for a Target in a binary tree with the ordering property. Note that, to take particular advantage of the ordering property, a Precedes function parameter will have to be added to the parameter list given in the definition of the Retrieve operation for generic binary trees (see Section 7.1).

8. Repeat Exercise 7 except write the procedure in a nonrecursive fashion.

9. In the style of Example 7.4, implement the Delete operation for a binary tree with the ordering property. For an added challenge, use the "mirror image" of the three cases discussed in this section.

10. Write a nonrecursive version of the procedure Add from Example 7.4.

11. Provide PSEUDO code for the Add, Delete, and Retrieve operations assuming that the linear representation of an ordered binary tree is used (see Section 7.2.)

12. Suppose that you are given an array of data arranged in increasing order. Develop a procedure that will load the data from this array into an optimal binary search tree.

13. Suppose that we change the definition of the ordering property for a binary search tree to stipulate that nodes that are equal in value to a given node may appear in either the left or right subtree of the given node. Is this change acceptable or does it cause unreasonable complications? Explain your answer.

7.4 APPLICATION: HEAPS, PRIORITY QUEUES, AND SORTING

Recall from Example 7.1 that we defined a heap as a binary tree in which each node's value was greater than or equal to the values of all items in its left and right subtrees. For generality, we assume that "greater than" is relative to some Precedes relation that the heap operations receive as an additional parameter. Moreover, the heaps we will discuss in this section and the remainder of the text will also have the property that they are full binary trees of level m such that

1. All nodes with two children at level $m - 1$ appear to the left of any node with only one child at level $m - 1$.

2. Any node with only one child at level $m - 1$ appears to the left of all nodes with no children at level $m - 1$.

3. There is at most one node with only one child at level $m - 1$.

Let us call this property *denseness*. Note that the heap in Example 3.1 is not dense, nor, in general, will a full tree necessarily be dense. Figure 7.25

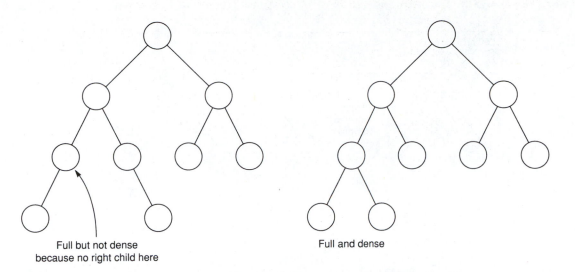

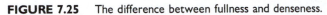

Full but not dense
because no right child here

Full and dense

FIGURE 7.25   The difference between fullness and denseness.

illustrates two full trees with nine nodes; the one on the left is not dense while the one on the right is. By maintaining the denseness of the heaps we manipulate, we can embed them in an array using the linear representation strategy described in Section 7.2 and not pay any price in wasted storage.

Hence, our implementation of a heap will rely on the following encapsulated record declaration:

```
type (* Assume that NodeLimit is a constant establishing
          maximum number of nodes in the tree *)
  TreeNodes: array [NodeLimit] of BinaryTreeData;
  BinaryTree: record
                  NumberNodes: integer; (* Number of nodes in
                                            tree *)
                  Node: TreeNodes        (* Data nodes *)
              endrecord;
```

We will also develop two subordinate procedures that will be particularly helpful in implementing the add and delete operations for a heap and in formulating a nonrecursive, $O(n \log_2 n)$ sorting algorithm. Because these subordinate procedures have applications in our general sorting interface, they will be stated in terms of an array instead of the prior encapsulated record declaration. However, keep in mind that we shall tie them into our heap implementation as well as a sorting algorithm.

We will call the first procedure WalkUp. The essence of WalkUp relies on your viewing an array of N values as having a dense binary tree embedded in it. Clearly, such an interpretation can be placed on any array of N items under the relationships

Left child of node at index K is at index $2 \times K$

Right child of node at index K is at index $2 \times K + 1$

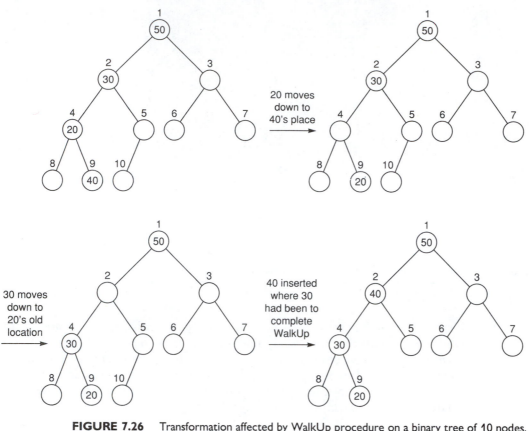

FIGURE 7.26   Transformation affected by WalkUp procedure on a binary tree of 10 nodes, with the ninth node (having value 40) being "walked up." Numbers outside circles indicate array index positions.

which were introduced in Section 3.2. Given this perspective, WalkUp takes a given node in the underlying binary tree and "walks it up" the path leading to it in the tree until its parent on that path is greater than it.

Figure 7.26 illustrates this transformation on a binary tree of 10 nodes with the ninth node designated as the node to be "walked up." Note that, if the node walked up is the only node that is out of place with respect to the heap property, then the tree will be a heap after the WalkUp operation is performed. Because of this, WalkUp will play a critical subordinate role in adding a new element to our heap structure.

```
procedure WalkUp
  ( given A: TreeNodes        (* Array viewed as full binary tree,
                                 with all indices in 1...N containing
                                 tree data *);
         N: integer          (* Number of values in the tree, less than
                                 or equal to NodeLimit *);
         J: integer          (* 1 <= J <= N; to be viewed as the index
                                 of a child node within the tree *);
         Precedes: Comparison (* Order relationship underlying tree *);
```

```
return A: TreeNodes          (* Array with data originally at index J
                                "walked" up a path within the tree.
                                That is, the data are repeatedly
                                exchanged with parent until that
                                original child is less than the parent
                                according to Precedes parameter *) );
var
  L, K: integer;
  Key: BinaryTreeData;

start WalkUp
  L := J;
  Key := A[L];
  (* A[L] will move along the appropriate path in tree *)
  K := L / 2; (* Initially K references parent *)
  while (K >= 1) and Precedes(A[K], Key) do   (* Move parent down *)
    A[L] := A[K];
    L := K;
    K := L /
  endwhile;
  A[L] := Key
end WalkUp;
```

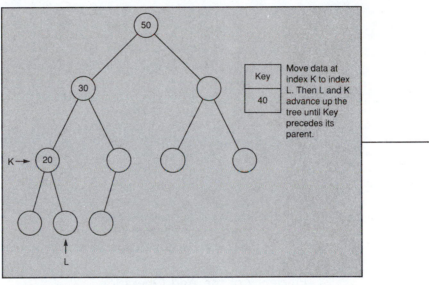

We can now use WalkUp to make short work of the Add operation for a binary tree that is to be maintained as a heap. Given a heap with NumberNodes nodes and a new Item to add, we will temporarily attach the new Item to the end of the array, that is, in the index following those nodes that have been arranged previously as a heap. Then, merely calling upon WalkUp for the new node will shift the entire tree into a heap. Hence, the Add operation is implemented as

```
procedure Add (* for binary tree with heap property implemented via linear
                 array representation *)
  ( given B: BinaryTree          (* A binary tree heaped by Precedes
                                    relationship *);
```

```
            Item: BinaryTreeData      (* A data item to be added to B *);
            Precedes: Comparison      (* Ordering relationship underlying heap *);
   return B: BinaryTree               (* B with Item inserted according to the
                                         Precedes relationship on which
                                         the heap is based *);

            Success: boolean          (* Set to true if Item successfully
                                         inserted; set to false if Item could
                                         not be inserted because there is no
                                         space in B *) );

start Add
   if Full(B) then
     Success := false
   else
     Success := true;
     B.NumberNodes := B.NumberNodes + 1;
     B.Node[B.NumberNodes] := Item;
     WalkUp(B.Info, B.NumberNodes, B.NumberNodes, Precedes)
   endif
end Add;
```

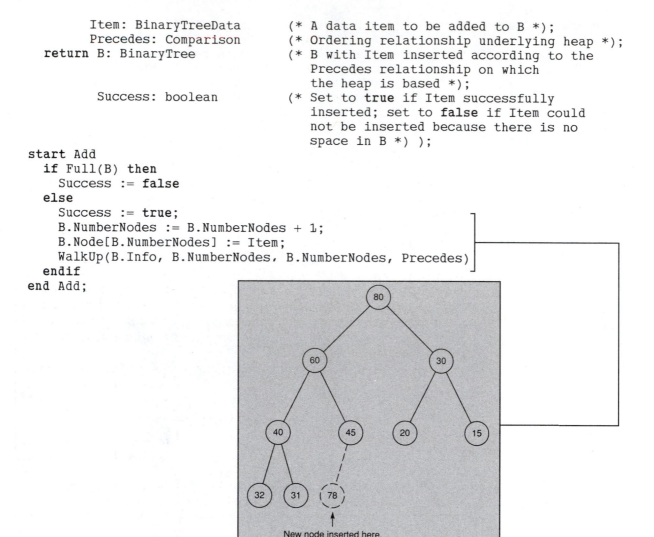

New node inserted here,
then walked up the tree

Efficiency of the Add Operation

The number of comparisons required to add a node to this implementation of a heap is clearly proportional to the length of the path that the new item travels as it is "walked up." But, since the tree is dense, our previous discussion of the number of levels in a full binary tree implies that this path length is $O(\log_2 n)$ for a tree with n nodes. Hence, we conclude that the add efficiency is also $O(\log_2 n)$.

The Heap as a Priority Queue and the Delete Operation

To implement the delete operation for a binary tree that is a heap, we are not concerned with finding a particular item to remove. If this were a concern, we should be using a binary tree with the ordering property for better search

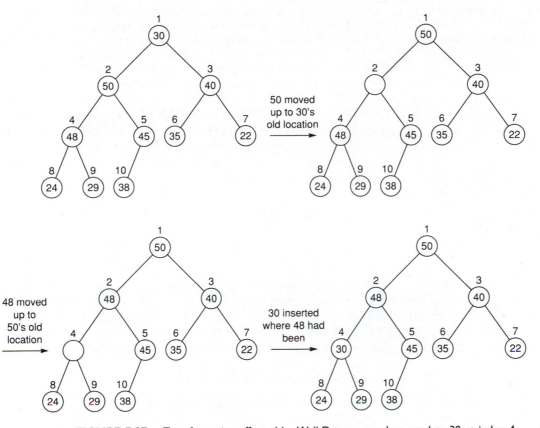

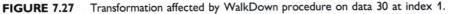

FIGURE 7.27   Transformation affected by WalkDown procedure on data 30 at index 1.

efficiency. Instead, we choose to view the heap as a means of implementing a priority queue (Section 4.5). Since removing from a priority queue always implies removing the item of highest priority, deletion from a heap simply means removing the item at the root (the item of greatest value) and then shuffling the remaining tree nodes back into a heap.

To achieve this shuffling, we use a subordinate procedure called Walk-Down, which does the opposite of WalkUp. That is, WalkDown takes a node in the binary tree embedded in the array and walks that node down an appropriate path in the tree until it is greater than both of its children. Figure 7.27 illustrates the tree transformation affected by WalkDown. As with the WalkUp procedure, if WalkDown is applied to the only node in a tree that is out of place with respect to the heap property, then the tree will be a heap after the WalkDown operation is performed. The following PSEUDO version of WalkDown is provided in array terms, rather than tree terms, so that we may reuse it conveniently when we turn our attention to sorting via heaps.

```
procedure WalkDown
    ( given A: TreeNodes      (* Array to be viewed as full binary tree, with
                                 all indices in 1...N containing tree data *);

           N: integer         (* Number of values in the tree, less than
                                 or equal to NodeLimit *);
```

```
        J: integer            (* 1 <= J <= N; to be viewed as the index
                                 of a parent node within the tree *);
       Precedes: Comparison (* Order relationship underlying tree *);
  return A: TreeNodes         (* Array with data originally at index J
                                 "walked down" a path within the tree.
                                 That is, the data are repeatedly
                                 exchanged with the child of greatest
                                 value (according to Precedes) until
                                 that original parent is greater than
                                 both of its children *) );
var
  L, K: integer;
  Key: BinaryTreeData;
  FoundSpot: boolean;

start WalkDown
  FoundSpot := false;
  L := J;
  Key := A[L];
  (* A[L] will move along the appropriate path in tree *)
  K := 2 * L; (* Initially K references left child *)
  while (K <= N) and not FoundSpot do
    if K < N then   (* Have K reference largest child  *)
      if not Precedes(A[K + 1], A[K]) then
        K := K + 1
      endif
    endif;
    if not Precedes(A[K], Key) then (* Child must move up *)
      A[L] := A[K];
      L := K;
      K := 2 * L
    else  (* Appropriate spot has been found *)
      FoundSpot := true
    endif
  endwhile;
  A[L] := Key
end WalkDown;
```

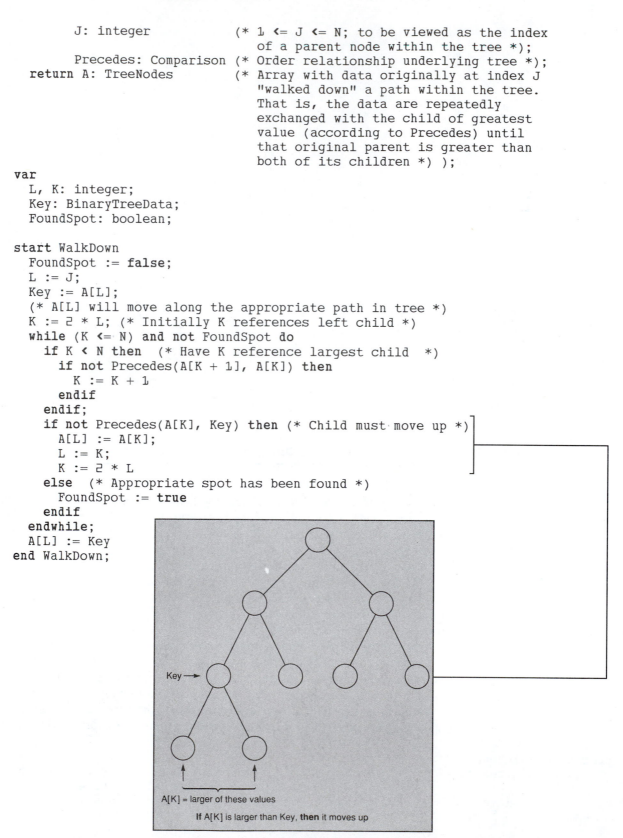

A[K] = larger of these values

If A[K] is larger than Key, **then** it moves up

We can now delete a node from a heap (priority queue) by

1. Removing the root (the item of greatest priority)
2. Moving the last item temporarily to the root position
3. Walking the new root down the remaining tree until it is reformed as a heap

The full Delete procedure, which invokes WalkDown, follows.

```
procedure Delete (* for binary tree with the heap property implemented via
                    linear array representation *)
  ( given B: BinaryTree        (* A binary tree B with the heap property *);
         Precedes: Comparison  (* Order relationship on which heap is based *);
    return B: BinaryTree       (* B with its original root, that is, its
                                  greatest value according to the
                                  Precedes relation, removed. B is then
                                  reshaped into a heap again *);
           Item: BinaryTreeData (* The value removed from B *);
           Success: boolean    (* false if an item could not be deleted
                                  from B; true otherwise *) );
  start Delete
    if Empty(B) then
      Success := false
    else
      Success := true;
      Item := B.Node[1];
      B.Node[1] := B.Node[B.NumberNodes];
      B.NumberNodes := B.NumberNodes - 1;
      WalkDown(B.Info, B.NumberNodes, 1, Precedes)
    endif
  end Delete;
```

Efficiency of Delete Operation for a Heap

Since the WalkDown procedure, like WalkUp, performs comparisons limited to one path within a dense binary tree, deleting a node is an $O(\log_2 n)$ operation.

Sorting via Heaps—The Heap Sort Algorithm

We have just seen that a heap, embedded in an array via the linear representation for a binary tree, becomes a very efficient priority queue. The utility of heaps does not end there, however. We will now see that viewing an array of n items as a binary tree that can be transformed into a heap provides the inspiration for a sorting algorithm that does the following:

- Guarantees $O(n \log_2 n)$ efficiency (hence, putting it in the same big-O class as the merge and quick sort algorithms)
- Avoids the overhead associated with recursion (unlike merge and quick sorts)
- Sorts the array in place, not requiring an extra copy of the values (unlike merge sort)

These features make the *heap sort* algorithm an attractive alternative when space is at a premium or when your programming language does not support recursion. The method, originally described by R. W. Floyd, has two phases. If you want to read Floyd's description of this method, see his article, entitled "Algorithm 245: Tree Sort 3" (*Communications of the ACM*, 7, December 1964, p. 701). In the first phase, the array containing the n data items is transformed into a linear heap.

As an example, suppose we wish to sort the following array:

11	1	5	7	6	12	17	8	4	10	2

The tree now appears as shown in Figure 7.28. In phase 1, to transform the embedded tree structure into a heap, we take the following steps:

1. Process the node that is the parent of the rightmost node on the lowest level. Call the WalkDown procedure with this node.
2. Move left on the same level. Again call the WalkDown procedure for this new node.
3. When the left end of this level is reached, move up a level, and, beginning with the rightmost parent node, repeat step 2. That is, call WalkDown with this node and then move left along the same level.

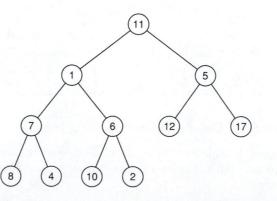

FIGURE 7.28
Full binary tree
corresponding to array.

4. Repeat step 3 until the root node has been processed.

Figure 7.29 shows these steps applied to the data in Figure 7.28.

Phase 2 of the heap sort finds the node with the largest value in the tree and cuts it from the tree. This is then repeated to find the second largest value, which is also removed from the tree. Then process continues until only two nodes are left in the tree; they are then exchanged if necessary. The precise steps for phase 2 are as follows:

1. Swap the root node with the bottom rightmost child, and sever this new bottom rightmost child from the tree. This is the largest value.

2. Call WalkDown on the new root value. That is, the tree is being restored to a heap.

3. Repeat steps 1 and 2 until only one element is left.

Phase 2 of the heap sort begun in Figure 7.29 is shown in Figure 7.30 for the three highest values.

The WalkDown procedure we developed earlier in this section is clearly a critical subalgorithm in both phases. Don't forget that each time we call on

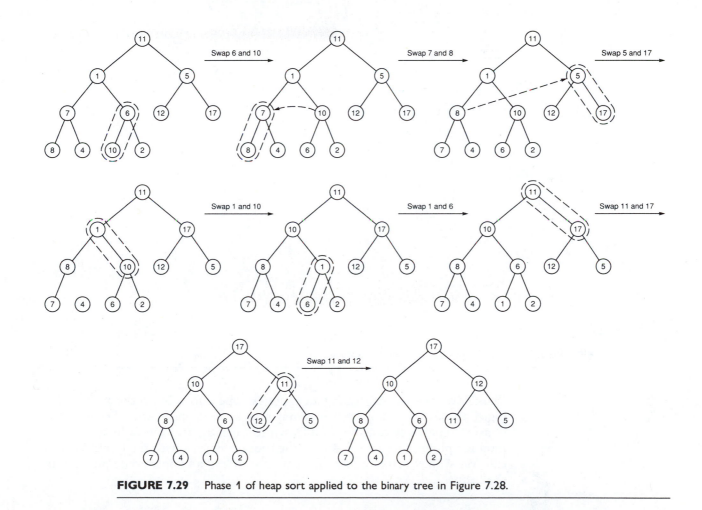

FIGURE 7.29   Phase 1 of heap sort applied to the binary tree in Figure 7.28.

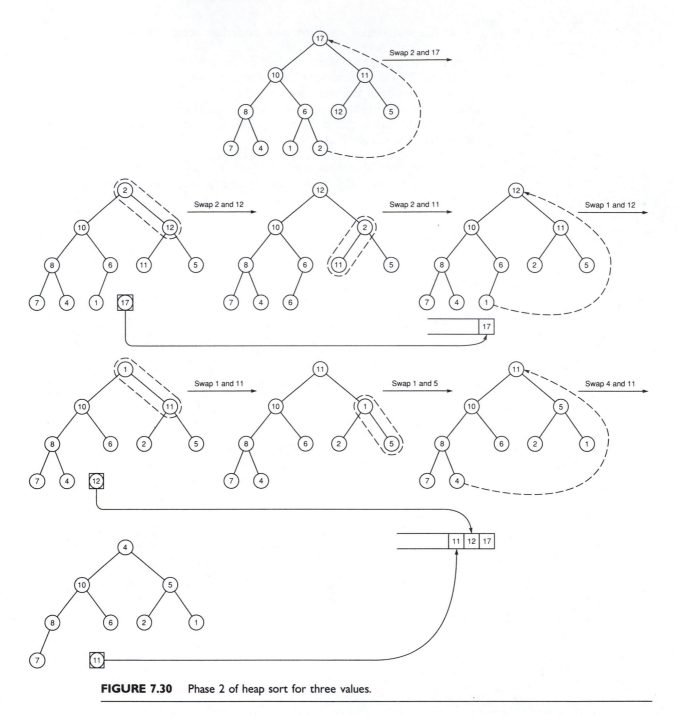

FIGURE 7.30   Phase 2 of heap sort for three values.

WalkDown we are performing an $O(\log_2 n)$ operation. Given the WalkDown logic, phases 1 and 2 of HeapSort may now be developed easily. The loop for phase 1 repeatedly calls on WalkDown to form the tree into a heap. Then a loop for phase 2 repeatedly swaps the root of the tree with the last child and calls on WalkDown to allow this new root to find an appropriate position in the heap.

```
type  (* Assume IndexLimit is constant determining array size *)
  ElementType: (* May be anything with an order relationship between
                  elements *);
  ElementArray: array [IndexLimit] of ElementType;
  Comparison: function
                  ( given A, B: ElementType  (* Values to compare *);
                    return: boolean          (* true if A precedes B in the order
                                                relationship on ElementType; false
                                                otherwise *) );
  (* Establish type equivalences that allow WalkDown to be used with
     ElementArray and ElementType *)
  BinaryTreeData: ElementType;
  TreeNodes: ElementArray;

procedure Sort  (* Heap sort implementation *)
  ( given A: ElementArray        (* Array with at most IndexLimit entries *);
          N: integer             (* Number of entries; assume 1 <= N
                                    <= IndexLimit *);

          Precedes: Comparison   (* An order relationship on elements in A *);
    return A: ElementArray       (* The array of values arranged in order
                                    according to Precedes relation *) );
  var
    Y: integer;
    Temp: ElementType;

  start Sort
    (* First phase 1 arranges the tree into a heap *)
    Y := N / 2;  (* Y starts at the last node to have child *)
    while Y > 0 do
      WalkDown(A, N, Y, Precedes);
      Y := Y - 1
    endwhile;
    (* Phase 1 done;  now begin phase 2 *)
    (* In phase 2, Y is used to point at the current last array slot *)
    Y := N;
    while Y > 1 do
      (* Interchange root with bottom right leaf node *)
      Temp := A[1];
      A[1] := A[Y];
      A[Y] := Temp;
      Y := Y - 1;
      WalkDown(A, Y, 1, Precedes)
    endwhile
  end Sort;
```

Swap these two, remove leaf node from further consideration, and walk down new root

Efficiency of the Heap Sort

It is relatively easy to deduce that the heap sort requires $O(n \log_2 n)$ comparisons. To see this, note that the phase 1 loop in the preceding PSEUDO procedure will execute $n/2$ times. Inside this loop we call WalkDown, which in turn has a loop that will execute at most $\log_2 n$ times (because it merely follows a path down a full binary tree). Hence, phase 1 requires at most

$$(n/2) \log_2 n$$

iterations at its deepest level. Phase 2 may be similarly analyzed. The phase 2 loop iterates n times. Within each iteration, WalkDown is called, again resulting in at most $\log_2 n$ operations. Thus, phase 2 requires at most $n \log_2 n$ iterations at its deepest level. Overall, we get

$$1.5n \log_2 n$$

as an upper bound for the number of iterations required by the combination of phases 1 and 2.

Thus, both quick sort and heap sort yield $O(n \log_2 n)$ efficiencies. In his book *Searching and Sorting*, Knuth has shown that, on the average, quick sort will be slightly faster since its big-O constant of proportionality will be smaller than that for heap sort. However, heap sort offers the advantage of guaranteeing an $O(n \log_2 n)$ efficiency regardless of the data being sorted. As we have already noted for quick sort, worst-case data can cause its performance to deteriorate to $O(n^2)$.

Exercises 7.4

1. Given the heap implementation described in this section, trace the status of the heap as each of the following operations are processed

   ```
   Add 14
   Add 40
   Add 26
   Add 32
   Add 12
   Add 45
   Add 28
   Add 9
   Add 8
   Add 16
   Delete
   Delete
   ```

2. Repeat Exercise 1 using the following operations

   ```
   Add 5
   Add 10
   Add 20
   Add 30
   Add 40
   Add 50
   Add 60
   Add 70
   ```

```
Add 80
Add 90
Delete
Delete
```

3. Consider the following heap:

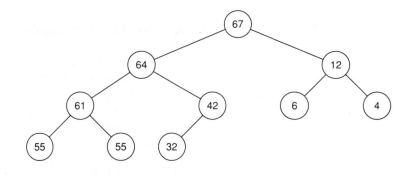

Specify an order in which these values could have arrived for insertion into this heap assuming the implementation described in this section.

4. One of the drawbacks of the linear array representation of a heap is that it places a static bound on the size of the heap. To avoid this, suppose that you decide to implement a heap using dynamically allocated pointer variables. Provide an encapsulated record description for such an implementation and then write PSEUDO code algorithms for each heap operation. (Hint: include a parent pointer in each node of the binary tree.)

5. What assumption is made about the evaluation of the boolean condition in the **while** loop of procedure WalkUp? Suppose that you work in a programming language that does not support this assumption. Indicate how the algorithm should be rewritten in such a language.

6. Consider the HeapSort procedure given in this section. Note that WalkDown is called at two points in the procedure: once in phase 1 and again in phase 2. Suppose that we were to trace the contents of the array being sorted after each call to WalkDown. What would we see as output if we called HeapSort with an array that initially contained

60 12 90 30 64 8 6

7. Repeat Exercise 6 for a six-element array that initially contains

1 8 2 7 3 6

8. Is a heap sort always better than a quick sort? When is it? When is it not?

9. What is the worst-case and average-case efficiency of the heap sort?

10. Give examples of arrays that generate the best and worst performances for the heap sort algorithm.

11. In Chapter 2, PointerSort used an index of pointers to sort data logically without rearranging it. Adapt the pointer sort procedure to the heap sort algorithm.

12. In Exercise 6 of Section 6.3, you evaluated the appropriateness of a collection of sorting algorithms for a particular application. Now evaluate the appropriateness of heap sort for that same application.

13. In Exercise 9 of Section 6.2 the notion of a stable sorting algorithm is defined. Is heap sort stable? If so, explain why. If not, provide an example of a data set that demonstrates its instability.

7.5 THREADING A TREE TO ELIMINATE RECURSION

We have seen that an ordered binary search tree can present an efficient alternative to ordered arrays and linked lists as a means of implementing the ordered-list ADT. One potential drawback to this strategy is that the algorithms to process binary trees are apparently recursive. This means that you must work in a language that supports recursion and that sufficient stack space must be allocated to support the recursive calling sequence. However, the results of Exercises 8 and 10 from Section 7.3 imply that nonrecursive algorithms exist for the Add, Retrieve, and Delete operations on an ordered binary tree. In this section, we shall examine a technique called *threading* to eliminate the recursion from our InOrderTraversal algorithm. Hence, for an ordered tree, *all* necessary operations may be implemented in a nonrecursive fashion.

Threading eliminates recursion at a very small price because it merely utilizes leaf node pointers that would otherwise be NULL. Consider the linked representation of a binary tree in Figure 7.31. There are ten wasted fields taken up by NULL pointers. These could be effectively used to point to significant nodes chosen according to a traversal scheme for the tree. For the inorder traversal of the binary tree in Figure 7.31, note that node A comes before − and that node B is preceded by − but followed by the root node +. With an inorder traversal, we could therefore adjust the RightChild pointer field of the node containing B (presently, NULL) to point to the node containing +, and the LeftChild pointer field of the node containing B to point to its predecessor node (−). The inorder traversal of this tree yields the expression A − B + C * E / F. Notice that B comes after − but before +. Similarly, because E is preceded by * but followed by /, the NULL left link of the node containing E should, in our scheme, point to *. The NULL right link of E should point to /.

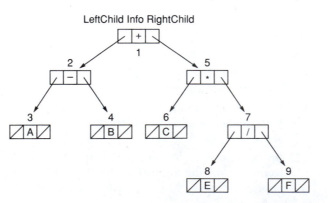

FIGURE 7.31
Example of binary expression tree to be threaded.

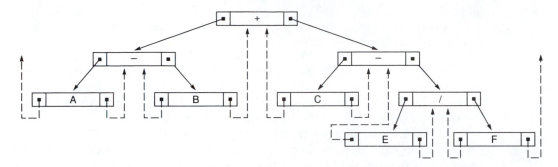

FIGURE 7.32   Threaded version of binary tree in Figure 7.31. Threads (indicated by a dashed line) that take the place of a left child pointer indicate the inorder predecessor, while threads that take the place of a right child pointer indicate the inorder successor.

Because we are arranging pointers to the inorder predecessor and successor of a leaf node, we call the pointers *inorder threads*. Following a thread pointer allows us to ascend strategically one or more appropriate levels in the tree without relying on recursion. Figure 7.32 is the transformed version of Figure 7.31 with threads indicated by dotted lines. Threads that take the place of a left child pointer indicate the inorder predecessor, whereas those that take the place of a right child pointer lead to the inorder successor.

The two threads on the far left and right of Figure 7.32 are the only loose threads at this stage. To correct this situation, we assume that a threaded binary tree is the left subtree of a dummy root node whose right child pointer points to itself. An empty, threaded binary tree drawn according to this convention is shown in Figure 7.33. We will also follow the convention of initializing the data field in this dummy header to a value guaranteed to be greater than any other item that could be added to the tree. This choice of a dummy root node for a threaded binary tree is similar to the strategy of using a dummy header for a linked list to eliminate consideration of special cases (see Section 3.4). By initially setting the pointers as indicated in Figure 7.33, we avoid having to treat the empty tree as a special case in our algorithm.

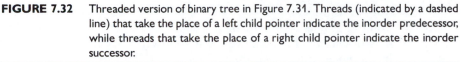

FIGURE 7.33

An empty, threaded binary tree. By using a dummy root node, initialized as shown, we can avoid treating the empty tree as a special case in our algorithm.

To keep track of which pointers are threads, we include two additional boolean fields in each node. One of these fields, LeftThread, indicates whether the left link of the node is an actual pointer or a thread. RightThread is used analogously for the right link. Let P be a pointer to a node. We follow the convention that

Ref(P).LeftThread = **false**

means that LeftChild is a normal pointer. Similarly

Ref(P).LeftThread = **true**

means that the left link of the node pointed to by P is a thread pointer. Similar interpretations hold for

Ref(P).RightThread = **false**

and

```
Ref(P).RightThread = true
```

The purpose of this boolean information as a means of identifying various pointers is only to help facilitate algorithms for different modes of traversing the tree. When we incorporate the header and boolean information into the tree of Figure 7.32, it takes the form of Figure 7.34.

To achieve an inorder traversal of the tree in Figure 7.34, we must proceed from each given node to its inorder successor. The inorder successor of a node is determined by one of two methods, depending upon whether or not the right child pointer of the node in question is a thread or a normal pointer. If it is a thread, then it leads us directly to the inorder successor. If it is not a thread, then we must follow the right child pointer to the node it references and, from there, follow left child pointers until we encounter a left thread.

To convince yourself of this last step, consider the threaded tree that is given in Figure 7.35. In this tree, to get the inorder successor of the node containing M, we must first follow the right child pointer from M to V and then go left as deeply as possible in the tree, finally arriving at the node containing Q. Note that this general strategy of proceeding one to the right, then left as deeply as possible, in combination with the initial setting of the right child pointer to the header node, ensures that the inorder traversal begins with the proper node. Trace the process shown in Figure 7.35 to find Q as the inorder successor of M.

Example 7.5   The following PSEUDO procedure more formally expresses the algorithm for the threaded inorder traversal operation just discussed. Note that it is achieved without any need for recursion or the use of a stack to simulate recursion.

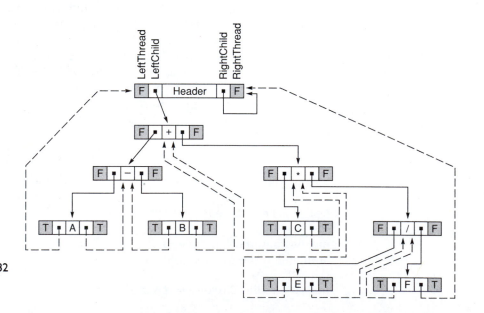

FIGURE 7.34

Threaded tree of Figure 7.32 with header and boolean information.

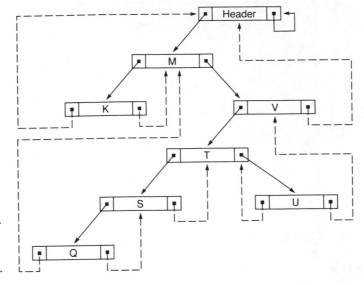

FIGURE 7.35

Threaded tree. To get the inorder successor of the node containing M, we must follow the right child pointer from M to V and then go left as deeply as possible in the tree, finally arriving at Q.

```
type
   BinaryTreeData: (* type of data stored in each tree node *);
   BinaryTree: pointer to BinaryTreeNode;
   BinaryTreeNode: record
                     LeftThread: boolean;
                     LeftChild: BinaryTree;
                     Info: BinaryTreeData;
                     RightChild: BinaryTree;
                     RightThread: boolean
                  endrecord;

procedure InOrderTraversal (* for threaded implementation *)
   ( given B: BinaryTree              (* A binary tree *);
          ProcessNode: NodeOperation (* This procedure determines the
                                        process applied to each
                                        BinaryTree node *);

     return B: BinaryTree             (* B with each node in its left
                                        subtree recursively affected
                                        by ProcessNode, then its root
                                        affected by ProcessNode, and
                                        finally each node in its right
                                        subtree recursively affected
                                        by ProcessNode *) );

   var
     P: BinaryTree;

   start InOrderTraversal
     P := B;
     repeat
        (* The following if statement alters P to point to its inorder
           successor *)
        if Ref(P).RightThread then
           P := Ref(P).RightChild
```

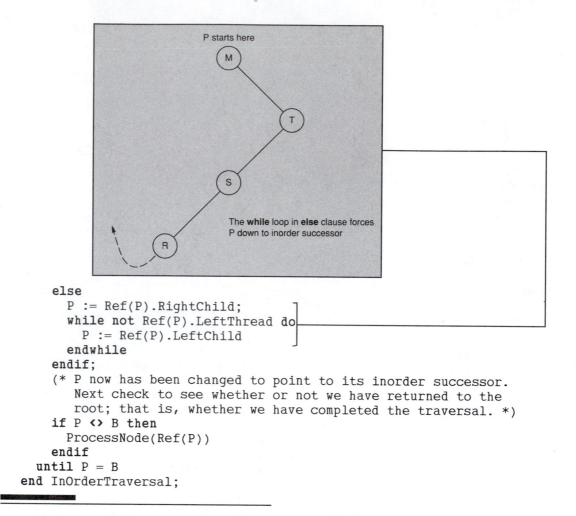

P starts here

M

T

S

The **while** loop in **else** clause forces
P down to inorder successor

R

```
      else
        P := Ref(P).RightChild;
        while not Ref(P).LeftThread do
          P := Ref(P).LeftChild
        endwhile
      endif;
      (* P now has been changed to point to its inorder successor.
         Next check to see whether or not we have returned to the
         root; that is, whether we have completed the traversal. *)
      if P <> B then
        ProcessNode(Ref(P))
      endif
    until P = B
  end InOrderTraversal;
```

We encourage you to trace carefully through the procedure of Example 7.5 on the tree appearing in Figure 7.35. You should also verify that the procedure gracefully prints nothing when the root pointer refers to an empty tree.

A few minor modifications to the procedure yields a new one that employs the predecessor threads to perform a reverse inorder traversal. Note that, if a given application required only forward traversing of the tree, there would be no need to maintain these predecessor threads. In that case, the left child pointers of the leaf nodes could remain NULL or perhaps even thread the tree for a preorder traversal. (See the exercises at the end of this section.)

A valid question at this stage is: Where do the threads come from? In our examples so far, they have merely been drawn as dotted-line pointers in the context of an already existing tree. However, we stress that, in practice, threads cannot exist unless they are continually maintained while nodes are added to the tree.

In the following discussion, we develop a procedure to insert a node into a threaded binary tree. In performing insertions, we preserve the ordering property cited in Section 7.3. For any given node, its left subtree contains only data less than it, whereas its right subtree contains only data greater

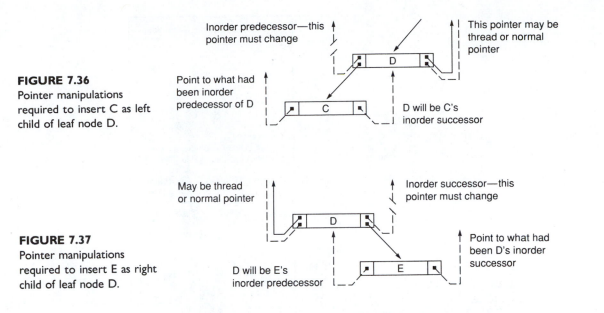

FIGURE 7.36
Pointer manipulations required to insert C as left child of leaf node D.

Inorder predecessor—this pointer must change

This pointer may be thread or normal pointer

Point to what had been inorder predecessor of D

D will be C's inorder successor

FIGURE 7.37
Pointer manipulations required to insert E as right child of leaf node D.

May be thread or normal pointer

Inorder successor—this pointer must change

Point to what had been D's inorder successor

D will be E's inorder predecessor

than or equal to it. To ensure that this property is met for the dummy root node, we specify that the data portion of the dummy root node be initialized to a value greater than any other data that will appear in the tree.

Given this criterion, insertion requires that the node to be inserted travel down a branch of the tree following the insertion rule (that we saw in Section 7.3): less than, go left; greater than, go right. Upon reaching a thread (that is, where a NULL pointer would be in an unthreaded tree), the new node is inserted appropriately as the left or right child. Figures 7.36 and 7.37 illustrate the pointer manipulations that must occur in each of these cases.

Example 7.6   The pointer manipulations just described are achieved by the following procedure Add for a threaded implementation of a binary tree. As is essential to any efficient insertion algorithm, no actual data are moved within the tree.

```
procedure Add  (* for threaded binary tree with ordering property *)
  ( given B: BinaryTree        (* A binary tree ordered by Precedes
                                  relationship *);
          Item: BinaryTreeData (* A data item to be added to B *);
          Precedes: Comparison (* The order relationship underlying B *);
    return B: BinaryTree        (* B with Item inserted according to the
                                  hierarchical relationship on which
                                  the tree is based *);
           Success: boolean     (* Set to true if Item successfully
                                  inserted; set to false if Item could
                                  not be inserted because there is no
                                  space in B *) );

  var
    Q, P, ParentQ: BinaryTree;
    Left: boolean;
```

until conditional controlling **repeat**

Leaf node may be reached with
Left **and** Ref(ParentQ).LeftThread
or
Leaf node may be reached with
not Left **and** Ref(ParentQ).RightThread

```
start Add
  if Full(B) then
    Success := false
  else
    Success := true;
    GetNode(P);
    Ref(P).Info := Item;
    (* Next allow this pointer to travel down appropriate
       branch of the tree until an insertion spot is found *)
    Q = B;
    ParentQ := NULL;
    repeat
      if Precedes(Item, Ref(Q).Data) then
        ParentQ := Q;
        Q := Ref(Q).LeftChild;
        Left := true
      else
        ParentQ := Q;
        Q := Ref(Q).RightChild;
        Left := false
      endif
    until (Left and Ref(ParentQ).LeftThread) or (not Left and
                                    Ref(ParentQ).RightThread);
    (*  Now insert P as the left or right child of ParentQ  *)
    Ref(P).LeftThread := true;
    Ref(P).RightThread := true;
    if Left then
      Ref(P).LeftChild := Ref(ParentQ).LeftChild;
      Ref(P).RightChild := ParentQ;
      Ref(ParentQ).LeftChild := P;
      Ref(ParentQ).LeftThread := false
    else
      Ref(P).RightChild := Ref(ParentQ).RightChild;
      Ref(P).LeftChild := ParentQ;
      Ref(ParentQ).RightChild := P;
      Ref(ParentQ).RightThread := false
    endif
  endif  (* for successful Add *)
end Add;
```

Efficiency Considerations for Threading a Tree

Deletion of a node from a threaded tree may be handled by considering the same cases discussed in Section 7.3. The only additional consideration is the maintenance of the boolean thread indicators. The only new fields required are the threads. Moreover, in practice, if space limitations are severe, the thread indicators may be incorporated into a bit of the left and right child pointers (though the methods for doing this are highly system-dependent). Thus, threading represents a true bargain. By spending very little, one regains both the time and stack space required for recursion.

ses 7.5

1. Consider the representation of a binary tree via an array of records as pictured in the table below (with zero indicating a NULL pointer).

BinaryTree

Location	LeftChild	Data	RightChild
1	3	A	5
2	7	B	11
3	6	C	0
4	0	D	0
5	8	E	10
6	4	F	2
7	0	G	0
8	0	H	0
9	0	K	0
10	0	L	9
11	0	I	0

Root
1

Location	LeftChild	Data	RightChild	RightThread
1		A		
2		B		
3		C		
4		D		
5		E		
6		F		
7		G		
8		H		
9		K		
10		L		
11		I		
12				

Root

ation
ersal)

ummy
your

l.
ry tree

has the

t main-
still be
nly lose
uld this
ied if no

the tree.
gested in

ay *not* be
ties intro-

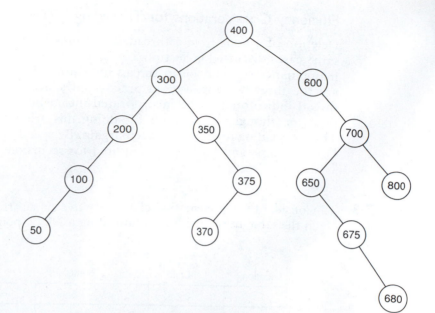

FIGURE 7.38
Tree for Exercise 2.

      a. Draw the binary tree represented by this implementation.

      b. By filling in the spaces in the table show the full memory represent
for this tree with a header node and right threads (for an inorder trav
added. Also indicate a new value for the root pointer.

2. Redraw the tree in Figure 7.38 as a threaded binary tree. Show the d
header, inorder predecessor threads, and inorder successor threads i
drawing.

3. Explain why it is not possible to thread a tree for a postorder traversa

4. Write a procedure that uses the predecessor pointers in a threaded bin
to generate a reverse inorder traversal.

5. Write a procedure to delete a node from a threaded binary tree that
ordering property.

6. If the inorder predecessor pointers appearing in Figure 7.34 were no
tained, that is, if NULL pointers were stored in their place, it would
possible to compete a threaded inorder traversal. Indeed, we would c
the ability to complete a threaded reverse inorder traversal. How wo
section's procedure for a threaded inorder traversal need to be modi
predecessor threads were maintained?

7. Redraw the threads in Figure 7.34 to indicate a preorder traversal of

8. Write a PSEUDO procedure for the preorder traversal diagram sug
Exercise 7.

7.6 HEIGHT-BALANCED TREES

Height-balanced binary trees represent an alternative that often m
worth the additional storage space and developmental complexi

duced for the sake of increasing speed. After describing the method, we shall cite some statistics that may help in deciding whether or not to height-balance a tree in a particular application. The height-balancing technique was developed in 1962 by researchers G. M. Adelson-Velskii and Y. M. Landis (Adelson-Velskii, G. M., and Y. M. Landis, "An Algorithm for the Organization of Information," *Dokl. Acad. Nauk SSSR, 146, 1962,* pp. 263–66). In credit to their work, height-balanced trees are also referred to as *AVL trees.* The AVL method represents an attempt to maintain trees that possess the ordering property of Section 7.3 in a form close to fullness, thereby ensuring rapid insertions and searches. One of the costs involved in doing this is that each node of the tree must store an additional item called its *balance factor,* which is defined to be the difference between the height of its left subtree and the height of its right subtree. In this context, the *height* of a tree is the number of nodes visited in traversing a branch that leads to a leaf node at the deepest level of the tree. An example of a tree with computed balance factors for each node is given in Figure 7.39.

A tree is said to be *height-balanced* if all of its nodes have a balance factor of 1, 0, or −1. Hence, the tree appearing in Figure 7.39 is not height-balanced. Note that every tree that is full is also height-balanced. However, the converse of this statement is not true (and you can convince yourself of this by constructing an example.) The AVL technique used to keep a tree in height-balance requires that each time an insertion is made according to the insertion rule specified in Section 7.3 one must

1. Let the node to be inserted travel down the appropriate branch, keeping track along the way of the deepest-level node on that branch that has a balance factor of +1 or −1. (This particular node is called the *pivot node* for reasons that will soon be apparent.) Insert the node at the appropriate point.

2. Inclusive of and below the pivot node, recompute all balance factors along the insertion path traced in step 1. It will be shown that no nodes other than these can possibly change their balance factors using the AVL method.

3. Determine whether the absolute value of the pivot node's balance factor switched from 1 to 2.

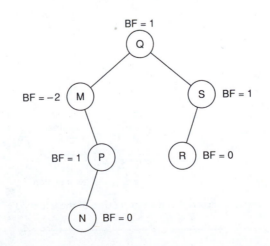

FIGURE 7.39

A tree with computed balance factors. A balance factor is the difference between the height of a node's left subtree and the height of its right subtree.

4. If there was such a switch as indicated in step 3, perform a manipulation of tree pointers centered at the pivot node to bring the tree back into height-balance. Since the visual effect of this pointer manipulation will be to "rotate" the subtree whose root is the pivot node, the operation is frequently referred to as an *AVL-rotation*.

We shall cover these steps in reverse order because, until one fully understands the nature of the AVL-rotation, it is not apparent why the pivot node is chosen as specified in step 1.

AVL-Rotations

In the following discussion we assume that steps 1, 2, and 3 above have all been completed and that we have a pointer, Pivot, to the deepest-level node whose balance factor has switched from an absolute value of 1 to 2. In practice, Pivot may be the root pointer for the entire tree or the child pointer of a parent node inside the tree. The pointer manipulations required to rebalance the tree necessitate division into four cases distinguished by the direction of the "guilty" insertion relative to the pivot node.

Case I The insertion that unbalanced the tree occurred in the left subtree of the left child of the pivot node. In this case, the situation pictured in Figure 7.40 must have occurred. Our only criterion for rebalancing the tree is the preservation of the ordering property for binary trees. Hence, if we could force a rotation (merely through changes in pointers) that made the tree pointed to by Pivot appear as in Figure 7.41, the rebalancing would be complete. The procedure to achieve this rotation is given below.

```
type
   BinaryTreeData: (* type of data stored in each node of tree *);
   BinaryTree: pointer to BinaryTreeNode; (* height-balanced implementation *)
   BinaryTreeNode: record
                   LeftChild: BinaryTree;
                   Info: BinaryTreeData;
```

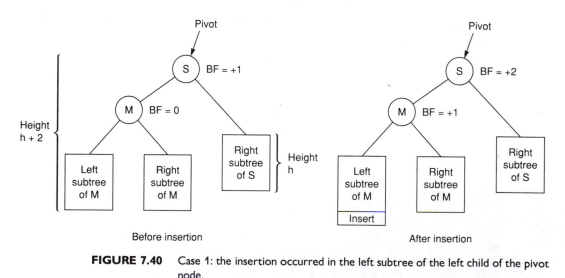

FIGURE 7.40   Case 1: the insertion occurred in the left subtree of the left child of the pivot node.

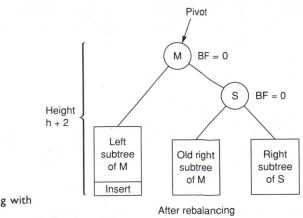

FIGURE 7.41
Case 1 after rebalancing with a LeftOfLeft rotation.

```
              BalanceFactor: integer;
              RightChild: BinaryTree
         endrecord;

procedure LeftOfLeft  (* for height-balanced binary tree *)
  ( given Pivot: BinaryTree  (* A binary tree rooted at the pivot
                                node in overall tree *);
    return Pivot: BinaryTree (* The pivotal subtree with the "left of
                                left" rotation performed on it *) );

  var
    P, Q: BinaryTree;
  start LeftOfLeft
    (* Begin by altering the necessary pointers *)
    P := Ref(Pivot).LeftChild;
    Q := Ref(P).RightChild;
    Ref(P).RightChild := Pivot;
    Ref(Pivot).LeftChild := Q;
    Pivot := P;
    (* Then readjust the balance factors that have been affected *)
    Ref(Pivot).BalanceFactor := 0;
    Ref(Ref(Pivot).RightChild).BalanceFactor := 0
  end LeftOfLeft;
```

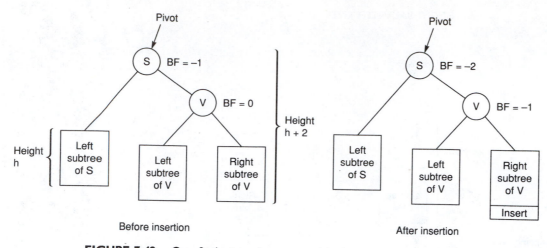

Before insertion   After insertion

FIGURE 7.42   Case 2: the insertion occurred in the right subtree of the right child of the pivot node.

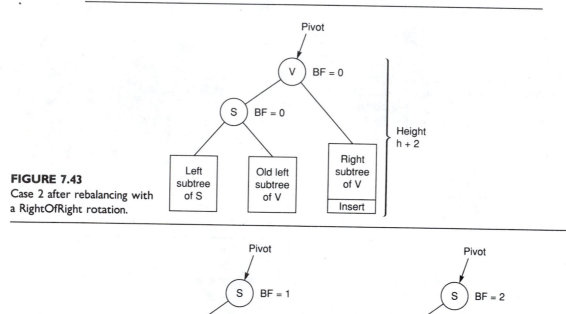

FIGURE 7.43

Case 2 after rebalancing with a RightOfRight rotation.

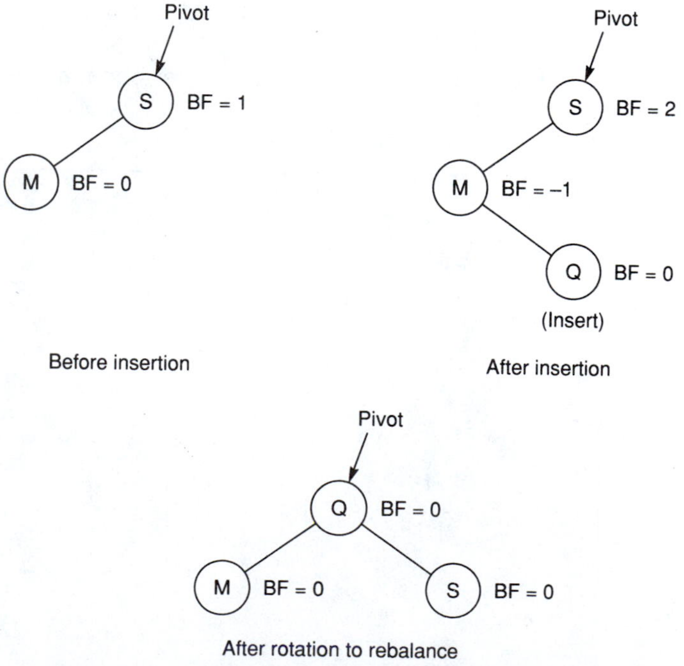

Before insertion   After insertion

FIGURE 7.44

Case 3, subcase 1: neither Pivot node nor its left child have a right child. Insertion occurs as the right child of the left child of the Pivot node.

After rotation to rebalance

Case 2 The insertion that unbalanced the tree occurred in the right subtree of the right child of the pivot node. In this case, the situation pictured in Figure 7.42 must have occurred. Figure 7.43 indicates the rebalancing that should occur. Again, the idea is to rotate the tree around the pivot node, except that this time the rotation must occur in the opposite direction. The procedure RightOfRight, necessary to achieve this rotation, remains as an exercise; it is essentially a mirror image of the LeftOfLeft procedure.

Case 3 The insertion causing the imbalance occurred in the right subtree of the left child of the pivot node. In this case, the procedure to perform the pointer manipulations necessary to rebalance the tree will require subdivision into three subcases, portrayed in diagrammatic form in Figures 7.44, 7.45, and 7.46, respectively.

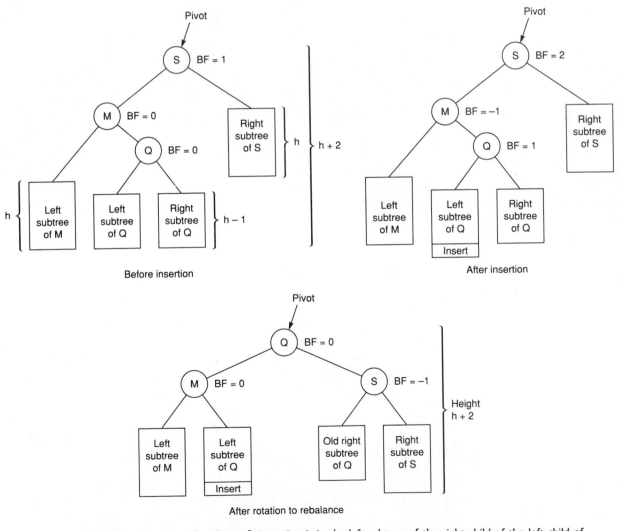

FIGURE 7.45 Case 3, subcase 2: insertion is in the left subtree of the right child of the left child of the Pivot.

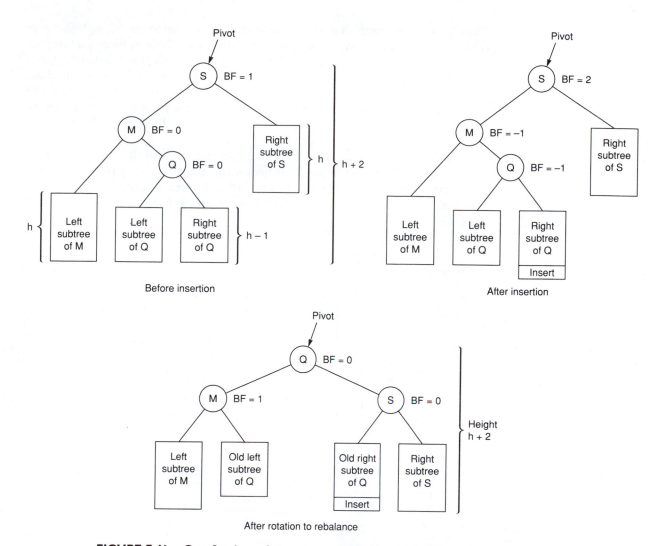

FIGURE 7.46   Case 3, subcase 3: insertion occurs in the right subtree of the right child of the left child of the Pivot.

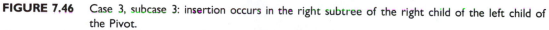

At first glance, the need for splitting Case 3 into three subcases may not be apparent. Indeed, all three subcases require nearly identical pointer changes. However, the subtle point of differentiation lies in how the balance factors are reset after the rotation has occurred. This subtlety is illustrated in the figures and is taken into account in the following procedure.

```
procedure RightOfLeft  (* for height-balanced binary tree *)
  ( given Pivot: BinaryTree  (* A binary tree rooted at the
                               pivot node in overall tree *);
    return Pivot: BinaryTree (* The pivotal subtree with the
                               "right of left" rotation
                               performed on it *) );
  var
    X, Y: BinaryTree;
```

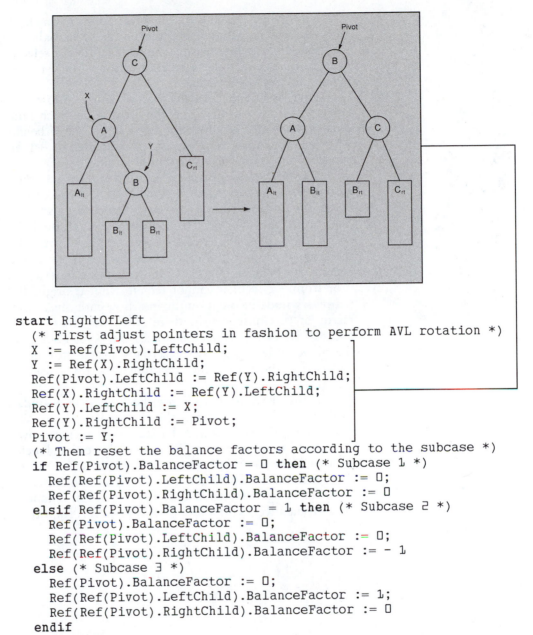

```
start RightOfLeft
   (* First adjust pointers in fashion to perform AVL rotation *)
   X := Ref(Pivot).LeftChild;
   Y := Ref(X).RightChild;
   Ref(Pivot).LeftChild := Ref(Y).RightChild;
   Ref(X).RightChild := Ref(Y).LeftChild;
   Ref(Y).LeftChild := X;
   Ref(Y).RightChild := Pivot;
   Pivot := Y;
   (* Then reset the balance factors according to the subcase *)
   if Ref(Pivot).BalanceFactor = 0 then (* Subcase 1 *)
      Ref(Ref(Pivot).LeftChild).BalanceFactor := 0;
      Ref(Ref(Pivot).RightChild).BalanceFactor := 0
   elsif Ref(Pivot).BalanceFactor = 1 then (* Subcase 2 *)
      Ref(Pivot).BalanceFactor := 0;
      Ref(Ref(Pivot).LeftChild).BalanceFactor := 0;
      Ref(Ref(Pivot).RightChild).BalanceFactor := - 1
   else (* Subcase 3 *)
      Ref(Pivot).BalanceFactor := 0;
      Ref(Ref(Pivot).LeftChild).BalanceFactor := 1;
      Ref(Ref(Pivot).RightChild).BalanceFactor := 0
   endif
end RightOfLeft;
```

Case 4 The insertion that causes the imbalance in the tree is made in the left subtree of the right child of the pivot node. Case 4 is to Case 3 as Case 2 is to Case 1; it remains as an exercise to write the procedure LeftOfRight.

Why Does the AVL Height-Balancing Technique Work?

Upon first studying the AVL algorithm, it is often not apparent why the pivot node must be the *deepest* node along the path of insertion that has a balance factor of $+1$ or -1. After all, it would seem that the Figures 7.42 through

7.46 work equally well as long as Pivot points to any node along the insertion path that has a change in the magnitude of its balance factor from 1 to 2. However, three subtle reasons are involved in the selection of the pivot node to be *not just any* node of balance factor +1 or −1 along the insertion path but the deepest such node.

First, it is quite evident that we must choose a node whose original balance factor is +1 or −1 as the pivot node. Such nodes are the only candidates for points at which the tree can go out of height-balance. Any node with balance factor zero can at worst change to +1 or −1 after insertion, therefore not requiring any rotation at all.

Second, whether or not a rotation takes place, *the only balance factors in the entire tree that will be affected are those of nodes inclusive of and below the pivot node along the insertion path.* In situations where a rotation does occur, this is evident from Figures 7.42 through 7.46. In all four cases of AVL-rotations, the overall height of the subtree pointed to by Pivot is the same after the rotation as it was before. In situations where no rotation occurs, the balance factor of the pivot node must change from either 1 to 0 or from −1 to 0; it cannot remain what it originally was. The reason is that every node below it on the insertion path must have an original balance factor of 0. Consequently, there is no way that an insertion may "hide" and not affect the balance factor of the pivot node. However, the fact that the pivot node changes to a zero balance factor in such situations again means that the rest of the tree above the pivot node is unaffected by the insertion.

Third, if we do not choose the deepest-level node with balance factor equal to +1 or −1, we run the risk of having an AVL-rotation that only partially rebalances the tree. Figure 7.47 indicates how this could occur. In this figure, if we choose a pivot node above that labeled S, that portion of the tree rooted at S will remain out of balance.

With this rationale in mind, we can now convincingly present a complete procedure to process an insertion into a height-balanced tree, recompute all affected balance factors, and perform an AVL-rotation if necessary.

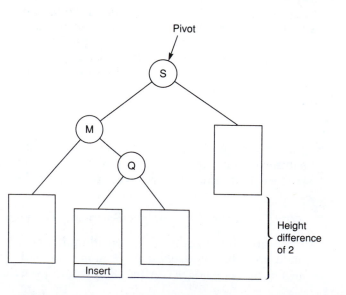

FIGURE 7.47
Case 3 incorrectly handled by not choosing proper pivot. AVL-rotation only partially rebalances the tree.

```
procedure Add  (* for height-balanced binary tree *)
  ( given B: BinaryTree          (* A binary tree ordered by Precedes
                                    relationship *);
         Item: BinaryTreeData    (* A data item to be added to B *);
         Precedes: Comparison    (* The order relation on which B is based *);
    return B: BinaryTree         (* B with Item inserted according to the
                                    hierarchical relationship on which the tree is
                                    based. Any AVL rotations necessary to maintain
                                    height-balance have been performed *);
         Success: boolean        (* Set to true if Item successfully inserted;
                                    set to false if Item could not be inserted
                                    because there is no space in B *) );

var
  P, Piv, PivParent, InP, InParent, Q: BinaryTree;

start Add
  Success := true;  (* To avoid a level of if-then-else nesting, assume
                       the implementation of pointers will find space
                       and hence guarantee success *)
  GetNode(P); (* Create a new node *)
  Ref(P).Info := Item;
  Ref(P).BalanceFactor := 0;
  Ref(P).LeftChild := NULL;
  Ref(P).RightChild := NULL;
  if B = NULL then
    B := P
  else
     (* Pointer InP keeps track of insertion point, with its parent InParent.
        Pointer Piv keeps trace of pivot node, with its parent PivParent *)
     InP := B;
     Piv := B;
     InParent := NULL;
     PivParent := NULL;
     (* Search for insertion point and pivot node *)
     repeat
       if Ref(InP).BalanceFactor <> 0 then
         Piv := InP;
         PivParent := InParent
       endif;
       InParent := InP;
       if Precedes(Item, Ref(InP).Info) then
         InP := Ref(InP).LeftChild
       else
         InP := Ref(InP).RightChild
       endif
     until InP = NULL;
```

At conclusion of **repeat** loop

PivParent

Piv

InParent

InP

```
(* Insert the node as the left or right child of InParent *)
if Precedes(Item, Ref(InParent).Info) then
   Ref(InParent).LeftChild := P
else
   Ref(InParent).RightChild := P
endif;

(* Now recompute the balance factors between Piv and InParent.
   By definition of a pivot node, all these balance factors must
   change by 1 in the direction of the insertion *)
Q := Piv;
repeat
   if Precedes(Item, Ref(Q).Info) then
      Ref(Q).BalanceFactor := Ref(Q).BalanceFactor + 1;
      Q := Ref(Q).LeftChild
   else
      Ref(Q).BalanceFactor := Ref(Q).BalanceFactor - 1;
      Q := Ref(Q).RightChild
   endif
until Q = P;

(* Need to rotate?  If not, then we're done! *)
if (-1 > Ref(Piv).BalanceFactor) or (Ref(Piv).BalanceFactor > 1) then
   (* AVL rotation is necessary. Call on the appropriate
      procedure, passing one of B, Ref(PivParent).LeftChild, or
      Ref(PivParent).RightChild as the pointer to the pivot node. *)
   if Precedes(Item, Ref(Piv).Info) then
      if Precedes(Item, Ref(Ref(Piv).LeftChild).Info) then
         if Piv = B then
            LeftOfLeft(B)
         elsif Piv = Ref(PivParent).LeftChild then
            LeftOfLeft(Ref(PivParent).LeftChild)
         else
            LeftOfLeft(Ref(PivParent).RightChild)
         endif
      elsif Piv = B then
         RightOfLeft(B)
      elsif Piv = Ref(PivParent).LeftChild then
         RightOfLeft(Ref(PivParent).LeftChild)
      else
         RightOfLeft(Ref(PivParent).RightChild)
      endif
   elsif not Precedes(Item, Ref(Ref(Piv).RightChild).Info) then
      if Piv = B then
         RightOfRight(B)
      elsif Piv = Ref(PivParent).LeftChild then
         RightOfRight(Ref(PivParent).LeftChild)
      else
         RightOfRight(Ref(PivParent).RightChild)
      endif
   elsif Piv = B then
      LeftOfRight(B)
   elsif Piv = Ref(PivParent).LeftChild then
      LeftOfRight(Ref(PivParent).LeftChild)
```

```
      else
         LeftOfRight(Ref(PivParent).RightChild)
      endif
   endif (* paired with test for absolute value of BF > 1 *)
  endif (* paired with initial else that tests B = NULL *)
end Add;
```

A subtle question that arises from this procedure is the following. Namely, consider the segment,

```
if Piv = B then
   LeftOfLeft(B)
elsif Piv = Ref(PivParent).LeftChild then
   LeftOfLeft(Ref(PivParent).LeftChild)
else
   LeftOfLeft(Ref(PivParent).RightChild)
endif
```

Why couldn't this lengthy segment from Add be replaced by the single procedure call LeftOfLeft(Piv)? The answer lies in the fact that the procedure LeftOfLeft alters the argument sent to it. It is for this reason that the argument to LeftOfLeft must by passed by reference. What we wish to alter in the segment above is *not* the pointer variable Piv but rather one of the pointer variables B, Ref(PivParent).LeftChild, or Ref(PivParent).RightChild. The simple procedure call LeftOfLeft(Piv) would leave the variables we really wish to change unaffected.

Height Balancing—Is It Worth It?

This is clearly a nontrivial algorithm. Moreover, the algorithm to delete a node from a height-balanced tree is no easier and is left for an exercise. In their paper, Adelson-Velskii and Landis were able to demonstrate that their method would guarantee a maximum branch length proportional to $\log_2 n$ where n is the number of nodes in the tree. In particular, they determined a constant of proportionality between 1.4 and 1.5. This means that the insertion efficiency for a height-balanced tree will be, in terms of orders of magnitude, roughly equivalent to that for a full tree. Compared to the worst case efficiency of $O(n)$ for a nonbalanced tree, it is clear that the AVL method can make a difference. However, one critical question is whether it is likely that arbitrary random data will generate such worst-case performance in a nonbalanced tree. This is a question you can explore empirically in the programming problems at the end of this chapter.

Whether the difference made by height balancing is worth the added developmental costs is, as always, a consideration tied to a particular application. The real problem in this regard, however, is that it is often impossible to have a realistic appraisal during the design stage of how height balancing will influence overall run-time efficiency. Consequently, if one does employ height balancing and it then turns out that system performance would have been adequate without it, a considerable amount of development time may have been wasted. We recommend a rather empirical approach to this dilemma. Unless the need for height balancing is obvious, design and write the application without height balancing. However, leave enough storage space in the tree nodes to accommodate balance factors. (You can get by with a mere two bits, if storage is at a real premium.) After empirically testing the performance of your application without height balancing, make the decision whether or not to rewrite routines to incorporate height balancing. If you've followed the ADT Use and Implementation rules from Chapter 2, your AVL routines should be "plug-compatible" with the ones they are replacing.

Exercises 7.6

1. Convince yourself that a height-balanced tree is not necessarily full by constructing an example that is height-balanced but not full.

2. Repeat Exercise 1 from Section 7.3 for a height-balanced tree.

3. Repeat Exercise 2 from Section 7.3 for a height-balanced tree.

4. Repeat Exercise 3 from Section 7.3 for a height-balanced tree.

5. Complete the procedures RightOfRight and LeftOfRight for insertion into a height-balanced tree.

6. Write a PSEUDO procedure to delete a node from a height-balanced tree. Provide an enumeration of the cases you must consider for such a procedure.

7. Write a PSEUDO procedure to add a node to an ordered binary search tree that is *both* threaded and height-balanced.

8. Consider the following alphabetical binary tree. Draw the tree after the data item A has been inserted and the tree has been height-balanced.

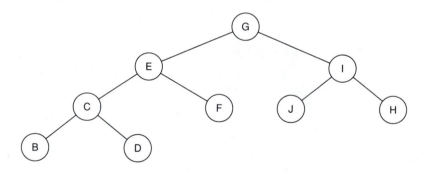

9. Repeat Exercise 8 for the insertion of D and the corresponding height balancing of the following tree.

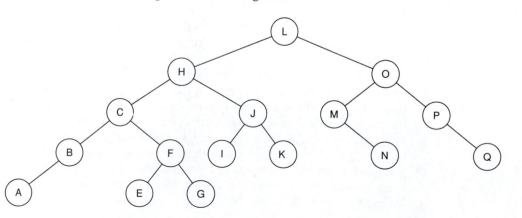

Chapter Summary   In this chapter we introduce some of the basic terminology of trees and define the *binary tree* ADT, where a binary tree is one whose nodes have at most two subtrees. Similarities between the binary tree ADT and ordered-list ADT of Chapter 3 are discussed, and Section 7.3 gives a binary tree implementation of an ordered list, together with a consideration of its efficiency. Both linear and linked representations for binary trees are considered and the storage efficiencies of each analyzed. Preorder, inorder, and postorder traversals are among the operations contained in the definition of the binary tree ADT, and an implementation for each is given.

The first application of binary trees examined is a heap, which is a binary tree in which each node's value is greater than or equal to the values of all items in its left and right subtrees. Add and delete operations for heaps are developed. In doing the latter we are not concerned with finding a particular item to remove, but instead we view the heap as a means of implementing a priority queue (priority queues were introduced in Chapter 4; only the item of highest priority is removed). Therefore, deletion from a heap simply means removing the item at the root and reshuffling the remaining tree nodes back into a heap. This approach is justified on the grounds that if the deletion of a particular node is a concern, then a binary tree with the *ordering property* (the data in each node of the tree are greater than all the data in the left subtree and less than or equal to all the data in the right subtree) would be more suitable because of the improved search efficiency it would provide. Heaps are then used as the basis for a nonrecursive sorting algorithm—the heap sort, which sorts an array and guarantees $O(n \log_2 n)$ efficiency, making it an attractive alternative when space is at a premium or the language used does not support recursion.

The notion of threading is introduced in Section 7.5 as a way to eliminate recursion from the InorderTraversal algorithm for ordered binary trees, allowing all necessary operations for this type of tree to be implemented nonrecursively. Finally, AVL trees are introduced to increase the speed of insertions and searches for ordered trees, and important issues are outlined for determining whether the added complexity of AVL trees makes it worthwhile to implement them.

Key Words

AVL-rotation	heap property	parent node
AVL trees	heap sort	pivot node
balance factor	height-balanced	postorder traversal
binary search tree	inorder traversal	preorder traversal
binary tree	inorder threads	right subtree
branch	insertion rule	root node
child node	leaf node	sibling
denseness	left subtree	subtree
full tree	level	threading
general tree	ordering property	tree traversal
heap		

Programming Problems/Projects

1. In Problem 11 of Chapter 4, you developed a program to store customer records for the Fly-by-Night credit card company in a priority queue based upon the promptness with which a customer pays his or her bill. Revise that program using a heap to implement the priority queue.

2. In previous chapters we have developed parsers for algebraic expressions—a stack-based parser with priority functions in Section 5.3 and a recursive descent parser in Section 6.4. Extend either or both of these parsers so that a binary expression tree is returned from the parser for a valid infix expression. Then write a procedure that traverses the tree and evaluates the expression represented by the tree.

3. In Problem 10 of Chapter 6 you developed a program that would allow you to empirically compare the sorting methods we had studied to that point. Extend this program by adding heap sort to the methods that can be chosen. Use your new program to empirically compare heap sort to other "fast" sorting methods such as Shell, quick, and merge sorts. In a written report, summarize your findings on the performance of heap sort compared to those other methods.

4. Develop a program to empirically test the search efficiency of a binary tree with the ordering property. Your program should load such a binary search tree with either

   a. a specific data set designed by the user, or

   b. a randomly generated data set for a user-specified number of values.

   Then your program should compute the average length of a search path required to find an item in the tree. This average search efficiency should then be output along with the theoretical upper and lower bounds on the search efficiency, that is, n and $\log_2 n$. Finally, have your program destroy the current tree before it iterates and allows the user to create another.
   Use your program to design an experiment that allows you to determine the likelihood of a given data set approaching the worst case $O(n)$ behavior. What kind of properties must a data set have before it seems to cross the line from $O(\log_2 n)$ to $O(n)$ behavior? Write your conclusions in a report in which you use the results from your program to back up your findings.

5. Extend your program from the previous problem so that it loads a given data set into a height-balanced tree as well as a nonbalanced tree. Have your program output comparative statistics for the average search efficiency for the two implementations.
   Use your program to design an experiment that allows you to reach some general conclusions regarding the difference in search efficiencies for these two implementations on specific kinds of data sets. Write your conclusions in a report using statistics from your program to back up your findings. Your report should also address the concerns addressed at the end of Section 7.6. That is, for what types of applications might the additional design and implementation time required for height balancing be worthwhile for achieving a significant gain in performance in the resulting system?

6. The definition given in Section 7.1 for the binary tree ADT should not be considered the only definition possible for this ADT. For instance, it is possible to

define the binary tree ADT without traversal operations if a collection of more primitive operations is provided that allows you to write your own traversals. For instance, you could maintain a *current node* and MoveLeft, MoveRight, MoveToParent, and MoveToRoot operations that are always performed relative to the current node. Write a complete ADT definition that employs such an alternate perspective. Then implement the ADT in your favorite programming language. Finally, use your new binary tree library to solve any of the programming problems presented here.

7. Modify the airline reservation system you developed for Wing-and-a-Prayer Airlines in Problem 1 of Chapter 3 so that the alphabetized lists are maintained with binary trees instead of linked lists.

8. Write a program that sorts the records of the Fly-by-Night credit card company file (Problem 2, Chapter 3) in alphabetical order by the last name and then the first name of the customer. Use a binary tree and its inorder traversal to accomplish the sort.

9. Recall the roster maintenance system that you wrote for the Bay Area Brawlers in the Programming Problems for Chapter 3. The system has been so successful that the league office would like to expand the system to include all the players in the league. Again the goal is to maintain the list of players in alphabetical order, allowing for frequent insertions and deletions as players are cut, picked up, and traded among teams. In addition to storing each player's height, weight, age, and university affiliation, the record for each player should be expanded to include team affiliation, years in league, and annual salary. Because the data base for the entire league is many times larger than that for just one team, maintain this list as a binary tree to increase efficiency.

10. Write a program that reads an expression in its prefix form and builds the binary tree corresponding to that expression. Then write procedures to print the infix and postfix forms of the expression using inorder and postorder traversals of this tree. Then see if you can extend the program to evaluate the expression represented by the tree.

11. Given a file containing some arbitrary text, determine how many times each word appears in the file. Your program should print out in alphabetical order the words that appear in the file, with their frequency counts. For an added challenge, do not assume any maximum word length; this will enable you to combine trees with the string handling methods you have already learned.

12. Here is a problem you will encounter if you write statistical analysis software. Given an arbitrarily long list of unordered numbers with an arbitrary number of different values appearing in it, determine and print out the marginal distribution for this list of numbers. That is, count how many times each different value appears in the list and then print out each value along with its count (frequency). The final output should be arranged from smallest to largest value. This problem can be solved elegantly using trees.

   An example of such output as produced by the COSAP (Conversationally Oriented Statistical Analysis Package) of Lawrence University appears at the top of page 364. Here the data file contained 838 occurrences of the values 1, 2, 3, and 5. Each value was a code number assigned to a particular judge.

```
                    Outagamie County Criminal Cases

                          MARGINAL FREQUENCIES

        Variable Judge          JUDGE BEFORE WHOM CASE BROUGHT (2)

        Value label             Value    Absolute      Relative
                                          frequency    frequency
          SMITH                    1         677         80.8%
          JONES                    2          88         10.5%
          DAVIS                    3          26          3.1%
          MILLER                   5          47          5.6%


          838 Valid        0 Missing   838 Total Observations
```

13. Many compilers offer the services of a cross-referencing program to aid in debugging. Such a program will list in alphabetical order all the identifiers that appear in a program and the various lines of the program that reference them. Write such a cross-referencer for your favorite language using a binary tree to maintain the list of identifiers that are encountered.

14. A relatively easy game to implement with a binary tree is to have the computer try to guess an animal about which the user is thinking by asking the user a series of questions that can be answered by *yes* or *no*. A node in the binary tree to play this game could be viewed as

    YES/NO pointers leading to

    1. Another question.

    2. The name of the animal.

    3. NULL.

    If NULL, have your program surrender and then ask the user for a new question that uniquely defines the animal. Then add this new question to the growing binary tree data base.

15. For this problem, you are to write a program that will differentiate expressions in the variable X. The input to this program will be a series of strings, each representing an infix expression to be differentiated. Each such expression is to be viewed as a stream of tokens. Valid tokens are integers, the variable X, the binary operators ($+$, $-$, $*$, $/$, $\uparrow$), and parentheses. To make scanning for tokens easy, you may assume that each token is followed by exactly one space, with the exception of the final token, which is followed by an end-of-line mark.

    First your program will have to scan the infix expression, building up an appropriate binary tree representation of it. For this you should be able to borrow significantly from the work you did with parsing expressions in Chapters 5 and 6. The major difference here is that the end result of this parse is to be a binary tree instead of a postfix string.

    Once the binary expression tree is built, traverse it, building up another binary expression tree that represents the derivative of the original expression. The following differentiation rules should be used in this process.

Suppose C is a constant, and S and T are expressions in X:

```
Diff(C) = 0
Diff(X) = 1
Diff(S + T) = Diff(S) + Diff(T)
Diff(S - T) = Diff(S) - Diff(T)
Diff(S * T) = S * Diff(T) + T * Diff(S)
Diff(S / T) = ((T * Diff(S)) - (S * Diff(T))) / (T ↑ 2)
Diff(S ↑ C) = (C * S ↑ (C - 1)) * Diff(S) { the infamous
                                            chain rule }
```

Finally, once the binary expression tree for the derivative has been built, print the expression. Print it in completely parenthesized infix notation to avoid ambiguity.

Note that there are three distinct phases to this problem.

• Parsing of the original infix expression into a binary tree representation

• Building a binary tree representation of the derivative

• Printing out the derivative in completely parenthesized infix notation

For an added challenge on this problem, simplify the derivative before printing it out. Simplify the expression for the derivative according to the following rules:

```
S + 0 = S
0 + S = S
S - 0 = S
S * 0 = 0
0 * S = 0
S * 1 = S
1 * S = S
0 / S = 0
S ↑ 0 = 1
S ↑ 1 = S
S - S = 0
S / S = 1
S / 0 = 'DIVISION BY ZERO'
0 / 0 = 'UNDEFINED'
```

16. A *mobile* is an object of a specified weight or a beam of a specified weight with a submobile attached to each end. Also, mobiles must be *balanced;* that is, submobiles suspended from opposite ends of each beam in the mobile should be equal in weight. Write a function that receives a potential mobile and returns a negative flagging value if the potential mobile is not balanced. If the mobile is balanced, your function should return the overall weight of the mobile. Test your function in an appropriate driver program.

8

GENERAL TREES

A tree's a tree. How many more
do you need to look at?

Ronald Reagan

CHAPTER OUTLINE

We began the last chapter with a discussion of the many ways in which hierarchical structures are used to organize information around us. We then quickly imposed a "birth control" dictate of at most two children, which focused all of our attention on the seemingly restricted case of the binary tree. But what about all those applications requiring a hierarchy in which a parent may have an unrestricted number of children? In this chapter we will examine techniques to implement those more general tree structures. In Sections 8.3 and 8.4, we will look at two applications of such general trees. The first of these applications, the two-three tree, leads to a very efficient implementation of the ordered-list ADT we introduced in Chapter 3. The second application consists of a series of refinements that use general trees to achieve an increasingly efficient implementation of the union-find ADT (Sections 2.4 and 3.7).

8.I   THE GENERAL TREE ADT

In trying to provide a complete definition of a general tree as an abstract data type, we find ourselves in the same predicament as with binary trees. That is, the applications of general trees are so varied in nature that it is impossible to provide a set of abstract operations that proves suitable for all situations. As with binary trees, we will take the approach of including only a small set of generic operations in our basic definition. Then, as we look at specific applications, ways of extending and tailoring these operations to optimize efficiency will be examined.

• **Definition:** A *general tree* is a set of nodes that is either empty (the recursive terminating condition) or has a designated node, called the root, from which zero or more subtrees descend. Each subtree itself satisfies the definition of a tree. Moreover, the collection of subtrees of the root is ordered in that there is a first subtree, second subtree, and so forth. The operations to be performed on a general tree are shown in terms of the following PSEUDO pre- and postconditions.

```
type
   GenTreeData: (* The type of each data item in the general tree *);
   GenTreeNode: (* Data type giving the structure of each node in the general
                   tree *);
   MatchCriterion: function (* The signature of a function that determines whether
                                two general tree data items match each other *)
                   ( given Target,
                          AnyData: GenTreeData (* Two data items, with
                                                  Target containing data to
                                                  be matched in some sense
                                                  as determined by Match
                                                  function *);
                     return: boolean          (* true if Target and AnyData
                                                  satisfy the Match
                                                  criterion *) );
   NodeOperation: procedure (* The signature of a procedure that can be
                                applied to an individual tree node *)
                     ( given Item: GenTreeNode    (* Arbitrary node in general
                                                     tree *);
                       return Item: GeneralTreeNode (* Item as affected by
                                                       NodeOperation *) );
procedure Create
   ( given T: GenTree              (* An arbitrary general tree variable in
                                      unknown state *);
     return T: GenTree             (* T initialized to the empty general
                                      tree *) );

procedure Destroy
   ( given T: GenTree              (* An arbitrary general tree T *);
     return T: GenTree             (* All dynamically allocated storage
                                      associated with T is returned to
                                      available space; T itself is in
                                      unreliable state *) );
```

```
function Empty
  ( given T: GenTree              (* A previously created general
                                     tree T *);

      return: boolean             (* true if T is empty; false
                                     otherwise *) );

function Full
  ( given T: GenTree              (* A previously created general
                                     tree T *);

      return T: GenTree           (* true if there is no space to insert
                                     additional nodes in T; false
                                     otherwise *) );

procedure Assign
  ( given Source: GenTree         (* A general tree whose contents are to
                                     be copied to Destination *);

      return Destination: GenTree (* Contains a copy of Source *) );

procedure Retrieve
  ( given T: GenTree              (* A general tree *);
         Target: GenTreeData      (* Node containing data to be matched *);
         Match: MatchCriterion    (* This function determines which general
                                     tree node is being sought *);

      return Item: GenTreeData    (* The "first" data in T satisfying the
                                     criterion established by Match *);

         Success: boolean         (* false if no data in T satisfied the
                                     Match criterion; true otherwise *) );

procedure Update
  ( given T: GenTree              (* A general tree *);
         Target: GenTreeData      (* Data to be matched *);
         Match: Comparison        (* This function determines which
                                     GenTreeNode is to be updated *);

         NewValue: GenTreeData    (* The new value to be assigned to the
                                     first node in T whose data satisfy the
                                     Match criterion. Assume that NewValue
                                     does not alter the logical position of
                                     the node in T *);

      return T: GenTree           (* The general tree T with the "first"
                                     data satisfying the Match criterion
                                     replaced by NewValue *);

         Success: boolean         (* false if no data satisfied the Match
                                     criterion; true otherwise *) );

procedure PreOrderTraversal
  ( given T: GenTree              (* A general tree *);
         ProcessNode: NodeOperation (* This procedure determines the process
                                     applied to each general tree node *);

      return T: GenTree           (* T's root is affected by ProcessNode;
                                     then each node in its first subtree is
                                     recursively affected by ProcessNode,
                                     then each node in its second subtree
                                     is recursively affected by
                                     ProcessNode, and so forth *) );

procedure PostOrderTraversal
  ( given T: GenTree              (* A general tree *);
         ProcessNode: NodeOperation (* This procedure determines the process
                                     applied to each general tree node *);
```

```
    return T: GenTree               (* Each node in T's first subtree is
                                       recursively affected by ProcessNode,
                                       then each node in its second
                                       subtree is recursively affected by
                                       ProcessNode, and so forth. Finally,
                                       after nodes in all subtrees of
                                       T are affected by ProcessNode,
                                       T's root node is affected by
                                       ProcessNode *) ):

procedure Add
  ( given T: GenTree                (* A general tree *);
         Item: GenTreeData          (* A data item to be added to T *);

    (* Additional parameters may be needed here, depending on the
       hierarchical relationship on which the tree is based *)

    return T: GenTree               (* T with Item inserted according to the
                                       hierarchical relationship on which
                                       the tree is based *);

         Success: boolean           (* Set to true if Item successfully
                                       inserted. Set to false if Item could
                                       not be inserted because there is no
                                       space in T *) );

procedure Delete
  ( given T: GenTree                (* A general tree *);
         Target: GenTreeData        (* Data to be matched for deletion *);
         Match: MatchCriterion      (* This function determines which
                                       GenTreeNode is to be deleted
                                       from T *);

    (* Additional parameters may be needed here, depending on the
       hierarchical relationship on which the tree is based *)

    return T: GenTree               (* General tree T with the first
                                       GenTreeNode whose data satisfy the
                                       Match criterion deleted. Only the
                                       first such GenTreeNode is deleted. *);

         Success: boolean           (* false if no GenTreeNode in T satisfied
                                       the Match criterion; true
                                       otherwise *) );
```

Not surprisingly, the operations provided by the above definition closely parallel those for binary trees. The main difference occurs in the traversal strategies, where only preorder and postorder make sense in the context of a general tree.

Example 8.1   Given the genealogical tree for the JONES family in Figure 8.1, indicate the order that nodes would be processed in a preorder traversal. Since a preorder

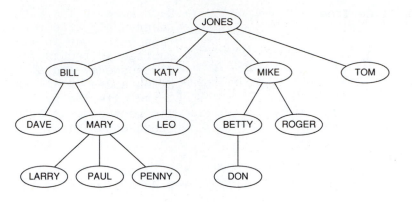

FIGURE 8.1
A genealogical tree.

traversal processes the parent first and then, recursively, all the children, we would have

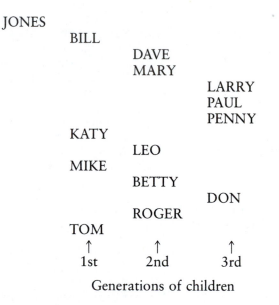

Generations of children

The indentation here has been added to highlight the fact that the preorder traversal will

- Process a parent node, and then
- Recursively process the child nodes from left to right

Relative to the general tree pictured in Figure 8.1, we see that the effect of the preorder traversal is to fix on a node at one level of the tree and then run through all of that node's children before progressing to the next node at the same level (the sibling). There is a hint here of a generalized nested-loop situation, which has some interesting applications, described in Chapter 10.

Example 8.2 Indicate the order that nodes in the tree of Figure 8.1 would be processed by a postorder traversal.

In general, the postorder traversal works its way up from the leaf nodes of a tree, ensuring that no given node is processed until all nodes in the subtree below it have been processed. Moreover, the subtrees of a given node are processed in first-to-last, that is, left-to-right, fashion. Hence, a postorder traversal yields the listing

DAVE

LARRY

PAUL

PENNY

MARY

BILL

LEO

KATY

DON

BETTY

ROGER

MIKE

TOM

JONES

Exercises 8.1 1. Indicate the order that nodes would be processed by a preorder traversal of the following general tree:

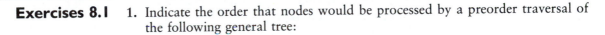
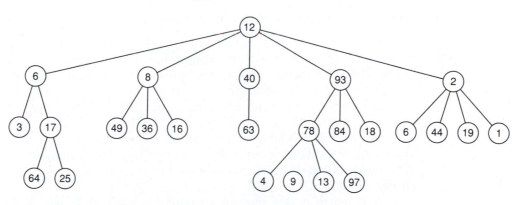

2. Indicate the order that nodes would be processed in a postorder traversal of the tree in Exercise 1.

3. Explain why an inorder traversal is not an applicable operation for a general tree.

4. Assuming the existence of the PreOrderTraversal operation, write an algorithm that would print out the preorder traversal of a tree in the indented format appearing in Example 8.1.

5. Assuming the existence of the PostOrderTraversal operation, write an algorithm to count the number of nodes in a general tree.

6. There are certainly alternative methods for defining the general tree ADT. One such method is to not provide explicit traversal operations but rather to provide operations that allow you to "navigate" your position within the tree from a continually changing "current node." For example, you could provide operations that allow you to

   a. Move to the root of the tree, that is, establish the root as the current node

   b. Move to the Kth child of the current node, where K would be a parameter for the operation

   c. Move to the parent of the current node

   Provide an ADT definition of a general tree based on this approach, then, using the operations from your definition, write preorder and postorder traversal algorithms.

8.2 IMPLEMENTATIONS OF GENERAL TREES

Because, in a general tree, a node may have any number of children, the implementation of a general tree is more complex than that of a binary tree. One alternative is to use a maximum but fixed number of children for each node. This strategy, however, has the disadvantage of being very wasteful of memory space taken up by NULL nodes. Hence, it is only effective in applications where you have prior knowledge regarding a realistic limit on the number of children a tree node may have (such as the application we will encounter in Section 8.3).

Binary Tree Representation of General Trees

A more practical way of implementing a completely general tree is to use a binary tree representation. This requires that each node have only two pointer fields. The first pointer points to the leftmost (that is, first) child of the node, and the second pointer identifies the next sibling to the right of the node under consideration. Since the children form an ordered set of nodes in this context, we can regard the leftmost child of a node as FirstChild and the sibling to the right of this node as Sibling. We will henceforth adopt this terminology for the two link fields involved with the binary tree representation of a general tree. Figure 8.2 gives the binary representation of the genealogical tree shown in Figure 8.1.

It is worth noting that an array of records with integer pointer fields can still be used to implement the FirstChild and Sibling pointers, just as it was for a linked list in Section 3.3. Indeed, because this array perspective allows us to specify some actual values for pointers, we have portrayed the tree of Figure 8.1 as an array of records in Figure 8.3. You should carefully check all FirstChild and Sibling values to convince yourself that the scheme

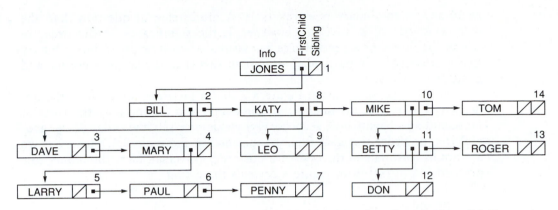

FIGURE 8.2   Binary tree representation of the genealogical tree in Figure 8.1. The numbers above the nodes refer to locations used in the array implementation of this tree in Figure 8.3.

Location	Info	First Child	Sibling
1	JONES	2	0
2	BILL	3	8
3	DAVE	0	4
4	MARY	5	0
5	LARRY	0	6
6	PAUL	0	7
7	PENNY	0	0
8	KATY	9	10
9	LEO	0	0
10	MIKE	11	14
11	BETTY	12	13
12	DON	0	0
13	ROGER	0	0
14	TOM	0	0

FIGURE 8.3

Tree in Figure 8.1 stored in array of records for data and pointers.

used to fill this array was to store a node before any of its children and then recursively store the leftmost child.

The analogous representation in terms of pointer variables requires the following type declarations:

```
type (* Declarations for binary tree representation of
          general tree *)
  GenTreeData: (* The type of each data item in the general
                  tree *);
  GenTree: pointer to GenTreeNode;
  GenTreeNode: record
                  Info: GenTreeData;
                  FirstChild: GenTree;
                  Sibling: GenTree
               endrecord;
```

Traversal of a General Tree Implemented via a Binary Tree

Because the binary scheme for a general tree is nothing more than a special interpretation of a binary tree, a traversal for a general tree can be established using any of the binary tree traversals. A more relevant question than the mere existence of a traversal, however, is the significance of the order in which the nodes of a general tree are visited when its representative binary tree is traversed. Of particular interest in this regard are the preorder and postorder traversals.

You should verify using Figure 8.2 that a preorder traversal of the underlying binary tree (assuming that FirstChild and Sibling play the roles of LeftChild and RightChild, respectively) yields precisely the order of the general tree preorder traversal that we specified in Example 8.1. However, we are not as fortunate in the case of a postorder traversal. Here the binary tree postorder traversal from Figure 8.2 yields the listing

PENNY

PAUL

LARRY

MARY

DAVE

LEO

DON

ROGER

BETTY

TOM

MIKE

KATY

BILL

JONES

This is *not* the general tree postorder traversal we obtained in Example 8.2. We will leave as a creative exercise the problem of generating a postorder traversal for a binary tree implementation of a general tree.

Ternary Tree Representation of General Trees

The ternary tree representation of a general tree can be effective for situations in which siblings always form an ordered list according to some specified Precedes relation. In such a representation, the informational field in each tree node is supplemented with the three pointers, which we call LeftSibling, Children, and RightSibling (see Figure 8.4). Also,

1. LeftSibling is either NULL or points to a node whose data precedes that of the given node in the ordered list of siblings at this level.

FIGURE 8.4

A node in a ternary tree representation of a general tree.

| LeftSibling | Info | Children | RightSibling |

2. RightSibling is either NULL or points to a node whose data equals or follows that of the given node in the ordered list of siblings at this level.

3. Children is a pointer to the ordered list of children of a given node.

Thus, a ternary tree representation of the general tree of Figure 8.1 that maintains the left-to-right order of siblings is given by Figure 8.5.

Interestingly enough, a perusal of the ternary tree representation of Figure 8.5 will show that it is composed of strategically located binary trees (encircled with dashes). For instance, an inorder traversal of the binary tree encircled by the dashed line numbered 2 yields the listing

BILL

KATY

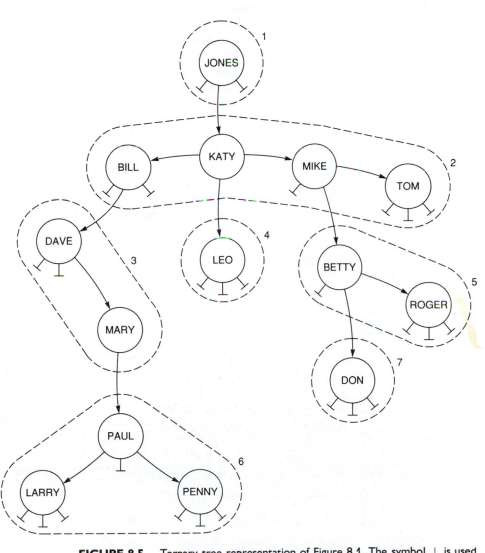

FIGURE 8.5 Ternary tree representation of Figure 8.1. The symbol ⊥ is used to emphasize NULL pointers.

MIKE

TOM

This is precisely the alphabetical order of the siblings that are the children of JONES in Figure 8.1. Similarly, an inorder traversal of the binary tree encircled by the dashed line numbered 6 yields the alphabetical order of the children of MARY in Figure 8.1. Thus, the LeftSibling and RightSibling pointers are tied to the ordering of children relative to an inorder traversal of an appropriate binary subtree of the entire structure. The Children pointer, on the other hand, is actually the root pointer to a binary tree which, in turn, represents an ordered list of children at the next deeper level.

The implications of the ternary tree representation in the area of data base management are significant. At first glance, it would seem that the only difference is that we are charged for one extra pointer per node. However, consider for a moment the following application, which is typical of the type of problem encountered in data base management. A university has a list of departments that it wishes to maintain in alphabetical order and each department has a list of professors to be kept in alphabetical order. Each professor teaches a list of courses; this list is to be kept in order by course number. Finally, each course has a list of students enrolled, also to be kept in alphabetical order. Figure 8.6 illustrates such a data base.

Consider the maintenance that is likely to be necessary for this tree-structured data base. Insertions and deletions will frequently occur at the class-section and student-enrollment levels. Depending upon the percentage of tenured faculty at this institution, this type of processing may not occur as often at the higher levels of the tree. Insertions and deletions in a large data base necessarily lead to considerations of efficiency. If this tree is implemented via the binary tree representation of a general tree, then each class list, each list of courses taught, and each list of departmental faculty becomes essentially a linked list. As such, each list's insertion and search efficiency is proportional to the number of members in the list. However, with the ternary

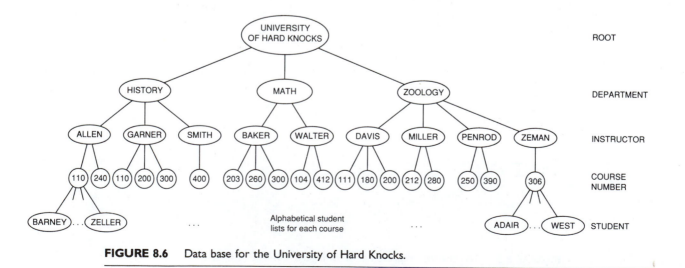

FIGURE 8.6   Data base for the University of Hard Knocks.

tree representation of this general tree, each sublist within the data is implemented with the binary tree method described in 7.3. Hence, insertion and deletion efficiency could well be proportional to the $\log_2 n$ figure we have cited previously. To ensure maximum efficiency, each binary tree sublist could be threaded and/or height-balanced. Clearly, for such a list-oriented data base, the third pointer of the ternary tree representation seems a relatively small price to pay for the added efficiency achieved.

In regard to traversing a general tree represented by the ternary tree method, we can duplicate the order of nodes visited by the preorder and postorder traversals of a binary tree representation. However, although the order can be duplicated, the method is slightly different. Suppose, for instance, that we wish to achieve the equivalent of a preorder traversal with a ternary representation. We must ensure that, immediately after processing a given node, we process *in order* all the children of that node. But to process in order all the children of a node, we need merely call on an inorder traversal procedure, with the root pointer being the Children pointer of a given node. That is, we essentially duplicate the effect of a preorder traversal for a binary representation by recursively calling on an inorder traversal for the tree of children! The procedure may be written quite elegantly in PSEUDO:

```
type (* Declarations for ternary tree implementation of general tree *)
  GenTreeData: (* The type of each data item in the general tree *);
  GenTree: pointer to GenTreeNode;
  GenTreeNode: record
                 Info: GenTreeData;
                 LeftSibling: GenTree;
                 RightSibling: GenTree;
                 Children: GenTree
               endrecord;

procedure PreOrderTraversal
  ( given T: GenTree                 (* A general tree *);
         ProcessNode: NodeOperation  (* This procedure determines the process
                                        applied to each general tree node *);
     return T: GenTree               (* T's root is affected by ProcessNode;
                                        then each node in its first subtree is
                                        recursively affected by ProcessNode,
                                        then each node in its second subtree
                                        is recursively affected by ProcessNode,
                                        and so forth *) );

  start PreOrderTraversal
    if T <> NULL then
      PreOrderTraversal(Ref(T).LeftSibling, ProcessNode);
      (* Then apply process to root node *)
      ProcessNode(Ref(T));
      (* Then visit the children *)
      PreOrderTraversal(Ref(T).Children, ProcessNode);
      (* Finally continue on at the sibling level *)
      PreOrderTraversal(Ref(T).RightSibling, ProcessNode)
    endif
  end PreOrderTraversal;
```

See the illustration at the top of page 378.

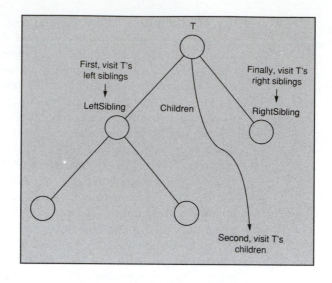

Exercises 8.2

1. Consider the following abstract graphical representation of a general tree. Draw specific pictures of how this tree would actually be stored using the binary and ternary tree implementations.

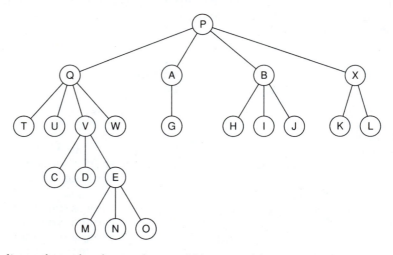

2. Indicate the order that nodes would be visited by a preorder traversal of the general tree in Exercise 1.

3. Indicate the order that nodes would be visited by a postorder traversal of the general tree in Exercise 1.

4. Write a PSEUDO version of the PostOrderTraversal operation for a general tree using the binary tree implementation.

5. Assume that the children of any given node in a general tree form an ordered list. Write a PSEUDO code version of the PostOrderTraversal operation for such a tree using the ternary tree implementation.

6. Assume that the children of any given node in a general tree form an ordered list. Write a PSEUDO version of the Retrieve operation for a general tree using the binary tree implementation.

7. Repeat Exercise 6, but now use a ternary implementation.

8. Analyze and compare the efficiencies of the algorithms you developed for Exercises 6 and 7. See Problem 8 at the end of the chapter.

9. In Exercise 6 of Section 8.1 you developed an alternate version of the ADT definition for a general tree. Now provide PSEUDO code procedures/functions for each of the operations in your definition under the assumption that a binary tree implementation of the general tree is used.

10. Repeat Exercise 9, but now assume that the children of any node in the tree form an ordered list and that a ternary tree implementation is used.

11. A *forest* is defined as a collection of general trees. A preorder traversal of a forest is a preorder traversal of the first tree in the forest, followed by a preorder traversal of the second, and so forth. Explain how a binary or ternary tree could be used to implement a forest. Then, for one of these implementations, provide the PSEUDO version of a preorder forest traversal.

8.3 APPLICATION: 2-3 TREES

We have seen in Section 7.3 that an ordered binary search tree can be used to implement an ordered list. The primary drawback of such an implementation is that, though the search efficiency may be as good as $O(\log_2 n)$, this fast search efficiency cannot be guaranteed. It is dependent upon the order that data arrive for insertion into the tree. In Section 7.6, we examined height-balancing as an implementation strategy for guaranteeing an $O(\log_2 n)$ search efficiency. We also noted that the constant of proportionality involved in this big-O efficiency figure is approximately 1.5.

In this section we shall examine another tree-based technique for implementing an ordered list. Called a *2-3 tree*, this technique can improve upon the efficiency of a height-balanced tree by guaranteeing a search path that never exceeds $\log_2 n + 1$. That is, it matches the efficiency of a full binary tree. The price paid for this efficiency is space—a price we will analyze more fully after examining the technique. Formally, we can define a 2-3 tree as follows.

• **Definition:** A *2-3 tree* consists of a general tree and a Precedes relationship with the following properties.

1. Every node in the 2-3 tree has room to store two informational fields. Call these informational fields FirstInfo and SecondInfo. Typically, these informational fields can represent two full-fledged data records.

2. Every node in the 2-3 tree has room for three pointers to other nodes. Call these pointers FirstChild, SecondChild, and ThirdChild.

3. Every node in the 2-3 tree has either
   • FirstInfo with active data and SecondInfo with an empty flag, or
   • The data in FirstInfo preceding that in SecondInfo according to the Precedes relationship for the tree

4. In any given nonleaf node:
   a. All data in the subtree referenced by FirstChild must precede FirstInfo, and all data in the subtree referenced by SecondChild must follow FirstInfo in the Precedes relationship for the tree.
   b. If SecondInfo has active data, then all data in the subtree referenced by SecondChild must precede SecondInfo, and all data in the subtree referenced by ThirdChild must follow SecondInfo.
5. All leaf nodes are on the same level.

According to this definition, we can think of a 2-3 tree node that is *not* at leaf level as the record structure in Figure 8.7. An example of a three-level 2-3 tree with integer informational keys appears in Figure 8.8. Those nodes in which the SecondInfo field is not active appear simply as data nodes with only one integer in them.

Search Algorithm

The search algorithm for 2-3 trees is similar to that for an ordered binary tree. That is, we start at the root of the tree. Comparing the target item to the informational fields indicates whether the target is in the current node or, based on the relationship of the target to First- and SecondInfo, which child pointer to follow. For instance, to find 650 in the tree of Figure 8.8, you should verify that

1. We follow the ThirdChild pointer from the root, because 650 follows 500

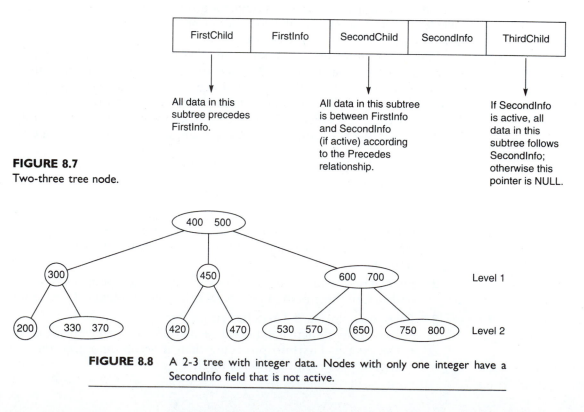

FIGURE 8.7
Two-three tree node.

FIGURE 8.8   A 2-3 tree with integer data. Nodes with only one integer have a SecondInfo field that is not active.

2. From the level-1 node containing 600 and 700 we follow the SecondChild pointer, because 650 is between 600 and 700

3. At level 2 we find the target

This algorithm is formalized in the following PSEUDO procedure. Note that the procedure does a bit more than the usual search. When the target is not found, Search also returns a pointer to the leaf node where it expected the target to be. This additional information will later allow us to use Search in the insert algorithm for 2-3 trees.

```
type
  TwoThreeData: (* The data in First- and SecondInfo in each TwoThreeNode;
                    admits a value identified by EmptyFlag, which is used to
                    indicate a field with no active data *);
  TwoThreeTree: pointer to TwoThreeNode;
  TwoThreeNode: record
                    (* Parent pointer facilitates moving up the tree *)
                    FirstChild, SecondChild, ThirdChild, Parent: TwoThreeTree;
                    FirstInfo, SecondInfo: TwoThreeData
                endrecord;
  Comparison: function (* The signature of a function that
                          determines the ordering of the 2-3 tree *)
                    ( given Item1, Item2: TwoThreeData (* Two data items to be
                                                          compared *);
                      return: boolean              (* true if Item1 is to be
                                                       considered as preceding
                                                       Item2 in ordering for the
                                                       tree; false otherwise *) );
  MatchCriterion: function (* The signature of a function that determines
                             whether two tree data items match each other *)
                    ( given Target,
                            AnyData: TwoThreeData (* Two data items, with
                                                     Target containing data to
                                                     be matched in some sense
                                                     as determined by Match
                                                     function *);
                      return: boolean           (* true if Target and
                                                    AnyData satisfy the Match
                                                    criterion *) );

procedure Search (* For 2-3 tree *)
  ( given T: TwoThreeTree        (* An arbitrary 2-3 tree *);
          Target: TwoThreeData   (* Data item being sought in T *);
          Precedes: Comparison   (* Order relationship for the tree *);
          Match: MatchCriterion  (* This function determines which tree
                                    node is being sought *);
    return Item: TwoThreeData    (* The information associated with Target *);
           Where: TwoThreeTree   (* If Target is found, this is a pointer to
                                    tree node where Target is located.
                                    Otherwise this is a pointer to the leaf
                                    node where Target would have been located
                                    if it were in the tree *);
           Found: boolean        (* true if Target is found; false otherwise *) );
```

```
var
   AtLeastOneItem, TwoItems: boolean;

start Search
   Found := false;
   if T <> NULL then
      AtLeastOneItem := not Match(Ref(T).FirstInfo, EmptyFlag);
      TwoItems := not Match(Ref(T).SecondInfo, EmptyFlag);
      if AtLeastOneItem then
         if Match(Ref(T).FirstInfo, Target) then (* check first info field *)
            Item := Ref(T).FirstInfo;
            Found := true
         elsif TwoItems then
            if Match(Ref(T).SecondInfo, Target) then (* check second info field *)
               Item := Ref(T).SecondInfo;
               Found := true
            endif
         endif
      endif;
      (* Assume LeafNode function returns true for LeafNode *)
      if Found or LeafNode(T) then (* return pointer *)
         Where := T
      elsif AtLeastOneItem then (* make recursive call to
                                    search appropriate subtree *)
         if Precedes (Target, Ref(T).FirstInfo) then
            Search(Ref(T).FirstChild, Target, Precedes,
                   Match, Item, Where, Found)
         elsif not TwoItems then
            Search(Ref(T).SecondChild, Target, Precedes,
                   Match, Item, Where, Found)
         elsif Precedes (Target, Ref(T).SecondInfo) then
            Search(Ref(T).SecondChild, Target, Precedes,
                   Match, Item, Where, Found)
         else
            Search(Ref(T).ThirdChild, Target, Precedes,
                   Match, Item, Where, Found)
         endif
      endif
   else (* tree is empty *)
      Where := T
   endif
end Search;
```

FirstInfo   SecondInfo

Call recursively with this tree if Target precedes FirstInfo

Call recursively with this tree if SecondInfo is empty or Target precedes SecondInfo

Call recursively with this tree if SecondInfo precedes Target

Search Efficiency

Stipulation 5 in our definition of a 2-3 tree is critical in an analysis of search efficiency for this data structure. By its guarantee that all leaf nodes are at the same level, it assures us that a 2-3 tree with N information items will have a maximal search path no longer than that in a *full* binary search tree with the same N items. From our earlier analysis of binary search trees, we know that this maximal path length is $\log_2 N + 1$.

Hence, provided we can develop add and delete operations that maintain a tree in a fashion dictated by the five stipulations in our definition of a 2-3 tree, we have a scheme for implementing ordered lists that is evidently on a par with full binary search trees and slightly better than height-balanced trees. What price have we paid? As usual, the trade-off is space. Here, we run the risk of having numerous SecondInfo fields filled with the empty flag. (You will explore how many such fields can be wasted in the exercises and problems for this chapter.) If these fields are actually large data records, you may decide the wasted space is not worth the relatively minor gain in speed over height-balanced trees.

Add Algorithm

To ensure that stipulation 5 of the definition is met, 2-3 trees exhibit the rather curious behavior of adding a new level to the tree by sprouting a new root instead of a leaf at a deeper level. We can illustrate this phenomenon and the algorithm that controls it by making a few insertions on the tree of Figure 8.8.

Example 8.3   Insert 250 as an informational item in the tree of Figure 8.8 on page 380.

Here a search algorithm would dictate that, if 250 were in the tree, it should have been found in the same node as 200. Since there is room for another informational field in the node containing 200, the place to insert 250 is obvious—as the SecondInfo field in that same node. The resulting tree is shown in Figure 8.9.

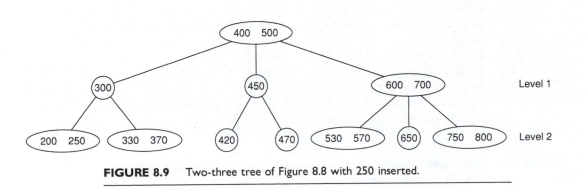

FIGURE 8.9   Two-three tree of Figure 8.8 with 250 inserted.

Example 8.4   Add 850 to the 2-3 tree of Figure 8.9.

The situation in this example is a bit more complex. As in Example 8.3, the search algorithm tells us that 850 should have been in the level-2 node containing 750 and 800 if it were in the tree. But it cannot fit there since we already have two data items. So, we will look at the tree items 750, 800, and 850; choose the middle one (800) to pass back up to the parent node; and then create two nodes containing one item each (for 750 and 850). Item 800 and the one-node tree containing 850 will then be passed back to the node containing 600 and 700. This is illustrated in Figure 8.10. If there were only one informational item here, 800 could be added as SecondInfo field and the node containing 850 added as the ThirdChild. Unfortunately, there is not enough room, so the splitting process must be repeated with 600, 700, and 800. This time 700 is chosen as the middle value with two subtrees rooted at 600 and 800 also created. This is highlighted in Figure 8.11. Item 700 is then passed back up the tree along with the subtree rooted at 800 for an encore of the splitting phenomenon. At the root, 400, 500, and 700 are compared. We split at 500, forming subtrees rooted at 400 and 700 and creating a new root with 500 as its FirstInfo data item. The resulting tree, now with a level added at the top, is shown in Figure 8.12.

The following PSEUDO procedure Add considers the two possibilities illustrated in Examples 8.3 and 8.4, that is, adding an item in a leaf

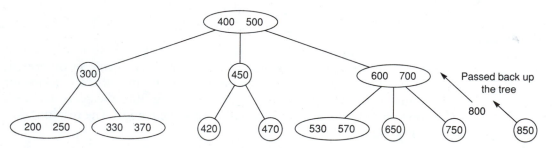

FIGURE 8.10   As leaf-level nodes become crowded, they are split with data being passed back up the tree to parent node.

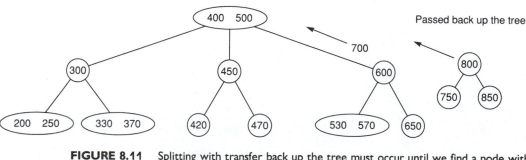

FIGURE 8.11   Splitting with transfer back up the tree must occur until we find a node with enough room to expand.

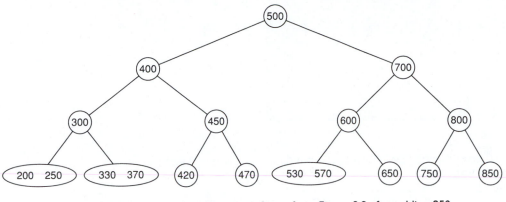

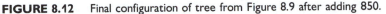

FIGURE 8.12   Final configuration of tree from Figure 8.9 after adding 850.

node with room to expand or forcing a split with data being passed recursively back up the tree until we find a node with room to store additional data. The details of splitting a node (perhaps recursively) are deferred to a subordinate procedure Split. Finally, note that, as a third possibility, Add must consider insertion of the first item in the empty tree as a special case.

```
procedure Add (* For 2-3 tree *)
  ( given T: TwoThreeTree        (* An arbitrary 2-3 tree *);
         NewData: TwoThreeData   (* Data item to be added in T *);
         Precedes: Comparison    (* Order relationship for the tree *);
         Match: MatchCriterion   (* This function determines whether NewData is
                                    already in the tree *);
    return T: TwoThreeTree       (* T with NewData added if NewData was not
                                    found. If NewData found in original tree,
                                    T is left unchanged *);
         Success: boolean        (* true if NewData is added; false
                                    otherwise *) );

  var
    Info: TwoThreeData;
    Found, TwoItems: boolean;
    Leaf: TwoThreeTree;

  start Add
    Search(T, NewData, Precedes, Match, Info, Leaf, Found); (* Find leaf for
                                                               key *)

    if Leaf = NULL then (* make initial root *)
      Success := true;
      (* MakeTreeNode will initialize tree node to two empty flags and three
         NULL pointers *)
      MakeTreeNode(T);
      Ref(T).FirstInfo := NewData
    elsif Found then (* NewData already in tree *)
      Success := false
    else (* Add new data node if it will fit in Leaf; call Split to
            split Leaf otherwise *)
      Success := true;
```

Leaf

No room in Leaf,
so it must split

40   50

NewData

35

```
        TwoItems := not Match(Ref(Leaf).SecondInfo, EmptyFlag);
        if TwoItems then
          (* Use Split procedure given below *)
          Split(T, Leaf, Leaf, NewData, false, Precedes, Match)
        elsif Precedes(Ref(Leaf).FirstInfo, NewData) then
          Ref(Leaf).SecondInfo := NewData
        else
          Ref(Leaf).SecondInfo := Ref(Leaf).FirstInfo;
          Ref(Leaf).FirstInfo := NewData
        endif
      endif
    end Add;
```

Leaf

50   Empty   →Transformed to→   40   50

NewData

40

```
procedure Split (* Subordinate procedure to Add *)
  ( given  T: TwoThreeTree        (* Root pointer for entire 2-3
                                     tree containing node to be split *);
           Tree: TwoThreeTree     (* Pointer to root of current subtree
                                     that must be split to add Data
                                     parameter *);
           Branch: TwoThreeTree   (* If AddBranch parameter is true, this
                                     is a pointer to a subtree to be added
                                     to the Tree node that is splitting.
                                     If AddBranch is false, this parameter
                                     has no well-defined value upon entry
                                     to the procedure *);
           Data: TwoThreeData     (* Data item forcing split of current root
                                     node in Tree *);
           AddBranch: boolean     (* true if a branch must be added to
                                     splitting node as well as Data item. This
                                     parameter is false when a leaf node is
                                     being split and true when an interior node
                                     is being split *);
           Precedes: Comparison   (* Order relationship for the tree *);
           Match: MatchCriterion  (* Used to test for EmptyFlag *);
```

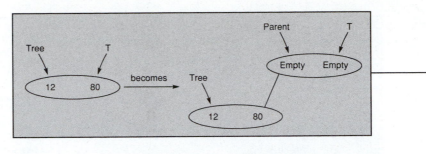

```
    return T: TwoThreeTree        (* Pointer to a new root for entire
                                     2-3 tree if Tree parameter is without
                                     a parent node. Otherwise T is unchanged *);
          Tree: TwoThreeTree      (* Original Tree is split based on the value
                                     in Data. Tree will now contain just one
                                     informational field and have a new sibling
                                     to its right *) );

var
  Parent, Sibling: TwoThreeTree;
  Middle, Key: TwoThreeData;

start Split
  if Tree = T then (* Tree is root, so make new parent (root) node *)
    MakeTreeNode(Parent); (* Returns new Parent with EmptyFlags and NULL
                                        children *)
    Ref(Tree).Parent := Parent;
    Ref(Parent).FirstChild := Tree;
    T := Parent
  else
    Parent := Ref(Tree).Parent
  endif;
  MakeTreeNode(Sibling); (* Make sibling node with EmptyFlags and NULL
                                     children *)
  Ref(Sibling).Parent := Parent;

  (* Determine which of the three key values is the middle one in terms of
     Precedes relation and assign it to Middle. Put (or leave) the smallest
     one in the current node (Tree), put the largest one in the new node
     (Sibling). *)
```

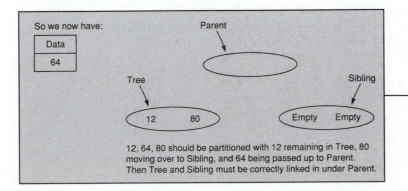

So we now have:

Data
64

12, 64, 80 should be partitioned with 12 remaining in Tree, 80 moving over to Sibling, and 64 being passed up to Parent. Then Tree and Sibling must be correctly linked in under Parent.

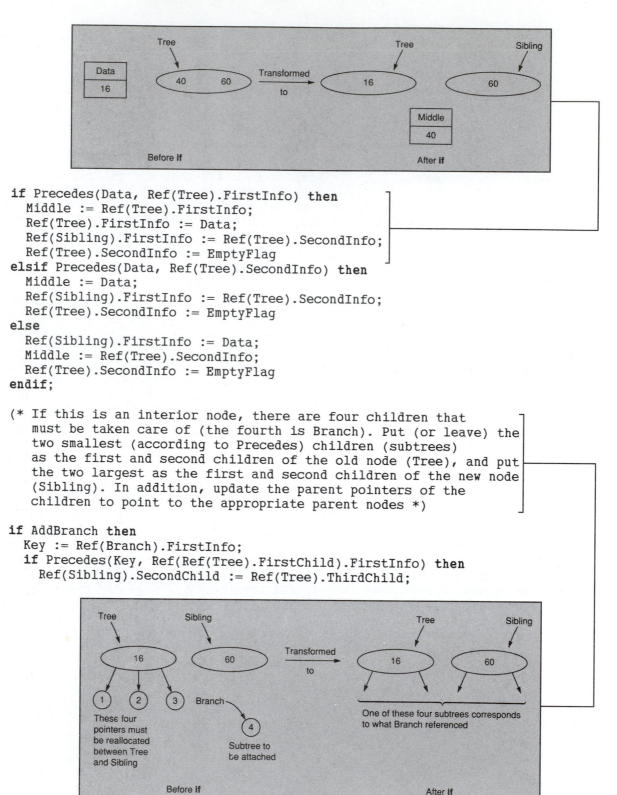

```
if Precedes(Data, Ref(Tree).FirstInfo) then
  Middle := Ref(Tree).FirstInfo;
  Ref(Tree).FirstInfo := Data;
  Ref(Sibling).FirstInfo := Ref(Tree).SecondInfo;
  Ref(Tree).SecondInfo := EmptyFlag
elsif Precedes(Data, Ref(Tree).SecondInfo) then
  Middle := Data;
  Ref(Sibling).FirstInfo := Ref(Tree).SecondInfo;
  Ref(Tree).SecondInfo := EmptyFlag
else
  Ref(Sibling).FirstInfo := Data;
  Middle := Ref(Tree).SecondInfo;
  Ref(Tree).SecondInfo := EmptyFlag
endif;

(* If this is an interior node, there are four children that
   must be taken care of (the fourth is Branch). Put (or leave) the
   two smallest (according to Precedes) children (subtrees)
   as the first and second children of the old node (Tree), and put
   the two largest as the first and second children of the new node
   (Sibling). In addition, update the parent pointers of the
   children to point to the appropriate parent nodes *)

if AddBranch then
  Key := Ref(Branch).FirstInfo;
  if Precedes(Key, Ref(Ref(Tree).FirstChild).FirstInfo) then
    Ref(Sibling).SecondChild := Ref(Tree).ThirdChild;
```

```
            Ref(Sibling).FirstChild := Ref(Tree).SecondChild;
            Ref(Tree).ThirdChild := NULL;
            Ref(Tree).SecondChild := Ref(Tree).FirstChild;
            Ref(Tree).FirstChild := Branch;
            Ref(Ref(Sibling).SecondChild).Parent := Sibling;
            Ref(Ref(Sibling).FirstChild).Parent := Sibling;
            Ref(Ref(Tree).FirstChild).Parent := Tree
         elsif Precedes(Key, Ref(Ref(Tree).SecondChild).FirstInfo) then
            Ref(Sibling).SecondChild := Ref(Tree).ThirdChild;
            Ref(Sibling).FirstChild := Ref(Tree).SecondChild;
            Ref(Tree).ThirdChild := NULL;
            Ref(Tree).SecondChild := Branch;
            Ref(Ref(Sibling).SecondChild).Parent := Sibling;
            Ref(Ref(Sibling).FirstChild).Parent := Sibling;
            Ref(Ref(Tree).SecondChild).Parent := Tree
         elsif Precedes(Key, Ref(Ref(Tree).ThirdChild).FirstInfo) then
            Ref(Sibling).SecondChild := Ref(Tree).ThirdChild;
            Ref(Sibling).FirstChild := Branch;
            Ref(Tree).ThirdChild := NULL;
            Ref(Ref(Sibling).SecondChild).Parent := Sibling;
            Ref(Ref(Sibling).FirstChild).Parent := Sibling
         else
            Ref(Sibling).SecondChild := Branch;
            Ref(Sibling).FirstChild := Ref(Tree).ThirdChild;
            Ref(Tree).ThirdChild := NULL;
            Ref(Ref(Sibling).SecondChild).Parent := Sibling;
            Ref(Ref(Sibling).FirstChild).Parent := Sibling
         endif
      endif;

      (* Now "promote" Middle up to Tree's parent node and determine
         whether that node must be split. If Middle will fit, arrange
         the parent node accordingly and return. If not, then make
         a recursive call to Split with the Parent node as Tree, the
         Sibling node as Branch, and Middle as Data *)

      if Match(Ref(Parent).FirstInfo, EmptyFlag) then
         Ref(Parent).FirstInfo := Middle;
         Ref(Parent).FirstChild := Tree;
         Ref(Parent).SecondChild := Sibling
      elsif Match(Ref(Parent).SecondInfo, EmptyFlag) then
         if Precedes(Ref(Parent).FirstInfo, Middle) then
            Ref(Parent).SecondInfo := Middle;
            Ref(Parent).ThirdChild := Sibling
         else
            Ref(Parent).SecondInfo := Ref(Parent).FirstInfo;
            Ref(Parent).FirstInfo := Middle;
            Ref(Parent).ThirdChild := Ref(Parent).SecondChild;
            Ref(Parent).SecondChild := Sibling
         endif
      else (* Split parent *)
         Split(T, Parent, Sibling, Middle, true, Precedes, Match)
      endif
   end Split;
```

Exercises 8.3

1. Repeat Exercise 1 of Section 7.3 for a 2-3 tree.

2. Repeat Exercise 2 of Section 7.3 for a 2-3 tree.

3. Repeat Exercise 3 of Section 7.3 for a 2-3 tree.

4. What is the percentage of informational fields wasted by storing empty flags for each of the final 2-3 trees from Exercises 1, 2, and 3?

5. What is the relationship of the distribution of data items in the nodes of a 2-3 tree to the order of their arrival for insertion in the tree? Explain your answer.

6. Develop a quasi-traversal algorithm for the data in a 2-3 tree. This algorithm should apply a procedural parameter ProcessNode to all items in the tree that follow a specified lower bound and precede a specified upper bound.

7. Develop a Delete algorithm for an ordered list implemented by a 2-3 tree.

8. Could the definition of a 2-3 tree be extended to a 3-4 tree in which each node had up to three informational fields and four subtrees? If so, provide such a definition. What would be the advantage of using this new structure to implement an ordered list? What would be the drawbacks?

8.4 APPLICATION: THE UNION-FIND PROBLEM

As a final example of the wide variability of tree applications and implementations, we return to the union-find ADT, which was first introduced in Section 2.4. We will assume for this discussion that the universe must be a finite subrange of some ordinal data type. Thus, as in Section 2.4, we have an identifiable *FirstValueInUniverse* and *LastValueInUniverse*. We also have the functions Index, Successor, and Predecessor that were defined in Section 2.4. In our analyses of efficiency, we will assume that each of these functions is $O(1)$.

This assumption will allow us to view the sets in the union-find partition as a collection of trees whose node values correspond to array indices and in which each tree is identified by the index value of its root. Because we only have two operations—UFUnion and UFFind—to consider, we can choose an implementation for these trees that is expressly tailored to optimize efficiency for this application. The implementation used is a simple one—an array Parent indexed by the elements of the universe. Parent[Index(X)] is the parent of X in the tree (that is, set) containing X. If X is the root of that tree, then Parent[Index(X)] is set to a special flagging value designated by NULL. Example 8.5 shows this correspondence between the union-find partition, the representation of each set in the partition by a tree, and the Parent array used to implement the tree.

Example 8.5

Suppose that the union-find universe consists of the eight integers 1, 2, 3, 4, 5, 6, 7, 8. Then trace the status of the union-find ADT for the following sequence of UFUnion operations. Assume that UFUnion(X, Y, P) results in the root of the tree containing Y becoming a child of the root of the tree containing X. Assume also that if X is the root of a tree then Parent[Index(X)] = 0, that is, NULL is zero.

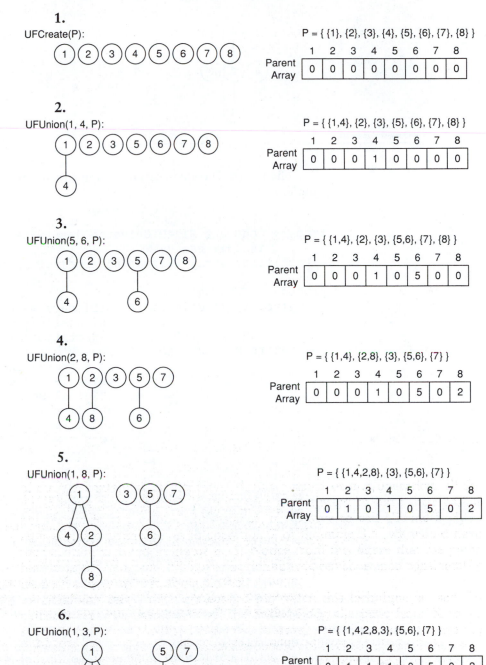

1.

UFCreate(P):

P = { {1}, {2}, {3}, {4}, {5}, {6}, {7}, {8} }

	1	2	3	4	5	6	7	8
Parent Array	0	0	0	0	0	0	0	0

2.

UFUnion(1, 4, P):

P = { {1,4}, {2}, {3}, {5}, {6}, {7}, {8} }

	1	2	3	4	5	6	7	8
Parent Array	0	0	0	1	0	0	0	0

3.

UFUnion(5, 6, P):

P = { {1,4}, {2}, {3}, {5,6}, {7}, {8} }

	1	2	3	4	5	6	7	8
Parent Array	0	0	0	1	0	5	0	0

4.

UFUnion(2, 8, P):

P = { {1,4}, {2,8}, {3}, {5,6}, {7} }

	1	2	3	4	5	6	7	8
Parent Array	0	0	0	1	0	5	0	2

5.

UFUnion(1, 8, P):

P = { {1,4,2,8}, {3}, {5,6}, {7} }

	1	2	3	4	5	6	7	8
Parent Array	0	1	0	1	0	5	0	2

6.

UFUnion(1, 3, P):

P = { {1,4,2,8,3}, {5,6}, {7} }

	1	2	3	4	5	6	7	8
Parent Array	0	1	1	1	0	5	0	2

7.

UFUnion(6, 2, P):

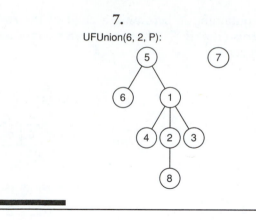

$P = \{\ \{1,4,2,8,3,5,6\},\ \{7\}\ \}$

	1	2	3	4	5	6	7	8
Parent Array	5	1	1	1	0	5	0	2

The PSEUDO code necessary to implement this union operation is quite simple:

```
type (* Constant SizeOfUniverse determines number of elements
         in universe *)
   Partition: array [SizeOfUniverse] of integer;

procedure UFUnion
   ( given X, Y: Universe (* Arbitrary members of the
                             universe *);
             P: Partition  (* A partition of the universe *);
      return P: Partition  (* The sets containing X and Y
                              in P are unioned. If the
                              union is different from the
                              original sets containing X
                              and Y, this union must be
                              added to P and the original
                              sets removed *) );

   var J, K: integer;

   start UFUnion
     J := Index(X);
     K := Index(Y);
     (* Move J to root of tree containing X *)
     while P[J] <> NULL do
       J := P[J]
     endwhile;
     (* Move K to root of tree containing Y *)
     while P[K] <> NULL do
       K := P[K]
     endwhile;
     (* If J and K are not the same roots, then attach tree
        rooted at K as child of tree rooted at J *)
     if J <> K then
       P[K] := J
     endif
   end UFUnion;
```

Efficiency of the UFUnion and UFFind Operations

The UFFind algorithm is similar to UFUnion in that, to determine if X and Y are in the same set, we must climb paths from X and Y to the roots of their respective trees and then check whether these roots are the same. Hence, the efficiency of both algorithms is proportional to the depth of the trees that are used to represent sets. This depth, in turn, is quite dependent upon how we choose to attach one tree as the subtree of another when unions are formed. For instance, in operation 7 of Example 8.5, when performing UFUnion(6, 2, P), the resulting tree would have been more efficient if the tree rooted at 5 had been attached to the tree rooted at 1 to form:

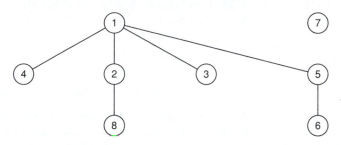

The worst-case search efficiency would then have been 3 instead of 4. In the exercises at the end of this section you will verify by example, that when the UFUnion operation is performed without any consideration of the depth of the two trees that are unioned, then the efficiency of the UFUnion and UFFind operations for a universe of N elements can deteriorate to $O(N)$.

Improving Efficiency of Union-Find Trees by Weight Balancing

The discussion above implies that an "intelligent" choice made in the UFUnion algorithm can improve significantly the efficiency of UFFind and other UFUnion operations that may follow. "Intelligent" here means that we should select the "smaller" of the two trees being joined and attach that as a subtree to the "bigger" tree's root. Of course, we must define precisely what is meant by "smaller" and "bigger," and we want to be sure that this definition does not involve a great deal of computational effort. Otherwise, the expense of choosing which tree to attach may outweigh any gain derived from the more efficient structure that results. One strategy that is often used is to maintain a count of the number of nodes in each tree. Thus, the array of parent pointers would become an array of records, each containing a parent pointer and a counter. For those array indices that correspond to a root, the counter would indicate the number of nodes in the tree rooted at that index. The counter field in other indices would be undefined. In the UFUnion operation, we would choose the tree with fewer nodes as the one to attach to the root of the other. Note that in operation 7 of Example 8.5 this would have resulted in the rooting of the tree at 1 instead of 5.

The technique described above is called *weight balancing*, with the weight of a tree corresponding to the number of nodes in the tree. Although weight balancing clearly should enhance the efficiency of the union-find implementation, the question arises whether it does so significantly. The answer is yes, as the following argument will show.

Suppose that we have N elements in our universe. Each time a set in the union-find partition is unioned with another set, the path length necessary to find each of the elements in the set being attached will increase by one. This phenomenon is illustrated in Figure 8.13. Hence, the question reduces to finding a limit on the number of times a set containing a particular element X may be attached to another set in a UFUnion operation. *When weight balancing is used,* each UFUnion operation will at least double the size of the set that is being attached. Hence, the maximum number of times X could be involved in a UFUnion operation, *as a member of the set being attached,* before it is in a set containing all N elements of the universe is $\log_2(N)$. Figure 8.14 illustrates such a series of occurrences. Since each of these unions could add at most 1 to the path length from X to the root, we conclude that $\log_2(N)$ is the worst-case efficiency for the UFUnion and UFFind operations when weight balancing is used.

Improving Efficiency of Union-Find Trees by Path Compression

Yet another strategy for improving the efficiency of the union-find operations is known as *path compression.* By this scheme, whenever we locate the root

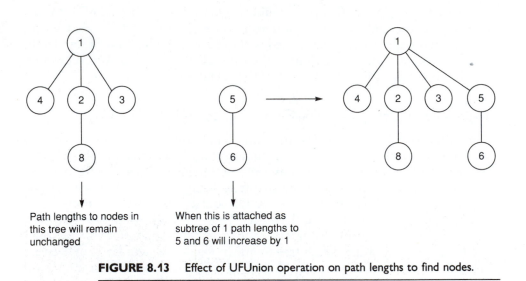

Path lengths to nodes in this tree will remain unchanged

When this is attached as subtree of 1 path lengths to 5 and 6 will increase by 1

FIGURE 8.13   Effect of UFUnion operation on path lengths to find nodes.

| X | Union #1 → with X in smaller set | New set must have at least 2 elements | Union #2 → with X in smaller set | New set must have at least 4 elements | Union #3 → with X in smaller set | ... ... | Union #$\log_2 N$ → with X in smaller set | New set must have at least N elements, that is, be the entire universe |

X starts out in set by itself

FIGURE 8.14   With weight-balancing, each Union with X in the set being attached will at least double the size of the set containing X.

of the tree containing an element X during a union or find operation, all the nodes along the path from X to its root are adjusted to have their parent pointer aimed at the root. For instance, if we were to call UFFind(8, 3, P) after performing the union in operation 7 of Example 8.5, we would have the partition pictured in Figure 8.15. Notice from this figure that the paths for future UFUnion and UFFind operations have been shortened considerably from what they were in Example 8.5.

Unfortunately, there is a cost to pay when this technique is used. To adjust the parent pointers of all the nodes along the path from X to its root, we must first traverse the path to locate the root and then traverse the path again, this time adjusting all the parent pointers to reference the now-known root. The hope is that this double traversal done once will pay off in much shorter paths and therefore greater efficiency in future operations. The efficiency of this method is very difficult to analyze formally and is dependent upon a large number of operations being performed so that, in the average case, we are able to benefit from these early double traversals. R. E. Tarjan ("Efficiency of a Good but Not Linear Set Union Algorithm," *Journal of the ACM, 22,* April 1975, pp. 215–225) has shown that the following interesting result holds when weight-balancing and path compression are combined.

If M UFUnion and/or UFFind operations are performed in sequence, where M exceeds N, the number of elements in the universe, then the worst-case efficiency of this sequence of operations is bounded by $O(M \times S(N))$.

Here $S(N)$ is a function of N, which grows so slowly that, for any reasonable value of N storable on a modern computer, $S(N)$ will be less than 4. The definition of $S(N)$ itself is beyond the scope of this text. However, the significance of the result is that, for all practical purposes, the combination of weight balancing and path compression enhances the efficiency of M union-find operations to $O(M)$ instead of the $O(M \log_2 N)$, which we might encounter with weight balancing alone.

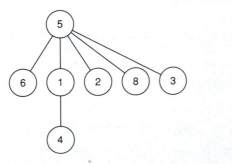

	1	2	3	4	5	6	7	8
Parent Array	5	5	5	1	0	5	0	5

FIGURE 8.15   Trees from operation 7 of Example 8.5 after UFFind (8, 3, P) with path compression. The nodes along the path from 8 to 5 and along the path from 3 to 5 become children of 5.

Exercises 8.4

1. Suppose we have a universe given by the set { 1, 2, 3, 4, 5, 6, 7, 8, 9, 10 }. Via diagrams, trace the union-find trees that would develop for the following sequence of operations if no weight balancing or path compression is used.

   UFCreate(P)
   UFUnion(9, 1, P)
   UFUnion(5, 2, P)
   UFUnion(5, 1, P)
   UFUnion(7, 3, P)
   UFUnion(8, 1, P)
   UFUnion(1, 10, P)
   UFUnion(1, 4, P)
   UFUnion(6, 3, P)
   UFUnion(9, 10, P)

2. Repeat Exercise 1 under the assumption that only weight balancing is used.

3. Repeat Exercise 1 under the assumption that only path compression is used.

4. Repeat Exercise 1 under the assumption that both weight balancing and path compression are used.

5. Develop PSEUDO code for UFFind assuming that neither weight balancing nor path compression is used.

6. Develop PSEUDO code for UFFind and UFUnion under the assumption that weight balancing is used.

7. Develop PSEUDO code for UFFind and UFUnion under the assumption that only path compression is used.

8. Develop PSEUDO code for UFFind and UFUnion under the assumption that path compression and weight balancing are used.

9. Show by an example that the worst case for the union and find operations deteriorates to $O(N)$ when neither path compression nor weight balancing is used.

10. Weight balancing seems to double the space required for the union-find structure, because both counters and a parent pointer must be allocated for each index. Develop a scheme that achieves weight balancing without doubling the space requirements.

11. Implement UFFind and UFUnion for a strategy that parallels weight balancing but uses the depth of a tree as a guide for the union operation instead of number of nodes. Recall that the depth of a tree is the maximal level at which a node occurs in the tree.

Chapter Summary

In Chapter 7 we discussed several ways in which the binary tree can be used to organize information. In this chapter we examine techniques for implementing more general trees, ones wherein a node may have an unrestricted number of children. The first such method, discussed in Section 8.2, uses

A RELEVANT ISSUE

Computer Security and Tree-Structured File Systems

One of the prime concerns in developing operating systems for multi-user computers is to ensure that a user cannot, in an unauthorized fashion, access system files or the files of other users. A convenient data structure to implement such a file directory system is a general tree such as pictured in Figure 8.16.

Each interior node of the tree can be viewed as a directory containing various system information about those files or subdirectories that are its descendants. Leaf nodes in the tree are the actual files. Hence, in the diagram, files can be broken down into system files and user files. System files consist of the Pascal Development Tools, the C Development Tools, and the Text Editor. User directories are called Vera, David, and Martha. One of the very convenient features of such a system is that it allows the user to extend this tree structure as deeply as desired. For instance, in the given tree directory structure, we see that user Vera has created subdirectories for files related to Payroll and Inventory. David and Martha could have similarly partitioned subdirectories to organize their work.

In addition to offering users the convenience of being able to appropriately group their files into subdirectories, such a file system offers a very natural solution to the problem of file security. Since each individual user is, in effect, the root of a miniature subordinate file system, a user has free access to every node in his or her subtree. That is, the user is viewed as the owner of every node in the subtree. To jump outside of this subtree of naturally owned files and directories requires that special permissions be given to the user by other users or by the operating system itself. Hence, the tree structure offers convenience as well as a means of carefully monitoring the integrity of the file system.

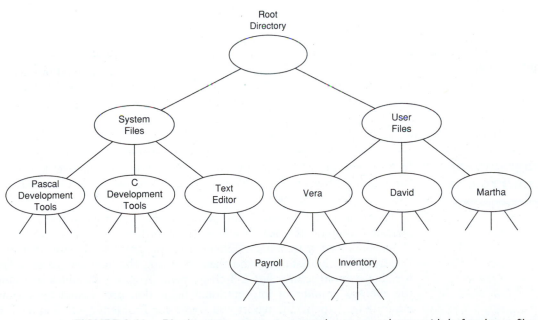

FIGURE 8.16   File directory system represented as a general tree with leaf nodes as files and interior nodes as directories.

AT&T's UNIX operating system, developed at Bell Laboratories in the early 1970s, was one of the first to use such a tree-structured directory system. The widespread popularity of UNIX today and the adoption of this scheme by a significant number of other operating systems is evidence of the attractive way in which it combines user convenience with system security. However, this is not to say that such systems are completely free of security problems. Once the security of such a system is slightly compromised, the tree structure lends itself to a cascade of far-reaching security breaks. Brian Reid's article "Reflections on Some Recent Widespread Computer Break-ins" (*Communications of the ACM*, 30, February 1987, pp. 103–105) provides an interesting account of how such security problems surfaced at Stanford University and how they spread to an entire network of computers. An entertaining narrative of another security incident is presented by Clifford Stoll in *The Cuckoo's Egg* (Doubleday, New York, 1989).

a binary tree to implement any general tree. On the other hand, for situations in which siblings can be organized as an ordered list, a ternary tree representation may be more effective and we follow our discussion of binary tree representations with one using this approach. In Section 8.3 we consider a technique based on 2-3 trees for implementing an ordered list as a way to improve on the efficiency of the height-balanced approach described in Section 7.6, though with the potential risk of having more wasted space than occurs with such binary trees. We conclude the chapter by using general trees to implement the Union-Find ADT of Section 2.4 and include a discussion of the techniques of weight balancing and path compression to improve the efficiency of the union-find operations.

Key Words

general tree	ternary tree	union-find problem
path compression	2-3 tree	weight balancing

Programming Problems/Projects

1. In Problems 11, 12, or 13 of Chapter 6 you wrote a recursive descent parser for a context-free grammar. Now extend that parser so that it builds a parse tree for valid expressions.

2. In Problem 5 of Chapter 7 you wrote a program that allows you to empirically compare the search efficiency of ordered binary search trees and height-balanced search trees. Extend that program by having it also build 2-3 trees for the data sets and then reporting the average search efficiency for this new structure. For 2-3 trees, your program should also report on the average amount of informational fields that are wasted by storing the empty flag. Expand the report you wrote for Problem 5 of Chapter 7 to include an analysis of 2-3 tree performance in comparison with the other two methods.

3. Wing-and-a-Prayer Airlines is expanding their record-keeping data base. This data base may now be pictured hierarchically as

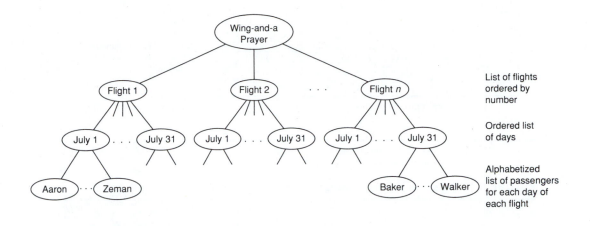

Write a program to maintain this data base. Your program should process requests to add, delete, or list the following:

- Specified flight number
- Specified day of the month (for a given flight number)
- Specified passenger or all passengers (for a given flight number and day of the month)

4. Many statistical analysis packages support a cross-tabulation command designed to explore the relationship between statistical variables. A cross-tabulation between two variables produces a two-dimensional table containing a frequency count for each possible ordered pair of values of the two variables. However, these statistical packages typically allow this type of analysis to proceed even further than merely exploring two variables. For instance, in a legal-system data base, we might be interested in cross-tabulating a defendant's age with the judge before whom the defendant stood trial. We may then wish to cross-tabulate this result with the sex of the defendant. Sex in this case is called the control variable. We would output a cross-tabulation table for both possible values of sex. Note that this type of output is not limited to just one control variable. There may be an arbitrary number of control variables and tables to cycle through. Moreover, the variables have an arbitrary number of observations and are all in arbitrary order. Yet for each variable, the list of possible values is always printed out in smallest-to-largest order.

   The general tree structure that emerges for handling cross-tabulations is pictured in Figure 8.17. Write a program to handle the task of producing statistical cross-tabulations.

5. Write a program to print out the nodes of a tree level by level; that is, all level-0 nodes, followed by all level-1 nodes, followed by all level-2 nodes, and so

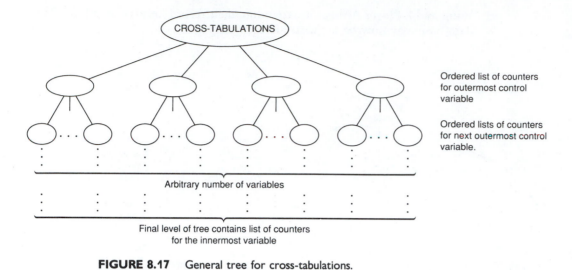

Ordered list of counters for outermost control variable

Ordered lists of counters for next outermost control variable.

Arbitrary number of variables

Final level of tree contains list of counters for the innermost variable

FIGURE 8.17   General tree for cross-tabulations.

on. Hint: this program will afford an excellent opportunity to practice using a queue in addition to a tree.

6. Operating systems often use general trees as the data structure on which their file directory system is based. Leaf nodes in such a system represent actual files or empty directories. Interior nodes represent nonempty directories. For instance, consider the following situation:

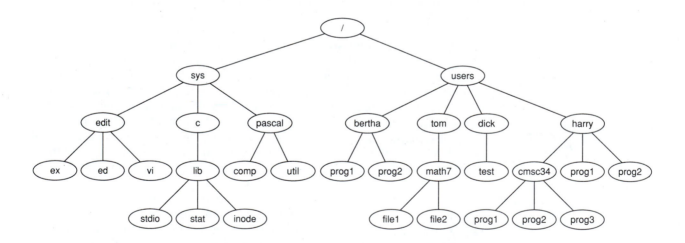

A directory entry is specified by the name of its path. A *pathname* consists of tree node names separated by slashes. Such a pathname is absolute if it starts at the root; that is, if it starts with a slash. It is relative to the current directory if it does not start with a slash.

In this assignment, you are to write a command processor that will allow a user to manipulate files within such a directory structure. The commands accepted by your processor will be in the form of numbers associated with particular operations and pathnames, as shown in the following table:

Number	Operation	Pathname
1	Change Directory	Absolute pathname, relative pathname, or ".." for parent
2	Make a new directory	Absolute or relative pathname
3	Make a new file	Absolute or relative pathname
4	Remove a file	Absolute or relative pathname
5	Remove a directory, but only if it is empty	Absolute or relative pathname
6	Remove a directory and, recursively, everything below it	Absolute or relative pathname
7	Print directory entries in alphabetical order	Absolute or relative pathname
8	Recursively print directory entries in alphabetical order	Absolute or relative pathname
9	Print current directory name	
10	Quit processing commands	

Since even intelligent tree-walking users can easily get lost, your command processor should be prepared to trap errors of the following variety:

- Specifying a nonexistent pathname
- Specifying a pathname that is a file when it should be a directory
- Specifying a pathname that is a directory when it should be a file

Upon detecting such an error, have your command processor print an appropriate error message and then return to accept the next user command.

7. In Section 8.4 several strategies were considered for implementing the union-find data structure via trees:

- Trees without any additional efficiency considerations
- Trees with weight balancing
- Trees balanced by depth (see Exercise 11 of Section 8.4)
- Trees with path compression

Develop a program that implements each of these individual strategies along with the combinations of weight balancing and path compression and depth-balancing and path compression. Your program should also count the number of operations executed by UFUnion and UFFind for each of these implementations. Finally, have your program generate a long sequence of random calls to UFFind and/or UFUnion. For each of the methods implemented, your program should report the average efficiency and the worst case. Use the results of your program to develop a written report in which you compare all of these strategies, reaching conclusions about their relative effectiveness for particular sequences of operations. Does your program empirically verify the result of Tarjan, which we cited in Section 8.4?

8. In Exercises 6 and 7 of Section 8.2 you developed PSEUDO code versions of the Retrieve operation for the binary and ternary tree implementations of a general tree in which the children of any given node formed an ordered list relative to a Precedes relation. Now incorporate each of these implementations of Retrieve into a program that lets you empirically compare Retrieve efficiences. Your program should randomly generate a data set, load each tree implementation with that data set, and then determine the average Retrieve efficiency for each item in the tree. Using the output of your program for a variety of data sets, write a report in which you summarize the difference in the efficiency of the Retrieve operation for these two implementations.

9 GRAPHS AND NETWORKS

As for that famous network of Vulcan, which
enclosed Mars and Venus, and caused that
unextinguishable laugh in heaven, since
the gods themselves could not discern it,
we shall not pry into it.

Sir Thomas Browne, *The Garden of Cyrus*

CHAPTER OUTLINE

403

9.1   BASIC CONCEPTS OF GRAPHS AND NETWORKS

A key characteristic of a tree is the hierarchical organization of its nodes resulting from the requirement that, except for the root node (which has no parent), every node must have exactly one parent node. Also, since the relationship between a parent node and a child node is expressed solely by pointers from parent to child, this hierarchical relationship is traditionally a one-way relationship. That is, there is no information within a child node that allows us to ascend directly to its parent. In many information storage applications such a one-way relationship is not sufficient.

Consider, for instance, the relationship between students and courses at a university. Since typically a student enrolls in several courses, each student could be viewed as a parent node whose children are the courses he or she is taking. On the other hand, since each course normally enrolls several students, a given course could justifiably be viewed as a parent node whose children are the students enrolled. Since it is likely that information retrieval requirements of the university will sometimes require moving from a course node to a related student node and sometimes vice versa, the information storage needs of any application doing such retrievals would be more effectively served by using a data structure that admits a nonhierarchical, bidirectional relationship between courses and students instead of using two trees. The data structure that supports this type of bidirectional relationship is called a *graph*. In Figure 9.1 we show a graph that represents some student-course relationships of the type we just described. In this figure the rectangles containing the names of a student or a course make up what are known as the nodes of the graph. The lines connecting various student and course rectangles are known as *edges*.

Using this example as a model, we shall define a *graph* as a structure comprised of two sets of objects, a set of *nodes* (or *vertices*) and a set of *edges*. Furthermore, with each edge we can associate two nodes (not necessarily distinct) called the *endpoints* of the edge. We say the endpoints are *directly connected* by the edge. A *loop* is an edge whose endpoints consist of one node. An example of a graph with a loop is shown in Figure 9.2.

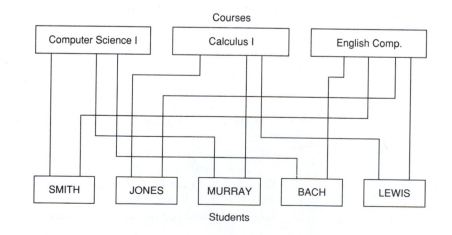

FIGURE 9.1
Bidirectional relationship between students and courses.

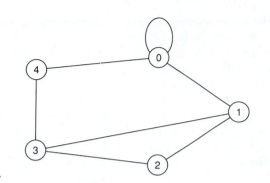

FIGURE 9.2

An example of a graph with nodes 0, 1, 2, 3, 4; edges between nodes 0 and 1, 1 and 2, 1 and 3, 2 and 3, 3 and 4; and a loop at node 0.

Another example of a graph can be given using a collection of cities and an airline's routes between them. Each city will be a node of the graph, and two cities will be related (that is, be directly connected by an edge) if the airline has a route between them. Such a relationship is not hierarchical because routes between cities will normally exist in both directions. An example of such a graph is shown in Figure 9.3. Note that in this graph, the routes between cities have been assigned a numerical value—representing the distance between cities for that route. A graph in which each edge has an associated numerical value (or *weight*) is called a *network*.

In this chapter, following some further discussion of the basic concepts and terminology of graphs, we shall define graphs and networks as ADTs, examine ways of implementing them, and explore some of the many algorithms that are derived from their fundamental operations. We will also indicate how such algorithms find application in many diverse areas, including arti-

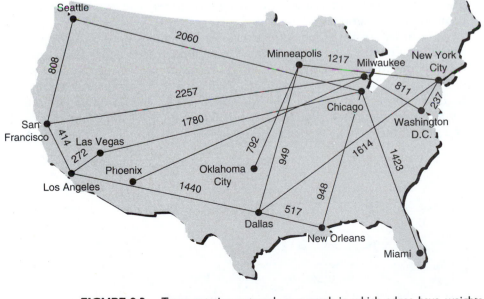

FIGURE 9.3   Transportation network as a graph in which edges have weights (distances).

ficial intelligence, communications, transportation, analysis of programming languages, and scheduling of projects.

In a sense, graphs are the most general data structures we shall discuss. Why? Because the relationships between items in a graph are completely arbitrary. With lists, queues, and stacks, the relationships between data items were linear; with trees, they were hierarchical; but, with graphs, any data item is potentially connected to any other. Even though the situation did not arise in Figure 9.1, the formal definition of a graph does not rule out the possibility of an edge connecting two courses or connecting two students. It is merely the nature of a course-student relationship that prevents the user from establishing a course-to-course edge or a student-to-student edge. In other applications, such as the transportation network pictured in Figure 9.3, it may be entirely feasible for any node in the graph to have an edge connecting it to any other node.

Because of the intrinsic generality of graphs, additional terminology is often needed to describe precisely particular relationships underlying a given graph. In a *directed graph* (or *digraph*) each edge establishes a directional orientation between its endpoints. Terminology such as "the edge from node A to node B" or "the edge AB" is used to describe this orientation. In digraphs the edges are known as *directed edges*, or more commonly, *arcs*, and are represented pictorially with arrows. In the directed graph of Figure 9.4, AB is an arc but there is no arc BA. There are also arcs from B to C, C to D, and D to E. The digraph of Figure 9.4 can be looked upon as expressing the alphabetical order relationship between the letters. In this text, we shall denote an arc from node x to node y by $x \rightarrow y$.

An *undirected graph* is a graph in which an edge between two nodes is not directionally oriented. Thus, in an undirected graph, the edge from node A to node G (also called the edge between A and G or the edge AG) is the same as the edge from G to A (edge between G and A, or GA). Undirected graphs typically are drawn without arrows on edges. The graph in Figure 9.5 is an undirected graph.

In order to use graphs effectively, we sometimes need to know which nodes are directly connected by an edge and also those nodes that are indirectly connected by a sequence of edges. For example, in the directed graph in Figure 9.4, A is directly connected to B, while B is indirectly connected to E via the arcs $B \rightarrow C$, $C \rightarrow D$, and $D \rightarrow E$. In a digraph, therefore, we say that there is a *directed path* of length n from node I to node J if and only if there is a sequence of nodes $I = I_0, I_1, I_2, \ldots, I_n = J$ such that for

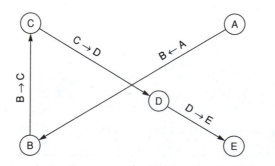

FIGURE 9.4
A directed graph.

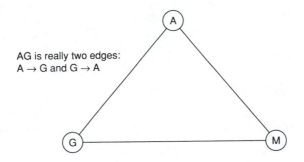

AG is really two edges:
A → G and G → A

FIGURE 9.5
An undirected graph.

$k = 1, \ldots, n$, node I_{k-1} is directly connected to I_k via an arc. In Figure 9.4, there is no directed path from node E to node A, but there is a directed path of length 4 from node A to E. A digraph is said to be *strongly connected* if, for any nodes I and J in the graph, there is a directed path from I to J *and* a directed path from J to I. A digraph is said to be *weakly connected* if, for any two nodes I and J, there is a directed path from I to J *or* from J to I. The digraph in Figure 9.4 is weakly connected but it is not strongly connected since there is no directed path from E to C (or from E to D, or B to A, etc.). The digraph shown in Figure 9.6 is strongly connected. Clearly, any digraph that is strongly connected is also weakly connected.

By the *outdegree* of a node in a digraph we mean the number of arcs extending from the node, whereas the *indegree* of a node is the number of arcs entering the node. In Figure 9.6, the indegree of node D is 2 and its outdegree is 1. The indegree and the outdegree of node B are 1 and 2 respectively. When a directed graph is applied to some data processing tasks, the indegree and the outdegree of a node sometimes indicate its relative importance in the data processing activity. A node whose outdegree is 0 largely acts as a depository of information and hence is called a *sink node*; on the other hand, a node whose indegree is 0 largely acts as a source of information and consequently is called a *source node*. In Figure 9.7 we use a digraph to illustrate the fundamental input-to-output operation common to all data processing activity.

By a *cycle* in a directed graph, we mean a directed path of length at least 1 that originates and terminates at the same node in the graph. In Figure 9.6, D → C → A → D is a cycle of length 3. An *acyclic graph* is one having no cycles.

The concepts and terms discussed in the preceding paragraphs for digraphs can generally be extended to analogous concepts for undirected

FIGURE 9.6

A strongly connected graph. For any nodes I and J in the graph there is a directed path from I to J and a directed path from J to I.

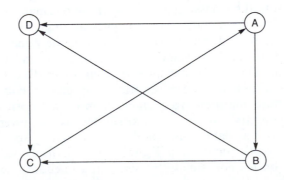

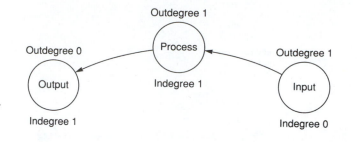

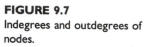

FIGURE 9.7
Indegrees and outdegrees of nodes.

graphs. For example, we can define a (undirected) path between two nodes to be a sequence of edges that directly or indirectly connects the two nodes. In Figure 9.5 there is a path between any two nodes. Although the concept of indegree and outdegree cannot apply to a node in an undirected graph, we can define the *degree* of a node to be the number of edges connected directly to the node; if the node is the endpoint of a loop, however, we count the loop as two edges. In Figure 9.5, the degree of each node is 2.

Since a network is a graph, all of the terminology we have defined for graphs applies to networks as well. For instance, a directed path between nodes I and J in a network may be thought of as a sequence of edges

$$I = I_0 \rightarrow I_1 \rightarrow I_2 \cdots \rightarrow I_{n-1} \rightarrow I_n = J$$

However, since now each edge $I_{k-1} \rightarrow I_k$ has a numerical weight associated with it, we can define the *total path weight* between I and J as the summation:

$$\sum_{k=1}^{n} \text{EdgeWeight}(I_{k-1} \rightarrow I_k)$$

Therefore, in Figure 9.3, the total path weight of the path

$$\text{San Francisco} \rightarrow \text{Los Angeles} \rightarrow \text{Las Vegas} \rightarrow \text{Chicago}$$

is $414 + 272 + 1{,}780 = 2{,}466$.

Many network problems revolve around finding paths that satisfy some specified criteria relative to their total weight. Many of these problems have been solved by classic algorithms whose originators have often used the term *length* as synonymous with weight. Although we do not object to such usage and, indeed, will often employ it in the remainder of this chapter, you should realize that "length" taken in this context does not necessarily mean Euclidean geometric distance between nodes. Euclidean distance is only one interpretation that an application may give to edge weight. Other applications may interpret edge weights as monetary cost, time units, and so forth. This potential for confusion arises because we often visualize the notion of a network as data points (nodes) connected by straight lines (edges). Hence, the network pictured in Figure 9.8 is perfectly valid, though the numeric labels on the edges make no sense in a Euclidean geometric context.

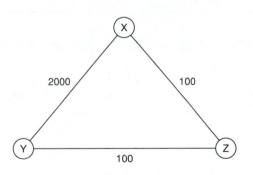

FIGURE 9.8
A network showing that edge weight does not necessarily correspond to Euclidean distance between nodes.

Exercises 9.1

1. Is a general tree a graph? Is a graph a general tree? Justify your answers to both of these questions.

2. Consider the directed graph in Figure 9.9.

   a. Is this graph weakly connected?

   b. Is it strongly connected?

   c. What are the outdegrees of each node in the graph?

   d. What are the indegrees of each node in the graph?

   e. Does the graph have any sink nodes or source nodes? If so, what are they?

3. The *total degree* of a node in a digraph is the sum of that node's indegree and outdegree. Show that the sum of the total degrees of all the nodes in a digraph is an even number. What can you say about the number of nodes in a digraph that have a total degree that is odd?

4. What is the maximum number of (nonloop) edges that can be present in a graph with four nodes, assuming only one edge joins a given pair of points? Suppose the graph has five nodes? Six nodes? Conjecture as to the maximum number of such edges that can be present in a graph with N nodes and prove your conjecture. A graph that contains the maximum number of such edges is said to be a *complete graph*.

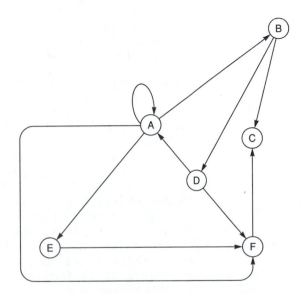

FIGURE 9.9
Graph for Exercises 9.2.4 and 9.2.5.

9.2 DEFINITION OF GRAPH AND NETWORK ADTS

Since a network is merely a graph with additional numeric information, it makes sense to first define the graph ADT. The definition of the network ADT will then be presented as a natural extension of the graph ADT.

The Graph ADT

• **Definition:** A *graph* is a structure comprised of two sets of objects: a set of *nodes* (or *vertices*) and a set of *edges*. A node is a data element of the graph in that it stores a data value, whereas an edge indicates a direct relationship between two nodes. A node is also called a *vertex* of the graph. If an edge exists between two nodes, we say the nodes are *adjacent*, or that one node is adjacent to another. The operations associated with the graph ADT are specified in terms of the following PSEUDO pre- and postconditions.

```
type
   GraphNode: (* Data type of each node in the graph. Identify the node
                 with the data in that node *);
   NodeOperation: procedure (* The signature of a procedure that can be
                             applied to an individual graph node *)
                 ( given Item: GraphNode  (* Arbitrary node in graph *);
                   return Item: GraphNode (* Item as affected by
                                           ProcessNode *) );

procedure Create
   ( given G: Graph            (* An arbitrary graph variable *);
     return G: Graph           (* Graph G initialized to a state with no
                                 edges. That is, no nodes are
                                 connected to any other nodes,
                                 including themselves *) );

procedure Destroy
   ( given G: Graph            (* An arbitrary graph variable *);
     return G: Graph           (* All dynamically allocated storage
                                 associated with G is returned to
                                 available space. G itself is in an
                                 unreliable state *) );

procedure AddEdge
   ( given G: Graph            (* An arbitrary graph that has been
                                 initialized by Create and, potentially,
                                 affected by other operations *);

         Node1, Node2: GraphNode  (* Two nodes in graph G *);
     return G: Graph           (* G with an edge from Node1 to Node2.
                                 If an edge already existed from Node1
                                 to Node2, G is not affected *) );

procedure RemoveEdge
   ( given G: Graph            (* An arbitrary graph that has been
                                 initialized by Create and, potentially,
                                 affected by other operations *);

         Node1, Node2: GraphNode  (* Two nodes in graph G *);
     return G: Graph           (* If there is an edge from Node1 to
                                 Node2, it is removed. Otherwise G is
                                 not affected *) );
```

```
function Edge
  ( given G: Graph                    (* An arbitrary graph that has been
                                         initialized by Create and, potentially,
                                         affected by other operations *);

         Node1, Node2: GraphNode      (* Two nodes in graph G *);
    return: boolean                   (* true if there is an edge from Node1 to
                                         Node2; false otherwise *) );

procedure DepthFirstTraversal
  ( given G: Graph                    (* An arbitrary graph that has been
                                         initialized by Create and, potentially,
                                         affected by other operations *);

         Start: GraphNode             (* A node at which the traversal is to
                                         start *);
         ProcessNode: NodeOperation   (* This procedure determines the process
                                         applied to each Graph node *);
    return G: Graph                   (* G has each node that can be reached
                                         from Start affected by ProcessNode.
                                         The order in which nodes are affected:
                                         first, Start itself is affected;
                                         then, recursively, the first node
                                         adjacent to Start and all nodes
                                         adjacent to that first node are
                                         affected; then, recursively, the
                                         second node adjacent to Start and all
                                         nodes adjacent to that second node
                                         are affected; and so on, until
                                         ProcessNode is applied to the last
                                         node adjacent to Start and,
                                         recursively, to all nodes adjacent to
                                         that last node. ProcessNode is not
                                         applied to any node more than
                                         once *) );

procedure BreadthFirstTraversal
  ( given G: Graph                    (* An arbitrary graph that has been
                                         initialized by Create and, potentially,
                                         affected by other operations *);

         Start: GraphNode             (* A node at which the traversal is to
                                         start *);
         ProcessNode: NodeOperation   (* This procedure determines the process
                                         applied to each Graph node *);
    return G: Graph                   (* G has each node that can be reached
                                         from Start affected by ProcessNode.
                                         The order in which nodes are affected:
                                         first, Start itself is affected;
                                         then, all nodes adjacent to Start are
                                         affected;  then, nodes adjacent to
                                         nodes affected in the previous step
                                         are affected; and so on, until
                                         ProcessNode has been applied to all
                                         nodes that can be reached from Start.
                                         ProcessNode is not applied to any node
                                         more than once *) );
```

Before extending our formal definition of the ADT graph to that of a network, we should identify a point of potential ambiguity in the definition of the depth-first and breadth-first traversal operations. In particular, neither of these operations establishes a *unique* order in which nodes will be visited from the Start node parameter for these operations. This lack of uniqueness is due to the potential variety of ways in which the phrase "first node adjacent to" can be interpreted in these definitions. The following examples will clarify these operations and how they can result in different orders of traversal from the Start parameter.

Example 9.1   Consider a depth-first traversal from Start node A in the graph of Figure 9.6 on page 407. The essential strategy of a depth-first traversal dictates that a given path starting at A be explored as deeply as possible before another path is probed. *If we assume that B is the first node adjacent to A*, then the traversal will proceed from A to B. *If we then assume that C is the first node adjacent to B*, the traversal will continue from B to C. From C, it is not possible to visit any nodes that have not already been visited. Hence, we will backtrack to B and, from there, continue the traversal to D. Hence, the overall order in which nodes would be visited by a depth-first traversal under the assumptions of this example are

A   B   C   D

However, as the next example will show, if we change our interpretation of "first node adjacent to," then we arrive at a different depth-first traversal from the same Start node.

Example 9.2   Consider the order in which nodes would be visited in a depth-first traversal starting at A under the assumption that *D is the first node adjacent to A*. Now the traversal will proceed initially from A to D. From D, we can proceed only to C. No new nodes can be visited from C, so we backtrack to D. Again, no new nodes can be visited from D, so we backtrack to A, from where B can now be visited. The overall order in which nodes are visited by a depth-first traversal under the assumption of this example is

A   D   C   B

The difference in the order of visited nodes in the depth-first traversals of this example and that of Example 9.1 is an indication that the underlying implementation of the graph ADT may affect a depth-first traversal—particularly in situations where there is not a well-defined ordering among graph nodes.

Example 9.3   Indicate the order that nodes would be visited in a breadth-first traversal starting at node B in the graph of Figure 9.6. *Assume that C is the first node adjacent to B.*

Since the breadth-first strategy does not probe one path as deeply as possible but rather fans out to all nodes adjacent to a given node, we would proceed from B to C and then to D, the next node adjacent to B. Since all nodes adjacent to B have been exhausted, we would fan out from C—the first node we visited from B. This takes us to A by the edge C → A, completing the traversal in the overall order:

B   C   D   A

The Network ADT

To define the network ADT requires only slight modifications of the graph definition. These modifications merely reflect that a network is a graph in which the edges carry a numerical weight.

• **Definition:** A *network* is a graph in which each edge has an associated positive numerical weight. The operations associated with the network ADT are specified in terms of the following PSEUDO pre- and postconditions.

```
type
  NetworkNode: (* Data type of each node in the network. Identify the node
                  with the data in that node *);
  WeightType:  (* Numeric data type--integer or real *);
  NodeOperation: procedure (* The signature of a procedure that can be
                              applied to an individual network node *)
                  ( given Item: NetworkNode  (* Arbitrary node in network *);
                    return Item: NetworkNode (* Item as affected by
                                                ProcessNode *) );

procedure Create
  ( given N: Network                    (* An arbitrary network variable *);
    return N: Network                   (* Network N initialized to a state with
                                           no edges. That is, no nodes are
                                           connected to any other nodes,
                                           including themselves *) );

procedure Destroy
  ( given N: Network                    (* An arbitrary network variable *);
    return N: Network                   (* All dynamically allocated storage
                                           associated with N is returned to
                                           available space. N itself is in an
                                           unreliable state *) );

procedure AddEdge
  ( given N: Network                    (* An arbitrary network that has been
                                           initialized by Create and, potentially,
                                           affected by other operations *);

        Node1, Node2: NetworkNode       (* Two nodes in network N *);
        Wt: WeightType                  (* A positive number representing the
                                           weight of an edge to be added from
                                           Node1 to Node2 *);

    return N: Network                   (* N has an edge of weight Wt from Node1
                                           to Node2. If an edge already existed
                                           from Node1 to Node2, the weight of
                                           that edge is now Wt *) );
```

procedure RemoveEdge
  (**given** N: Network   (* An arbitrary network that has been
                                                   initialized by Create and,
                                                   potentially, affected by other
                                                   operations *);
        Node1, Node2: NetworkNode   (* Two nodes in network N *);
    return N: Network   (* If there is an edge from Node1 to
                                                     Node2, it is removed. Otherwise N is
                                                     not affected *));

function EdgeWeight
  (**given** N: Network   (* An arbitrary network that has been
                                                     initialized by Create and,
                                                   potentially, affected by other
                                                   operations *);
        Node1, Node2: NetworkNode   (* Two nodes in network N *);
    return: WeightType   (* Zero if there is no edge from Node1
                                                     to Node2 and the numerical value of
                                                   the edge if it exists *));

procedure DepthFirstTraversal
  (**given** N: Network   (* An arbitrary network that has been
                                                     initialized by Create and,
                                                   potentially, affected by other
                                                   operations *);
        Start: NetworkNode   (* A node at which the traversal is to
                                                   start *);
        ProcessNode: NodeOperation (* This procedure determines the process
                                                   applied to each Network node *);
    return N: Network   (* N has each node that can be reached
                                                   from Start affected by ProcessNode.
                                                   The order in which nodes are affected:
                                                   first, Start itself is affected;
                                                   then, recursively, the first node
                                                   adjacent to Start and all nodes
                                                   adjacent to that first node are
                                                   affected; then, recursively, the
                                                   second node adjacent to Start and all
                                                   nodes adjacent to that second node
                                                   are affected; and so on, until
                                                   ProcessNode is applied to the last
                                                   node adjacent to Start and,
                                                   recursively, to all nodes adjacent to
                                                   that last node. ProcessNode is not
                                                   applied to any node more than
                                                   once *));

procedure BreadthFirstTraversal
  (**given** N: Network   (* An arbitrary network that has been
                                                     initialized by Create and, potentially,
                                                     affected by other operations *);
        Start: NetworkNode   (* A node at which the traversal is to
                                                   start *);
        ProcessNode: NodeOperation (* This procedure determines the process
                                                   applied to each Network node *);

```
return N: Network
```
                                    (* N has each node that can be reached
                                       from Start affected by ProcessNode.
                                       The order in which nodes are affected:
                                       first, Start itself is affected;
                                       then all nodes adjacent to Start are
                                       affected; then nodes adjacent to
                                       nodes affected in the previous step
                                       are affected; and so on, until
                                       ProcessNode has been applied to all
                                       nodes that can be reached from Start.
                                       ProcessNode is not applied to any
                                       node more than once *));

Exercises 9.2

1. Redo Example 9.3 under the assumption that D is the first node connected to B.

2. Provide the order in which nodes would be visited in a depth-first traversal starting at D in the graph of Figure 9.6. State any assumptions you made in arriving at your answer.

3. Provide the order that nodes would be visited in a breadth-first traversal starting at D in the graph of Figure 9.6. State any assumptions you made in arriving at your answer.

4. Provide the order in which nodes would be visited in a depth-first traversal starting at A in the graph of Figure 9.9. State any assumptions you made in arriving at your answer.

5. Provide the order that nodes would be visited in a breadth-first traversal starting at A in the graph of Figure 9.9. State any assumptions you made in arriving at your answer.

6. Write a procedure that uses the operations provided with the graph ADT to compute the indegree and outdegree of a node that is passed as a parameter to the procedure. Did you have to make any assumptions about the GraphNode data type in writing your procedure? If so, state them.

7. Does the AddEdge operation for the graph ADT correctly add an edge between Node1 and Node2 if the graph G is an undirected graph? If not, explain why and write a procedure AddUndirectedEdge that uses AddEdge to add an edge in an undirected graph.

8. Consider the digraph

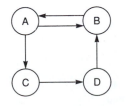

How many paths of length 3 are there from A to B?

9.3   IMPLEMENTATIONS OF THE GRAPH AND NETWORK ADTs

A graph may be implemented conveniently using a two-dimensional table of boolean values. For instance, the information in the graph of Figure 9.6 is contained in the two-dimensional table of Figure 9.10. In this figure, the value **true** at row J, column K indicates the presence of an edge from J to K, and the value **false** indicates the absence of such an edge. When used as an implementation technique for graphs, a two-dimensional table such as that in Figure 9.10 is often called the *adjacency matrix*.

In the case of a network, the adjacency matrix implementation still applies. Now, however, the data stored in the matrix are WeightType. Such a two-dimensional table implementation of the transportation network from Figure 9.3 is given in Figure 9.11. Note that, since this network is not directionally oriented, the data are mirrored across the diagonal of the table.

Figure 9.11 illustrates a quality typically found in adjacency matrix implementations of large graphs and networks: the sparseness of nontrivial data. Thus, the techniques we discuss for implementing sparse matrices (see Sections 2.1, 3.5, and 11.4) actually provide alternate implementation strategies for graphs and networks. In particular, when the linked list scheme of Section 3.5 is used for implementing the adjacency matrix of a graph or network, the resulting lists are often called *adjacency lists*. For example, the adjacency list representation corresponding to Figure 9.10 appears in Figure 9.12.

FIGURE 9.10

Adjacency matrix implementation of the graph from Figure 9.6. A value **true** in the matrix entry at row J and column K indicates the presence of an edge from node J to node K. A value **false** indicates the absence of such an edge.

	A	B	C	D
A	false	true	false	true
B	false	false	true	true
C	true	false	false	false
D	false	false	true	false

FIGURE 9.11

Matrix implementation of the network from Figure 9.3. Only nonzero weights are shown.

	NYC	Wash	Miam	Milw	Chi	NOrl	Mpls	OklC	Dals	LVeg	Phex	StL	SFran	LA
NYC		237					1,217		1,614					
Wash	237			811										
Miam					1,423									
Milw		811									1,771		2,257	
Chi			1,423			948				1,780		2,060		
NOrl					948				517					
Mpls	1,217							792	949					
OklC							792							
Dals	1,614					517	949							1,440
LVeg					1,780									272
Phex				1,771										
StL					2,060								808	
SFran				2,257								808		414
LA									1,440	272			414	

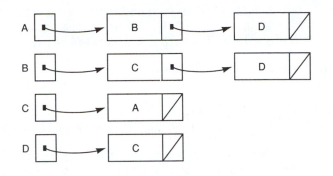

FIGURE 9.12

Adjacency lists corresponding to Figure 9.10.

Clearly, at the highest level of abstraction, there is a direct correspondence between graphs/networks and their adjacency matrices. Our algorithms will typically be expressed at this highest level. That is, a call to the Edge operation for a graph (or EdgeWeight operation for a network) may be considered an access to a particular row and column of a matrix. We must, however, realize that, at a level below this abstraction, the efficiency of our algorithm will be affected by the sparse matrix implementation we choose. If space needs will allow us to use a row-major implementation (such as that provided by most compilers), then the Edge operation will be O(1). If, however, the number of nodes in the graph makes a row-major implementation impractical from a space perspective, then the adjacency list representation will result in a worst-case efficiency of O(NumberOfNodes) for the Edge operation. The sparse table implementation presented in Section 11.4 will provide yet another time/space alternative to consider. For the graph and network algorithms presented in this chapter, we must always remember to factor a consideration of the graph or network implementation into an efficiency analysis.

Implementation of the Depth-First Traversal Operation

To provide implementations of the traversal operations, we will need some means of iterating through all nodes adjacent to a given node. As we indicated in Examples 9.1 and 9.2, the order that this iteration takes will influence the visiting of nodes in the traversal algorithm. Here, and throughout the remainder of the chapter, we will assume that this order is determined by defining the type GraphNode (or NetworkNode) as a finite data type with an ordering that allows data to be put into a one-to-one correspondence with the range of integers between 1 and NumberOfNodes. Thus, as we did when discussing universes for the set ADT in Section 2.4, we can assume the existence of first and last values for data of type GraphNode. We will call these first and last values *FirstNode* and *LastNode*, respectively, and assume the existence of appropriate Index, Node, Successor, and Predecessor functions satisfying the following pre- and postconditions:

```
(* Assume that NumberOfNodes is a constant equal to the number of nodes
   in the graph or network *)


function Index
  ( given N: GraphNode (* An arbitrary graph node *);
```

```
    return: integer     (* A value in a subrange of the integers between
                           1 and NumberOfNodes with the property that M < N
                           implies Index(M) < Index(N) *) );
function Node
  ( given K: integer    (* 1 <= K <= NumberOfNodes *);
    return: GraphNode    (* The graph node with Index value K *) );
function Successor
  ( given N: GraphNode  (* Any GraphNode value except LastNode *);
    return: GraphNode    (* The value that immediately follows N *) );
function Predecessor
  ( given N: GraphNode  (* Any GraphNode value except FirstNode *);
    return: GraphNode    (* The value that immediately precedes N *) );
```

Given these operations on data of type GraphNode, we can conveniently move between the data at graph/network nodes and the integers that correspond to these data. The DepthFirstTraversal operation from a specified start node may now be implemented by using an auxiliary boolean array Visited, which is indexed from 1 to NumberOfNodes. The Visited array is used to mark those nodes that have already been visited at any given stage of the traversal. Initially, this array must be set to all **false**. The actual traversal is then accomplished by calling recursively on a subordinate procedure Search-From which continues to probe along paths that can be reached from nodes adjacent to the Start node, marking as **true** each node that is visited to ensure that no node is visited twice.

```
(* Assume that NumberOfNodes is a constant equal to the number of nodes
   in the graph or network *)


procedure DepthFirstTraversal
  ( given G: Graph                  (* An arbitrary graph that has been
                                       initialized by Create and, potentially,
                                       affected by other operations *);

          Start: GraphNode          (* A node at which the traversal is to
                                       start *);

          ProcessNode: NodeOperation (* This procedure determines the process
                                       applied to each graph node *);

    return G: Graph                 (* G has each node that can be reached
                                       from Start affected by ProcessNode.
                                       The order in which nodes are affected:
                                       first, Start itself is affected;
                                       then, recursively, the first node
                                       adjacent to Start and all nodes
                                       adjacent to that first node are
                                       affected; then, recursively, the
                                       second node adjacent to Start and all
                                       nodes adjacent to that second node
                                       are affected; and so on, until
                                       ProcessNode is applied to the last
                                       node adjacent to Start and,
                                       recursively, to all nodes adjacent to
                                       that last node. ProcessNode is not
                                       applied to any node more than once *) );
```

```
var
  K: integer;
  Visited: array [NumberOfNodes] of boolean;

procedure SearchFrom
  ( given Start: GraphNode          (* Node at which to initiate a depth-first
                                        traversal *);
    return Start: GraphNode         (* Start, marked as visited and having
                                        ProcessNode applied to it and,
                                        recursively, to all nodes that can be
                                        reached from it *) );

  var
    K: integer;

  start SearchFrom
    ProcessNode(Start);
    Visited[Index(Start)] := true;
    for K := 1 to NumberOfNodes do
      if not Visited[K] and Edge(G, Start, Node(K)) then
        SearchFrom(Node(K))
      endif
    endfor
  end SearchFrom;

start DepthFirstTraversal
  for K := 1 to NumberOfNodes do
    Visited[K] := false
  endfor;
  SearchFrom(Start)
end DepthFirstTraversal;
```

Original Start

The recursive call will successively pass in Start as graph nodes
along this path, ensuring that this path is completely probed
before any other nodes adjacent to the original Start are visited

Efficiency Analysis of This Implementation of DepthFirstTraversal

Although the preceding algorithm presents a clear statement of the depth-first logic, it may be quite inefficient for a graph with a large number of nodes because the recursive call in the subordinate procedure SearchFrom could potentially be invoked NumberOfNodes times. You will devise a graph that generates this worst-case scenario in the exercises at the end of the section. Each time the recursive call is made, we will iterate NumberOfNodes times through the loop in procedure SearchFrom. Hence, in the worst case,

$O(\text{NumberOfNodes}^2)$ operations will be performed. If adjacency lists are used to implement the graph, the structure of these lists can be used to eliminate performing operations on nodes that are not connected to the Start node in procedure SearchFrom. You will explore developing such an implementation of DepthFirstTraversal in the exercises at the end of the section.

Implementation of the Breadth-First Traversal Operation

The essence of the breadth-first traversal is to begin exploration of many paths from the Start node before following any of them more deeply. Figure 9.13 highlights the fan-out nature of the breadth-first traversal compared to the probing strategy of the depth-first traversal. To achieve this fanning out, nodes adjacent to a visited node must be put on hold while we continue to visit nodes adjacent to the current Start node. In general, the earlier that a node is visited, the earlier nodes adjacent to it will be visited. This suggests that a queue is the natural data structure to hold nodes that are adjacent to visited nodes. Hence, the following PSEUDO implementation of BreadthFirstTraversal relies on operations from the queue ADT of Chapter 4.

```
type
   QueueData: GraphNode   (* To allow queue of graph nodes *);

procedure BreadthFirstTraversal
   ( given G: Graph              (* An arbitrary graph that has been
                                    initialized by Create and, potentially,
                                    affected by other operations *);

        Start: GraphNode         (* A node at which the traversal is to
                                    start *);
```

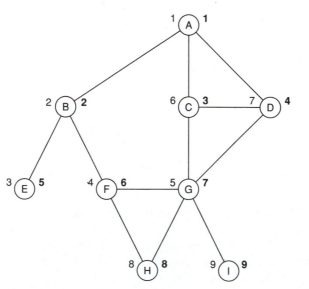

Number on left represents order of visiting in depth-first traversal

Number on right (bold) is for breadth-first traversal

FIGURE 9.13
Difference in order of visiting nodes in depth-first and breadth-first traversals from A, assuming adjacency ordering is alphabetic.

Depth-first: A B E F G C D H I
Breadth-first: A B C D E F G H I

```
              ProcessNode: NodeOperation (* This procedure determines the process
                                            applied to each graph node *);
      return G: Graph                    (* G has each node that can be reached
                                            from Start affected by ProcessNode.
                                            The order in which nodes are affected:
                                            first, Start itself is affected;
                                            then all nodes adjacent to Start are
                                            affected; then nodes adjacent to
                                            nodes affected in the previous step
                                            are affected; and so on, until
                                            ProcessNode has been applied to all
                                            nodes that can be reached from Start.
                                            ProcessNode is not applied to any node
                                            more than once *) );

var
  K: integer;
  CurrentNode: GraphNode;
  NodesToVisit: Queue;
  InQueue: array [NumberOfNodes] of boolean;

start BreadthFirstTraversal
  for K := 1 to NumberOfNodes do
    InQueue[K] := false
  endfor;
  Create(NodesToVisit);
  Enqueue(NodesToVisit, Start);
  InQueue[Start] := true;
  while not Empty(NodesToVisit) do
    Dequeue(NodesToVisit, CurrentNode);
    ProcessNode(CurrentNode);
    for K := 1 to NumberOfNodes do
      if not InQueue[K] and Edge(G, CurrentNode, Node(K)) then
        Enqueue(NodesToVisit, Node(K));
        InQueue[K] := true
      endif
    endfor
  endwhile;
  Destroy(NodesToVisit)
end BreadthFirstTraversal;
```

CurrentNode

These nodes potentially added to queue of nodes to visit

Efficiency Analysis of This Implementation of BreadthFirstTraversal

This analysis is similar to the one we carried out for DepthFirstTraversal. If it is possible to reach every node from the original Start node, then every node will be put on the NodesToVisit queue. When dequeued, all nodes are checked for adjacency to the CurrentNode—a check involving $O(NumberOfNodes)$ operations. Hence, the overall efficiency of the algorithm for this implementation is $O(NumberOfNodes^2)$. As with DepthFirstTraversal, this efficiency can be improved for many graphs by direct use of an adjacency-list implementation of the graph. You will explore this improvement in the following exercises.

Exercises 9.3

1. What are the time efficiencies of the Edge, AddEdge, and RemoveEdge operations for a graph if

   a. An adjacency matrix is used to implement the graph?

   b. Adjacency lists are used to implement the graph?

2. In our definition of the Graph ADT we provide operations for adding and removing edges from a graph but have no parallel operations for nodes. Instead, upon completion of the Create operation, we obtain a graph with an established node structure and an empty structure for representing the edges. Suppose we wanted to modify our definition of the Graph ADT so that Create returns an empty graph to which nodes may be added (up to a maximum number MaxNodes) via an AddNode operation and later removed via a RemoveNode operation. Assuming the data values for each node will be taken from a subrange of an ordinal type:

   a. Specify PSEUDO pre- and postconditions for an AddNode operation and a RemoveNode operation. With regard to the RemoveNode operation, provide a rationale for any assumptions made pertaining to the existence of edges incident with the node to be removed.

   b. Give a PSEUDO implementation for the AddNode operation using an adjacency matrix.

   c. Give a PSEUDO implementation for the AddNode operation using an adjacency list.

3. Given the implementation of DepthFirstTraversal appearing in this section, provide an example of a graph that leads to the worst-case efficiency of $O(\text{NumberOfNodes}^2)$. Then provide another graph for which this worst-case efficiency would not be realized.

4. Assuming an adjacency-list implementation of a graph, write a DepthFirstTraversal that takes advantage of this implementation to avoid the $O(\text{NumberOfNodes}^2)$ worst-case efficiency of an adjacency-matrix implementation. What is the worst-case efficiency of your new implementation of the DepthFirstTraversal? Are there graphs for which the worst-case efficiency of your new implementation will be worse than that for the adjacency-matrix implementation? Identify general conditions under which the adjacency-list strategy seems to provide a more efficient implementation for DepthFirstTraversal.

5. Repeat Exercise 4 for the BreadthFirstTraversal operation.

6. Suppose that the data type GraphNode is not a type for which well-defined Index, Node, Successor, and Predecessor operations exist. For example, GraphNode may be a string data type. Develop an implementation of the Graph ADT under these circumstances. Provide PSEUDO code for each graph operation under your implementation. What is the time efficiency of each of these operations?

7. Write a procedure that will apply a ProcessNode operation to all nodes in a graph, not just those nodes that can be reached from a given Start node.

8. A graph that is not strongly connected is composed of disjoint subgraphs that are strongly connected. Each subgraph is called a *connected component* of the original graph. Write a procedure that takes as input a graph G and

returns a count of the number of connected components in G. Analyze the time efficiency of your procedure.

9. Write a procedure that receives a graph G and a designated Start node and then determines whether or not the graph contains a cycle that begins and ends at the Start node. Analyze the time efficiency of your procedure.

10. Write a procedure that will count the number of edges in a graph

   a. Assuming an adjacency matrix implementation.

   b. Assuming an adjacency list implementation.

   Analyze the time efficiency of each of these procedures.

9.4 PATH ALGORITHMS

Shortest Path Algorithms

In a transportation network such as in Figure 9.3, a typical question is how to find the shortest distance between two nodes in the network. This question may be asked from two perspectives. First, given two nodes in the network—a Start node and a Destination node—we may ask for the shortest path from Start to Destination. Second, we could ask to find the shortest path between all pairs of nodes in the network. An efficient algorithm to answer the first question was first discovered by E. W. Dijkstra. For further reading on this, see Dijkstra's work "A Note on Two Problems in Connection with Graphs," (*Numerische Mathematik*, 1, pp. 269–272). Although the second question could certainly be answered by iterating pairs of nodes through Dijkstra's algorithm, a more efficient method of answering this was devised by R. W. Floyd. (More on this can be found in *Communications of the ACM*, 1962 Algorithm 97: "Shortest Path," 5, p. 345.)

Dijkstra's Algorithm to Find the Shortest Path between Two Nodes

Given a small network such as that in Figure 9.14, a careful examination reveals that the shortest path from node 1 to node 3 is not the direct edge

FIGURE 9.14
Network with edge weights. Note that the shortest path from node 1 to node 3 is not the direct edge 1 → 3, but rather the path 1 → 2 → 3.

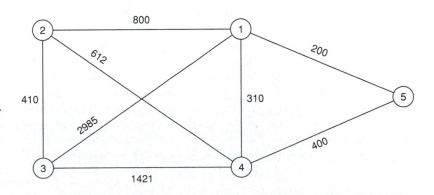

connecting these nodes, but rather the path $1 \rightarrow 2 \rightarrow 3$. That is, starting at node 1, it requires less total edge weight to reach node 3 by going through node 2 than it does to follow the edge directly linking 1 and 3. This is not surprising if you recall the caution about edge weights we mentioned at the end of Section 9.1. Remember that edge weights are not necessarily Euclidean distances; hence, if we visualize conceptual edge weights as the lengths of straight lines between nodes, we may possibly observe the "phenomenon" where the sum of two sides of a triangle has a smaller total edge weight than the third side. Indeed, this phenomenon is at the core of Dijkstra's algorithm to determine the shortest distance between two nodes.

In discussing Dijkstra's algorithm, we shall make the same assumptions about the NetworkNode data type as we did about the GraphNode data type in Section 9.3. That is, the values of the nodes are from a finite data type with an ordering that allows it to be put into a one-to-one correspondence with the range of integers between 1 and NumberOfNodes. Again, we assume the existence of first and last values for data of type NetworkNode. We will call these first and last values *FirstNode* and *LastNode*, respectively, and will use appropriate Index, Node, Successor, and Predecessor functions to move between a node's value and the integer corresponding to it. Given such a collection of nodes, Dijkstra's algorithm requires three arrays in addition to a suitable implementation of the network N. These three arrays are identified as follows:

```
var
   Distance: array [NumberOfNodes] of WeightType;
   Path: array [NumberOfNodes] of NetworkNode;
   Included: array [NumberOfNodes] of boolean;
```

Identifying one node as the Start, the algorithm proceeds to find the shortest distance from Start to other nodes in the network until the shortest distance to the Destination node is known. At the conclusion of the algorithm, the shortest distance from Start to Destination is stored in Distance[Index(Destination)] while Path[Index(J)] contains the immediate predecessor of node J on the path determining the shortest distance. While the algorithm is in progress, Distance[Index(J)] and Path[Index(J)] are being continually updated until Included[Index(J)] is switched from **false** to **true**. Once this switch occurs, it is known definitely that Distance[Index(J)] contains the shortest distance from Start to J. The algorithm progresses until the Destination node has been so included. Hence, it actually gives the shortest distance from Start to Destination. The algorithm may be easily extended to give us the shortest distance from Start to every other node in the network.

Given the Start node in the network N, the algorithm may be divided into two phases: an initialization phase followed by an iteration phase in which nodes are included one by one in the set of nodes for which the shortest distance from Start is known definitely.

During the initialization phase, we must

1. Initialize Included[Index(Start)] to **true** and Included[Index(J)] to **false** for all other J.

2. Initialize the Distance array via the rule

$$
Distance[Index(J)] = \begin{cases} 0 & \text{if } J = Start \\ EdgeWeight(N, Start, J) & \text{if } EdgeWeight <> 0 \\ \infty & \text{if } J \text{ is not connected to Start} \\ & \text{by a direct edge; that is, if} \\ & EdgeWeight(N, Start, J) = 0 \end{cases}
$$

3. Initialize the Path array via the rule

$$
Path[Index(J)] = \begin{cases} Start & \text{if } EdgeWeight(N, Start, J) <> 0 \\ Undefined & \text{otherwise} \end{cases}
$$

Given this initialization, the iteration phase may be expressed in a generalized PSEUDO form as follows:

```
repeat
    Find the node J having minimal Distance among those nodes not yet Included;
    Mark J as now Included;
    for each node R not yet Included
        if R is connected by an edge to J then
            if Distance[Index(J)] + EdgeWeight(N, J, R) < Distance[Index(R)] then
                Distance[Index(R)] := Distance[Index(J)] + EdgeWeight(N, J, R);
                Path[Index(R)] := J
            endif
        endif
    endfor
until destination node is Included
```

The crucial part of the algorithm occurs within the innermost **if** of the **for** loop. Figure 9.15 provides a pictorial representation of the logic involved here. The encircled nodes represent those nodes already Included prior to a given iteration of the **repeat** loop. The node J in Figure 9.15 represents the node found in the first step of the **repeat** loop; R represents another arbitrary node that has not yet been Included. The lines emanating from

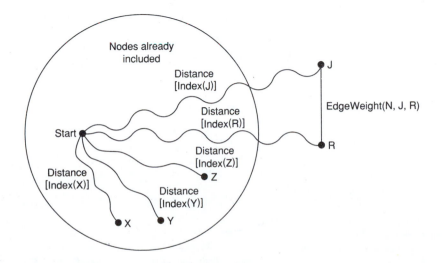

FIGURE 9.15
Repeat loop logic in shortest-path (Dijkstra's) algorithm.

Start represent the paths corresponding to the current entries in the Distance array. For nodes within the circle—that is, those already Included— these paths are guaranteed to be the shortest-distance paths. If J is the node having the minimal entry in the Distance array among those not yet Included, we will add J to the circle of Included nodes and check to see if J's connections to other nodes in the network that are not yet Included may result in a newly found shorter path to such nodes.

Referring to Figure 9.15 again, the sum of two sides of a triangle

$$Distance[Index(J)] + EdgeWeight(N, \ J, \ R)$$

may in fact be shorter than the third side, Distance[Index(R)]. As we have hinted earlier, this geometric contradiction is possible because these are not true straight-sided triangles, but "triangles" whose sides may be very complicated paths through a network.

It is also apparent from Figure 9.15 why Dijkstra's algorithm works. As the node J in this figure is found to have the minimal Distance entry from among all those nodes not yet Included, we may now Include it among the nodes whose minimal distance from the Start node is *absolutely* known. Why? Consider any other path from P from Start to J that contains nodes not yet Included at the time J is Included. Let X be the first such non-Included node on the path P. Then clearly, as the first non-Included node on the path P, X must be adjacent to an Included node. However, as Figure 9.16 indicates, the criterion that dictated the choice of J as an Included node ensures that

$$Distance[Index(J)] \leq \ \text{The total edge weight through node X on the path P}$$
$$\leq \ \text{Total edge weight of Path P}$$

The above inequality demonstrates that once J is included there exists no other path P to J through a non-Included node that can yield a shorter overall distance. Hence, we have verified our claim that Including a node guarantees our having found a path of shortest-possible distance to that node.

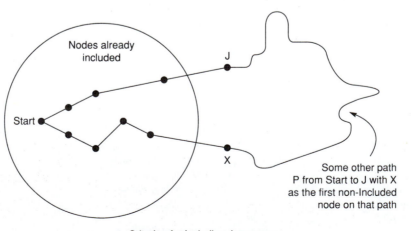

FIGURE 9.16
Guaranteeing the minimality of Distance to J once it is Included.

Criterion for Including J ensures
Distance[Index(J)] ≤ Distance[Index(X)] ≤ Length of path P

Example 9.4   To be sure you understand Dijkstra's algorithm before you attempt to implement it, trace it through the network of Figure 9.14 with FirstNode = 1, LastNode = 5, and Start = FirstNode.

Initially, we would have

Distance[2] = 800   Path[2] = 1
Distance[3] = 2985   Path[3] = 1
Distance[4] = 310   Path[4] = 1
Distance[5] = 200   Path[5] = 1

in accordance with steps 2 and 3 of the initialization phase. According to the iteration phase of the algorithm, we would then, in order

1. Include node 5; no change in Distance and Path needed
    Distance[2] = 800   Path[2] = 1
    Distance[3] = 2985   Path[3] = 1
    Distance[4] = 310   Path[4] = 1
    Distance[5] = 200   Path[5] = 1
2. Include node 4; update Distance and Path to
    Distance[2] = 800   Path[2] = 1
    Distance[3] = 1731   Path[3] = 4
    Distance[4] = 310   Path[4] = 1
    Distance[5] = 200   Path[5] = 1
    (Note that it is shorter to go from node 1 to node 4 to node 3 than to follow the edge directly connecting node 1 to node 3.)
3. Include node 2; update Distance and Path to
    Distance[2] = 800   Path[2] = 1
    Distance[3] = 1210   Path[3] = 2
    Distance[4] = 310   Path[4] = 1
    Distance[5] = 200   Path[5] = 1
    (Now we find that traveling from node 1 to node 2 to node 3 is even better than the path determined in step 2.)
4. Finally node 3 is included with no changes made in Distance or Path.

Efficiency of Dijkstra's Algorithm

If we assume an implementation of the EdgeWeight operation that is $O(1)$, then an inspection of the iterative control structure in our statement of Dijkstra's algorithm implies a worst-case $O(\text{NumberOfNodes}^2)$ efficiency for the algorithm. The reason is that the steps to find the minimal Distance among nodes not yet Included and then to update the Distance array are both O(NumberOfNodes) and they are nested sequentially inside the outer **repeat** loop, which is also O(NumberOfNodes). We shall see in the next chapter that, for sparse networks (i.e., those with relatively few edges compared to the number of nodes), we can achieve a somewhat better efficiency by using an adjacency-list implementation of the network and a priority queue to assist in finding the minimal distance.

Floyd's All-Pairs Shortest Path Algorithm

Dijkstra's algorithm is appropriate for finding the shortest distance between two specified nodes in a graph. However, if we want to use iteration of Dijkstra's algorithm to find the shortest distance between every possible pair of nodes in the network, we would have to nest Dijkstra's $O(\text{NumberOfNodes}^2)$ algorithm in another $O(\text{NumberOfNodes}^2)$ looping structure—one for each ordered pair of nodes in the graph. The resulting efficiency would be $O(\text{NumberOfNodes}^4)$. Floyd's algorithm is designed specifically to find the shortest distance between all pairs of nodes in a network. With this as its goal, it is able to compute all of these shortest paths in $O(\text{NumberOfNodes}^3)$ runtime. However, it remains inferior to Dijkstra's algorithm for finding the shortest distance between a single pair of nodes. Depending upon the pair of nodes, it may require $O(\text{NumberOfNodes}^3)$ time to do this single-pair computation.

The essence of Floyd's algorithm is to use information from the network to compute a sequence of matrices that have rows and columns indexed from 1 to NumberOfNodes. We will call this matrix the Distance matrix. At the Kth stage of Floyd's algorithm ($1 \leq K \leq \text{NumberOfNodes}$), Distance[I, J] is computed to contain the distance of the shortest path satisfying the two following criteria:

1. The path must start at Node(I) and end at Node(J).
2. Internal nodes on the path (i.e., excluding the start and end nodes) must come from the set of nodes having Index values between 1 and K inclusive.

Provided that such a succession of matrices can be computed, we are guaranteed that, at the final stage of the algorithm, Distance[I, J] contains the length of the shortest path from Node(I) to Node(J) because, by satisfying the second criterion, it contains the length of the shortest path whose internal nodes are selected from the set of all possible nodes.

Hence, we must merely ensure that the Distance matrix satisfying the two criteria above can be computed. Floyd discovered a surprisingly easy algorithm to do this. During an initialization phase of Floyd's algorithm, each entry of the Distance matrix is defined by the follow rule:

$$
\text{Distance[I, J]} = \begin{cases}
0 & \text{if } I = J \\
\text{EdgeWeight(N, Node(I), Node(J))} & \text{if network N contains an edge} \\
& \text{from Node(I) to Node(J)} \\
\infty & \text{otherwise}
\end{cases}
$$

Then, the following iterative step recomputes the Distance matrix through a succession of NumberOfNodes stages.

```
for K := 1 to NumberOfNodes do
  for I := 1 to NumberOfNodes do
    for J := 1 to NumberOfNodes do
      Distance[I, J] := minimum(Distance[I, J],
                                Distance[I, K] + Distance[K, J])
    endfor
  endfor
endfor
```

To see why this computation of the Distance matrix will satisfy the two criteria we have established as goals, consider the situation pictured in Figure 9.17. In the figure, the solid-line path from Node(I) to Node(J) represents the path of shortest length between those two nodes at the $(K - 1)$st stage of Floyd's algorithm. At the Kth stage of the algorithm, we compare the solid-line path from Node(I) to Node(J) with the path formed by joining the dashed-line path from Node(I) to Node(K) with the dotted-line path from Node(K) to Node(J). If the joining of these two paths results in a path from Node(I) to Node(J) whose overall length is less than the length of the solid-line path, we can adjust Distance[I, J] since, at the Kth stage of the algorithm, we allow node K to be an internal node on the shortest path.

The $O(\text{NumberOfNodes}^3)$ efficiency of Floyd's algorithm can be deduced immediately from its three-deep nested loop structure. It is also evident why Floyd's algorithm cannot be used efficiently to answer the single-pair shortest path question. The algorithm has no way of guaranteeing that it has found the shortest path between a specified pair of nodes until it checks

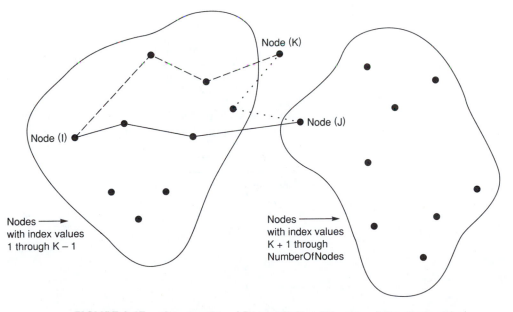

FIGURE 9.17   Computation of Distance[I, J] at Kth stage of Floyd's algorithm.

whether LastNode should be part of that path, and it cannot perform this check without iterating through $O(\text{NumberOfNodes}^3)$ operations.

Example 9.5   To be sure that you understand Floyd's algorithm before you attempt to implement it in the exercises, trace through the contents of the Distance matrix for the directed network of Figure 9.18.

1. During the initialization phase, the Distance array would be set to the following values:

		1	2	3
Distance	1	0	8	5
	2	3	0	∞
	3	∞	2	0

2. During the first iteration of the algorithm, we would determine whether any Distance values from step 1 can be decreased by using a path that has node 1 as an interior node. Since the path

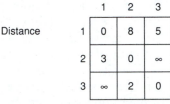

is certainly less than ∞ presently in Distance[2, 3], the Distance array is updated to

		1	2	3
Distance	1	0	8	5
	2	3	0	8
	3	∞	2	0

3. In the second iteration, we seek paths that are shorter than those we presently have and that contain 2 as an interior node. The path

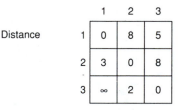

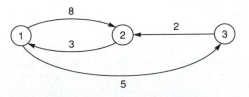

FIGURE 9.18
Network for tracing Floyd's algorithm in Example 9.5.

yields such a smaller value for the Distance [3, 1]. Hence, the matrix becomes

	1	2	3
1	0	8	5
2	3	0	8
3	5	2	0

4. The final iteration considers paths with node 3 as an interior node. In this case, we note that the path

$$1 \longrightarrow 3 \longrightarrow 2$$

Length 5 Length 2

is shorter than the direct edge $1 \rightarrow 2$ whose value is presently recorded in Distance[1, 2]. Hence, the Distance array is determined to be

	1	2	3
1	0	7	5
2	3	0	8
3	5	2	0

Transitive Closure and Warshall's Algorithm

In our previous discussion we were interested in finding the shortest path between given nodes in a graph. Sometimes, however, we may only be interested in discerning whether paths exist between two nodes and not what the shortest path is. One way to expedite answering queries about the existence of a path between two nodes of a graph G is to augment the edge structure of G by adding an edge directly between two nodes in G if there is a path between those nodes. The graph that results is known as the *transitive closure* of G. In this section we give an algorithm for converting a graph to its transitive closure. This algorithm is an adaptation of an algorithm formulated by Stephen Warshall in 1962 (S. Warshall, "A Theorem on Boolean Matrices," *Journal of the ACM*, 9(1), 1962, pp. 11–12). In outline form our algorithm is as follows

```
repeat
    choose a node N of graph G;
    repeat
        choose a node M of graph G;
        if there is an edge from M to N then
            repeat
                choose a node P of graph G;
```

> **if** *there is an edge from N to P* **then**
>   *add an edge from M to P*
>   **endif**
> **until** *all nodes P of graph G have been examined*
> **endif**
> **until** *all nodes M of graph G have been examined*
> **until** *all nodes N of graph G have been examined*

The key observation behind Warshall's algorithm is that one can eventually derive the transitive closure of a graph by looking only at nodes N that are at the center of paths of length 2, and then adding an edge between the first and third nodes of this path, bypassing the center node. Once this edge is added, it has the potential for being part of another path of length 2 that may come up later if one or both of its edges are chosen as a new value for N. This approach certainly seems nonintuitive and may lead one to inquire why it works (an "intuitive" approach might lead one to systematically select each node in the graph, examine paths that run through the node, and then make direct connections to the endpoints of each edge in this path). Although we shall not formally prove that Warshall's algorithm does produce the transitive closure of graph G, we can develop some further understanding of how (and why) the algorithm works by considering the following simple graph G consisting of a path of length 3.

$$N_1 \rightarrow N_2 \rightarrow N_3 \rightarrow N_4$$

One of the edges that will appear in the transitive closure of G is the edge $N_1 \rightarrow N_4$. A complete discussion of how the edge would be produced would have us consider the 24 different ways that three nodes among N_1 through N_4 could be selected in the nested loop structure of Warshall's algorithm. We shall consider only the case in which the nodes are selected in the order N_1, N_2, N_3, N_4. In so doing we shall be examining a case in which the edges that have to be added for N_1 will not be added at the time that N_1 is selected in the outer control loop of Warshall's algorithm (which again seems the intuitive place to add them), but later, when N_2 and N_3 are selected.

When $N = N_1$, no edges are added to the graph because N_1 is not the center of a path of length 2.

$$N_1 \rightarrow N_2 \rightarrow N_3 \rightarrow N_4$$
$$\uparrow$$
$$N$$

On the other hand, when $N = N_2$, the edge $N_1 \rightarrow N_3$ will be added:

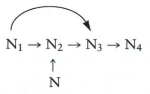

$$N_1 \rightarrow N_2 \rightarrow N_3 \rightarrow N_4$$
$$\uparrow$$
$$N$$

And when $N = N_3$, the algorithm takes advantage of this newly added edge to determine that N_3 is the center node of the path $N_1 \rightarrow N_3 \rightarrow N_4$, so the path $N_1 \rightarrow N_4$ is added to the graph (later, edge $N_2 \rightarrow N_4$ will also be added):

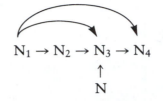

$$N_1 \rightarrow N_2 \rightarrow N_3 \rightarrow N_4$$
$$\uparrow$$
$$N$$

With this overview for Warshall's algorithm behind us, we now give a complete algorithm in PSEUDO, incorporating into it our previous assumptions about the nodes' values coming from a finite data type that can be ordered to achieve a one-to-one correspondence with the range of integers between 1 and NumberOfNodes inclusive.

```
procedure FindTransitiveClosure
  ( given G: Graph       (* An arbitrary graph *);
    return TC: Graph     (* The transitive closure of G *) );

  var M, N, P: integer;

  start FindTransitiveClosure
    Create(TC);
    (* Initially give TC the same edge structure as G *)
    for N := 1 to NumberOfNodes do
      for M := 1 to NumberOfNodes do
        if Edge(G, Node(M), Node(N)) then
          AddEdge(TC, Node(M), Node(N))
        endif
      endfor
    endfor;
    (* Now start adding edges to TC *)
    for N := 1 to NumberOfNodes do
      for M := 1 to NumberOfNodes do
        if Edge(TC, Node(M), Node(N)) then
          for P := 1 to NumberOfNodes do
            if Edge(TC, Node(N), Node(P)) then
              AddEdge(TC, Node(M), Node(P))
            endif
          endfor
        endif
      endfor
    endfor
  end FindTransitiveClosure;
```

Example 9.6   Find the transitive closure of the graph G of Figure 9.19.
Following Warshall's algorithm, we first include all edges from the original graph in the transitive closure. Now, starting with N = 1 and continuing

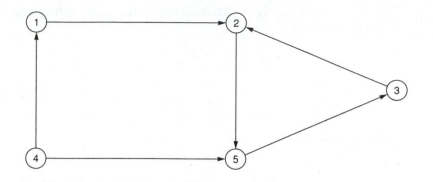

FIGURE 9.19
Graph for Example 9.6.

on through 2, 3, 4, and 5, we seek in the current transitive closure paths of length 2 centered about node N:

1. For $N = 1$, there is one path of length 2 centered about node 1, the path $4 \to 1 \to 2$; hence, we add the path $4 \to 1$ to the transitive closure.

2. For $N = 2$ we have the following paths of length 2 centered about node 2: $1 \to 2 \to 5$, $3 \to 2 \to 5$, and $4 \to 2 \to 5$. Consequently, we "add" the paths $1 \to 5$, $3 \to 5$, and $4 \to 5$ to the transitive closure, though in the case of the path $4 \to 5$ nothing new is being added since the path was already in the transitive closure by virtue of its being one of the paths of G.

3. For $N = 3$, there is one path of length 2 centered at node 3, the path $5 \to 3 \to 2$; hence, we add the path $5 \to 2$ to the transitive closure.

4. For $N = 4$ there are no paths of length 2 centered about node 4.

5. For $N = 5$ we have six paths of length 2 centered about node 5: $1 \to 5 \to 2$, $1 \to 5 \to 3$, $2 \to 5 \to 3$, $3 \to 5 \to 2$, $4 \to 5 \to 2$, and $4 \to 4 \to 3$. Consequently, we "add" the paths $1 \to 2$, $1 \to 3$, $2 \to 3$, $3 \to 2$, $4 \to 2$, and $4 \to 3$ to the transitive closure, though the only arcs added that were not in the transitive closure already are the arcs $1 \to 3$, $2 \to 3$, and $4 \to 3$. The transitive closure for G is shown in Figure 9.20.

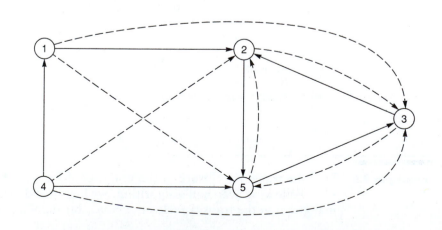

FIGURE 9.20

Transitive closure of the graph in Figure 9.19. The dashed arcs indicate those added to those of G to arrive at the transitive closure.

Warshall's Algorithm as a Special Case of Floyd's Algorithm

The alert reader may have noticed some similarities between our discussion of Warshall's algorithm, with its search for paths of length 2 centered about a node N, and our discussion of Floyd's algorithm and its concern with nodes K, which are interior to paths between other pairs of nodes. In fact, these similarities are more than just coincidental. Suppose we are given a directed graph G. Now let G' be the directed network that has the same node structure as G and in which each pair of nodes is connected by an arc in each direction. Furthermore, for each arc E of G', we shall assign it a weight of 0 if there is a corresponding arc in G and a weight of 1 otherwise. Now given Node(I) and Node(J) in G, the arc connecting these nodes will be in the transitive closure of G if the shortest path between Node(I) and Node(J) in G' is of length 0. Furthermore, if we represent the edges of G with an adjacency matrix, then the determination of the correct boolean value for the entry in row I, column J of the transitive closure of G corresponds to the calculation of the value of Distance[I, J] for the network G' in Floyd's algorithm. Consequently, assuming the edges of G and its transitive closure TC are represented with adjacency matrices, an alternative implementation of FindTransitiveClosure could have been given by

```
type   (* Assume adjacency matrix implementation *)
  Graph: array [NumberOfNodes, NumberOfNodes] of boolean;

procedure FindTransitiveClosure
  ( given G: Graph      (* An arbitrary graph *);
    return TC: Graph    (* The transitive closure of G *) );

  var M, N, P: integer;

  start FindTransitiveClosure
    Create(TC);
    (* Initially give TC the same edge structure as G *)
    for N := 1 to NumberOfNodes do
      for M := 1 to NumberOfNodes do
        TC[M, N] := G[M, N]
      endfor
    endfor;
    (* Now start adding edges to TC *)
    for N := 1 to NumberOfNodes do
      for M := 1 to NumberOfNodes do
        for P := 1 to NumberOfNodes do
          (* The next boolean computation corresponds to
             taking the minimum in Floyd's algorithm *)
          TC[M, P] := TC[M, P] or (TC[M, N] and TC[N, P])
        endfor
      endfor
    endfor
  end FindTransitiveClosure;
```

We should point out that it is the triple **for** loop of this procedure that is traditionally referred to as Warshall's algorithm. The algorithm we gave earlier offers an overall improvement in run-time efficiency by making the execution of the third **for** loop conditional and dependent upon the initial number of edges in the graph. Moreover, this earlier algorithm for calculating the transitive closure uses only operations from the Graph ADT and, hence, does not depend on the method used to represent the graph's edges.

We shall consider issues related to the efficiency of Warshall's algorithms in Exercise 13.

Exercises 9.4

1. Trace the contents of the Distance, Path, and Included arrays as Dijkstra's shortest path algorithm is applied to the transportation network of Figure 9.3. Use Phoenix as the Start node and Chicago as the Destination node.

2. Repeat Exercise 1 with Milwaukee as the Start node and Oklahoma City as the Destination node.

3. Only a skeletal form of Dijkstra's shortest path algorithm was presented in this section. Expand this skeletal version to a complete PSEUDO implementation.

4. Modify your answer to Exercise 3 so that the PSEUDO procedure you developed in that exercise finds the shortest path from a designated Start node to all other nodes in the network. How does this modification affect the time efficiency of the algorithm?

5. Suppose that the transportation network of Figure 9.3 is restricted to the nodes Chicago, New Orleans, Dallas, Las Vegas, Los Angeles, and the edges that exist between them. Define an appropriate ordering for these nodes and then trace the contents of the Distance matrix in Floyd's all-pairs shortest path algorithm for this five-node network.

6. Repeat Exercise 5 for the network of Figure 9.21.

7. Only a skeletal form of Floyd's all-pairs shortest path algorithm was presented in this section. Extend it to a compete PSEUDO implementation.

8. Modify your PSEUDO procedure of Exercise 7 so that the nodes on each path, as well as the lengths of the paths, are retrievable.

9. Trace the contents of the data structures involved in your algorithm from Exercise 8 when it is executed on the network of Exercise 5. Your trace should indicate how your recording of nodes on each path progresses as well as your recording of the lengths of these paths.

10. Repeat Exercise 9 for the network of Figure 9.21.

11. Using the underlying graph structure for the network of Exercise 5 and assuming that an edge between two nodes indicates the existence of an arc in each direction between the nodes, find the transitive closure of this graph.

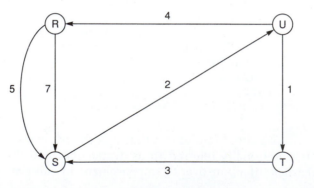

FIGURE 9.21
Network for Exercises 6, 10, and 12.

12. Repeat Exercise 11 for the network of Figure 9.21.

13. Analyze the efficiency of both versions of Warshall's algorithm. What effect does the density of the edges have on these efficiencies? In the case of a sparse graph, discuss the potential trade-offs in space/time efficiency for the first version of the algorithm that would result from using adjacency lists to represent the edges of the graph.

9.5 MINIMUM SPANNING TREES

A problem different in nature from those of the previous section is often faced by the designers of communications networks. Because of the high speed at which electronic communications travel, the length of a communications path between two nodes in such a network may not be a terribly critical issue. However, construction of the network itself can be a very expensive proposition, involving the installation of costly, high-speed data links between network nodes. Hence, a more crucial issue for designers is to minimize the cost of network construction, *not* to find the shortest path between any two nodes. That is, being able to link *all* nodes in the network for the least possible cost is much more crucial than being able to link any two nodes in the most economical fashion.

A *minimal spanning tree* is a subnetwork constructed from a larger network to address this issue. In particular, given an original undirected network in which there is a path between any two nodes, the edges for a minimum spanning tree are chosen in such a way that two properties result:

1. Every node in the network must be included in the spanning tree.
2. The total edge weight of the spanning tree is the minimum possible that will allow the existence of a path between any two nodes in the tree.

Two algorithms exist for the construction of minimal spanning trees. The first, discovered by R. C. Prim ("Shortest Connection Network and Some Generalizations," *Bell System Technical Journal*, 36, 1957, pp. 1389–1401), is effective for networks that are dense, meaning they have relatively few edges missing from the maximum number they can have. The second, originated by J. B. Kruskal ("On the Shortest Spanning Tree of a Graph and the Traveling Salesperson Problem," *Proceedings of the AMS*, 7:1, 1956, pp. 48–50) is designed for sparse networks; that is, for networks that have relatively few edges with respect to the maximum numbers of edges they can have. To simplify our discussion of both these algorithms, we shall again assume that the data type NetworkNode is a finite data type that can be ordered to achieve a one-to-one correspondence with the range of integers between 1 and NumberOfNodes inclusive.

Prim's Algorithm

Prim's algorithm parallels Dijkstra's shortest path algorithm (Section 9.4) in that it divides network nodes into two sets: *included* and *nonincluded* nodes. A node is included when we decide which edge will connect it into the minimum spanning tree. As in Dijkstra's algorithm, we *include* nodes (and corresponding edges) one at a time until all nodes have been *included*. In PSEUDO, Prim's algorithm may be stated as follows:

```
type
  NetworkNode: (* The data type of the value of each node in the network.
                  We assume that this is a subrange type that can be
                  enumerated to correspond to the range of integers between
                  1 and the constant NumberOfNodes *);
  (* The next type declaration provides a means of storing an encapsulated
     edge in the algorithm *)
  Edgetype: record
              Node1, Node2: NetworkNode;
              Weight: WeightType
            endrecord;

procedure ConstructMST  (* Construction of minimum spanning tree by
                           Prim's algorithm *)
  ( given N: Network     (* A strongly connected network *);
    return MST: Network  (* A subnetwork of N with minimum spanning tree
                            properties *) );
  var
    Included: array [NumberOfNodes] of boolean;
    K: integer;
    E: Edgetype;
  start MST
    Create (MST);
    (* Begin by including any node in the MST. Here the first node is chosen *)
    Included[1] := true;
    for K := 2 to NumberNodes do
      Included[K] := false
    endfor;
    (* Next enter a loop in which a different node is Included on each
       iteration. Since the loop is executed NumberOfNodes - 1 times, all
       nodes are Included upon exit from the loop *)
    for K := 1 to NumberNodes - 1 do
      FindMinimum(E);  (* Call on procedure to return the edge E
                          of minimum weight connecting a
                          non-Included node to an Included node *)

      Included[Index(E.Node1)] := true;
      Included[Index(E.Node2)] := true;
```

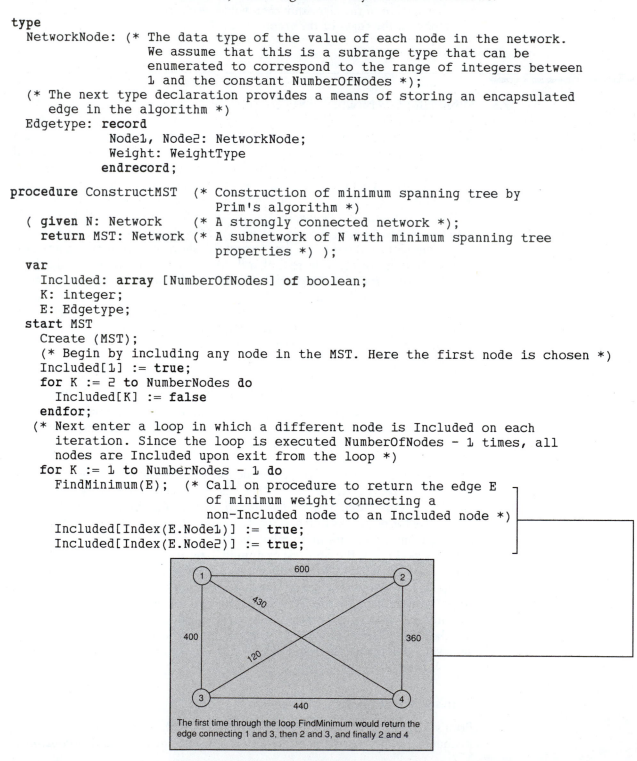

The first time through the loop FindMinimum would return the edge connecting 1 and 3, then 2 and 3, and finally 2 and 4

```
        AddEdge(MST, E.Node1, E.Node2, E.Weight);
        AddEdge(MST, E.Node2, E.Node1, E.Weight)
    endfor
end MST;
```

The procedure FindMinimum, which you will develop in the exercises as a procedure subordinate to ConstructMST, is critical to understanding how Prim's algorithm works. To illustrate, we will trace it on a small network.

Example 9.7   Consider the network in Figure 9.22. Trace the order in which edges would be added to its minimum spanning tree.

1. After the initialization of the Included array, only node 1 is Included.

2. On the first pass through the construction loop, FindMinimum would select the edge connecting nodes 1 and 5 and node 5 would be included. The current state of the MST would be

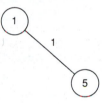

3. On the second iteration of the construction loop, FindMinimum would select the edge connecting nodes 4 and 5. Hence, node 4 would be included and the MST is updated to

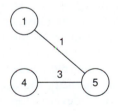

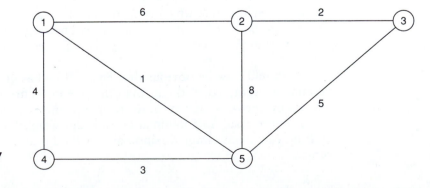

FIGURE 9.22
Network for Examples 9.7 and 9.8.

4. On the next iteration, the edge connecting nodes 3 and 5 is selected, expanding the MST to

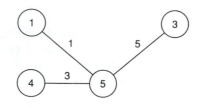

5. On the final iteration, the edge connecting nodes 2 and 3 is chosen, yielding a final MST of the form

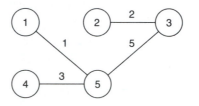

You should verify that this final MST satisfies the two minimum spanning tree properties that we established at the beginning of this section.

It is obvious that, if the original network has a path between any two nodes, the minimum spanning tree constructed by Prim's method will also have a path between any two nodes. It is perhaps not as obvious that the method will necessarily produce a tree of the minimum total edge weight allowing the existence of a path between any two nodes. The following argument gives an intuitive rationale for why this indeed must be so. Consider any other method for choosing nodes and edges that belong to the minimal spanning tree. Since Prim's method allows us to start with any node, we could easily identify the choice at which Prim's algorithm and the proposed other method deviate. Let us group the nodes and edges for which the two methods dictate the same choice, as indicated in Figure 9.23. The edge leaving the circled edges in Figure 9.23 identifies the choice at which the proposed method and Prim's would deviate. That is, this edge cannot be an edge of minimal weight connecting a node outside the circle to one within the circle. There must be an edge of lesser weight connecting a node outside the circle to one within the circle. Such an edge is indicated by a dotted line in Figure 9.24.

It should now be obvious that Figure 9.24 has given us a spanning tree of smaller overall edge weight than the one in Figure 9.23. Hence, we have informally shown that any other proposed method of selecting nodes and edges *cannot* result in a minimal overall edge weight! The method prescribed by Prim can always improve upon any method that would dictate a different choice.

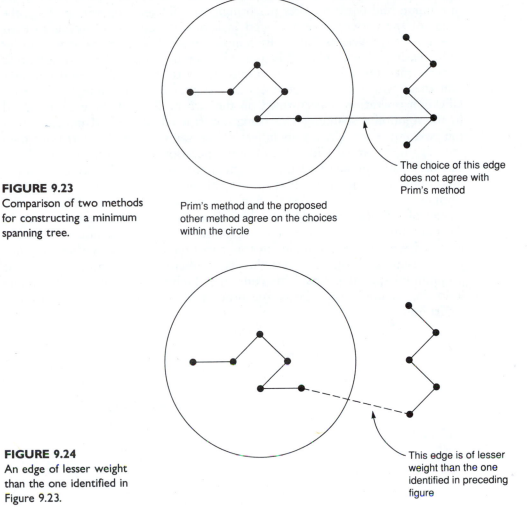

FIGURE 9.23
Comparison of two methods for constructing a minimum spanning tree.

Prim's method and the proposed other method agree on the choices within the circle

The choice of this edge does not agree with Prim's method

FIGURE 9.24
An edge of lesser weight than the one identified in Figure 9.23.

This edge is of lesser weight than the one identified in preceding figure

Efficiency of Prim's Algorithm

In the exercises at the end of this section, you will develop an implementation of the FindMinimum procedure (called by Prim's ConstructMST algorithm) that is $O(\text{NumberOfNodes})$ in its runtime. Given such a procedure, it is trivial to conclude that Prim's algorithm itself is $O(\text{NumberOfNodes}^2)$. Notice that the efficiency of Prim's algorithm is not dependent on the number of edges in the graph, only the number of nodes. This makes it the algorithm of choice for networks that are dense with edges. For sparse networks, we shall turn our attention to Kruskal's alternative algorithm for constructing a network's minimum spanning tree.

Kruskal's Algorithm

Kruskal's algorithm initially views the nodes of the network as existing in a union-find partition (Section 2.4) in which each set in the partition contains exactly one node. That is, the nodes of the network initially exist as members of a union-find partition after performing the UFCreate operation. Then the edges of the network are arranged in a priority queue according to their respective edge weights. Edges are removed from this priority queue in order of increasing edge weights. When an edge is removed, the UFFind operation is performed on the two nodes connected by the edge. If UFFind indicates that these two nodes are members of disjoint sets in the partition, then a UFUnion operation is performed on the two nodes and the edge is added to the minimum spanning tree being constructed. If UFFind indicates that the two nodes are already members of the same set in the partition, then the edge is discarded with no UFUnion operation being performed. Why is this the case? The fact that the two edges are already in the same set of the union-find partition means that we have already found a path between them composed of edges whose individual weights are less than or equal to the weight of the edge currently being examined. To include the current node in the minimum spanning tree at the expense of removing a node previously included would link the nodes in this partition set in a way that may not yield the minimal total edge weight—contradicting the defining property of a minimum spanning tree. This concept is highlighted in Figure 9.25. The following example will clarify the process of selecting edges in Kruskal's algorithm.

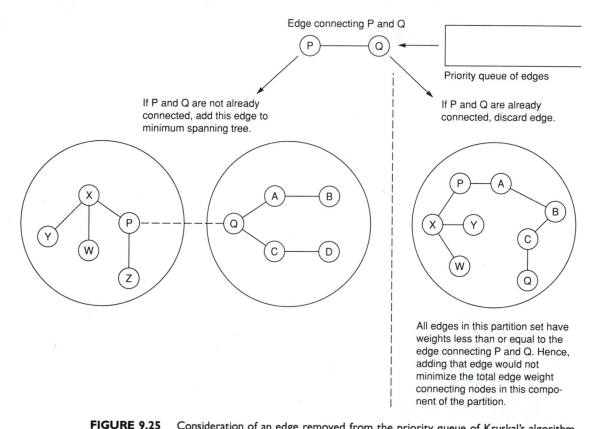

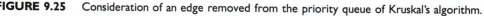

FIGURE 9.25   Consideration of an edge removed from the priority queue of Kruskal's algorithm.

Example 9.8 Trace the order of edge selection as Kruskal's algorithm executes on the network of Figure 9.22 on page 439.

1. Initially create a priority queue of edges and the partition formed by the UFCreate operation.

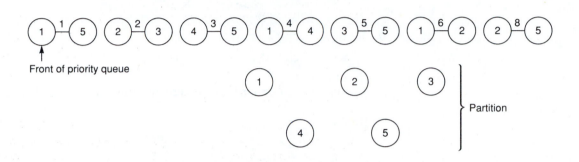

Front of priority queue

Partition

2. Successively remove edges from the priority queue, apply UFFind to nodes connected by each edge.

a. Remove

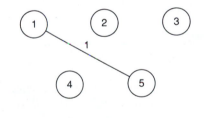

from priority queue; UFFind returns **false**, so partition becomes

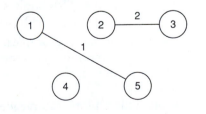

b. Remove

from priority queue; UFFind returns **false**, so partition becomes

c. Remove

from priority queue; UFFind returns **false**, so partition becomes

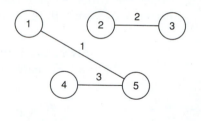

d. Remove from priority queue; UFFind returns **true**, so discard this edge.

e. Remove from priority queue; UFFind returns **false**, so partition becomes

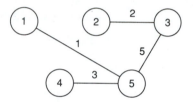

The construction of the minimum spanning tree is complete.

In comparing the selection of edges by Prim's and Kruskal's algorithms (Examples 9.7 and 9.8, respectively), we make the following observations and pose some questions.

1. Prim's and Kruskal's algorithms do not select edges in the same order.
2. Both algorithms terminate upon selecting (NumberOfNodes − 1) edges. This implies that a minimum spanning tree will always contain (NumberOfNodes − 1) edges. Why must this be the case?
3. In these examples, Prim's and Kruskal's algorithms arrive at the same minimal spanning tree upon completion. Will this always be the case?

You will explore the answers to these questions and develop a complete Pascal implementation of Kruskal's algorithm in the exercises at the end of this section. We now turn our attention toward analyzing the efficiency of Kruskal's algorithm.

A RELEVANT ISSUE

The Traveling Salesperson Problem

A well-known problem of classical graph theory, which is easy to state but difficult to solve, is the *traveling salesperson problem*. The problem tries to minimize the round-trip cost of visiting once and only once every city on the business route of the salesperson. This problem was first proposed by the Irish mathematician Sir William Rowan Hamilton (1805–1865).

The problem can be looked upon as a network such as in Figure 9.3. The cities to be visited are the nodes in the network, and the weighted edges are the distances between the cities. Prim's minimum spanning tree algorithm discussed in this section is not the solution to this problem, but it can be adapted to yield the solution in the following way:

1. Set the total cost of traveling to 0.
2. Select a home node (home city of the salesperson), and designate it as X.
3. Find an unused node that minimizes the sum of the edge weight connecting it to X plus the remaining round trip distance. Add this edge weight to the total cost.
4. Designate the node found in step 3 as the new home node; that is, as node X.
5. Repeat steps 3 and 4 until all nodes are visited and the salesperson is back at home; that is, until X is the home node chosen in step 2.

Although the algorithm described above solves the traveling salesperson's problem, it is slow because of the extensive computation involved in step 3. When the number of cities on the salesperson's tour is moderately large, the solution is annoyingly slow, but nothing better is known that will *guarantee* finding a solution to the problem.

Prototypes of this classical algorithm find frequent application in the design of computer operating systems. For instance, suppose we have a collection of processes all waiting to access a popular disk file. The operating system designer is concerned with scheduling these processes in a fashion that minimizes the total disk access time. By viewing each process P_i as a network node and the edge weight connecting node P_i to node P_j as the disk access time required if process P_j immediately follows process P_i in the scheduling, the solution to this operating system problem is essentially the traveling salesperson problem. A complicating factor is that the slowness of the algorithm cited above may make it impractical to incorporate into an interactive operating system.

The complexity of the traveling salesperson problem places it in a class of problems known as NP-complete problems. This theoretical class of problems has the following interesting property. If we can find for any one such problem a solution that has a polynomial time efficiency, then we will automatically have polynomial time solutions to all other problems in this class and an even larger theoretical class of problems known as NP problems. A thorough discussion of NP and NP-complete problems may be found in *Theory of Computation: Formal Languages, Automata, and Complexity* by J. Glenn Brookshear (Menlo Park, CA: Benjamin/Cummings, 1989).

Efficiency of Kruskal's Algorithm

The efficiency of Kruskal's algorithm will clearly be dependent upon the efficiency of the implementations we choose for the priority queue and union-find ADTs. In this regard, recall from Section 7.4 that a priority queue implemented by a heap provides $O(\log_2 n)$ efficiency for the enqueue and dequeue operations. Also recall from Section 8.4 that a union-find structure implemented by weight-balanced trees yields $O(\log_2 n)$ time efficiency for both the UFFind and UFUnion operations. In the argument that follows, we will assume these efficiencies for the priority queue and union-find operations. We will also assume that an adjacency-list implementation is used for the network; this will allow us to go through all edges in $O(\text{NumberEdges})$ times.

Under these assumptions, the initial formation of the priority queue of edges will require $O(\text{NumberEdges} \times \log_2(\text{NumberEdges}))$ time. During the second phase of Kruskal's algorithm, when each edge is removed from the queue and one or two union-find operations are performed on the nodes that it connects, we also have an $O(\text{NumberEdges} \times \log_2(\text{NumberEdges}))$ efficiency. The rationale is that, potentially, each edge must be removed from the priority queue—an $O(\log_2(\text{NumberEdges}))$ operation for each edge. Then, each of the one or two union-find operations that follow for that edge are also $O(\log_2(\text{NumberEdges}))$. Hence, the algorithm can be broken up into two phases, each of which is $O(\text{NumberEdges} \times \log_2(\text{NumberEdges}))$ in its efficiency—resulting in an overall $O(\text{NumberEdges} \times \log_2(\text{NumberEdges}))$ efficiency. Note that, as we claimed at the beginning of this section, this efficiency will make Kruskal's algorithm faster than Prim's for sparse networks with relatively few edges.

Exercises 9.5

1. In the style of Examples 9.7 and 9.8, trace both Prim's and Kruskal's algorithms for constructing minimal spanning trees from the following network.

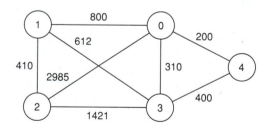

2. In the style of Examples 9.7 and 9.8, trace both Prim's and Kruskal's algorithms for constructing minimal spanning trees from the network at the top of page 447.

3. Complete Prim's version of the ConstructMST algorithm by writing the FindMinimum procedure called in the second **for** loop of that algorithm. Recall that this procedure must find the edge of minimum weight that connects a non-Included node to an Included node. Be sure that your algorithm is $O(\text{NumberOfNodes})$. (Hint: if necessary, introduce auxiliary data structures and update them as the algorithm executes.)

4. Suppose that we change the specification for the FindMinimum procedure in Prim's version of the ConstructMST algorithm to the following: find the edge of minimum weight that connects a non-Included node to the node

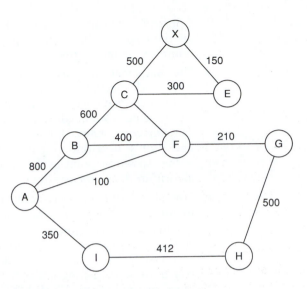

most recently Included. Show by an example that the algorithm may now fail to construct a minimum spanning tree.

5. Write a PSEUDO procedure ConstructMST to completely implement Kruskal's algorithm. Assume an adjacency-list implementation of networks to ensure $O(NumberOfEdges \times \log_2(NumberOfEdges))$ efficiency.

6. How would an adjacency-matrix implementation of the network affect the run-time efficiency of the procedure you wrote for Kruskal's algorithm in Exercise 5?

7. In our observations following Examples 9.7 and 9.8, we stated that a minimum spanning tree will always contain $(NumberOfNodes - 1)$ edges. Provide a logical argument to prove this claim. (Hint: use a proof by contradiction.)

8. Given a network N, is there necessarily a unique minimum spanning tree for the network? If not, provide an example of a network that has two different minimum spanning trees.

9. In our observations following Examples 9.7 and 9.8, we stated that Prim's and Kruskal's algorithms arrived at the same minimum spanning tree for the network of Figure 9.22. Will this always be the case? If not, provide an example where the two algorithms arrive at different minimum spanning trees.

10. Is the following statement true or false? In any network with three or more nodes and no two edges having equal weights, the two edges that have the smallest weights among all edges will always be part of the minimal spanning tree. If false, provide a counterexample.

11. Is the following statement true or false? In any network with four or more nodes and no two edges having equal weights, the three edges with the smallest weights among all edges will always be part of the minimal spanning tree. If false, provide a counterexample.

12. Is it possible for a minimum spanning tree to contain a cycle? Justify your answer.

13. In our tracing of Kruskal's algorithm in Example 9.8, we were able to stop removing edges from the priority queue before the queue became empty.

Construct an example in which Kruskal's algorithm would have to examine all the edges in the priority queue before completing construction of the minimum spanning tree.

14. Use mathematical analysis to estimate the point at which the sparseness of a network dictates the use of Kruskal's algorithm instead of Prim's. That is, the maximal edge density that a network can have is NumberOfNodes^2 edges—a network in which every node has edges connecting it to every node. The adjacency matrix for such a network would have only nonzero entries, and Prim's algorithm clearly will be more efficient than Kruskal's. What is the cross-over point in the ratio of edges to nodes that makes Kruskal's algorithm more efficient than Prim's?

15. You are constructing a communications network of computers at over 1,000 remote sites. You wish to minimize construction costs for the network and still make it possible for any computer to get a message to or from any other computer. In theory, it is possible to directly link any two computers, and you have a cost estimate for each possible link. From these cost estimates, you must write a program that extracts the minimum spanning tree with respect to total cost. Which MST algorithm should you use? Why?

9.6   TOPOLOGICAL ORDERING

One area where directed graphs find frequent application is in establishing precedence relations among activities that must be scheduled. For instance, consider the directed graph of Figure 9.26. This graph indicates a prerequisite structure among courses in a computer science curriculum. A directed edge from node X to node Y means that course X is a prerequisite for course Y. Analogous directed graphs can be developed to portray scheduling patterns for many large projects that can be broken down into subordinate activities. Such graphs can even be used to coordinate the execution of a main program's subordinate modules on a computer with multiple processors.

We can make three important observations about directed graphs that reflect such scheduling patterns. First, we note that it makes no sense for such

FIGURE 9.26

Course prerequisites in a computer science (CS) curriculum.

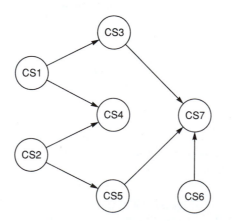

a graph to contain a cycle. That is, if we had a path such as X → Y → Z → X in such a graph, it would imply that activity X must be completed before activity Y could be started. Similarly, Y must be completed before Z could be started. However, the edge Z → X will not allow us to start X before Z is completed. We have an impossible scheduling task; none of the tasks in the cycle can be completed. Consequently, we conclude that directed graphs that portray a feasible precedence relationship among subactivities in a large project must be *acyclic*, that is, contain no cycles.

A second observation about directed acyclic graphs is that the precedence relationships in such a graph define a *partial ordering* on the set of graph nodes. A partial ordering on a set S is a relation $<$ having the following three properties:

1. Irreflexivity: for each element s in S, $s \not< s$.
2. Assymmetry: for elements s and t in S, if $s < t$, then $t \not< s$.
3. Transitivity: for elements r, s, and t in S, if $r < s$ and $s < t$, then $r < t$.

You should verify that in a directed acyclic graph with nodes belonging to a set S the relationship defined by

$$s < t \qquad \text{if and only if there is a path from } s \text{ to } t$$

satisfies the irreflexivity, asymmetry, and transitivity properties. Hence, we can conclude that the nodes in a directed acyclic graph form a partially ordered set.

Our third observation about directed acyclic graphs is related to the scheduling problems they often depict. For such problems, it is important that we be able to specify a linear sequence of graph nodes corresponding to the order in which subactivities may be completed, one after the other, and still comply with all of the precedence relationships in the graph. Such a linear ordering is called a *topological ordering* of the graph nodes. For example, in Figure 9.26, the sequence

$$\text{CS1} \quad \text{CS2} \quad \text{CS3} \quad \text{CS4} \quad \text{CS5} \quad \text{CS6} \quad \text{CS7}$$

is such a topological ordering. Notice that topological orderings are not unique for a given graph. You should verify that

$$\text{CS2} \quad \text{CS1} \quad \text{CS5} \quad \text{CS4} \quad \text{CS3} \quad \text{CS6} \quad \text{CS7}$$

and

$$\text{CS6} \quad \text{CS2} \quad \text{CS5} \quad \text{CS1} \quad \text{CS4} \quad \text{CS3} \quad \text{CS7}$$

are also topological orderings for the graph of Figure 9.26.

We now turn our attention to developing an algorithm that will find a topological ordering of the nodes for a given directed acyclic graph. To introduce the algorithm, we recall from Section 9.1 the notion of the *indegree* of a graph node—the number of edges entering a node. Clearly, a topological ordering may begin with any node that has an indegree of zero. Hence, we begin by adding all such nodes to a queue. As a node is removed from the queue of nodes with indegree 0, we record it as the next node in the topological ordering. We also subtract one from the indegree of all nodes connected by an edge from the node just removed. If this subtraction results in nodes having an adjusted indegree of zero, these nodes are then added to the queue. Because all predecessors of these nodes have been recorded previously in the topological ordering, the activities corresponding to these nodes may now be completed.

In the following complete TopologicalOrder algorithm, we again assume that type GraphNode is a subrange of some enumerated data type with finite Node and Index functions that establish a one-to-one correspondence between GraphNode values and the range of integers between 1 and NumberOfNodes inclusive.

```
type
   GraphNode: (* The data type of each node in the graph. We assume
               that this is a type that can be enumerated to correspond
               to the range of integers between 1 and the constant
               NumberOfNodes *);
   QueueData: GraphNode;
   NodeArray: array [NumberOfNodes] of GraphNode;

procedure TopologicalOrder
   ( given G: Graph                   (* A directed acyclic graph *);
     return T: NodeArray              (* A linear arrangement of graph
                                         nodes corresponding to a
                                         topological ordering for G *) );

   var
      ZeroQ: Queue;                          (* Holds nodes with adjusted
                                                indegree zero *)

      InDeg: array [NumberOfNodes] of integer;  (* Stores adjusted indegree
                                                of nodes *)

      TNode: GraphNode;
      N, OrderCount: integer;

   start
      ComputeInitialInDegree(G, InDeg)   (* Call a procedure that computes
                                            the indegree of each node in the
                                            graph G. The indegree of a node is
                                            stored at its Index position in
                                            the InDeg array *);
      Create(ZeroQ);                     (* Create the queue of nodes with zero
                                            indegree *)
      (* Place all nodes with zero indegree on ZeroQ *)
      for N := 1 to NumberOfNodes do
         if InDeg[N] then
            Enqueue(ZeroQ, Node(N))
         endif
      endfor;
      (* Now move nodes from ZeroQ to topological order array and check
         if additional nodes have an adjusted indegree of zero *)
      OrderCount := 0;
```

```
while not Empty(ZeroQ) do
   Dequeue(ZeroQ, TNode);
   OrderCount := OrderCount + 1;
   T[OrderCount] := TNode;
   for N := 1 to NumberOfNodes do
      if Edge(G, TNode, Node(N)) then
         InDeg[N] := InDeg[N] - 1;
         if InDeg[N] = 0 then
            Enqueue(ZeroQ, Node(N))
         endif
      endif
   endfor
endwhile;
Destroy (ZeroQ)
end TopologicalOrder;
```

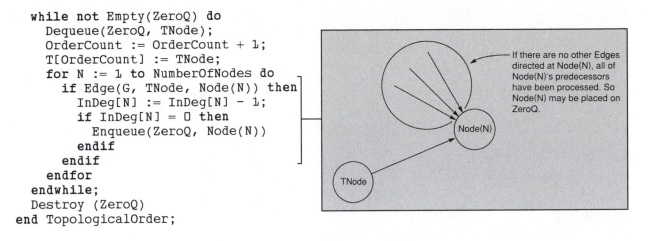

If there are no other Edges directed at Node(N), all of Node(N)'s predecessors have been processed. So Node(N) may be placed on ZeroQ.

Efficiency of the Topological Order Algorithm

The version of the topological order algorithm presented above makes no assumptions about the implementation of the graph G. Hence, the overall efficiency of the nested loop structure within the procedure is $O(\text{NumberOfNodes}^2)$. The CompleteInitialInDegree procedure would also be $O(\text{NumberOfNodes}^2)$ if the implementation of G does not provide an effective way to process edges. In the following exercises you will explore several different topological order algorithms that enhance this efficiency for graphs with specific properties and implementations.

Exercises 9.6

1. Trace the states of the topological order array T and the queue ZeroQ as the procedure TopologicalOrder would execute on the directed acyclic graph in Figure 9.26. Assume the following enumeration of graph nodes:

   CS1 CS2 CS3 CS4 CS5 CS6 CS7

2. Repeat Exercise 1 except now assume the following enumeration of graph nodes:

   CS7 CS6 CS5 CS4 CS3 CS2 CS1

3. Provide a logical, written argument that all graph nodes will eventually pass through the queue ZeroQ in procedure TopologicalOrder. (Hint: your argument should use the precondition you are given regarding graph G's being acyclic.)

4. What behavior will procedure TopologicalOrder display if the graph G contains a cycle?

5. Explain how the behavior you describe in Exercise 4 could be used to detect the existence of a cycle in a graph. Write a function that is given a directed graph G and returns **true** if G contains a cycle and **false** otherwise.

6. Provide a written rationale supporting the claim made in this section that the nodes in a directed acyclic graph form a partially ordered set under the relation

   $s < t$ if and only if there is a path from s to t

   Your rationale must contain logical arguments that demonstrate that this relation is irreflexive, asymmetric, and transitive.

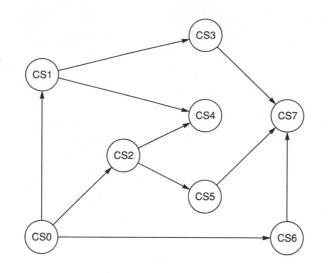

FIGURE 9.27
Directed acyclic graph for
Exercise 8.

7. Suppose that an adjacency-list implementation of the graph G is used in procedure TopologicalOrder. Rewrite the internal code of the procedure to directly access this adjacency-list implementation. How does the different implementation affect the efficiency of the algorithm? Provide a big-O analysis of the resulting efficiency. Under what circumstances would this new version of the algorithm be more efficient than the version given in this section? Under what circumstances would it be less efficient?

8. For this exercise, work under the assumption that a directed acyclic graph G has exactly one node with indegree zero. (Clearly, if more than one such node exists, we can add an artificial node that is a predecessor of all and only those nodes having indegree 0 and hence satisfy this assumption with the augmented graph.) Consider a modified depth-first traversal operation that does not apply the ProcessNode procedure to the Start node until after it returns from the recursively called traversals of nodes adjacent to the Start node. Suppose that ProcessNode merely prints the Start node.

   a. What will be the order in which nodes are printed by this modified depth-first traversal if it is called with the directed graph of Figure 9.27 using CS0 as the original Start node?

   b. What is the relationship between the order in which nodes are printed by this modified depth-first traversal and the linear arrangement of nodes in a topological ordering?

   c. Will the relationship you observed in part b always hold? If so, use it to develop an alternative version of procedure TopologicalOrder.

   d. Analyze the efficiency of the TopologicalOrder procedure you developed in part c. How is this efficiency contingent upon whether an adjacency matrix or adjacency lists are used to implement the graph?

Chapter Summary

In many information storage applications the hierarchical organization brought by trees is insufficient and a data structure that allows for two-way relationships among data entities is needed. In this chapter we introduce the concepts of a graph and a network (or weighted graph). Because relationships between items in a graph are completely arbitrary (as opposed to

A RELEVANT ISSUE

Critical Path Analysis, PERT, and CPM

In the late 1950s techniques based on directed networks were developed to assist managers of large-scale projects in the planning, scheduling, and coordinating of numerous and interrelated activities. A project's activity is represented in a network by an edge, with the weight of the edge designating an estimated time for completing the activity. A node of the network, on the other hand, represents an event with the property that all activities leading to the node/event must be completed before any activity emanating from the node can commence.

The network shown below represents roughly the activities involved in building a small house.

The events are labeled 0 through 10, with node 0 representing the starting time for the project and node 10 representing completion time for the project. The dashed edges, marked dummy, are used to establish precedence relationships only and do not represent real activities of the project. They have an associated weight of 0. We associate the following completion times with each activity: prepare lot—3; lay foundation—4; erect external frame—10; erect roof—3; install plumbing—9; install electrical wiring—7; external walls—7; cover roof—2; interior walls, floor, and ceiling—5; finish exterior—5; and finish interior—8. Then an examination of the network will show that there is one path in the network, $0 \to 1 \to 2 \to 3 \to 5 \to 8 \to 9 \to 10$, such that any delay in the completion of an activity in this path will delay the whole project. The length of this path is 39. Paths such as this are known as *critical paths* of the network. Possessed with a knowledge of a project's critical paths, a project manager can analyze it to determine where the greatest attention should be focused to keep the project on schedule; to predict what effects, if any, a delay in the completion of a given activity will have on the completion time of the entire project; and to locate activities where an improvement in performance would have to occur in order to improve the project's completion time.

Two well-known techniques using such a critical path analysis are PERT (Program Evaluation and Review Technique) and CPM (Critical Path Method). In PERT, three estimates are used for the completion time of each activity—a most

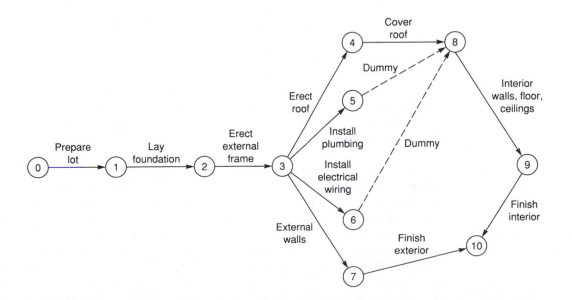

likely estimate, an optimistic estimate, and a pessimistic estimate. This trio is then used to calculate an expected time and a variance for each activity. These times and variances in turn allow one to calculate an expected completion time and variance for the project, which are used to give a probability that a scheduled completion time can be met. PERT is often used for evaluating schedules for research and development projects, where the completion times of activities are not well known. It was originally developed for the *Polaris* missile project.

CPM, on the other hand, assumes that the completion times of a project's activities are well known. A time-versus-cost relationship is established for each activity and a critical path analysis applied to the CPM network to determine a time-cost trade-off for each activity so that a scheduled completion time can be met at a minimum cost. CPM is especially appropriate for construction and maintenance projects, where experience allows activity times to be estimated with a high degree of certainty.

Although originally developed independently, the techniques of PERT and CPM are now merged into a single method of analysis often referred to as a *PERT-type* analysis. An overview of the PERT-CPM techniques can be found in Hillier and Lieberman, *Introduction to Operations Research* (second edition), San Francisco: Holden-Day, 1974, pp. 229–241).

the linear relationships of lists, stacks, and queues, or the hierarchical relationships of trees), they represent the most general data structure we discuss in this book. We begin by introducing the basic concepts and terminology of graphs and networks in Section 9.1 and move on to a formal definition of both as abstract data types in Section 9.2. Examples of depth-first and breadth-first traversals are shown.

Implementations of graphs and networks are taken up in Section 9.3, with adjacency matrices and adjacency lists being discussed as ways for representing the edges of a graph and network. To avoid weighting down the rest of our discussion with cumbersome implementation details, we assume for the rest of the chapter that the values of the nodes of our graphs and networks come from an enumerated set that can be placed into one-to-one correspondence with the range of integers between 1 and NumberOfNodes. Such an ordering is necessary for providing algorithms that implement depth-first and breadth-first traversals.

Section 9.4 deals with path algorithms. Shortest path algorithms are concerned with finding the shortest distance between two nodes in a network. Dijkstra's algorithm allows us to find the shortest distance between two specified nodes of a network, but does not extend efficiently to find the shortest distance between every possible pair of nodes in the network. Floyd's algorithm, on the other hand, deals effectively with the all-pairs shortest path problem but remains inferior to Dijkstra's for finding the shortest path between a single pair of nodes. For some applications, it is not the shortest path between two nodes that is of interest, but merely the existence of a path between two nodes. One way to expedite answering queries about the existence of a path between two nodes of a graph G is to augment the edge structure of G by adding an edge directly between two nodes in G if there is a path between those nodes. The resulting graph is known as the transitive closure of G. Warshall's algorithm for finding the transitive closure of a graph is given and later shown to be a special case of Floyd's algorithm.

A problem different in nature from those of Section 9.4 is that of finding a minimal spanning tree for a network, which is subnetwork of a given network such that the total of all the edge weights of the subnetwork is minimal, all nodes of the original network are included in the subnetwork, and any two nodes in the subnetwork have a path between them that is within this subnetwork. Algorithms by Prim and Kruskal are given for finding a minimal spanning tree. Kruskal's algorithm views the nodes of a network as existing in a union-find partition of single node sets, hence allowing us to use the operations of the Union-Find ADT from Section 2.4.

We conclude the chapter with a discussion of topological ordering in Section 9.6.

Key Words

adjacency lists	edges	partial ordering
adjacency matrix	Floyd's algorithm	Prim's algorithm
adjacent	graph	strongly connected
arc	indegree	topological ordering
breadth-first traversal	Kruskal's algorithm	total path weight
cycle	length	transitive closure
degree	loop	Warshall's algorithm
depth-first traversal	minimal spanning tree	weakly connected
digraph	network	weight
Dijkstra's algorithm	nodes	
directed path	outdegree	

Programming Problems/Projects

1. Write a program that provides an implementation of the transportation network in Figure 9.3 and then uses that implementation to allow a user to find the shortest path (and its length) between two cities, which are input by the user.

2. Write a program that provides an implementation of the transportation network in Figure 9.3 and then uses that implementation to find the shortest paths (and their lengths) between all pairs of cities.

3. Write a program that provides an implementation of the network in Figure 9.3 and then uses that implementation to find a minimal spanning tree of the network.

4. Recall that a directed graph is said to be strongly connected if, for any two nodes A and B, there is a path from A to B and one from B to A. Write a program that provides an implementation of the graph in Figure 9.28 and then uses that implementation to detect whether the graph is strongly connected. If your program determines that the graph is not strongly connected, it should report those pairs of nodes that are not connected by a path. What is the time efficiency of your algorithm?

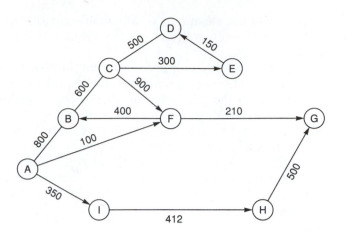

FIGURE 9.28
Directed graph for Problem
4.

5. The Bay Area Brawlers professional football team is considering building a new stadium. The entire process of building the stadium has been broken down into a series of subtasks as specified in this diagram:

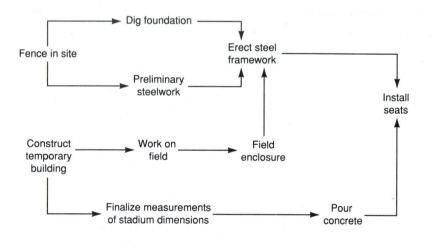

One subtask preceding another in this graph means that the first subtask must be completed before the second can be started. Write a program that will topologically order the subtasks in the preceding graph. Note that this ordering represents a possible ordering in which the subtasks could be performed by the workers.

6. Many language compilers allow separate compilation of external modules that may be linked to form a complete executable program. Write a program that allows a user to enter a graph of dependency relationships between separately compiled modules, for example, a graph such as that in Figure 9.29. The user should then be able to enter one module's identifier—representing a module in which edits were made and therefore had to be recompiled. Your program should consequently output an ordering of all other modules that need to be recompiled because of the changes made by the user in the input module. This ordering should represent a sequence in which the dependent modules could be recompiled.

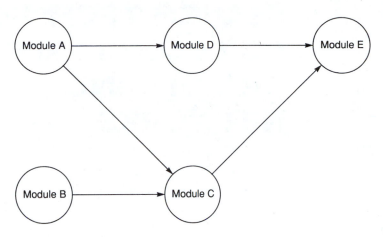

FIGURE 9.29

Graph of dependency relationships between externally compiled modules. An edge from one module to another indicates that the compilation of the latter is dependent upon the former.

7. Implement a procedure that is given a directed graph G and indicate whether or not G contains a cycle. What is the time efficiency of your algorithm?

8. Begin this problem by writing a procedure that randomly generates a specified number of points within rectangular boundaries of the Euclidean plane. Then your procedure should randomly generate weighted edges connecting these points. The weight of an edge is merely the Euclidian distance between points. The number of edges generated should be user-specified and should ensure that the resulting network is strongly connected.

   Given this network, develop separate procedures that find its minimal spanning tree by Prim's and Kruskal's algorithms. Additionally, your procedures should count the number of operations performed by each algorithm. Write out these counts at the completion of both algorithms.

   Now use the resulting program to experiment with the relationship between the sparseness of a graph (i.e., ratio of nodes to edges) and the corresponding efficiency of Prim's and Kruskal's algorithms. Do your experimental results confirm your answer to Exercise 14 in Section 9.5?

9. Write a program that implements both of the topological sort algorithms discussed in Section 9.6 (i.e., the one for which PSEUDO code is given and the one you deduced in Exercise 8 of that section). Then augment each of the implemented algorithms by maintaining counters that keep track of the number of operations performed by these algorithms. Use the counters to empirically compare the performance of the two algorithms for a variety of directed acyclic graphs. Write a report in which you summarize the conclusions that you reach from this empirical testing of the algorithms. Under which condition does one algorithm tend to outperform the other? Provide an explanation of such differences in performance.

10

SEARCH TECHNIQUES FOR CONCEPTUAL GRAPHS AND NETWORKS

Attempt the end, and never stand to doubt;
Nothing's so hard, but search will find it out.

Robert Herrick

CHAPTER OUTLINE

In the last chapter we examined some ways of finding paths through a graph or network. For instance, Dijkstra's algorithm finds a path from a designated start node to a goal node in a fashion that ensures the shortest possible path. In this chapter we will pursue the problem of finding paths from a start node to a goal node. However, we will also add some variations to this general theme. First, we will not always require that the path we find be the shortest path from the start node to the goal node; we hope that we may be able to find a path from the start to the goal *faster* if we settle for any path rather than the shortest one. That is, we will switch the emphasis from how long it takes to traverse the path found by our algorithm to how long it takes our algorithm to find a path. Second, though we will still be searching through graphs and networks in theory, such graphs and networks will be viewed as purely conceptual search structures—structures that may never exist entirely as data in computer memory. Both of these adaptations on the path-finding motif are motivated by the existence of abstract graphs and networks so large that no implementation will squeeze them into a reasonable amount of space. Consider, for instance, the conceptual graph that underlies a game of strategy such as chess. A designated start node in such a graph is a representation of the initial state of a chessboard. That node is adjacent to each possible chessboard configuration that could be realized by the first player's making one move. Each configuration attainable by the first player's move is similarly adjacent to each possible configuration achieved by the opponent's first countermove. This interpretation of adjacent nodes in the graph representing a chess game extends for second moves, third moves, and so forth as indicated in Figure 10.1. It has been estimated that the number of possible paths in such a graph is on the order of 10^{120}. Clearly, one cannot store a graph of this size in memory, though it is certainly possible to develop an algorithm for computing all nodes "adjacent" to a given game state. It is also clear that if we seek a path from the starting configuration of the chessboard to a goal state—that is, a winning configuration for a designated player—we are not necessarily concerned with the shortest such path. We would be happy merely to find a winning path as opposed to beating our opponent in the smallest possible number of moves.

Such is the framework from which we will approach graph and network search algorithms. The methods we will describe are often applied in such

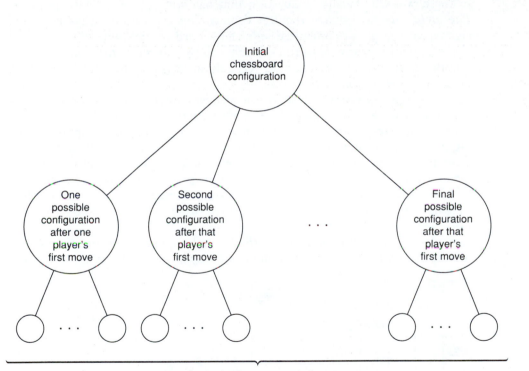

Configuration possible after opponent's first countermove

And so forth . . .

We seek a path to a goal node that represents a win
for a designated player.

FIGURE 10.1   Graph of game states in a chess game.

areas as artificial intelligence and natural language processing. In Section 10.1 we will develop a brute-force technique that blindly generates paths radiating from the start node until the goal node is encountered. Though suitable for some type of problems, the method of the first section has a time efficiency that is exponential and hence is often not practical. In Section 10.2 we will study ways of refining the technique from Section 10.1 in the hope of making such search algorithms polynomial instead of exponential in their run time. Finally, in Section 10.3, we will look at the application of such techniques in the area of strategic game playing—one of the first endeavors in which computers were able to demonstrate "intelligent" behavior.

10.1 RECURSIVE BRUTE-FORCE SEARCHES OF CONCEPTUAL GRAPHS AND NETWORKS

As an example of a problem that can be attacked by the so-called brute-force strategy, we will consider a question that has long intrigued chess fanatics. The *eight queens problem* requires determining the various ways in which eight queens could be configured on a chessboard so that none of them could access any other queen. (The rules of chess allow a queen to move an arbitrary number of squares in a horizontal, vertical, or diagonal fashion.) Figure 10.2 illustrates one such configuration.

The logic we propose to solve this problem involves trial-and-error backtracking of the sort you might use to find a path out of a maze. You must explore numerous paths before you find the appropriate one. Upon exploring a given path and determining that it can lead only to a dead end, you must retrace the points on the path in reverse order—backtrack—until you reach a point at which you can try an appropriate new path. This concept of trial-and-error backtracking is illustrated in Figure 10.3. Retracing points that have been visited previously in reverse order allows recursion to come into play.

Applying backtracking logic to the eight queens problem, we could attempt to find a "path" to a configuration by successively trying to place a

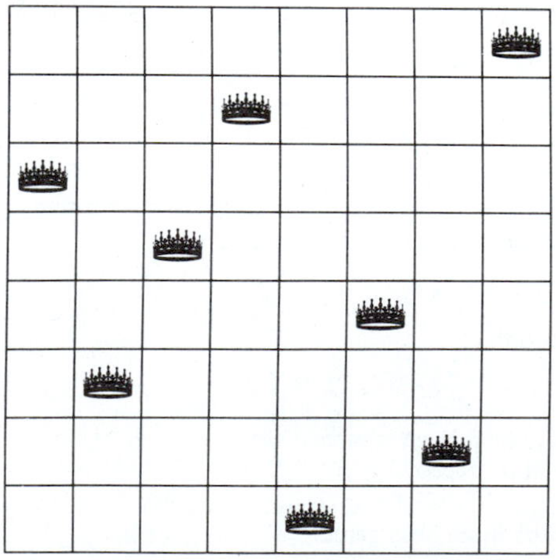

FIGURE 10.2
One successful eight queens configuration; no queen has access to any other.

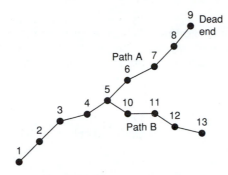

FIGURE 10.3 The backtracking problem as illustrated by maze solution. Upon reaching a dead end for path A, you must retrace steps 9 through 5 before you can try path B.

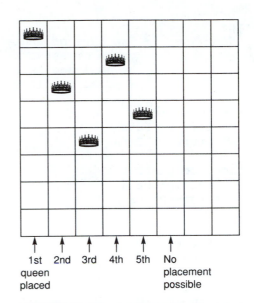

FIGURE 10.4 Dead end in queen placement. Given the previous 5 placements, a queen cannot be placed in the sixth column. You must backtrack and attempt to reposition the queen in column 5. If that fails, you must backtrack to column 4, and so on.

queen in each column of a chessboard until we reach a dead end: a column in which the placement of queens in prior columns makes it impossible to place the queen being moved. This situation is pictured in Figure 10.4. When we reach this dead end, we must backtrack one column (to column 5 in the case of Figure 10.4) and attempt to find a new placement for the queen in this column. If placement in the previous column is impossible, we must backtrack yet another column to attempt the new placement. This backtracking through previous columns continues until we finally are able to reposition a queen. At that point, we can begin a new path by again attempting to position queens on a column-by-column basis until another dead end is reached or until a successful configuration is developed.

Rather than develop an algorithm specifically to solve the eight queens problem, we will extend our perspective to generating an algorithm for solving a general class of problems that could all be viewed analogously to the maze situation previously described. We will then discuss how the general algorithm could be used in the specific context of the eight queens problem and allow you to explore similar questions in the exercises and problems. Our general algorithm will require the following *Path* abstract data type.

- **Definition of the Path ADT:** A Path is a sequence of adjacent nodes (states) in a conceptual graph or network. In a nonempty path, the first node in the sequence is called the *Start node* and the last node is called the *Final node*. The operations we wish to perform on the ADT Path can be defined in terms of the following PSEUDO pre- and postconditions.

```
type
   NodeType: (* The type of individual nodes within a conceptual
               graph or network. Has a special value NULL that can
               be assigned to variables of type NodeType to signal a
               special condition *);

procedure Create
   ( given P: Path              (* An arbitrary path *);
     return P: Path             (* P initialized to the empty path *) );

procedure Destroy
   ( given P: Path              (* An arbitrary path *);
     return P: Path             (* All storage dynamically allocated to P
                                   is returned to available space.  P
                                   itself is in an unreliable state *) );

function FirstNode
   ( given P: Path              (* A nonempty path *);
     return: NodeType           (* The first node in path P) );

function FinalNode
   ( given P: Path              (* A nonempty path *);
     return: NodeType           (* The final node in path P) );

procedure GetSuccessor
   ( given P: Path              (* An arbitrary path *);
           Succ: NodeType       (* Either NULL or a node that is adjacent
                                   to the final node on the path P *);

     return Succ: NodeType      (* If Succ is NULL upon entry to
                                   GetSuccessors, then Succ is returned as
                                   the first node adjacent to the final
                                   node on path P. Otherwise Succ is
                                   returned as the next node adjacent to
                                   the final node on the path P. Here
                                   "first" and "next" imply that we have a
                                   method for generating in sequence nodes
                                   adjacent to the final node in P *);
           MoreSuccessors: boolean  (* true if we could generate an adjacent
                                   node; false otherwise *) );
procedure ExtendPath
  ( given P: Path               (* An arbitrary path *);
          N: NodeType           (* A node adjacent to the final node
                                   on P *);

     return Q: Path             (* A path formed by extending P to include
                                   N as its final node *) );
procedure ContractPath
  ( given P: Path               (* A nonempty path *);
     return P: Path             (* P with its final node removed *) );

function PathLength
  ( given P: Path               (* An arbitrary path *);
     return: integer            (* The length of the path P. If P is a
                                   path in a conceptual graph, then the
                                   length of P is the number of nodes in
                                   the path minus 1, that is, the number
                                   of edges *) );
```

```
function GoalReached
  ( given P: Path                  (* An arbitrary path *);
    return: boolean                (* true if the path P represents a path to
                                      a goal state in the conceptual graph or
                                      network being explored; false
                                      otherwise *) );
```

Example 10.1   Let us consider how some of these operations might be implemented and used in the conceptual search graph underlying the eight queens problem. In this problem, a node in the graph being explored for a solution might be represented as an ordered pair (Row, Col), where Row and Col are chessboard coordinates for the placement of a queen. A path P is a sequence of these ordered pairs, such as

$$P = (\ (3,1)\ (6,2)\ (4,3)\ (2,4)\ )$$

This path P is the partial path of the first four nodes in the successful configuration of Figure 10.2. The FirstNode and FinalNode operations on P would return (3, 1) and (2, 4) respectively. The PathLength operation would return 3, and the GoalReached operation would return **false**, since these four placements do not constitute a complete eight queens configuration. An invocation of ExtendPath(P, (8, 5), Q) would return Q as the path

$$Q = (\ (3,1)\ (6,2)\ (4,3)\ (2,4)\ (8,5)\ )$$

ContractPath (P) would reduce P to the path

$$P = (\ (3,1)\ (6,2)\ (4,3)\ )$$

Finally, the GetSuccessor operation is dependent on the fashion in which we generate the nodes adjacent to the final node of the path currently under exploration. For instance, if we were extending the path

$$P = (\ (3,1)\ (6,2)\ (4,3)\ (2,4)\ )$$

into the fifth column, then there are two valid nodes adjacent to the final node on this path—(5, 5) and (5, 8). *Valid* here means that an extension of the path by such a node must preserve the property that no queen can access any other queen. Two successive invocations of the GetSuccessor operation would return these two adjacent nodes. There is no specific requirement with respect to the order in which the adjacent nodes would be returned. For instance, (5, 5) could be returned from the first invocation (when the parameter Successor is passed in as NULL), and (5, 8) could be returned from the second invocation (when Successor is passed in as (5, 5)). The implementor of the GetSuccessor operation is free to determine the order of generation of adjacent nodes; the only requirement is that successive invocations of Get-Successor must eventually return all possible adjacent nodes. For instance, the following PSEUDO code represents one possible implementation of Get-Successor for the eight queens problem.

```
procedure GetSuccessor
  ( given P: Path                  (* An arbitrary path *);
         Succ: NodeType            (* Either NULL or a node that is
                                      adjacent to the final node on the
                                      path P *);

    return Succ: NodeType          (* If Succ is NULL upon entry to
                                      GetSuccessor, then Succ is returned
                                      as the first node adjacent to the
                                      final node on path P. Otherwise
                                      Succ is returned as the next node
                                      adjacent to the final node on the
                                      path P. Here "first" and "next"
                                      imply that we have a method for
                                      generating in sequence nodes
                                      adjacent to the final node in P *);
           MoreSuccessors: boolean (* true if we could generate an adjacent
                                      node; false otherwise *) );
```

```
(* This implementation of GetSuccessor assumes the existence of a
   function Conflict, which takes the path P and a candidate for a node
   adjacent to the final node on P.  Conflict returns false if the
   candidate for the adjacent node does not cause a conflict with any
   other queen placement that already exists on path P. If the candidate
   for the adjacent node causes a conflict, true is returned. *)
```

```
start GetSuccessor
  if Succ = NULL then   (* Start at first row *)
    Succ.Row := 1
  else                  (* Continue with next row *)
    Succ.Row := Succ.Row + 1
  endif;
  Succ.Col := FinalNode(P).Col + 1;  (* Probe into the next column *)
  while Conflict(P, Succ) and Succ.Row <= 8 do
    Succ.Row := Succ.Row + 1
  endwhile;
  MoreSuccessors := not (Succ.Row = 9)
end GetSuccessor;
```

1st   2nd   3rd   4th   GetSuccessor
queen   iterates from 1st
placed   row through 8th,
                            seeking valid
                            placement.

Using the Path ADT, we are now ready to describe a generalized search algorithm that could be used to probe a conceptual graph or network seeking a path to a particular goal node. The algorithm relies on two procedures—FindPath and FindPathAux. FindPath is a front-end procedure that prepares a one-node path containing the Start node for FindPathAux—the workhorse portion of the algorithm. FindPathAux takes the path it is given and then uses the GetSuccessor operation to iterate through nodes adjacent to the final node on the given path. For each adjacent node, it adds the node to the given path (via the ExtendPath operation) and then recursively calls itself with this new path, hoping to extend it even further—perhaps all the way to a goal state; the strategy used by FindPathAux is to extend recursively one path as far as it will go—to a goal state or a dead-end state. In this respect, the algorithm resembles the depth-first traversal we introduced in the last chapter. If the goal state is reached, we are done and the resulting path can be returned. If a dead-end is reached, the path that was extended and probed deeper must be contracted and the next adjacent node added to it, so that we may probe this alternative path. A formal statement of this recursive probing appears in the following two procedures.

```
procedure FindPath
  ( given Start: NodeType    (* The node from which exploration toward goal
                                is to start *);
    return P: Path           (* A path from Start to a goal determined
                                by the GoalReached function. If no such
                                path exists, P is unreliable *);
           Found: boolean    (* true if path from Start to goal has been
                                found; false if no path is found *) );
  start FindPath
    Found := false;
    Create(P);
    ExtendPath(P, Start, P);
    FindPathAux(P, Found)
  end FindPath;

procedure FindPathAux
  ( given P: Path            (* A partial path to goal as determined by
                                GoalReached function *);
           Found: boolean    (* Initially false since FindPathAux called only
                                when a path has not yet been reached *);
    return P: Path           (* An extension of path P to a goal state as
                                determined by GoalReached function. If such
                                a goal cannot be reached by extending P,
                                then P is returned unchanged *);
           Found: boolean    (* true if path P can be extended to reach goal;
                                false otherwise *) );

  var
    MoreSuccessors: boolean;
    Succ: NodeType;

  start FindPathAux
    Succ := NULL;
    GetSuccessor(P, Succ, MoreSuccessors);
```

```
while not Found and MoreSuccessors do
  ExtendPath(P, Succ, P);
  if GoalReached(P) then
    Found := true
  else
    FindPathAux(P, Found);
    if not Found then
      ContractPath(P);
      GetSuccessor(P, Succ, MoreSuccessors)
    endif
  endif
endwhile
end FindPathAux;
```

Example 10.2   Partially trace the FindPath and FindPathAux procedures for the eight queens problem, assuming that the Start node is (1, 1). Assume also that the Get-Successor operation generates adjacent nodes by placing queens in the next column. Within the next column, adjacent nodes are generated from first row to last (eighth) row, as the implementation in Example 10.1 suggested. GetSuccessor only returns a node if it is not in conflict with queen placements in prior columns.

A convenient way to trace such an algorithm is to use a graphic called a *search tree*. A partial search tree for this example appears in Figure 10.5. A given node within the search tree contains two items of information—the node added to the path currently being probed and a counter indicating the order in which nodes are received from GetSuccessor for deeper exploration. The various paths are arranged from left to right descending from the start node, corresponding to the order in which they are explored. This implies that the order in which nodes are returned from GetSuccessor corresponds to a preorder traversal of the search tree. A path reaching the goal occurs when we reach a node at level 7 of the search tree, that is, a branch with eight nodes and seven edges. Note that such search trees are conceptual trees only—just as the graph being explored in this type of problem is an intangible graph that never exists as a complete data structure in memory. They are analogous to the tree of recursive calls that we used to analyze the efficiency of recursive algorithms in Chapter 6. You should attempt to fill the partial tree in Figure 10.5. However, be forewarned that actual completion of the search tree—tracing all paths explored before the goal state is reached—may take a while!

Efficiency Analysis of the FindPath Algorithm

In the preceding example, we remarked that the search tree corresponds to the tree of recursive calls that are made to the FindPathAux algorithm. For the eight queens problem, each call to the FindPathAux procedure potentially results in eight new probes generated by placing the queen in each row of the next column. Although many of these probes are never returned from Get-Successor as valid probes because they generate a conflict with queens placed in prior columns, a brute-force approach to implementing the GetSuccessor

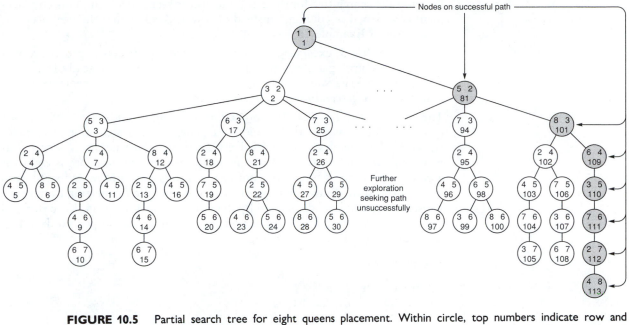

FIGURE 10.5 Partial search tree for eight queens placement. Within circle, top numbers indicate row and column of queen placement and bottom number indicates order in which nodes (board positions) are explored.

operation must still consider a queen placement in each of the eight rows before deciding that placement in certain rows is not valid. Hence, an upper bound on the number of operations performed by the FindPath algorithm for the eight queens problem is 8^7—eight possible row placements to consider for each of the seven columns in which we must place a queen through a recursive extension of the current path. In general, the brute-force strategy we have described here will be bounded by an $O(N^M)$ efficiency, where N is an upper bound on the number of possible extensions that GetSuccessor will consider for each attempt to extend a path one node deeper, and M is the maximal depth to which we must probe before reaching a goal node or concluding a goal cannot be reached. Clearly, this brute-force approach generates algorithms whose time efficiencies are exponential; and thus it can only be used to solve problems of relatively small magnitude.

Exercises 10.1

1. Complete the implementation of the Path ADT for the eight queens problem begun in Example 10.1. Provide specific PSEUDO declarations for NodeType and Path. Then write procedures/functions for each of the operations, including the Conflict function, which was invoked by GetSuccessor in Example 10.1. Analyze the time efficiency of your Conflict function.

2. Complete the partial search tree for the eight queens problem in Figure 10.5. Assume that the GetSuccessor procedure of Example 10.1 is used. That is, assume a GetSuccessor implementation that generates viable placements in ascending row number order.

3. Develop the search tree for the eight queens problem if the initial queen placement is in row 4 of column 1 instead of row 1. Assume that the GetSuccessor procedure of Example 10.1 is used.

4. Repeat Exercise 3, except now assume that the GetSuccessor procedure will begin by attempting a queen placement in the eighth row (instead of the first) and then work its way up to the first row. That is, it will generate viable placements in *descending* row number order.

5. The logic of the FindPathAux procedure in concert with the GetSuccessor procedure of Example 10.1 achieves a generalized nested looping control structure that enables us to control the depth to which iteration is nested at program *runtime*. In the eight queens problem this nesting depth is eight for a conventional chess board, but notice that loops were not nested eight deep in our procedure. Rather, our procedure could handle the nesting of iterative constructs to the level demanded by the GoalReached function. Keep in mind this generalized nested looping as you try to predict the output produced by the following PSEUDO procedure.

```
program Easy;

  procedure Tough
    ( given B, C, D: integer;
      return        (* nothing *) );

    var K: integer;

    start Tough
      if B <= C then
        write(D);
        for K := B to C do
          Tough(B + 1, C, K)
        endfor
      endif
    end Tough;

  start Easy
    Tough(1, 4, 12)
  end Easy;
```

6. A maze could be viewed as an ADT, which is a matrix of records of the form

```
record
  NorthBlocked,
  EastBlocked,
  SouthBlocked,
  WestBlocked: boolean
endrecord;
```

At each square in the array, the boolean fields are set to indicate whether or not we can proceed in the suggested direction. Implement the Path ADT for the problem of finding an exit from a maze of the above form. Analyze the efficiency of the FindPath procedure for the implementation you develop.

7. (Knight's Tour Problem) Another classic chess problem that can be solved by trial-and-error backtracking is known as the Knight's Tour. Given a chessboard with a knight initially placed at coordinates x_0, y_0, specify a series of moves for the knight that will result in each board location being visited

exactly once. From a given square on the chessboard, a knight may move to any one of the eight numbered squares in the following diagram:

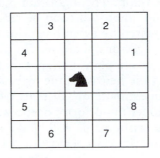

Implement the Path ADT for the Knight's Tour problem. Analyze the efficiency of the FindPath procedure for your implementation.

8. How would the FindPath and FindPathAux procedures have to be modified to find all possible paths from the start node to the goal instead of just one path?

10.2 GUIDING THE SEARCH OF CONCEPTUAL GRAPHS AND NETWORKS

The recursive brute-force search method of the last section is severely limited by its exponential efficiency. It can only be applied to problems whose search space is sufficiently small. In this section, we will examine methods of "guiding" graph and network searches in the hope of bringing their efficiency into the realm of polynomial time. Our method for doing this will involve following the path that is most likely to lead to a goal. To determine this "most likely" criterion, we will need a function that can be applied to a path and quickly return an estimate of the distance remaining from that path's final node to the goal node. Such a function, often called a *heuristic,* should guide us to a solution as quickly as possible. Heuristics are similar to the rules of thumb that humans use to help themselves solve problems. For instance, when playing chess, a human does not mentally play through all possible scenarios, looking for a final state in which she wins. Instead, she will look at the current state of the board, mentally generate the relevant successor states, and evaluate them quickly using a heuristic to decide where to move next. Unfortunately, heuristics are not guaranteed to succeed. Following a bad rule of thumb can lead to your quickly being defeated in a game of chess and pursuing paths that lead to dead ends in other types of search endeavors. The same is true of computerizable heuristics. Often they cannot provide a mathematical guarantee of reducing a search's efficiency from exponential to polynomial time. However, in practice, a good heuristic can usually produce this result. The determination of a good heuristic is usually a matter of time-consuming experimentation with a variety of methods.

Best-First Search Algorithm

A priority queue provides the key to the heuristic search algorithm we will develop. The algorithm is known as the best-first search algorithm, for reasons that will soon be clear. We will use this priority queue to store paths created by extending prior paths with adjacent nodes returned from the Get-Successor operation. The arrangement of paths within the priority queue will give the path that appears to be closest to reaching the goal state (according to the heuristic) the highest priority. That is, given that the heuristic returns an estimate of "distance" from the current final node on a path to the goal node, the priority queue will be arranged so that the item with the smallest heuristic value will be the first to be removed. Using this priority queue, the algorithm to perform a search guided by the heuristic function can be stated in the following skeletal terms:

Initialize a path to contain solely the start node;
Add this path to the priority queue of paths;
`while` *the goal has not been found* `and` *the priority queue is* `not` *empty* `do`
  Remove the first path on the priority queue as the current path;
  `while` *the goal is* `not` *found* `and` *there are nodes adjacent to current path* `do`
    Get such a node using the GetSuccessor operation;
    `if` *the node obtained is the goal* `then`
      A complete path to the goal has been found
    `else`
      Form a new path by extending the current path with the node obtained;
      Add this new path to the priority queue
    `endif`
  `endwhile`
`endwhile`

Before proceeding to detailed PSEUDO code for this algorithm, one potential problem must be recognized. Remember that underneath this algorithm a conceptual graph is being searched. That conceptual graph may have cycles in it. If so, it would be possible to return to a node whose successors had already been generated via the GetSuccessor operation. In turn, that would lead to an infinite looping situation, where we just continue to generate paths reaching the same node over and over again. Each path would be longer than the previous one because it would contain one or more repetitions of a cycle embedded in it. However, relative to our heuristic, which estimates the distance from the path's final node to the goal, the path may continually appear to be a wise choice.

Example 10.3 To illustrate the complication described above, consider the network pictured in Figure 10.6. Suppose that we are starting at node B in this network and wish to find a path to node C. Suppose also that we use the following heuristic to estimate the distance from the final node on a path to the goal node:

$$\text{Heuristic(P)} = \begin{cases} \text{Absolute value of the difference between the ordinal values} \\ \text{of the letters that label the goal node and the final node} \\ \text{on the path} \end{cases}$$

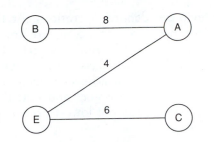

FIGURE 10.6

Network to illustrate possibility of infinite looping in Example 10.3.

For instance, the heuristic value of the path B → A with goal node C is 2, since the ordinal distance between A and C is 2. Granted, this may not be a good heuristic, but not all heuristics will be good in practice. We use it here merely to illustrate the dilemma that can occur with the algorithm as stated. If we now trace execution of the preceding algorithm to find a path from B to C, we have the following infinite iteration.

Initially, the priority queue appears as the single path

$$(B)$$

We then generate successors of B, which in this case leads only to the path B → A. Hence, the priority queue becomes

$$(B \rightarrow A)$$

This path is then removed from the priority queue, and the GetSuccessor operation returns two nodes adjacent to A, namely, B and E. Thus, there are two paths to add to the priority queue: B → A → B and B → A → E. The heuristic arranges the priority queue as

$$(B \rightarrow A \rightarrow B, B \rightarrow A \rightarrow E)$$

The path B → A → B is removed from the queue, and the infinite looping situation emerges.

The process of generating the successors of the last node on a path is called *expanding* that node. The cure for the predicament illustrated by Example 10.3 is to keep a set of nodes that have been expanded at any given time in the algorithm's execution. This set is called the set of *closed nodes;* the set of nodes that occur as final nodes on paths in the priority queue are the *open nodes*. The open nodes are primed to be expanded when they are removed from the priority queue. If GetSuccessor returns a node on the closed list, we discard it instead of extending the current path by it, because further exploration from a closed node can seldom reveal any substantive new path to a goal. (To see whether further exploration from a closed node could ever find a useful path, consider Exercises 10 and 11 at the end of this section.)

Using our previously defined operations for the Path, PriorityQueue, and Set ADTs, we can now provide a complete implementation of the Find-Path procedure for a heuristically guided search. The procedure receives a heuristic function, which is then passed to the priority queue PriorityEn-queue operation. We assume that a lower-valued heuristic is "better," since it suggests that we are closer to a goal and that the priority queue is thus implemented to dequeue the item of lowest priority.

```
type
  Universe: NodeType;                (* To enable a set of closed nodes *)
  PriorityQueueData: Path;           (* To enable a priority queue of paths to
                                        expand *)

  Heuristic: function               (* Signature of a heuristic function *)
          ( given P: Path           (* A path whose distance from Goal is
                                        to be estimated *);

              return: real          (* The heuristic value of P *) );

procedure FindPath                  (* Best-first algorithm *)
  ( given Start: NodeType           (* The node from which exploration toward
                                        goal is to start *);

          Goal: NodeType            (* The goal node to which we seek a
                                        path *);

          H: Heuristic             (* The heuristic function *);
    return P: Path                  (* A path from Start to Goal if such a
                                        path exists. If no such path exists, P
                                        is unreliable *);

          Found: boolean            (* true if path from Start to Goal is
                                        found; false otherwise *) );

  var
    Closed: Set;
    Open: PriorityQueue;
    Current, NewPathToExplore: Path;
    Succ: NodeType;
    MoreSuccessors: boolean;

  start FindPath
    Found := false;
    Create(Current);
    ExtendPath(Current, Start, Current);  (* Current path has start node *)
    Create(NewPathToExplore);
    Create(Open);                         (* Create priority queue *)
    PriorityEnqueue(Open, Current, H);    (* Put current path on it *)
    Create(Closed);                       (* Initially, set of closed nodes
                                             is empty *)

    while not Found and not Empty(Open) do
      PriorityDequeue(Open, H, Current);  (* Prepare to expand new current
                                             path *)
      if not IsElementOf(Closed, FinalNode(Current)) then
                                          (* Expand only nodes that are not
                                             already closed *)

        if FinalNode(Current) = Goal then  (* Check if goal reached *)
          Found := true;
          P := Current
```

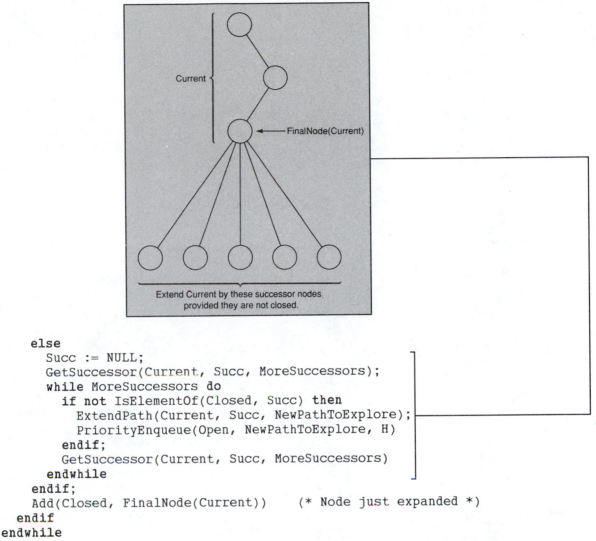

```
        else
            Succ := NULL;
            GetSuccessor(Current, Succ, MoreSuccessors);
            while MoreSuccessors do
                if not IsElementOf(Closed, Succ) then
                    ExtendPath(Current, Succ, NewPathToExplore);
                    PriorityEnqueue(Open, NewPathToExplore, H)
                endif;
                GetSuccessor(Current, Succ, MoreSuccessors)
            endwhile
        endif;
        Add(Closed, FinalNode(Current))    (* Node just expanded *)
    endif
  endwhile
end FindPath;
```

To illustrate the execution of the best-first search algorithm, consider the network in Figure 10.7. The following examples discuss the search trees that result from employing a best-first search strategy on this network for various choices of start and goal nodes and heuristic functions.

Example 10.4   Suppose that we use the heuristic function of Example 10.3 (absolute value of the difference between the ordinal numbers of the letters labeling the goal node and the final node on the path) to search for a path from Q to N in Figure 10.7. Then Figure 10.8 illustrates the search tree that results from the best-first search algorithm. Compare this to the search tree in Figure 10.9. This latter tree results from an unguided recursive search in which successors of a node were generated in alphabetical order of node labels. Note that in the search tree of Figure 10.9, 15 nodes must be removed from the queue

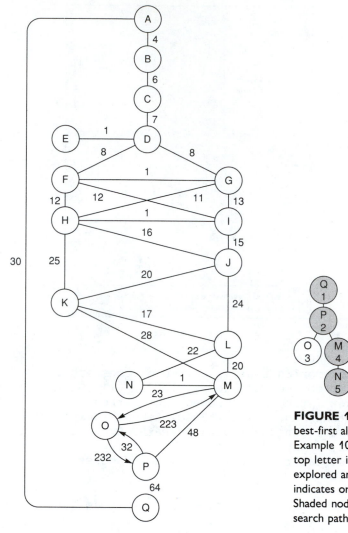

FIGURE 10.7
Network to explore by best-first search.

FIGURE 10.8 Search tree for best-first algorithm in Example 10.4. Within circle, top letter indicates node being explored and bottom number indicates order of exploration. Shaded nodes comprise the search path found by the algorithm.

of open nodes before the goal node is reached. The search tree of Figure 10.8 indicates that only five nodes must be dequeued before reaching the goal when guided by the heuristic. This is an indication of how the best-first search can speed the execution of the search.

Example 10.5   Suppose that we wish to find a path from node B to node P in the network of Figure 10.7. In this example, we will experiment with different heuristic functions to guide us to the goal. The first heuristic, which we will designate as H_1, is the same heuristic used in Example 10.4. The second heuristic, H_2, we define as

$$H_2(P) = H_1(P) + \text{PathLength}(P)$$

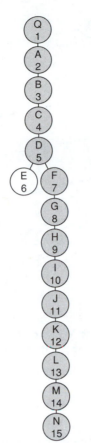

FIGURE 10.9

Search tree for recursive brute-force search in Example 10.4. Within circle, top indicates node being explored and bottom number indicates order of exploration. Shaded nodes comprise the search path found by the algorithm.

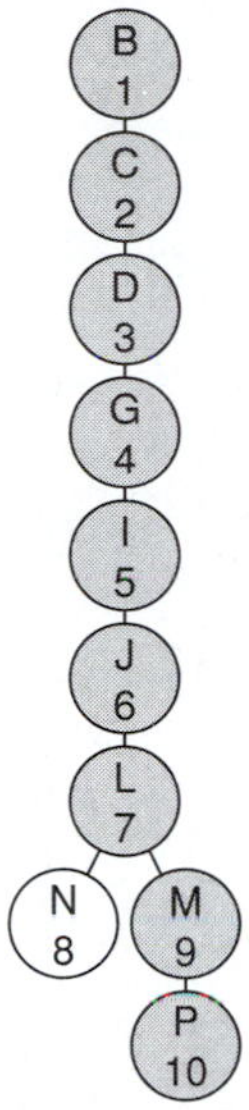

FIGURE 10.10

Search tree for Example 10.5 using H_1 heuristic. Within circle, top letter indicates node being explored and bottom number indicates order of exploration. Shaded nodes comprise the search path found by the algorithm.

That is, the second heuristic is taken to be the sum of the first heuristic and the length of the path already traversed. The reason for doing this is to give equal weight to the two criteria of finding a path quickly and finding the shortest path. The PathLength portion of the sum gives weight to the shortness of path criterion, and the H_1 portion contributes to finding a path quickly. The search trees for H_1 and H_2 are presented in Figures 10.10 and 10.11, respectively. These figures demonstrate the cost paid in execution time for attempting to find the shortest path instead of merely any path. In Figure 10.10, only 10 nodes must be removed from the open queue before a path is found. In Figure 10.11, the weight given to shortness of path leads to 69 nodes being dequeued before a path is found. In the exercises at the end of this section and the programming problems and projects at the end of the chapter, you will explore how a relatively small adjustment on the best-first algorithm presented here can lead to an alternate version of Dijkstra's shortest path algorithm.

Analysis of Best-First Search Algorithm

These two examples illustrate the great degree of control the heuristic exercises over the best-first search algorithm. In the worst case, when the heuristic

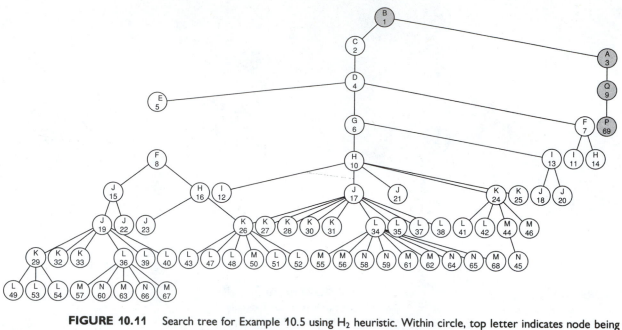

FIGURE 10.11　Search tree for Example 10.5 using H_2 heuristic. Within circle, top letter indicates node being explored and bottom number indicates order of exploration. Shaded nodes comprise the search path found by the algorithm.

is bad and guides the search astray, the efficiency of the search algorithm is no better than the exponential efficiency of the recursive brute-force search technique developed in Section 10.1. However, a good heuristic can dramatically improve the efficiency of the search algorithm. Usually, in complex search spaces such as those arising in artificial intelligence applications, much experimentation must be done before an effective heuristic is found.

Exercises 10.2

1. Suppose that we replace the priority queue in the best-first search algorithm with a stack. Describe the search strategy that results.

2. Suppose that we replace the priority queue in the best-first search algorithm with an ordinary queue. Describe the search strategy that results.

3. In implementing the priority queue for the best-first search algorithm, a path's heuristic value could be stored in the priority queue along with the path itself, or this heuristic value could be computed whenever it is needed. Discuss the trade-offs between these two alternatives.

4. In this section we defined an open node as one that is the final node of a path on the priority queue during execution of the best-first algorithm. Is it possible for a node to be an open node on more than one path in the priority queue, or does the set of closed nodes rule out this possibility? Explain.

5. By developing a search tree similar to that in Figure 10.8 (see Example 10.4), trace the execution of the best-first search algorithm as it attempts to find a path from node Q to node M in the network from Figure 10.7. Assume that we use the heuristic given in Example 10.3. How does the execution of the best-first search algorithm for this set of parameters compare to the brute-force recursive method of Section 10.1, assuming that successor nodes are generated in alphabetical order?

6. Discuss how the ADT Path could be implemented to allow the priority queue in the best-first search algorithm to store only open nodes instead of the complete paths ending at the open nodes. Incorporate the ideas from your discussion into a version of the best-first search that is more space efficient than the one given in the text.

7. Is the heuristic function given in Example 10.3 always effective for the network of Figure 10.7? If not, construct an example where the best-first search guided by this heuristic would actually explore more nodes than the brute-force recursive algorithm of Section 10.1.

8. In Example 10.5 suppose we adjust the heuristic function H_2 to be

$$H_2(P) = W * H_1(P) + PathLength(P)$$

where W is a constant "weight" factor intended to weight the H_1 heuristic more than the path length in the hope of finding a path more quickly. By developing search trees for several values of W, trace the execution of the best-first algorithm in seeking a path from node B to node P. Can you find a value for W that results in fewer open nodes than we found in Example 10.5? Does this choice of W still find the shortest path, or have you weighted execution speed in finding a path too heavily?

9. Suppose that we use the best-first search algorithm with a heuristic function that is the length of a path; that is, we use the length of the path already constructed instead of an estimate of distance to the goal as a guide for ordering the priority queue. By weighting path length so heavily, does the best-first search algorithm now guarantee that we will find the shortest path from start node to goal node? If not, find an example in which the heuristic is taken to be path length and in which the shortest path still is not found by the algorithm.

10. Modify the best-first search algorithm so that by choosing the heuristic function to be path length instead of an estimate of distance to the goal, it will now find the shortest path from the start node to the goal node. (Hint: Consider your answer to Exercise 9 before you start the modifications for this exercise.) What is the time efficiency of your new algorithm? How does this compare to the implementation of Dijkstra's shortest path algorithm developed in Section 9.4? Under what circumstances would you use this new implementation of the shortest path algorithm instead of that developed in Section 9.4? Why?

11. In the discussion following Example 10.3, we said that exploration from a closed node can seldom reveal any substantive new paths to a goal. Under what circumstances might you want to reopen a closed node for further exploration? Why? In what sense would you be revealing a substantive new path to the goal that was not apparent when the node was originally closed?

10.3 SEARCH TREES IN GAMES OF STRATEGY—
THE MINIMAX ALGORITHM

Grundy's game matches two opponents who are presented initially with one stack of seven pennies on a table in front of them. On a given move, a player must divide one of the stacks of pennies currently on the table into two *unequal* stacks. The player who is unable to find a stack that can be divided into two unequal stacks loses the game. Figure 10.12 illustrates a complete search tree for Grundy's game. (Search trees specific to games are often called

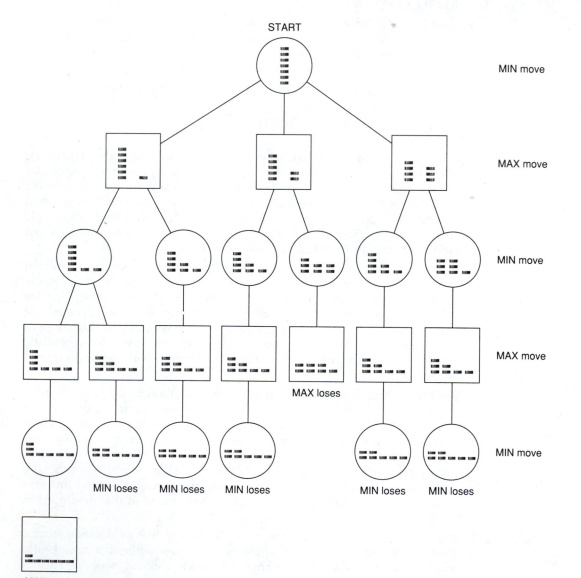

FIGURE 10.12 A complete search tree for Grundy's game, beginning with seven pennies.

game trees.) The alternating moves of the opposing players, identified by the names MAX and MIN, are indicated by square and circular tree nodes, respectively. Square nodes represent game states at which MAX is choosing a move, and circular nodes represent MIN's moves. The reason for this particular choice of names will soon become apparent. Because MIN moves first in Figure 10.12, even levels of the tree have circular nodes, while odd levels have only square nodes.

From the game tree in Figure 10.12, note that it is always possible for MAX to win if she moves second—no matter what initial move MIN may devise. This is apparent because we have a representation of the entire game in a compact tree that can be completely traversed to scan all possible outcomes. More challenging games of strategy do not allow a representation and traversal of a complete game tree. Space limitations usually rule out the former, and time limitations make the latter practically impossible.

When playing games of strategy, humans rarely search an entire game tree. Rather, we have heuristic rules, similar to those introduced in the last section, that guide us intuitively toward making smart moves from a given game state. Of course, sometimes the moves aren't smart enough, and we lose. But that shouldn't surprise us—it's the nature of heuristics to be imperfect. One of the differences, however, between searching a game tree and using the best-first strategy developed in the last section is that with game trees we can only dictate the path at alternating levels. In the search trees of the last section, we were in control of the search at each level of the tree—at each node we could choose the successor node that appeared to be best according to the heuristic. With game trees, we only have this luxury at alternating levels. If we put ourselves in the perspective of the MAX player, we can only choose the moves dictated by our heuristic at game states where it is MAX's move. At levels of the tree where it is MIN's move, we must presume that MIN will choose the move that is actually the worst from MAX's perspective. In other words, our game-playing strategy should take into account the supposition that MIN will always try to force MAX into the worst possible situation at a given point in the game.

The game-playing algorithm emerging from these considerations is called the *minimax algorithm*. The minimax algorithm assumes the following:

1. We are playing the game from MAX's perspective; that is, we are attempting to develop a winning strategy for MAX.

2. We have a heuristic function (often called a *static evaluator* in game-playing contexts) that is given a game state and returns a number corresponding to that game state. The larger the number returned, the better the state is from MAX's perspective.

3. Time and space constraints will not allow a search of the entire game tree descending from a particular state. We will instead search only to a specified depth from a particular game state. In the vernacular of game-playing programs, the levels that we search are often called *plies*. Thus, a four-ply search would search the game tree four levels beyond the current game state. Upon reaching the *ply limit*, four in this case, search would be cut off and the static evaluator called upon to obtain an approximate characterization of the state. The

deeper the ply to which we can carry out a game-playing search, the better our game playing strategy should be. Why? Because a deeper ply allows us to get closer to searching the entire game tree below our current state. As the game nears its end, this means that we may actually reach winning or losing states in our search efforts. In the early stages of the game, a deeper ply will hopefully result in a more accurate heuristic value. Hence, our goal will always be to search to the deepest possible ply in the time allowed.

To illustrate the concepts behind the minimax algorithm, consider the game of Fifteen. In this game, opposing players alternatively choose digits between 1 and 9 with the goal of selecting a combination of digits that adds up to 15. Once a digit is chosen, it may not be chosen again by either player. Hence, to win Fifteen you must choose digits that include one of the following eight combinations:

1 5 9
1 6 8
2 4 9
2 5 8
2 6 7
3 4 8
3 5 7
4 5 6

This game could be represented by two sets of digits—those currently chosen by MAX and MIN, respectively. We suggest the following heuristic to guide MAX's moves. Remember, the larger the heuristic's value, the better the game state supposedly will be for MAX.

$$H(S) = \begin{cases} +\infty & \text{if game state S is a win for MAX} \\ -\infty & \text{if game state S is a loss for MAX} \\ & \text{otherwise, using S, compute the following} \\ & \text{difference : (the number of winning combinations} \\ & \text{that remain open for MAX)} - \text{(the number of} \\ & \text{winning combinations that remain open for MIN)} \end{cases}$$

For example, if game state S were ({5} , {2}), where the first and second sets represent the chosen digits of MAX and MIN respectively, then H(S) would be 1, since five winning combinations are still possibilities for MAX and four are possible for MIN.

The essence of the minimax algorithm is to explore the game tree descending from the present state to leaf levels if the ply limit will allow. If the ply limit is reached before a leaf level is encountered, then we explore to the ply limit and apply the heuristic to approximate the worth of a state. As we descend through levels of the tree, we must distinguish from those levels at which MAX is choosing a move and those levels at which MIN is making a move. At a game state where MAX is making a move, we should choose the successor state of maximum value because the heuristic is designed to produce larger values for states that are better from MAX's perspective. Because we assume that MIN will try to force MAX into the least advantageous states, a game state from which MIN is making a choice should be guided by the perspective that MIN will choose the minimum move among all possible successor states. To summarize, the minimax value of a game state S, dependent on the ply limit to which we will search, may be defined by the following rule:

$$
\text{MINIMAX(S, PlyLimit)} = \begin{cases}
\text{The maximum of MINIMAX applied, with PlyLimit reduced by one, to each successor state of S } \textit{if S is a maximizing node, that is, a node at which MAX is selecting a move} \\
\\
\text{The minimum of MINIMAX applied, with PlyLimit reduced by one, to each successor state of S } \textit{if S is a minimizing node, that is, a node at which MIN is selecting a move} \\
\\
\text{H(S) } \textit{if game state S occurs at a depth whose level has reached the ply limit, that is, if PlyLimit has been reduced to zero} \\
\\
\text{H(S) } \textit{if game state S is a leaf in the overall game tree, that is, S is a win, lose, or draw state for MAX}
\end{cases}
$$

Example 10.6   Compute MINIMAX(S, 2) in the game of Fifteen, where S is the state given by S = ({4, 5} , {6, 9}) and H is the heuristic defined above.

Figure 10.13 highlights the work involved in this computation. We must descend from the current state to each of the possible choices that could be made by MAX: 1, 2, 3, 7 or 8. For each of these choices we must descend to each of the four options that MIN has. At this level, we have reached the ply limit. Hence, the heuristic H would be invoked at this level. Because this level represents a move made by MIN, the minimum value according to the heuristic would be returned to the prior level. In Figure 10.13, the minimum values 0, 0, −1, 0, and 0 are returned to ply level 1 from ply level 2. At ply level 0, we select the maximum of these five returned minimums. Therefore, the MINIMAX value of S would evaluate to 0. This implies that, *according to this particular heuristic,* choices of 1, 2, 7, or 8 are all equally likely to optimize MAX's chances of winning. Remember, these choices are predicated upon the heuristic H that we use and the ply limit to which time allows us to search. Searching to a deeper ply limit or changing the heuristic may well change the MINIMAX value and hence the move that MAX selects.

Example 10.7   Consider the hypothetical partial game tree in Figure 10.14. Suppose that MAX is choosing a move from game state A. Use the minimax algorithm to determine MAX's best move. Assume that time considerations allow a ply limit of three and the numbers at the leaf levels of the tree in Figure 10.14 represent the values of the heuristic function at this level.

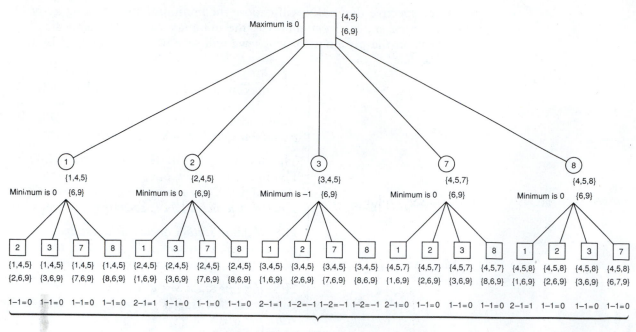

Evaluation of heuristic H occurs when ply limit 2 is reached.

FIGURE 10.13   Computation of MINIMAX value for game state ({4, 5}, {6, 9}) with ply limit 2. Values inside circles and squares indicate number that is selected.

Because MAX is choosing a move at the nodes labeled E through K, we would seek to find the maximal value of the successors of each of these nodes. Hence, the values 7, 8, 3, 0, 6, 8, and 9 would be recursively returned to nodes E, F, G, H, I, J, and K respectively. Since the nodes labeled B, C, and D are nodes at which MIN is selecting a move, their minimax values are the minimums of (7, 8, 3), (0, 6), and (8, 9), respectively. That is, the minimax value of B is 3; the minimax value of C is 0; and the minimax value of D is 8. At node A, MAX would now choose the maximum among 3, 0,

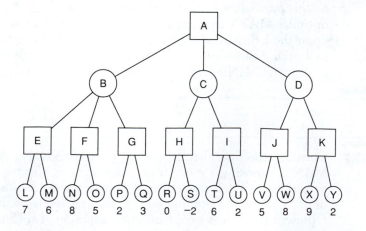

FIGURE 10.14
Partial game tree for
Example 10.7.

and 8. Hence, MAX would choose to move to D, whose minimax value is 8. Note this essentially implies that, if MAX moves to D, it can be guaranteed a position two levels deeper with a heuristic value of 8—even if MIN plays to its optimal strategy according to the heuristic being used.

The ADT Path may be conveniently used to represent the state of a game. This state may be regarded as the sequence of moves that has occurred in the game. Using a path to represent that sequence, the minimax algorithm may be implemented by the following PSEUDO code.

```
type
  Heuristic:  function  (* The signature of the heuristic (static
                           evaluator) function *)
            ( given T: Path  (* A possible game state *);
              return: real  (* The heuristic value of state T *) );

procedure Minimax
  ( given S: Path          (* A path representing the current state of
                               the game *);

         H: Heuristic      (* The heuristic function *)
         Max: boolean      (* true if MAX is choosing the next move to extend
                               state S; false if MIN is choosing the move *);

         Ply: integer      (* The level to which minimax searching is to
                               occur. If zero, merely return the heuristic
                               applied to the game state *);

   return Move: NodeType   (* The move selected by the minimax algorithm when
                               applied to state S *);

         Value: real       (* The minimax value associated with Move *) );

  var
    MoreSuccessors: boolean;
    Succ, X: NodeType;
    NewValue: real;

  start Minimax
    Succ := NULL;
    GetSuccessor(S, Succ, MoreSuccessors);
    if Ply = 0 or not MoreSuccessors then  (* Ply limit reached or leaf
                                               level *)
      Move := FinalNode(S);
      Value := H(S)
    else
      (* Find the value of the first successor state *)
      ExtendPath(S, Succ, S);
      Minimax(S, H, not Max, Ply - 1, X, Value);  (* X used to fill parameter
                                                      slot *)
      Move := Succ;
      ContractPath(S);
      (* Now compare to values of other successors *)
```

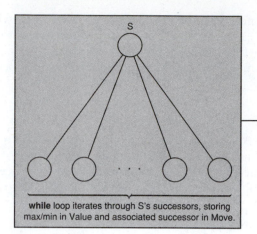

while loop iterates through S's successors, storing max/min in Value and associated successor in Move.

```
while MoreSuccessors do
   GetSuccessor(S, Succ, MoreSuccessors);
   ExtendPath(S, Succ, S);
   Minimax(S, H, not Max, Ply - 1, X, NewValue); (* X used to fill
                                                     parameter slot *)

   if Max then  (* MAX or MIN node? *)
     if NewValue > Value then
       Move := Succ;
       Value := NewValue
     endif
   else
     if NewValue < Value then
       Move := Succ
       Value := NewValue
     endif
   endif;
   ContractPath(S)
 endwhile
endif
end Minimax;
```

Analysis of the Minimax Technique

A higher-level program would call on Minimax and use the Move parameter that Minimax returns as a basis for selecting the next move in a game of strategy. Our analysis of Minimax is based upon its usage in this context. If we were to call on it expecting its recommendation for a move from a given state of the game, how long would we have to wait for a response? This is typical of the way game programs are used in computer chess tournaments, for instance. A limit is placed on the time the computer has to select each move in the game.

This time efficiency is dependent upon two factors—the ply limit to which we are willing to carry out our analysis and the average number of successor moves possible from a given state. If N represents this average number of moves, then the generalized iteration caused by the recursive calls in Minimax results in a time efficiency of N^{Ply} for one external call to the algorithm. The goal in using Minimax to play a game of strategy is to push the ply limit to the deepest possible value allowed by the time limits which are imposed. The deeper the ply limit, the better the chance of being able to search all the way to leaf nodes in the overall game tree or, at least, getting a more accurate estimate from the heuristic when it finally is invoked.

Refinements to the minimax algorithm allow certain subtrees to be skipped during the process of checking for the maximum or minimum of all states which succeed a given state. You will explore one of these techniques, called *alpha-beta pruning*, in the exercises for this section and in the problems at the end of the chapter.

Exercises 10.3

1. In the game of Nim, two players alternate in selecting one, two, or three pennies from a pile of five pennies. The person who forces his or her opponent to select the final penny is the winner. Construct a complete search tree for this game. Can one of the players be assured a win if he or she makes the appropriate moves? Which player? Construct a fail-safe heuristic to guide this player's moves.

2. Develop a heuristic for a more general game of Nim (see Exercise 1), in which the pile initially contains N pennies, the players are free to choose 1, 2, 3, . . . , or M pennies on a given move.

3. Compute MINIMAX(S, 2) in the game of Fifteen, where S is ({2, 8},{4, 6}). Use the heuristic employed in Example 10.6. Does the computed value of MINIMAX guarantee that MAX will choose 5 as its next move and consequently win the game?

4. Develop a heuristic for the game of tic-tac-toe. Then use your heuristic to compute the minimax value of the following game state to a ply level of 2.

Assume that MAX marks its moves with X and is to make the next move from this state. What move does your heuristic dictate for MAX?

5. Try the heuristic you developed for Exercise 4 to compute the minimax value of the following state to a ply level of 2.

Does your heuristic dictate that MIN moves to block MAX's win?

A RELEVANT ISSUE

Computer Chess

More than any other game of strategy, chess has attracted the attention of many computer scientists. Computer chess tournaments are quite commonplace, and, in 1968, British chess master David Levy issued a challenge that no computer chess program would be able to beat him in a best-of-seven match. Artificial intelligence experts Donald Michie, Seymour Papert, and John McCarthy raised the money to cover Levy's challenge, and in 1978 the match took place between Levy and Chess 4.7—a program developed by David Slate and Larry Atkin of Northwestern University. Although Chess 4.7 was trounced, winning only one game in the match, the publicity surrounding the event served to arouse a new crop of chess programs in the 1980s.

The early part of the 1980s was the era of the Cray Blitz program. Developed by Cray Research of Wisconsin and Minnesota, the Blitz program was powered by the fastest supercomputer of the decade and went four years without being defeated by another program. Unfortunately, it actually fared worse against David Levy than its Chess 4.7 predecessor. Levy walloped the Blitz program 4 to 0 in a $5000 rematch of his earlier human-computer confrontation.

The year 1985 marked the end of the Blitz's domination of the computer chess world; in the North American Computer Chess Championship, the Blitz was defeated by the Hitech program developed by Hans Berliner of Carnegie-Mellon University. The Hitech program was the first chess program to take real advantage of parallel processing. The program ran on a Sun minicomputer augmented by 64 microprocessors—one for each square of the chessboard. This configuration allowed Hitech to process 200,000 game states per second—a number doubling the state processing speed of the Cray Blitz but still paling when faced with the 10^{120} possible game states in chess.

Hitech in turn has been overtaken by a chess-playing machine known as Deep Thought. A combination of software and specialized hardware, Deep Thought was developed by Feng-hsiung Hsu, Thomas Anantharaman, Murray Campbell, and Andreas Nowatzyk while they were doctoral students at Carnegie-Mellon. Its main hardware components were two processors, each capable of searching 500,000 positions per second. In January, 1988, Deep Thought defeated U.S. Grandmaster Brent Larson, a former contender for the world title, in a major tournament held in Long Beach, California (in fact, Deep Thought tied for first place in the tournament with Grandmaster Anthony Miles). In March, 1991, it became the first computer to compete in a round-robin tournament for grandmasters and placed seventh out of eight participants in the IBM Cup, held in Hanover, Germany.

The next generation of Deep Thought, based on a single chip designed to examine 1 billion positions per second and expected to be ready in early 1992, is expected to pose a serious challenge to world champion Gary Kasparov (Kasparov defeated the current Deep Thought in a match in late 1989). Kasparov begs to differ, however, maintaining that "human creativity and imagination (in particular, *his* creativity and imagination) will surely triumph over silicon and wire." (Quote taken from the article "A Grandmaster Chess Machine" by Hsu, Anantharaman, Campbell and Nowatzyk, which appeared in *Scientific American*, 263: 4, October 1990, pp. 44–52).

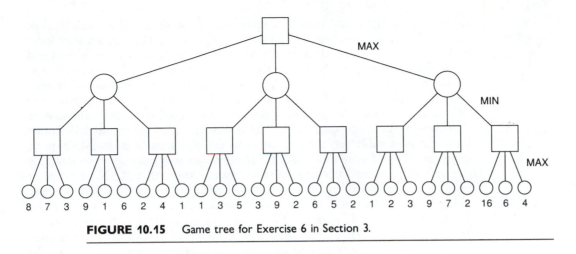

FIGURE 10.15   Game tree for Exercise 6 in Section 3.

6. Consider the game tree in Figure 10.15. Suppose that MAX is to choose one of the three possible moves at level one of this tree. Apply the minimax algorithm to a ply level of 3 to determine MAX's move and its minimax value. The numbers at the leaves of the tree indicate values returned by the heuristic function.

7. Consider the game tree in Figure 10.16. Suppose that MAX is to choose one of the three possible moves at level one of this tree. Apply the minimax algorithm to a ply level of 3 to determine MAX's move and its minimax value. The numbers at the leaves of the tree indicate values returned by the heuristic function.

8. Suppose that you are MAX and that your opponent has been paid by gamblers to purposely lose. Hence your opponent is always choosing the worst possible move among the options open to her. How will the minimax algorithm perform under these circumstances? How would you adjust the minimax algorithm to allow you to defeat your opponent as rapidly as possible?

9. (Alpha-Beta Pruning) A technique known as *alpha-beta pruning* can reduce the number of nodes that must be explored when the minimax algorithm is invoked for a particular ply limit. When using this technique, two values,

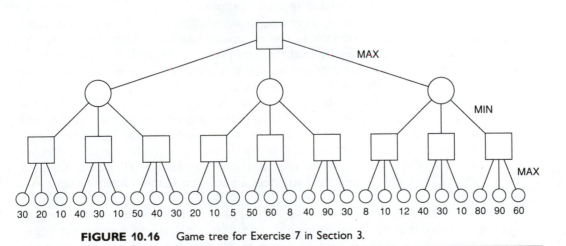

FIGURE 10.16   Game tree for Exercise 7 in Section 3.

designated as alpha and beta by convention, are maintained at each level of the game tree as it is being searched. During search, the alpha value for a MAX node (that is, a node at which MAX is choosing a move) is maintained to be the maximum of the values that have been returned from exploration of successor nodes. Similarly, at a MIN node, the beta value is maintained to be the minimum of the values that have been returned from exploration of successor nodes. With these definitions of alpha and beta values, note that generation of successor nodes can be discontinued below any MIN node having a beta value less than or equal to the alpha value of its MAX node ancestor. Why? Further generation of successors will only serve to decrease the beta value at the MIN node, and we already know that MAX, at the prior level, has found an alternative better (from MAX's perspective) than the beta value of this MIN node. Hence, MAX would never want to choose a move to this MIN state. It is thus a waste of time to explore it further. Similar reasoning dictates that generation of successor nodes can be discontinued below any MAX node having an alpha value greater than or equal to the beta value of its MIN node ancestor. Apply alpha-beta pruning to the game trees in Exercises 7 and 8. How many tree nodes can be avoided in each case because of the cutoff? Finally, modify the Minimax algorithm presented in the text to take alpha-beta pruning into account.

Chapter Summary

In Chapter 9 we examined ways of finding paths through a graph or network. In this chapter we have pursued further the problem of finding paths from a start node to a goal node, but we have not required that the path we find be the shortest path from the start node to the goal node as we did in Dijkstra's algorithm. Rather, we have sought to expedite the search for a path between two nodes by settling for any path rather than the shortest one. Second, though we have been searching through graphs and networks in theory, such graphs and networks have been viewed as purely conceptual search structures—structures that may never exist entirely as data in computer memory. Both of these adaptations on the path-finding motif have been motivated by the existence of abstract graphs and networks so large that no implementation will squeeze them into a reasonable amount of space.

In Section 10.1 we have applied a brute-force technique involving backtracking logic that blindly generates paths radiating from the start node until the goal node is encountered. The technique has been illustrated using the search graph underlying the eight queens problem. Though suitable for some types of problems, the method of this first section has an exponential time efficiency and is thus often not practical.

In Section 10.2 we have refined the technique from Section 10.1 in the hope of making the run time of such search algorithms polynomial instead of exponential. The method we have used, known as the best-first search algorithm, involves applying a heuristic function that quickly calculates an estimate of the distance remaining from a given path's final node to the goal node. This value is then used to select a path that is most likely to lead to a goal.

Finally, in Section 10.3, we have applied heuristic search techniques, in particular the minimax algorithm, in the area of strategic game playing—one of the first endeavors in which computers were able to demonstrate "intelligent" behavior.

Key Words	alpha-beta pruning game trees path ply

Key Words

alpha-beta pruning   game trees   path ply
best-first search   Grundy's game   ply limit
eight queens problem   heuristic   search tree
Fifteen game   minimax algorithm   static evaluator

Programming Problems/Projects

1. Implement a program that determines the number of possible eight queens configurations existing on a standard chessboard.

2. In Exercise 7 of Section 10.1 you were introduced to the knight's tour problem. Implement a program that searches for a knight's tour using the recursive brute-force strategy of Section 10.1. What is the time efficiency of this algorithm? Does your program find a solution to the knight's tour in a reasonable amount of time for an 8 by 8 chessboard? If not, what is the maximum board size for which your program is able to find a knight's tour solution on your computer?

3. Develop a heuristic to guide the choice of the knight chess piece as it searches for a valid knight's tour (see Problem 2). Develop a program that then uses this heuristic in a best-first search for the knight's tour problem. Compare the performance of this program to the program you wrote for Problem 2. Is there a measurable increase in efficiency? If not, try adjusting the heuristic. Write up the results of your experimentation in a formal report.

4. In Exercise 6 of Section 10.1, you developed a Maze ADT. Now implement that ADT in a program that randomly generates mazes and then uses a recursive brute-force strategy to find a path through the maze. Experiment with the program to determine the types of mazes that the program is able to solve in a reasonable amount of time.

5. Retain the random maze generator you developed for Problem 4, but now develop one or more heuristics to find paths through the mazes generated. Using a best-first search employing these heuristics, experiment with the heuristics you formulate. Write up the results of your experimentation to summarize the strengths and weaknesses of each heuristic. Include empirical evidence from runs of your program to substantiate your written conclusions.

6. In Problem 1 of Chapter 9 you implemented Dijkstra's shortest path algorithm using the Network ADT operations introduced in that chapter. Now modify that program to use the version of the shortest path algorithm that you formulated in your answer to Exercise 10 of Section 10.2. Which program (the one from Problem 1 of Chapter 9 or the new one) runs faster on the network of Figure 9.3? Can you find a network that reverses these results; that is, will the program that is slower on the network of Figure 9.3 run faster on the new network you've found? If so, to what do you attribute this difference in performance? Develop some general criteria for the type of networks likely to be processed faster by each of these programs.

7. Develop a program that performs a best-first search for a path from Start node to Goal node in the network of Figure 10.7. Use your program to experiment with a variety of heuristics that guide the selection of nodes on this path. Include in your experimentation heuristics that weigh both the path length (that is, distance already covered) along with an estimate of the distance remaining to the goal node. Write up the results of your experimentation, including a discussion of which heuristics find the goal

nodes fastest, which find the shortest path, and which produce a desirable blend of usually finding the shortest path in the least amount of time.

8. In Exercise 2 of Section 10.3 we described a generalized form of the game of Nim. Write a program that pits a computer against a human opponent in this game. The computer's moves should be guided by the minimax algorithm. Experiment with various heuristics and ply limits in this program. What heuristics seem to produce the best results in a reasonable amount of time?

9. Generalize the game of Fifteen described in Section 10.3 to a game in which two opponents alternately select different digits from among 1, 2,..., M, attempting to collect a combination of digits adding up to some specified N. Develop heuristics for this game and then implement those heuristics in a program that enables a computer to play a human opponent. In a written report, discuss the success (or lack thereof) of your program. What heuristics are most likely to lead to computer wins?

10. Write a computer program to play tic-tac-toe against a human opponent. Use the minimax algorithm with a variety of heuristics and ply limits. In a written report, discuss the level of tic-tac-toe expertise your program is able to attain. This report should include empirical evidence indicating the success your program has in defeating human opponents. Note that one way of viewing the game of tic-tac-toe is to assign the digits from 1 to 9 to board positions in the following pattern:

$$4 \quad 9 \quad 2$$

$$3 \quad 5 \quad 7$$

$$8 \quad 1 \quad 6$$

Then observe that playing tic-tac-toe is equivalent to playing the game of Fifteen as described in Section 10.3.

11. Modify any of the programs you developed for Problems 8, 9, or 10 to include the alpha-beta pruning technique described in Exercise 9 of Section 10.3. Given the time limits you establish for selecting a move in these games, to what extent does the alpha-beta technique allow you to search to a deeper ply? To what extent does this deeper search allow your program to play the game better?

12. Most of us have worked a sliding tile puzzle. In such a puzzle, there are 8 (or 15) numbered tiles in a 3 by 3 (or 4 by 4) grid. One grid position is unoccupied by a tile, so that tiles adjacent to that position may be moved into it. The object of the game is to manipulate the puzzle from its initial configuration into a specified final configuration. For instance, a series of moves to proceed from the following initial configuration (with X marking an unoccupied position) to the goal represents one possible way of "solving" the puzzle.

Initial Configuration				Goal		
1	2	3		1	2	3
4	5	6	$\rightarrow$	8	X	4
7	8	X		7	6	5

Develop a program that accepts an initial puzzle configuration and a goal arrangement for the tiles. Using a variety of heuristics, have your program search for a path to a particular goal using the best-first search strategy. Write up the results of experimenting with your program. This report should include a discussion of which heuristics proved most effective, whether the time limit you imposed on the computer's selection of a move allowed a 4 by 4 puzzle to be solved, and whether the heuristics you developed solved the puzzle with a path that included the minimum possible number of moves (as opposed to merely solving the puzzle by finding any path).

11

ADDITIONAL SEARCH STRATEGIES

He who would search for pearls must dive below.

John Dryden

CHAPTER OUTLINE

In Chapter 3 we introduced the list ADT. Three pivotal operations on this ADT are the add, delete, and retrieve operations. The efficiency of each of these operations is contingent upon the method we use to search for items within the list.

The sequential search, though easy to implement and applicable to short lists, is limited in many practical situations by its $O(n)$ search efficiency. The binary search offers a much faster $O(\log_2 n)$ search efficiency but also has limitations. Foremost among these limitations are the need to maintain the list in physically contiguous order and the need to maintain a count of the number of records in the list. Both of these limitations are particularly restrictive for volatile lists—that is, lists in which additions and deletions are frequently made. In Chapter 7 a binary search tree emerged as offering the best of both worlds. Additions and deletions can be done on a binary search tree by merely manipulating pointers instead of moving data, and an $O(\log_2 n)$ search efficiency can be achieved if the tree remains nearly full. Unfortunately, to guarantee that the tree remains nearly full and thus ensure the $O(\log_2 n)$ efficiency, height balancing (see Section 7.6) is required. The complications involved in implementing this technique frequently dictate that it not be used. Essentially, you must weigh the significant cost in development time to implement a height-balanced tree against the risk that the order in which data arrive for insertion may cause search efficiency to deteriorate from $O(\log_2 n)$ to $O(n)$. If data items arrive in a relatively random order, then taking the risk may well be the prudent choice. In Chapter 8, a 2-3 tree was introduced as a means of implementing an ordered list. Although this technique guarantees $O(\log_2 n)$ search efficiency and $O(1)$ data interchanges for adds and deletes, it can be relatively inefficient in its use of space because many data records within the tree are potentially filled with an empty flag.

In this chapter we shall look at additional strategies for implementing the retrieve, add, and delete operations on a list. We begin with a section that further develops the idea of using trees to facilitate searching; in it we consider the advantages gained by moving from 2-3 trees to 2-3-4 trees and then from 2-3-4 trees to red-black trees. We conclude the section with a discussion of splay trees, which do not yield a worst-case performance as efficient as one can obtain from various balanced trees, but nevertheless, compare favorably with balanced trees when the efficiency of their operations is analyzed over sequences of such operations. They also employ simpler restructuring algorithms to achieve this level of performance. Should you wish to do so, Section 11.1 may be skipped without affecting your understanding of later sections.

The efficiency of all the search techniques considered up to this point and in Section 11.1 depends on the number of items in the list being searched. In Section 11.2 we study another search strategy called *hashing*. Its efficiency is contingent upon the amount of storage you are willing to waste. Hashing can achieve phenomenally fast search times, regardless of how much data you have, provided that you can afford to keep a relatively large amount of unused list space available. On the surface, the drawback to hashing would appear to be in the list traversal operation. Hashing renders it impossible to go through a list in order without augmenting the basic method. We shall see in Section 11.3 that one such adaptation of hashing to ordered traversals involves a combination of linked lists and hashing. In Sections 11.4 and 11.5

we shall also see how variations on hashing can be used to implement sparse matrices and the search operation for the string ADT.

We close the chapter by exploring some of the special considerations that enter into searching for data stored in a disk file instead of main memory. These considerations lead to a variety of search schemes, all of which employ some variations of a data structure known as an *index*.

II.I   ADDITIONAL TREE-BASED SEARCH TECHNIQUES

2-3-4 Trees

We begin our discussion in this section by generalizing 2-3 trees one more degree to allow for nodes with four children. Known as a *2-3-4 tree,* this type of tree offers an advantage over 2-3 trees in that insertions and deletions can be performed using one pass from the tree's root to a leaf, instead of requiring a root-to-leaf pass followed by a pass from the leaf back to the root. On the other hand, the overall storage requirements for a 2-3-4 tree will increase because each node will now have to accommodate three data fields and four pointer fields, not all of which will be used necessarily in each node in the tree; this means a potentially greater waste of storage than you have with 2-3 trees. It turns out, however, that a 2-3-4 tree can also be represented as a binary tree (known as a *red-black tree*), allowing us to allocate space more efficiently than in 2-3-4 trees while still retaining the simplicity of a single root-to-leaf pass for data insertion and deletion. We shall discuss red-black trees later in this section.

Formally, we can define a 2-3-4 tree as follows.

• **Definition:** A *2-3-4 tree* consists of a general tree and a Precedes relationship with the following properties.

1. Every node in the 2-3-4 tree has room for three informational fields. We call these fields FirstInfo, SecondInfo, and ThirdInfo. Typically each such field represents a data record.

2. Every node in the 2-3-4 tree has room for four pointers to other nodes. We call these pointers FirstChild, SecondChild, ThirdChild, and FourthChild.

3. Every node in the 2-3-4 tree has one of the following arrangements of data:
   a. FirstInfo with active data, and SecondInfo and ThirdInfo with a special value, EmptyFlag, which indicates that those fields have no active data. Such a node is called a 2-node.
   b. The data in FirstInfo preceding that in SecondInfo according to the Precedes relationship for the tree, and ThirdInfo with the value EmptyFlag. Such a node is called a 3-node.
   c. The data in FirstInfo preceding that in SecondInfo according to the Precedes relationship and the data in SecondInfo preceding that of ThirdInfo. Such a node is called a 4-node.

4. In any given nonleaf node:
   a. If only FirstInfo has active data, then all data in the subtree referenced by FirstChild must precede FirstInfo, and all data in the subtree referenced by FourthChild must follow FirstInfo in the Precedes relationship for the tree. Note our convention here that the two subtrees of a 2-node are referenced by the FirstChild and FourthChild pointer, respectively. We will later see that this is done to minimize data movement.
   b. If only FirstInfo and SecondInfo have active data, then all data in the subtree referenced by FirstChild must precede FirstInfo; all data in the subtree referenced by SecondChild must precede SecondInfo and follow FirstInfo; and all data in the subtree referenced by FourthChild must follow SecondInfo. Note the convention that the three subtrees of a 3-node are referenced by the First-, Second-, and FourthChild pointers in the node.
   c. If FirstInfo, SecondInfo, and ThirdInfo have active data, then all data in the subtree referenced by FirstChild must precede FirstInfo; all data in the subtree referenced by SecondChild must precede SecondInfo and follow FirstInfo; all data in the subtree referenced by ThirdChild must precede ThirdInfo and follow SecondInfo; and all data in the subtree referenced by FourthChild must follow ThirdInfo.

We can picture the structure of a 2-3-4 node as follows:

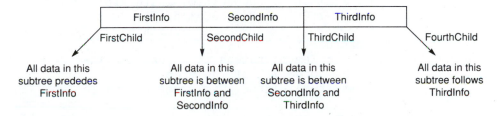

An example of a 2-3-4 tree with integer data fields is given in Figure 11.1.

Search Algorithm for 2-3-4 Trees The search algorithm for 2-3-4 trees is similar to those for ordered binary trees and 2-3 trees. We start at the root of the tree. Comparing the target item to the informational fields indicates whether the target is in the current node or, based on the relationship of the

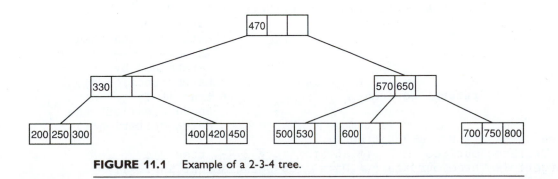

FIGURE 11.1 Example of a 2-3-4 tree.

target to FirstInfo, SecondInfo, and ThirdInfo, which child pointer to follow. For instance, to find 600 in the tree of Figure 11.1:

1. Compare 600 to the value in FirstInfo: 470. Since 600 follows 470 and since SecondInfo is empty, we follow the FourthChild pointer from the root.
2. From the level-1 node containing 570 and 650, we follow the SecondChild pointer because 600 is between 570 and 650.
3. At level 2 we find the target in the FirstInfo field.

Suppose now that instead of 600 the search value was 610. Then our search would proceed as in steps 1 and 2 above, except that at the level-2 node, a comparison of 600 and 610 would show that 610 did not precede 600. Upon finding that SecondInfo is empty, we begin a search of the subtree reached from the FourthChild pointer of the level-2 node. Since this is NULL, however, our search now terminates unsuccessfully.

This algorithm is formalized in the following PSEUDO procedure.

```
type
  TwoThreeFourData: (* The type of each information field in the 2-3-4 tree;
                 admits a value identified by EmptyFlag, which is used
                 to indicate a field with no active data *);
  TwoThreeFourTree: pointer to TwoThreeFourNode;
  TwoThreeFourNode: record
             FirstInfo, SecondInfo, ThirdInfo: TwoThreeFourData;
             FirstChild, SecondChild, ThirdChild,
                            FourthChild: TwoThreeFourTree
           endrecord;
  Comparison: function (* The signature of a function that determines the
                 ordering of the tree *)
        ( given Item1, Item2: TwoThreeFourData (* Two data items to
                                    be compared *);
           return: boolean              (* true if Item1 is to
                                    be considered as
                                    preceding Item2 in
                                    ordering for the
                                    tree; false
                                    otherwise *) );
  MatchCriterion: function (* The signature of a function that determines
                   whether two tree data items match each other *)
        ( given Target,
           AnyData: TwoThreeFourData (* Two data items, with
                              Target containing
                              data to be matched
                              in some sense as
                              determined by
                              Match function *);
           return: boolean              (* true if Target and
                                    AnyData satisfy the
                                    Match criterion *) );
procedure Search234  (* For 2-3-4 tree *)
  ( given T: TwoThreeFourTree        (* An arbitrary 2-3-4 tree *);
        Target: TwoThreeFourData  (* Data item being sought in T *);
```

```
          Precedes: Comparison       (* The order relationship on tree data *);
          Match: MatchCriterion      (* This function determines which tree
                                         node is being sought *);
  return Item: TwoThreeFourData      (* The information associated with
                                         Target *);
          Found: boolean             (* true if Target is found; false
                                         otherwise *) );

start Search234
  Found := false;
  if T <> NULL then
    if Match(Ref(T).FirstInfo, Target) then (* Check first info field *)
      Item := Ref(T).FirstInfo;
      Found := true
    elsif Precedes(Target, Ref(T).FirstInfo) then      (* Make recursive
                                                           call to search
                                                           appropriate
                                                           subtree *)

      Search234(Ref(T).FirstChild, Target, Precedes, Match, Item, Found)
    elsif not Match(Ref(T).SecondInfo, EmptyFlag) then  (* The current node
                                                            is a 3-node or
                                                            4-node *)

      if Match(Ref(T).SecondInfo, Target) then          (* Check second
                                                            info field *)

        Item := Ref(T).SecondInfo;
        Found := true
      elsif Precedes(Target, Ref(T).SecondInfo) then    (* Make recursive
                                                            call to search
                                                            appropriate
                                                            subtree *)

        Search234(Ref(T).SecondChild, Target, Precedes, Match, Item, Found)
      elsif not Match(Ref(T).ThirdInfo, EmptyFlag) then (* The current node
                                                            is a 4-node *)

        if Match(Ref(T).ThirdInfo, Target) then         (* Check third info
                                                            field *)

          Item := Ref(T).ThirdInfo;
          Found := true
        elsif Precedes(Target, Ref(T).ThirdInfo) then   (* Make recursive
                                                            call to search
                                                            appropriate
                                                            subtree *)

          Search234(Ref(T).ThirdChild, Target, Precedes, Match, Item,
                    Found)
        else
          Search234(Ref(T).FourthChild, Target, Precedes, Match, Item,
                    Found)
        endif
      else  (* The current node is a 3-node! *)
        Search234(Ref(T).FourthChild, Target, Precedes, Match, Item, Found)
      endif
    else  (* The current node is a 2-node! *)
      Search234(Ref(T).FourthChild, Target, Precedes, Match, Item, Found)
    endif
  endif (* T <> NULL *)
end Search234;
```

Search Efficiency for 2-3-4 Trees   Suppose we had a 2-3-4 tree of height h, all of whose nodes are 2-nodes. Such a tree could hold a maximum of $2^{h+1} - 1$ data items. Similarly, if the tree contained only 4-nodes, the tree could hold a maximum of $4^{h+1} - 1$ data items. Thus, given a 2-3-4 tree storing N data items in a mixture of 2-, 3-, and 4-nodes, the height of the tree will be between $\log_4(N + 1) - 1$ and $\log_2(N + 1) - 1$. Consequently, searching in a 2-3-4 tree storing N data items will involve visiting no more than $\log_2(N + 1) - 1$ nodes, so 2-3-4 searching is $O(\log_2 N)$.

Add Algorithm for 2-3-4 Trees   As noted in the opening remarks about 2-3-4 trees, one of their merits is that they allow insertions to be made with their structure preserved in one pass from the root to a leaf. The key insight permitting this is that, in the process of searching for the proper place to insert a data item, we "split" any 4-nodes we find along the way; that is, we form two additional 2-nodes and pass the data in SecondInfo of the node being split up to its parent. The newly formed 2-nodes are attached to the parent node via the proper child pointers and the value passed back to this parent is inserted in its proper place in the information fields. If the 4-node encountered is the tree's root, we handle the situation differently, creating two new nodes to be attached to the root.

Two other observations should be made:

1. Because we do this splitting as we are searching for a place to attach the node, the parent of a 4-node will always be a 2- or 3-node (and hence capable of holding the value being passed up to it from the 4-node). Also, because we make the split before advancing further in the tree, there will always be a leaf node available to hold the new data.

2. The manner in which 4-nodes are split and reattached to the tree allows it to remain "balanced," assuring that searches, as well as insertions and deletions, can be done in $O(\log_2 N)$ time.

Let us now examine the different situations that must be considered for splitting nodes and illustrate how they are handled.

A.   The node to be split is the root of the 2-3-4 tree.

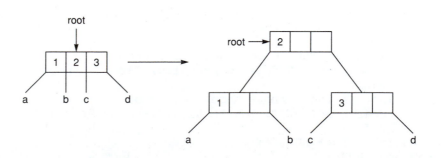

B. The parent of the node to be split is a 2-node. There are two subcases:

1. The 4-node is accessed by the FirstChild pointer of the parent.

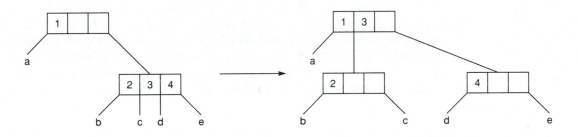

2. The 4-node is accessed by the FourthChild pointer of the parent.

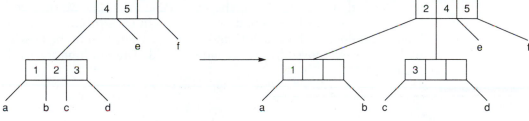

C. The parent of the node to be split is a 3-node. There are three subcases:

1. The 4-node is accessed by the FirstChild pointer of the parent.

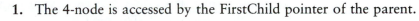

2. The 4-node is accessed by the SecondChild pointer of the parent.

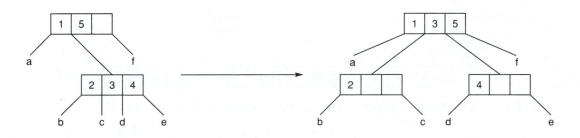

3. The 4-node is accessed by the FourthChild pointer of the parent.

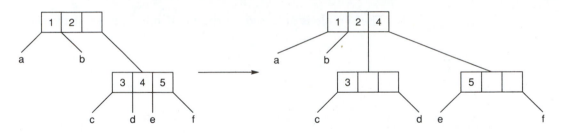

We now consider a few examples to show how these splittings work together.

Example 11.1   Insert 620 as a data item in the tree of Figure 11.1 on page 495.
Since 620 follows the value of the root node of our tree, 470, we advance to the node with data values 570 and 650. Since 620 is between these two values, we follow the SecondChild pointer of this node to the leaf node with the single value 600. We now insert 620 into the SecondInfo field of this node because it follows 600. The resulting tree appears in Figure 11.2. No nodes needed to be split in this insertion.

Example 11.2   Add 790 to the 2-3-4 tree of Figure 11.2.
Our search proceeds as in Example 11.1, but this time at the level-1 node containing the values 570 and 650 we follow the FourthChild pointer since 790 follows 650. The next node we encounter is a 4-node. Since its parent is a 3-node, we are in the situation of case C.3. Splitting the node as described there, we obtain the tree in Figure 11.3. We now follow the FourthChild of the level-1 node with data values 570, 650, and 750 to the level 2 leaf node with value 800 and insert the value 790 in the FirstInfo field, with 800 being moved to the SecondInfo field. The resulting tree is shown in Figure 11.4.

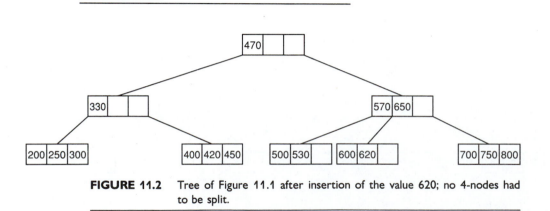

FIGURE 11.2   Tree of Figure 11.1 after insertion of the value 620; no 4-nodes had to be split.

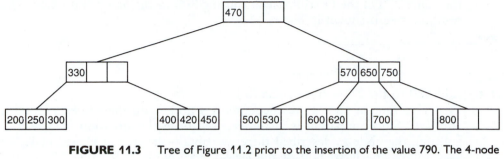

FIGURE 11.3   Tree of Figure 11.2 prior to the insertion of the value 790. The 4-node with values 700, 750, and 800 in the Figure 11.2 tree was split and the value 750 passed to the parent node.

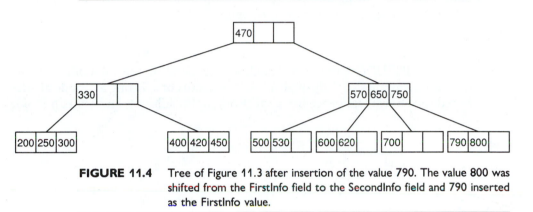

FIGURE 11.4   Tree of Figure 11.3 after insertion of the value 790. The value 800 was shifted from the FirstInfo field to the SecondInfo field and 790 inserted as the FirstInfo value.

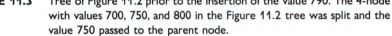

Example 11.3   Add 270 to the 2-3-4 tree of Figure 11.4.

Because 270 precedes 470, our search takes us to the 2-node at level 1 containing the value 330. We then follow the FirstChild pointer to the 4-node with values 200, 250, and 300. Since its parent is a 2-node, we are in the situation of case B.1. Splitting the node as described there, we obtain the tree in Figure 11.5. We now follow the FirstChild of the level-1 node with data values 250 and 330 to the level-2 leaf node with value 300 and insert

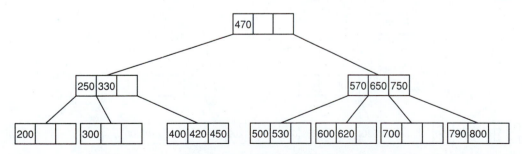

FIGURE 11.5   Tree of Figure 11.4 during insertion of the value 270. The 4-node with values 200, 250, and 300 in the Figure 11.4 tree was split and the value 250 was inserted in the parent node after the value 330 was shifted to the SecondInfo field.

the value 270 in the FirstInfo field, shifting 300 to the SecondInfo field. The resulting tree is shown in Figure 11.6.

Example II.4   Add 480 to the 2-3-4 tree of Figure 11.6.

This time at level 1 we encounter a 4-node with the values 570, 650, and 750. Since its parent is a 2-node, we are in the situation of case B.2. Splitting the node as described there, we obtain the tree in Figure 11.7. We now follow the FirstChild of the level-1 node with data value 570 to the level-2 leaf node with values 500 and 530 and insert the value 480 in the FirstInfo field, moving 500 to the SecondInfo field and 530 to the ThirdInfo field. The resulting tree is shown in Figure 11.8.

The PSEUDO procedure Add234 considers all the possibilities illustrated in Examples 11.1 through 11.4. The details of splitting a 4-node are deferred to subordinate procedures SplitRoot, SplitChildof2, and SplitChildof3.

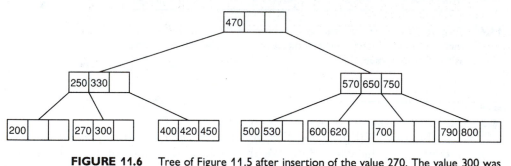

FIGURE 11.6   Tree of Figure 11.5 after insertion of the value 270. The value 300 was shifted from the FirstInfo field to the SecondInfo field and 270 inserted as the FirstInfo value.

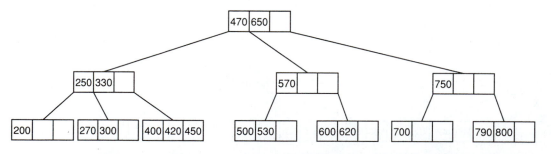

FIGURE 11.7   Tree of Figure 11.6 during insertion of the value 480. The 4-node with values 570, 650, and 750 in the Figure 11.6 tree was split and the value 650 inserted into the parent node (here the root of the tree) in the SecondInfo field.

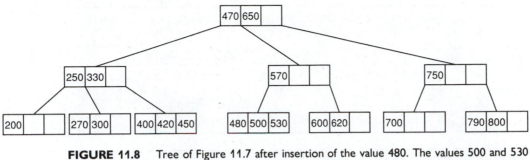

FIGURE 11.8 Tree of Figure 11.7 after insertion of the value 480. The values 500 and 530 were shifted from the FirstInfo field and SecondInfo field, respectively, to the SecondInfo field and ThirdInfo field, and 480 was inserted as the FirstInfo value.

The specifications for these splitting procedures, as well as other subordinate modules needed by Add234, are given in the form of pre- and postconditions with accompanying graphic documentation. The writing of the subordinate modules is left for the exercises.

```
(* Specifications for subordinate modules SplitRoot, SplitChildOf2,
   SplitChildOf3, NodeType, InsertData, LeafNode, and Compare follow. These
   modules are all invoked by Add234. *)


procedure SplitRoot
   ( given T: TwoThreeFourTree      (* A non-NULL pointer to a 2-3-4
                                        tree node with 3 keys *);

     return T: TwoThreeFourTree     (* SplitRoot will create two new
                                        2-3-4 nodes and use these to split
                                        the initial node into three nodes,
                                        each with one key. T will be
                                        returned as a pointer to the root
                                        of a 2-3-4 subtree and will have
                                        two children *) );
```

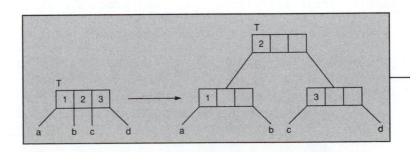

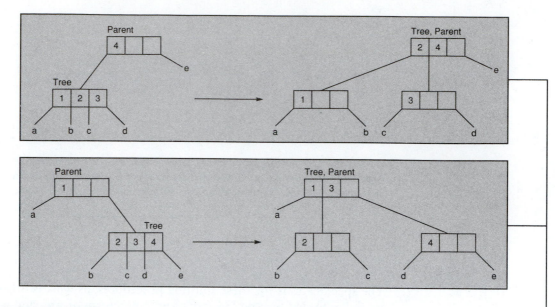

procedure SplitChildOf2
  (**given** Tree,
        Parent: TwoThreeFourTree   (* Tree is pointer to a 2-3-4 tree
                                            4-node, which stores three data
                                            values, and whose parent node,
                                            accessible through the pointer
                                            Parent, has one data value *);

    return Tree,
        Parent: TwoThreeFourTree   (* The procedure will split the node
                                              pointed to by Tree into two nodes,
                                            each of which will have one data
                                            value. The middle value will be
                                            promoted to the parent node. Upon
                                            return, Tree will point to the
                                            parent node *));

procedure SplitChildOf3
  (**given** Tree,
        Parent: TwoThreeFourTree   (* Tree is a pointer to a 2-3-4 tree
                                              4-node, which stores three data
                                            values, and whose parent node,
                                            accessible through the pointer
                                            Parent, has two data values *);

    return Tree,
        Parent: TwoThreeFourTree   (* The procedure will split the tree
                                              node pointed to by Tree into two
                                            tree nodes, each of which will have
                                            one data value. The middle value
                                            will be promoted to the parent node.
                                            Upon return, Tree will point to the
                                            parent node *));

See the three illustrations
on page 505.

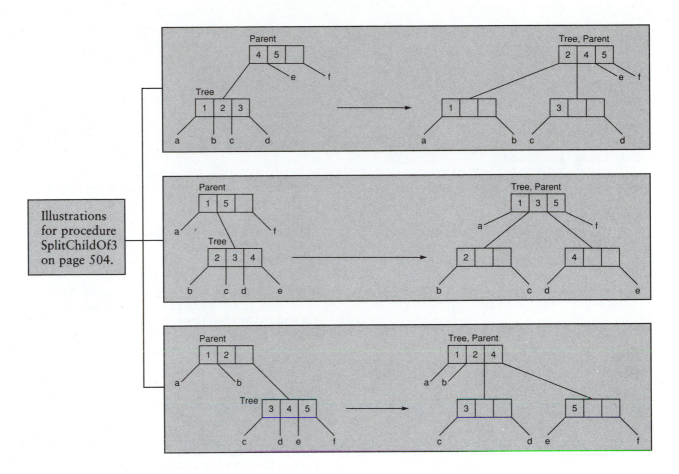

Illustrations for procedure SplitChildOf3 on page 504.

```
procedure  MakeTreeNode
  ( given Node: TwoThreeFourTree          (* Arbitrary pointer *);
    return Node: TwoThreeFourTree         (* Node initialized with
                                             EmptyFlags in Info fields
                                             and NULL pointers in Child
                                             fields *) );


function  NodeType
  ( given T: TwoThreeFourTree             (* Pointer to a 2-3-4 tree node;
                                             presumed to be non-NULL *);

            Match: MatchCriterion         (* This function used to determine if
                                             an Info field contains EmptyFlag *);

    return: integer                       (* A value indicating the type of
                                             node--2 for two-node, 3 for
                                             three-node, 4 for four-node *) );


procedure  InsertData
  ( given T: TwoThreeFourTree             (* Pointer to a non-NULL 2-3-4 tree
                                             node. T is assumed to have values
                                             in one or two data fields *);

            Precedes: Comparison          (* Order relationship on
                                             TwoThreeFourData *);

            Match: MatchCriterion         (* This function used here to determine
                                             NodeType *);
```

```
         NewData: TwoThreeFourData)    (* Data to be inserted into the 2-3-4
                                          tree node pointed to by T. It is
                                          assumed that NewData is not already
                                          in the node *);

    return T: TwoThreeFourTree         (* T will have NewData inserted into a
                                          data field of this node at an
                                          appropriate Info field, possibly
                                          requiring that existing records be
                                          moved to make room *) );

function LeafNode
  ( given T: TwoThreeFourTree          (* Pointer to a 2-3-4 tree node *);
    return: boolean                    (* true if the node is a leaf node;
                                          false otherwise *) );

function Compare
  ( given T: TwoThreeFourTree          (* Pointer to a non-NULL 2-3-4 tree
                                          node *);

         Data: TwoThreeFourData        (* Data value to be compared to the
                                          data items stored in node T *);

         Precedes: Comparison          (* Order relationship for the tree *);
         Match: MatchCriterion         (* This function determines if Data is
                                          already in the tree *);

    return: integer                    (* Return a value indicating whether
                                          the given data value occurs in the
                                          current node or not. If a match,
                                          returns the value -1; if not,
                                          returns the value 0 if the current
                                          node is a leaf, otherwise returns a
                                          value indicating which child to
                                          follow to the appropriate next node
                                          where the data value may occur. Here
                                          1 implies FirstChild, 2 implies
                                          SecondChild, 3 implies ThirdChild, 4
                                          implies FourthChild *) );
```

(* Procedure Add234 uses the preceding modules to implement a complete
   algorithm for inserting into a 2-3-4 tree. Note that, in an attempt to
   insert into a 2-3-4 tree a value that is already in the tree, nodes may be
   split en route to the node where the existing value is stored *)

```
procedure Add234 (* For 2-3-4 tree *)
  ( given T: TwoThreeFourTree          (* An arbitrary 2-3-4 tree *);
         NewData: TwoThreeFourData     (* Data item to be added in T *);
         Precedes: Comparison          (* Order relationship on
                                          TwoThreeFourData *);

         Match: MatchCriterion         (* This function determines if NewData
                                          is already in the tree *)

    return T: TwoThreeFourTree         (* Will have NewData added if NewData
                                          was not found. If NewData found
                                          in original tree, T is left
                                          unchanged, unless a nonleaf FourNode
                                          was encountered in the search, in
                                          which case it is split *)

         Success: boolean              (* true if NewData is added; false
                                          otherwise *) );
```

```
var
 Done: boolean;
 P, Parent: TwoThreeFourTree;
 CompareResult: integer;

start Add234
   if T = NULL then
     MakeTreeNode(T);
     Ref(T).FirstInfo := NewData;
     Success := true
   else
     if NodeType(T, Match) = 4 then   (* Root is a 4-node and must be
                                          split *)
       SplitRoot(T)
     endif;
     P := T;
     Parent := NULL                    (* Parent is parent of P *)
     Done := false;
     while not Done do
       if NodeType(P,Match) = 4 then  (* P is a 4-node *)
         if NodeType(Parent, Match) = 3 then   (* Parent is a 3-node *)
           SplitChildOf3(P, Parent)
         else
           SplitChildOf2(P, Parent)
         endif
       endif;
       (* After returning from SplitChildOf procedure, P has been reset to
          Parent *)
       CompareResult := Compare(P, NewData, Precedes, Match);
       if CompareResult < 0 then      (* NewData already in tree *)
         Done := true;
         Success := false
       elsif CompareResult = 0 then    (* P is a leaf node; can insert
                                          value *)
         InsertData(P, Precedes, Match, NewData);
         Done := true;
         Success := true   .
       (* Otherwise determine child pointer to follow *)
       elsif CompareResult = 1 then  (* First child *)
         Parent := P;
         P := Ref(P).FirstChild
       elsif CompareResult = 2 then  (* Second child *)
         Parent := P;
         P := Ref(P).SecondChild
       elsif CompareResult = 3 then  (* Third child *)
         Parent := P;
         P := Ref(P).ThirdChild
       else                            (* Fourth child *)
         Parent := P;
         P := Ref(P).FourthChild
       endif
     endwhile
   endif
end Add234;
```

Efficiency of Add for a 2-3-4 Tree   For a 2-3-4 tree with N data elements, the Add234 operation will require $O(\log_2 N)$ comparisons and splittings to reach the leaf where a new element can be added. Since the splittings themselves are $O(1)$, the efficiency of the Add234 operation for a 2-3-4 tree is $O(\log_2 N)$.

Red-Black Trees

In our initial remarks on 2-3-4 trees, we indicated that it was possible to represent any 2-3-4 tree with a binary tree known as a *red-black tree*. Such a representation will give us the worst-case search efficiency of balanced search trees along with the economical storage utilization of binary trees. The price we pay for this is minimal; two additional boolean fields called LeftBlack and RightBlack to tell us if the child pointers of our binary tree node are being used (1) to represent child pointers from a 2-3-4 node, or (2) to map a 2-3-4 node structure to its binary tree representation. Pointers used in the first sense are known as "black" pointers, and those used to map 2-3-4 nodes into binary tree nodes are known as "red" pointers.

In the following discussion on mapping 2-3-4 trees into a binary tree structure, we shall assume the following type definitions:

```
type
   RedBlackData: (* The data in each RedBlackNode; admits a value identified by
               EmptyFlag, which is used to indicate a field with no active
               data *);
   RedBlackTree: pointer to RedBlackNode;
   RedBlackNode: record
                Info: RedBlackData;
                LeftChild, RightChild: RedBlackTree;
                LeftBlack, RightBlack: boolean  (* true if the corresponding
                                                   pointer is a black
                                                   pointer and false if
                                                   red *)
         endrecord;
```

We consider separately the cases of 2-nodes, 3-nodes, and 4-nodes:

1. A 2-node, P, can be represented by a node Q of type RedBlackNode that will have both of its color fields Black (indicated in the following illustration by a solid line), Ref(Q).Info = Ref(P).FirstInfo, Ref(Q).LeftChild = Ref(P).FirstChild, and Ref(Q).RightChild = Ref(P).FourthChild.

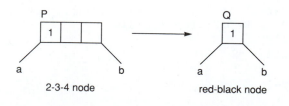

2-3-4 node   red-black node

2. A 3-node, P, is represented by two RedBlack nodes Q1 and Q2 connected by a red pointer (represented in the following diagram by a broken line). This representation can be done in either of two ways. In the first form, known as a "left 3-node" (because the left child pointer uses a red link), we have
   - For Q1: Ref(Q1).Info = Ref(P).FirstInfo, Ref(Q1).LeftChild = Ref(P).FirstChild, Ref(Q1).RightChild = Ref(P).SecondChild, Ref(Q1).LeftBlack = **true**, and Ref(Q1).RightBlack = **true**
   - For Q2: Ref(Q2).Info = Ref(P).SecondInfo, Ref(Q2).LeftChild = Q1, Ref(Q2).RightChild = Ref(P).FourthChild, Ref(Q2).LeftBlack = **false**, and Ref(Q2).RightBlack = **true**

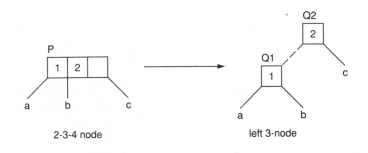

2-3-4 node   left 3-node

Alternatively, we have the following representation, known as a "right 3-node" because of the use of a red right child pointer:
- For Q1: Ref(Q1).Info = Ref(P).SecondInfo, Ref(Q1).LeftChild = Ref(P).SecondChild, Ref(Q1).RightChild = Ref(P).FourthChild, Ref(Q1).LeftBlack = **true**, and Ref(Q1).RightBlack = **true**
- For Q2: Ref(Q2).Info = Ref(P).FirstInfo, Ref(Q2).LeftChild = Ref(P).FirstChild, Ref(Q2).RightChild = Q1, Ref(Q2).LeftBlack = **true**, and Ref(Q2).RightBlack = **false**

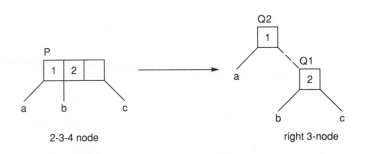

2-3-4 node   right 3-node

3. A 4-node, P, is represented by three RedBlack nodes Q1, Q2, and Q3 as follows:
   - For Q1: Ref(Q1).Info = Ref(P).FirstInfo, Ref(Q1).LeftChild = Ref(P).FirstChild, Ref(Q1).RightChild = Ref(P).SecondChild, Ref(Q1).LeftBlack = **true**, and Ref(Q1).RightBlack = **true**
   - For Q2: Ref(Q2).Info = Ref(P).SecondInfo, Ref(Q2).LeftChild = Q1, Ref(Q2).RightChild = Q3, Ref(Q2),LeftBlack = **false**, and Ref(Q2).RightBlack = **false**

- For Q3: Ref(Q3).Info = Ref(P).ThirdInfo, Ref(Q3).LeftChild = Ref(P).ThirdChild, Ref(Q3).RightChild = Ref(P).FourthChild, Ref(Q3).LeftBlack = **true**, and Ref(Q3).RightBlack = **true**

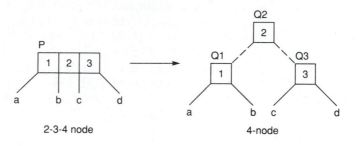

Search Algorithm for Red-Black Trees Since a red-black tree is a binary search tree, searches can be carried out using the same algorithm that was used for a binary tree search—the colors of the pointers never come into play.

Add Algorithm for Red-Black Trees A red-black tree is a representation of a 2-3-4 tree. Consequently, we can use the same fundamental algorithm to insert nodes into this tree that we used for adding nodes to a 2-3-4 tree. In particular, the splitting algorithms used for the insertion of a node into a 2-3-4 tree will be used here; we need only reformulate the algorithms in terms of left and right children and colors instead of FirstChild, SecondChild, and so on. As we shall see, in some cases, splitting a 4-node in a red-black tree is simpler than in 2-3-4 trees, involving nothing more than changing the colors of at most 3 links. To illustrate, let us review, pictorially, the different types of splits used in adding a node to a 2-3-4 tree and reformulate the before and after pictures of the splits in terms of red-black nodes in order to describe what must be done solely in red-black terms.

A. Splitting a root, T, which is a four-node: In the case of a 2-3-4 node, we would represent the splitting as

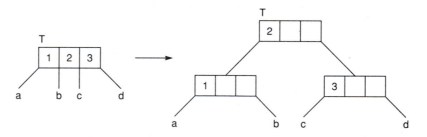

If we reformulate this diagram in terms of a red-black representation of the nodes, we get

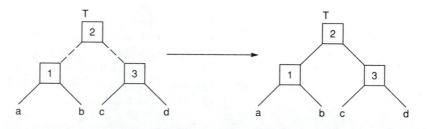

This shows us that splitting a red-black representation of a 4-node referenced by T involves nothing more than a change of colors (from red to black) of the pointers of T.

B. Splitting a 4-node, T, whose parent is a 2-node. Here we consider two subcases.

1. The 4-node is a first child of the 2-node. In the 2-3-4 case we represent the splitting as

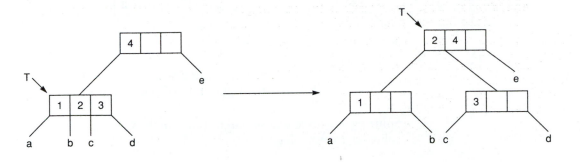

In terms of a red-black reformulation, this diagram becomes

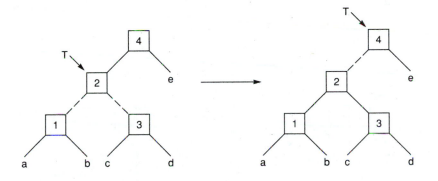

Here again, the only changes required were changes in the colors of the pointers of T and the left child of the parent of T; the pointer values themselves remain unaltered.

2. The 4-node is a fourth child of the 2-node. In the 2-3-4 case we represent the splitting as

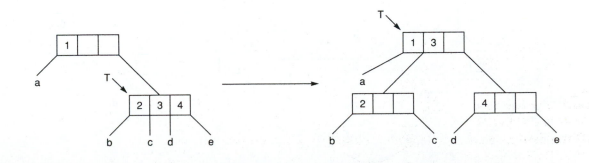

In terms of a red-black reformulation, this diagram becomes

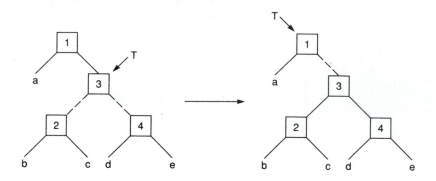

Again the only changes required were changes in the colors of the pointers of T and the right child of the parent of T.

C. Splitting a 4-node whose parent is a 3-node. Once more we have several subcases to consider.

1. The 4-node is the first child of the 3-node:

In the 2-3-4 case we represent the splitting as

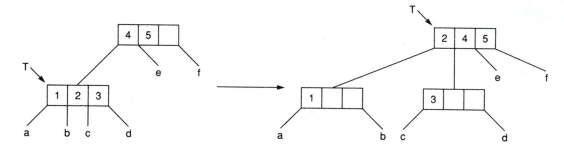

In terms of a red-black reformulation, we have two additional cases to consider. First we have the case where the 3-node is a left 3-node:

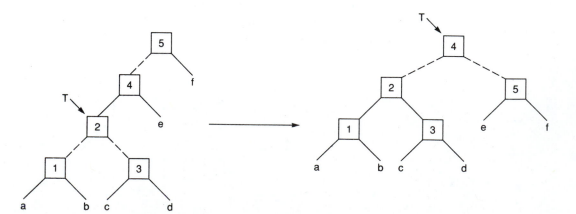

On the other hand, if the 3-node is represented using a right 3-node, the splitting would look like this:

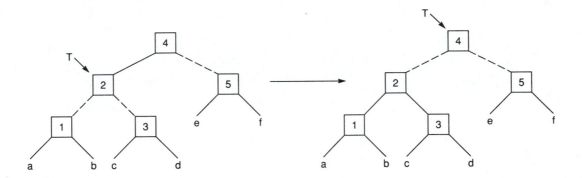

2. The 4-node is the second child of the 3-node. In the 2-3-4 case we represent the splitting as

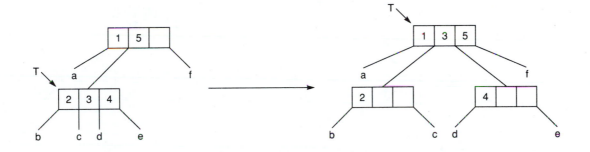

In terms of a red-black reformulation, we have two cases to consider. First we have the case where a left 3-node is used:

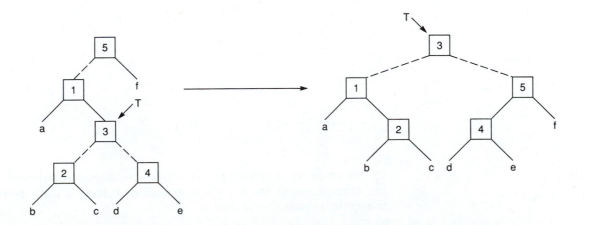

On the other hand, for a right 3-node the splitting would look like

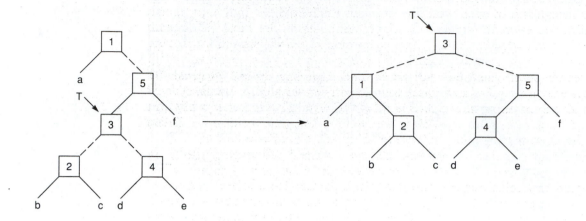

3. The 4-node is the fourth child of the 3-node. In the 2-3-4 case we represent the splitting as

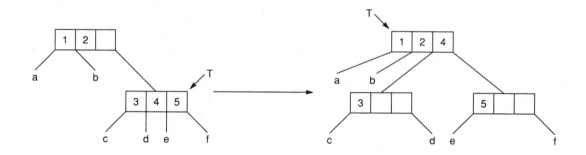

In terms of a red-black reformulation, we again have two cases to consider. In the case where the 3-node is represented using a left 3-node, we have

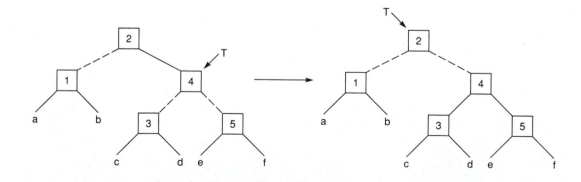

In this case only a change of some color indicators is required. On the other hand, if the 3-node is represented using a right 3-node, the splitting would look like

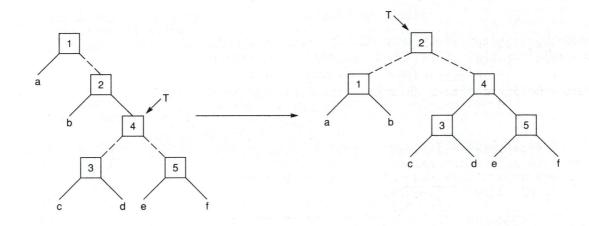

We now give a high-level algorithm for adding new data to a red-black tree. You will notice that, at this high level, the logic for red-black trees is virtually identical to that for 2-3-4 trees. This is not surprising since red-black trees are merely an alternative representation scheme for 2-3-4 trees. As with our description of the Add algorithm for 2-3-4 trees, we defer many of the details to modules that are left for the exercises.

```
type
  RedBlackData: (* The data in each RedBlackNode; admits a value identified by
                    EmptyFlag, which is used to indicate a field with no active
                    data *);
  RedBlackTree: pointer to RedBlackNode;
  RedBlackNode: record
                  Info: RedBlackData;
                  LeftChild, RightChild: RedBlackTree;
                  LeftBlack, RightBlack: boolean  (* true if the corresponding
                                                     pointer is a black
                                                     pointer and false if
                                                     red *)
                endrecord;
  Comparison: function (* The signature of a function that determines the
                          ordering of the tree *)
                ( given Item1, Item2: RedBlackData (* Two data items to be
                                                      compared *);
                  return: boolean           (* true if Item1 is to be
                                               considered as preceding
                                               Item2 in ordering for
                                               the tree; false
                                               otherwise *) );
  MatchCriterion: function (* The signature of a function that determines
                              whether two tree data items match each
                              other *)
                ( given Target,
                        AnyData: RedBlackData (* Two data items, with
                                                 Target containing data to
                                                 be matched in some sense
                                                 as determined by Match
                                                 function *);
```

```
                    return: boolean              (* true if Target and
                                                    AnyData satisfy the
                                                    Match criterion *) );
procedure AddRedBlack                (* For red-black tree *)
  ( given T: RedBlackTree            (* An arbitrary red-black tree *);
         NewData: RedBlackData       (* Data item to be added in T *);
         Precedes: Comparison        (* Order relationship on RedBlackData *);
         Match: MatchCriterion       (* This function determines whether NewData is
                                        already in the tree *);
    return T: RedBlackTree           (* Will have NewData added if NewData was
                                        not found. If NewData found in original
                                        tree, T is left unchanged, unless a
                                        nonleaf 4-node was encountered in the
                                        search, in which case it is split *);
         Success: boolean            (* true if NewData is added; false otherwise *) );
  var
   Done: boolean;
   P, Parent: RedBlackTree;
   CompareResult: integer;

  start  AddRedBlack
    if T = NULL then                 (*  Need to create a tree node  *)
      MakeTreeNode(T);
      Ref(T).Info := NewData;
      Success := true
    else
      (* T is the root of the red-black tree *)
      if NodeType(T) = 4 then (* Assume NodeType returns 4 for a four-node *)
        SplitRoot(T)
      endif;
      P := T;
      Parent := NULL;    (* Parent is parent of P *)
      Done := false;
      while not Done do (* Descend in tree looking for a match with NewData
                           or for a leaf where NewData can be inserted. Any
                           4-nodes encountered along the way are split in a
                           manner dependent on the structure of its parent *)
        if NodeType(P) = 4 then (* Assume NodeType returns 4 for four-node *)
          if NodeType(Parent) = 2 then (* Assume NodeType returns 2 for
                                          two-node *)
            SplitChildOf2(P, Parent) ]
```

Example of transformation effected by SplitChildOf2

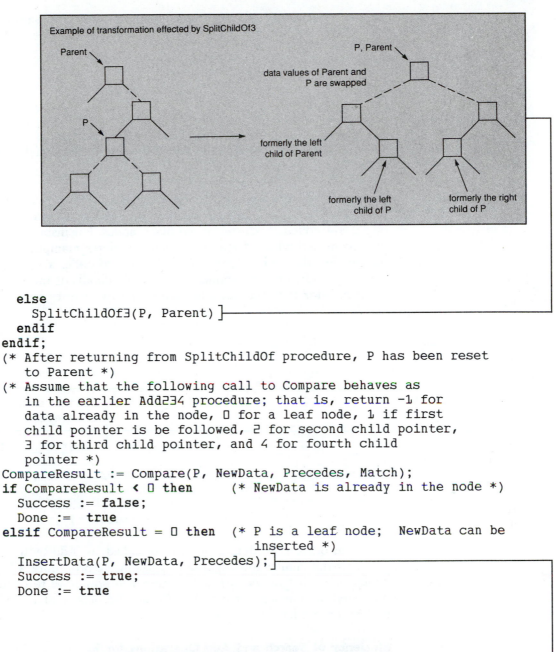

Example of transformation effected by SplitChildOf3

```
      else
         SplitChildOf3(P, Parent)
      endif
   endif;
   (* After returning from SplitChildOf procedure, P has been reset
      to Parent *)
   (* Assume that the following call to Compare behaves as
      in the earlier Add234 procedure; that is, return -1 for
      data already in the node, 0 for a leaf node, 1 if first
      child pointer is be followed, 2 for second child pointer,
      3 for third child pointer, and 4 for fourth child
      pointer *)
   CompareResult := Compare(P, NewData, Precedes, Match);
   if CompareResult < 0 then     (* NewData is already in the node *)
      Success := false;
      Done := true
   elsif CompareResult = 0 then   (* P is a leaf node;  NewData can be
                                         inserted *)
      InsertData(P, NewData, Precedes);
      Success := true;
      Done := true
```

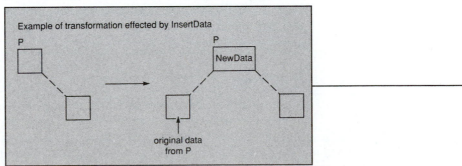

Example of transformation effected by InsertData

```
     else  (* First, second, third, or fourth child--look for another
              node to examine as to whether it is a leaf or has a value
              that matches NewData *)
        AdvancePointers(P, Parent, CompareResult)
     endif
  endwhile
 endif
end AddRedBlack;
```

The AdvancePointers procedure called in AddRedBlack mimics, in red-black logic, the advancing of the P and Parent pointers that occurred in our earlier Add234 procedure. Here we choose to defer the advancing of these pointers to a separate procedure, rather than providing them in the Add procedure itself, because of the complications caused by the mapping of a 2-3-4 node to a cluster of red-black nodes. For instance, the advancing of P to its second child requires different pointer manipulations depending on whether the node referenced by P is a two-node, a right three-node, a left three-node, or a four-node. We leave the details of the AdvancePointers procedure for the exercises and merely specify its pre- and postconditions here.

```
procedure AdvancePointers
 ( given Current,
        Previous: RedBlackTree     (* Pointers to Current and Previous tree
                                      nodes that will be advanced *);
        Next: integer              (* Indicator of which pointer to follow
                                      next--from a 2-3-4 tree perspective.
                                      1 implies first child, 2 second child,
                                      3 third child, and 4 fourth child *);
  return Current,
        Previous: RedBlackTree     (* The Previous pointer points at what was
                                      the current node, and the Current
                                      pointer points at the child indicated
                                      by the Next parameter *) );
```

The other subordinate procedures called by AddRedBlack all follow specifications similar to their counterparts in the procedure Add234. In particular, note that the NodeType function will now have to distinguish right three-nodes from left three-nodes. Again, the details of these subordinate procedures are left for the exercises.

Efficiency of Search and Add Operations for Red-Black Trees Since red-black trees are simply binary-tree representations of 2-3-4 trees, the search and add operations will have $O(\log_2 N)$ efficiency for a tree storing N data items.

Splay Trees

In our analyses of binary search tree operations—in particular searching and insertion—we determined that the use of balancing techniques can reduce the worst-case times for these operations from $O(n)$ to $O(\log_2 n)$ for a tree with n data items. This reduction comes at a price, of course. First, the restructuring algorithms used to keep the trees balanced are somewhat complex. Second, additional storage is required in each node to accommodate the structure of the balanced trees, be it balance factors for AVL trees, multiple information and pointer fields for 2-3 and 2-3-4 trees, or pointer color information for red-black trees.

In this section we describe another type of binary search tree in which a search, insert, or delete operation is carried out in exactly the same manner as for ordinary binary search trees, but in which these operations are followed by *splays*, which are sequences of rotations (called *splay rotations*) about nodes located between a given node and the tree's root. Their purpose is to move this given node—typically, one just accessed or one just inserted—to the root of the tree. At the same time the tree is restructured along the path from the root to the given node in such a way that, not only does the tree remain a binary search tree, but some of the nodes along this path may be moved closer to the root.

As we shall see, splay trees exchange the comparatively complex readjustments needed to maintain height-balanced binary search trees for simpler rotations. Although they may leave the tree with a suboptimal overall structure for carrying out efficient search and insertion operations, splay rotations readjust portions of the tree to improve the efficiency of future operations in those regions.

The rationale behind splay trees is that, in situations where a sequence of tree operations exhibits a phenomenon known as *locality of reference*, the time spent performing a splay rotation will be compensated for by improved performance in future operations involving the same data element. Locality of reference is exhibited when the references to data elements in a sequence of operations seems to favor *a small subset* of the data elements being referenced. Moreover, membership in this favored set *may change gradually* as one advances through the sequence of operations. In performing a splay after accessing or inserting a data element, one is gambling that this same element will be frequently referenced in the near future. If that is the case, the additional time taken to move the element to the root and readjust the tree will in the long run become less detrimental because of the improved future access times. Thus, over the entire sequence of operations, the self-adjusting structure of the splay tree produces an overall efficient performance.

In our discussion of splay rotations and insertions into splay trees, we shall assume the following type definitions:

```
type
  SplayData: (* The type of data used in the Info field
               of each SplayNode *);
  SplayTree: pointer to SplayNode;
  SplayNode: record
               Info: SplayData;
               RightChild: SplayTree;
               LeftChild: SplayTree;
               Parent: SplayTree
             endrecord;
```

The inclusion of the Parent pointer in a splay node will assist us in readjusting the tree along the path backward from a given node to the tree's root.

We describe six types of splay rotations, each of which is designed to move a given node, T, to the root of a particular subtree. Successive rotations will then enable T to be advanced to the root of the entire splay tree.

A. The first type of splay rotation, known as an *L rotation*, will be used when node T is a left child of the root of the splay tree; it will make T the root.

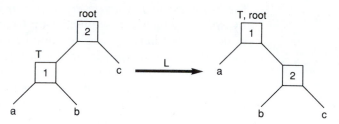

In our implementation, the L rotation will be performed via the following sequence of pointer transfers:

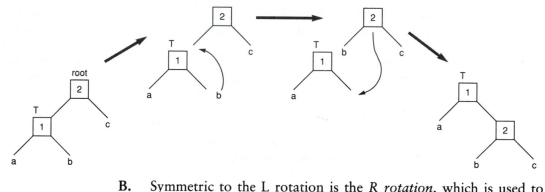

B. Symmetric to the L rotation is the *R rotation*, which is used to move the right child of the tree's root so that it becomes the new root.

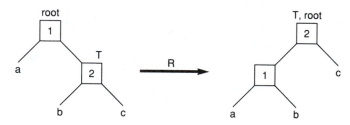

Its implementation will be similar to that of the L rotation:

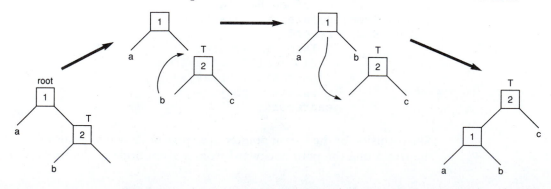

C.   The next rotation is the first of the double rotations. All are intended to move a given node T two levels higher in the tree. The rotation we show here is known as an *LL rotation* because the given node is the left child of the left child of the node whose position it will assume.

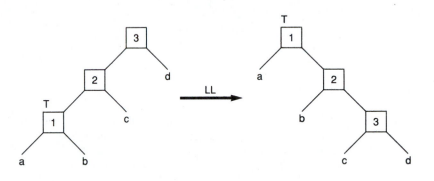

Its implementation will be carried out via the following sequence of pointer transfers:

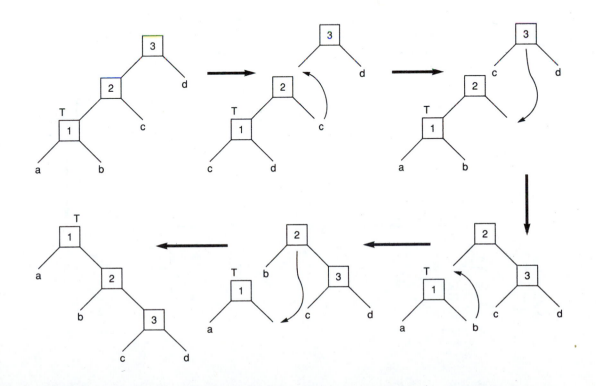

D. Symmetric to the LL rotation is the *RR rotation.*

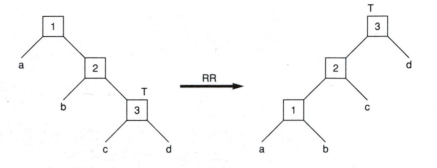

Its implementation is illustrated by the following diagram:

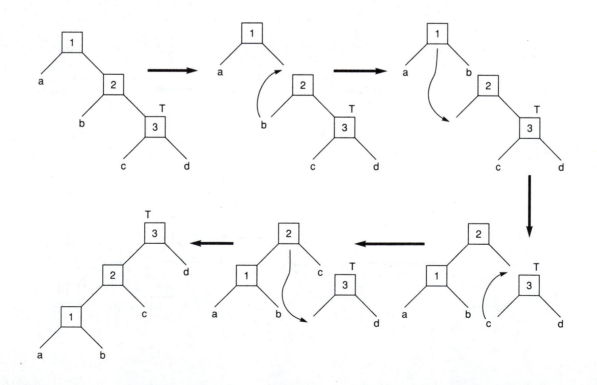

E. Our next rotation is the first of the two "zig-zag" rotations, and is labeled the *LR rotation*.

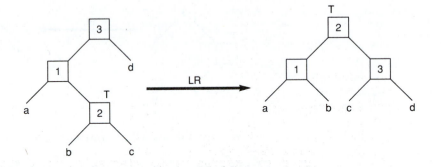

Its implementation, more complex than the others, can be illustrated as follows:

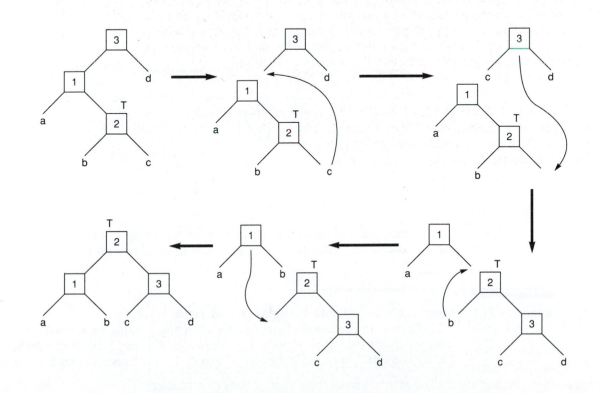

F.   Our last rotation is the second of the "zig-zag" rotations, the *RL rotation.*

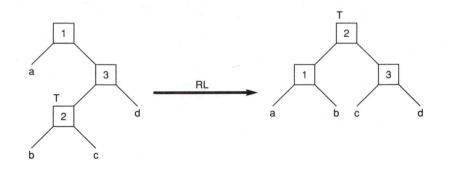

Its implementation is, of course, similar to that of the LR rotation:

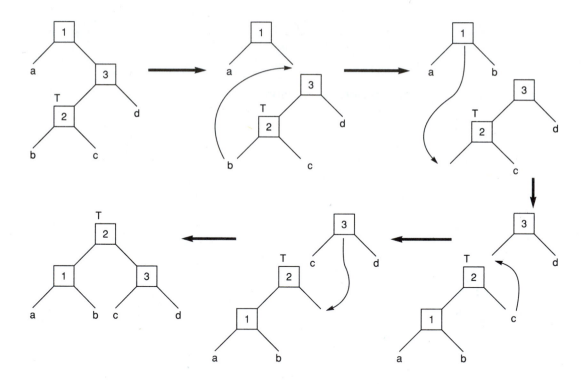

Before proceeding to the algorithms for searching a splay tree or inserting a node in one, we illustrate the behavior of a splay with some examples.

Example 11.5   Insert the value 55 into the splay tree of Figure 11.9.

Following the usual algorithm for inserting a value in a binary search tree, we insert the value in node T as shown in Figure 11.10. Performing an LR rotation at T, we obtain the tree of Figure 11.11. Executing an R rotation

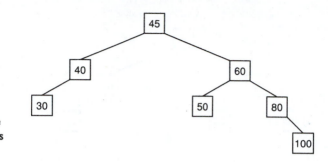

FIGURE 11.9
Tree to be used for illustrating splay rotations in Example 11.5. The value 55 will be inserted into this splay tree.

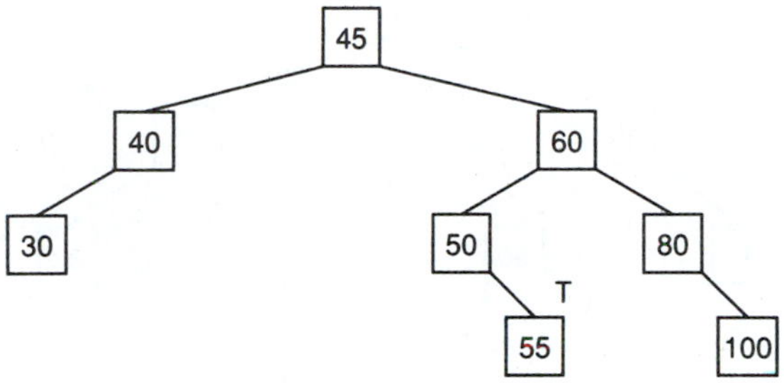

FIGURE 11.10
Splay tree of Figure 11.9 with the value 55 inserted into node T. The splay rotations have not yet been performed.

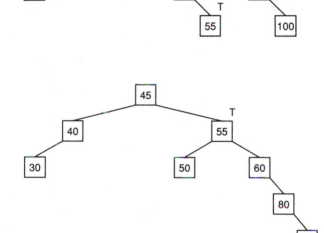

FIGURE 11.11
Splay tree of Figure 11.10 following an LR rotation at node T.

at T will then move 55 to the root, completing our splay and giving us the tree of Figure 11.12.

Example 11.6   Insert the value 90 into the splay tree of Figure 11.12.

Again following the algorithm for inserting a value in a binary search tree, we insert the value 90 into node T as shown in Figure 11.13. Executing an RL rotation at T, we obtain the tree of Figure 11.14. Following this with an RR rotation will move T to the root of the tree. The final tree is shown in Figure 11.15.

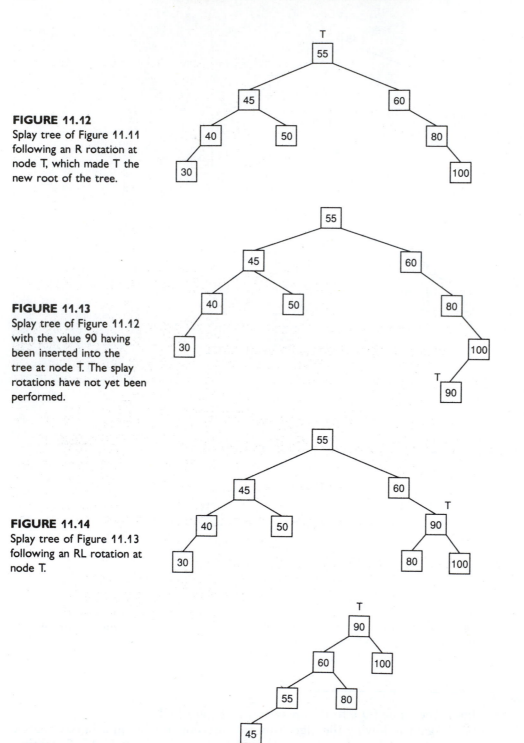

FIGURE 11.12
Splay tree of Figure 11.11 following an R rotation at node T, which made T the new root of the tree.

FIGURE 11.13
Splay tree of Figure 11.12 with the value 90 having been inserted into the tree at node T. The splay rotations have not yet been performed.

FIGURE 11.14
Splay tree of Figure 11.13 following an RL rotation at node T.

FIGURE 11.15
Splay tree of Figure 11.14 following an RR rotation at node T, which made T the new root of the tree.

We now give PSEUDO code for implementing a splay, as well as the code for searching a splay tree and for inserting a node in a splay tree. The PerformSplay procedure invokes a subordinate procedure for each of the six possible rotations. The details of these subordinate procedures are left for the exercises.

```
type
   SplayData: (* The type of data used in the Info field of each SplayNode *);
   SplayTree: pointer to SplayNode;
   SplayNode: record
                  Info: SplayData;
                  RightChild: SplayTree;
                  LeftChild: SplayTree;
                  Parent: SplayTree
              endrecord;
   Comparison: function (* The signature of a function that determines the
                            ordering of the tree *)
                  ( given Item1, Item2: SplayData (* Two data items to be
                                                     compared *);
                    return: boolean          (* true if Item1 is to be
                                                 considered as preceding
                                                 Item2 in ordering for
                                                 the tree; false
                                                 otherwise *) );
   MatchCriterion: function (* The signature of a function that determines
                               whether two tree data items match each other *)
                      ( given Target,
                              AnyData: SplayData (* Two data items, with Target
                                                    containing data to be
                                                    matched in some sense as
                                                    determined by Match
                                                    function *);
                        return: boolean         (* true if Target and AnyData
                                                    satisfy the Match
                                                    criterion *) );
procedure PerformSplay
   ( given Root: SplayTree    (* Pointer to the root of a splay tree *);
           Node: SplayTree    (* Pointer to node at which to perform the
                                  splay *);
     return Root: SplayTree   (* A sequence of splay rotations is performed on
                                  tree referenced by Root until Node has been
                                  moved to the root of the tree *) );
   var
      GP, P: SplayTree;
      Done: Boolean;

   start PerformSplay
      Done := false;
      while not Done do
        if (Node = NULL) or (Node = Root) then
          Done := true
        else
          P := Ref(Node).Parent;
          GP := Ref(P).Parent;
```

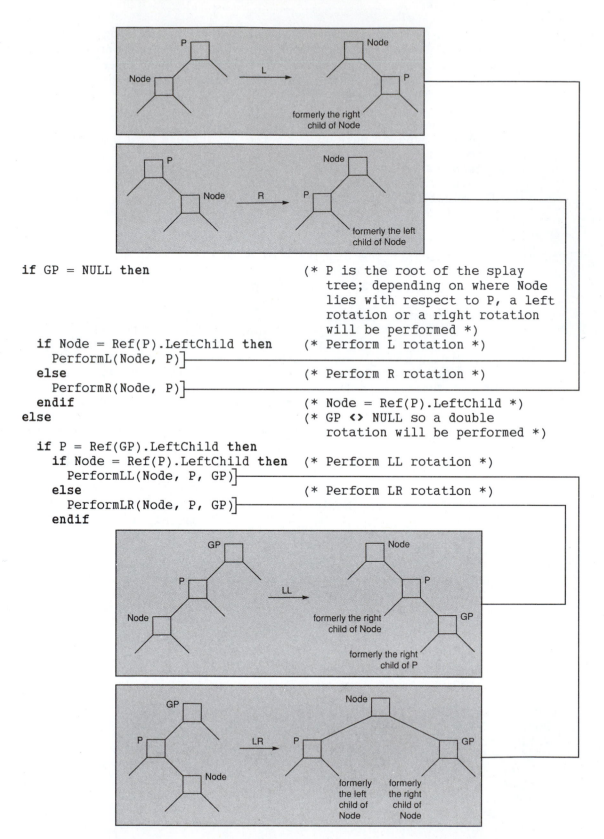

```
if GP = NULL then                          (* P is the root of the splay
                                              tree; depending on where Node
                                              lies with respect to P, a left
                                              rotation or a right rotation
                                              will be performed *)
  if Node = Ref(P).LeftChild then          (* Perform L rotation *)
    PerformL(Node, P)
  else                                     (* Perform R rotation *)
    PerformR(Node, P)
  endif                                    (* Node = Ref(P).LeftChild *)
else                                       (* GP <> NULL so a double
                                              rotation will be performed *)

  if P = Ref(GP).LeftChild then
    if Node = Ref(P).LeftChild then        (* Perform LL rotation *)
      PerformLL(Node, P, GP)
    else                                   (* Perform LR rotation *)
      PerformLR(Node, P, GP)
    endif
```

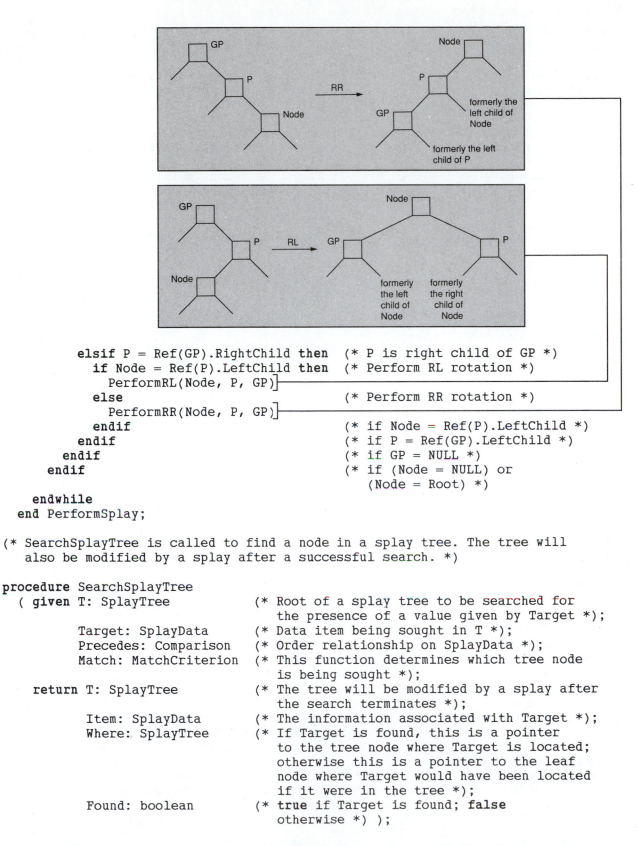

```
        elsif P = Ref(GP).RightChild then  (* P is right child of GP *)
          if Node = Ref(P).LeftChild then  (* Perform RL rotation *)
            PerformRL(Node, P, GP)
          else                             (* Perform RR rotation *)
            PerformRR(Node, P, GP)
          endif                            (* if Node = Ref(P).LeftChild *)
        endif                              (* if P = Ref(GP).LeftChild *)
      endif                                (* if GP = NULL *)
    endif                                  (* if (Node = NULL) or
                                              (Node = Root) *)

  endwhile
end PerformSplay;
```

(* SearchSplayTree is called to find a node in a splay tree. The tree will
   also be modified by a splay after a successful search. *)

```
procedure SearchSplayTree
  ( given T: SplayTree          (* Root of a splay tree to be searched for
                                   the presence of a value given by Target *);
         Target: SplayData      (* Data item being sought in T *);
         Precedes: Comparison   (* Order relationship on SplayData *);
         Match: MatchCriterion  (* This function determines which tree node
                                   is being sought *);
    return T: SplayTree         (* The tree will be modified by a splay after
                                   the search terminates *);
         Item: SplayData        (* The information associated with Target *);
         Where: SplayTree       (* If Target is found, this is a pointer
                                   to the tree node where Target is located;
                                   otherwise this is a pointer to the leaf
                                   node where Target would have been located
                                   if it were in the tree *);
         Found: boolean         (* true if Target is found; false
                                   otherwise *) );
```

```
var
  SearchLoc: SplayTree;

procedure SearchForNode            (* Subordinate to SearchSplayTree *)
  ( given Current: SplayTree       (* Pointer to a current tree node *);
          Parent: SplayTree        (* Parent node of Current *);
          Target: SplayData        (* Target value to find *);
          Precedes: Comparison     (* Order relationship on SplayData *);
          Match:MatchCriterion     (* This function determines which tree node
                                      is being sought *);
    return Where: SplayTree        (* If Target is found, this is a pointer to
                                      the tree node where Target is located; if
                                      Current is NULL, this will point to
                                      the parent of the current node; otherwise,
                                      if the search can continue, Where is
                                      determined by a recursive call made with
                                      the appropriate subtree *);
           Found: boolean          (* true if Target found; false
                                      otherwise *) );

  start SearchForNode
    if Current = NULL then
      Where := Parent;
      Found := false
    else
      if Match(Target, Ref(Current).Info) then
        Where := Current;
        Found := false
      else
        if Precedes(Target, Ref(Current).Info) then
          SearchForNode(Ref(Current).LeftChild, Current, Target, Precedes,
                    Match, Where, Found)
        else
          SearchForNode(Ref(Current).RightChild, Current, Target, Precedes,
                    Match, Where, Found)
        endif
      endif
    endif
  end SearchForNode;

start SearchSplayTree
  SearchForNode(T, NULL, Target, Precedes, Match, SearchLoc, Found);
  if Found then
    PerformSplay(T, SearchLoc)
  endif
end SearchSplayTree;

(* The procedure AddSplayNode is called to add a data item to the
   splay tree. It relies on a subordinate procedure InsertNode *)

procedure AddSplayNode
  ( given Root: SplayTree          (* A pointer to a splay tree);
          NewData: SplayData       (* Value to be inserted in the splay tree
                                      referenced by Root *);
```

```
            Precedes: Comparison    (* Order relationship on SplayData *);
            Match: MatchCriterion   (* This function determines which tree node
                                       is being sought *);
    return Root: SplayTree          (* Will have a node with NewData added to the
                                       tree, preserving the ordering structure.
                                       After the new data is inserted, or if it
                                       is already in the tree, a splay will be
                                       performed from Root to the node containing
                                       NewData *) );

var
  InsertLoc: SplayTree;

procedure InsertNode              (* Subordinate to AddSplayNode *)
  ( given T: SplayTree            (* Pointer to current node in tree T.
                                     Initially T is the root of a splay
                                     tree *);

        Parent: SplayTree         (* Pointer to the parent of T; will be NULL
                                     if T is the root of a tree *);
        NewData: SplayData        (* Item to be inserted *);
        Precedes: Comparison      (* Order relationship on SplayData *);
        Match: MatchCriterion     (* This function determines which tree node
                                     is being sought *);
    return T: SplayTree           (* Will be recursively searched for the
                                     appropriate spot to insert NewData.
                                     When that spot is found, NewData will
                                     be inserted into the tree *);

        Where: SplayTree          (* Pointer to newly created node with data
                                     item in it. If NewData was already in
                                     the tree, Where points to this spot *) );

  var
    Node: SplayTree;

  start InsertNode
    if T = NULL then (* Add a new node *)
      GetNode(Node);
      Ref(Node).LeftChild := NULL;
      Ref(Node).RightChild := NULL;
      Ref(Node).Info := NewData;
      Ref(Node).Parent := Parent;
      Where := Node;
      T := Node
    elsif Match(NewData, Ref(T).Info) then
      Where := T
    elsif Precedes(NewData, Ref(T)Info) then (* Move down the list *)
      InsertNode(Ref(T).LeftChild, T, NewData, Precedes, Match, Where)
    else
      InsertNode(Ref(T).RightChild, T, NewData, Precedes, Match, Where)
    endif
  end InsertNode;

start AddSplayNode
  InsertNode(Root, NULL , NewData, Precedes, Match, InsertLoc);
  PerformSplay(Root, InsertLoc)
end AddSplayNode;
```

Analysis of Splay Trees Since the rationale behind a splay tree is that it performs a "localized" restructuring designed to improve the efficiency of future operations in the tree rather than improve the worst-case time per operation, it is important to analyze its efficiency with respect to sequences of operations. Using a method known as amortized complexity, Sleator and Tarjan show that splay trees are as efficient as balanced trees when total running time for a sequence of operations is the measure of interest (see D. D. Sleator, and R. E. Tarjan, "Self-Adjusting Binary Search Trees," *Journal of the ACM,* 32, July 1985, pp. 652–686).

Exercises 11.1

1. Repeat Exercise 1 in Section 7.3 for 2-3-4 trees.

2. Repeat Exercise 2 in Section 7.3 for 2-3-4 trees.

3. Repeat Exercise 3 in Section 7.3 for 2-3-4 trees.

4. Complete the development of modules for 2-3-4 trees by writing SplitRoot, SplitChildOf2, SplitChildOf3, NodeType, InsertData, LeafNode, and Compare. Recall that detailed specifications of these modules were given in our discussion of the Add algorithm for 2-3-4 trees.

5. Write a PSEUDO procedure to delete an item from an ordered list implemented with a 2-3-4 tree.

6. Repeat Exercise 1 in Section 7.3 for red-black trees.

7. Repeat Exercise 2 in Section 7.3 for red-black trees.

8. Repeat Exercise 3 in Section 7.3 for red-black trees.

9. Complete the development of modules for red-black trees by writing SplitRoot, SplitChildOf2, SplitChildOf3, NodeType, InsertData, LeafNode, Compare, and AdvancePointers. Specifications for these modules were given in our discussion of the Add algorithm for red-black trees.

10. Write a PSEUDO procedure to delete an item from an ordered list implemented using a red-black tree.

11. If, instead of using LeftBlack and RightBlack fields for red-black nodes, we use a field to represent the color of the pointer from the parent of a node (if any) to the node, we need only use one color field in a node. Write the corresponding AddRedBlack procedure for this alternative structure.

12. Repeat Exercise 1 in Section 7.3 for splay trees.

13. Repeat Exercise 2 in Section 7.3 for splay trees.

14. Repeat Exercise 3 in Section 7.3 for splay trees.

15. Find a sequence of insertions that will lead to the splay tree in Figure 11.9.

16. Complete the development of the PerformSplay procedure by writing the subordinate procedures PerformL, PerformR, PerformLL, PerformLR, PerformRL, and PerformRR that carry out the six possible splay rotations.

17. Write a PSEUDO procedure to delete an item from an ordered list implemented with a splay tree.

11.2 DENSITY-DEPENDENT SEARCH TECHNIQUES

In an ideal data-processing world, all identifying keys such as product codes, Social Security numbers, and so on would start at 1 and follow in sequence thereafter. Then, in any given list, we would merely store the key and its associated data at the position that matched the key. The search efficiency for any key in such a list would be one access to the list. Unfortunately, in the real world users desire keys that consist of more meaningful characters, such as names, addresses, region codes, and so on. For instance, it may be that in an inventory-control application, product codes are numbered in sequence beginning with 10,000 instead of 1. A moment's reflection should indicate that this is still a highly desirable situation since, given a key, we need merely locate the key at position (KeyValue − 9999) in the list, and we still have a search efficiency of 1. What we have done here is to define what is known as a key-to-address transformation, or *hashing function*. The idea behind a hashing function is that it acts upon a given key in such a way as to return the relative position in the list at which we expect to find the key.

Most hashing functions are not as straightforward as the preceding one and present some additional complications. Suppose we use the following hashing function:

$$\text{Hash(KeyValue)} = (\text{KeyValue } \textbf{mod } 4) + 1$$

Then the set of keys 3, 5, 8, and 10 will be scattered as illustrated here:

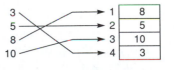

However, if we happen to have 3, 4, 8, and 10 as keys instead of 3, 5, 8, and 10, a problem arises: 4 and 8 hash to the same position. They are said to be *synonyms*, and the result is termed a *collision*. In this situation, there is a collision at position 1, as shown in the following illustration.

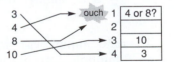

Clearly, one of the goals of the hashing functions we develop should be to reduce the number of collisions as much as possible.

The Construction of Hashing Functions

The business of developing hashing functions can be quite intriguing. The essential idea is to build a mathematical black box that will take a key value as input and issue as output the position in the list where that key value should be located. This position should have a minimal probability of colliding with the position that would be produced for any different key. In addition, the black box we create must ensure that a given key will always produce the same position as output. You should begin to note a similarity between some of the properties possessed by a good hashing function and a good *random number generator* such as that used in our simulation of users sharing a resource in an operating system environment (Section 4.4). Indeed, list access by means of a hashing function is sometimes called *randomized storage*, and the first type of hashing function we discuss makes direct use of a random number generator.

Method 1: Use of a Random Number Generator   Many high-level languages provide a random number generator to produce random sequences of real or integer values. If one is not provided, you may easily write one using a method such as that described in Appendix A. (For readable discussions of other methods of random number generation see Chapter 7 of *Numerical Recipes* by William H. Press, Brian P. Flannery, Saul A. Teukolsky. and William T. Vetterling, Cambridge, England: Cambridge University Press, 1986.) Typically, these methods rely on having a global seed to start the process of generating random numbers. Computations done on this seed produce the random number. At the same time, the computations alter the value of the seed so that the next time the random number generator is called, a different random number will almost surely be produced.

    In typical applications of random number generation, you need merely initialize the seed to some arbitrary value to start the random sequence. Once the seed is supplied, the random sequence is completely determined. If you have access to a system procedure that returns the current time, day, month, and year, this procedure can be called to initialize the seed in a fashion that ensures there is only a very small likelihood of generating the same random sequence twice.

    How does all of this relate to hashing? For a hashing application, we must slightly alter the definition of our random number generator so that the seed is supplied as a value parameter. Then we supply the values of search keys as the seeds. The nature of the random number algorithm ensures that

- Each time the same key is passed to the function, the same random value will be returned.
- It is unlikely that two different keys will yield the same random value.

The random number that is correspondingly produced can then be appropriately multiplied, truncated, and shifted to produce a hash value within the range of valid positions.

Method 2: Folding In situations where the key to be positioned is not a pure integer, some preliminary work may be required to translate it into a usable form. Take, for instance, the case of a Social Security number such as 387-58-1505. Viewed as one integer, this would cause overflow on many machines. By a method known as *shift folding*, however, this Social Security number would be viewed as three separate numbers to be added: 387 + 58 + 1505, producing the result 1950. This result could be regarded as either the hash position itself or, more likely, as a pure integer that could be further acted upon by Method 1 or 4 to produce a final hash position in the desired range.

Another often-used folding technique is called *boundary folding*. The idea behind boundary folding is that, at the boundaries between the numbers making up the key under consideration, every other number is reversed before being accumulated into the total. Applying this method to our Social Security number example, we would have 387 + 85 (58 reversed) + 1505, yielding a result of 1977. Clearly, the two methods do not differ by much, and a choice between them must often be made on the basis of experimentation to determine which will produce more scattered results for a given application.

Regardless of whether shift or boundary folding is used, one of the great advantages of the folding method is its ability to transform noninteger keys into an integer suitable for further hashing action. For keys such as names, which contain alphabetic characters, the type of folding just illustrated may be done by translating characters into their ASCII (or other appropriate) codes.

Method 3: Digit or Character Extraction In certain situations, a given key value may contain specific characters that are likely to bias any hash value arising from the key. The idea in *digit* or *character extraction* is to remove such digits or characters before using the result as a final hash value or passing it on to be further transformed by another method. For instance, a company may choose to identify the various products it manufactures by using a nine-character code that always contains either an A or a B in the first position and either a 1 or a 0 in the fourth position, with the rest of the characters in the code tending to occur in less predictable fashion. Character extraction would remove the biased first and fourth characters, leaving a seven-character result to pass on for further processing.

Method 4: Division Remainder Technique All hashing presupposes a given range of positions that can be valid outputs of the hash function. In the remainder of this section, we assume the existence of a global constant, TableSize, which represents the upper limit of our hashing function. That is, the function should produce values between 1 and TableSize. It should then be evident that

$$Hash(KeyValue) = (KeyValue \bmod TableSize) + 1$$

is a valid hashing function for integer KeyValue.

To begin examining criteria for choosing an appropriate TableSize, we load the keys 41, 58, 12, 92, 50, and 91 into a list with TableSize = 15. Table 11.1 shows the results. In this table, zeros are used to denote empty positions. However, if we keep TableSize the same and try to load the keys 10, 20, 30, 40, 50, 60, and 70, we have many collisions, as shown in Table

Position	Key
1	0
2	91
3	92
4	0
5	0
6	50
7	0
8	0
9	0
10	0
11	0
12	41
13	12
14	58
15	0

TABLE 11.1
Array with TableSize 15 loaded using a division remainder hashing function.

Position	Key	
1	30	← 60 (collision)
2	0	
3	0	
4	0	
5	0	
6	20	← 50 (collision)
7	0	
8	0	
9	0	
10	0	
11	10	← 40 ← 70 (collision)
12	0	
13	0	
14	0	
15	0	

TABLE 11.2
Array from Table 11.1, loaded with other values and having several collisions.

11.2. With this choice of TableSize, a different set of keys causes disastrous results even though the list seemingly has plenty of room available. On the other hand, if we choose TableSize to be 11, we have a list with considerably less room but no collisions. Table 11.3 indicates the hashing positions when the same set of keys is acted upon by 11 instead of by 15.

Although these examples are far from conclusive, they suggest that choosing a prime number for TableSize may produce a more desirable hashing function. You will continue to explore this question in the Exercises 11.2. Also, in Section 11.5 we will investigate more deeply the issue of how to choose TableSize to produce an optimal hashing function for keys that are strings. Apart from considerations of whether or not TableSize should be prime, it is clear that the nature of a particular application may dictate against the choice of certain TableSize values. For instance, in a situation where the rightmost digits of key values happen to follow certain recurring patterns, it would be unwise to choose a power of 10 for TableSize. (Why?)

Despite such TableSize cautions, no hashing function can preclude the possibility of collisions; it can only make them less likely. You should be able quickly to imagine a key value that will produce a collision for the hashing function used in determining the list of Table 11.3. Notice that, as the list becomes more full, the probability that collisions will occur increases. Hence,

Position	Key
1	0
2	0
3	0
4	0
5	70
6	60
7	50
8	40
9	30
10	20
11	10

TABLE 11.3
Array with same keys as Table 11.2 but with TableSize 11. No collision results.

when using hashing as a search strategy, one must be willing to waste some positions in the list; otherwise search efficiency will drastically deteriorate. How much space to waste is an interesting question that we will discuss later in this section. Further, since no hashing function can eliminate collisions, we must be prepared to handle them when they occur.

The Keyed Collection ADT

Before discussing collision-processing strategies, we should put hashing into the context of abstract data types. Because hashing scatters keys within the search table, hashing is not *by itself* an appropriate implementation technique for the ordered list ADT introduced in Chapter 3. The traverse operation provided as part of the interface to the list ADT assumes that the list will be processed in order; the randomized placement of keys by a good hashing function is directly opposed to this requirement. Consequently, we will define a new ADT—the keyed collection—that is more directly suited to an implementation by hashing.

• **Definition:** A *keyed collection* is an unordered group of records, each of which has one field designated as a *key field*, along with other fields that are grouped as a subrecord. Records within the collection are identified by the value of their key field. Hence a record within a keyed collection may be viewed as follows:

```
type
  KCRecord: record
          Key: KeyType (* A data type appropriate for identifying
                          the record *);
          OtherData:   (* The data associated with a
                          particular key *)
        end;
```

The operations provided with a keyed collection are defined by the following PSEUDO pre- and postconditions.

```
procedure Create
  ( given KC: KeyedCollection    (* An arbitrary keyed collection variable
                                    in an unknown state *)
    return KC: KeyedCollection   (* KC as an initialized empty keyed
                                    collection *) );
procedure Destroy
  ( given KC: KeyedCollection    (* An arbitrary keyed collection variable
                                    that has been acted upon by Create and
                                    other operations *);
    return KC: KeyedCollection   (* KC in unknown state, with any storage
                                    dynamically allocated for KC now available
                                    for future invocation of Create *) );
procedure Add
  ( given KC: KeyedCollection    (* An arbitrary keyed collection variable
                                    previously acted upon by Create and,
                                    possibly, other operations *);
         Item: KCRecord          (* A data item to be added to KC *);
    return KC: KeyedCollection   (* KC with Item added if possible, that is, if
                                    there is room in the collection and if no
                                    item already exists in the collection with
                                    the same key value. KC is returned
                                    unchanged if Item could not be added to the
                                    collection *);
        Success: boolean         (* Set to true if Item successfully added to
                                    KC; set to false if Item could not be
                                    added *) );
procedure Delete
  ( given KC: KeyedCollection    (* An arbitrary keyed collection variable
                                    previously acted upon by Create and,
                                    possibly, other operations *);
        Target: KeyType          (* Target key being sought for deletion *);
    return KC: KeyedCollection   (* KC has record associated with Target
                                    removed if possible, that is, if such a
                                    record existed in the collection. KC is
                                    returned unchanged if Target could not be
                                    found in the collection *);
        Success: boolean         (* false if no item in the collection matched
                                    Target; true otherwise *) );
procedure Retrieve
  ( given KC: KeyedCollection    (* An arbitrary keyed collection previously
                                    acted upon by Create and, possibly other
                                    operations *);
        Target: KeyType          (* Target key being sought for retrieval of
                                    information *);
    return Item: KCRecord        (* The item in the collection associated with
                                    the target key value if it can be found.
                                    If it can't be found, Item is
                                    unreliable *) );
        Success: boolean         (* false if an item associated with Target
                                    cannot be found in the collection; true
                                    otherwise *) );
```

Note that the keyed collection ADT could be considered a restricted form of the list ADT introduced in Chapter 3. We have add, delete, and retrieve operations similar to the list ADT; however, the traverse operation furnished with lists is not part of the keyed collection ADT. This makes the keyed collection an appropriate ADT for information retrieval systems in which individual records must be accessed frequently (and quickly) but the entire collection of records must never be processed sequentially. It should be evident that hashing is potentially an ideal way to implement a keyed collection—once we resolve what to do with the problem of collisions.

Collision Processing—Implementation of a Keyed Collection by Hashing

The essential problem in collision processing is to develop an algorithm that will position a key in a table when the position dictated by the hashing function itself is already occupied. Ideally, this algorithm should minimize the possibility of future collisions; that is, the problem key should be located at a position that is not likely to be the hashed position of a future key.

However, the nature of hashing makes this latter criterion difficult to meet with any degree of certainty, since a good hashing function does not allow prediction of where future keys are likely to be placed. We shall discuss five methods of collision processing: linear, quadratic, rehashing, linked, and buckets. In all of the methods it will be necessary to detect when a given list position is not occupied. To signify this, we use a global constant Empty to distinguish unoccupied positions. As you read, give some thought to the question of how the Delete operation could be accomplished in a keyed collection implemented by one of these hashing methods. In particular, will the Empty flag suffice to denote positions that have never been occupied *and* positions previously occupied but now vacant? This question is explored in the Exercises and Programming Problems.

Linear Collision Processing The linear method of resolving collisions is the simplest to implement (and, unfortunately, the least efficient). *Linear collision processing* requires that, when a collision occurs, we proceed down the list in sequential order until a vacant position is found. The key causing the collision is then placed at this first vacant position. If we come to the physical end of our list in the attempt to place the problem key, we merely wrap around to the top of the list and continue looking for a vacant position. For instance, suppose we use the hashing function

$$\text{Hash(KeyValue)} = (\text{KeyValue } \textbf{mod } \text{TableSize}) + 1$$

with TableSize = 7 and attempt to insert the keys 18, 31, 67, 36, 19, and 34. The sequence of lists in Table 11.4 shows the results of these insertions. When a collision occurs at the third insert, it is processed by the linear method; 67 is thus loaded into position 6.

Example 11.7 Suppose that a hashing implementation of a keyed collection has been loaded with data using the linear collision processing strategy illustrated in Table

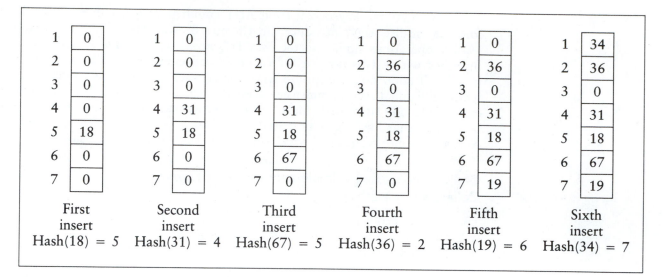

TABLE 11.4   Insertion with linear collision processing.

11.4. Write an implementation of the Retrieve operation *under the assumption that no delete operations will be performed on the collection.*

```
(* Assumptions for the hashing implementation of a keyed collection are
   that we have constants Empty, to flag unoccupied locations in the hash
   table, and TableSize, to establish the maximum possible number of
   entries in the hash table. We also assume the existence of a hashing
   function, Hash, which takes data of type KeyType and returns an
   address between 1 and TableSize *)

type
   KeyedCollection = array [TableSize] of KCRecord;

procedure Retrieve
   ( given KC: KeyedCollection   (* An arbitrary keyed collection previously
                                    acted upon by Create and, possibly, other
                                    operations *);
            Target: KeyType      (* Target key being sought for retrieval of
                                    information *);
     return Item: KCRecord       (* The item in the collection associated
                                    with the target key value if it can be
                                    found. If it can't be found, Item is
                                    unreliable *);
            Success: boolean     (* false if an item associated with Target
                                    cannot be found in the collection; true
                                    otherwise *) );
   var
     K, J: integer;
     Traversed: boolean;

   start Retrieve
     Success := false;
     Traversed := false;       (* Toggled to true if entire table is
                                  traversed *)
```

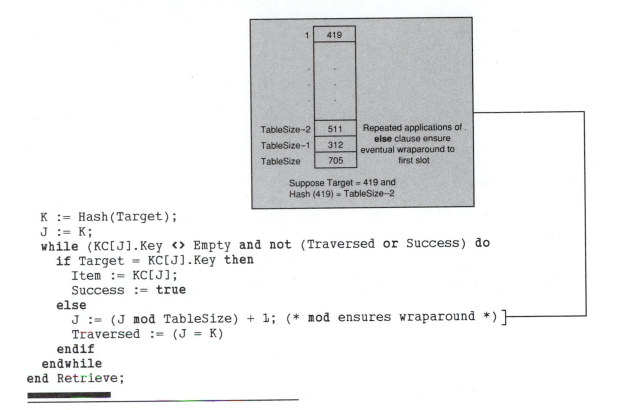

```
K := Hash(Target);
J := K;
while (KC[J].Key <> Empty and not (Traversed or Success) do
  if Target = KC[J].Key then
    Item := KC[J];
    Success := true
  else
    J := (J mod TableSize) + 1; (* mod ensures wraparound *)
    Traversed := (J = K)
  endif
endwhile
end Retrieve;
```

Several remarks are in order concerning the procedure in Example 11.7. First, we emphasize that the procedure as it stands would not handle keyed collection processing in which it was necessary to process deletions. You will explore the problem of deletions from a keyed collection maintained by hashing in greater detail in the Exercises and Programming Problems.

Second, note that the linear method is not without its flaws. In particular, it is prone to a problem of *clustering* (or *primary clustering*). Clustering occurs when a collision resolution strategy relocates keys that have a collision at the same initial hashing position to the same region (known as a *cluster*) within the storage space. This usually leads to further collisions with relocated values and further relocations until everything gets resolved. With linear resolution the clustering problem becomes compounded because as one cluster expands it can run into another cluster, immediately creating a larger cluster. This one big cluster ultimately causes collision resolutions from both initial hashing points to be drawn out longer than they would otherwise be. The occurrence of such clustering phenomena brought on by linear collision resolution is shown in Figure 11.16.

Efficiency Considerations for Linear Hashing A final point to note about the linear hashing method is its search efficiency. Knuth has shown that the average number of list accesses for a successful search using the linear method is

$$\left(\frac{1}{2}\right)\left(1 + \frac{1}{1 - D}\right)$$

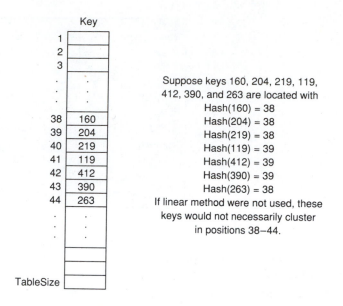

FIGURE 11.16

Clustering due to linear collision processing. As the primary clusters from locations 38 and 39 merge, the value 263 is located even farther from the initial hash point than dictated by just the collisions at location 38.

where

$$D = \frac{\text{Number of currently active records}}{\text{TableSize}}$$

(See Donald E. Knuth, *Searching and Sorting*, Vol. 3 of *The Art of Computer Programming*, Menlo Park, CA: Addison-Wesley, 1973.) An interesting fact about this search efficiency is that it is not solely dependent on the number of records currently in the list, but rather on the *density ratio (D)* of the number of records currently in the list to the total record space available. In other words, no matter how many records there are, a highly efficient result can be obtained if one is willing to waste enough vacant records. This is what is meant by a *density-dependent search technique*. In the case of searching for a key that cannot be found, Knuth's results indicate that the average search efficiency will be

$$\left(\frac{1}{2}\right)\left(1 + \frac{1}{(1-D)^2}\right)$$

Table 11.5 illustrates the effectiveness of linear collision resolution by showing the computed efficiencies for a few strategic values of D.

D	Efficiency for successful search (number of accesses)	Efficiency for unsuccessful search (number of accesses)
0.10	1.06	1.18
0.50	1.50	2.50
0.75	2.50	8.50
0.90	5.50	50.50

TABLE 11.5

Average search efficiency for linear collision processing.

Quadratic and Rehashing Methods of Collision Processing Both the quadratic and rehashing collision-processing methods attempt to correct the problems of primary clustering caused by linear collision resolution. The *quadratic method* examines locations whose distance (excluding the effects of any wraparound) from the initial collision point increases as the square of the number of previous locations tried. Thus, suppose that a key value initially hashes to position K and a collision results. Then, on its first attempt to resolve the collision, the quadratic algorithm attempts to place the key at position $K + 1^2$. Then, if a second attempt is necessary to resolve the collision, position $K + 2^2$ is probed. In general, the Rth attempt to resolve the collision probes position $K + R^2$. Each of these values may have to be adjusted, however, if it extends beyond the upper limit of the hash table and needs to be wrapped around to the table's lower end. By leaving increasingly larger gaps between successive relocation positions, quadratic collision processing prevents formation of the contiguous relocation regions that characterizes primary clustering. Figure 11.17 illustrates this type of dispersal. At this point you should verify that if the hashing function

$$\text{Hash}(\text{KeyValue}) = (\text{KeyValue } \mathbf{mod} \text{ TableSize}) + 1$$

is used with TableSize equal to 7, then the quadratic method will locate keys 17, 73, 32, and 80 in positions 4, 5, 6, and 1 respectively.

Although quadratic collision resolution effectively eliminates primary clustering, there is another problem, known as *secondary clustering*, that arises. Note that any two values having a collision at a given location, say K, will subsequently examine the same sequence of alternative locations— $K + 1^2, K + 2^2, K + 3^2, \ldots$—until the collision is resolved. Such a sequence of locations, which is examined by a key that has a collision at location K, is known as a *secondary cluster*. Though not as deleterious to the effectiveness of collision processing as primary clusters (secondary clusters cannot merge to

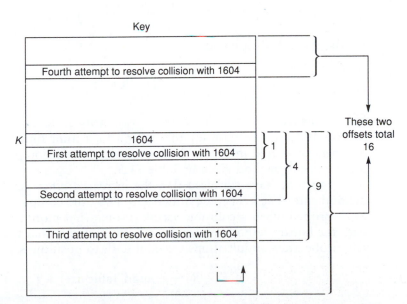

FIGURE 11.17
Quadratic collision processing.

form larger secondary clusters), secondary clustering can generate undesirable sequences of additional collisions before a resolution is attained.

If we want to avoid secondary clustering, it will be necessary to generate different sequences of collision resolution locations for each value that becomes involved in a collision at a given location. Under a collision processing method known as *rehashing*, additional hashing functions are applied to a given key each time a collision occurs. If a collision results from the first hashing function, a second is applied, then a third, and so on, until the key can be successfully placed. If the key exhausts the entire sequence of hashing functions, we could (perhaps prematurely) declare the hash table to be full or resort to linear collision processing from the final hash position. Ideally, the rehashing sequences for each key would have a random pattern that is independent of that of any other key so that no primary or secondary clustering would occur. Unfortunately, this approach appears to be difficult to implement in general, but there is a rehashing scheme, known as *double hashing*, which has been shown by empirical studies to provide behavior that is almost as good (see page 523 of Knuth, *Sorting and Searching*, cited earlier in this section).

The idea behind double hashing is to define a second hashing function, r, that for a given key K, calculates an integer, $r(K)$, that is relatively prime to TableSize. If h is the original hash function, then the entire sequence of table locations to be examined, where L_i is the ith location in the sequence, is given by

$$L_i(K) = (((h(K) + i \times r(K)) - 1) \bmod \text{TableSize}) + 1$$

Efficiency Considerations for the Quadratic and Rehashing Methods
Knuth's results (see *Searching and Sorting*, cited earlier in this section) demonstrate the effectiveness of the rehashing and quadratic methods versus the linear method. For the quadratic method, average search efficiencies improve to

$$1 - \log_e(1 - D) - \frac{D}{2}$$

for the successful case and

$$\frac{1}{1 - D} - D - \log_e(1 - D)$$

for an unsuccessful search, where D is density ratio defined earlier in this section and e is the base for the natural logarithm function. Compare the numbers presented in Table 11.6 for quadratic collision processing to those for the linear method given in Table 11.5.

You may have surmised that the increased efficiency of the quadratic method entails at least some drawbacks. First, the computation of a position to be probed when a collision occurs is somewhat more obscure than it was with the linear method. We leave it for you to verify that the position for the Rth probe after an initial unsuccessful hash to position K is given by

$$[(K + R^2 - 1) \bmod \text{TableSize}] + 1$$

D	Efficiency for successful search (number of accesses)	Efficiency for unsuccessful search (number of accesses)
0.10	1.05	1.11
0.50	1.44	2.19
0.75	2.01	4.64
0.90	2.85	11.40

TABLE 11.6
Average search efficiency for quadratic collision processing.

A more significant problem, however, is that the quadratic method seemingly offers no guarantee that we will try every position in the list before concluding that a given key cannot be inserted. With the linear method, the only way that the insertion could fail is for every position in the list to be occupied. The linear nature of the search, although inefficient, ensured that every position would be checked. However, with the quadratic method applied to the TableSize in Figure 11.18, you can confirm that an initial hash to position 4 will lead to future probing of positions 4, 5, and 8 only; it will never check positions 1, 2, 3, 6, or 7.

Fortunately, a satisfactory answer to the question of what portion of a list will be probed by the quadratic algorithm was provided by Radke for values of TableSize that are prime numbers satisfying certain conditions. Radke's results and their application to the quadratic algorithm are explored in the Exercises at the end of the section. (If you wish to read Radke's results, see C. E. Radke, "The Use of Quadratic Residue Research," *Communications of the ACM*, 13, February 1970, pp. 103–105.)

For rehashing with a random sequence of rehashing locations for each key that are independent from those of other keys we get efficiencies on the order of

$$-\frac{1}{D}\log_e(1 - D)$$

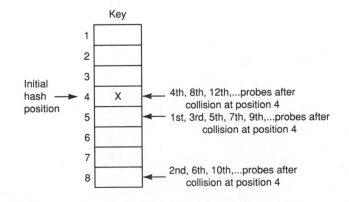

FIGURE 11.18
Quadratic probing after initial hash to 4.

for the successful case and

$$\frac{1}{1-D}$$

for an unsuccessful search. As we noted in our discussion of double hashing, empirical tests indicate that its performances compare favorably with these results. Compare the numbers presented in Table 11.7 for double hashing and (ideal) random rehashing to those in Tables 11.5 and 11.6. Finally, we point out that choosing r in the double hashing scheme so that its values are relatively prime to TableSize ensures that all entries of the table will be tried before determining that a particular key is not in the table or that it cannot be inserted.

Linked Method of Collision Processing The logic of this method completely eliminates the possibility that one collision begets another. It requires a storage area divided horizontally into two regions: a *prime hash area* and an *overflow area*. Each record requires a Link field in addition to the Key and OtherData fields. The constant TableSize is applicable to the prime hash area only. This storage concept is illustrated in Figure 11.19.

D	Efficiency for successful search (number of accesses)	Efficiency for unsuccessful search (number of accesses)
0.10	1.05	1.11
0.50	1.39	2.00
0.75	1.84	4.00
0.90	2.56	10.00

TABLE 11.7
Average search efficiency for collision processing using double hashing, or rehashing.

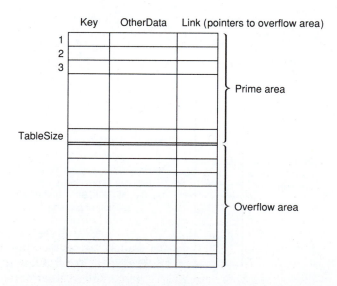

FIGURE 11.19
Storage allocation for linked collision processing.

	Key	Link
1	0	NULL
2	22	8
3	0	NULL
4	31	NULL
5	67	10
6	0	NULL
7	0	NULL
8	36	9
9	29	NULL
10	60	NULL
11	0	NULL
12	0	NULL
13	0	NULL
14	0	NULL
15	0	NULL
16	0	NULL
17	0	NULL

FIGURE 11.20
Loading keys with (KeyValue **mod** 7) + 1 and linked collision procession.

Initially, the hashing function translates keys into the prime hashing area. If a collision occurs, the key is inserted into a linked list with its initial node in the prime area and all following nodes in the overflow area (no dummy header is used). Figure 11.20 shows how this method would load the keys 22, 31, 67, 36, 29, and 60 for TableSize = 7 and hashing function

$$\text{Hash(KeyValue)} = (\text{KeyValue } \textbf{mod} \text{ TableSize}) + 1$$

Example 11.8 Suppose that a hashing implementation of a keyed collection has been loaded with data using the linked collision processing strategy illustrated in Figures 11.19 and 11.20. Write an implementation of the Retrieve operation *under the assumption that no delete operations will be performed on the collection.*

```
(* Assumptions for the hashing implementation of a keyed collection with
   linked collision processing are that we have constants Empty, to flag
   unoccupied locations in the hash table; TableSize, to establish the
   maximum possible number of entries in the prime hash area; OverflowSize,
   to establish the maximum possible number of entries in the overflow
   area; and NULL, to flag the end of a linked list of records. We also
   assume the existence of a hashing function, Hash, which takes data of
   type KeyType and returns an address between 1 and TableSize *)

type
  LinkedRecord: record
                  Data: KCRecord;
                  Link: integer   (* Links are being maintained as integer
                                     pointers to other array locations.
                                     They could also be other abstract
                                     pointer types *)
                endrecord;
  KeyedCollection: array [TableSize + OverflowSize] of LinkedRecord;
```

```
procedure Retrieve
  ( given KC: KeyedCollection  (* An arbitrary keyed collection previously
                                  acted upon by Create and, possibly, other
                                  operations *);
          Target: KeyType      (* Target key being sought for retrieval of
                                  information *);
   return Item: KCRecord        (* The item in the collection associated
                                  with the target key value if it can be
                                  found. If it can't be found, Item is
                                  unreliable *);
          Success: boolean      (* false if an item associated with Target
                                  cannot be found in the collection; true
                                  otherwise *) );
var
  K: integer;

start Retrieve
  Success := false;
  K := Hash(Target);
  repeat
    if Target = KC[K].Data.Key then
      Item := KC[K].Data;
      Success := true
    else
      K := KC[K].Link
    endif
  until Success or (K = NULL)
end Retrieve;
```

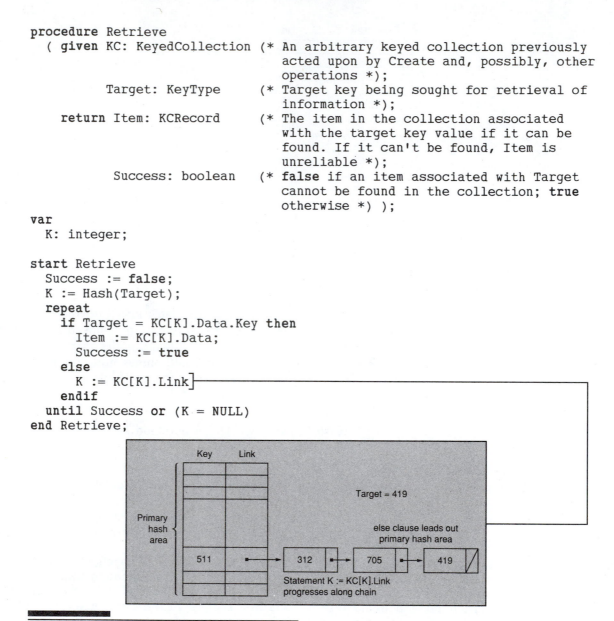

Efficiency Considerations for Linked Hashing Knuth's efficiency results for the linked hashing method depend on a density factor (D) computed using the TableSize in the prime hashing area only. Hence, unlike the other hashing methods we have discussed, the linked method allows a density factor greater than 1. For example, if the TableSize for the primary hash area is 200 and the overflow area contains space for 300 additional records, then 400 active records will yield a density factor of 2. Given this variation, average search efficiencies for the successful and unsuccessful cases are $1 + (D/2)$ and D, respectively. Table 11.8, which shows computations of this search efficiency for selected values of D, should be compared to the corresponding results for the linear, quadratic, and rehashing methods, which were presented in Table 11.5, Table 11.6, and Table 11.7, respectively.

	D	Efficiency for successful search (number of accesses)	Efficiency for unsuccessful search (number of accesses)
	2	2	2
	5	3.5	5
	10	6	10
	20	11	20

TABLE 11.8
Average search efficiency for
the linked method.

Bucket Hashing In the bucket hashing strategy for collision processing, the hashing function transforms a given key to a physically contiguous region of locations within the list to be searched. This contiguous region is called a *bucket*. Thus, instead of hashing to the Kth location, a key would hash to the Kth bucket of locations. The number of locations contained in this bucket would depend on the bucket size (we assume that all buckets in a given list are the same size). Figure 11.21 illustrates this concept for a list with seven buckets and a bucket size of 3.

Having hashed to a bucket, the Target must then be compared sequentially to all of the keys in that bucket. On the surface, it would seem that this strategy could do no better than duplicate the efficiency of the linked hash method discussed earlier. Indeed, because a sequential search is conducted in both cases after the initial hash is made, the average number of list accesses for a successful or unsuccessful search cannot be improved by using buckets. Moreover, provisions for linking to some sort of overflow area must still be made in case a series of collisions consumes all of the space in a given bucket.

What then could be a possible advantage of using buckets? If the list to be searched resides entirely in main memory, there is no advantage. However, if the list resides in a disk file, the bucket method will allow us to take advantage of some of the physical characteristics of the storage medium itself. To illustrate this, let us assume a one-surface disk divided into concentric *tracks* and pie-shaped *sectors* as indicated in Figure 11.22.

There are two ways in which the bucket hashing strategy may take advantage of the organization of the data on the disk. First, when records in a contiguous random access file are stored on a disk, they are generally located in relative record number order along one track, then along an adjacent track, and so on. The movement of the read-write head between tracks is generally the cause of the most significant delays in obtaining data from a disk. The farther the movement, the greater is the delay. Hence, if our knowledge of the machine in question allows us to make a bucket coincide with a track on the disk, then hashing to the beginning of a bucket and proceeding from there using a sequential search within the bucket (that is, the track) will greatly reduce head movement. A linked hashing strategy, on the other hand, could cause considerable movement of the read-write head between tracks on the disk, thereby slowing program execution. This consideration is an excellent example of how one must examine more than just the number of list accesses when measuring the efficiency of a program involving disk files.

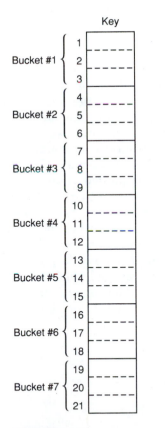

FIGURE 11.21
Storage allocation for bucket hashing.

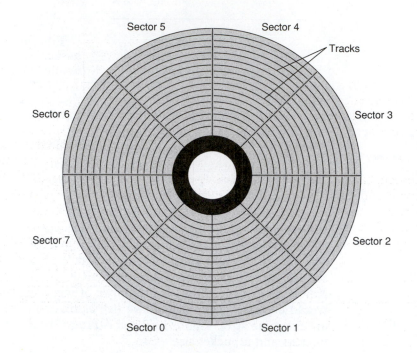

FIGURE 11.22
One-surface disk.

A second advantage in using the bucket hashing algorithm when disk files are being searched is related to the way in which records are transferred between the disk and main memory. Frequently, programming languages create the illusion that each record accessed requires a separate disk access. However, records are frequently blocked—that is, positioned in contiguous regions on a track of the disk—so that a fixed number of them are brought into main memory when a record in that block is requested. This means that, if the record requested happens to be part of the block presently in main memory, a program statement that requests a record may not even require a disk access but only a different viewing window applied to the block already in main memory. Since main memory manipulations are orders of magnitude faster than the rate of data transfer to and from a disk, positioning buckets to coincide with a disk block will necessitate only one disk access each time an entire bucket is sequentially searched. Here again, the more scattered nature of a purely linked hashing algorithm would not allow this disk-oriented efficiency consideration to be taken into account.

Exercises 11.2

1. Assume a hashing function has the following characteristics:

   Keys 459 and 333 hash to 1.

   Key 632 hashes to 2.

   Key 1090 hashes to 3.

   Keys 1982, 379, 238, and 3411 hash to 10.

   Assume that insertions into a hashed file are performed in the order 1982, 3411, 333, 632, 1090, 459, 379, and 238.

a. Indicate the position of the keys if the linear method is used to resolve collisions.

Index   Key

1	
2	
3	
4	
5	
6	
7	
8	
9	
10	
11	

b. Indicate the position of the keys if the quadratic method is used to resolve collisions.

Index   Key

1	
2	
3	
4	
5	
6	
7	
8	
9	
10	
11	

c. Indicate the position of the keys and the contents of the link fields if the chaining (that is, linked) method is used to resolve collisions. Use zeros to represent NULL links and assume that the first record used in the overflow area is 12, then 13, then 14, and so on.

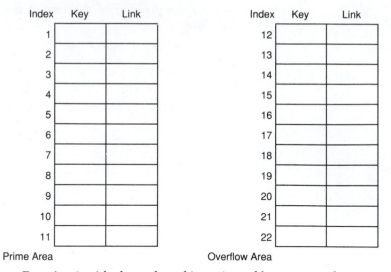

2. Repeat Exercise 1 with the order of insertion of keys reversed.

3. **a.** Given the arrival of integer keys in the order 67, 19, 4, 58, 38, 55, and 86 and TableSize = 9 with

$$\text{Hash(KeyValue)} = (\text{KeyValue } \textbf{mod } \text{TableSize}) + 1$$

trace the insertion steps of linearly processing collisions.

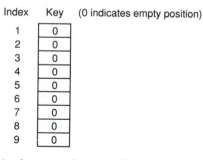

b. Given the arrival of integer keys in the order 32, 62, 34, 77, 6, 46, and 107 and TableSize = 15 with

$$\text{Hash(KeyValue)} = (\text{KeyValue } \textbf{mod } \text{TableSize}) + 1$$

trace the insertion steps of quadratically processing collisions.

Index	Key	(0 indicates empty position)
1	0	
2	0	
3	0	
4	0	
5	0	
6	0	
7	0	
8	0	
9	0	
10	0	
11	0	
12	0	
13	0	
14	0	
15	0	

c. Given the arrival of integer keys in the order 5, 3, 16, 27, 14, 25, and 4 and TableSize = 11 with initial hashing function

$$\text{Hash}_1(\text{KeyValue}) = (\text{KeyValue} \bmod \text{TableSize}) + 1$$

trace the insertion steps of the rehashing collision-processing method where the secondary hashing function is

$$\text{Hash}_2(\text{KeyValue}) = [(5 \times \text{KeyValue}) \bmod \text{TableSize}]) + 1$$

Assume that, if the secondary hashing function is not successful in locating a position for the key, linear collision processing is used from the address indicated by the secondary hashing function. Comment on the effectiveness of rehashing with this particular secondary hashing function. Can you think of a better one?

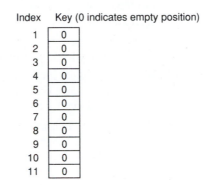

Index	Key (0 indicates empty position)
1	0
2	0
3	0
4	0
5	0
6	0
7	0
8	0
9	0
10	0
11	0

d. Given the arrival of integer keys in the order 6, 21, 9, 20, 88, 42, 7, 51, and 72 and TableSize = 11 with initial hashing function

$$\text{Hash}_1(\text{KeyValue}) = (\text{KeyValue} \bmod \text{TableSize}) + 1$$

trace the insertion steps using the double hashing collision-processing method with the second hashing function defined by

$$\text{Hash}_2(\text{KeyValue}) = \begin{cases} 1 & \text{if } (\text{KeyValue} / \text{TableSize}) \bmod \text{TableSize} = 0 \\ (\text{KeyValue} / \text{TableSize}) \bmod \text{TableSize} & \text{otherwise} \end{cases}$$

Note that, since TableSize = 11 is a prime number, the values of Hash_2 are automatically relatively prime to TableSize.

4. What search strategy would you use for each of the following applications? Justify your choices of strategy in a short essay.

a. The list to be maintained is the card catalog of a library. Frequent additions to and deletions from this catalog are made by the library. Additionally, users are frequently searching for the data associated with a given book's key. However, the library rarely prints out an ordered list of all its holdings; ordering the list is therefore not to be considered a high priority.

b. You are writing a program that maintains the lists of passengers on flights for an airline company. Passengers are frequently added to these lists. Moreover, passengers quite often cancel flight plans and must be removed from a list. You are also told that the airline frequently wants alphabetized listings of the passengers on a given flight and often needs to search out a particular passenger by name when inquiries are received from individuals.

c. You are writing a program that will access a large customer data base and build up counts for the numbers of customers from each of the 50 states (plus the District of Columbia). To do this you will use a list of records consisting of the two-character state abbreviation and an integer representing the count of customers from that state. For each customer you read in from the data base, you must find the customer's home state in your list and increase the corresponding count field. At the end, you must print out the counts in order, alphabetized by the two-character state abbreviation.

5. Write a complete implementation for the keyed collection ADT using hashing with linear collision processing. Unlike Example 11.7, make sure that your implementation correctly processes deletions.

6. Write a complete implementation for the keyed collection ADT using hashing with rehashing by separate hash functions to resolve collisions. Make sure that your implementation allows for deletion of keys from the collection.

7. Write a complete implementation for the keyed collection ADT using double hashing to resolve collisions. Make sure that your implementation allows for deletion of keys from the collection.

8. Write a complete implementation for the keyed collection ADT using hashing with linked collision processing. Unlike Example 11.8, make sure that your implementation correctly processes deletions.

9. In Section 11.2 we mentioned a result by Radke that answered the question of how many array slots would be probed by the quadratic hashing algorithm for certain values of TableSize. In particular, Radke showed that if TableSize is a prime number of the form $4m + 3$ for some integer m, then half of the array slots would be probed by the sequence

$$K, \ K + 1^2, \ K + 2^2, \ K + 3^2, \ldots$$

where K is the original hash position. Radke also showed that the other half would be probed by the sequence

$$K - 1^2, \ K - 2^2, \ K - 3^2, \ldots$$

Use Radke's result to write a complete implementation for the keyed collection ADT using hashing with quadratic collision procession. Make sure that your implementation correctly processes deletions and does not prematurely declare a hash table full when the Add operation is invoked.

10. Explain how hashing could be used to implement a variation of a keyed collection in which keys were not unique. For example, we might have several people identified by the same name.

11.3   APPLICATION: USING HASHING TO IMPLEMENT THE ORDERED LIST ADT

Our discussion of hashing in Section 11.2 introduced a new ADT, the keyed collection, with an eye toward hashing as an implementation technique. The keyed collection is essentially a restriction of the ordered list ADT introduced in Section 3.1. The limitation of a keyed collection is that arrangement of data in order is not a required operation.

Hashing is an implementation technique for a keyed collection that can virtually guarantee $O(1)$ efficiency for the Add, Delete, and Retrieve operations—regardless of the amount of data in the collection. With this kind of performance, it seems natural to ask whether we can extend hashing to provide an implementation of the ordered list ADT, that is, to allow ordered list traversals and updates. Although the requirement that a good hashing function scatter keys seems directly at odds with ordered traversals, there are strategies that can be used to allow hashing and ordering of data to coexist. One such strategy is simply to use a pointer sort algorithm (see Section 2.3) to sort the data logically when an ordered list is needed. This strategy has the drawback of not maintaining the list in order but actually performing a potentially costly sort algorithm each time an ordering is requested. Clearly, this strategy is not wise if such an ordering is to be requested frequently and irregularly. However, it is appropriate if requests for ordered lists come only at a relatively few, regularly scheduled intervals. In such situations, the time required to perform a pointer sort will not normally be a negative factor from a user's perspective.

In situations where requests for ordering would come frequently enough to make maintaining the list in order (as opposed to sorting) a necessity, we could follow a strategy that would combine the search speed of hashing with the ordered list advantages offered by a linked list implementation. This combination uses hashing to search for an individual record but adds link fields to each record so that a linked list for each desired ordering can be woven through the collection of hashed records. Implementing this combination of hashing and linked list entails the following considerations with respect to the ordered list operations:

- *Add.* In effect, the hashing/collision-processing algorithm will provide us with an available node to store data. That is, the implementation of the new operation for the pointer ADT will be the algorithm that finds an empty slot in the hash table. Each linked list involved will then have to be traversed to link the node into each ordering in the appropriate logical location.

- *Update.* Hashing could be used to find the record to be altered. If the change occurs in a field by which the record is ordered, the links will have to be appropriately adjusted. For this purpose, the use of a doubly linked list might offer a substantial advantage. (Why?)

- *Retrieval.* There is no problem here because the hash algorithm should find the desired record quickly.

- *Delete.* This is similar to the change operation. Hashing can be used to find the record to be deleted; then the link field will be adjusted appropriately. Here again, a doubly linked list could prove to be particularly valuable. (Why?)

- *Traverse.* There is no problem here because the linked lists constantly maintain the appropriate orderings.

Exercises 11.3

1. Suppose that we combine hashing with a linked list in the fashion described in Section 11.3 so that all ordered list operations can be performed efficiently. Which of the variations on a linked list structure described in Section 3.4 would be most effective in this context? Why?

2. Write a complete implementation of the ordered list ADT from Section 3.1 that uses hashing combined with a pointer sort to achieve the Traverse operation.

3. Write a complete implementation of the ordered list ADT from Section 3.1 that uses hashing combined with a linked list to achieve the Traverse operation.

11.4 APPLICATION: USING HASHING TO IMPLEMENT THE SPARSE MATRIX ADT

Recall the sparse matrix problem introduced in Section 2.1. Given a matrix with a high percentage of a certain uniform value, say 0, how can we implement this matrix in a space-efficient fashion without completely sacrificing processing speed? We have already suggested two implementation strategies for such matrices.

1. In Section 2.1 we described a strategy that would simply create a list of the (row, column) pairs of indices corresponding to nontrivial (that is, nonzero) values in the matrix. Along with each (row, column) pair, we maintain the nontrivial value stored at that position of the matrix. Thus, determining the value of the data at a conceptual row/column location is simply a matter of searching this list.

2. In Section 3.5 we described a strategy that would form a linked list of the nontrivial columns in each row. Here, determining the value of the data at a conceptual row/column location is reduced to the problem of sequentially searching a relatively small linked list.

At the time we explored these two strategies, the first one appeared to be less attractive. Because the data in the list of the row/column coordinates of nonzero values are likely to be volatile, physically ordering the data for a binary search would not be practical. Yet, without a binary search, requests to inspect the value at any given location are met with the $O(n)$ response time of a sequential search. Hashing allows us to search for a row/column coordinate in the list of the first strategy in a very efficient fashion, probably faster than the sequential search along the linked list representing a given row required by the second strategy. Moreover, since the order of the data in the list is not important for this application, the scattered nature of hashed storage does not present any obstacle at all. Figure 11.23 illustrates how a hash table could be used as the implementation underlying a sparse table.

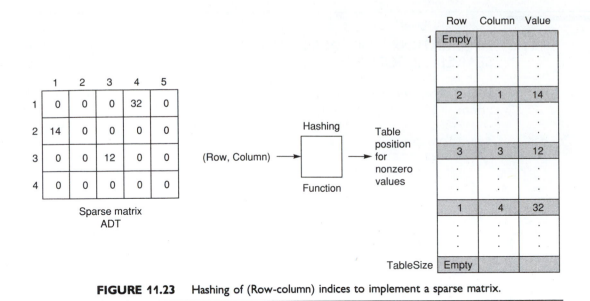

FIGURE 11.23   Hashing of (Row-column) indices to implement a sparse matrix.

Exercises 11.4

1. Write a complete PSEUDO implementation for the sparse matrix ADT using the hashing technique described in this section.

2. Suppose that we have a 3,000 × 4,000 matrix of real values that contain no more than 15 percent nonzero values. Suppose also that we wish to resolve any request to retrieve or assign a value in an average of three probes into an underlying hash table implementation. How large would you declare the hash table? Provide a rationale for your choice of size.

3. Suppose that we implement a sparse matrix by the hashing technique described in this section but use a hashing function that involves only the row index in its computation of a table position for a (row, column) pair. Is this implementation likely to fare better, worse, or as well as the linked list implementation for sparse matrices described in Section 3.5? Justify your answer.

4. You are considering hashing as an implementation technique for a sparse matrix of real values. The following are parameters that will influence your deliberations.

   $R =$ the number of bytes to store a real

   $I =$ the number of bytes to store an integer (such as a row or column coordinate)

   $P =$ the percentage of matrix locations that store a nontrivial value

   $N =$ the average number of hash table probes you are willing to tolerate for resolving collisions

   In terms of the other parameters, what must P be before the hashing implementation actually becomes more space efficient than the standard row major implementation of the matrix? Assume linear collision processing is used. What if quadratic collision processing is used? Linked collision processing?

11.5 **APPLICATION: THE RABIN-KARP STRING SEARCH ALGORITHM**

Recall, from the definition of the string ADT (Section 2.2), the Search operation:

```
function Search
  ( given Master,
          Sub: String      (* Two strings with Sub potentially
                               contained in Master *);
          Start: integer   (* Represents a character position
                               in Master. Master is to be
                               searched for Sub from this
                               position onward *);
    return: integer        (* The position of the first
                               occurrence of Sub in Master at
                               position Start or after. Zero
                               returned if Sub is not found in
                               this portion of Master *) );
```

In the worst case, the straightforward implementation of this algorithm, presented in Section 2.2, can deteriorate to $O(\text{Length}(\text{Master}) \times \text{Length}(\text{Sub}))$ efficiency. A variation on hashing, however, can virtually guarantee an efficiency of $O(\text{Length}(\text{Master}) + \text{Length}(\text{Sub}))$ for this same operation. This adaptation of hashing to string searching requires the notion of a *perfect* hashing function for strings.

A Perfect Hashing Function for Strings

We will assume that our strings are drawn from an alphabet with C possible characters. Then we can easily define an Index function that maps each character to a different integer in the range from 0 to $C - 1$. Now suppose that we have a string S of length N. Then, via the Index function, the characters of S can be viewed as the digits of a number in the base-C number system. Hence, corresponding to S, we have the number

$$\text{Index}(S_1) \times C^{N-1} + \text{Index}(S_2) \times C^{N-2} + \cdots + \text{Index}(S_{N-1}) \times C^1$$
$$+ \text{Index}(S_N) \times C^0$$

where S_i represents the ith character in the string S. Note that this number is uniquely associated with this string; no other string drawn from the same C characters can have this as its number. We will designate the number associated with a string in this fashion as Number(S). The uniqueness property cited above implies that, for strings S and T with $S \neq T$, we have Number(S) $\neq$ Number(T). Given a hash table of infinite size, we thus have a perfect hash function for strings from this particular alphabet of C characters. Namely, Number(S) + 1 will give us an address for S (in a table starting with address 1) that no other string could claim.

Example 11.9   Consider strings drawn from uppercase alphabetic characters with an Index function that maps A to 0, B to 1, C to 2, and so forth. Compute Number("ZETA"). Since $C = 26$ for strings under consideration, and since the characters 'Z', 'E', 'T', and 'A' are mapped to the numbers 25, 4, 19, and 0, respectively, we have

$$\text{Number}(\text{"ZETA"}) = (25)26^3 + (4)26^2 + (19)26^1 + (0)26^0$$
$$= 442,598$$

Limitations to Perfection

Unfortunately, computers are not machines with infinite resources. Hence, the perfect hashing function described above is not realizable on any machine. First, we cannot declare a hash table of infinite size. Second, the computation of Number(S) would quickly cause integer overflow on strings of reasonable size. So a compromise must be reached. Instead of working with an infinite table, we declare a hash table of a particular TableSize, designed to fit within the limits of our application. To map a string to a particular location in this table, we compute

$$(\text{Number}(S) \ \textbf{mod} \ \text{TableSize}) \ + \ 1$$

Even this computation, however, is not without its problems. First, note that Number(S) is a polynomial in powers of C. To compute this efficiently, we can use an algorithm known as *Horner's method*. This algorithm views the definition of Number(S) for a string of length 4,

$$\text{Index}(S_1) \times C^3 \ + \ \text{Index}(S_2) \times C^2 \ + \ \text{Index}(S_3) \times C^1 \ + \ \text{Index}(S_4) \times C^0$$

as the equivalent expression:

$$(((((\text{Index}(S_1) \times C) + \text{Index}(S_2)) \times C) + \text{Index}(S_3)) \times C) + \text{Index}(S_4)$$

In general, after initializing Number(S) to Index(S_1), Horner's method reduces the computation of Number(S) to a loop involving $N - 1$ multiplications (by C) and $N - 1$ additions (of the Index corresponding to the next character in the string). This is illustrated in the following iterative control structure.

```
NumberS  := Index(S1);
for K := 2 to Length(S) do
   NumberS := NumberS * C + Index(SK)
endfor
```

Example 11.10 To evaluate Number ("ZETA") by Horner's method, we would perform the following computations:

$$
\begin{array}{c}
\underbrace{25 * 26} \\
\underbrace{650 + 4} \\
\underbrace{654 * 26} \\
\underbrace{17004 + 19} \\
\underbrace{17023 * 26} \\
\underbrace{442598 + 0} \\
442598
\end{array}
$$

Although Horner's method provides an $O(Length(S))$ algorithm for the computation of Number(S), it will not by itself solve the problem of overflow in the computation of the hash function value, (Number(S) **mod** TableSize) + 1. The computation of Number(S) may overflow before the **mod** operation is performed. To remedy this, we note that we may **mod** Number(S) by TableSize after each iteration of the loop in Horner's algorithm to arrive at the computation of Number(S) **mod** TableSize. That is, we modify Horner's algorithm so that it becomes

```
NumberS  := Index(S₁) ;
for K  := 2  to Length(S) do
   NumberS  := (NumberS  * C  + Index(Sₖ))  mod TableSize
endfor
```

Now Number(S) will always be less than TableSize as we iterate the loop. Hence the expression

$$\text{NumberS} \times C + \text{Index}(S_I)$$

will be less than

$$\text{TableSize} \times C + C = (\text{TableSize} + 1) \times C$$

So choosing TableSize small enough to ensure that (TableSize + 1) × C will not overflow guarantees that no overflow will occur in the iterative computation of our hash function value.

The choice of TableSize should also be made to minimize the chance that two different strings will hash to the same position. In this regard, we want to be sure that the effect of each term in the expression for Number(S),

$$\text{Index}(S_1) \times C^{N-1} + \text{Index}(S_2) \times C^{N-2} + \cdots + \text{Index}(S_{N-1}) \times C^1$$
$$+ \text{Index}(S_N) \times C^0$$

is not canceled when we **mod** by TableSize. Such cancellation will occur if the **mod** TableSize operation reduces a nonzero term to zero, that is, if the term is a nonzero multiple of TableSize. We can guarantee that this won't happen if TableSize is chosen to be a prime number larger than C. Since C will usually be relatively small, this criterion should be easy to satisfy.

In summary, here is the recommended compromise to the perfect hashing function for strings.

1. Choose TableSize to be a prime number that is (a) larger than C, (b) small enough to ensure that (TableSize + 1) × C will not cause overflow on your machine, and (c) within the range of a hash table size that your application will allow.

2. Then compute the "compromised" value of Number(S) by a Horner's algorithm loop that **mod**s by TableSize in each iteration. Hereafter we will refer to this value as CompNumber(S).

Example 11.11   You have an application in which the keys being hashed are composed of uppercase letters and spaces, so C is 27. The application is running on a 16-bit computer, which implies an integer overflow point of 32,767. Hence, TableSize should be chosen to be a prime number larger than 27 and small enough to ensure that (TableSize +1) × 27 ≤ 32,767.

The Rabin-Karp Algorithm

We are now ready to attack the string search problem that initiated our discussion. Suppose that we wish to search the Master string KOKOMO for the Sub string KOM. Then KOM must be compared against all the three-character substrings of KOKOMO: KOK, OKO, KOM, and OMO. If any of these comparisons returns a successful match, then the search succeeds; otherwise it fails. The Rabin-Karp algorithm suggests that we imagine KOK, OKO, KOM, and OMO as the only four strings stored in an exceptionally large hash table determined by the hashing function CompNumber(S). This concept is illustrated in Figure 11.24. How large can this table be? Since it is a conceptual table that is never allocated in computer memory, it must meet only criteria 1(a) and 1(b) above; that is, TableSize must be larger than C (the number of characters in the alphabet for our strings) and small enough to insure that (TableSize + 1) × C will not cause overflow. To determine whether or not Sub is contained in Master, we must merely determine whether or not Sub is contained in the conceptual hash table of Figure 11.24. But this is the same as determining whether or not CompNumber(Sub) equals the CompNumber of any of the substrings of Master that are "contained" in this table. Since TableSize can be chosen extremely large, we ignore, for the time being, the remote possibility that CompNumber(Sub) could equal the CompNumber of another one of the substrings of Master. That is, because of the large TableSize and relatively small number of strings stored in it, the possibility of a hashing collision is so small that we temporarily pretend

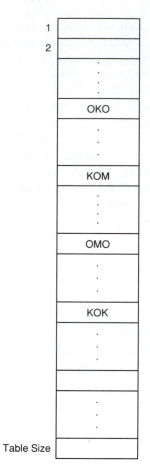

FIGURE 11.24

Substrings of length 3 of KOKOMO as the sole occupants of a large hash table.

it cannot happen. Hence, the Rabin-Karp string search algorithm can be formalized as follows:

```
function Search              (* Rabin-Karp algorithm *)
  ( given Master,
         Sub: String        (* Two strings with Sub potentially contained
                               in Master *);
        Start: integer      (* Represents a character position in Master.
                               Master is to be searched for Sub from this
                               position onward *);
       return: integer      (* The position of the first occurrence of Sub
                               In Master at position Start or after. Zero
                               returned if Sub is not found in this portion
                               of Master *) );

var
  Temp: String;
  Target, Candidate, Position: integer;
  Found: boolean;
```

```
start Search
  Target := CompNumber(Sub);
  Substring(Master, 1, Length(Sub), Temp);
  Candidate := CompNumber(Temp);
  Position := Start;
  Found := false;
  while (Position <= Length(Master) - Length(Sub) + 1) and not Found do
    if Target = Candidate then
      Found := true
    else
      Position := Position + 1;
      Substring(Master, Position, Position + Length(Sub) - 1, Temp);
      Candidate := CompNumber(Temp)
    endif
  endwhile;
  if Found then
    Search := Position
  else
    Search := 0
  endif
end Search;
```

Analysis of the Rabin-Karp Algorithm

Clearly the **while** loop in the Rabin-Karp algorithm is $O(\text{Length(Master)})$. The repeated computations of CompNumber nested within the loop are each $O(\text{Length(Sub)})$ under the assumption that Horner's algorithm is used. However, under the special circumstances of the string search, we may achieve a more efficient computation of CompNumber within the **while** loop. In particular, note that, from one iteration of this loop to the next, the substring Temp shifts only by one character. Hence much of the computation of Candidate from one iteration of the loop can be used again in the next iteration. For instance, if LS is used to denote Length(Sub), Candidate will be on the Kth pass through the loop,

$$(\text{Index}(\text{Master}_K) \times C^{LS-1} + \text{Index}(\text{Master}_{K+1}) \times C^{LS-2}$$
$$+ \cdots + \text{Index}(\text{Master}_{K+LS-1}) \times C^0) \bmod \text{TableSize}$$

and, on the $(K + 1)$st pass,

$$(\text{Index}(\text{Master}_{K+1}) \times C^{LS-1} + \text{Index}(\text{Master}_{K+2}) \times C^{LS-2}$$
$$+ \cdots + \text{Index}(\text{Master}_{K+LS}) \times C^0) \textbf{ mod } \text{TableSize}$$

Note that the latter value of Candidate may be computed from the former by

$$\text{Candidate} = (\text{Candidate} \times C - \text{Index}(\text{Master}_K) \times C^{LS}$$
$$+ \text{Index}(\text{Master}_{K+LS})) \textbf{ mod } \text{TableSize}$$

To avoid problems with the **mod** operation when $(\text{Candidate} \times C - \text{Index}(\text{Master}_K) \times C^{LS} + \text{Index}(\text{Master}_{K+LS}))$ is negative, we must add a $\text{TableSize} \times C$ term

$$\text{Candidate} = (\text{Candidate} \times C - \text{Index}(\text{Master}_K) \times C^{LS} + \text{TableSize} \times C$$
$$+ \text{Index}(\text{Master}_{K+LS})) \textbf{ mod } \text{TableSize}$$

Thus, we can obtain a better algorithm by computing C^{LS} prior to the **while** loop and replacing the two lines

```
Substring(Master, Position, Length(Sub), Temp);
Candidate := CompNumber(Temp)
```

by the more efficient computation of Candidate presented above. This refined version of the Rabin-Karp algorithm is incorporated into the following:

```
(* Assume constant C represents number of possible characters in strings *)

function Search          (* Rabin-Karp algorithm *)
  ( given Master,
          Sub: String    (* Two strings with Sub potentially contained
                             in Master *);
          Start: integer  (* Represents a character position in Master.
                             Master is to be searched for Sub from this
                             position onward *);
      return: integer    (* The position of the first occurence of Sub in
                             Master at position Start or after. Zero returned
                             if Sub is not found in this portion of Master *) );
  var
    Temp: String;
    Target, Candidate, Position, CPower, LS, I: integer;
    Found: boolean;

  start Search
    LS := Length(Sub);
    CPower := 1;
    for I := 1 to LS do
      CPower := CPower * C mod TableSize (* C is the number of possible
                                            characters *)
    endfor;
```

```
      Target := CompNumber(Sub);
      Substring(Master, 1, LS, Temp);
      Candidate := CompNumber(Temp); (* CompNumber called only outside loop *)
      Position := Start;
      Found := false;
      while (Position <= Length(Master) - LS + 1) and not Found do
        if Target = Candidate then
          Found := true
        else
          Candidate := (Candidate * C - Index(Master[Position]) * CPower
                                + TableSize * C
                                + Index(Master[Position + LS])) mod TableSize;
          Position := Position + 1
        endif
      endwhile;
    if Found then
      Search := Position
    else
      Search := 0
    endif
end Search;
```

With these modifications, the **while** loop will have $O(\text{Length}(\text{Master}))$ efficiency. Because CompNumber(Sub) and CompNumber(Master) are computed before the loop, the entire procedure will have $O(\text{Length}(\text{Sub}) + \text{Length}(\text{Master}))$ efficiency.

The only problem that remains is that the present implementation of the Rabin-Karp algorithm could fail under the *highly improbable* occurrence that CompNumber(Sub) equals the CompNumber of one of Master's substrings even though the two strings are not identical. The modifications necessary to handle this possibility are left for the exercises.

Exercises 11.5

1. Suppose that we are drawing strings from the set of uppercase letters and the space character. Compute Number("ZEBRA").

2. You are working on a 16-bit computer with strings drawn from the set of uppercase letters and the space character. What should the TableSize be for the Rabin-Karp algorithm? Given this choice, compute CompNumber("ZEBRA").

3. What would be the effect of choosing TableSize equal to C in the computation of a string's CompNumber?

4. Complete the Rabin-Karp string search algorithm presented in this section by adding code to handle the remote possibility that a substring of the Master string and Sub will have the same CompNumber even when they are not identical as strings.

5. The Rabin-Karp algorithm can also be modified to search for patterns in two-dimensional tables. Suppose that we have a large matrix of 1s and 0s representing a graphic image. A 1 indicates that the screen dot (pixel) corresponding to that position in the matrix should be black; a 0 indicates white. We want to determine whether a certain subimage, represented as a smaller two-dimensional array of 1s and 0s is contained in this larger image. Write

a variation of the Rabin-Karp algorithm that will search the larger image for an occurrence of the smaller image.

6. When searching strings for a particular pattern, it is often convenient to allow certain characters to count as *wildcards*. A wildcard character matches any other character. Suppose that * were designated as a wildcard character. Then a wildcard string search for "M*T" in "METAMATEMATICS" would turn up both "MET" and "MAT" (twice) as matches. Modify the Rabin-Karp algorithm to accept wildcard characters in the Sub string.

11.6 INDEXED SEARCH TECHNIQUES

All the search strategies we have studied up to this point could be applied to lists implemented in main memory or on a random access disk. However, with the exception of bucket hashing, none of the methods we have studied take into account physical characteristics of actual disk storage in an attempt to enhance their efficiency. In practice, because retrieval of data from a disk file is orders of magnitude slower than retrieval from main memory, we often cannot afford to ignore these special characteristics of disk files if we want reasonable response time for our searching efforts. The indexing schemes we discuss in this section are primarily directed toward file-oriented applications and will thus take into account the operational properties of this storage medium. We encourage you to reread the discussion of bucket hashing at the end of Section 11.2 for a short analysis of file storage considerations.

The idea behind the use of an index is analogous to the way in which we routinely use an address book to find a person we are seeking. That is, if we are looking for a person, we do not simply knock on the doors of numerous houses until we find the one where that person lives. Instead, we apply a search strategy to an address book. There we use the name of the person as a key to find a pointer—that is, an address—that swiftly leads us to where the person can be found. Only one actual "house access" must be made, even though our search strategy may require numerous accesses into the address book index.

In a computer system, records (or more precisely blocks) could play the role of houses in the search scenario just described. Data records on disk are (when compared to main memory) terribly slow and awkward creatures to access. One reason for this is that a large amount of data must often be moved from disk to main memory when a record is accessed. Because of this, we must revise the conceptual picture we have of the general setup for an indexed search so that our list of keys is no longer parallel to the actual data the keys are logically associated with but rather is parallel to a list of pointers that will lead us to the actual data. This revised picture is presented in Figure 11.25.

The general strategy of an indexed search is to use the key to search the index efficiently, find the relative record position of the associated data, and then make only one access into the actual data. Because the parallel lists of keys and relative record positions require much less storage than the list data, the entire index can frequently be loaded and permanently held in main memory, necessitating only one disk access for each record being sought.

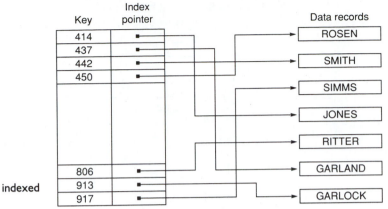

FIGURE 11.25

General setup for an indexed search.

For larger indices, it is still true that large blocks of keys and associated pointers may be manipulated in main memory, thereby greatly enhancing search efficiency.

Indexed Sequential Search Technique

The *indexed sequential search* technique is also commonly recognized by the acronym ISAM, which stands for Indexed Sequential Access Method. This technique involves carefully weighing the disk-dependent factors of blocking and track size to build a partial index.

The partial index, unlike some other index structures we shall study, does not reduce to one the number of probes that must be made into the actual data. To continue the analogy between searching for data and searching for a person, the indexed sequential strategy is somewhat like an address book that would lead us to the street on which a person lives but leave it to us to check each house on that street. The ISAM method correspondingly leads us to an appropriate region (often a track or a cylinder containing multiple tracks within a disk pack), leaving it for us to search sequentially within that region.

As an example, let us suppose that we can conveniently fit the partial index, or directory, pictured in Figure 11.26 into main memory and that the organization of our disk file allows six records per track. This directory contains the highest key value in each six-record track along with a pointer indicating where that track begins. Here our pointers are simply relative record numbers; in practice they could well be more disk-dependent. The strategy to conduct an indexed sequential search is as follows:

1. Search the main memory directory for a key that is greater than or equal to the Target.
2. Then follow the corresponding pointer out to the disk and there search sequentially until finding a match (success) or the high key within that particular region (failure).

For the data given in Figure 11.26, this technique would mean that the 36-record file would require no more than six main memory index accesses plus six disk accesses, all of which are located in the same track.

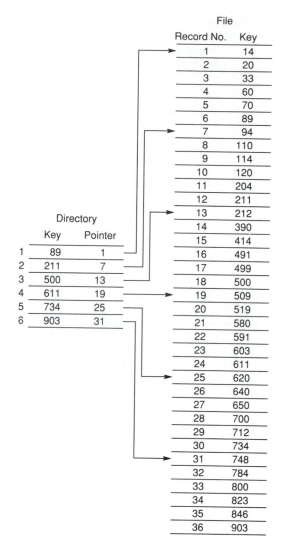

FIGURE 11.26
One-level indexed sequential
file.

For larger files, it may be advantageous to have more than one level of these directory structures. Consider, for instance, the two-level directory structure for a file with 216 records given in Figure 11.27. Here we suppose that storage restrictions allow the entire primary directory to be kept in main memory, the secondary directory to be brought in from a disk file in blocks of six key–pointer pairs each, and the actual data records to be stored six per track. The primary directory divides the file into regions of 36 records each. The key in the primary directory represents the highest-valued key in a given 36-record region, but the pointer leads us into the subdirectory instead of the actual file. We therefore search the primary directory for a key greater than or equal to the target we are seeking. Once this is done, we follow the primary directory pointer into the secondary directory. Beginning at the position indicated by the primary directory's pointer, we again search for a key greater than or equal to the target. Notice that fetching one block of six key–pointer pairs from the subdirectory has necessitated one disk access in

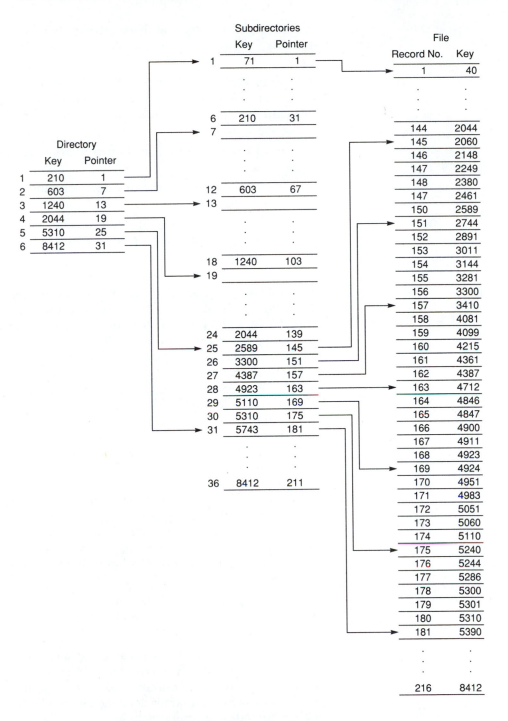

FIGURE 11.27

Two-level directory structure.

our hypothetical situation. In return for this single disk access, we are able to subdivide the 36-record region determined by the primary directory into six 6-record regions, each of which will lie entirely on one track by the time we get out to the actual disk file. Following the subdirectory's pointer to the file, we end up with a fairly short sequential search on the storage medium itself. In this example, the maximum number of disk accesses required to find any record would be seven, and six of those would be isolated on one track of the disk.

Efficiency Considerations for the Indexed Sequential Search It should be clear from the preceding discussion that the search efficiency of the indexed sequential technique depends on a variety of factors, including

- To what degree the directory structures are able to subdivide the actual file
- To what degree the directory structures are able to reside in main memory
- The relationship of data records to physical characteristics of the disk such as blocking factors, track size, cylinder size, and so on

It should also be clear that the indexed sequential method may not be ideal for a highly volatile file. This is true because, as implicitly indicated in Figures 11.26 and 11.27, the actual data records must be physically stored in increasing (or decreasing) key order. The requirement for physical ordering is obviously not conducive to frequent insertions and deletions. In practice, the solution to this problem is that each file subregion that is ultimately the subject of a sequential search is equipped with a pointer to an overflow area. Insertions are located in this overflow area and linked to the main sequential search area. As the overflow area builds up, the search efficiency tends to deteriorate. In some applications this deterioration can be so severe that data-processing personnel have been known to refer to the ISAM technique as the Intrinsically Slow Access Method.

The way to avoid deterioration is to periodically reorganize the file into a new file with no overflow. However, such reorganization cannot be done dynamically. It requires going through the file in key sequential order and copying it into a new one. Along the way the indices must be rebuilt, of course. These types of maintenance problems involved with the ISAM structure have led to the development of several more dynamic indexing schemes.

Binary Tree Indexing

The concept of a binary tree search has already been covered in Chapter 7. The only twist added when the binary tree plays the role of an index is that each node of the tree contains a key and a pointer to the record associated with that key in some larger data aggregate. The advantages of using a binary tree as an index structure include

- A potential search efficiency of $O(\log_2 n)$
- The ability to traverse the list indexed by the tree in key order
- Dynamic insertion and deletion capabilities

These qualities make the binary tree the ideal index structure for situations in which the entire tree can fit in main memory. However, if the data collection is so large that the tree index must itself be stored on disk, the efficiency of the structure is less than optimal. This is true because each node of the index may lie in a different disk block and hence require a separate disk access. For example, with 50,000 keys a search of a *binary tree index* could require 16 disk accesses. To solve this problem, we would like to cluster the nodes along a given search path into one, or at least relatively few, disk blocks. The *B-tree* index structure is a variation on the tree index that accomplishes this.

B-Tree Indexing

We begin this discussion of B-trees with a reminder that one index entry is nothing more than a pair consisting of a key and a pointer. Moreover, we have assumed that both the key and the pointer are integers, and we continue to operate under this assumption during our discussion of B-trees. In a B-tree a given tree node will in fact contain many such key–pointer pairs because a B-tree node will in fact coincide with one disk block. The idea behind a B-tree is that we will somehow group related key–pointer pairs in the search algorithm into a few strategic B-tree nodes, that is, disk blocks. At this point, we make a formal definition; later, we'll clarify this definition via some examples.

- **Definition** A *B-tree of order n* is a structure with the following properties:

  1. Every node in the B-tree has sufficient room to store $n - 1$ key–pointer pairs.
  2. Additionally, every node has room for n pointers to other nodes in the B-tree (as distinguished from the pointers within key–pointer pairs, which point to the position of a key in the file).
  3. Every node except the root must have at least $(n - 1)/2$ (integer division) key–pointer pairs stored in it.
  4. All terminal nodes are on the same level.
  5. If a nonterminal node has m key–pointer pairs stored in it, then it must contain $m + 1$ non-NULL pointers to other B-tree nodes.
  6. For each B-tree node, we require that the key value in key–pointer pair KP_{i-1} be less than the key value in key–pointer pair KP_i, that all key–pointer pairs in the node pointed to by pointer P_{i-1} contain keys that are less than the key in KP_i, and that all key–pointer pairs in the node pointed to by pointer P_i contain key values that are greater than the key in KP_i.

According to property 5 of the definition, we can think of a B-tree node as a list

$$P_0, KP_1, P_1, KP_2, P_2, KP_3, \ldots, P_{m-1}, KP_m, P_m$$

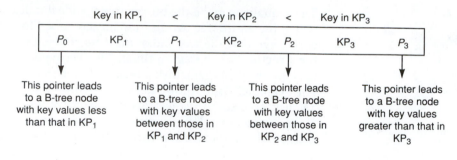

FIGURE 11.28

Example of a B-tree node with three key–pointer pairs.

where P_i represents the ith pointer to another B-tree node and KP_i represents the ith key–pointer pair. Note that a B-tree node will always contain one more pointer to another B-tree node than it does key–pointer pairs. If you keep this picture in mind, the sixth property of our definition makes sense. Figure 11.28 illustrates how this rather involved definition applies to a B-tree node with three key–pointer pairs.

As a further illustration of this definition, a complete B-tree of order 6 serving as an index structure for the 36-record file of Figure 11.26 appears in Figure 11.29. (In this figure, the slash between numbers denotes a key–pointer pair; ⊢ denotes a NULL pointer.) Carefully verify that all six defining properties are satisfied.

The choice of order 6 for Figure 11.29 was made only for the purposes of making the figure fit on a page of text. In practice, the order chosen would be the maximum number of B-tree pointers and key–pointer pairs that we could fit into one disk block. That is, the choice should be made to force a disk block to coincide with a B-tree node.

Efficiency Considerations for B-Tree Indexing Let us now consider what is involved in searching a B-tree for a given key. Within the current node (starting at the root), we must search sequentially through the key values in the node until we come to a match, a key value that is greater than the one being sought, or the end of the key values in that particular node. If a match is not made within a particular B-tree node, we have a pointer to follow to an appropriate follow-up node. Again, you should verify this algorithm for several of the keys appearing at various levels of Figure 11.29. The sequential search on keys within a given node may at first seem unappealing. However, it is important to remember that each B-tree node is a disk block that is loaded entirely into main memory. Hence, it may be possible to search sequentially on hundreds of keys within a node in the time it would take to load one new node from disk. Our main concern is to minimize disk accesses, and here we have achieved a worst-case search for our 36-entry file in three disk accesses. What, then, in general is the search efficiency for a B-tree tree index? It should be clear from the nature of the structure that the maximum number of disk accesses for any particular key will simply be the number of levels in the tree. Thus, the efficiency question really amounts to knowing the maximum number of levels that the six defining criteria will allow for a B-tree containing n key–pointer pairs; this number is the worst-case search efficiency. To determine this number, we use the minimum number of nodes

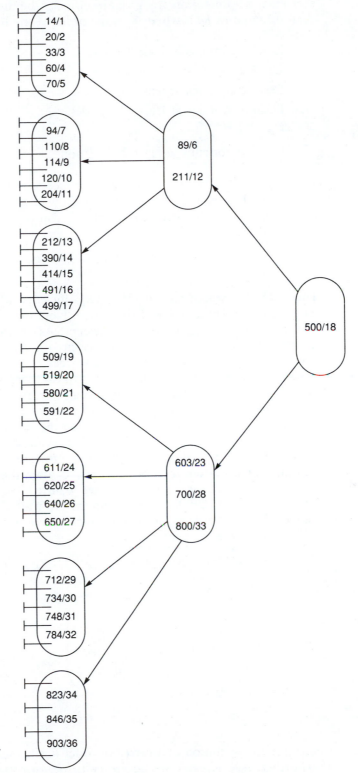

FIGURE 11.29

B-tree index of order 6 for file in Figure 11.26.

that must be present on any given level. Let L be the smallest integer greater than or equal to $K/2$, where K is the order of the B-tree in question. Then

Level 0 contains at least 1 node.
Level 1 contains at least 2 nodes.
Level 2 contains at least $2L$ nodes.
Level 3 contains at least $2L^2$ nodes.
$\vdots$
Level m contains at least $2L^{m-1}$ nodes.

An argument based on Knuth's research (see *Searching and Sorting,* cited in Section 11.1) uses this progression to show that the maximum number of levels (and thus the worst-case search efficiency) for n key–pointer pairs is

$$\log_K \frac{n + 1}{2}$$

Thus, a B-tree search has an $O(\log_K n)$ efficiency where n is the number of records and K is the order of the B-tree. Note that this can be considerably better than an $O(\log_2 n)$ search efficiency. As an example, the index for a file of 50,000 records, which would require on the order of 16 disk accesses using a binary tree structure, could be searched with three disk accesses using a B-tree of order 250. Note that, given typical block sizes for files, the choice of order 250 for this example is not at all unrealistic.

Unlike ISAM, the B-tree index can dynamically handle insertions and deletions without a resulting deterioration in search efficiency. We next discuss how B-tree insertions are handled; making deletions is left for an exercise. The essential idea behind a B-tree insertion is that we must first determine which bottom-level node should contain the key–pointer pair to be inserted. For instance, suppose that we want to insert the key 742 into the B-tree of Figure 11.29. By allowing this key to walk down the B-tree from the root to the bottom level, we could quickly determine that this key belongs in the node presently containing

712/29
734/30
748/31
784/32

Since, by the definition of a B-tree of order 6, this node is not presently full, no further disk accesses are necessary to perform the insertion. We merely need to determine the next available record space in the actual data file (37 in this case) and then add the key–pointer pair 742/37 to this terminal node, resulting in a node containing in order,

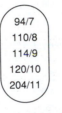

712/29
734/30
742/37
748/31
784/32

A slightly more difficult situation arises when we find that the key–pointer pair we wish to add should be inserted into a bottom-level node that is already full. For instance, this would occur if we attempted to add the key 112 to the B-tree of Figure 11.29. We would load the actual data for this key into file position 38 (given the addition already made in the preceding paragraph) and then determine that the key–pointer pair 112/38 belongs in the bottom-level node containing

94/7
110/8
114/9
120/10
204/11

The stipulation that any B-tree node except the root have at least $(6 - 1) / 2 = 2$ key–pointer pairs allows us to split this node, creating one new node with two key–pointer pairs and one with three key–pointer pairs. We also have to move one of the key–pointer pairs up to the parent of the present node. The resulting B-tree is given in Figure 11.30.

Although it does not happen in this particular example, note that it is entirely possible that the moving of a key–pointer pair up to a parent node that is already full would necessitate a split of this parent node using the same procedure. Indeed, it is possible that key–pointer pairs could be passed all the way up to the root and cause a split of the root; this is how a new level of the tree would be introduced. A split of the root would force the creation of a new root which would only have one key–pointer pair and two pointers to other B-tree nodes. At the root level, however, this is still a sufficient number of pointers to retain the B-tree structure. Because the insertion algorithm for a B-tree requires checking whether a given node is full and if so, moving back up to a parent node, it is convenient to allow space within a node to store both of the following:

- A count of the number of key–pointer pairs in the node
- A back pointer to the node's parent

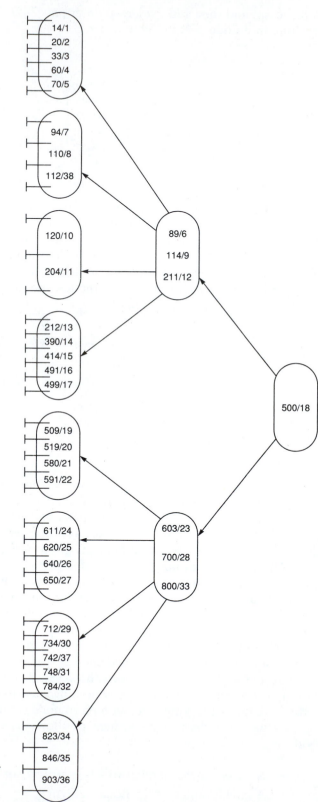

FIGURE 11.30
B-tree of Figure 11.29 after
insertion of 742/37 and
112/38.

Trie Indexing

In all the indexing applications we have discussed so far, the keys involved have been integers. In practice, however, we must be prepared to deal with keys of different types. Perhaps the worst case is that of keys that are variable-length character strings. *Trie indexing* has developed as a means of retrieving keys in this worst case. (The term is derived from the four middle letters of *retrieve* but is usually pronounced "try.")

Let us suppose that the strings in the following list represent a set of keys. Each string may be thought of as a last name followed by initials and a delimiting $.

ADAMS BT$

COOPER CC$

COOPER PJ$

COWANS DC$

MAGUIRE WH$

MCGUIRE AL$

MEMINGER DD$

SEFTON SD$

SPAN KD$

SPAN LA$

SPANNER DW$

ZARDA JM$

ZARDA PW$

Here is an individual node in a trie structure for these keys:

$ ♭ A B C D E F H I J K L M N O P Q R S T U V W X Y Z

Trie Node
(♭ denotes the space character)

It is essentially a fixed-length array of 28 pointers: one for each letter of the alphabet, one for a blank, and one for the delimiter. Each pointer within one of these nodes can lead to one of two entities—either another node within the trie or the actual data record for a given key. Hence it may be convenient to embed a boolean flag in each pointer indicating the type of entity to which it is pointing. The trie structure for the preceding list of keys is given in Figure 11.31. In this figure, pointers to nodes labeled as data records lead us outside the trie structure itself.

The logic behind a trie structure may best be seen by tracing through an example. The search algorithm involves examining the target key on a character-by-character basis (see Figure 11.31). Let us begin by considering the easy case of finding the data record for ADAMS BT$. In this case, we look at A, the first character in the key, and follow the A pointer in the root node to its destination. We know that its destination will be either another node

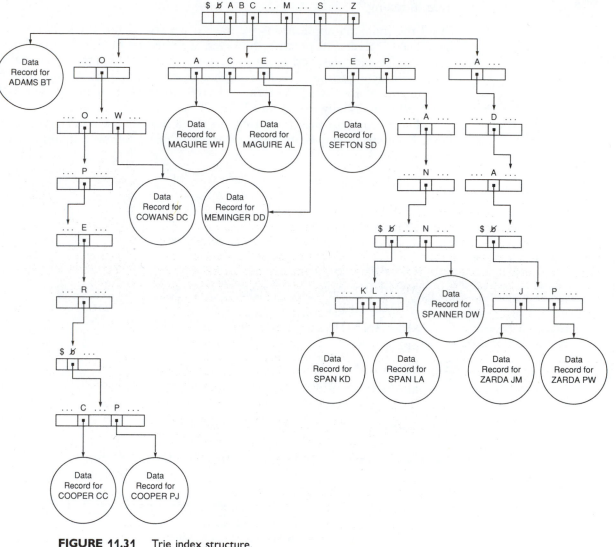

FIGURE 11.31   Trie index structure.

within the trie structure or an actual data record. If it were a node within the trie, it would be a node on the search path for all keys that begin with A. In this case, there is only one key in our list that begins with A, so the A pointer in the root node leads us directly to the actual data record for ADAMS BT$. On the other hand, the search path to find the key COOPER CC$ in the trie is somewhat longer. We follow the C pointer from the root node down a level to a node shared by all keys starting with C. From there, the O pointer is followed to a trie node shared by all keys that start with CO. The process continues down level by level, following the O pointer to a trie node shared by all keys starting with COO, the P pointer to a node for all keys starting with COOP, the E pointer to a node for all keys starting with COOPE, the R pointer to a node for all keys starting with COOPER, and the blank pointer to a node shared by all keys starting with COOPER followed by a blank. Notice that, as each character is read in, we must continue following these pointers from trie node to trie node (instead of from trie node to actual data record) until we finally reach a point where the next character to be read will uniquely define the key. At this point, the key in question no longer needs to share its pointer with other keys that match it on an initial substring, so the pointer may now lead to an actual data record. This is what happens in our example when we read in the next C to form the uniquely defined substring COOPER C.

Efficiency Consideration for Trie Indexing The search efficiency for the trie index is quite easily determined. The worst case occurs when a key is not uniquely defined until its last character is read in. In this case, we may have as many disk accesses as there are characters in the key before we finally locate the actual data record. You may have observed, however, that there is another efficiency consideration to take into account when using the trie method. This is the amount of wasted storage in the trie nodes. In our example using a short list of keys, only a small percentage of the available pointers are ever used. In practice, however, a trie would be used only for an extremely large file, such as the list represented by a phone book with names as keys. In such a situation, a much larger number of character combinations occurs, and the resulting trie structure is correspondingly much less sparse.

A final point to consider about trie indexes is their ability to handle insertions and deletions dynamically. Here we discuss insertions; deletions are left as an exercise. Insertions may be broken down into two cases. For both we must begin by reading the key to be inserted, character by character, and following the appropriate search path in the trie until we come to either of the following:

- A trie node that has a vacant pointer in the character position corresponding to the current character of the insertion key
- An actual data record for a key different from the one being inserted.

The first case is illustrated by trying to insert the key COLLINS RT$ into the trie of Figure 11.31: We follow the search path pointers until we come to the trie node shared by all keys starting with CO. At this point, the L pointer is NULL. The insertion is completed by merely aiming the presently NULL L pointer to a data record for the key COLLINS RT$. The second case is illustrated by trying to insert the key COOPER PA$ into the trie of Figure 11.31. Here, following the search path of the trie eventually leads us to the data record for the key COOPER PJ$. The dynamic solution is to get a new trie node, aim the P pointer presently leading to the data record for COOPER PJ$ to this new trie node, and use the A and J pointers in the new trie node to lead us to data records for COOPER PA$ and COOPER PJ$, respectively. Both the COLLINS RT$ and COOPER PA$ insertions are shown with the resulting trie in Figure 11.32.

Exercises 11.6

1. a. Suppose that the records associated with keys 810, 430, 602, 946, 289, 106, and 732 are stored in positions 1, 2, 3, 4, 5, 6, and 7 of a file, respectively. Draw a B-tree index of order 8 for this file.

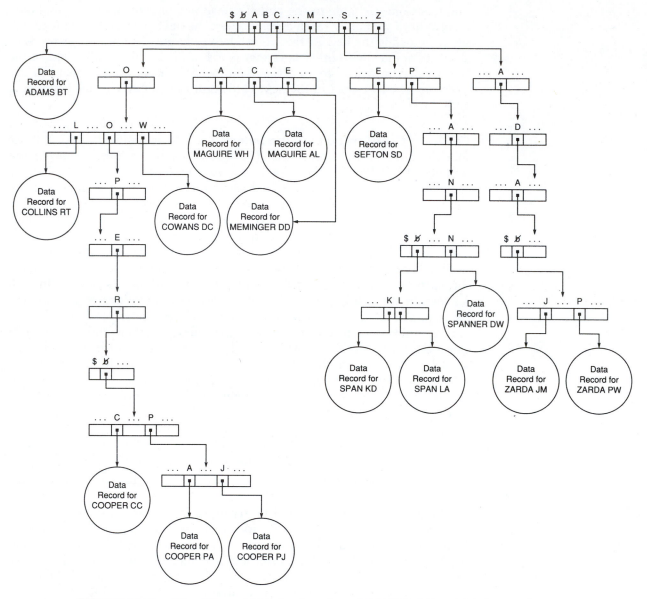

FIGURE 11.32 Trie of Figure 11.31 after insertions of COLLINS RT$ and COOPER PA$.

b. Suppose the key 538 then arrives for insertion in position 8. Redraw your B-tree of order 8 after this insertion.

2. Suppose that the following strings arrive for insertion into a trie index.

CARTER
HERNANDEZ
HERMAN
HERMANSKI
HERSCHEL
HALL

CARSON

CARSWELL

CARSEN

a. Draw the trie index.

b. Draw the index after CARSWELL and HERMANSKI have been deleted.

3. Discuss a key deletion strategy for B-trees. Write a procedure that implements your strategy.

4. Discuss a key deletion strategy for trie indexes. Write a procedure to implement your strategy.

5. Carefully read your system reference material concerning the specifics of how disk file records are blocked. Then explain how this knowledge would influence your decisions in the construction of

a. An ISAM index structure

b. A B-tree index structure

c. A trie index structure

d. A bucket hashing structure

6. All the search strategies we have discussed assume a key that is uniquely valued. That is, no two records have the same value for their key field. In practice this will not always be the case; we may have duplicate keys. For instance, a list of personnel records may contain two records for different people with the same name. Discuss how each of the search strategies we have covered would have to be modified to perform a duplicate key search. What effect would these modifications have on the performance of the algorithm?

7. Write a PSEUDO implementation of the ordered list ADT, introduced in Section 3.1, assuming that the data in the list is stored in a random access disk file and uses the indexed sequential access method as a means of efficiently processing this data. Since PSEUDO has no random access file statements per se, assume that you have an implementation of the pointer ADT in which the pointers returned by new actually refer to record positions in a random access file.

8. Repeat Exercise 7 but use a B-tree index instead of the indexed sequential access method.

9. Repeat Exercise 7 but use a trie index instead of the indexed sequential access method.

Chapter Summary

In this chapter we examine additional strategies for searching for items, for adding items to, and for deleting items from a list. In Section 11.1 we look at three more types of trees that can be used to facilitate searching: 2-3-4, red-black, and splay trees. Two-three-four trees offer an advantage over the 2-3 trees discussed in Chapter 8 in that insertions and deletions can be performed using one pass from the tree's root to a leaf, rather than requiring a root-to-leaf pass followed by a pass from the leaf back to the root. On the other hand, the overall storage requirements for a 2-3-4 tree will increase because each node has to accommodate three data fields and four pointer fields. A red-black tree offers a way to implement a 2-3-4 tree as a binary tree, allowing

A RELEVANT ISSUE

Relational Database Management Systems

A *database* is a collection of related files. For example, the registrar's system at a large university may contain a file of professor records, a file of class records, and a file of student records. These files do not exist in isolation because records in one file are related to one or more records in the other files. For instance, each professor teaches classes and advises students. Each class has many students enrolled and may have many sections, each of which is taught by a different professor. Each student takes several classes. Software that allows users to conveniently manage all of the files in a database and make queries of them is called a *database management system* (DBMS). For instance, in a database management system, a user may make a query such as "During what hours of the day is Mary Jones in class?" Although this information may not be a part of Mary Jones' record in the student file directly, the DBMS will be able to consult the student file to determine what classes Mary Jones is enrolled in and, from there, move to the file of course records to determine the times at which these classes meet. Hence, the user's query is answered because of the ability of the DBMS to associate records in one file with those in another.

Many models have been proposed for DBMS, but the *relational model* appears to be emerging as the winner. The relational model was originated in 1970 by E. F. Codd ("A Relational Model of Data for Large Shared Data Banks," *Communications of the Association of Computing Machinery*, 13, June 1970). The most appealing characteristic of Codd's model is its simplicity. In the relational model, files are typically called relations. A relation is simply a table of rows and columns. Each column corresponds to a field in a record (though it is called an *attribute* in relational terminology), and each row corresponds to a record (though it is called a *tuple* in relational terminology). Codd then defines a collection of operations on relations that allow the construction of new conceptual relations based on queries made by the user. Hence, the user could request to see the courses taken by each student and the DBMS would construct the relation below.

Name	Course
Emerson, I	BOT422 A
Emerson, I	MAT444 B
Emerson, I	PHI309 A
Emerson, I	CPS110 B
Kupper, D	MAT111 C
Kupper, D	MAT111 C
Smart, B	PHI723 B
Smart, B	PSY388 A
Smart, B	ZOO910 A
Smart, B	CPS310 B
Smart, B	ENG222 B
Smart, B	MAT311 A

Note that Codd's relational example is data abstraction at its purest. There is no hint provided by Codd as to how these relations and the operations on them are to be implemented. For instance, in the conceptual student/course relation above, each student's name appears many times. This does not imply that these names would be stored redundantly in the database. It is left to the implementer to decide how to present to the user this image of relations consisting of rows and columns of data while at the same time providing performance that does not cripple a system from a time or space perspective. Although Codd defined his relational model in 1970, it was not until the 1980s that hardware and software technology combined to make it a practical tool. Many of the information retrieval techniques presented in this chapter have played instrumental roles in moving Codd's relational database model from a purely theoretical existence to a high degree of functionality.

us to allocate space more efficiently than in 2-3-4 trees while still retaining the simplicity of a single root-to-leaf pass for data insertion and deletion. Splay trees provide an alternative to balanced trees for carrying out searching operations. Although they may not always yield as efficient a worst-case search performance as the various balanced trees, they compare favorably when their efficiency is analyzed over sequences of searches. An advantage is that they employ simpler restructuring algorithms than the balanced trees to achieve this level of performance.

The efficiency of all the search techniques considered up to this point and in Section 11.1 depend on the number of items in the list being searched. In Section 11.2 we study another search strategy, called hashing, whose efficiency is measured in terms of the amount of storage you are willing to waste. Hashing can achieve phenomenally fast search times regardless of how much data you have, provided that you can afford to keep a relatively large amount of unused list space available. On the surface, hashing makes it impossible to go through a list in order without augmenting the basic method. In our discussion we describe different ways of constructing hashing functions: a random number generator, folding, digit or character extraction, and division remainder. Because hashing scatters keys within a search table, it is not by itself an appropriate implementation technique for the ordered list ADT introduced in Chapter 3. We therefore define a new ADT—the keyed collection—that is similar to the ordered list ADT but does not require an ordering among its elements or a traversal operation for processing these elements in order. In Section 11.3, however, we look at an adaptation of hashing to ordered traversals using a combination of linked lists and hashing.

The keyed collection ADT is suited to an implementation by hashing that can virtually guarantee $O(1)$ efficiency for the add, delete, and retrieve operations—regardless of the amount of data in the collection. We conclude Section 11.2 with a discussion of the various collision-processing methods that such an implementation may employ: the linear, quadratic, rehashing, linked, and bucket collision-processing methods.

In Section 11.4 we see how variations on hashing can be used to implement sparse matrices, and in Section 11.5 hashing is applied, via the Rabin-Karp algorithm and Horner's method, to the Search operation for the string ADT.

We close the chapter by exploring some of the special considerations that enter into searching for data stored in a disk file instead of main memory. These considerations lead to a variety of search schemes, all of which employ some variations of a data structure known as an index. Indexed sequential search and tree indexing (especially B-tree indexing) are effective when the search keys are of a fixed size, such as integer data. Indexed sequential searching can be effective in situations where the data being stored are relatively stable, but its performance can deteriorate rapidly if it must handle frequent insertions or deletions. B-tree indexing provides a way to handle insertions and deletions dynamically without a resulting deterioration in search efficiency. Perhaps the worst search keys are variable-length character strings. Trie indexing has developed as a means of retrieving keys in this worst case.

Key Words

B-tree	Horner's method	Rabin-Karp algorithm
binary tree index	index	red-black tree
boundary character	indexed sequential search	rehashing
bucket hashing	key field	secondary hashing
character extraction	keyed collection	sectors
clustering	linear collision processing	shift folding
collision processing	linked hashing	splay
density ratio	locality of reference	splay rotations
density-dependent search	overflow area	tracks
digit extraction	primary cluster	trie indexing
double hashing	prime hash area	2-3-4 tree
folding	quadratic collision	
hashing	processing	

Programming Problems/Projects

1. Wing-and-a-Prayer Airlines has the records of all its customers stored in the following form:

   • Last name

   • First name

   • Address

   • Arbitrarily long list of flights on which reservations have been booked

   Using a trie index, write a search-and-retrieval program that will allow input of a customer's last name (and, if necessary, the first name and address to resolve conflicts created by matching last names) and then output all flights on which that customer has booked reservations.

2. SuperScout Inc. is a nationwide scouting service for college football talent to which the Bay Area Brawlers professional team subscribes. As the pool of college talent increases in size, SuperScout has found that its old record-keeping system has deteriorated considerably in its ability to quickly locate the scouting record associated with a given player in its file. Rewrite the scouting record system using a trie to look up the record location of the data associated with a given player's name.

3. Using a large collection of randomly generated keys, write a series of programs that will test various hashing functions you develop. In particular, your programs should report statistics on the number of collisions generated by each hashing function. This information could be valuable in guiding future decisions about which hashing functions and techniques are most effective for your particular system.

4. Repeat Problem 3 but test different collision-processing strategies instead of different hashing functions.

5. Consider a student data record that consists of

   - Student identification number
   - Student name
   - State of residence
   - Sex

   Choose an index structure to process a file with such records. Then write a program to maintain such a file in a fashion that allows retrieval and traversal of records by both the identification number and name fields.

6. Suppose that data records for a phone book file consist of a key field containing both name and address, and a field containing the phone number for that key. Devise an appropriate index for such a file. Then write a program that calls for input of (a) a complete key or (b) if a complete key is not available, as much of the initial portion of a key as the inquirer is able to provide. In the case of situation (a), your program should output the phone number corresponding to the unique key. In the case of situation (b), have your program output all keys (and their phone numbers) that match the provided initial portion.

7. Consider the following problem faced in the development of a compiler. The source program contains many character-string symbols such as variable names, procedure names, and so on. Each of these character-string symbols has associated with it various attributes such as memory location, data type, and so on. However, it would be too time-consuming and awkward for a compiler to manipulate character strings. Instead, each string should be identified with an integer that is viewed as an equivalent to the string for the purpose of compiler manipulation. In addition to serving as a compact equivalent form of a string symbol within the source program, this integer can also serve as a direct pointer into a table of attributes for that symbol. Devise such a transformation that associates a string with an integer, and in turn serves as a pointer into a table of attributes. Test the structure(s) you develop by using them in a program that scans a source program written in your favorite programming language. You will, in effect, have written the symbol table modules for a compiler.

8. Write a spelling-check program. Such a program must scan a file of text, looking up each word it finds in a dictionary of correctly spelled words. When a word cannot be found in the dictionary, the program should convey this fact to its user, giving the user the opportunity to take one of the following steps:

   - Change the spelling of the word in the text file
   - Add the word to the dictionary so it will not be reported as incorrectly spelled in the future

   Since the dictionary for such a program will be searched frequently and is likely to become quite large, an efficient search algorithm is an absolute necessity. One possibility in this regard is to use a trie index with pointers into a large string workspace instead of the pointers to data records. Test your program with a text file and a dictionary large enough to handle all the possibilities your algorithm and data structure may encounter.

9. If you did one of the problems from Chapter 3 that involved maintaining an ordered list, redo that problem using hashing combined with linked lists

as an implementation technique. When finished, write a report in which you empirically compare the performance of your two implementations.

10. If you did one of the problems from Chapter 2 that involved maintaining a sparse matrix, redo that problem using hashing of row and column indices as an implementation technique. When finished, write a report in which you empirically compare the performance of your two implementations.

11. If you did one of the problems in Chapter 2 that involved an implementation of the string search operation, redo that problem using the Rabin-Karp algorithm. When finished, write a report in which you empirically compare the performance of your two algorithms.

12. Implement in a test program the wildcard version of the Rabin-Karp algorithm you formulated in your answer to Exercise 6 of Section 11.5.

13. Implement in a test program the two-dimensional version of the Rabin-Karp algorithm you formulated in your answer to Exercise 5 of Section 11.5.

14. If you did one of the problems from Chapter 3 that involved maintaining an ordered list, redo that problem using 2-3-4, red-black, or splay trees. When finished, write a report in which you empirically compare the performance of your two implementations.

12

SORTING—REVISITED AND EXTENDED

We shall now proceed to construct the socialist order.

Lenin

CHAPTER OUTLINE

12.1 Internal Sorting Algorithms –A Theoretical Bound on Efficiency
12.2 External Sorting
The Two-Way Merge Sort
Analysis of Two-Way Merge Sort
Two-Stream Polyphase Merge Sort

We have already covered a wide variety of sorting algorithms—selection, insertion, radix, quick, merge, and heap sorts. Often we presented a sorting algorithm because it happened to provide an excellent illustration of another topic such as big-O analysis or recursion. In this chapter, we will focus only on sorting. In Section 12.1, we will present an overview of the methods already covered. We will demonstrate that no sorting method based on making comparisons can improve upon the $O(n \log_2 n)$ performance that we have been able to achieve with the heap, merge, and quick sort algorithms.

In Section 12.2, we will shift our attention from *internal sorting*, that is, sorting data within main memory, to *external sorting*, that is, sorting data stored in sequentially accessible secondary memory such as disk and tape files. The methods used for external sorting often involve a combination of a main memory algorithm, such as quick sort, with a variation on the merge logic that we introduced in Section 6.3.

12.1 INTERNAL SORTING ALGORITHMS—A THEORETICAL BOUND ON EFFICIENCY

The criteria we use to evaluate sorting algorithms are the same that we use to evaluate any algorithm—time and space efficiency. Table 12.1 presents a concise summary of what we have already learned about sorting, with references to the chapter in which a particular method was studied. The question of particular interest at this point in our study of sorting is whether any sorting algorithm can better the $O(n \log_2 n)$ efficiency of the heap, merge, and quick sorts. Radix sort is excluded from consideration for two reasons:

1. The disadvantages cited in the comments column of Table 12.1 dictate a choice other than radix sort in most applications.

2. Radix sort is different than other sorting algorithms in that it is not based on making comparisons between values in the array being sorted. Instead it works by iteratively categorizing *individual* values and then appending categories until the entire array is sorted.

We claim that *no sort based on comparisons between array values can be more efficient than* $O(n \log_2 n)$.

To prove this claim, we need to introduce the notion of a decision tree for comparison-based sorting algorithms. Such a tree is illustrated for a three-element insertion sort algorithm in Figure 12.1. To interpret such a tree, observe that all interior nodes represent comparisons made between elements of the array X relative to the original position of these elements in the array. Hence, at the root of the tree, we compare the original X[1] to the original X[2]. If the former is smaller, then we follow the true (T) branch and compare the original X[2] to the original X[3]; otherwise we follow the false (F) branch and compare the original X[1] (which would now be in the second array position) to the original X[3]. When we reach a leaf node of the tree, we have made sufficient comparisons to determine the sorted order of the array. Consequently, there are six leaf nodes in the tree of Figure 12.1, corresponding to the six possible arrangements of data in a three-element array.

Although it may not be easy to do manually, it is evident that such a decision tree can be constructed for any comparison-based sorting algorithm applied to an *n*-element array. In this general case, there must be *n*! leaf nodes in the decision tree, since there are *n*! possible arrangements of data in the array. From our work with binary trees in Chapter 7 we know that, even if it is full, a binary tree with *n*! leaf nodes must contain at least $\log_2(n!)$ levels. This implies that the sort efficiency for any comparison-based algorithm must be at least $O(\log_2(n!))$ since potentially all comparisons corresponding to the longest path in the decision tree must be made. However, in the exercises at the end of the section, you will prove the following inequality:

$$n! \geq (n/2)^{n/2}$$

Hence, $\log_2(n!) \geq \log_2((n/2)^{n/2}) = (n/2)\log_2(n/2)$. This last inequality implies that the number of comparisons must indeed be $O(n \log_2 n)$, and the proof of our claim is complete.

Sorting method	Chapter	Number of comparisons proportional to the number of data items being sorted (n)	Space requirement	Additional comments
Binary tree	7	Between $O(n^2)$ and $O(n \log_2 n)$ depending on original data and whether tree is height-balanced	Pointers for tree and possible stack space for recursive traversals	
Heap	7	$O(n \log_2 n)$	No additional overhead	
Insertion	1	$O(n^2)$	No additional overhead	Loop check allows early exit as soon as item is correctly placed
Merge	6	$O(n \log_2 n)$	Requires duplicate array and stack space for recursion	Since only requires sequential access, can be used for linked lists and sequential files
Pointer	2	Depends on method with which it is combined	Requires list of pointers to maintain logical order	Can be combined with any method to substantially reduce size of data items being interchanged
Radix	4	$O(n)$ but with a large constant of proportionality	Minimal extra storage if queues are allocated dynamically	Large constant of proportionality often makes it slower than $O(n \log_2 n)$ algorithms; highly dependent on type of data being sorted and machine representations of that data, so a difficult method to generalize
Quick	6	$O(n \log_2 n)$ on the average but $O(n^2)$ for worst case	Stack space for recursion	Variations on choosing pivot can make worst case almost impossible to generate
Selection	1	$O(n^2)$	No additional overhead	Only $O(n)$ data interchanges
Shell	1	Between $O(n(\log_2 n)^2)$ and $O(n^{1.5})$ depending on increments used	No additional overhead	

TABLE 12.1   Summary of sorting methods we have studied.

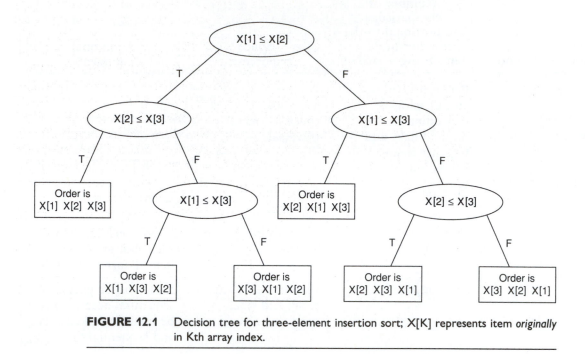

FIGURE 12.1   Decision tree for three-element insertion sort; X[K] represents item *originally* in Kth array index.

This result establishes a lower bound for the efficiency of all comparison-based sorting algorithms. Such an algorithm simply cannot handle all cases in time faster than $O(n \log_2 n)$—it is logically impossible. So, if you hoped to make a name for yourself in computer science by discovering a comparison-based sorting algorithm that is an order of magnitude faster than those already known, it is a hopeless endeavor!

Exercises 12.1

1. Prove the inequality used in our proof of the lower bound on the efficiency of comparison-based sorting algorithms, that is,

$$n! \geq (n/2)^{n/2}$$

(Hint: use induction.)

2. Produce a decision tree for a three-element selection sort. Does it have more, less, or the same number of nodes as the corresponding tree for insertion sort?

3. Construct a decision tree for a seven-element heap sort.

4. Show that we cannot find the minimum or maximum element in an array with fewer than $O(n)$ comparisons.

5. Suppose that we alter the specifications for a sorting algorithm as follows. The algorithm is to produce an array of sorted *distinct* elements. If the original array contains duplicates, the new algorithm must remove those duplicates from the final sorted array. Is the lower bound for the efficiency of this new algorithm less than, equal to, or greater than the lower bound we established for ordinary sorting? Justify your claim with a proof analogous to that presented for ordinary sorting.

6. A sorting method is said to be *stable* if two data items of matching value are guaranteed *not* to be rearranged with respect to each other as the algorithm progresses. For example, in the four element array

$$60 \quad 42_1 \quad 80 \quad 42_2$$

a stable sorting method would guarantee a final ordering

$$42_1 \quad 42_2 \quad 60 \quad 80$$

Classify each of the sorting algorithms in Table 12.1 as to their stability. For the binary tree method, assume that the data is loaded into the binary tree by reading array indices 1 through n; then the data is written back into the array by doing an inorder traversal of the tree. (To see why stability may be important, consider Programming Problem 1 at the end of the chapter.)

12.2 EXTERNAL SORTING

The sorting algorithms we have studied so far assume that the list being sorted is randomly accessible. That is, we may access the Kth entry in the list without going through the first $K - 1$ entries. Such access is typical of arrays that are stored in main memory. However, data on permanent storage devices such as disk and tape frequently are accessible only in a sequential fashion. In this section we shall turn our attention to sorting data that is organized sequentially. Algorithms that sort data maintained in sequentially accessible streams are called *external sorting* algorithms—as opposed to the *internal sorting* algorithms that operate within the confines of main memory.

The merge procedure that we developed as a subordinate algorithm to the merge sort procedure in Section 3 of Chapter 6 is noteworthy because it only requires sequential access to each of the lists being merged. This feature makes merging an essential ingredient of virtually all external sorting algorithms. In broad terms, these algorithms take a sequentially accessible data stream and partition it into runs—sequentially accessible sublists that are sorted. These runs are then merged into larger runs, with this process continuing until we are left with just one large run containing all records in the original data stream.

To more formally describe external sorting algorithms, we require the definition of a sequentially accessible data stream as an abstract data type. It should be apparent how the operations described below can be mapped to the file and tape processing commands of your favorite programming language.

• **Definition:** A *data stream* is a sequence of homogenous records that may be accessed only by starting at the first record in the sequence and then reading the second, third, and so forth. A *run* is a subsequence of a stream arranged in order according to a specified Precedes relationship between records. The operations on a stream are defined in the following PSEUDO pre- and post-conditions. Note that these operations imply that a given stream may either be read from or written to. After the Create operation is performed on a stream, records may be sequentially written to the stream; once the First operation is performed, records may only be read from the stream.

```
type
  StreamRec: (* The type of record composing the stream *);

procedure Create
  ( given S: Stream           (* An arbitrary stream *);
    return S: Stream          (* S initialized as an empty stream and ready
                                 to be written to via the Put operation *) );
procedure First
  ( given S: Stream           (* A stream that has been previously created
                                 and acted upon by other operations *);
    return S: Stream          (* Stream S in read mode; the next call to Get
                                 will return the second record in S. S may
                                 not be written to again unless it is
                                 re-created *);
         SRec: StreamRec      (* The first record in stream S if EOStream is
                                 false. If EOStream is true, then SRec is
                                 unreliable *);
         EOStream: boolean    (* false if S contains a first record; true if
                                 S is empty *) );
procedure Get
  ( given S: Stream           (* A stream that has been previously created
                                 and accessed at least once by First or Get *);
    return S: Stream          (* Stream S in read mode; the next call to Get
                                 will return the record in S that follows the
                                 one returned by this invocation of Get. S
                                 may not be written to again unless it is
                                 re-created *);
         SRec: StreamRec      (* If EOStream is false, then SRec is the record in
                                 stream S that follows the one returned by
                                 the most recent invocation of First or Get. If
                                 EOStream is true, then SRec is unreliable *);
         EOStream: boolean    (* false if S contains a valid record to be
                                 returned in SRec; true if there are no more
                                 records in S *) );
procedure Put
  ( given S: Stream           (* A stream that has been created and
                                 potentially acted upon by previous
                                 invocations of Put.  S must not have been
                                 accessed by First or Get after its
                                 creation *);
         SRec: StreamRec      (* A record to append to the end of S *);
    return S: Stream          (* S with SRec appended *) );
```

Example 12.1 To illustrate the use of streams, consider the following procedure, which merges runs beginning with the most recently accessed records on streams In1 and In2. The run resulting from merging these two runs is written out to stream Out, which we assume to have been previously created. The internal logic of the procedure follows closely that of the Merge procedure we developed in conjunction with the merge sort algorithm in Section 6.3. The particular interface we have chosen for this procedure is designed so that the procedure may be strategically called in the external sorting algorithms we will soon discuss.

```
type
   Comparison: function (* The signature of a function establishing an
                          order relationship on stream records *)
                  ( given A, B: StreamRec   (* Records to compare *);
                    return: boolean         (* true if A precedes B in the
                                               order relationship underlying a
                                               run *) );
procedure MergeRuns
   ( given In1, In2: Stream              (* Two streams, each of which
                                            has been previously
                                            accessed by First or
                                            Get *);

           Current1, Current2: StreamRec (* The most recently accessed
                                            records from In1 and In2
                                            respectively. These
                                            respective records are
                                            unreliable if EOS1 or EOS2
                                            is true *);

           EOS1, EOS2: boolean           (* The end of stream boolean
                                            values returned by the most
                                            recent invocation of First
                                            or Get for In1 and In2,
                                            respectively *);

           Precedes: Comparison          (* The order relationship for
                                            stream records *);

     return Out: Stream                  (* A previously created stream
                                            to which has been appended
                                            the merging of the two
                                            runs beginning with
                                            Current1 and Current2
                                            from In1 and In2,
                                            respectively *);

            In1, In2: Stream             (* Positioned at the record
                                            (or end of stream) that
                                            terminated their
                                            respective runs *);

            Current1, Current2: StreamRec (* Contain the records that will
                                            begin a new run on In1 and
                                            In2, respectively, provided
                                            the end-of-stream indicator
                                            is not true for that
                                            stream *) );
```

This run is written to stream Out. On exit from procedure, Current1 contains 4 and In2 is at end of stream.

```
var
   Done1, Done2: boolean;          (* Used to signal end of run in In1
                                      and In2 *)
   Prev1, Prev2: StreamRec;        (* Retain record last written from
                                      In1 and In2 *)

start MergeRuns
   Done1 := EOS1;
   Done2 := EOS2;
   while not Done1 and not Done2 do  (* Choose first among two current
                                        records *)
      if Precedes(Current1, Current2) then
         Prev1 := Current1;
         Put(Out, Current1);
         Get(In1, Current1, EOS1);
         Done1 := EOS1 or Precedes(Current1, Prev1)
      else
         Prev2 := Current2;
         Put(Out, Current2);
         Get(In2, Current2, EOS2);
         Done2 := EOS2 or Precedes(Current2, Prev2)
      endif
   endwhile;
   if Done1 then  (* Flush the run that remains on one stream *)
      while not Done2 do
         Prev2 := Current2;
         Put(Out, Current2);
         Get(In2, Current2, EOS2);
         Done2 := EOS2 or Precedes(Current2, Prev2)
      endwhile
   else
      while not Done1 do
         Prev1 := Current1;
         Put(Out, Current1);
         Get(In1, Current1, EOS1);
         Done1 := EOS1 or Precedes(Current1, Prev1)
      endwhile
   endif
end MergeRuns;
```

We will now use the MergeRuns procedure of Example 12.1 in developing two external sorting algorithms: the N-way merge sort and the N-stream polyphase merge sort. We will discuss both algorithms for the case in which N = 2 and leave their generalizations for you to ponder in the exercises.

The Two-Way Merge Sort

Both of the external sorting algorithms we will consider assume that we have streams with embedded runs. In the extreme case, the size of these embedded runs could be as small as 1. However, more typically, the runs are larger, having been put on the stream by loading a large amount of data into main memory, sorting it by invocation of an efficient internal sorting algorithm, and then writing the sorted data out to a stream. The external sorting algorithms work regardless of the size of the runs on the initial streams; however, they become more efficient with larger runs. We will use M to designate the size of runs on the initial input streams; this value will then be factored into our efficiency analyses of the external sorting algorithms.

The two-way merge sort requires five streams—two with the original data split between them, arranged in runs of size M; two scratch streams; and one stream to return the sorted data. Figure 12.2 depicts this situation for a stream originally containing 25 items. Using an appropriate internal sorting algorithm with size M = 2 (an unrealistically small value for M, but convenient for illustration), this original data is split over two streams S_1 and S_2. The runs of size 2 on S_1 and S_2 are then merged, via repeated calls to MergeRuns, producing streams S_3 and S_4—each with runs of size 4. We now cascade back and forth between S_3, S_4 and S_1, S_2—each time

Original Stream: (14, 2, 57, 6, 3, 28, 45, 1, 30, 4, 9, 31, 23, 35, 12, 8, 11, 13, 19, 18, 21, 5, 37, 89, 77)

$\downarrow$ Use internal sort to produce runs of size M = 2

S_1: ((2, 14), (3, 28), (4, 30), (23, 35), (11,13), (5, 21))

S_2: ((6, 57), (1, 45), (9, 31), (8, 12), (18,19), (37, 89), (77))
S_3:
S_4:

$\downarrow$ Merge runs on S_1 and S_2 to produce runs of size 4 on S_3 and S_4

S_1:
S_2:
S_3: ((2, 6, 14, 57), (4, 9, 30, 31), (11,13, 18, 19))
S_4: ((1, 3, 28, 45), (8, 12, 23, 35), (5, 21, 37, 89), (77))

$\downarrow$ Merge runs on S_3 and S_4 to produce runs of size 8 on S_1 and S_2

S_1: ((1, 2, 3, 6, 14, 28, 45, 57), (5, 11, 13, 18, 19, 21, 37, 89))
S_2: ((4, 8, 9, 12, 23, 30, 31, 35), (77))
S_3:
S_4:

$\downarrow$ Merge runs on S_1 and S_2 to produce runs of size 16 on S_3 and S_4

S_1:
S_2:
S_3: ((1, 2, 3, 4, 6, 8, 9, 12, 14, 23, 28, 30, 31, 35, 45, 57))
S_4: ((5, 11, 13, 18, 19, 21, 37, 77, 89))

FIGURE 12.2

Two-way merging where the original data stream is split into two streams S_1 and S_2. The data in S_1 and S_2 are arranged in runs of size 2.

$\downarrow$ Merge runs on S_3 and S_4 to produce sorted file on S_1

S_1: (1, 2, 3, 4, 5, 6, 8, 9, 11, 12, 13, 14, 18, 19, 21, 23, 28, 30, 31, 35, 37, 45, 57, 77, 89)
S_2:
S_3:
S_4:

producing runs that double the size of the previous runs. Eventually we are left with just one large run on one of the streams. This is the stream we must return as the sorted stream. The version of the two-way merge sort presented below assumes that the original data stream has already been split into two streams with an equal number of runs, although potentially the last run on one of the streams could be empty. The real work of the procedure TwoWayMergeSort is done in the subordinate procedure MergeStreams. Here the merging of all runs from two input streams onto two output streams is accomplished. TwoWayMergeSort merely must control the back-and-forth cascading of MergeStreams until we are left with one long run, which is then copied onto the stream to be returned.

```
procedure TwoWayMergeSort
  ( given S1, S2: Stream       (* Two streams each containing a number of
                                  runs. Ideally, the number of runs on
                                  the two streams will differ by at most
                                  one, although this is not necessary for
                                  the algorithm to work correctly *);
        Precedes: Comparison    (* Order relationship on stream records *);
    return S: Stream            (* A sorted stream containing the data
                                  originally on S1 and S2 *) );

  var
    Count: integer;
    S3, S4: Stream;  (* Scratch streams *)

(* Procedure MergeStreams called as subordinate by TwoWayMergeSort *)

  procedure MergeStreams
    ( given F1, F2: Stream       (* Two streams each containing a number
                                    of runs. Ideally, the number of runs
                                    on the two streams will differ by at
                                    most one, although this is not
                                    necessary for the algorithm to work
                                    correctly *);
          Precedes: Comparison    (* Order relationship on stream records *);
      return F3, F4: Stream       (* F3 contains runs consisting of the
                                    merging of the 1st, 3rd, 5th,...runs
                                    on F1 and F2. F4 contains runs
                                    consisting of the merging of the 2nd,
                                    4th, 6th,...runs on F1 and F2 *);
            NumberRuns: integer   (* The number of runs on each of F1 and F2.
                                    If the two streams do not have the same
                                    number of runs, the number for the
                                    stream with more runs is returned *) );

    var
      Current1, Current2: StreamRec;
      EOS1, EOS2: boolean;

    start MergeStreams
      NumberRuns := 0;
      First(F1, Current1, EOS1);
      First(F2, Current2, EOS2);
```

```
      Create(F3);
      Create(F4);
      while not EOS1 or not EOS2 do      (* More data on one of the streams? *)
        NumberRuns := NumberRuns + 1;
        (* Call procedure from Example 12.1 *)
        MergeRuns(F1, F2, Current1, Current2, EOS1, EOS2, Precedes, F3);
        if not EOS1 or not EOS2 then    (* More data on one of the streams? *)
          NumberRuns := NumberRuns + 1;
          MergeRuns(F1, F2, Current1, Current2, EOS1, EOS2, Precedes, F4)
        endif
      endwhile
    end MergeStreams;

start TwoWayMergeSort
  Create(S3);
  Create(S4);
  Count := 0;
  repeat
    Count := Count + 1;
    if Count mod 2 <> 0 then    (* Use odd-even test on Count to flip-flop *)
      MergeStreams(S1, S2, Precedes, S3, S4, NumberRuns)
    else
      MergeStreams(S3, S4, Precedes, S1, S2, NumberRuns)
    endif
  until NumberRuns <= 1;
  if Count mod 2 <> 0 then      (* Did S1 or S3 end up with the sorted list? *)
    CopyStream(S3, S)           (* Assume existence of trivial procedure to
                                   copy first stream onto second *)
  else
    CopyStream(S1, S)
  endif
end TwoWayMergeSort;
```

Analysis of Two-Way Merge Sort

The procedure MergeStreams is clearly $O(NumberRec)$, where NumberRec is the number of records in the original stream. Observe that, because the number of runs is halved on each iteration of the **repeat** loop in **procedure** TwoWayMergeSort, this loop is $O(\log_2(\text{Maximum of number of runs in original S1 and S2}))$. Under the assumption that S1 and S2 are created by producing runs equal in size to M (the maximum number of values that we can sort internally at one time), then it follows that the **repeat** loop in TwoWayMergeSort is $O(\log_2(\text{Number Rec}/M))$. Hence, the overall efficiency of the two-way merge is $O(NumberRec \times \log_2(NumberRec/M))$. Of course, this does not take into account the cost of originally producing the runs on S1 and S2. You will analyze the price paid for this factor in the exercises. The exercises will also allow you to explore how much the algorithm increases in efficiency if more than two input streams are provided initially (so that the algorithm becomes an N-way merge instead of a two-way merge).

Two-Stream Polyphase Merge Sort

The two-way merge sort required five streams to sort one stream. Although the algorithm could be modified to use only four streams by using the stream to be returned as one of the scratch streams, the number of streams is still a considerable price to pay in resources—particularly if a separate tape drive must be allocated for each stream. The polyphase merge algorithm represents an attempt to reduce this resource cost. It only requires one scratch stream in addition to the two streams with embedded runs provided as input to the algorithm. Figure 12.3 highlights the essence of the algorithm. The same original stream of 25 values used in Figure 12.2 is distributed in runs of size $M = 2$ over streams S_1 and S_2. Stream S_1 contains five runs and S_2 contains eight runs. This choice for distributing runs over the two input streams works nicely for reasons that will soon become apparent. The first five runs on S_1 and S_2 are merged, producing five runs on S_3 and leaving three runs on

Original Stream: (14, 2, 57, 6, 3, 28, 45, 1, 30, 4, 9, 31, 23, 35, 12, 8, 11, 13, 19, 18, 21, 5, 37, 89, 77)

$\downarrow$ Use internal sort to produce runs of size M = 2, with 5 runs on S_1 and 8 runs on S

S_1: ((2, 14), (3, 28), (4, 30), (23, 35), (11,13))
S_2: ((6, 57), (1, 45), (9, 31), (8, 12), (18,19), (5, 21), (37, 89), (77))
S_3:

$\downarrow$ Merge 5 runs from each stream onto S_3

S_1:
S_2: ((5, 21), (37, 89), (77))
S_3: ((2, 6, 14, 57), (1, 3, 28, 45), (4, 9, 30, 31), (8, 12, 23, 35), (11,13, 18 19))

$\downarrow$ Merge 3 runs from each stream onto S_1

S_1: ((2, 5, 6, 14, 21, 57), (1, 3, 28, 37, 45, 89), (4, 9, 30, 31, 77))
S_2:
S_3: ((8, 12, 23, 35), (11, 13, 18, 19))

$\downarrow$ Merge 2 runs from each stream onto S_2

S_1: ((4, 9, 30, 31, 77))
S_2: ((2, 5, 6, 8, 12, 14, 21, 23, 35, 57), (1, 3, 11, 13, 18, 19, 28, 37, 45, 89))
S_3:

$\downarrow$ Merge 1 run from each stream onto S_3

S_1:
S_2: (1, 3, 11, 13, 18, 19, 28, 37, 45, 89))
S_3: ((2, 4, 5, 6, 8, 9, 12, 14, 21, 23, 30, 31, 35, 57, 77))

FIGURE 12.3
Polyphase merging with two input streams, each of which has its data arranged in runs of size 2.

$\downarrow$ Merge 1 run from each stream onto S_1

S_1: (1, 2, 3, 4, 5, 6, 8, 9, 11, 12, 13, 14, 18, 19, 21, 23, 28, 30, 31, 35, 37, 45, 57, 77, 89)
S_2:
S_3:

S_2. Then the first three runs on S_2 and S_3 are merged, producing three larger runs on S_1 and leaving two runs on stream S_3. Now we merge runs from S_3 and S_1 onto S_2, and so forth, until we finish with just one run which, in this example, is produced on S_1. We will not delve into a detailed analysis of the polyphase merge sort because it is quite complex. The interested reader is referred to Knuth (*The Art of Computer Programming: Searching and Sorting*) for these particulars. However, note the following interesting facts about the polyphase algorithm. First, the distribution of runs on the initial two input tapes is determined by the famous Fibonacci sequence—the same sequence that arose in our discussion of interpolative search strategies in Chapter 1 (Section 1.3, Exercise 6). Recall that this sequence has the property that each member of the sequence is the sum of the two preceding members, with the first two members initialized to one. In the polyphase merge algorithm, runs should be distributed on the original input streams in a way that ensures that the number of runs on S_1 and S_2 are successive members of the Fibonacci sequence. (If necessary, one of the streams may be padded with empty runs to guarantee this.) Second, a careful comparison of Figures 12.2 and 12.3 indicates that, on the same set of data, the two-way merge sort will require four iterations of merging input streams whereas the two-stream polyphase merge will require five. This is evidence that polyphase will be somewhat less efficient in time—a fact that should not be surprising given its greater efficiency in terms of resources.

Exercises 12.2

1. Complete the efficiency analysis for sorting a stream using a two-way merge sort by determining the cost of initially producing runs of size M from a stream with NumberRec records. In practice, is this cost likely to be more or less than the cost of actually performing the two-way merge sort? Remember that, since streams usually exist on secondary storage devices, accessing the next record in a stream could well be an order of magnitude slower than accessing an item in a main memory array.

2. In the MergeRuns procedure of Example 12.1, the boolean variable Done1 is assigned by the statement

   ```
   Done1 := EOS1 or Precedes(Current1, Prev1)
   ```

   What assumption does this statement make about the way in which a logical **or** will be evaluated? What could go wrong with this statement?

3. Modify the TwoWayMergeSort procedure so that only four streams are used instead of five.

4. Write an NWayMergeSort procedure that receives N input streams (instead of two) and uses N scratch streams. Assume that you can declare an array of streams for this purpose. This is not an unrealistic assumption since the implementation of a stream or file variable in an actual programming language typically does not associate the entire stream with the variable. Rather, the stream variable is only a pointer to the memory address of the current record for that stream. How does the expansion of this algorithm to encompass N input streams instead of two affect the algorithm's efficiency?

5. Write an implementation of the two-stream polyphase merge sort algorithm.

6. The two-stream polyphase merge sort can be generalized to an N-stream algorithm that receives N input streams, each containing an appropriate number

of runs, and still requires only one scratch stream. How should runs be distributed over the input streams for this more general form of the algorithm? (Hint: think about ways of generalizing the Fibonacci sequence.) Illustrate how the method would work by tracing a three-stream polyphase merge sort for the list of keys in Figure 12.3.

A RELEVANT ISSUE

Virtual Memory System and External Sorting

The more sophisticated operating systems of today will often allow a user to apply an internal sorting algorithm to an entire file through what is known as *virtual memory*. In such systems, a programmer is able to view main memory as virtually limitless. That is, such systems give the programmer "infinite" main memory. Given this perspective, the programmer can sort a relatively large file by loading it into a virtually infinite array, applying an internal sorting algorithm to it, and then writing the array back out to permanent storage in a file.

Does this mean that external sorting algorithms are, or soon will be, obsolete? They will not be completely obsolete for two reasons. First, such "infinite" memory systems are not really infinite. They are limited by the memory address size of the computer. For instance, on a computer with a 32-bit architecture, this memory address size is $2^{32} - 1$, or 2,147,483,647. Such a computer can access that many bytes of virtual memory. If a file does not fit in that many bytes, then it cannot be loaded in virtual memory and cannot have an internal sorting algorithm applied to it. Although there are techniques to push this maximum memory address to higher limits, all computers have such a limit. A file that surpasses the limit simply cannot be loaded all at once into virtual memory.

The second argument against using a large amount of virtual memory to sort a data stream internally centers around the "virtual" portion of virtual memory. Virtual memory is not true main memory. Rather, it is memory divided into pages—some of which actually reside in main memory while others reside on disk storage. When you write a program that accesses a virtual-memory page not presently in main memory, the operating system must execute a *paging algorithm*—an algorithm responsible for bringing into main memory the page your program requests and deciding which page presently in main memory should be swapped out to disk storage to make room for the new page.

Paging is the hidden price paid for the programming convenience offered by virtual memory systems. Any internal sorting algorithm applied to a virtually infinite array will cause paging to occur. Since paging represents a disk access, it will take longer than a pure memory access, which does not generate a page swap. The key to the efficiency of a virtual internal sorting algorithm is whether the algorithm forces an excessive amount of paging to occur. That is, does the algorithm frequently require the operating system to fetch back from disk storage a page just recently swapped out? If so, an $O(n \log_2 n)$ sorting algorithm may well take longer than a theoretically based estimate would predict. Such an estimate will not include the paging costs.

What is the cure for this problem? Consult local system references to determine the paging algorithm your system uses and then try to tailor the sorting algorithm you choose to take advantage of this information. Or, resort to an external sorting algorithm that allows you to have more direct control over the paging that occurs.

Chapter Summary

In this chapter we focused only on sorting. In Section 12.1, we gave an overview of the methods already covered and demonstrated that no sorting method based on making comparisons can improve upon the $O(n \log_2 n)$ performance that we were able to achieve with the heap, merge, and quick sort algorithms.

In Section 12.2, we shifted our attention from internal sorting, that is, sorting data within main memory, to external sorting, which is sorting data stored on sequentially accessible secondary memory such as disk and tape files. The two methods we presented for external sorting rely on the merge procedure developed as a subordinate algorithm to the merge sort in Section 3 of Chapter 6. Both algorithms take a sequentially accessible data stream and partition it into runs—sequentially accessible sublists that are sorted. These runs are then merged into larger runs, with this process continuing until we are left with just one large run containing all records in the original data stream. The two-way merge sort requires five streams—two with the original data split between them, arranged in runs of size M; two scratch streams; and one stream to return the sorted data. The two-stream polyphase merge algorithm reduces this resource cost by requiring one scratch stream in addition to the two streams with embedded runs that are provided as input to the algorithm. The price paid for the increased efficiency in resource cost of the polyphase algorithm is a poorer run-time efficiency.

Key Words

data stream	run	two-way merge sort
external sorting	two-stream polyphase	
internal sorting	merge sort	

Programming Problems/Projects

1. Consider a list of records, each containing four fields:

   Name

   Month of birth

   Day of birth

   Year of birth

   Write a program to sort this list in oldest-to-youngest order. People with the same birth date should be arranged alphabetically. One strategy you could employ would be to concatenate strategically the four fields into one, and then just sort that one field. Another strategy would be to sort the list four times, each time by a different field. (Think carefully about which field to sort first.) Which of the strategies would require that you choose a stable sorting algorithm?

2. In Table 12.1, the quick sort procedure is identified as an $O(n \log_2 n)$ algorithm that can occasionally degenerate to $O(n^2)$. Write a program in which you throw a large number of random data sets at quick sort. Use this program to empirically estimate the percentage of time that quick sort will degenerate to its worst-case efficiency.

3. Develop a program to sort external data files using the two-way merge sort algorithm. Your program should allow the user to input M, the size of the initial runs that are produced by an internal sorting algorithm. Insert timing statements into your program so that you can experiment to determine which value of M produces the fastest execution time. In a short essay, relate your experimental findings to the answer you gave for Exercise 1 in Section 2.

4. Develop a program to sort external data files using the two-stream polyphase merge algorithm. Your program should allow the user to input M, the size of the initial runs that are produced by an internal sorting algorithm. Race this program against the program that you (or a classmate) developed for Problem 3. Write up the results of your experimentally racing these two algorithms. Your write-up should address the question of what execution-time price was paid for the more efficient use of resources achieved by the polyphase algorithm.

5. Pivotal to the execution-time efficiency of both the two-way merge sort and the polyphase merge sort is the size M of the runs that are present on the initial input streams. The larger these runs are, the more efficient the external sorting algorithm becomes. In this section we assumed that the runs would be produced by invoking an internal sorting algorithm on an array of size M, which is loaded by getting the next M items from the original data stream. Consider the following alternative strategy, known as *replacement selection,* for producing these runs using an internal array with room for M values. Instead of getting a block of M values from the original stream and sorting these M values, use the array to provide a modified implementation of a priority queue that can accommodate up to M items at a time. Begin by loading M values from the original input stream into this priority queue. Then remove the first item in the priority queue and put it out to the run that is currently being produced. There is now room to bring another item into the priority queue from the original input stream; so do this. If the item brought in precedes the item that was just dequeued, then "mark" it so that it will not move to the front of the priority queue and, hence, not be removed with the next invocation of the dequeue operation for the priority queue. (Think about the need for this marking. Its necessity explains why the priority queue used in the replacement selection algorithm to create runs is a slightly modified priority queue.) If the item that is brought in does not precede the item that had previously been dequeued, then it may be enqueued in the normal fashion. Continue dequeueing unmarked items and bringing in additional items from the original stream until the marking of items dictates that a new run must be started.

   Given an internal array of size M, implement the replacement selection strategy to create runs in the streams initially fed to the two-way merge sort or the polyphase merge sort. Incorporate this implementation into the program you developed for Problem 4 or 5 above. Execute a series of experimental tests to determine the average size of a run produced in terms of M, the internal array size used for the modified priority queue. By running your new program against the program you developed previously for Problem 4 or 5, determine the effect of the replacement selection strategy on the actual execution time of the overall sorting algorithm. Write up the results of your experimentation in a report.

6. Use a high-level language to create a program that will complete the following steps. Artificially create a stream S of 1,000 randomly chosen names. Read

into a separate stream S_1 all those names from S whose last names begin with A through G. Sort this stream with heap sort, and store this sorted stream in another stream Large. Now read into S_1 all those names from S whose names begin with H through N; sort it, and append it to the end of Large. Repeat this process until all names from S are exhausted. The file Large will be the sorted version of the original stream S. Observe the execution time of your program. Provide a general efficiency analysis of this external sorting method in terms of the size of the streams S and S_1.

13

MEMORY MANAGEMENT TECHNIQUES

A government that is big enough to give you all you want
is big enough to take it all away.

Barry Goldwater

CHAPTER OUTLINE

In Section 3 of Chapter 3, we described a method for implementing the pointer ADT. That strategy employs a linked list of available data nodes, from which the GetNode operation, when invoked, supplies the first available node on the list. The ReturnNode operation places the node being returned at the head of this available space list. Essentially, the available space list used by this strategy is a stack—the node most recently returned to the list is the one that will be allocated next by GetNode.

   In this chapter we will examine, in greater detail, methods for allocating memory to applications that need it and then effectively reclaiming the memory when the application explicitly or implicitly declares it is no longer needed. In Section 13.1, we will use the example of memory allocation among users in a time-sharing environment to illustrate how memory resources can be managed when users are requesting blocks of varying sizes—a complication avoided in our simple implementation of Section 3.3. The discussion of Section 13.1 will also indicate how the allocation of variably sized blocks complicates the problem of *garbage collection*—the rather colorful term applied to algorithms that effectively recover memory from users who no longer need it.

In Section 13.2, we will pursue the example of a multiuser, time-sharing environment to illustrate three variations of memory management strategies identified by the common term *buddy systems*. The three buddy systems we will explore are the binary, Fibonacci, and boundary tag systems. All of these methods are designed to allow fast garbage collection with a minimum of wasted space.

Finally, in Section 13.3, we will switch from the example of allocating memory among users in a time-sharing environment to the problem of providing a completely general implementation of the pointer ADT. This problem, as faced by the implementors of programming languages that provide a pointer type, requires extending the memory management techniques discussed in Sections 1 and 2 to handle one additional complication—the potential of multiple pointer references to a particular data node. The techniques that encompass this complication are specific to an area of memory management often referred to as *heap management*. Note again that the use of the term *heap* in this context is somewhat unfortunate since it bears no relationship to our earlier discussion of the heap ADT in Section 4 of Chapter 7.

13.1 MEMORY ALLOCATION AND THE FRAGMENTATION PROBLEM

Perhaps the most precious commodity in a multiuser, time-sharing environment is memory. The designers and implementors of operating systems must have as their overriding goal a distribution scheme that ensures that each user gets the amount of resource needed but not more. Because different users have vastly different requirements, the simple implementation of the pointer ADT discussed in Section 3.3 is totally inadequate. Recall that this implementation assumed that all memory blocks doled out by the GetNode operation would be the same size. Now we must fit the block of memory returned by the GetNode operation to the particular needs of the user. Moreover, as users finish with a block of memory, it must be immediately reclaimed by the operating system so that it may be reallocated to other users. As an example of the complications that arise in this allocate-reclaim-reallocate cycle, consider the sequence of user requests for memory presented in Figure 13.1.

This figure illustrates what is known as the *fragmentation problem*. That is, as memory is allocated to users and then returned, the resulting overall pattern of available memory contains relatively small, disconnected fragments of available space. The problem with this fragmented pattern is that we cannot honor a user request for a contiguous memory area exceeding the size of the largest available memory block, even though overall we may have more than enough memory to grant the request. This dilemma is illustrated by the 10K request in the final memory snapshot of Figure 13.1.

One solution to this fragmentation problem would be to move all used memory blocks down in memory, resulting in just one large free block whose size is equal to the sum of the sizes of all the original smaller free blocks. This strategy is called *compaction* and is not acceptable from an operating system

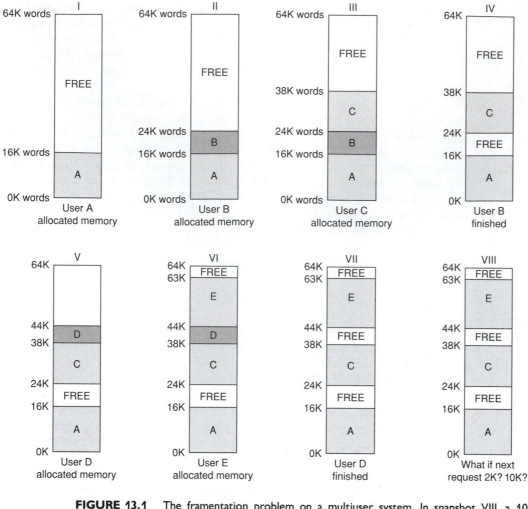

FIGURE 13.1   The framentation problem on a multiuser system. In snapshot VIII, a 10K request could not be met even though a total of 15K is unused.

perspective because operating systems must be extremely time-efficient in their responses to users. The compaction process would require stopping all user activity while memory is reorganized by moving large amounts of data. Compaction would therefore inevitably result in periodic and time-consuming interruptions in service that would be sure to annoy system users.

Another attempt at solving this problem is to generalize the algorithm behind the implementations of GetNode and ReturnNode procedures in Chapter 3, enabling them to handle variable-length records. For instance, the free blocks pictured in the last memory snapshot of Figure 13.1 could be linked into an available list by allocating two words in each block to store the size of the block and a pointer to the next available block. (See Figure 13.2.)

When a user request is made of the list in Figure 13.2, our generalized implementation of GetNode could search the list for a block whose size satisfies the request. This search could employ one of two algorithms:

1. A *first-fit* algorithm in which the list is searched until we find the first block whose size meets or exceeds the request

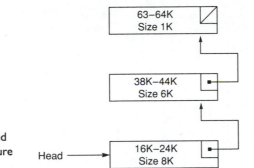

FIGURE 13.2
Available block list derived from snapshot VIII of Figure 13.1.

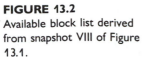

2. A *best-fit* algorithm in which the list is searched for the block whose size surpasses the request by the least amount

Having determined the block to allocate to the user, next it would be wise to check whether or not the user actually requires the entire block. If not, it could be split, giving the user what is requested and keeping what remains of the block in the available block list. This strategy, applied to the available block list of Figure 13.2 for a request of 2K memory, yields the result displayed in Figure 13.3.

Unfortunately, this scheme will lead to another problem when it comes time to collect the memory blocks no longer needed by users. Consider, for instance, what happens if the 2K memory block allocated in Figure 13.3 is returned by its user before any other changes are made in the available space structure. The new available space list now contains one additional 2K block as indicated in Figure 13.4.

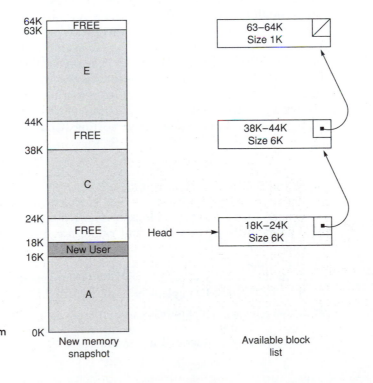

FIGURE 13.3
Honoring a 2K request from the available block list of Figure 13.2.

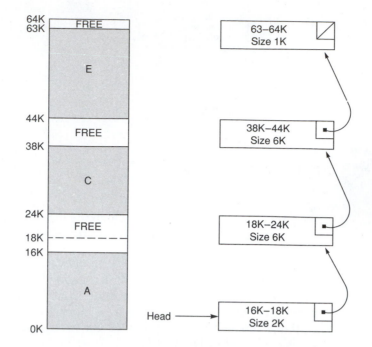

FIGURE 13.4
Available block list after
returning the 2K block.

As more and more of these relatively small blocks are returned, the available list will have an excessive number of very small blocks. This is not desirable because it will eventually become impossible to fill the legitimate request of a user needing one large memory block. We will have small neighboring blocks, the sum of whose sizes may collectively surpass the total memory needed by the large request. However, their being partitioned into many small blocks instead of relatively few large blocks will make it impossible to fill the request. To remedy this problem, we must devise a method that will allow a block being returned to the available list to be *coalesced* with any other block(s) in the list that is (are) the physical neighbor(s) of the returning block. Interestingly, one of the solutions we are about to describe makes use again of the sequence of numbers from mathematics known as the Fibonacci sequence, which arose in our discussions of interpolative search strategies (Chapter 1) and polyphase merge sorting (Chapter 12).

Exercises 13.1

1. In the operating system routines responsible for file management, users are typically allocated a fixed-size disk block, such as 512 bytes, each time they extend a file. Hence, the blocks associated with a given file may not be contiguous on the disk surface but rather are linked blocks scattered over the entire disk. Which implementation of the GetNode operation would be most appropriate for the file management portion of an operating system: the implementation of Section 3.3, the first-fit implementation discussed in this section, or the best-fit implementation discussed in this section? Why?

2. Extend the implementations of GetNode and ReturnNode originally developed in Section 3.3 to manage memory nodes of varying size by using the first-fit strategy described in Section 13.1.

3. Extend the implementations of GetNode and ReturnNode originally developed in Section 3.3 to manage memory nodes of varying size by using the best-fit strategy described in Section 13.1.

4. Given a memory region of 128K words, trace the blocks allocated to users and the status of the list of available blocks for the following sequence of user requests:

   User 1 requests 47K

   User 2 request 39K

   User 3 request 4K

   User 4 requests 34K

   User 1 finishes

   User 5 requests 6K

   User 4 finishes

   User 6 requests 18K

   User 7 requests 32K

   User 8 requests 30K

   Assume that the list of available blocks is traversed from the available block at the lowest address to that at the highest address. Assume also that the best-fit algorithm is used.

5. How is your tracing of the scenario in Exercise 4 affected if

   a. The first-fit algorithm is used?
   b. The available block list is maintained in order of *descending* block sizes and the first-fit algorithm is used?
   c. The available block list is maintained in order of *ascending* block sizes and the first-fit algorithm is used?

6. Will the best-fit algorithm always manage memory more space-efficiently than the first-fit algorithm? If yes, explain why; otherwise, provide a sequence of user requests for which the first-fit algorithm would perform better from a space perspective.

7. Specify the additional data that must be maintained to implement the compaction strategy mentioned at the beginning of this section. Then supply full declarations for this data and use these declarations to implement a compaction algorithm. Analyze the time efficiency of your algorithm.

13.2 BUDDY SYSTEMS

A common method to avoid fragmentation and ensure that a returning block coalesces with neighboring available memory is to designate for each block one or two buddy blocks. A buddy block must reside next to its corresponding block in memory. When a block is ready to be returned, we check the available space list for its buddy. If the buddy is also available, we coalesce the two before returning them as one block to available space. This is not quite as easy as it seems. To determine the buddy of a given block, it is necessary to impose certain restrictions upon block sizes and/or to store a fair amount of bookkeeping data in each block. We shall examine three buddy schemes.

1. Binary buddies
2. Fibonacci buddies
3. Boundary tag buddies

These schemes differ in the data structures used for their implementation. After stating the general algorithms in skeletal pseudocode, we shall give a more detailed discussion of these data structures.

```
procedure Allocate
    ( given S: integer     (* The size of the memory block for a
                               particular request *);
      return P: pointer    (* A pointer to a memory block that
                               meets the request with a minimum
                               amount of waste *) );

      start Allocate
        call a search procedure to search the available block list(s) and find
             a block that surpasses the size requested with the least possible
             amount of excess;
        if no such block can be found then
          call InsufficientMemory
        elsif the block found cannot be split into buddies (one of
              which would satisfy the size requested) then
          Return the block found by the search procedure, referenced by the
          pointer P
        else (* The buddy system being used allows splitting *)
          Split the block into two buddies;
          Return one buddy to appropriate available block list(s);
          Return P as the pointer to the other buddy
        endif
      end Allocate;
```

The search procedure called upon to find a block in this procedure would be dependent upon the data structure used by a particular buddy system to store available blocks. Whether a block, once found, can be further split is determined by the restrictions the given buddy system imposes on block sizes.

A similar skeletal pseudocode algorithm for restoring a returning memory block to available space is presented here in recursive form. The recursion expresses the fact that, once a returning block has been coalesced with its buddy on the left or right, we have a larger block that may itself be a candidate for coalescing with another buddy.

```
procedure ReturnBlock
    ( given P: pointer      (* A pointer to a memory block being returned to
                               available space *);
            Avail           (* The available space structure used by the buddy
                               system in question *);
```

```
      return P: pointer     (* Now unreliable since the memory referenced by P
                               has been returned to available space *);
              Avail         (* The available space structure with the block
                               referenced by P included and appropriately
                               coalesced with its buddies *) );
   start ReturnBlock
     (* Begin by recursively coalescing P with its buddies *)

     Coalesce(P, Avail);(* See procedure Coalesce following *)

     (* Upon return from Coalesce, P may be pointing to a much larger
        block than it was before. The final step is now to attach this
        potentially larger block to the available space structure *)

     Attach (P, Avail)
   end ReturnBlock;


procedure Coalesce
   ( given P: pointer       (* A pointer to a memory block *);
           Avail            (* The available space structure used by the
                               particular buddy system *);
     return P: pointer      (* P now pointing to a potentially larger block formed
                               by coalescing the original block with its buddies
                               on the left and/or right *);
              Avail         (* Buddies of P in the available space structure have
                               been coalesced with P *) );
   start Coalesce
     (* The call to CheckBuddies represents a call to a procedure that will
        determine whether buddies of P exist in the available space structure.
        If a left buddy of P is available, then a pointer to it is returned in
        LBuddy. Otherwise, LBuddy is returned as NULL. A similar convention is
        followed for a right buddy and its pointer RBuddy *)

     CheckBuddies(P, Avail, LBuddy, RBuddy);

     (* If both LBuddy and RBuddy come back as NULL, both of the conditional
        tests that follow will fail and an immediate return will result.
        Otherwise coalescing must occur on left and/or right *)

     if RBuddy <> NULL then
       Remove RBuddy from Avail structure;
       Change appropriate fields in P to coalesce P with RBuddy;
       (* Fields dependent upon buddy system being used *)
       Coalesce(P, Avail)
       (* Recursively attempt to coalesce the new, larger P with its buddies  *)
     endif;
     if LBuddy <> NULL then
       Remove LBuddy from Avail structure;
       Change appropriate fields in LBuddy to coalesce P with LBuddy;
       (* Fields dependent upon buddy system being used *)
       Set P to LBuddy;          (* P now references larger block *)
       Coalesce(P, Avail)
       (* Recursively attempt to coalesce the new, larger P with its buddies *)
     endif
   end Coalesce;
```

We now explain in more detail the methodology of each of the three previously cited buddy systems. From the generic procedures Allocate and ReturnBlock given above, it is clear that a detailed exposition must describe both the data structure used to store available blocks and the bookkeeping data (for example, the size of the block, a flag to indicate whether or not it is free, and so on) that must be stored within and about each memory block.

Binary Buddy System

The logic of the *binary buddy system* method requires that all blocks be of size 2^i for some *i*. Whenever a block is split, the resulting two buddies must be of equal size. That is, if a block of size 2^i is split, then the resulting buddies will each be of size 2^{i-1}. As an example, let us suppose that we have 2^{16} (64K) words of memory to manage and that we wish to allocate no blocks smaller than 2^{10} (1K) words. Then, at any given time, we could potentially have free blocks of size 2 raised to the 10th, 11th, 12th, 13th, 14th, 15th, and 16th power. The available space structure in this case will consist of a doubly linked list of free blocks for each of the seven potential block sizes. Hence, we would need head pointers as follows:

Avail(1) $\rightarrow$ Head of list for blocks of size 2^{10}
Avail(2) $\rightarrow$ Head of list for blocks of size 2^{11}
Avail(3) $\rightarrow$ Head of list for blocks of size 2^{12}
.
.
.
Avail(7) $\rightarrow$ Head of list for blocks of size 2^{16}

Each block would need to contain the following bookkeeping information:

- A boolean flag to indicate whether or not it is free
- An integer field to store its size
- Left and right links used when it is a node in an Avail list

An illustration of such a node is given in Figure 13.5.

Initially, all 2^{16} words of memory would be viewed as one free block; that is, Avail(7) would point to the beginning of memory and all other Avail

FIGURE 13.5
Bookkeeping information in block for binary buddy system.

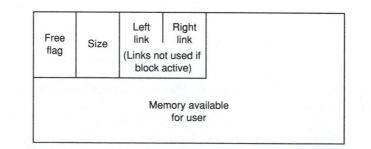

pointers would be NULL. Now let us suppose that a sequence of user requests came in the following order:

   a. Request for memory block of size 2^{14}
   b. Request for memory block of size 2^{13}
   c. Request for memory block of size 2^{14}
   d. Request for memory block of size 2^{14}
   e. Block from request a no longer needed
   f. Block from request b no longer needed

The dynamic processing of these requests can best be described pictorially. In Figure 13.6, we use tree diagrams to represent the splitting and coalescing that would occur as requests a through f are processed. Memory addresses in this figure are given as 0, 1, 2, . . . , 62, and 63; i represents the beginning of the $(i + 1)$st K memory block (of which there are 64 in all).

Three comments are needed to explain more fully the actions highlighted in Figure 13.6. First, the reason for coalescing is that one available block of size $2n$ is always preferred over two available blocks of size n. The whole is greater than the sum of its parts. This is why, in returning the block from request b in Figure 13.6, we coalesce two 8K blocks into a 16K block and then immediately take advantage of an available 16K left buddy to coalesce further into a 32K block.

Second, the binary splitting scheme means that, when a block is to be returned, the address of its buddy can be immediately determined. For instance, the block of size 2^{14} (16K) that begins at address 0 (relative to 1K blocks) has a right buddy of the same size that begins at address 16 (relative to 1K blocks). The location of this block's buddy is purely a function of the block's own size and location. In absolute terms, a block of size 2^i with starting address $n \times 2^i$ will have a right buddy with starting address $(n+1) \times 2^i$ if n is even and a left buddy starting at address $(n-1) \times 2^i$ if n is odd. This means that, as a block is being returned, a simple computation allows us to find its buddy, whose free flag is then checked to determine whether or not coalescing is possible. Notice that, in a binary buddy system, a given block has either a left or a right buddy but not both.

Third, if the buddy of the block to be returned is free, the doubly linked nature of the available block lists becomes crucial because we have essentially jumped into the middle of an available space list in accessing the buddy of the block to be returned. Without the double linking, we would not have the back pointer necessary to remove this buddy from the available list of which it is presently a part. Of course, once a returning block has been coalesced with its buddy, we have a new returning block that may recursively undergo further coalescing as indicated in our generic Coalesce procedure.

Fibonacci Buddy System

Let us begin a consideration of Fibonacci systems by analyzing the binary buddy system. Contradictory as this may seem, the rationale consists of defining the relationships between block sizes that must exist in a buddy system

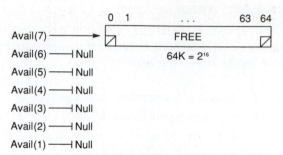

Initial status

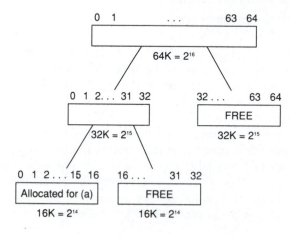
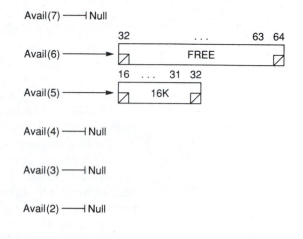

Request (a) process—allocate block of size 2^{14}

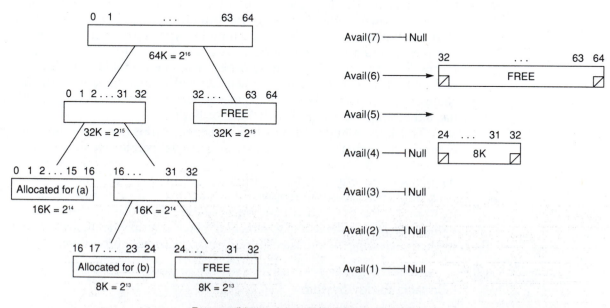

Request (b) process—allocate block of size 2^{13}

FIGURE 13.6 Processing requests using the binary buddy system.

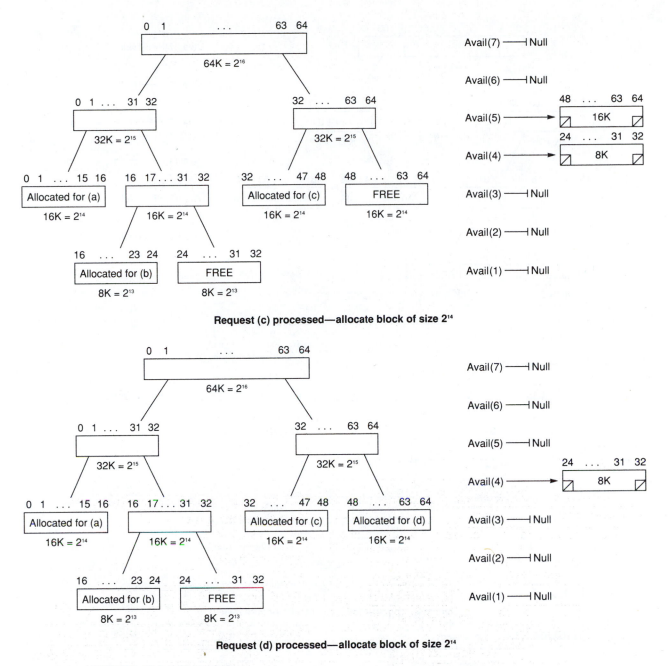

FIGURE 13.6 (continued)

of this type. Examining the sequence of possible block sizes in the binary system,

$$2^1, 2^2, 2^3, \ldots, 2^{10}, 2^{11}, \ldots$$

we notice that every member of the sequence except the first is the result of adding the previous member to itself. Since any block size (except the smallest

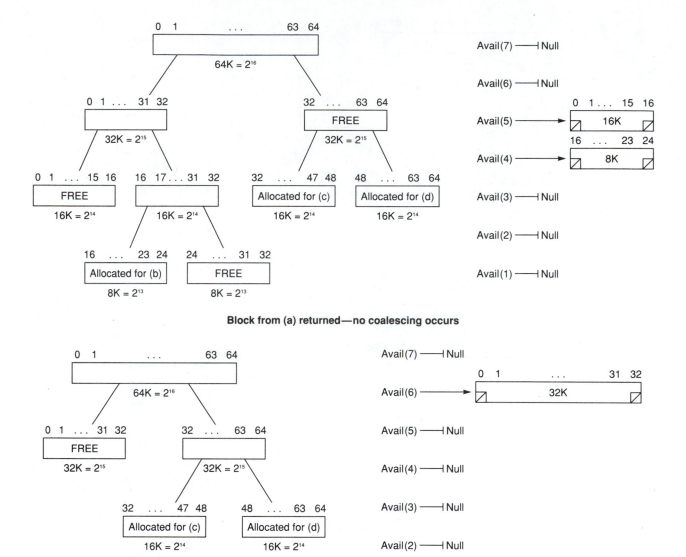

Block from (a) returned—no coalescing occurs

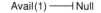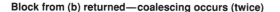

Block from (b) returned—coalescing occurs (twice)

FIGURE 13.6   (continued)

possible) may result from coalescing two smaller blocks, it becomes clear that any sequence of possible block sizes for a buddy system of this variety must have the property that any size element within the sequence is the sum of two preceding members of the sequence. In the binary buddy system, this sum is always obtained by adding the size of the immediately prior member of the sequence to itself. However, the binary system is a special case; all that is really required is that any size can be represented as the sum of two smaller sizes.

Perhaps the most famous sequence of numbers having this property is the Fibonacci sequence. The ith member of the Fibonacci sequence can be recursively defined as

$$F_1 = 1$$
$$F_2 = 1$$
$$F_i = F_{i-1} + F_{i-2} \quad \text{for } i > 2$$

Hence, the initial members of the Fibonacci sequence are

$$1, 1, 2, 3, 5, 8, 13, 21, 34, \ldots$$

Suppose, for instance, that we were managing 21K memory using Fibonacci block sizes and were faced with the following requests for storage:

a. Request for 7K
b. Request for 7K
c. Request for 2K
d. 7K from request c no longer needed
e. 2K from request a no longer needed
f. 7K from request f no longer needed

Figure 13.7 illustrates the allocation, deallocation, and resulting coalescing that would occur as these requests were processed. Naturally, some additional overhead (beyond that required for the binary buddy system) is required when the Fibonacci buddy system is used. First, depending upon the implementation scheme, it may be necessary to store the Fibonacci numbers themselves in an array to allow quick access to data necessary to allocate, split, and coalesce blocks. The alternative would be to recompute the sequence each time it is needed. Second, unlike the binary system, it is not clear from a block's size and location whether it is the left buddy or right buddy of another block. Consequently, it becomes necessary to store some additional bookkeeping data within each block, in the form of a left buddy count field as indicated in Figure 13.8. The left buddy count maintains a record of how deeply a given block is nested as the left buddy of other blocks. In Figure 13.7, the left buddy count is indicated by the circled digit appearing above each block. The algorithm for maintaining this left buddy count involves these steps.

1. As a block is split, the resulting left buddy has its left buddy count field increased by one. The resulting right buddy has its left buddy count field set to zero.

2. As coalescing occurs, the left buddy must always have its left buddy count field decreased by one.

Given the increase in overhead involved in the Fibonacci system, it is certainly a valid question to ask whether or not it offers any advantage

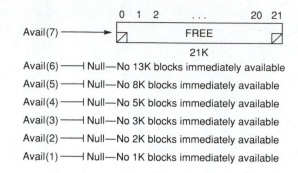

Initial state of memory—21K free

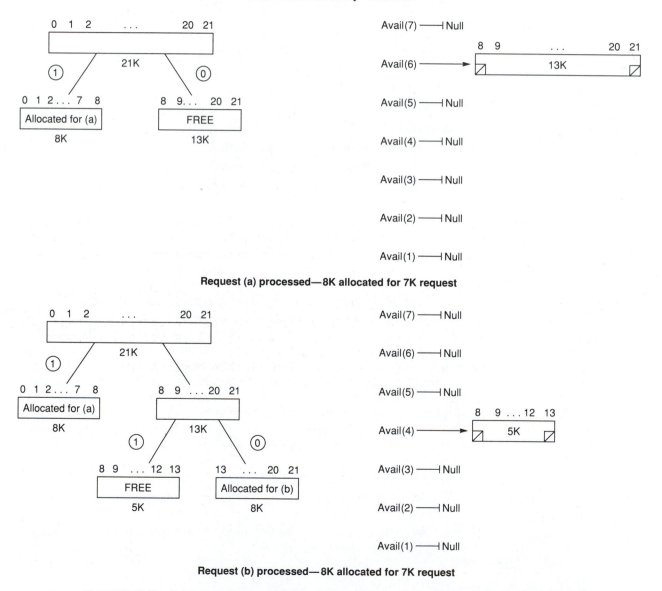

Request (a) processed—8K allocated for 7K request

Request (b) processed—8K allocated for 7K request

FIGURE 13.7 Processing requests using the Fibonacci buddy system. Circled digits represent left buddy counts.

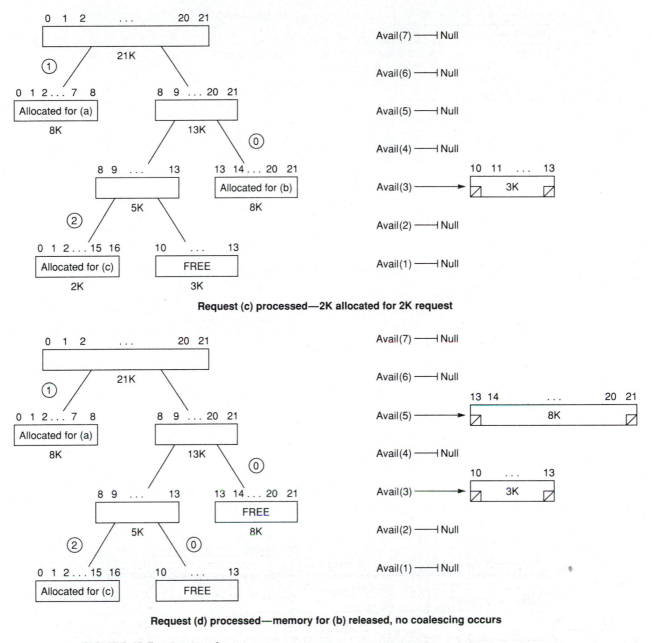

Request (c) processed—2K allocated for 2K request

Request (d) processed—memory for (b) released, no coalescing occurs

FIGURE 13.7   *(continued)*

over the binary system. Its primary advantage is that it allows for a greater variety of possible block sizes in a given amount of memory than its binary counterpart. For instance, in 64K words of memory, the Fibonacci system would allow block sizes of 1K, 2K, 3K, 5K, 8K, 13K, 21K, 34K, and 55K; nine sizes in all. Clearly, a greater variety of sizes allows us to allocate memory in a way that minimizes the difference between what the user actually needs and what our block sizes force us to give.

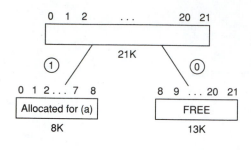

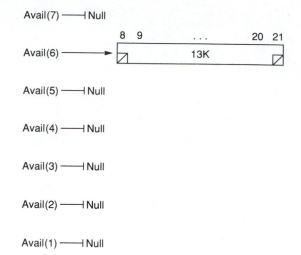

Request (e) process—memory for (c) released, coalescing occurs up to 13K block

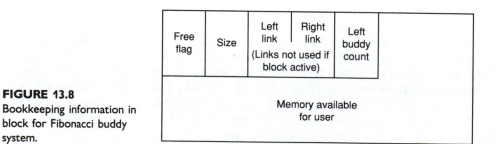

Request (f) processed—memory for (a) released, coalescing occurs—one free 21K block results

FIGURE 13.7   (continued)

Free flag	Size	Left link Right link (Links not used if block active)		Left buddy count	
Memory available for user					

FIGURE 13.8
Bookkeeping information in block for Fibonacci buddy system.

In fact, if one uses a more generalized kth Fibonacci sequence defined by

$$F_j = 1 \qquad \text{for } j = 1, 2, \ldots, k$$
$$F_j = F_{j-1} + F_{j-k} \qquad \text{for } j > k$$

then it can be readily seen that, the larger k becomes, the finer our partitioning of block sizes will be. (Notice that by this definition, the binary buddy system is in fact generated by the first Fibonacci sequence.) Of course, with each increase in k comes a corresponding increase in the overhead of bookkeeping information that must be balanced against the greater selection of block sizes.

For a more theoretical discussion of which k may be appropriate to choose in a given situation, see J. A. Hinds, "A Design for the Buddy System with Arbitrary Sequences of Buddy Sizes," Technical Report no. 74. (Buffalo, NY: State University of New York at Buffalo, 1973).

Boundary Tag Buddies

Both the binary and Fibonacci systems have the disadvantage of not allowing an arbitrary selection of block sizes, thereby forcing the waste of some memory each time a user's request does not precisely match one of the specified block sizes. The *boundary tag buddy system* overcomes this drawback but only at the expense of requiring even more bookkeeping data than either of the other methods.

The reason that the binary and Fibonacci schemes limit us to a finite number of block sizes and splitting possibilities is that, without such a limitation, it would be impossible to determine where a block's buddy begins. For instance, suppose that we were using the Fibonacci buddy system and were about to return a block of size 13K whose left buddy count field was found to be zero. Because of the limitations on the sizes into which a block may be split under the Fibonacci method, we know that this block must have a left buddy of size 8K with which it could possibly coalesce. Using the starting address of the block to be returned and the fact that its left buddy has size 8K, the starting address of the left buddy can be obtained.

The problem of determining the size and starting location of a returning block's buddy is less complicated if the returning buddy has a right buddy instead of a left buddy. The distinction between finding the size and starting location of right and left buddies in the binary and Fibonacci systems can be seen in Figures 13.9 and 13.10. As highlighted in Figure 13.9, in a block with a right buddy, the starting location and size of the returning block would tell us the starting address of the right buddy. Then, provided we have stored the bookkeeping information for that right buddy precisely at its starting location, the size field and free flag are immediately available for our inspection. Here, the bookkeeping information for the right buddy can be accessed at memory address (S + Size).

As shown in Figure 13.10, the bookkeeping information for this block's left buddy can be accessed at one of the following memory addresses:

- (S − Size)   for binary buddy system
- (S − Fibonacci number preceding Size)   for Fibonacci buddy system

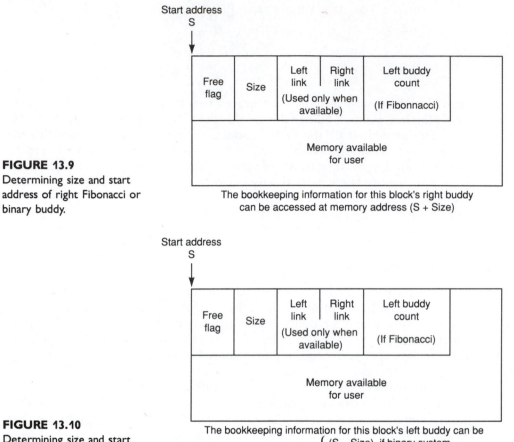

Start address
S

The bookkeeping information for this block's right buddy
can be accessed at memory address (S + Size)

FIGURE 13.9

Determining size and start address of right Fibonacci or binary buddy.

Start address
S

The bookkeeping information for this block's left buddy can be
accessed at memory address $\begin{cases} \text{(S – Size) if binary system} \\ \text{(S – Fibonnacci number preceding Size)} \\ \text{if Fibonacci system} \end{cases}$

FIGURE 13.10

Determining size and start address of a left Fibonacci or binary buddy.

Figures 13.9 and 13.10 should make it apparent that if we are willing to store duplicate copies of a block's size and free flag at its right boundary as well as its left boundary, then the problem of determining the starting address of a left buddy does not require prior knowledge of what its size must be. Its size can be found by checking the bookkeeping information along the right boundary. The effect of this concept is that sizes can be chosen arbitrarily to specifically meet a user's request. No longer is it necessary to allocate 13K to meet an 11K request because the available choices of block sizes demand it. This is the primary motivation behind the boundary tag buddy system. A block and the bookkeeping information within it appears as in Figure 13.11.

The boundary tag technique has advantages and disadvantages that you must carefully consider before choosing it to use in a particular context. The major advantage is that it allows a user's request to be granted precisely, with no excess memory being allocated and therefore wasted. The logic of the method also implies that a given block is not a left or right buddy per se. Rather, any block except one starting or ending at a memory boundary has both a left and a right buddy with which it could coalesce. The primary disadvantages of the boundary tag method are the additional bookkeeping

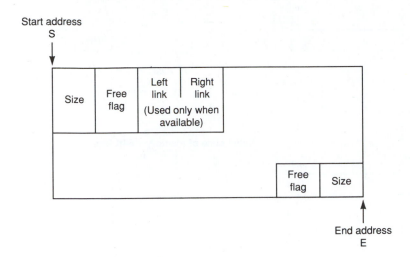

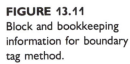

FIGURE 13.11

Block and bookkeeping information for boundary tag method.

information that must be stored and maintained within each block and the fact that the available space structure now must be stored as one long doubly linked list instead of as a sequence of doubly linked lists for each of the respective block sizes allowed. This second disadvantage means that, in determining whether a user's request can be met, the boundary tag method requires sequentially searching a single available space list, clearly a slower process than that required for either the binary or Fibonacci schemes.

Trace through the actions diagrammed in Figure 13.12, highlighting the allocation and deallocation of memory as the following requests are processed:

a. Initially all memory, 64K, is free.

b. User requests 7K.

c. User requests 9K.

d. User requests 4K.

e. Memory requested in request c is no longer needed.

f. Memory requested in request b is no longer needed.

g. Memory requested in request d is no longer needed.

The three memory management methods discussed in this section provide an excellent illustration of the application of data structures at the operating system level. Notice in particular that all three methods require the use of one or more doubly linked lists to store available memory blocks. The elegance of this relatively simple data structure allows us to delete a given block from the middle of an available list without having to traverse the entire list to find a back pointer as we would be forced to do with a singly linked list. In the next section we will examine memory management from the perspective of the developer of a programming language. In particular, we will consider the implementation of a completely general pointer system for such a language. Although the techniques we have described in Sections 13.1 and 13.2 are applicable in this context, one further complication is also introduced—the referencing of a single memory area by multiple pointers.

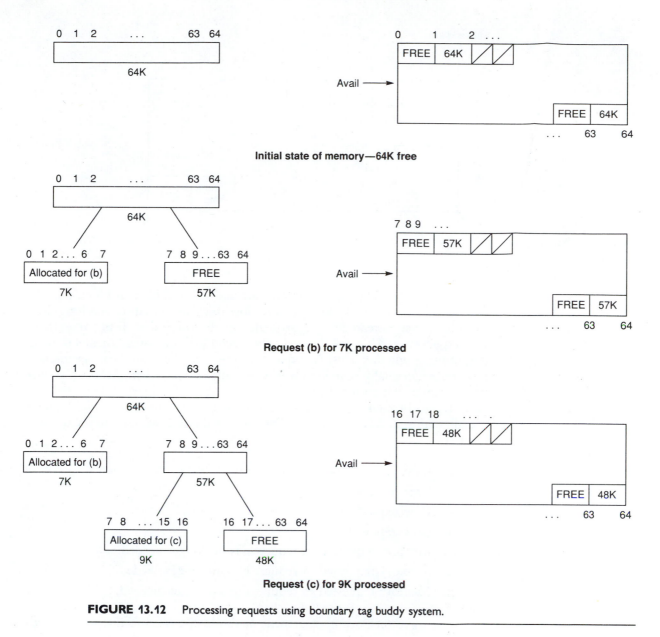

FIGURE 13.12   Processing requests using boundary tag buddy system.

Exercises 13.2   1. Suppose that you have a 128K memory and receive the following sequence of requests from users for memory allocation/deallocation

User A requests 32K
User B requests 19K
User C requests 6K
User D requests 22K
User B finishes
User E requests 12K

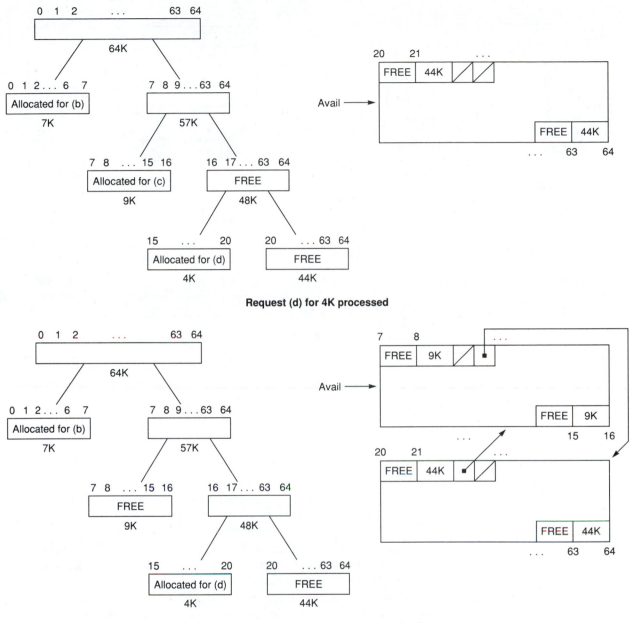

Request (d) for 4K processed

(e) Processed—memory for (c) released, no coalescing occurs

FIGURE 13.12 *(continued)*

User C finishes
User F requests 13K
User D finishes
User E finishes
User A finishes
User F finishes

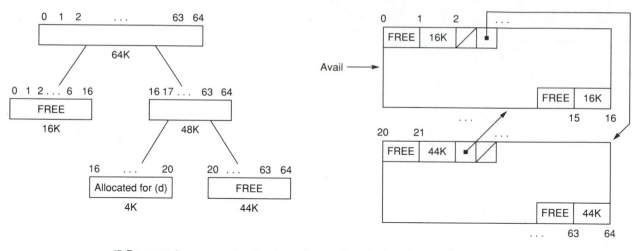

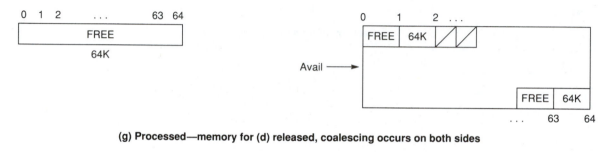

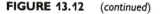

(f) Processed—memory for (b) released, returning block coalesces with right buddy

(g) Processed—memory for (d) released, coalescing occurs on both sides

FIGURE 13.12   *(continued)*

Trace the status of available and allocated memory blocks as these requests are processed using the binary buddy system. Of the memory allocated by the system, what percentage is not actually needed by the user?

2. Repeat Exercise 1 for the standard Fibonacci buddy system. Treat the difference between 128 and the Fibonacci number preceding 128 as the size of a block that cannot be further subdivided.

3. Repeat Exercise 1 for a Fibonacci buddy system using the general Fibonacci sequence with $k = 3$. Treat the difference between 128 and the Fibonacci number preceding 128 as the size of a block that cannot be further subdivided.

4. Repeat Exercise 1 for the boundary tag buddy system, assuming a best-fit algorithm is used to search the list of available blocks. Do this again under the assumption that a first-fit algorithm is used to search the list of available blocks.

5. The Fibonacci buddy system allows a finer degree of block sizes than the binary buddy system. You have memory of 512K at your disposal. Devise a sequence of user requests that could be met by the Fibonacci buddy system but not by the binary buddy system.

6. A Fibonacci buddy system based on the third Fibonacci sequence allows a finer degree of block sizes than one based on the standard Fibonacci sequence.

You have 1,000K memory at your disposal. Devise a sequence of requests that could be met by a buddy system based on the third Fibonacci sequence but not by a buddy system based on the standard (that is, the second) Fibonacci sequence.

7. The Allocate and ReturnBlock algorithms described in this section are given in skeletal PSEUDO code, which is general enough to apply to all the buddy systems discussed in the section. Complete this skeletal PSEUDO code by providing full PSEUDO implementations for any or all of the binary, Fibonacci, and boundary tag systems. For each system you implement, try to make your interface as compatible as possible with the GetNode and ReturnNode operations defined in Chapter 3. Where such compatibility is not completely possible, be sure to specify why it is not completely possible and how you have worked around the incompatibility, for example, by using a global storage area.

<table>
<tr><td>

A RELEVANT ISSUE

</td><td>

Computer Viruses: Corrupting the Memory Resource

It is becoming increasingly evident that operating system software must not only manage memory efficiently for well-intentioned users, but it must also provide security against corruption of the memory resource by malicious users whose intent is to spread viruses. According to John McAfee and Colin Haynes (*Computer Viruses, Worms, Data Diddlers, Killer Programs, and Other Threats to Your System*, NY: St. Martin's Press, 1989), a virus is a program created to infect other programs with copies of itself. Having achieved this, it may do nothing other than continue spreading itself within the infected system and systems networked to that system. More malicious viruses may destroy valuable data while they continue to spread.

Self-replicating programs have long intrigued computer scientists. As early as the 1960s, researchers at the Massachusetts Institute of Technology, AT&T's Bell Laboratories, and Xerox Corporation's research center in Palo Alto entertained themselves by engaging in so-called Core Wars. In these contests, the programmers developed self-replicating programs that infected and devoured the programs of opponents. The winner was the player whose program rendered all other players' programs to a state of total inoperability.

From such harmless beginnings, self-replicating programs have grown to a very serious hazard, particularly to networked computing. Perhaps the most famous incident involving such a virus was the InterNet virus created by Cornell graduate student Robert Morris, Jr., in November 1988. This virus took advantage of a loophole in operating system software to spread itself to a variety of computers on the InterNet network. Having infected a computer, the InterNet virus replicated itself on the host system until so many resources were consumed by the virus that other users were totally ignored by the system. Although not malicious in the sense of destroying data, Morris's virus did force numerous computer centers to shut down and to reboot an estimated 42,000 machines. The resulting loss in human and machine time is estimated by McAfee and Cohen to have a monetary value of over $98 million!

</td></tr>
</table>

13.3   HEAP MANAGEMENT FOR PROGRAMMING LANGUAGES

Thus far we have examined memory allocation from the perspective of an operating system designer who must meet the requests of users for memory blocks of various sizes. Let us now work from the perspective a programming language implementor who must manage the memory nodes associated with pointers in the language. Such memory management is often termed *dynamic memory management* or *heap management*. The former term derives from the fact that this management of the memory resource takes place as your program runs, not at compilation time. To understand the origin of the latter term, we must examine the configuration of memory when your program is loaded into it from an external file. As indicated in Figure 13.13, there are memory costs that must be paid in addition to the storage space required for the object code of your program. In particular, memory must have room to accommodate

- Various operating system requirements
- A stack used by the operating system for subroutine processing (as explained in Chapter 6)
- The object code of your program, that is, the machine-language version of your program's instructions
- Static data areas, that is, the globally declared arrays and other variables used by your program

Notice that the four memory components listed will generally not consume all of the available computer memory. What is left over is called the *heap*. (This usage of the term *heap* is not to be confused with the heap ADT discussed in Chapter 7.) It is in the heap area that memory associated with pointer-based variables is allocated.

What are the similarities and differences between the heap management required of a programming language implementor and the memory

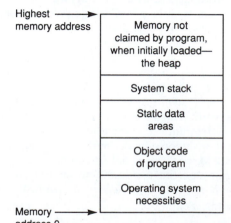

FIGURE 13.13

Computer memory configuration for typical program.

management issues that we have already discussed from an operating system perspective? Like an operating system, a heap management system must often allocate nodes of different sizes. The reason is that different pointer variables within the same program in languages such as Pascal and C may be associated with record structures having dissimilar size requirements. That is, a pointer variable P could reference a structure requiring 18 bytes, while another pointer variable Q points at a structure consuming 1,800 bytes. Hence, the techniques already discussed for managing nodes of various sizes apply to general heap management just as they do in an operating system environment.

What sets heap management apart are the complexities arising from the possibility of a node in the heap being referenced by more than one pointer. Consider, for instance, the following PSEUDO code.

```
var
  P, Q: pointer to integer;
  .
  .
  .
  GetNode(P);
  Ref(P) := 14;
  Q := P;
  write(Ref(Q));
```

Certainly, there is nothing wrong with this code, and it is evident that the *write* instruction will produce 14 as its output. However, suppose that we now append the following two instructions to the preceding code.

```
ReturnNode(P);
write(Ref(Q));
```

What should the second *write* instruction produce? Is the call to ReturnNode even valid; that is, should we be allowed to return a node to available space when it is still referenced by another pointer? The authors have worked with one implementation of Pascal that would flag the Pascal analogue of the call to ReturnNode as a run-time error and another implementation of Pascal that happily executed both write instructions, producing 14 each time.

These questions revolve around the issue of how much explicit responsibility is placed upon the programmer to control the return of nodes to available space. Granting the programmer completely explicit control would dictate that the call to ReturnNode(P) in the above coding should actually return the node to available space despite its also being referenced by the pointer Q—an approach that assumes that the programmer always knows what he or she is doing no matter how unorthodox it may be. A lesser degree of explicit programmer control would be to use the call to ReturnNode(P) to indicate that the node referenced by P can be returned to available space when the pointer Q is also finished with it, that is, when all pointers in addition to P no longer need access to the node.

There are even languages, such as Lisp and SNOBOL, that make the return of nodes to available space in the heap completely implicit—not providing a programmer-callable operation to release nodes. To illustrate how such implicit garbage collection might be invoked, consider the following code.

```
var
  P, R: pointer to integer;
  .
  .
  .
  GetNode(P);
  GetNode(R);
  P := R;
```

In a language that requires the programmer to explicitly return nodes to the heap, the assignment statement P := R will render the portion of the heap originally referenced by P inaccessible for future use, even though it is no longer used by the program. The implementation of a language in which garbage is collected implicitly would detect the inaccessibility of this node and return it to an available heap without an explicit request to do so by the programmer.

We will discuss two methods for garbage collection, *reference counting* and *marking*, which take into account the complexities associated with multiple pointers referencing a node in the heap. The first of these strategies is simpler and more efficient but has loopholes that make it inappropriate in some contexts. It should be emphasized that both strategies augment the space management algorithms already discussed in the first two sections of this chapter and that neither strategy is needed in a language where control over returning nodes to the heap is under the total, explicit control of the programmer. In the latter case, we simply obey the programmer's dictate. ReturnNode means precisely that—regardless of how many other pointers may be referencing the node.

Reference Counting

This strategy merely retains in each node a RefCount field that is used by the heap management system to keep track of the number of pointers that reference a given node. This concept is highlighted in Figure 13.14. As indicated in this figure, an invocation of ReturnNode(P) cannot restore a node to available space if the RefCount field is more than 1, that is, if pointers other than P currently reference the node. Instead, Ref(P).RefCount is merely reduced to 1. The assignment statement Q := R in Figure 13.14 must reduce by 1 the RefCount field in the node originally referenced by Q and increase by 1 the RefCount field in the node referenced by R. Since the RefCount field in the node originally referenced by both P and Q is now zero, it is this assignment statement that actually restores the node to available space, not the earlier invocation of ReturnNode(P). Table 13.1 summarizes the effect of GetNode, ReturnNode, and pointer assignment operations when the reference counting technique is used.

Although relatively simple to implement, the reference counting strategy described above has the serious drawback that it will not correctly return to available space nodes that are linked in a circular structure. Convince yourself that the circular list consisting of one node in Figure 13.15 can *never* be

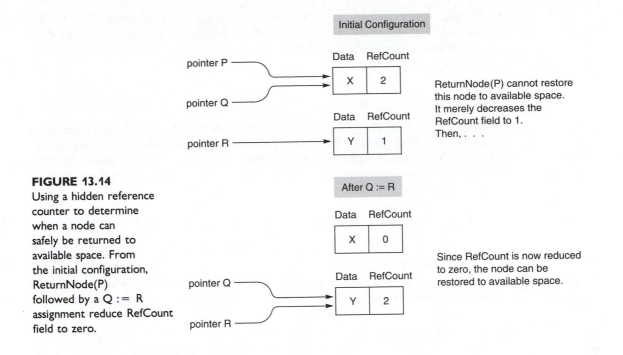

FIGURE 13.14
Using a hidden reference counter to determine when a node can safely be returned to available space. From the initial configuration, ReturnNode(P) followed by a Q := R assignment reduce RefCount field to zero.

Operation	Effect on RefCount and available space
GetNode(P)	Reduce by 1 the RefCount field in the node previously referenced by P. If this RefCount field is now zero, return the node to available space. Finally, establish P's new pointer value, and set Ref(P).RefCount to 1.
ReturnNode(P)	Reduce Ref(P).RefCount by 1. If the RefCount is now zero, it may be returned to available space.
Pointer assignment Q := R	Reduce by 1 the RefCount field in the node previously referenced by Q. If this RefCount field is now zero, return it to available space. Finally, increase by 1 the RefCount field in the node referenced by R.

TABLE 13.1   Effect of pointer operations on available space pool when reference counting is used.

FIGURE 13.15
A data structure for which the reference count technique will render a node inaccessible for future use.

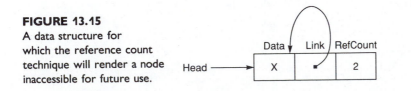

returned to available space when reference counting is used. This implies that, ideally, reference counting should be employed only for applications in which you know beforehand that circular structures will not be created in the heap.

Marking

Marking has arisen as a more comprehensive garbage collection strategy; it avoids the flaw we have found with respect to reference counting and circular lists. The marking technique dictates that we do no actual garbage collection until we apparently run out of heap. When this occurs, the following three steps are invoked:

1. All heap nodes are initially marked as available.
2. Then each heap node reachable through an active pointer is marked as in use.
3. Those nodes that remain marked as available after step 2 are then linked into an appropriate, available space structure.

Since all nodes in the heap will be visited at least once during this marking phase, this technique is clearly O(NumberNodes) in its time efficiency. However, unlike the compaction strategy cited in Section 13.1, this strategy necessitates no movement of data and hence will require substantially less time than compaction.

It is the second step of the marking phase that requires more discussion. The symbol tables maintained by the programming language will provide us with a record of each active pointer variable. Given such an active pointer variable P, we view the heap node referenced by P as a graph node. The non-NULL pointers embedded in this graph node lead us to other graph nodes (that is, heap nodes) adjacent to the node referenced by P. For instance, in Figure 13.16, if the programmer had developed a binary tree referenced by

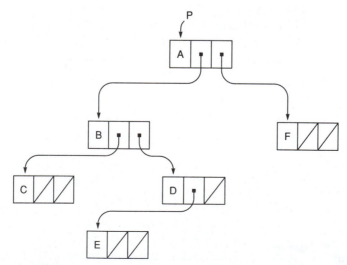

FIGURE 13.16
Nodes reachable through the pointer P may be obtained by a depth-first traversal starting at A, that is, A, B, C, D, E, F.

the pointer variable P, then the nodes B and F are adjacent to A, nodes C and D are adjacent to B, and node E is adjacent to D under this graph interpretation of nodes in the heap. To mark the nodes reachable through P as being in use, we could generate a depth-first traversal of the graph starting at the node referenced by P. As a node is visited in this traversal we mark it as in use. We would have to call this depth-first traversal for each active pointer to complete step 2 of the mark-and-collection process.

To implement this depth-first traversal, we must make some assumptions about the structure of the heap nodes being visited. Clearly a heap node will contain some user data and, quite possibly, some pointers to other heap nodes that are maintained by the programmer. From the perspective of the programming language implementor, we are not interested at all in the user's data. The pointers in the heap node can be viewed as an array of pointers. Additionally, we will need to add a boolean InUse field to indicate whether or not a heap node is currently reachable through an active pointer. These considerations give rise to the following heap node structure.

```
type  (* NumberPtrs is a constant that limits the number of
         pointers in a node *)
  HeapNodePtr: pointer to HeapNode;
  HeapNode: record
                Data: (* Appropriate user data type *);
                Ptrs: array [NumberPtrs] of HeapNodePtr;
                InUse: boolean
            endrecord;
```

The following PSEUDO algorithm, called for each active pointer variable, will then accomplish step 2 of the marking phase via a depth-first traversal of all heap nodes reachable through the current pointer.

```
procedure MarkInUse
  ( given Current: HeapNodePtr  (* Pointer to an active heap
                                   node *);
    return Current: HeapNodePtr (* Current, and all nodes
                                   reachable through it,
                                   will be marked as in
                                   use *) );

  var
    K: integer;

  start MarkInUse
    if Current <> NULL then
      Ref(Current).InUse := true;
      for K := 1 to NumberPtrs do
        MarkInUse(Ref(Current).Ptrs[K])
      endfor
    endif
  end MarkInUse;
```

The marking technique for garbage collection, implemented by this version of the MarkInUse procedure, eliminates the circular structure loophole inherent in reference counting. However, this particular implementation of MarkInUse has, potentially, a subtle flaw of its own. In practice, MarkInUse is only called when we are running short on space. However, the recursive implementation of this algorithm may require a relatively large amount of stack space—you will analyze how much stack space for the worst-possible scenario in the exercises. Hence, the algorithm we must execute to recover space may not be able to execute because of insufficient space to accommodate its run-time stack!

We need a nonrecursive version of the MarkInUse procedure that does not require a run-time stack. Fortunately, a nonrecursive version was discovered simultaneously by Deutsch and Bobrow (L. P. Deutsch and D. G. Bobrow, "An Efficient Incremental Automatic Garbage Collector," *Communications of the ACM*, 19:9, 1966, pp. 522–26) and by Schorr and Waite (H. Schorr and W. M. Waite, "An Efficient, Machine-Independent Procedure for Garbage Collection in Various List Structures," *Communications of the ACM*, 10:8, 1967, pp. 501–06). This nonrecursive version of the algorithm is reminiscent of the threading method we used in Section 7.5 to avoid the use of recursion in tree traversals. Essentially, we use the pointer fields within the heap nodes to embed the information that would be stored in the recursive stack. This embedding must be a temporary situation since it actually changes the contents of the heap nodes that are in use. The original contents of these nodes must be restored upon completion of marking or we will corrupt the data structures that the user has created in the heap.

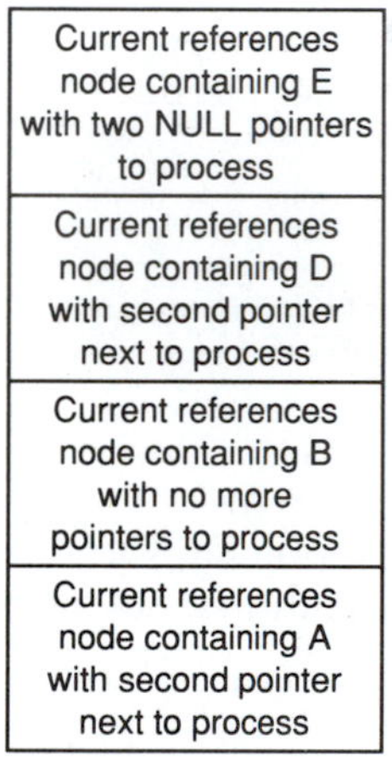

To illustrate the algorithm, we begin by carefully analyzing the contents of the run-time stack that would be used by the recursive version of the algorithm. Figure 13.17 illustrates a portion of the contents of this stack that would exist when the node containing E in Figure 13.16 is being marked as in use. Figure 13.17 tells us that, at this stage of execution of the recursive algorithm, the topmost Current pointer is referencing the node containing E. Below this topmost stack frame is another stack frame in which the Current pointer references the node containing D and the loop of recursive calls is set to resume at the second pointer field within the node. Similar information is replicated in deeper-level stack frames with the stack frame at the bottom having a Current pointer leading to the heap node by which the structure was entered.

This analysis of stack frames for the recursive version of the algorithm implies that, relative to any heap node being marked, we must always have two information items: a pointer to the node that preceded this node and an indication of which pointer within the node is being followed as we descend deeper into the structure. The latter item we can store in an integer WhichPtr field, which now must be included in each heap node. The former item we will store temporarily in the pointer field we have followed to descend deeper into the structure. Some fairly tricky coding involving a temporary variable can then be used to restore this pointer field to its original contents. Figure 13.18 indicates how the stack contents of Figure 13.17 can be embedded in the pointer fields of the structure being marked. In this figure, the dotted pointers indicate the return path to ascend in the structure being marked; the WhichPtr value indicates the pointer field that has been altered temporarily to store this path of ascent. The details of the nonrecursive marking algorithm are provided in the following PSEUDO code.

| Current references node containing E with two NULL pointers to process |
| Current references node containing D with second pointer next to process |
| Current references node containing B with no more pointers to process |
| Current references node containing A with second pointer next to process |

FIGURE 13.17
Status of system stack when node containing E in Figure 13.16 is being marked as Current node by recursive implementation. At each level, there may be additional pointers to process in the Current node.

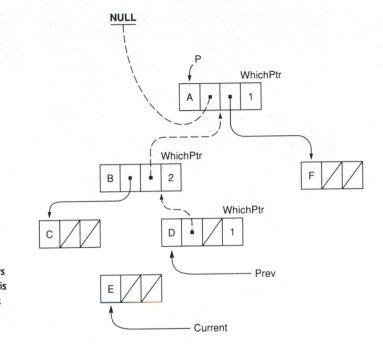

FIGURE 13.18

Status of internal pointers when node containing E is being marked as Current node by nonrecursive implementation.

```
type  (* NumberPtrs is a constant that limits the number of pointers in a node *)
  HeapNodePtr: pointer to HeapNode;
  HeapNode : record
                  Data: (* Appropriate user data type *);
                  Ptrs: array [NumberPtrs] of HeapNodePtr;
                  InUse: boolean;
                  WhichPtr: integer (* Additional field needed for nonrecursive
                                          version *)
             endrecord;

procedure MarkInUse  (* Nonrecursive version *)
  ( given Current: HeapNodePtr   (* Pointer to an active heap node *);
    return Current: HeapNodePtr  (* Current, and all nodes reachable through
                                    it, marked as in use *) );

  var
    Prev, Temp: HeapNodePtr;
    Descend: boolean;

  start MarkInUse
    Prev := NULL;
    Descend := true; (* To indicate we are descending from Current node *)
    repeat
      if Descend then
        if Current = NULL or Ref(Current).InUse then    (* NULL or already
                                                            marked? *)

          Descend := false                               (* Prepare to ascend *)
        else                                             (* Mark this node and
                                                            descend *)
```

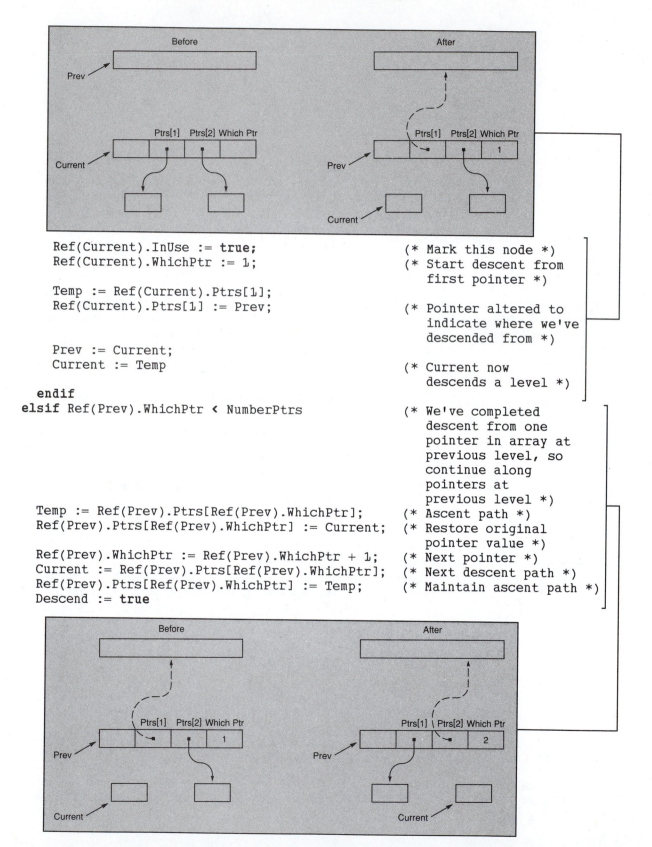

```
      Ref(Current).InUse := true;          (* Mark this node *)
      Ref(Current).WhichPtr := 1;          (* Start descent from
                                               first pointer *)

      Temp := Ref(Current).Ptrs[1];
      Ref(Current).Ptrs[1] := Prev;        (* Pointer altered to
                                               indicate where we've
                                               descended from *)

      Prev := Current;
      Current := Temp                       (* Current now
                                               descends a level *)

   endif
elsif Ref(Prev).WhichPtr < NumberPtrs      (* We've completed
                                               descent from one
                                               pointer in array at
                                               previous level, so
                                               continue along
                                               pointers at
                                               previous level *)

   Temp := Ref(Prev).Ptrs[Ref(Prev).WhichPtr];          (* Ascent path *)
   Ref(Prev).Ptrs[Ref(Prev).WhichPtr] := Current;       (* Restore original
                                                            pointer value *)

   Ref(Prev).WhichPtr := Ref(Prev).WhichPtr + 1;        (* Next pointer *)
   Current := Ref(Prev).Ptrs[Ref(Prev).WhichPtr];       (* Next descent path *)
   Ref(Prev).Ptrs[Ref(Prev).WhichPtr] := Temp;          (* Maintain ascent path *)
   Descend := true
```

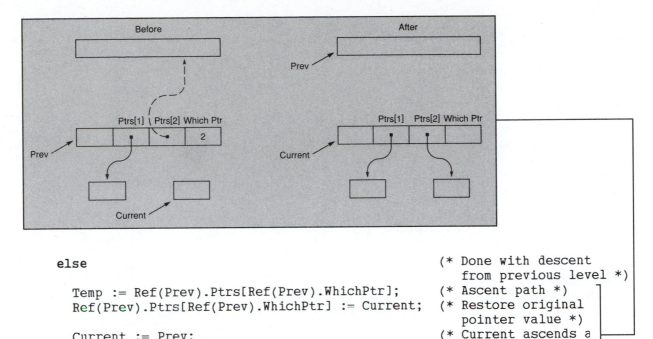

```
   else                                            (* Done with descent
                                                      from previous level *)

     Temp := Ref(Prev).Ptrs[Ref(Prev).WhichPtr];   (* Ascent path *)
     Ref(Prev).Ptrs[Ref(Prev).WhichPtr] := Current;(* Restore original
                                                      pointer value *)

     Current := Prev;                               (* Current ascends a
                                                      level *)

     Prev := Temp                                   (* Prev ascends a
                                                      level *)

   endif
 until Prev = NULL
end MarkInUse;
```

Exercises 13.3

1. In a brief essay, explain why the one-node circular list in Figure 13.15 can never be returned to available space when reference counting is used for garbage collection.

2. Consider the structure referenced by the pointer variable P in Figure 13.19. By a series of pictures that show the settings for Current, Prev, and pointers internal to the structure, trace how these pointers change as each node reachable through P is marked by the nonrecursive implementation of MarkInUse.

3. What is the maximal size to which the run-time stack could grow in the recursive version of procedure MarkInUse? What kind of structure in the heap generates this maximal-size stack? Does this maximal size provide a rationale for using a nonrecursive version of the algorithm? Explain why or why not.

4. Consider the following algorithm.

```
var
  P, Q: pointer to integer;
    .
    .
    .
  GetNode(P);
  Q := P;
  Ref(Q) := 14;
  write(Ref(Q));
```

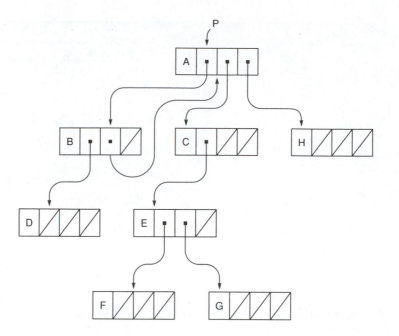

FIGURE 13.19
Structure to be marked as in use for Exercise 2.

```
ReturnNode(P);
write(Ref(Q));
GetNode(P);
Ref(P) := 16;
write(Ref(P));
write(Ref(Q));
```

What do you predict the output will be from this algorithm? Explain why in a short essay. Then implement the algorithm in your favorite programming language and execute it. Are there any discrepancies from what you predicted? If so, try to explain them.

5. In a short essay, explain why the nonrecursive version of the MarkInUse algorithm should *not* be used on nodes in a heap that stores data structures shared concurrently by several users in a time-sharing environment.

6. Another strategy for heap management is known as the *mark-and-release* method. This technique views the heap as a stack in which the GetNode operation always allocates a node on top of the stack. Rather than a ReturnNode operation, there are two operations—Mark and Release. The Mark operation marks the current top of the heap/stack. The Release operation restores to available space all heap/stack nodes down to the topmost mark. Develop PSEUDO implementations of the GetNode, Mark, and Release operations for this method of heap management. In an essay, discuss the benefits and drawbacks of this method compared to the other techniques you have studied in this section.

Chapter Summary   This chapter examined in greater detail methods for allocating memory to applications needing it and for later reclaiming the memory when no longer needed. Section 13.1 used the example of memory allocation among users in a time-sharing environment to illustrate how memory resources could be managed when users request blocks of varying sizes. The best-fit and first-fit strategies were described for allocating such variably sized blocks of memory, and compaction and coalescing were discussed as alternative methods for effectively recovering memory that is no longer needed.

In Section 2, we used the example of a multiuser, time-sharing environment again to illustrate three variations of memory management strategies identified by the term *buddy systems:* the binary, Fibonacci, and boundary tag systems. All of these methods are designed to allow fast garbage collection with a minimum of wasted space.

Section 3 switched from the example of allocating memory among users in a time-sharing environment to the problem of providing a completely general implementation of the pointer ADT. This problem, as faced by the implementors of programming languages that provide a pointer type, requires extending the memory management techniques discussed in Sections 1 and 2 to handle one additional complication—the potential of multiple pointer references to a particular data node. The techniques that encompass this complication are specific to an area of memory management often referred to as heap management. Two methods for garbage collection, reference counting and marking, were discussed. Both methods take into account the complexities associated with multiple pointers possibly referencing a node in the heap.

Key Words

best-fit searching	dynamic memory	garbage collection
binary buddy system	management	heap
boundary tag buddy	Fibonacci buddy system	heap management
system	first-fit searching	marking
coalescing	fragmentation	reference counting
compaction		

Programming Problems/Projects

1. Try to determine as much as you can about the heap management techniques used by the implementors of your favorite programming language. Do this by writing a series of short programs, similar to the algorithm of Exercise 4 in Section 13.3, that are designed specifically to exercise the heap management implementation. Write up the results of your experimentation in a report in which you state your conclusions about how heap management is conducted by your programming language. Justify each of your conclusions by citing results from running one or more of your test programs.

2. In Section 13.2, we described three memory management schemes that might be used by an operating system: binary buddy, Fibonacci buddy, and boundary tag buddies. Write a program in which random numbers are used to simulate users requesting and then returning memory. Interface this program with each of the three memory management schemes presented in Section 13.2 and accumulate statistics regarding various measures of space efficiency for each of these three methods.

3. Write a program in which random numbers are used to simulate users requesting and then returning memory. Interface your program with an implementation of a memory management system in which a best-fit algorithm is used. Then repeat, but use a first-fit algorithm. Accumulate statistics on the effectiveness of each algorithm and write up your conclusions, backed by empirical evidence from your runs, in a formal report.

4. Provide a complete implementation for the pointer ADT using the reference counting strategy for heap management. Then test your implementation with a variety of pointer-based programs that you have developed earlier in this course and, possibly, for other courses and applications.

5. Repeat Problem 4, but use a marking strategy to implement the pointer ADT.

6. If you did Problem 7 of Chapter 2 (a workspace-index implementation of string storage), extend your work from that problem to incorporate one of the heap management strategies discussed in Section 13.3.

A RANDOM NUMBERS: GENERATION AND USE IN EVENTS BASED ON PROBABILITIES

The discussion of computer simulation in Chapter 4 cited the use of random numbers in determining the occurrence of a particular event. There are really two issues involved here:

- How to generate a sequence of random numbers
- How to use that sequence to simulate the occurrence (or nonoccurrence) of a particular event

For the discussion that follows, a sequence of random numbers is a sequence of real numbers $x_1, x_2, x_3, \ldots$ such that:

1. For each x_i, $0 \leq x_i < 1$.
2. The x_i are not biased toward any particular subinterval of the reals between 0 and 1. That is, members of the sequence should be evenly distributed between 0 and 1.
3. It should not be possible to predict the value of x_i from prior members of the sequence. That is, members of the sequence occur in an unpredictable fashion.

Random numbers generated by computer are often called pseudo-random. The origin of this latter term is due to the fact that sequences of such computer-generated numbers appear to be random even though there is a fixed mathematical formula underlying their generation. If you know the formula, you can in principle compute the sequence—hence, it is not truly unpredictable. However, if you merely observe the sequence without knowledge of the formula, the sequence appears to satisfy the three properties of randomness cited above.

GENERATING A SEQUENCE OF RANDOM NUMBERS

Many compilers have a built-in random number generator. In case your compiler doesn't have such a function, we will describe a method for generating random numbers known as the *linear congruential algorithm*. This algorithm is dependent on an integer value called the *seed*. The seed is acted on by two other integers, called the *multiplier* and the *adder*, using the following formula:

$$\text{Multiplier} \times \text{Seed} + \text{Adder}$$

The result of this computation is then divided by another integer, called the *divisor*. The remainder of this division yields a new value for the seed, which is then divided by the divisor less 1 to yield a real value between 0 and 1. For appropriate choices of the divisor, multiplier, and adder, the sequence of real numbers produced by acting on a continually changing seed will give the appearance of a random sequence. The preceding discussion is formalized in the following PSEUDO function and procedure:

```
function Random
  ( given           (* Formally no parameter is given to the function. However, it
                       is necessary to declare a global integer variable Seed that
                       is modified by each invocation of Random. Some languages
                       allow declaration of Seed as a local variable whose value
                       is retained between function invocations *);
    return: real    (* Produce a real random value between 0 (inclusive) and 1. To
                       do so, a global variable Seed is used. Seed is modified on
                       each call to Random to ensure a (probably) different random
                       number on successive invocations of the function *) );

(* The method of generating random numbers used here is known as the linear
   congruential algorithm. The details of this method may be found in Knuth's
   "The Art of Computer Programming: Seminumerical Algorithms." The method is
   dependent on the word size of your computer. The choice of Divider below is
   appropriate for a 32-bit machine. In general, the Divider should be less than
   or equal to 2 raised to the power ( B/2 ) on a B-bit machine. If your machine
   does not flag integer overflow as a run-time error, then Divider may be 2
   raised to the power B. The best choices for Multiplier and Adder are
   relatively large, odd integers less than the Divider. By changing the Divider,
   Multiplier, and Adder constants in this function, you can tailor the
   generation of random numbers to your particular machine *)

var
  Divider, Multiplier, Adder: integer;
  XDivider, XSeed: real;                    (* Real representation of Divider and
                                               global Seed *)

start Random
  (* Regard Divider, Multiplier, and Adder as constants *)
  Divider = 65536;                          (* 2^16 *)
```

```
   Multiplier = 15625;
   Adder = 22221;
   (* Seed a global variable to ensure its value is retained between
      invocations of Random *)
   Seed := (Multiplier * Seed + Adder) mod Divider;
   XDivider := Divider - 1;
   XSeed := Seed;
   Random := abs(Seed / (Divider - 1))  (* Assume abs is absolute value *)
end Random;

procedure InitRandom;
   ( return  (* Initialize the value of the global variable Seed for use by
               the random number generator *) );

   (* The choice of Seed completely determines the random number sequence that
      is generated. The choice appearing here is one of many appropriate Seed
      initializations for a 32-bit machine. In general, Seed should be an odd
      positive integer less than or equal to 2 raised to the power ( B/2 ) on a
      B-bit machine. (This limit becomes 2 raised to the power B if your machine
      does not flag integer overflow as a run-time error that halts your
      program.) To generate a different random number sequence, merely adjust
      the value of the global variable Seed. More details on the "linear
      congruential" method for generating random numbers may be found in
      Knuth's "The Art of Computer Programming: Seminumerical Algorithms" *)

start InitRandom
   Seed := 44449;    (* An odd prime *)
end InitRandom;
```

Given this algorithm, you merely call **procedure** InitRandom at the beginning of a program in which you wish to generate random numbers. Thereafter, each call to the **function** Random will yield a random value between 0 and 1. Note that use of InitRandom and Random requires that you declare Seed as a global variable. This ensures that the value of Seed is retained from one invocation of Random to the next. Also, by choosing a different value for Seed in InitRandom, you can easily generate a different sequence of random numbers. Finally, the values for the Multiplier, Adder, and Divider used in the foregoing code are tailored to a compiler that uses 32 bits to store an integer. If your compiler uses 16 bits, you should adjust the method as described in the documentation that accompanies InitRandom and Random.

USING RANDOM NUMBERS TO SIMULATE EVENTS ACCORDING TO PROBABILITIES

Here we describe three situations in which the generation of a random number may be used to simulate the occurrence of an event in a simulation. Our description here is intended only to be brief and prescriptive in nature. An explanation of the theory underlying these and other applications of random number generation in simulation is given in *Modern Statistical, Systems, and*

GPSS Simulation by Zaven Karian and Edward Dudewicz (New York, NY: Computer Science Press, 1991).

Situation 1 An event occurs with a certain probability p. For example, in a given time unit of a simulation, there is a probability of 0.40 that a car will arrive in a queue waiting at a toll booth.

In this situation, generate a random number X. If X is less than p, declare that the event in question occurred; otherwise, declare that it did not occur. In the previous example, if X is less than 0.40, we process the event of a car's arrival; otherwise our simulation proceeds as if no car arrived.

Situation 2 The occurrence of an event is associated with a value, and that value is distributed uniformly over some interval $[a, b)$. Here the term *uniformly* means that the value associated with the event shows no bias to any portion of the interval $[a, b)$.

For instance, you must generate the time of day at which an event occurs, based on a 24-hour clock. The event is no more likely to occur at one time than another. Thus, you wish to generate a value in the interval $[0, 24)$.

In this situation, generate a random number X, $0 \le X < 1$. Then convert X to the desired value by the formula

$$a + (b - a)X$$

In our 24-hour clock example, if you generate a random value $X = 0.8125$, the formula above would convert it to 19.5, indicating a 7:30 PM time of occurrence.

A restricted case of this second situation occurs when the values to be generated are integers that are uniformly distributed over the range of integers given by Lo, Lo + 1, Lo + 2, ..., Hi − 1, Hi. For instance, you are rolling a die and hence must generate an integer value uniformly distributed over the range 1, 2, 3, 4, 5, 6, that is, Lo = 1 and Hi = 6. In this situation, create the integer you want by generating a real number in the interval [Lo, Hi + 1) and then truncating this real to produce an integer. For instance, a random value $X = 0.24$ would yield a die's value of 2, according to the following evaluation:

$$1 + (7 - 1)(0.24)$$

Evaluates to
2.44
↓ Truncates to
2

Situation 3 The occurrence of an event is associated with a value, and the value is *normally* distributed, with mean μ and standard deviation σ. We assume here a familiarity with the notion of a bell-shaped normal distribution and its associated mean and standard deviation. Such a distribution is used to model a variety of events in which values tend to aggregate around a middle value, known as the mean. For instance, test scores may be normally distributed around a mean of 70 with a standard deviation of 10, or temperature readings (in Fahrenheit) may be normally distributed around a mean of 60 with standard deviation of 15. For a precise definition of the normal distribution, consult any introductory statistics text.

In such a situation, the normally distributed value may be approximated by generating 12 random numbers $X_1, X_2, X_3, \ldots, X_{12}$ and then using them in the following formula:

$$\mu + \sigma \left(\left(\sum_{i=1}^{12} X_i \right) - 6 \right)$$

For instance, to generate a normally distributed temperature with mean 60 and standard deviation 15:

1. Generate 12 random values between 0 and 1 and form their sum. Suppose that this sum turns out to be 5.5.
2. Subtract 6 from the sum in step 1, obtaining -0.5.
3. Multiply the value in step 2 by the standard deviation 15, obtaining -7.5.
4. Add the result of step 3 to the mean 60, yielding a generated temperature of 52.5.

A justification of why the formula described above approximates a normally distributed variable is due to a famous theorem of statistics called the Central Limit Theorem. If you are interested in finding out more about this theorem, see Chapter 4 of the Karian and Dudewicz text cited earlier in this Appendix.

B EXPLICIT SOLUTIONS OF RECURRENCE RELATIONS

In Chapter 6 we cited explicit solutions to certain recurrence relations that were necessary to analyze the efficiency of the recursive algorithms studied in that chapter. In this Appendix, we give an overview of some general methods for finding explicit solutions to recurrence relations. The explicit solutions to recurrence relations cited in Chapter 6 represent specific cases of these general methods. The theoretical basis for these general methods is not presented here. A presentation of the theory underlying the methods may be found in *Applied Discrete Structures for Computer Science* by Alan Doerr and Kenneth Lavasseur (New York, NY: Macmillan, 1989).

Before discussing these general methods, some definitions are needed. We shall use E to represent a recurrence relation

$$E(N) = f(E(K_1), E(K_2), \ldots, E(K_n), g(N)) \qquad (B.1)$$

where all $K_i < N$. This equation implies that the evaluation of the recurrence relation E for the nonnegative integer N is defined in terms of the function f of $m + 1$ arguments. Substituted for the first m of these arguments are the results of prior evaluations of E, that is, evaluations of E for nonnegative integers smaller than N. Substituted for the last argument of f is the result of evaluating some explicit function g at N. Initially, this formula for $E(N)$ appears complicated, because it is stated in full generality. An example should help clarify matters.

Suppose f is a function of two arguments X and Y, defined by $f(X, Y) = X + Y$. Then if $K_1 = N - 1$ and $g(N) = 1$, the recurrence relation expressed by (B.1) is

$$E(N) = E(N - 1) + 1$$

This should be recognized as one of the particular recurrence relations we cited in Chapter 6.

Types of recurrence relations for which general methods of finding explicit solutions are known include a variety of situations in which f is a linear function.

Explicit solution to (B.1) when f is a linear function, $K_1 = N - 1$, $K_2 = N - 2, \ldots, K_m = N - m$, $g(N) = 0$.
In this case, equation (B.1) takes the form

$$E(N) = c_1 E(N - 1) + c_2 E(N - 2) + \cdots + c_m E(N - m) \qquad \text{(B.2)}$$

where $c_1, c_2, \ldots, c_m$ are constants, Equation (B.2) is called an *mth-order linear homogeneous recurrence relation*. The term *homogeneous* denotes that the function g is identically zero. Doerr and Lavasseur show that the general solution of such a recurrence relation may be obtained by

1. Finding all roots of the equation

    $$x^m - c_1 x^{m-1} - c_2 x^{m-2} - \cdots - c_{m-1} x - c_m = 0 \qquad \text{(B.3)}$$

    where the c_i come from (B.2). Equation (B.3) is called the *characteristic equation* of (B.2).

2. If equation (B.3) has m distinct roots $x_1, x_2, \ldots, x_n$, then the explicit solution of (B.2) is of the form

    $$E(N) = d_1 x_1^N + d_2 x_2^N + \cdots + d_m x_m^N$$

    where the d_i must be determined.

3. To determine the coefficients d_i, use the m initial conditions for the recurrence relation. These initial conditions specify the values of $E(1), E(2), \ldots, E(m)$.

Again, the notation can become imposing, so an example should help to clarify. If we have the recurrence relation

$$E(N) = 2E(N - 1) \qquad \text{with initial condition } E(1) = 1$$

then the method tells us to find a solution of the characteristic equation

$$x - 2 = 0$$

Clearly a solution to this is $x = 2$. Hence, all explicit solutions of the recurrence relation

$$E(N) = 2E(N - 1)$$

will be of the form

$$E(N) = d_1 2^N$$

Since the given initial condition is $E(1) = 1$, d_1 must be $\frac{1}{2}$. Hence for the initial condition $E(1) = 1$, we have the specific explicit solution

$$E(N) = (\tfrac{1}{2})2^N = 2^{N-1}$$

A complication in obtaining general solutions for linear homogeneous recurrence relations occurs when the corresponding characteristic equation has roots of multiplicity greater than 1. We omit discussion of the general solution for this more complicated case; it is covered in Doerr and Lavasseur.

Explicit solution to (B.1) when f is a linear function, $K_1 = N - 1$, $K_2 = N - 2$, ..., $K_n = N - m$, $g(N) \neq 0$.
In such a case, equation (B.1) takes the form

$$E(N) = c_1 E(N - 1) + c_2 E(N - 2) + \cdots + c_m E(N - m) + g(N) \qquad \text{(B.4)}$$

The appearance of the nonzero $g(N)$ function causes this type of recurrence relation to be called an *mth-order linear nonhomogeneous recurrence relation*. The method for solving such a nonhomogeneous recurrence relation is

1. First find the general explicit solution of the corresponding homogeneous recurrence relation—that is, the recurrence relation with $g(N) = 0$.
2. Then, often by taking an educated guess, find one particular solution of (B.4).
3. Obtain the general solution to (B.4) by adding the general solution obtained in step 1 and the particular solution from step 2.
4. Use the initial conditions to find the values of the constants in the general solution of step 3.

For example, to solve the nonhomogeneous recurrence relation

$$E(N) = 2E(N - 1) + 1 \qquad \text{initial condition } E(1) = 1$$

we would first obtain the general solution

$$E(N) = d_1 2^N$$

to the corresponding homogeneous equation. Observation also reveals that $E(N) = -1$ is one particular solution to the original nonhomogeneous relation. Hence, the general solution to the nonhomogeneous relation is

$$E(N) = d_1 2^N - 1$$

Since $E(1) = 1$, d must be 1, yielding a solution

$$E(N) = 2^N - 1$$

for the specified initial conditions. You should recognize this explicit solution as the one we used in analyzing the efficiency of the Towers of Hanoi algorithm in Chapter 6.

Explicit solution to (B.1) when f is of the form $f(X, Y) = aX + Y$, $K_1 = N$ div b for an integer $b > 1$, $g(N) = N^r$ for some integer $r \geq 0$, with initial condition $E(1) = c$.

This form of recurrence relation occurs in many divide-and-conquer algorithms, where the work involved in computing for input of size N may be recursively expressed as the amount of work done in computing for input of size N **div** b. Our analyses in Chapter 6 often have $b = 2$.

The assumptions for this case mean that the recurrence relation we are trying to solve appears as

$$E(N) = aE(N \text{ div } b) + N^r \qquad E(1) = c \qquad \text{(B.5)}$$

Doerr and Lavasseur show that an explicit solution to this recurrence relation is given by

$$E(N) = cN^{\log_b a} + \begin{cases} \dfrac{a^{\log_b N} - b^{r \log_b N}}{\dfrac{a}{b^r} - 1} & \text{if } a \neq b^r \\[2em] N^r \log_b N & \text{if } a = b^r \end{cases} \qquad \text{(B.6)}$$

For instance, if $E(N) = E(N \text{ div } 2) + 1$ with $E(1) = 1$ (as it was for the binary search), then the formula for $a = b_r$ in (B.6) tells us that

$$E(N) = 1 + \log_2 N$$

In a broader context, (B.6) implies the following:

- $E(N)$ is $O(N^{\log_b a})$ if $a > b^r$.
- $E(N)$ is $O(b^{r \log_b N}) = O(N^r)$ if $a < b^r$.
- $E(N)$ is $O(N^r \log_b N)$ if $a = b^r$.

C

PASSING PROCEDURES AS PARAMETERS

The Relevant Issue section of Chapter 1 described how to pass procedures and functions as parameters in standard Pascal programs. In particular, we saw that the signature of the procedure/function is included directly in the formal parameter list of the procedure that receives the procedure/function parameter. This appendix will describe how to achieve this same effect in a variety of other popular programming languages: Turbo Pascal, Object-Oriented Turbo Pascal, Modula-2, C, C++, and Ada. The approach will be to present a brief example for passing procedures (or functions) as parameters in each of these languages. What is provided here is not intended to be a complete treatment of this topic for these languages. Rather, the goal is to provide a template that can be used to serve as a quick reference for passing procedures as parameters in your particular programming language. You should also consult a comprehensive reference on your language to gain further insight into this usage of parameters.

TURBO PASCAL

Unlike standard Pascal, in which the signature of the procedure being passed is declared in the formal parameter list of the procedure that receives the parameter (see Relevant Issue for Chapter 1), Turbo Pascal requires that you establish the signature of the procedure being passed in a type declaration. For example:

```
type
  Comparison = function
               ( A, B: ElementType (* Values to compare *) )
```

```
                              : boolean        (* Return true if A
                                                  precedes B in
                                                  order relationship on
                                                  ElementType *);
```

A Sort procedure could then receive a parameter of type Comparison.

```
procedure Sort
  ( var A: ElementArray        (* Array of values to be
                                  returned in order
                                  according to Precedes
                                  relation *);
          N: integer           (* Number of values in
                                  array. Assume
                                  0 <= N <= IndexLimit *);
          Precedes: Comparison (* Determines order relationship
                                  between array entries *) );
    begin (* Sort *)
      :
      if Precedes(A[J], A[J - 1]) then...
        :
    end; (* Sort *)
```

A function adhering to this signature could then be defined as the actual parameter to pass to procedure Sort.

```
function GreaterThan       (* Used as the actual parameter for
                                  Precedes *)
  ( A, B: ElementType      (* Values to compare *) )
        : boolean          (* Return true if A > B *);
    begin
      GreaterThan := (A > B)
    end;  (* GreaterThan *)

begin (* Main program to demonstrate procedure call to sort
          in descending order *)
  :
  Sort(Data, Size, GreaterThan);
  :
end
```

OBJECT-ORIENTED TURBO PASCAL

The newer versions of Turbo Pascal are object-oriented and, as such, allow an object to "own" an operation (often called a *method* in object-oriented jargon). The advantage of this approach is that an operation such as Precedes can be invoked in a procedure without the necessity of passing it in as a separate parameter. This is possible because the object that the procedure receives as a parameter carries the operation with it. The following example illustrates this usage.

```
type
  ElementType = object
                ... (* Appropriate other fields *)
                function Precedes
                  ( A : ElementType) (* An object to be
                                        compared to the
                                        object that owns
                                        Precedes *)
                            : boolean;     (* true if the object
                                              that owns Precedes
                                              comes before A *)
            end;  (* object declaration *)
    :

procedure Sort
  ( var A: ElementArray  (* Array of values to be returned
                            in order according
                            to Precedes relation
                            owned by each object
                            in ElementArray *);
        N: integer        (* Number of values in array. Assume
                             0 <= N <= IndexLimit *) );

  begin (* Sort *)
    :
    if A[J].Precedes(A[J-1]) then... (* A[J] owns the Precedes
                                        relation *)
    :
  end; (* Sort *)
```

MODULA-2

Like Turbo Pascal, Modula-2 dictates that the signature of a function to be passed as a parameter be declared as a TYPE.

```
TYPE
  Comparison = PROCEDURE
                ( A, B: ElementType (* Values to compare *) )
                    : BOOLEAN      (* Return TRUE if A
                                      precedes B in
                                      order relationship
                                      on ElementType *);
```

A Sort procedure could then receive a parameter of type Comparison.

```
PROCEDURE Sort
  ( VAR A: ElementArray        (* Array of values to be
                                  returned in order
                                  according to Precedes
                                  relation *);
        N: integer             (* Number of values in
                                  array. Assume
                                  0 <= N <= IndexLimit *);
        Precedes: Comparison (* Determines order relationship
                                  between array entries *) );

  BEGIN (* Sort *)
    .
    .
    .
    IF Precedes(A[J], A[J-1]) THEN...
    .
    .
    .
  END Sort;
```

C

In C, functions may be passed as parameters to other functions through a feature that permits the definition of pointers to functions. The following example illustrates this usage for an array of C structs of type elementtype.

```
/* Define interface to the sort function */
sort(a, n, precedes)
struct elementtype a[];              /* Array of entries to
                                        sort */

int n;                               /* Number of elements
                                        in array */

int (*precedes) ();                  /* Pointer to precedes
                                        relationship */

{
  .
  .
  .
  if (*precedes)(a[j], a[j-1]) ...   /* Usage of precedes
                                        parameter */
  .
  .
  .
}
```

C++

C++ is a language that offers object-oriented extensions to standard C. One of the very nice extensions offered in C++ is the ability to overload operators.

This means that you can define what you want an operator such as less than (<) to mean for a particular class of data. Hence a "precedes" parameter does not have to be passed as an extra argument to a sort procedure; the objects being sorted "own" a less than (<) operation that will be appropriately invoked. The following example illustrates this usage.

```
class elementtype {
    ⋮
    elementtype operator < (elementtype k);   /* elementtype
                                                   objects own
                                                   < relation */
    ⋮
};

/* Now define < for objects belonging to class elementtype */
int elementtype::operator < (elementtype k)
{
 /* Return appropriately computed value based on data in
    elementtype */
    ⋮
};

/* Now define the interface to a function that sorts an array
   of elementtype objects */
sort(a, n)
class elementtype a[];    /* Array of entries to sort */
int n;                    /* Number of elements in array */

{
    ⋮
  if a[j] < a[j-1])...    /* Use the overloaded < operator */
    ⋮
}
```

ADA

Strictly speaking, Ada does not offer the capability to pass procedures as parameters. However, you can achieve the same effect by using what Ada calls generic subprograms. A generic subprogram is one written without respect to any particular data type. For instance, the partial coding for a GENERIC_SORT procedure is given below. Notice that this procedure uses a less than (<) operator to compare array elements.

```
generic
type ELEMENTTYPE is private;
type INDEX is (<>);
type ELEMENTARRAY is array (INDEX) of ELEMENTTYPE;
procedure GENERIC_SORT(LIST : in out ELEMENTARRAY) is
 LOWER_BOUND : LIST'FIRST;
 UPPER_BOUND : LIST'FIRST;
 INDEX_1 : LIST'RANGE;
 INDEX_2 : LIST'RANGE;
 OUTER_LIMIT : LIST'RANGE;
 INNER_BEGIN : LIST'RANGE;
 begin
    :
   if LIST(INDEX_1) > LIST(INDEX_2)
      then
    :
end GENERIC_SORT;
```

This generic subprogram can then be *instantiated* into an actual sort procedure for a particular kind of data with a statement such as the following:

```
procedure INTEGER_SORT is new GENERIC_SORT (INTEGER);
```

The < operator that is invoked within INTEGER_SORT will then be the appropriate operator for the INTEGER data type. For more complex data types, Ada allows operator overloading, thereby allowing you to define what < means for a structured type.

HINTS AND SOLUTIONS TO SELECTED EXERCISES

Exercises 1.1

1. No. The **repeat...until** loop is a posttest loop; that is, the loop body is always executed at least once before the boolean expression controlling the loop is evaluated. In a **for...to** loop, if the initial value is less than the final value, the body of the loop will not be executed.

3.
```
procedure BestWorst
  ( given BetterThan: Comparison;
          A, B, C: ElementType;
    return A, B, C: ElementType);

  start BestWorst
   if BetterThan(C, A) then
    Swap(C, A)
   endif;
   if BetterThan(B, A) then
    Swap(B, A)
   endif;
   if BetterThan(C, B) then
    Swap(C, B)
   endif
  end BestWorst;
```

Exercises 1.2

1. Selection sort:

```
18  90  40   9   3  92   6
 3  90  40   9  18  92   6
 3   6  40   9  18  92  90
 3   6   9  40  18  92  90
 3   6   9  18  40  92  90
 3   6   9  18  40  92  90
 3   6   9  18  40  90  92
```

3. Big-O: This version of the insertion sort has the same Big-O analysis as the "swap" version. The difference in efficiency between the two versions lies in data manipulation. Each call to swap in the original version requires three data transfers, whereas each comparison in the "move" version requires only one.

5. **a.** N^2 **b.** $N \log_2 N$ **c.** $N \log_2 N$

7. **a.** $n^3 \log_2 n$ **b.** 4^n **c.** 2^n

9. Insertion sort is stable. Selection sort as presented in the text is not stable. Consider the array

$$18 \quad 13_1 \quad 6 \quad 12 \quad 13_2 \quad 9$$

Exercises 1.3

1. 23 probes; 23 microseconds

3. The search is sequential, which is $O(N)$.

5. Assume that Index is a function that returns the ordinal value of the first character in an alphanumeric string, Float is a function that returns a real representation of an integer number, and Round is a function that rounds off a real number to the nearest integer. Then the Split function is determined as follows.

```
if Index(Target) < Index(A[Lo]) then
  Split := Lo
elsif Index(Target) > Index(A[Hi]) then
  Split := Hi
else
  Split := Lo + Round(Float(Hi - Lo)
            * Float((Index(Target)
            - Index(A[Lo])))
            / Float((Index(A[Hi])
            - Index(A[Lo]))))
endif
```

Note that this requires A[Lo] and A[Hi] (or the entire array A) to be parameters to Split.

Exercises 1.4

1.
```
60  12  90  30  64   8   6
 6  12   8  30  64  90  60
 6   8  12  30  60  64  90
```

3. The Shell sort is named after its inventor, D. L. Shell.
5. The advantage of using increments of prime value size lies in the fact that the increments will not divide evenly into each other; all of the segments are therefore distinct.
7. The best-case data set would have the data already in order. In the worst-case data set none of the data would be partially sorted at all; that is, each segment would initially be in descending instead of ascending order.
9. Insertion sort: 28 comparisons

    Shell sort (diminishing increments = **div** 2): 22 comparisons

    Shell sort (diminishing increments = 5, 3, 1): 20 comparisons

11. **a.** K := K / 2 + 1, after a preliminary loop to build K up to an appropriate initial value
    d. K := K / 3, after a preliminary loop to build K up to an appropriate initial value

Exercises 2.1

1. The term *information hiding* describes the ability of a package to meet the specifications of an abstract data type in a self-contained fashion, allowing use of the package without having to know how it achieves the implementation.

    The user of the operations defined for the sparse matrix has no knowledge of how the values of the matrix are stored or retrieved. There is no way, for example, for the user to see that zero values are, in fact, not stored at all.

3. $\text{NumCols} \times \text{Depth} \times (R - 1) + \text{Depth} \times (C - 1) + D$

    where R, C, D = row, column, and depth. For a matrix on n dimensions specified $(N_1, N_2, N_3, \ldots, N_n)$:

    $$\text{NumN}_2 \times \text{NumN}_3 \times \cdots \times \text{NumN}_n \times (N_1 - 1)$$
    $$+ \text{NumN}_3 \times \cdots \times \text{NumN}_n \times (N_2 - 1)$$
    $$+ \cdots$$
    $$+ \text{NumN}_n \times (N_{n-1} - 1)$$
    $$+ N_n$$

9. A sparse matrix using boolean data would store the row and column of an implied boolean value (such as **true**).

Exercises 2.2

1. Encapsulation is the bundling into a record of all data items necessary to implement the ADT. Encapsulation is necessary to completely separate the use of an ADT from its implementation.
3. No. Since the length is kept in the string record, a function to look up the length of a string does not add appreciably to the time efficiency. However, length could be called once and its value stored in a variable to avoid the overhead of many calls to length within the algorithm.
5. The algorithm is most efficient in the unsuccessful case if Align[P] is close to 0, and is most efficient for the successful case if Align[P] is close to P − 1.

Exercises 2.3

1. Final arrangement of pointers:

1	5138
2	4492
3	5300
4	5232
5	4016
6	3094

3. A pointer sort still requires the same number of data comparisons as the sort into which it is incorporated. The performance improvement lies in the savings in data interchanges, which are fewer in selection sort.

Exercises 2.4

3. Since the implementation of the set is an array, the most inefficient use would be when the set is from a large universe but has only a few elements.
5. Make Partition an array of pointers to some data type. UFCreate assigns a pointer value for each pointer in the partition; UFFind compares the pointers of P[X] and P[Y] and returns **true** if they are the same; UFUnion checks the entire array P and changes every pointer equal to P[Y] to be the same value as P[X].

Exercises 3.1

1. Retrieve the record with the old name; change the name in the record; delete the node with the old name; add a node with the new record.
5. Add the following operations:
    a. GetFirst, which returns the first node in a list if the list is not empty
    b. GetNext, which returns a node following a given node in a list if the given node has a successor
    c. EndOfList, which returns true if the end of the list has been reached
7. A general list is a collection of data items, each of which is the same data type. The elements of a list are related to each other by their absolute position in the list. That is, there is a first element, a second element, a third, and so on. The operations to be performed on a general list should include the following:
    • Add an element to the list at a given position
    • Assign a value to a list element at a given position
    • Search a list for the position of a given value
    • Return the number of nodes in the list
    • Retrieve the value of a given list element at a given position
    • Delete an element from the list at a given position
    • Sort the list in a specified order

9.
```
function Sum
  ( given L: List;
    return: integer);
  var
    Total: integer;
  procedure ProcessNode
    ( given Node: ListNode);
```

```
  start ProcessNode
    Total := Total + (* value of data item
                        in ListNode *)
  end ProcessNode;

  start Sum
   Total := 0;
   Traverse(L, ProcessNode);
   Sum := Total
  end Sum;
```

Exercises 3.2

3.

Create	$O(n)$	to initialize each element
Destroy	$O(1)$	
Assign	$O(n)$	(data moves)
Add	$O(\log_2 n)$	to find slot, $O(n)$ data moves
Delete	$O(\log_2 n)$	to find item, $O(n)$ data moves
Retrieve	$O(\log_2 n)$	
Update	$O(\log_2 n)$	
Traverse	$O(n)$	

9. Broccoli
   Corn
   Lima Beans
   Peas
   Spinach

11. A search for an item in an ordered array is $O(\log_2 n)$, but in a pointer-linked list the search must be sequential ($O(n)$). However, the data manipulation required for Adds and Deletes in an ordered array is $O(n)$. An addition or deletion requires a lot of data shifting. In the linked list, however, only pointers are manipulated. Therefore, the linked list is good for a volatile database, whereas an ordered array is better for a stable database.

17. In a linked list the pointer points to another node in the list. The pointers in the data structure for the pointer sort point to data values, not list nodes.

Exercises 3.3

1. a. head = 9   List = 79, 55, 89, 13, 19, 178

   b.

	Data	Link
1	47	3
2	89	5
3	66	7
4	883	2
5	912	10
6	55	2
7	112	4
8	912	0
9	79	6
10	912	8

3.

	DATA	LINK	
1	LOCKE	3	HEAD = 5 AVAIL = 2
2	MILLER	NULL (=0)	
3	SMITH	NULL (=0)	
4	FOSTER	1	
5	ALLEN	4	

5. Final status:

1	AARON	4	HEAD = 1	AVAIL = 5
2	WAGNER	NULL		
3	SEFTON	2		
4	LEE	3		
5				

7. $O(1)$ for both

Exercises 3.4

1. Final status:

1	DUMMY	2	HEAD = 1	AVAIL = 6
2	AARON	5		
3	WAGNER	NULL		
4	SEFTON	3		
5	LEE	4		
6		NULL		

3. Final status:

1	DUMMY	2	NULL	HEAD = 1	AVAIL = 6
2	AARON	5	1		
3	WAGNER	NULL	4		
4	SEFTON	3	5		
5	LEE	4	2		
6		NULL	NULL		

5. When a linked list is implemented using a dummy header, operations that involve empty lists are made easier. Further, the header can be used to store information about the list.

7. In a singly linked list, in order to delete a node or to insert a node before a given node, it is necessary to partially traverse the list to first identify the node preceding the node to be deleted, or the node that will precede the one being added. Such a traversal is not necessary with double linking.

Exercises 3.5

3. Assume that RowRange is a constant determining number of rows and that ColRange is a constant determining number of columns. Assume that MatrixData is integer.

```
procedure FormSums
  ( given M: Matrix;
    return S: array [RowRange] of integer
                          (* Row sums *));
  var
   J, K: integer;

  start FormSums
   for J := 1 to RowRange do
    S[J] := 0;
    for K := 1 to ColRange do
     S[J] := S[J] + Retrieve(M, J, K);
    endfor
   endfor
  end FormSums;
```

Since efficiency of Retrieve is $O(\text{ColRange})$, overall efficiency is $O(\text{RowRange} \times \text{ColRange2})$.

Exercises 3.6

3. When string2 is assigned to string1, no new copy is made of the 'COFFEE' string. Instead, the pointer for string2 is directed to the same location as the pointer for string1. When string1 changes, it is possible with this implementation that string2 also changes. So the output given would be 'TEA' and not the 'COFFEE' that we would expect.

5. Place a copy of T, rather than T itself, into string S. Use the Assign procedure. The cost in efficiency is that string T is traversed in Assign ($O(n)$) to copy it.

Exercises 3.7

5. a. **type**
```
    Set: pointer to Element;
    Element: record
                City: string;
                NextEl: Set
             endrecord;
```
   b. Partition: **array** [MaxCities] **of** Set;

7. The sets in the union-field problem are disjoint, so each element is unique and it is not necessary to compare every element of one set against every element of another set. The elements must be located ($O(N)$ comparisons) and the links established to join the two sets containing them (an $O(1)$ operation).

Exercises 4.1

1.
```
procedure Substitute
  ( given Q: Queue   (* Orig queue *);
         Old, New: QueueData;
    return Q: Queue (* Altered queue *));
 var
  Temp: QueueData;
 start Substitute
  if not Empty(Q) then
   Dequeue(Q, Temp);
   Enqueue(Q, -1);
   while Temp <> -1 do
    if Temp = Old then
     Enqueue(Q, New)
    else
     Enqueue(Q, Temp)
    endif;
    Dequeue(Q, Temp)
   endwhile
  endif
 end Substitute;
```

Exercises 4.2

1.

Front	Rear	Array
1	1	SMITH

Front	Rear	Array
1	2	SMITH
		JONES

Front	Rear	Array
1	3	SMITH
		JONES
		GREER

Front	Rear	Array
2	3	
		JONES
		GREER

Front	Rear	Array
2	4	
		JONES
		GREER
		CARSON

Front	Rear	Array
3	4	
		GREER
		CARSON

Front	Rear	Array
3	5	
		GREER
		CARSON
		BAKER

Front	Rear	Array
3	1	CHARLES
		GREER
		CARSON
		BAKER

QUEUE FULL—BENSON NOT ADDED

Front	Rear	Array
4	1	CHARLES
		CARSON
		BAKER

Front	Rear	Array
4	2	CHARLES
		MILLER
		CARSON
		BAKER

3.

Condition	Special Situation
Front = Rear	One-entry queue
(read mod ArraySize) + 1 = Front	Empty queue
((Rear + 1) mod ArraySize) + 1 = Front	Full queue

5. a. To create a queue, Rear should be equal to Front, and both should be equal to 1.
   To detect an empty queue, Rear should be equal to Front. A full array is detected when Rear + 1 = ArraySize.

b. To create a queue, Rear should be equal to Front, and both should be equal to 1.

To detect an empty queue, Rear should be equal to Front.

To detect a full queue, Rear will be one less than Front (depending on how the array wraps). Note that this will waste one open space.

c. In all cases, Rear will have to be a dummy pointer, an extra link.

Exercises 4.3

1. 1st Pass:

Digit	Sublist		
0			
1	9021		
2	1142		
3			
4	94		
5			
6	3216	416	3316
7			
8	9438		
9			

2nd Pass:

Digit	Sublist		
0			
1	3216	416	3316
2	9021		
3	9438		
4	1142		
5			
6			
7			
8			
9	94		

3rd Pass:

Digit	Sublist	
0	9021	94
1	1142	
2	3216	
3	3316	
4	416	9438
5		
6		
7		
8		
9	94	

4th Pass:

Digit	Sublist	
0	94	416
1	1142	
2		
3	3216	3316
4		
5		
6		
7		
8		
9	9021	9438

3. Rather than test the Master List at each digit to find if there are values at that digit level, it is better to search the Master List once to find the largest digit, which can be done during the first pass through RadixSort.

5. Since the length of each sublist is variable, a linked list implementation is preferable.

7. No. The resulting algorithm is $O(n^2/4)$, which is still $O(n^2)$, although with a smaller constant of proportionality.

9. RadixSort is inflexible for data of varying size. If a set of real numbers could be preprocessed to be presented to RadixSort in a uniform format (i.e., of uniform length to the right of the decimal point, and possibly with the decimal point removed), the list could be sorted by RadixSort just as any other list of strings of digits.

Exercises 4.4

1.

Time Slice	Ready Queue	Blocked Queue	Signal	Pause	Current Process
1	A(6)*				A(6)
2	B(4),A(5)				B(4)
3	A(5),B(3)			Y	A(5)
4	B(3),C(6),A(4)				B(3)
5	A(4),B(2)	C(6)		Y	C(6)
6	A(4),B(2)	C(6)			A(4)
7	B(2),A(3)	C(6),B(2)		Y	B(2)
8	A(3)	C(6),B(2)		Y	A(3)
9	A(3),C(4)	C(6),B(2)	Y		A(2)
10	C(4),A(2)	B(2)			C(6)

*The number in parentheses represents the remaining time slices available to that process.

3. Instead of using a boolean variable for the semaphore, use an integer variable that keeps track of the number of resources that are available for allocation from the pool. When the number available reaches 0 and a request is made, the requesting process must be enqueued.

Exercises 4.5

1. PriorityDequeue is very efficient. Removal of an item merely involves increasing the pointer to the front of the queue ($O(1)$). PriorityEnqueue, however, requires first a search to locate the position for insertion of the new element (average search is $N/2$ elements) and then shifting the preceding or succeeding elements of the array to the left or right, respectively. The average shift is of $N/2$ elements, depending on which shift direction would require the least data movement.

3. You can use a linked list to great advantage when implementing a priority queue. Whenever an item arrives to be inserted into a given priority level, the rear pointer for that priority gives us an immediately accessible pointer to the node after which the item is to be inserted. This avoids a costly sequential search for the insertion point. If a dummy header is included at the beginning, the empty conditions for any given priority are as shown:

Condition	Priority
Front = Rear1	For priority 1, the highest priority
Rear1 = Rear2	For priority 2
Rear$(n-1)$ = Rear n	For priority n

7.

Option	PriorityEnqueue	PriorityDequeue
1	yes	no
2	no	yes
3	yes	no
4	no	yes
5	yes	no

Assuming that the priority value is stored in PriorityQue-Node whenever the queue is ordered, PriorityEnqueue requires the Priority function to locate the insertion point. Since insertion in an unordered queue is always to the rear of the queue, no special insertion function is necessary. The reverse is true for PriorityDequeue. An unordered queue needs the Priority function to locate the first item of the highest priority to dequeue, whereas an ordered queue will always dequeue from the front.

   The argument for retaining the Priority function is to keep the ADT blind to the implementation option used.

9. If processes are to be processed FIFO with varying time bursts, the queue that presents the processes to the scheduler need not be a priority queue, as long as the scheduler can allot the proper number of time slices to each process.

   Alternatively, allow processes to be put on a priority queue with two priorities, in which only one process may occupy the high priority position at a time and all the other processes are of an equal lower priority. At each time slice, PriorityDequeue the item at the front of the queue (high priority position). If its run burst is greater than one, at the end of its time slice it is PriorityEnqueued, and its run burst decremented. If the process is not finished by the end of its run burst, it is put back on the end of the queue at the low priority, with its run burst restored to its original value. This involves, of course, keeping counters within the DataNode.

Exercises 5.1

1. In a stack structure, the first item in is the last item out. The most recent addition to the stack is always at the top of the stack.

3. A stack stores the return address and local variables (among other data) for each procedure/function when it is invoked. When the procedure/function returns to the calling routine, its data are popped from the stack and the return address retrieved. The local variables for this routine are now at the top of the stack.

Exercises 5.2

3.
```
Create(S);
while not at end of line do
  read(c);
  push(S, c)
endwhile;
while not Empty(S) do
  pop(S, c);
  write(c)
endwhile;
```

Exercises 5.3

1. Postfix notation: ABCD − PR − / * +
   Prefix notation: +A*B/−CD−PR

3. The stacks would vary as follows:

opStack	String
#	P
#+	P
#+(	P
#+(	PQ
#+(−	PQ
#+(−	PQF
#+	PQF−
#+/	PQF−
	PQF−Y/+

5. The stacks would vary as follows:

opStack	String
#	P
#*	P
#*(	P
#*(	PQ
#*(/	PQ
#*(/	PQY
#*	PQY/
#*+	PQY/
#*+	PQY/A
#* + −	PQY/A
#* + −	PQY/AB
#* + −+	PQY/ABD
#**	PQY/ABD+ − +
#**	PQY/ABD+ − +Y
	PQY/ABD+ − +Y**

7. When the infix priority of a given operator is greater than the stack priority of another given operator, the operator with the lower stack priority has a lesser overall algebraic priority. In the normal system we use, the + and − have a low stack priority when compared with the infix priority of the * or the /. Similarly, when the stack priority of a given operator is high, it will be performed before other "incoming" operators.

9. The comparison between stack and infix priorities determines how long an operator must wait on the stack before being popped. To correctly evaluate $3 \uparrow 2 \uparrow 3$ (3^{2^3}), 2^3 must be computed first, and then 3 raised to that power. In 3^{2^3}, the first symbol must have a higher priority than the second $\uparrow$ or the expression will be incorrectly evaluated as $(3^2)^3$ Therefore, for the operator $\uparrow$, the infix priority must be lower than the stack priority for the same operator, so that the $\uparrow$ on the stack will not be popped prematurely.

11. The operators $<, >, <>, \leq, \geq, =$ (comparisons) typically have a lower value than the arithmetic operators.

   The boolean logical operators AND, OR, NOT have a higher value than the comparison boolean operators. Typically, NOT has the highest value of all operators, except left parenthesis; AND has the same value as * and /; and OR has the same value as + and −. The left parenthesis must have the highest infix priority.

Exercises 6.1

1.
```
procedure ReverseTraverse
  ( given L: List;
          ProcessNode: NodeOperation;
    return L: List (* with nodes processed
                      in reverse order *));
  var
  L1, L2, Done: List;
  start ReverseTraverse
  if L <> NULL then
    Done := nil;
    L1 := L;
    while Done <> L1 do
    L2 := Ref(L1).Link;
    if (L2 = Done) then
      ProcessNode(Ref(L1));
      Done := L1;
      L1 := L
    else
      L1 := L2
    endif
    endwhile
  endif
  end ReverseTraverse;
```

3.

Return	M	N	Function Evaluation
1	0	1	2
2	1	0	2
3	0		2
2	1	1	3
3	0		3
2	1	2	4
3	1		4
0	1	3	5

5. First define a procedure:

```
procedure InsertValue
  ( given A: ElementArray;
          N: IndexRange;
          Value: ElementType;
          Precedes: Comparison;
    return A: ElementArray);
```

This procedure inserts the value Item into the array A of N values, where the values are already sorted according to the Precedes relationship.

For the procedure Sort:

```
if N > 1 then
  Sort(A, NumVals - 1, Precedes);
  InsertValue(A, N - 1, A[N], Precedes)
endif;
```

9.
```
function Reverse
  ( given S: string;
    return R: string);
  var T, V: string;
  start Reverse
  if Length(S) > 1 then
    Substring(S, 2, Length(S) - 1, T);
    Reverse(T, R);
    SubString(T, 1, 1, V);
    Concatenate(R, V)
  else
    Assign(S, R)
  endif
  end Reverse;
```

Exercises 6.2

1. The value output from the array would vary as follows:

Lo	Hi	Array
1	7	60 12 90 30 64 8 6
1	4	6 12 8 30
2	4	12 8 30
2	2	8
4	4	30
6	7	64 90
7	7	90

3. When the data are already in order.

5. When the data are in order or when there is a small data set.

7. The best-case behavior of QuickSort consists of a randomly distributed data set and a pivot that always divides the set evenly into two. This results in an $O(n \log_2 n)$ sort. The worst case is a completely sorted data set, for which the pivots chosen distribute the subarrays unevenly into sets of 0 and $n - 1$ elements for an ascending sort and into sets of $n - 1$ and 0 elements for a descending sort. This will be $O(n^2)$.

9. If the data set is randomly distributed, the choice of pivot will make no difference.

11. The worst-case space efficiency (i.e., stack size) occurs if the partitioning of the data is uneven and the bounds of the smaller subsets are consistently chosen to be stacked.

Exercises 6.3

1. The output values would be

Lower	Upper	Array
1	7	60 12 90 30 64 8 6
1	4	60 12 90 30
1	2	60 12
1	1	60
2	2	12
3	4	90 30
3	3	90
4	4	30
5	7	64 8 6

and so on.

5. MergeSort, as presented, is not stable. Consider the array

$$1_1 \quad 1_2 \quad 1_3$$

This would return from MergeSort as $1_1 \quad 1_3 \quad 1_2$.

Exercises 6.4

1a.

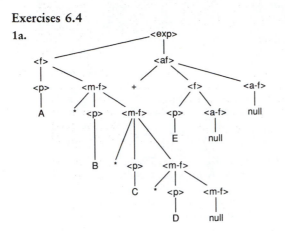

3a. yes

3b. (parse tree for expression of **1a**)

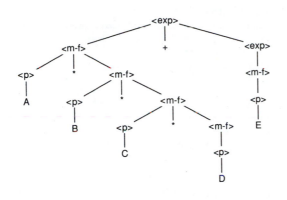

3d. Grammar of Exercise 3 has right to left associativity for + and *. Example 6.8 has left to right associativity for + and *.

5. <if-statement> := if <condition>
                         then <statement>
                      := if <condition>
                         then <statement>
                         else <statement>

We assume <statement> := <if-statement> is also defined.

Since two different parse trees may be derived from this grammar, this grammar is ambiguous.

(1) let <s> = <statement>, <c> = <condition>, and <ifs> = <if-statement>

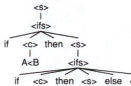

(2)

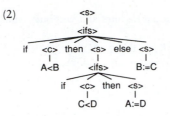

Pascal interpretation corresponds to parse tree (1).

Exercise 7.1

1. A * B − (C + D) * (P / Q)

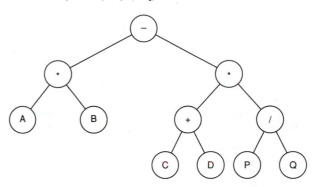

3. A tree structure is a hierarchical ordering of data.

5. a. This binary tree is a heap.
  b. The node containing 19 has a right subtree with a node containing 35. The node containing 36 has a left subtree with a node containing 39. In a heap, no descendent of a node may contain data greater than the node's data.
  c. This binary tree is a heap.

7.

binary-to-heap:	The data in any given node of the tree are greater than or equal to the data in its left and right subtrees.
binary-to-ordered:	The data value in each node of the tree is greater than all of the data in that node's left subtree and less than or equal to all the data in the right subtree.
binary-to-expression:	The relationship of binary operator to its two operands.

Exercises 7.2

1b.

Location	Data	Left Child	Right Child
1	C	3	nil
2	R	nil	3
3	G	nil	nil
4	F	nil	nil
5	X	9	4
6	Y	nil	nil
7	B	6	5
8	A	7	1
9	J	nil	nil

Root = 8; Avail = 2

3. Values will appear on separate lines and without commas in actual output.

OOPS, OOPS, OOPS, K, OOPS, I, OOPS, OOPS, OOPS, J, H, G, C, OOPS, OOPS, E, OOPS, OOPS, D, B, A

7.

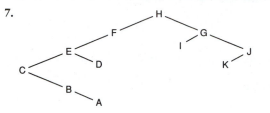

9. A, B, E, J, nil, nil, nil, K, nil, nil, nil, L, nil, nil, nil, nil, nil, C, F, nil, nil, nil, G, nil, nil, nil, H, nil, nil, nil, D, nil, nil, I, nil, M, O, nil, nil, nil, nil, nil, N, nil, nil, nil

Exercises 7.3

1. The resulting tree is not very full. Its big-O efficiency would be $O(n)$.

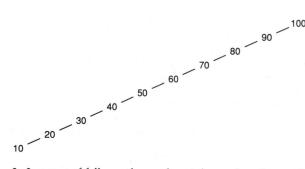

3. In terms of fullness, the tree here is better than the tree in Exercise 1. But since constants are not considered significant with large values of n, its big-O performance remains $O(n)$.

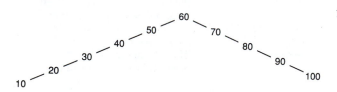

5. With any of these three implementations, the insertion of a node is relatively easy. To find the correct position in a single-linked list, two pointers have to be used: one to keep track of the previous node and the other to keep track of current node. In a doubly linked list and in a binary tree, this situation is avoided. However, in a doubly linked list, the entire list has to be sequentially searched to find the correct node. In a binary tree, the search is potentially equivalent to a binary search.

13. Complications arise when trying to develop insertion and deletion algorithms.

Exercise 7.4

1. Final tree:

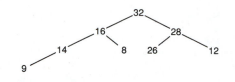

3. 67, 64, 12, 61, 42, 6, 4, 55, 55, 32

5. The assumption is made that evaluation of an **and** will be short-circuited upon evaluation of a component that is **false**. In a language that does not support this assumption, use the following code:

```
var Done: boolean;
 .
 .
 .
Done := false;
while (K >= 1) and not Done do
  if Precedes(A[K], Key) then
   Done := true
  else
   A[L] := A[K];
   L := K;
   K := L / 2
  endif
endwhile;
```

7. Phase I: 1 8 6 7 3 2
              1 8 6 7 3 2
              8 7 6 1 3 2

   Phase II: 7 3 6 1 2 8
               6 3 2 1 7 8
               3 1 2 6 7 8
               2 1 3 6 7 8
               1 2 3 6 7 8

9. Heap sort is $O(n \log_2 n)$ regardless of the data being sorted.

13. Heap sort is not stable. Consider the array

$$9 \quad 8 \quad 10_1 \quad 11 \quad 10_2$$

Heap sort will sort it to the array

$$8 \quad 9 \quad 10_2 \quad 10_1 \quad 11$$

Exercises 7.5

1a.

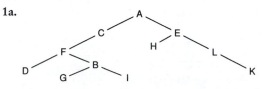

3. To thread a tree for postorder traversal, the threads of the rightmost nodes would have to point back to the header, but the header would also have to be pointed to by the left-

most nodes. So when the header was reached by traversing the threads, you would not know if you had really traversed all of the nodes.

Exercises 7.6

1. This tree is height-balanced but not full since F has no children.

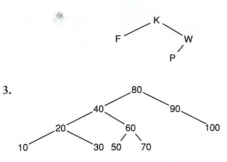

3.

Exercises 8.1

1. 12, 6, 3, 17, 64, 25, 8, 49, 36, 16, 40, 63, 93, 78, 4, 9, 13, 97, 84, 18, 2, 6, 44, 19, 1
3. An inorder traversal of a binary tree requires that you recursively visit all nodes in the left subtree, process the root node, and then recursively visit all nodes in the right subtree. Any node in a general tree may have more than two children, and therefore the terms *left* subtree and *right* subtree lose their meaning; thus, a general tree cannot be processed by an inorder traversal.
5. Use a global variable to keep count of the nodes visited. Have ProcessNode increase the count each time it is invoked by PostOrderTraversal.

Exercises 8.2

1. Tree stored in an array of records for data and pointers.

Location	Data	FirstChild	Sibling
1	P	2	nil
2	Q	3	13
3	T	nil	4
4	U	nil	5
5	V	6	12
6	C	nil	7
7	D	nil	8
8	E	9	nil
9	M	nil	10
10	N	nil	11
11	O	nil	nil
12	W	nil	nil
13	A	14	15
14	G	nil	nil
15	B	16	19
16	H	nil	17
17	I	nil	18
18	J	nil	nil
19	X	20	nil
20	K	nil	21
21	L	nil	nil

Ternary tree implementation:

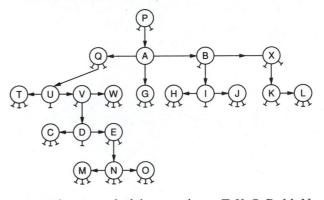

3. Postorder traversal of the general tree: T, U, C, D, M, N, O, E, V, W, Q, G, A, H, I, J, B, K, L, X, P
   Postorder traversal of the general tree using binary implementation: O, N, M, E, D, C, W, V, U, T, G, J, I, H, L, K, X, B, A, Q, P

Exercises 8.3

1.

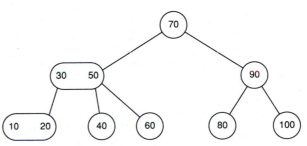

5. The order in which data arrive does not affect the distribution of data in a 2-3 tree, since insertion maintains a tree with all of its leaves on the same level. A new level is added by sprouting a new root rather than adding a leaf at a deeper level.

Exercise 8.4

1. Final configuration:

   P = {{7, 3, 6}, {8, 5, 2, 9, 1, 10, 4}}

Parent	1	2	3	4	5	6	7	8	9	10
Array	9	5	7	8	8	7	0	0	5	8

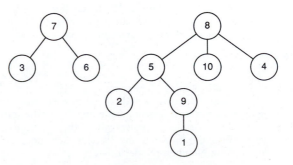

3. Final configuration:

P = {{7, 3, 6}, {8, 5, 2, 9, 1, 10, 4}}

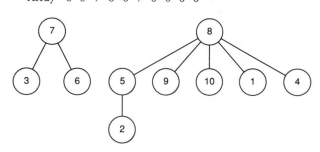

Parent 1 2 3 4 5 6 7 8 9 10
Array 8 5 7 8 8 7 0 0 8 8

9. Consider the set {1, 2, 3, 4, 5} and the operations

UFCreate(P);
UFUnion(1, 2, P);
UFUnion(2, 3, P);
UFUnion(3, 4, P);
UFUnion(4, 5, P);

Exercises 9.1

1. A nonempty general tree is a graph since it is a set of nodes connected by parent/child relationships, which are depicted as edges. Each edge has two end-points: the parent node and the child node. A graph, however, is not necessarily a general tree. A graph, for example, may have a loop or a cycle, which a tree may not have.

3. Since each edge in a graph has two endpoints, each edge contributes two degrees to the sum of the total degrees of all the nodes in a digraph. Therefore, the sum must be even. The number of nodes in a digraph that has an odd total degree must be even.

Exercises 9.2

1. B D C A
3. D C A B
5. A B D C. Assume that B is the first node adjacent to A.
7. The AddEdge operation does not correctly add an edge between Node1 and Node2 if the graph G is an undirected graph. In an undirected graph, an edge between two nodes is not directionally oriented. The edge from Node1 to Node2 is the same as the edge from Node2 to Node1. The AddEdge operation gives an edge from Node1 to Node2 but does not establish the edge from Node2 to Node1. Procedure AddUndirectedEdge needs to call AddEdge twice—first with the parameters (G, Node1, Node2), and then with the parameters (G, Node2, Node1).

Exercises 9.3

1. a. $O(1)$
   b. $O(\text{NumberofNodes})$ (worst case)
3. The worst-case efficiency is realized when every node in the graph is connected (directly or indirectly) to the start node. In that case the recursive call in the subordinate procedure SearchFrom will be involved for each connected node, totalling NumberofNodes times.

Exercises 9.4

1. Final structures:

	Distance	Path	Included
NYC	2819	WASH	True
WASH	2582	MILW	True
MIAM	∞	?	False
MILW	1771	PHEX	True
CHI	6494	LVEG	True
NORL	4950	DALS	False
MPLS	5382	DALS	False
OKLC	∞	?	False
DALS	4433	NYC	True
LVEG	4714	LA	True
PHEX	0	?	True
STL	4836	SFRAN	False
SFRAN	4028	MILW	True
LA	4442	SFRAN	True

5. Final structure:

	CHI	NORL	DALS	LVEG	LA
CHI	0	948	1465	1780	2052
NORL	948	0	517	2229	1957
DALS	1465	517	0	1712	1440
LVEG	1780	2229	1712	0	272
LA	2052	1957	1440	272	0

11.

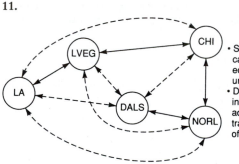

• Solid lines indicate the original edges of the underlying graph.
• Dotted lines indicate edges added in the transitive closure of the graph.

Exercises 9.5

1. Prim's algorithm: Final MST

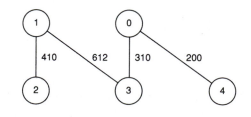

Kruskal's algorithm: Final MST

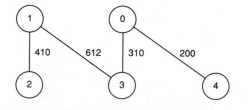

7. In a minimal spanning tree there is only one edge connecting any two nodes. If the number of edges is greater than or equal to the number of nodes, then some node is connected by more than one path, thus creating a cycle. This contradicts the definition of a minimal spanning tree, in which there may be only one path, the path of minimal weight, and no cycles connecting any two nodes.

11. False. For this network

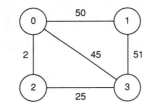

the minimal spanning tree would be

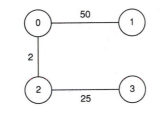

13.

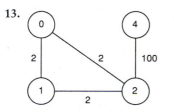

15. Since a cost estimate (a weighted edge) is given for each direct link between any two computers for all 1000 sites, the network can be considered dense: it has a maximum number of edges. Prim's algorithm is the most effective for this type of network.

Exercises 9.6

1. **a.** Initialize ZeroQ: ZeroQ = 1, 2, 6
   b. Loop: dequeue from ZeroQ and reduce indegree of all nodes connected to the dequeued item by one. Add any connected nodes of indegree zero to ZeroQ.
   Loop iteration:
   (1) ZeroQ = 2, 3, 6
       T[1] = 1
   (2) ZeroQ = 6, 3, 4, 5
       T[1] = 1, T[2] = 2
   (3) ZeroQ = 3, 4, 5
       T[1] = 1, T[2] = 2, T[3] = 6
   (4) ZeroQ = 4, 5
       T[1] = 1, T[2] = 2, T[3] = 6, T[4] = 3
   (5) ZeroQ = 5
       T[1] = 1, T[2] = 2, T[3] = 6, T[4] = 3,
       T[5] = 4

   (6) ZeroQ = 7
       T[1] = 1, T[2] = 2, T[3] = 6, T[4] = 3,
       T[5] = 4, T[6] = 5
   (7) ZeroQ = (empty)
       T[1] = 1, T[2] = 2, T[3] = 6, T[4] = 3,
       T[5] = 4, T[6] = 5, T[7] = 7

3. Since the graph is acyclic, there must exist one or more nodes in the graph of indegree zero. When these nodes are processed (removed from ZeroQ), they may be considered as having been removed from the graph, along with the edges connected to their successor nodes. As edges are removed, the indegree of the successor nodes is reduced. When all the predecessors of a node have been removed (placed on ZeroQ), the node will have an indegree of zero, and thus will be placed on the ZeroQ. Once a node is on ZeroQ, it has no predecessor nodes, so no other node will have an edge leading to it (i.e., it cannot be resubmitted to ZeroQ). Thus, all the nodes of a directed acyclic graph will be placed on ZeroQ once.

Exercises 10.1

3.

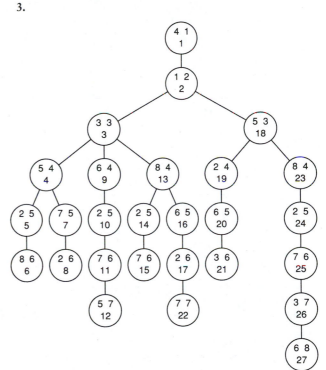

5. The output is the following (with each number on a separate line): 1, 2, 1, 2, 3, 4, 3, 3, 4, 4, 3, 4, 2, 2, 3, 4, 3, 3, 4, 4, 3, 4, 3, 2, 3, 4, 3, 3, 4, 4, 3, 4, 4, 2, 3, 4, 3, 3, 4, 4, 3, 4

Exercises 10.2

1. A depth-first strategy results. The stack ADT has no way of using any completed heuristic value to organize its elements.

3. The trade-offs are the time it takes to compute the heuristic value every time it is needed versus the memory space required to store the heuristic value in the priority queue.

7. The heuristic function is always effective.

9. The path from A to E chosen by the heuristic function of path weight will be A → B → C → D → E instead of the shorter path A → D → E.

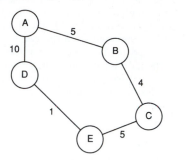

Exercises 11.1

3.

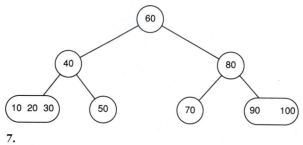

7.

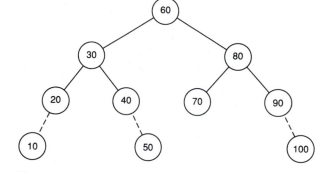

13.

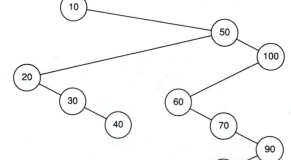

Exercises 11.2

1. a.

Index	Key
1	333
2	632
3	1090
4	459
5	379
6	238
7	
8	
9	
10	1982
11	3411

b.

Index	Key
1	333
2	632
3	1090
4	238
5	459
6	
7	
8	379
9	
10	1982
11	3411

c.

Index	Key	Link		Index	Key	Link
1	333	13		12	3411	14
2	632	0		13	459	0
3	1090	0		14	379	15
4				15	238	0
5				16		
6				17		
7				18		
8				19		
9				20		
10	1982	12		21		
11				22		

3. a.

Position	Key
1	0
2	19
3	38
4	55
5	67
6	4
7	58
8	86
9	0

b.

Position	Key
1	0
2	46
3	32
4	62
5	34
6	0
7	77
8	6
9	0
10	0
11	0

c.

Position	Key
1	0
2	0
3	0
4	4
5	16
6	5
7	27
8	14
9	25
10	20
11	0
12	107
13	0
14	0
15	0

d.

Position	Key
1	20
2	7
3	42
4	51
5	0
6	72
7	6
8	88
9	0
10	9
11	21

Exercises 11.3

1. The doubly linked list is the best choice for implementing linked lists with hashing. When the order of the list is disturbed during a change of a key field or during a deletion of an item in the list, the linked list must be rebuilt. If a doubly linked list is not used, the list would have to be tra-

versed to find the predecessor node in the linked list. The doubly linked list makes rebuilding lists more efficient.

Exercises 11.4

3. At best, hashing gives the same performance. It could give worse performance if the hashing function leads to collisions.

Exercises 11.5

1. 298,891,372
3. CompNumber reduces to Index(S_N).

Exercises 11.6

1. a.
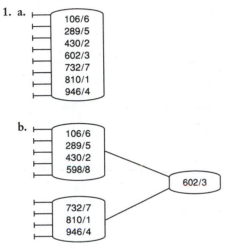

5. a. For the ISAM index, this knowledge will enable us to set the index so that the subsequent search on the disk will be more efficient.
   b. The size of each node on the B-tree can parallel the size of the blocks on the hard disk, making the B-tree efficient. If the nodes are too big, they may be broken up over different sections of the disk.
   c. The tree is constructed the same no matter what the disk structure may be.
   d. Knowing the block sizes of the disk allows us to set the bucket sizes appropriately.

Exercises 12.1

1. Using induction, at the induction step we determine that $(n+1)! = (n+1)n! > (n+1)(n/2)^{n/2}$. Using calculus, one can show that the function $f(n) = (n+1)(n/2)n/2 - [(n+1)/2]^{(n+1)/2}$ is positive and increasing; hence $(n+1)(n/2)^{n/2} > [(n+1)/2]^{(n+1)/2}$, completing the induction step.
5. Using a decision tree analysis as in the text, we determine that an algorithm to produce an array of sorted distinct elements would require $\log_2(n!)$ comparisons to sort the elements and another $n-1$ comparisons among adjacent values to remove duplicate values. Thus, a lower bound

for this algorithm is $(n/2)\log_2(n/2) + (n-1)$. Since, however, $n\log_2 n$ dominates n for large values of n, the lower bound is asymptotically equal to the lower bound established for ordinary sorting.

Exercises 12.2

1. The cost of initally producing runs of size M from a stream of NumberRec records requires that we perform NumberRec/M internal sorts of M records each. If we assume each sort is done with efficiency $M\log_2 M$, the overall efficiency of producing runs of size M becomes NumberRecs $\times \log_2 M$. This is likely to execute much faster than the subsequent merge sorting, since only $O(\text{NumberRecs})$ time-costly disk accesses need to be performed, whereas nearly all of the $O(\text{NumberRec} \times \log_2(\text{NumberRec}/M))$ operations of the two-way merge sort are disk accesses.

Exercises 13.1

1. The implementation of either Section 3.3 or first-fit seems most appropriate for file management using fixed-size disk blocks since it is already set up to allocate and reclaim fixed-size units of storage.
7. Relocation information must be maintained to identify those data values, such as address operands of instructions, that would have to be changed to perform correctly if they are moved during the compaction.

Exercises 13.2

1. Ratios of unused storage after each event: 0/32, 13/32, 15/72, 25/104, 12/72, 16/88, 14/80, 17/96, 7/64, 3/48, 3/16, 0
3. Ratios of unused storage after each event: 7/39, 9/60, 11/68, 44/123, 42/102, 51/123, 49/115, 49/128, 16/73, 7/52, 0/13, 0
5. Assuming the standard Fibonacci sequence, one would be left with blocks of size 377K and 145K. Hence, a pair of requests such as 300K, 100K could be satisfied by the Fibonacci buddy system, but not by the binary buddy system.

(1)
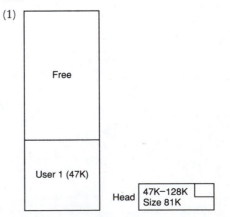

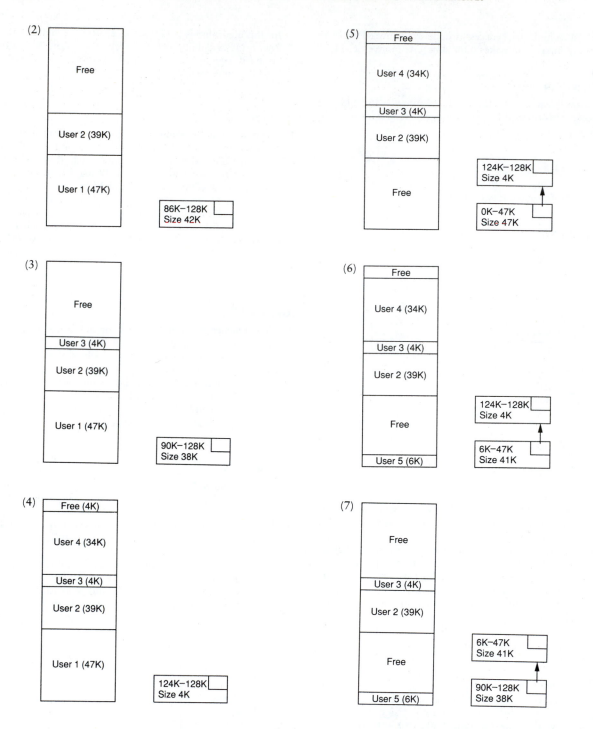

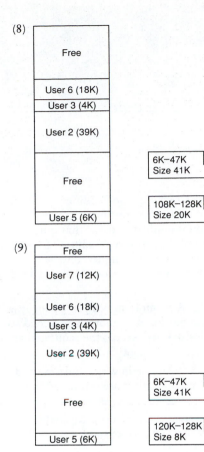

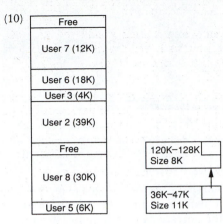

Exercises 13.3

3. O(SizeOfHeap); linked list

GLOSSARY

abstract data type A formal, language-independent description of data elements, the relationships among them, and the operations that act upon them.

abstraction The description of data structures at a conceptual level, apart from their implementation using a particular technique and language.

abstract syntax tree *See* parse tree.

acyclic graph A directed graph without any cycles.

adjacency list A method using linked lists to represent the edges of a graph or network.

adjacency matrix A method that uses a matrix to represent the edges of a graph or network.

adjacent Two nodes of a graph or network are adjacent if they are connected by an edge.

algorithm An unambiguous sequence of clear instructions that, when applied to a problem, will solve it in a finite amount of time and then stop.

alpha-beta pruning A technique employed in game tree searching for reducing the number of nodes that must be explored when the minimax algorithm is invoked for a particular ply limit.

ancestor A tree node that is hierarchically related to another tree node at a lower level in the tree.

arc An edge of a graph or network that establishes a directional orientation between its end points.

AVL rotation A rearrangement of the subtrees of a node of an AVL tree to restore the height balance of the tree at that node. A rotation follows an insertion into or deletion from the tree that has caused the tree to become unbalanced at a node.

AVL tree A tree in which, for each node, the difference between the height of its left subtree and the height of its right subtree is at most one.

balance factor For a node in a binary tree, the difference between the height of its left subtree and the height of its right subtree.

best case The arrangement of data items prior to beginning an algorithm that allows the algorithm to finish in the least amount of time for that particular set of items. *See also* worst case.

best-first search A technique for finding a path through a graph or network from a start node to a goal node. A heuristic function is applied to paths that quickly calculates an estimate of the distance remaining from a given path's final node to the goal node. This value is then used to select a path that is most likely to lead to a goal.

best-fit searching A memory allocation policy in which a list of available blocks of memory is searched so that the block whose size least exceeds the requested amount is allocated.

big-O analysis A technique in which the time and space requirements of an algorithm are estimated in order of magnitude terms.

binary buddy system System used to coalesce blocks of memory in which all blocks have size 2^k for some integer k.

binary search The process of examining a middle value of a sorted array to see which half contains the value in question and continuing to halve until the value is located.

binary search tree A binary tree with the ordering property.

binary tree A tree in which each node has exactly two subtrees, either or both of which may be empty.

binary tree index A binary tree with the ordering property used as an index for the positions of keys in a random access file.

binary tree search A search algorithm driven by the hierarchical relationships of data items in a tree with the ordering property.

bin sort *See* radix sort.

blocked queue In an operating system, the queue of processes that have requested a resource currently owned by another process.

boundary folding A variation on shift folding; in boundary folding the digits in every other numeric section are reversed before the addition is performed.

boundary tag buddy system System for coalescing blocks of memory in which each block contains bookkeeping information at both its upper and lower boundaries.

branch In a tree, a link between a parent and its child node.

breadth-first search A visiting of all nodes in a graph; it proceeds from each node by first visiting all nodes adjacent to that node.

B-tree An efficient, flexible index structure often used in database management systems on random access files.

bubble sort Rearranges elements of an array until they are in either ascending or descending order. Consecutive elements are compared to move (bubble) the elements to the top or bottom accordingly during each pass. *See also* insertion sort, selection sort, radix sort, Shell sort, heap sort, merge sort, and quick sort.

bucket In bucket hashing, a contiguous region of storage locations.

bucket hashing Method of handling collisions in which the hashing function sends the key to a bucket of locations rather than a single location. The key is then placed by performing a sequential search within the bucket.

buddy system Name applied to a variety of techniques that coalesce blocks of memory being returned from users.

children Nodes pointed to by an element in a tree.

circular linked list A linked list in which the last node of the list points to the first node in the list.

cluster In a linked list implementation of a character string, the placement of more than one character per data node forms a cluster of data.

clustering Occurs when a collision-resolution strategy causes keys that have a collision at an initial hashing position to be relocated to the same region within the storage space.

coalescing The process by which two adjacent available blocks of memory are combined into one larger block.

collision Condition in which more than one key hashes to the same position with a given hashing function.

column major Implementation of a two-dimensional array as a one-dimensional array so that the columns are arranged in sequential order with all entries of the same column being adjacent.

compaction The process of collecting fragments of available memory and moving them to one end of memory to create one large block.

component of a linked list *See* node.

constant of proportionality In a big-O analysis, the constant accompanying the dominant term.

context-free grammar A rigorous formalism for defining the syntax of expressions and other programming language constructs. In context-free grammars, no account needs to be taken of the context in which the elements of the construct being parsed are used.

cubic algorithm A polynomial algorithm in which the highest nonzero term is n^3.

cycle A directed path of a graph, with length at least 1, that originates and terminates at the same node.

data abstraction The formal definition of a data structure apart from its actual implementation in a specific language. This definition includes specification of the elements of the structure, the relationships between them, and the operations that may be performed on them.

data stream A sequence of homogenous records that may be accessed only by starting at the first record in the sequence and then reading the second, third, and so forth.

data structure An abstraction of the elementary data types provided by a language. Its values allow a decomposition into several components. Characteristic of a given data structure is the organization of each component and the relationships between components.

deadlock An infinite wait state in which each of two processes owns system resources the other needs and will not release them until it has obtained the remaining resources it needs. Also referred to as *fatal embrace*.

degree of a node The number of edges of a graph for which the node is an endpoint; if the node is the endpoint of a loop, we count the loop as two edges.

denseness A property of binary trees. A binary tree is dense at level m if (a) all nodes with two children at level $m - 1$ appear to the left of any node with only one child at level $m - 1$; (b) any node with only one child at level $m - 1$ appears to the left of all nodes with no children at level $m - 1$; and (c) there is at most one node with only one child at level $m - 1$.

density The density is the number of storage locations used divided by the number of total storage locations available.

density-dependent search technique Search technique whose efficiency is determined solely by the density of the data.

depth-first search A visiting of all nodes in a graph; this traversal proceeds from each node by probing as deeply as possible along one path leading from that node.

dereferencing Accessing the object being referenced by a pointer.

difference The difference of set A and set B is $A - B$, where $A - B$ contains the elements that are in A but not in B. *See also* intersection and union.

digit/character extraction In creating a hashing function, the process of removing from a key those digits or characters that may bias the results of the hashing function.

digraph/directed graph A graph in which each edge establishes a directional orientation between its endpoints.

Dijkstra's algorithm An algorithm for finding the shortest path between two nodes in a network.

diminishing increment sort A sort in which the number of segments on which the sort works on any one pass decreases with each successive pass. *See also* Shell sort.

directed path A sequence of directed edges from one node of a graph to another. Each pair of successive edges in the path contains a common endpoint.

divide-and-conquer A problem-solving strategy in which a problem is broken down into two or more subproblems, each of which is a simpler case of the original problem.

division remainder technique A technique used in creating hashing functions to ensure that the results will be a valid output. It uses the **mod** function to scale the value into the proper range.

dominant term The highest power of n in a polynomial. For large n the behavior of the entire polynomial will approach the behavior of the polynomial that contains only that term.

double hashing A collision-processing method in which a second hashing function is used to determine a sequence of storage locations to examine until an available spot is found.

doubly linked list A linked list in which each node has two pointers instead of one. One pointer points to the node preceding that node in the list and the other points to the node following that node in the list.

dummy header A node preceding the first actual data node in a list and often containing information about the list.

dynamic memory management The allocation and reclamation of computer memory locations as necessary during program execution.

edge One of the two main structures (along with a node) of a graph. The edges establish a relationship between two (not necessarily distinct) nodes of a graph.

efficiency ratio For a sparse matrix implementation method, the efficiency ratio is the number of storage locations used by that method divided by the number of storage locations used by standard row major form.

eight queens problem Requires one to determine the various ways in which eight queens could be configured on a chessboard so that none of them could access any other queen.

encapsulate To bundle into one unit, via a record, all data items necessary to specify the data structure of an abstract data type.

exponential algorithm An algorithm whose efficiency is dominated by a term of the form a^n.

external file A file used to store data in secondary storage between runs of a program. *See also* internal file.

external sort A sort in which the list being sorted resides in a file rather than in memory.

factorial The product of the first N positive integers (denoted $N!$).

fatal embrace *See* deadlock.

Fibonacci buddy system System of coalescing blocks of memory in which all blocks of memory have a size corresponding to one of the numbers in a Fibonacci sequence.

FIFO *See* queue.

fifteen game Opposing players alternately choose digits between 1 and 9 with the goal of selecting a combination of digits that adds up to 15. Once a digit is chosen, it may not be chosen again by either player.

first-fit searching A memory allocation policy in which a list of available blocks of memory is searched and the first block that can accommodate a memory request is allocated.

first-in first-out *See* queue.

fixed-length method A method of storing strings in which a fixed amount of space is allocated for each string regardless of its actual length.

Floyd's algorithm An algorithm for finding the shortest distance between any pair of nodes in a network.

folding A method of constructing a hashing function in cases where the key is not an integer value. The nonnumeric characters are removed and the remaining digits are combined to produce an integer value.

fragmentation problem Problem faced by an operating system where, after frequent allocation of memory to and reclamation of memory from users, the overall pattern of available memory is one of relatively small disconnected fragments of available space.

front pointer The pointer to the front of a queue.

full binary tree A binary tree such that all nodes with fewer than two children must occur at level m or $m - 1$, where m is the deepest level in the tree.

functionally cohesive A functionally cohesive module achieves one particular predefined task without having unexpected side effects on the performance of other modules in the system.

game tree A search tree specific to games. *See* search tree.

general list A collection of data items, all of the same type, that are related to each other by their relative positions in the list.

general tree A set of nodes that is either empty or has a designated node (called the root) from which descend zero or more subtrees.

graph A structure composed of two sets of objects: a set of nodes (or vertices) and a set of edges. Typically, a node is a data element of the graph in that it has an associated data value, whereas an edge indicates a direct relationship between two nodes.

Grundy's game Matches two opponents who are presented initially with one stack of seven pennies on a table in front of them. On a given move, a player must divide one of the stacks of pennies currently on the table into two *unequal* stacks. A player who is unable to make such a division loses the game.

hashing A density-dependent search technique in which the key for a given data item is transformed using a hashing function to produce the address in which that item is stored in memory.

hashing function A key-to-address transformation.

head pointer A pointer to the head or front of the list.

heap (1) The portion of computer memory not required to store the program instructions, pre-declared data storage locations, or various operating system requirements. The heap contains the memory used for dynamic memory requests. (2) A binary tree with the heap property.

heap management A dynamic memory management technique that allocates available memory from a heap upon a new request and reclaims memory upon a dispose command.

heap property A binary tree has the heap property when the data at any given node are greater than or equal to the data in its left and right subtrees.

heap sort Sort in which the array is treated like the array implementation of a binary tree and the items are repeatedly manipulated to create a heap from which the root is removed and added to the sorted portion of the array. *See also* insertion sort, selection sort, bubble sort, radix sort, Shell sort, quick sort, and merge sort.

height balancing A technique for ensuring that an ordered binary tree remains as full as possible in form.

heuristic A rule of thumb that cuts down on the number of possible choices to examine. Heuristics often lead to quick solutions but do not guarantee a solution the way an exhaustive search algorithm does.

hierarchy A relationship between nodes in which one node is viewed as above or prior to another.

Horner's method An efficient algorithm for calculating the value of a polynomial.

implementation A representation of an abstract model of a system and its abstract data types in terms of declarations and instructions in a particular computer language.

indegree of a node The number of directed edges that terminate at the node.

index A collection of entries for records in a file. Each index entry contains a key attribute and a reference pointer for a record to allow immediate access to that record.

indexed sequential access method (ISAM) The most common method of indexed sequential search.

indexed sequential search Use of a partial index based on disk-dependent factors to find the proper portion of the disk on which to search sequentially for the key.

infix Algebraic notation in which the arithmetic operator appears between the two operands to which it will be applied.

infix priority Function to hierarchically rank algebraic operators in order of precedence.

information hiding A characteristic of a package that allows it to be used by a calling program without that program's requiring knowledge of the implementation details of the package.

inorder predecessor The node preceding a given node in an inorder tree traversal.

inorder successor The node following a given node in an inorder tree traversal.

inorder threads Pointers to the inorder predecessor and inorder successor of a node.

inorder traversal A binary tree traversal in which, at any node, that node's left subtree is visited first, then that node is processed, and finally that node's right subtree is visited.

insertion rule For binary trees, a rule whereby a new item is placed in the left subtree of an item greater than it or in the right subtree of an item less than or equal to it.

insertion sort Sorts an array of elements in either ascending or descending order. Starts with an empty array and inserts elements one at a time in their proper order. *See also* bubble sort, heap sort, merge sort, quick sort, radix sort, selection sort, and Shell sort.

interface The lines of communication between a module and those that use it. The interface to a module is its parameter list.

internal sort A sort in which the list being sorted resides in memory.

intersection The intersection of set A and set B is $A * B$, where $A * B$ contains the elements that are in both A and B. *See also* difference and union.

key Field in a general list that is used to order or access elements of the list.

keyed collection An unordered group of records, each of which has one field designated as a key field, along with other fields that are grouped as a subrecord. Records within the collection are identified by the value of their key field.

keyed ordering Ordering imposed on the entries in a list by the value of a key field.

key-to-address transformation Transformation in which the key of the data item is transformed to provide the address at which the data are actually stored.

Kruskal's algorithm An algorithm for finding a minimal spanning tree of a network.

last-in first-out (LIFO) *See* stack.

leaf In a tree, a node that has no children.

left subtree One of two subtrees of a node in a binary tree. For a binary tree with the ordering property, the values of all nodes in the left subtree of a node will precede the value of the node. *See also* right subtree.

length (1) The number of edges in a path. (2) The weight of an edge in a network.

level All nodes in a tree whose paths are the same length from the root node.

lexical analysis The task of recognizing valid language tokens in an incoming stream of characters.

LIFO *See* stack.

linear algorithm A polynomial algorithm in which the highest nonzero term is n.

linear collision processing Method of handling a collision in which the storage space is searched sequentially from the location of the collision for an available location where the new key can be placed.

linear representation (of binary tree) An implementation of a binary tree in an array. For a given node stored at index position K, that node's left child is at position $2K$ and the right child is at position $2K + 1$.

link A pointer from one node to another.

linked collision processing Method of handling a collision in which the second key is stored in a linked list located in an overflow area.

linked list A collection of elements called nodes, each of which contains a data portion and a pointer to the node following that one in the linear ordering of the list.

list traversal The process of sequentially visiting each node in a list.

locality of reference Describes the behavior exhibited when, in examining the references to data elements in a sequence of operations, within any given interval the sequence seems to favor a small subset of the data elements being referenced. Membership in this favored set changes gradually as one advances through the sequence.

logarithmic algorithm An algorithm whose efficiency is dominated by a term of the form $\log_a n$.

logically sorted Data have been logically sorted when pointers to the data have been sorted even though the data have not been touched. Hence items that the sort places consecutively need not be physically adjacent.

$\log_2 n$ search algorithm A search algorithm whose efficiency is dominated by a term of the form $\log_2 n$.

loop An edge that starts and ends at a single node.

mapping function A function that transforms row-column array coordinates to the linear address of that array entry.

marking A garbage collection strategy for heap management that is invoked when the heap runs out of memory to allocate. When this occurs, all heap nodes are initially marked as available, each heap node reachable through an active pointer is marked as in use, and the nodes that remain marked as available after this are linked into an available space structure.

matrix A collection of data of the same type arranged as a rectangular grid whose rows and columns are each indexed by a separate contiguous range of an ordinal data type. Each entry in the grid can be specified by its row and column coordinates.

merge The process of combining lists; typically refers to files or arrays.

merge sort Sort in which the array is repeatedly split in half and then these pieces are merged together. *See also* insertion sort, selection sort, bubble sort, radix sort, heap sort, Shell sort, and quick sort.

minimal spanning tree A collection of edges connecting all of the nodes of a network—a spanning tree—such that the total edge weight of this spanning tree is at least as small as the total edge weight of any other spanning tree for the network.

minimax algorithm A game-playing algorithm based on the supposition that one player, **min,** will always try to force the other player, **max,** into the worst possible situation at a given point in the game.

multilinked list A linked list in which each node has two or more link fields.

network A graph in which the edges have weights associated with them.

node A structure storing a data item in a linked list, tree, graph, or network.

nonterminals In a grammar, symbols that represent various grammatical constructs within the language being represented by the grammar.

ordered list A collection of data nodes arranged in a linear sequence according to some ordering criterion between nodes.

ordering A means of arranging the elements in a list.

ordering property In a binary tree, the data in each node of the tree are greater than all of the data in that node's left subtree and less than or equal to all of the data in its right subtree.

order of magnitude Power of ten. Two numbers have the same order of magnitude if their representations in scientific notation have identical exponents to designate the power of ten.

outdegree of a node The number of directed edges that originate at the node.

overflow area In linked collision processing, the area in which keys that cause collisions are placed.

parent In a tree, the node that is pointing to its children.

parser A program that checks the syntax of an expression and represents that expression in a unique form.

parser generator A program that can take the input grammar for a language and produce the parser for that language.

parse tree Tree representation of the syntactic structure of a source program produced by a compiler; also referred to as *abstract syntax tree*.

parsing The procedure of checking the syntax of an expression and representing it in one unique form.

partial ordering A relation among pairs of elements of a set that is irreflexive (an element is not related to itself), asymmetric (if a is related to b then b is not related to a), and transitive (if a is related to b and b is related to c then a is related to c).

partition In quick sort, the process of moving the pivot to the location where it belongs in the sorted array and arranging the remaining data items to the left of the pivot if they are less than or equal to the pivot and to the right if they are greater than or equal to the pivot.

path A sequence of edges that connects two nodes in a graph or network.

path compression A strategy for improving the efficiency of the union and find operations of the union-find problem.

pivot (1) Item used to direct the partitioning of quick sort. (2) A node at which a rotation occurs in an AVL tree.

ply In game-playing algorithms, a level in a game tree.

ply limit In game-playing algorithms, a maximal depth to which one will search beyond a particular game state.

pointer A memory location containing the location of another data item.

pointer sort A sort in which pointers to the data are manipulated rather than the data themselves.

polynomial algorithm An algorithm whose efficiency can be expressed in terms of a polynomial.

pop A procedure that removes an item from the top of the stack.

postfix Unambiguous algebraic notation in which the arithmetic operator appears after the two operands to which it is to be applied.

postorder traversal A binary tree traversal in which, at any node, the node's left subtree is visited first, then the node's right subtree is visited, and finally the node is processed.

preorder traversal A binary tree traversal in which, at any node, the node is first processed, then the node's left subtree is visited, and finally the node's right subtree is visited.

primary cluster The relocation region arising from primary clustering.

primary clustering Occurs when a collision-resolution strategy causes keys that have a collision at an initial hashing position to be relocated to the same region within the storage space; same as clustering.

prime hash area In linked collision processing, the main storage area in which keys are placed if no collision occurs.

Prim's algorithm An algorithm for finding a minimal spanning tree of a network.

priority queue A queue in which the entries on the queue are ranked into groups according to priority. Such a queue requires a rear pointer for each different possible priority value.

productions Formal rules that define the syntactical composition of the nonterminals of a formal grammar.

quadratic algorithm A polynomial algorithm in which the highest nonzero term is n^2.

quadratic collision processing Method of handling a collision in which the storage space is searched in the k^2 place (for successive integer values of k) past the location of the collision, until an available spot is found.

queue A dynamic data structure in which elements are entered at one end, and removed from the other end. Referred to as a FIFO (first-in first-out) structure.

quick sort A relatively fast sorting technique that uses recursion and a partitioning subalgorithm. *See also* bubble sort, insertion sort, radix sort, heap sort, Shell sort, merge sort, and selection sort.

Rabin-Karp algorithm A string search algorithm based on the use of a conceptual hash table.

radix sort Sorts integer data by repeatedly placing the items into bins and then collecting the bins starting with the least significant digit for the first pass and finishing with the most significant digit. Also referred to as *bin sort*. *See also* bubble sort, insertion sort, quick sort, heap sort, Shell sort, merge sort, and selection sort.

randomized storage A name given to list access via a hashing function.

random number generator A function that returns a real number between 0 and 1 each time it is called. The numbers it returns are statistically random in that, after repeated calls to the function, the sequence of numbers returned is evenly distributed over the interval even though each one is completely unpredictable.

ready queue In an operating system, the queue of processes with cleared access to all the resources the processes require to run.

rear pointer The pointer to the rear of a queue.

recursion The process of a subprogram calling itself. A clearly defined stopping state must exist. Any recursive subprogram can be rewritten using iteration and a stack.

recursive descent parsing A parsing technique for grammars; it relies heavily upon recursive procedures, one for each nonterminal of the grammar.

recursive termination condition A condition that terminates a series of recursive calls and hence prevents an infinite series of such calls.

red-black tree A binary tree in which the pointers to the left and right subtrees of each node have an associated color of red or black used to map the node into a cluster of nodes representing one node in a 2-3-4 tree.

reference counting A garbage collection strategy for heap management. Each node contains a field to keep track of the number of pointers that reference the node. An invocation to dispose of the node will not restore a node to available space if the count field has a value greater than 1.

rehashing Method of handling a collision in which a sequence of new hashing functions is applied to the key that caused the collision until an available location for that key is found.

relatively prime Two numbers are relatively prime if and only if their only common factor is 1.

relative ordering An ordering imposed on the entries in a list by their relative positions in that list.

right subtree One of two subtrees of a node in a binary tree. For a binary tree with the ordering property, the values of all nodes in the right subtree of a node will equal or follow the value of the node. *See also* left subtree.

row major Implementation of a two-dimensional array as a one-dimensional array so that the rows are arranged in sequential order with all entries of the same row adjacent.

run A subsequence of a data stream arranged in order according to some ordering relationship between records.

search tree In graph search problems, a tree used to help systematically explore all possible paths.

secondary clustering A situation that arises in quadratic collision processing when two values that have a collision at a given location subsequently examine the same sequence of alternative locations—$K + 1^2$, $K + 2^2$, $K + 3^2$, etc.—until the collision is resolved.

sector A particular portion of a magnetic disk used at the machine-language level in addressing information stored on the disk.

selection sort A sorting algorithm that sorts the components of an array in either ascending or descending order. This process puts the smallest or largest element in the top position and repeats the process on the remaining array components. *See also* bubble sort, insertion sort, radix sort, heap sort, Shell sort, merge sort, and quick sort.

semaphore In an operating system, special flags that regulate the addition and removal of processes to and from the blocked and ready queues.

sequential access file A file whose components must be accessed in sequence, starting with the first component.

sequential search The process of examining the first element in a list and proceeding to examine the elements in order until a match is found.

set A structured data type that consists of a collection of distinct elements from an indicated base type (which must be ordinal).

Shell sort Sort that works by dividing the array into smaller noncontiguous segments. These segments are separately sorted using the insertion sort algorithm. The number of these segments is repeatedly reduced on each successive pass until the entire array has been sorted. *See also* insertion sort, bubble sort, selection sort, radix sort, heap sort, merge sort, and quick sort.

shift folding A variation on folding in which each numeric part of the key is treated as a separate number and these numbers are added to form an integer value. *See also* boundary folding.

siblings The child nodes of a given node.

signature The number, type, and order of parameters in a procedure's formal parameter list.

simulation of system stack Technique used to eliminate recursion by making a program explicitly perform the duties of the system stack.

software engineering A methodology of software design based on the structured methods of engineering in which the goal is to develop software that is both cost-effective and reliable. The emphasis is on making additions and modifications to the design of the system while it is still in the conceptual stage rather than during the physical implementation stage.

sparse matrix A matrix in which a high percentage of data storage locations will be of a uniform value.

splay A sequence of splay rotations about nodes of a binary search tree to move a given node—typically, one just accessed or one just inserted—to the root of the tree. At the same time the tree will be restructured along the path from the root to the given node so that the tree remains a binary search tree.

splay rotation A restructuring of a subtree of a binary search tree to move a given node—typically, one just accessed or one just inserted—to the root of the subtree, while at the same time preserving the binary search property of the subtree.

stack A data structure where access can be made from only one end. Referred to as a LIFO (last-in first-out) structure.

stack frame The information placed on the system stack by the operating system when a procedure call is made.

stack priority Function to hierarchically rank algebraic operators in order of precedence while they are held in the stack.

static evaluator In game-playing contexts, another name for a heuristic.

string A list of characters that are related in linear fashion and that can be manipulated using string operations.

strongly connected A property of a directed graph wherein, for any two nodes A and B in the graph, there is a path from A to B and one from B to A.

synonyms Two keys that hash to the same position and therefore cause a collision.

tail recursion A type of recursion in which an initial return operation triggers a series of returns uninterrupted by further recursive calls.

terminals *See* token.

ternary tree A tree in which each node can have at most three children.

thread A pointer contained in a tree node that leads to the predecessor or to the successor of the node relative to a specified traversal.

threaded tree A tree in which threading is used.

threading A technique of avoiding recursion in tree traversal algorithms whereby the pointers unused in tree formation are turned into pointers to the inorder predecessor and inorder successor of that node.

time/space trade-off The maxim that an attempt to make a program more efficient in terms of time will only come as a result of a corresponding decrease in efficiency in terms of space, and vice versa.

token A language symbol composed of one or more characters in an incoming stream of characters; the basic unit returned from lexical analysis.

top The end of a stack at which entries are added and removed.

topological ordering A linear ordering for the nodes in a directed, acyclic graph derived from the partial ordering on the nodes defined using the directional orientation of its edges.

total path weight The sum of the weights of all the edges of a network path.

track A particular portion of a magnetic disk used at the machine-language level in addressing information stored on the disk.

transitive closure A graph derived from a given graph, G, that has the same nodes and edges as G. In addition, the transitive closure of G will have an edge between two nodes if there is a path between those nodes in G.

tree *See* general tree.

tree of recursive calls A hierarchy representing the successive recursive calls that will be made by a recursive procedure for an initial set of parameters.

tree traversal A means of processing every node in the tree.

trial-and-error backtracking A recursive search technique in which a path is probed until a dead end is found; a return is then made to a previous decision point and an alternate path followed.

trie indexing A type of indexing used when the keys are variable-length character strings. Although taken from the word *retrieve*, trie is pronounced "try."

two-stream polyphase merge sort An external sorting algorithm similar to the two-way merge sort, but which requires only one scratch stream.

2-3 tree A general tree composed of two types of nodes—those that can have two children (2-nodes) and those that can have three children (3-nodes). 2-3 trees are maintained so that all leaf nodes occur at the bottom-most level.

2-3-4 tree A general tree composed of three types of nodes—those that can have two children (2-nodes), those that can have three children (3-nodes), and those that can have four children (4-nodes). 2-3-4 trees are maintained so that all leaf nodes occur at the bottom-most level.

two-way merge The process of merging two sorted lists.

two-way merge sort An external sorting algorithm similar to merge sort; requires five data streams in addition to one with the given data—two streams with the original data split between them, arranged in runs of a given size; two scratch streams; and one stream to return the sorted data.

union The union of set A and set B is $A + B$ where $A + B$ contains any element that is in A or that is in B. *See also* difference and intersection.

union-find problem In working with sets, the union-find problem requires that the members of the universe must be partitioned into sets such that each member of the universe is in one and only one set. The find problem requires that one be able to determine when two members of the universe are in the same set of a partition; the union problem requires that the union of sets containing two given elements of the universe be formed and that the sets that were joined be removed from the partition.

volatile list A list that undergoes frequent insertions and deletions.

Warshall's algorithm An algorithm for finding the transitive closure of a graph.

weakly connected A property of a digraph wherein, for any pair of (distinct) nodes, there is an arc between them.

weight A numeric value associated with an edge in a network.

weight balancing A strategy for improving the efficiency of the union and find operations of the union-find problem.

workspace index method A method of storing strings in which one large workspace is provided for storing all the strings and an index keeps track of the starting locations and lengths of each of the individual strings.

worst case The arrangement of data items prior to the beginning of an algorithm that causes the algorithm to take the longest amount of time for that particular set of items. *See also* best case.

INDEX